ALFRED PLUMMER

CONVERSATIONS WITH DR. DÖLLINGER

BIBLIOTHECA EPHEMERIDUM THEOLOGICARUM
LOVANIENSIUM

LXVII

ALFRED PLUMMER

CONVERSATIONS WITH DR. DÖLLINGER

1870-1890

Edited with Introduction and Notes

BY

ROBRECHT BOUDENS

with the collaboration of Leo Kenis

LEUVEN
UNIVERSITY PRESS

UITGEVERIJ PEETERS
LEUVEN

1985

C.I.P. KONINKLIJKE BIBLIOTHEEK ALBERT I

Alfred Plummer: conversations with Dr. Döllinger / edited with
introduction and notes by Robrecht Boudens; with the collaboration of Leo Kenis. – Leuven: Leuven University Press;
Peeters, 1985. – LV, 360 p.; 24 cm. – (Bibliotheca ephemeridum
theologicarum Lovaniensium; 67).

ISBN 90-6186-178-0: BF. 1.800.
SISO 237   UDC 2
Onderwerpen: Theologie [Katholieke]; Theologie [Angli-
kaanse]; Plummer, Alfred; Döllinger, Johann Joseph Ignaz von
(1799-1890).

D/1985/1869/6

© 1985 Leuven University Press/Presses Universitaires de Louvain
Universitaire Pers Leuven
Krakenstraat 3, B-3000 Leuven-Louvain (Belgium)

Uitgeverij Peeters, Bondgenotenlaan 153, B-3000 Leuven (Belgium)

PREFACE

In piam memoriam
R^i D^i Caroli Blockx
(1925-1983)

This publication of Alfred Plummer's *Conversations with Dr. Döllinger* is dedicated to the memory of Dr. Karel Blockx, professor of Modern Church History at the Theological Faculty of the Katholieke Universiteit of Leuven. The life and works of Ignaz von Döllinger was one of his favourite course subjects, and having come across the manuscript at Pusey House, Oxford, in 1976, he planned to prepare the edition of this text. He carefully kept his copy of the manuscript, but more urgent tasks prevented him from undertaking the editorial work. His wish to publish this important document was left unfulfilled, due to his unexpected death on February 11, 1983.

Alfred Plummer, the Anglican Church historian and Biblical scholar, is a well-known name, especially in the field of New Testament studies. Ignaz von Döllinger is not less known for his scholarly work and still more for the role he played in the infallibility debate just before, during and after the First Vatican Council. The Oxford manuscript contains the history of the contact between both men during the years 1870-1890, and especially reveals Plummer's impression of the famous professor of Munich.

We offer our heartfelt thanks to all who have helped us in the preparation of this edition. We would especially like to mention the efficient assistance of Lic. theol. Leo Kenis who has demonstrated a special talent for historical detection in identifying some of the persons and events mentioned in the text and, moreover, has provided considerable material help. We are equally grateful to Dr. John Muddiman, Oxford, for contributing a most valuable essay on Plummer's exegetical work. We also wish to express our gratitude to the Librarian of Pusey House, Oxford, who gave permission for the publication of the manuscript, and to Prof. F. Neirynck, who inspired the carrying out of this work and accepted it for publication in the series *Bibliotheca Ephemeridum Theologicarum Lovaniensium*.

Leuven, February 11, 1985   R. B.

TABLE OF CONTENTS

INTRODUCTION

In order to assist a better understanding of the importance and range of Plummer's *Conversations*, in the first part we will introduce the principal character, Dr. Döllinger: the person, the theologian, the historian, the evolution of his ideas, and his place in the history of the Church. In these pages no new information is offered, but such an introduction is necessary for an understanding of certain facts and allusions contained in Plummer's manuscript. In particular, an insight into the prehistory of Döllinger's conflict with Rome is helpful.

In the second part a closer look is taken at Plummer's person and activity, his contacts with the scholar of Munich, and the historical value of the *Conversations*.

I

IGNAZ VON DÖLLINGER (1799-1890)

Johann Joseph Ignaz von Döllinger, who ever more clearly appears to have been the most influential German Church historian of the 19th century, was born on February 28, 1799, in Bamberg (Franconia). His father was professor of medicine, first in Bamberg, then in Würzburg and Munich, and well known as an anatomist and embryologist. He experienced no great need of religion. Döllinger's mother on the other hand was pious, counterbalancing his father's positivistic orientation. As a student the young Döllinger was gifted and studious. In addition to Latin and Greek, he studied French, English and Italian and acquired a passive knowledge of Spanish and Portuguese. He began his university studies in Würzburg in 1816. His original choice of such a diverse selection of courses as history, philosophy, philology, natural sciences with a specialisation in botany, mineralogy, and entomology could suggest a wide range of interests, but was undoubtedly also an expression of intellectual gluttony.

There is no agreement among historians on the motives which led him, in 1817, to choose the priesthood. Whereas Friedrich contends that he began studying theology because no professor in the faculty of philosophy satisfied him and because he came under the influence of certain converts,[1] Conzemius and Schwaiger emphasize that he

---

1. J. FRIEDRICH, *Döllinger*, in *Allgemeine Deutsche Biographie* 48 (1904) 1-20, p. 1.

had a genuine calling to the priesthood.[2] The courses in theology he took in 1818-1819 in Würzburg also failed to arouse any great interest. The only classes he attended faithfully were biblical philology and exegesis. He became acquainted with the most prominent theologians of his time through personal reading. It is also noteworthy that at this time he read some fundamental works on Church history which were to form the basis for his later historical studies: Baronius' *Annales ecclesiastici* (1588-1607) and Paolo Sarpi's *Istoria del Concilio Tridentino* (1619).

In 1820 he entered the seminary in Bamberg where he took courses at the lyceum for a year and a half. He seems to have considered the professors at Bamberg more satisfactory than those at Würzburg. However, in later years he was to acknowledge that there had been lacunae in his early theological education. His dissatisfaction with some of his teachers led him to undertake his own private studies, especially in his preferred area of Church history. In fact, in this area he would remain largely self-taught.

On April 22, 1822, when Döllinger was ordained priest, he had not yet thought about a career as professor. According to Friedrich, his ideal was to undertake the spiritual guidance of a small parish using his free time for scientific research.[3] In November he was assigned as chaplain at Markt Scheinfeld in Middle Franconia, but then, through his father's intervention, he was appointed professor of Canon law and Church history in the lyceum at Aschaffenburg. Here he wrote *Die Lehre von der Eucharistie in den drei ersten Jahrhunderten*, which in 1826 was accepted by the University of Landshut as a doctoral dissertation and in which he opposed the position taken by liberal Protestant theologians. It was clear that, when treating theological subjects, he preferred the historical approach to the speculative. He had an extensive knowledge of sources, but he was not always sufficiently critical in his use of them. His writing, according to modern standards, was overly polemical and apologetical in character. His approach to the subject was insufficiently objective and serene. As would become clearer in his later life, he demonstrated even at this

---

2. V. CONZEMIUS, *Ignaz v. Döllinger: The Development of a XIXth Century Ecumenist*, in *Hundert Jahre Christkatholisch-theologische Fakultät der Universität Bern* (Beiheft zur "Internationalen Kirchlichen Zeitschrift", 64/4), Bern, 1974, pp. 110-127 (p. 111); G. SCHWAIGER, *Ignaz von Döllinger* (Münchener Universitätsreden. Neue Folge, 37), Munich, 1964, p. 6; more strongly expressed in ID., *Ignaz von Döllinger (1799-1890)*, in H. FRIES and G. SCHWAIGER (eds.), *Katholische Theologen Deutschlands im 19. Jahrhundert*, vol. III, Munich, 1975, pp. 9-43 (p. 13); and ID., *Ignaz von Döllinger (1799-1890)*, in H. FRIES and G. KRETSCHMAR (eds.), *Klassiker der Theologie*, vol. II, Munich, 1983, pp. 127-150 (p. 129).

3. J. FRIEDRICH, *Ignaz von Döllinger. Sein Leben auf Grund seines schriftlichen Nachlasses dargestellt*, vol. I, Munich, 1899, p. 134.

early period an unusually extensive knowledge, but it has correctly
been pointed out that he lacked the great vision characteristic of a
Möhler or a Newman, two eminent scholars whom he admired.[4]

On Johann Michael Sailer's recommendation he was appointed,
after obtaining his doctorate, to the professorship of Canon law and
Church history at the newly established University of Munich—moved
from Landshut by Ludwig I of Bavaria—where he would spend the
rest of his life. He turned down invitations to teach at Breslau and
Freiburg.

Most historians distinguish three periods in Döllinger's further development.[5] The first could be called his 'ultramontane' period, but this
term can lead to misunderstanding if one takes it to mean an enthusiasm
for Rome. It is perhaps more accurate to speak of a period in which
he devoted himself primarily to the renewal of the Catholic Church
in Germany. The second period began in the 1850's, when it had
become evident that historical criticism would play a greater role in
his whole attitude to life, an element which after 1860 was manifested
in a distinct anti-Romanism. One notes reactions against papal absolutism, a questioning of the temporal power of the Pope, a growing
indignation regarding the evolution of Pius IX's pontificate, a hostility
to the revival of scholastic theology. This led finally to his excommunication in 1871, which marked the beginning of a third period, a period
of increasing bitterness with regard to the Roman Catholic Church
which he continued to view as his mother Church, yet which continued
to disillusion him in so many aspects. He was convinced that he was
being unjustly treated, but at the same time we see his honest concern
and exertion for the reunion of separated Churches.

These three periods must be examined more closely. In the years
1820-1850 the German Catholic Church experienced an inner renewal.
It was not so much the official organisations which formed the basis
of this renewal as the personalities who worked against the rational
forces of the Enlightenment, and the small revival groups, the most
important of which were to be found in Münster, Mainz, Landshut,
and soon also in Munich. When Döllinger arrived in Munich he
became an active representative of the Görres circle. He owed much
to Joseph von Görres, perhaps especially his great urge to fight for
the freedom of the Church and his polemical approach to Church
problems. The Görres circle was active in the defence of Catholic
interests and the recovery of the Catholic Church in Germany. *Eos,*

---

4. Y. CONGAR, *Döllinger*, in *Catholicisme* 3 (1952) 972-974, col. 974.

5. See the survey in J. FINSTERHÖLZL, *Die Kirche in der Theologie Ignaz von
Döllingers bis zum ersten Vatikanum*, ed. J. BROSSEDER (Studien zur Theologie und
Geistesgeschichte des Neunzehnten Jahrhunderts, 9), Göttingen, 1975, p. 23.

Münchener Blätter für Poesie, Literatur und Kunst was their official publication. From 1828 to 1832 Döllinger contributed to this paper, treating both religious and literary questions.[6] His influence grew. In 1845-1846 he was rector of the University. In the periods 1845-1847 and 1849-1851 he represented the University in the Bavarian *Landtag*. Here he demonstrated an avid interest in religious affairs. When in 1847 the University came in conflict with King Ludwig I as a result of the Lola Montez affair, Döllinger was temporarily obliged to tender his resignation. In 1848-1849 he represented Lower Bavaria in the Frankfurt Parliament. His election was apparently due to the great popularity he found with the people when he fell from the king's favour and was removed from his position as professor. In Frankfurt he worked for the freedom of the Church. But it is noteworthy that he did not sympathize with the restoration of the Jesuits in Germany. This attitude would later become more adamant.

The Church showed its appreciation of Döllinger by making him a canon in 1840 and provost (*Stiftspropst*) of the Royal Chapel of St. Cajetan in 1847. Scientific recognition of his work can be seen in the fact that in 1837 he was made member extraordinary, in 1843 regular member, and in 1864 secretary, of the Bavarian Academy of Sciences. In 1873 he became its president.

From the time of his notorious speech in Parliament (August 21, 1848),[7] Döllinger was generally recognized as one of the most prominent Catholics. In this period he also published a brief anonymous text on *Kirche und Staat*,[8] in which he argued the case for the Church's independence, but not, however, for a separation of Church and State. He wanted Catholics in Germany to feel at home and be accepted. At the founding meeting of the *Katholischer Verein* in Mainz, Döllinger alluded to a German national Church which he did not view as being in conflict with Catholicity but rather as a uniting together of all the Catholic forces in the various German *Länder*. It is possible that when giving this address he had in mind the forthcoming bishops' conference of Würzburg, where all the German bishops would gather together for the first time. Earlier governments had forbidden on principle any form of episcopal co-operation. It was precisely for such co-operation, made possible since the gains of March '48, that the Church historian of Munich pleaded. The bishops themselves did

---

6. See the survey in S. Lösch, *Döllinger und Frankreich. Eine geistige Allianz 1823-1871* (Schriftenreihe zur bayerischen Landesgeschichte, 51), Munich, 1955, pp. 502-513. In the years 1828-1838 he also became known by his revised edition of J. N. Hortig's *Handbuch der christlichen Kirchengeschichte* (see Döllinger bibliography, p. LII).

7. Published in *Kleinere Schriften*, 1890, pp. 23-41.

8. *Kirche und Staat. Betrachtungen über den Artikel III des Entwurfs der Grundrechte des deutschen Volkes*, Frankfurt, 1848. Also in *Kleinere Schriften*, pp. 3-22.

not wish to go so far and some saw in Döllinger's speech, which in their opinion was inopportune, an indication that, however learned he may be, he was not a real politician, possessing the art of keeping the possible in view.[9]

When we turn to the historical aspect of his activities in this period, we must first of all say a few words about his voluminous but unfinished work, *Die Reformation, ihre innere Entwicklung und ihre Wirkungen im Umfange des Lutherischen Bekenntnisses*, published in 1846-1848. According to Conzemius, it "was the first Catholic treatment of the topic in modern times".[10] The work was impressive for the mass of documentation which it brought together, but a closer look reveals that he was very selective in his choice of documents. Although he did not ignore the Reformers' good intentions, he did not succeed in seeing the positive religious character of the Reformation. Instead he emphasized its unfavourable moral and cultural consequences. He was interested not so much in the facts as in the inner development of Protestantism, which he treated as an institution in opposition to Catholicism. The image given of the Reformation was shadowy and lacked nuance and that of Luther was distorted. For Döllinger the heart of Luther's teaching was justification which, according to him, was the most important root of the schism. Perhaps he treated this teaching too extrinsically and without examining its further implications. Only later would his judgment concerning Luther and the Reformation undergo a certain evolution.[11]

The fact that Döllinger had contact with many people within and outside Germany is also significant for this period. The importance of personal relations and intellectual exchange was one of his convictions. He had contact with the Rhine circle around Friedrich Schlosser, with professors in Tübingen and Mainz, with Lamennais and his collaborators in France, especially Montalembert, with Dupanloup, Bishop of Orléans, Maret, dean of the theological faculty of the Sorbonne, Meignan, who would later become Bishop of Châlons, F.X. De Ram, first rector of the newly re-established University of Louvain (1834), Newman and Wiseman in England, and with national leaders like Gladstone, as well as with a number of Anglicans such as Pusey and Liddon.

It can be useful to note how his long lasting interest in the religious life of England arose. When the later Cardinal Wiseman, at the time

9. See K. BUCHHEIM, *Ultramontanismus und Demokratie. Der Weg der deutschen Katholiken im 19. Jahrhundert*, Munich, 1963, pp. 61-65.

10. V. CONZEMIUS, *Ignaz v. Döllinger* (see n. 2), p. 116.

11. See G. SCHWAIGER, *Luther im Urteil Ignaz Döllingers*, in B. MOELLER (ed.), *Luther in der Neuzeit* (Schriften des Vereins für Reformationsgeschichte, 192), Gütersloh, 1983, pp. 70-83.

rector of the English College in Rome and professor in the *Sapienza*, had come to appreciate the need to give Catholicism in England a new elan, he believed that contact with the German clerical intelligentsia could prove enriching. In 1835 he went to visit Döllinger in Munich to discuss the situation and the future possibilities for the Catholic Church in England. Döllinger considered Wiseman so engaging that he visited him in England the following year. From that moment on his interest remained undiminished concerning all what took place there on the political, religious, or ecclesiastical levels. This interest found one notable expression in the fact that he frequently extended his hospitality to a number of English students whose studies he guided. It was as a result of this that the young student John Dalberg Acton took up residence with Döllinger. Acton would later become an intimate friend playing an important part in Döllinger's further personal evolution.

In this first period of his life, the scholar of Munich enjoyed the confidence of most German bishops. He was an influential adviser during the first German episcopal conference which took place in Würzburg in 1848. His emphasis on closer relations among the bishops and on the idea of a more nationally organized Church, aimed at opposing existing government interference in Church affairs (*Staatskirchentum*), was not gratefully received by some bishops, and especially not by the Roman curia.[12] All in all, it can be said that in the first decades of his career he had become a man of real influence inside as well as outside Germany. However, his historical writing was still mainly apologetical in character.

A change occurred in 1850. The works published between this year and the Vatican Council can be considered as the most scientific of his whole career. He devoted full attention to the norms of historical criticism and became more aware that Church history was the weak member among the Catholic disciplines and the rising strength of Protestant scholarship. More attention had to be given to the historical aspects of theological questions and less to the speculative thought of a sterile scholasticism. It is in the light of this conviction that one must judge the subjects which he treated in these years. In 1853 he published *Hippolytus und Callistus; oder die römische Kirche in der ersten Hälfte des dritten Jahrhunderts*, in 1857 *Heidenthum und Judenthum. Vorhalle zur Geschichte des Christenthums*, and in 1860 *Christenthum und Kirche in der Zeit der Grundlegung*. His method gradually led him to assume a more understanding stance with regard to the positions adopted by the separated Christians while he looked scepti-

---

12. See R. LILL, *Die ersten deutschen Bischofskonferenzen*, Freiburg/Basel/Vienna, 1964, pp. 14-56.

cally on the uncritical manner in which his own Catholic Church approached theological problems. He considered the dogmatic declaration of the Immaculate Conception of Mary (1854) as an unjustifiable victory of one particular theological school. Perhaps his animosity toward the person of Pius IX, who had championed the dogma, was also not foreign to his changing attitude.

If a precise date has to be given to the moment when this anti-Roman reaction appeared unequivocally for the first time, one would have to mention the Odeon Lectures held in Munich on April 5 and 6, 1861. During these he treated of the Roman Question which was much in the news at that time. He explained the origin and evolution of the Papal States and was not afraid to show the disadvantages associated with the Pope's temporal power. The Pope's mission was a spiritual mission; the papacy would continue to exist even if the Holy Father had to reign without his States. The lectures aroused great excitement. During the first conference the papal nuncio Chigi ostentatiously left the hall in protest against what he considered an insult to the Pope. Catholic opinion was also aroused, to a good extent due to the fact that many episcopal letters expressly stated that the Papal States belonged to the essence of the Church. It is clear that the historical context rendered Döllinger's pronouncements in this delicate area controversial. In the preceding years the pressure of the nationalistic movement for Italian unification had grown increasingly stronger so that the problem of the Pope's temporal power had become acute. The standpoints which Döllinger developed in the Odeon Lectures automatically made him a defender of the Italian *Risorgimento* and an advocate of liberalism. Indeed, since his visit to Rome in 1857, the curia's centralizing tendencies had been a thorn in his side, and he further considered Pius' papal absolutism to be the result of an unjustifiable historical evolution. But still he had not expected such a violent reaction to his conferences.

In 1861 he published *Kirche und Kirchen. Papstthum und Kirchenstaat* to clarify his standpoint.[13] In this book he emphasized that Churches which separate themselves from the Pope wander aimlessly and end in chaos. On the other hand, the ruling structure of the Papal States was in urgent need of reform. Then he repeated what he had already stressed in the Odeon Lectures, "that the Church can exist by and for herself, and that she did exist for seven centuries without the territorial possessions of the Popes".[14] He added that in later times this property had become a necessity to guarantee the Church's freedom

---

13. See Lord ACTON, *Döllinger on the Temporal Power*, in ID., *The History of Freedom and Other Essays*, ed. J.N. FIGGIS and R.V. LAURENCE, London, 1907, pp. 301-374.

14. *The Church and the Churches*, 1862, pp. 2-3.

and independence. The papacy's temporal power was not an ideal situation but was required by historical circumstances. He did not refer to the possibility of an irreparable end of the Papal States, as he had done in his second lecture.

Even though the Pope was not overly alarmed by the book, which could also be seen as an expression of pastoral concern to reassure frightened Catholics, attentive observers saw that Döllinger had not been able to hide his anti-Roman feelings completely. Looking back on Döllinger's life, Lord Acton wrote of this book : "The cold analysis, the diagnosis by the bedside of the sufferer, was not the work of an observer dazzled by admiration or blinded by affection. It was a step, a first unconscious, unpremeditated step, in the process of detachment. The historian here began to prevail over the divine, and to judge church matters by a law which was not given from the altar".[15] It seems incontrovertible that Döllinger's alienation from Rome was growing. But it is equally certain that the triumphalism of those who considered themselves obliged to accuse the forward-looking Church historian of betrayal of the Church encouraged this alienation.

Another element which played a part was the controversy between the proponents of a scholastic theology such as was primarily practised among the theologians in Mainz and the German scholars who did not look favourably on a revival of thomism. The latter preferred an historical approach to questions of faith rather than a speculative one. It is in this context that we should view the Assembly of Catholic Scholars which took place at Munich in 1863 on the initiative of Döllinger and a few of his colleagues and had as goal the promotion of a greater rapport between the various viewpoints. There Döllinger delivered his well-known *Rede über die Vergangenheit und Gegenwart der katholischen Theologie*.[16] He pointed out that Germany's hour in the evolution of theology had arrived, and he expressed the hope that the Protestant separation which had begun in his country would also find its end there thanks to efforts of German theologians. For this three conditions had to be fulfilled. First Catholic theology must have the courage to overcome all that had contributed to the separation and broken the continuity of the tradition. Next, it must view Catholic

---

15. Lord ACTON, *Doellinger's Historical Work*, in *The English Historical Review* 5 (1890) 700-744; reprinted in ID., *The History of Freedom and Other Essays*, pp. 375-435.

16. *Verhandlungen der Versammlung katholischer Gelehrten in München vom 18. September bis 1. Oktober 1863*, Ratisbon, 1863, pp. 25-39; reprinted in *Kleinere Schriften*, pp. 161-196, and in J. FINSTERHÖLZL, *Ignaz von Döllinger* (Wegbereiter heutiger Theologie), Graz/Vienna/Cologne, 1969, pp. 227-263. See J. HOFFMANN, *Théologie, magistère et opinion publique. Le discours de Döllinger au Congrès des Savants Catholiques de 1863*, in *Recherches de science religieuse* 71 (1983) 245-258.

teaching in its totality, in its organic cohesion, and in so doing separate the essential from the accidental. And finally, the science of theology must radiate a magnetic force which would draw to itself all that was good in the other Churches, while separating the wheat from the chaff.

Döllinger supported the notion that theology should be exercised as critically as were the other sciences and pleaded that dogmatics should be viewed in close association with critically judged history and philosophy. One must dare to confront the problem of a teaching's historical evolution. Moreover, he uttered a warning: a theological opinion did not have the authority of a generally valid doctrine of faith. It was a plea for an historical foundation of theology and was not regarded favourably in curia circles.

In fact, the address was intended to encourage understanding between the two theological tendencies in Germany. This result proved difficult to achieve. It was made even more difficult because Döllinger, shortly before the opening of the Assembly of Munich, published a book which by its nature could not but arouse the distrust of many. He had first contemplated writing a history of the papacy, but when he was gathering historical data he came across so much legendary material that he decided to limit his consideration to overthrowing a number of legends about the papacy. The result was *Die Papst-Fabeln des Mittelalters*, a study dealing with nine legends which to a greater or lesser extent influenced Church thinking in the Middle Ages. Some had ceased to have any importance, but the Donation of Constantine, for example, had a direct relation to the Pope's claim to temporal power, and the Honorius Question was to be constantly raised by the bishops of the Minority during the debate on papal infallibility at the First Vatican Council. It is evident that the book met more than normal criticism in ultramontane circles. Yet it must be noted that Döllinger was not the first to approach history critically. He was, it is true, ahead of the Catholic theologians, but among Protestants historical criticism was already accepted in ecclesiastical studies. Döllinger felt that the Church's suspicious attitude toward ecclesiastical sciences was out of date. When the Syllabus of Errors appeared in 1864 he could not, of course, have been pleased. Not only the notorious last sentence of the Syllabus was problematic. He felt himself personally struck by the condemnation of the 13th thesis: "The method and principles whereby the ancient scholastic doctors cultivated theology, are not suited to the necessities of our time and to the progress of the sciences".[17]

---

17. On several occasions Döllinger expressed his views on the Syllabus: in an article on *Die Speyerische Seminarfrage und der Syllabus*, composed in Jan. 1865, published in *Kleinere Schriften*, pp. 197-227; in a lecture delivered at Munich, Dec. 1866, *Die*

The atmosphere in which the Vatican Council was prepared was not of a nature to put him at ease. When the commissions were being formed, he was overlooked.[18] It became an almost exclusively ultramontane affair and the ultramontane press, with *Civiltà Cattolica* in the lead, referred repeatedly to papal prerogatives, so that it became increasingly clear that the goal was reinforcement of papal authority and—even though originally this was not explicitly stated—a possible proclamation of papal infallibility. It was in this period that Döllinger became ecclesiastically a displaced person. He published five unsigned articles in the *Augsburger Allgemeine Zeitung* (March 10-15, 1869) against the obviously tendentious contributions of the *Civiltà*.[19] In the same year these articles were expanded and appeared in book form under the title, *Der Papst und das Concil von JANUS*. The work demonstrated such a thorough knowledge of the papacy that readers having any familiarity with the subject had no difficulty identifying Janus with Döllinger. The Church historian of Munich intended to show that from the point of view of Church history a dogmatic declaration of papal infallibility was impossible. He did not, however, deny the infallibility of the Church: "The Church in its totality is secured against false doctrine; it will not fall away from Christ and the Apostles and will not repudiate the doctrine it has once received, and which has once been handed down within it".[20] This allows us to conclude that he opposed any definition of personal infallibility as it was defended at the Council by bishops such as Manning.

During the Council debates Döllinger was regularly kept informed of the discussions' progress by friends staying in Rome and particularly by Lord Acton. On the basis of this information he published 28 letters in the *Allgemeine Zeitung* from December 1869 to March 1870. All have the same title, *Römische Briefe vom Concil von QUIRINUS*. In the autumn of 1870 they were published in book form along with 41 other letters.[21] Döllinger himself overestimated the impact of these

Universitäten sonst und jetzt, Munich, 1867, reprinted in *Akademische Vorträge*, vol. II, 1888, pp. 3-55 (English translation: *Universities Past and Present*, Oxford, 1867); in several articles on the Inquisition in the *Allgemeine Zeitung* (1867) and the *Neue Freie Presse* (1868), reprinted in *Kleinere Schriften*, pp. 286-404.

18. See K. SCHATZ, *Kirchenbild und päpstliche Unfehlbarkeit bei den deutschsprachigen Minoritätsbischöfen auf dem I. Vatikanum* (Miscellanea Historiae Pontificiae, 40), Rome, 1975, p. 115; for further explanation of Döllinger's absence from the Council, pp. 132-138.

19. *Das Concilium und die Civiltà*, reprinted in W. BRANDMÜLLER, *Ignaz v. Döllinger am Vorabend des I. Vatikanums. Herausforderung und Antwort* (Kirchengeschichtliche Quellen und Studien, 9), St. Ottilien, 1977, pp. 147-180.

20. *The Pope and the Council by JANUS*, 1869, p. 411.

21. See V. CONZEMIUS, *Die "Römischen Briefe vom Konzil". Eine entstehungsgeschichtliche und quellenkritische Untersuchung zum Konzilsjournalismus Ignaz v. Döllingers und Lord Actons*, in *Römische Quartalschrift* 59 (1964) 186-229; 60 (1965) 76-119.

letters. Since he had to operate more on the level of council journalism than council theology, his influence among the bishops was less convincing than he had hoped. The approval came from people who had little interest in theological motives but who joined him because of his attacks against Rome.

Döllinger's campaign had little effect on subsequent events. On July 13, 1870, the much discussed text on papal prerogatives was put to a test vote of the Council Fathers. The result showed that unanimity was not imminent. Of those eligible to vote, 451 voted *placet*, 88 *non placet*, and 62 *placet juxta modum*. When the time came for the final vote, about 60 bishops left Rome. On July 18 the constitution *Pastor Aeternus* was adopted and promulgated.

In the weeks which followed most of the bishops who had belonged to the Minority suffered a crisis of conscience. Many felt themselves placed before a dilemma : either obey the Pope or follow one's own conscience. Pius IX demanded that all bishops explicitly submit. Some complied hesitantly and others only after repeated insistence. Archbishop von Scherr also sent a letter to the faculty of theology in Munich concerning the Council's decrees. He wanted a unanimous opinion from the faculty.[22] The answer required more than a month to prepare. The archbishop considered his wish well met but found it strange that Döllinger had not signed the document. Therefore, on January 4, 1871, he wrote him a personal letter to bring about a public submission.[23] Döllinger's answer is dated January 29, 1871. He said that it was impossible for him to submit but that he had begun a new thorough study of "the great question of the nature and extent of the papal authority and its relation to the Church". Further, he promised he would publicly submit if he came to the conclusion that he had erred, but asked for the time needed to study the affair thoroughly.[24] The archbishop, although disappointed by the answer, gave him until March 15.[25] Just before the end of this postponement was reached, Döllinger requested him to agree to an extension.[26] Scherr then gave him one last chance : the ultimate date for a public submission would be March 31, 1871. He was very formal : "after this date, I shall not be in a position to grant any further prolongation".[27] On March 28 Döllinger sent a moving letter to his archbishop, in which he explicitly rejected the new doctrine concerning the Pope's prerogatives. The

---

22. The letter is dated Oct. 20, 1870, and published in *Briefe und Erklärungen*, 1890, pp. 58-61; in the English translation, *Declarations and Letters*, 1891, pp. 65-69.

23. *Declarations and Letters*, pp. 70-73; in the German edition, pp. 62-65.

24. *Ibid.*, pp. 74-77; in the German edition, pp. 66-68.

25. *Ibid.*, p. 78; in the German edition, p. 69.

26. *Ibid.*, pp. 79-80; in the German edition, pp. 70-71.

27. *Ibid.*, p. 81; in the German edition, p. 72.

wording is well known: "As Christian, as theologian, as historian, as citizen, I cannot accept this doctrine".[28] Three days later, on March 31, the text appeared in the *Allgemeine Zeitung*.

The die was cast. Döllinger had definitively entered the last period of his life. On April 2 Archbischop von Scherr published a pastoral letter in which he condemned Döllinger's position,[29] and the following day the historian of the Ordinariate of Munich-Freising was informed that the archbishop forbade the further attendance of his lectures by any student of theology. On April 17 he was officially informed that he had incurred the greater excommunication.[30]

From his correspondence of these weeks it is clear that Döllinger experienced this excommunication as an injustice perpetrated against him and therefore invalid. Later attempts by Hefele and others to convince him to submit were to no avail. Whenever the rumour spread somewhere that he was on the verge of submission, he was the first to refute it. He began to doubt the validity of the Council itself where—as he wrote to Archbishop von Steichele, von Scherr's successor—"there was notoriously no freedom, no thorough examination, and no statement of actual tradition; a Council whose very unexampled order of business proclaimed the servitude of the bishops".[31]

The protest against the Vatican decrees in Germany led to the establishment of the Old Catholic Church. To know the real nature of Döllinger's ecclesiastical position, we must attend not only to his declarations but also to his concrete stance.[32] At the first meeting of the protest movement in Munich (September 1871), he expressly warned against the establishment of an "altar against altar". When, on July 4, 1873, the Old Catholics elected Prof. Reinkens bishop, Döllinger asked the Bavarian minister of public worship not to recognize the election. He dissuaded Lady Blennerhassett from following the path he himself had taken after the Council and advised Gladstone's sister Helen to stay in the Church of Rome while rejecting Vaticanism. When his best friend Lord Acton remained in the Catholic Church, he never objected. However, the Old Catholics continued to refer to him. So one can ask whether or not he was in fact the founder of a Church of which he did not want to be a member. When he ceased celebrating mass and administering the sacraments, it was because

---

28. *Declarations and Letters*, pp. 82-104; in the German edition, pp. 73-92.

29. *Ibid.*, pp. 105-110; in the German edition, pp. 93-97.

30. *Ibid.*, pp. 113-115; in the German edition, pp. 100-102.

31. *Ibid.*, pp. 141-157; in the German edition, pp. 129-143.

32. See V. CONZEMIUS, *Aspects ecclésiologiques de l'évolution de Döllinger et du Vieux-catholicisme*, in *Revue des sciences religieuses* 34 (1960) 247-279. In contrast, from the Old Catholic standpoint, W. KRAHL, *Döllinger als Altkatholik*, in *Internationale Kirchliche Zeitschrift* 62 (1972) 219-230.

he accepted the consequences of his excommunication. In the last years of his life he was often seen praying in a Roman Catholic church.

One can not point to any moment in his life in which he directly encouraged schism or heresy. He considered his stance a "protest" against something his conscience could not accept: a papal infallibility which was exercised independently of any communion with the faithful or an infallibility of the Church. The Pope's papalist behaviour made it difficult for him to submit to the decree, and he refused to accept something which he could not stand behind in all honesty. One can see in him the spiritual head of the Old Catholic movement, but it would be difficult to show that he had ever been a full member of this community. Although he did say once: "I belong by conviction to the Old Catholic Community",[33] he also wrote, on October 12, 1887, to the nuncio Ruffo Scilla: "Nor do I wish to be a member of a schismatic society: I am isolated. Convinced that the sentence decreed against me is unjust and legally null, I persist in regarding myself as a member of the great Catholic Church; and it is the Church herself, who, through her holy Fathers, tells me that such an excommunication cannot harm my soul".[34] These words, written two years before his death, seem to us to reflect best his ecclesiastical position.

He must have felt deeply the pain of separation. The problem of the reunification of all Christian Churches continued to occupy him and led to the so-called Bonn Reunion Conferences where in 1874 and 1875 he tried to bring together Orthodox, Protestants, Anglicans, and Old Catholics to discuss the existing differences of opinion.[35] But he soon came to appreciate the fact that the point of departure was too narrow to keep a continuous discussion going; the Roman Catholics were not represented at all, the Anglicans present were not sufficiently representative, the majority of the Protestants stayed home, and the discussions with the Orthodox did not always go smoothly, especially when fundamental questions of faith, such as the *Filioque*, were involved.

---

33. Letter of Oct. 18, 1874, to Pastor Widmann of Todtnau, in *Declarations and Letters*, pp. 117-120; in the German edition, pp. 104-107.

34. *Ibid.*, p. 167. The French text can be found on p. 163; the same, with German translation, in the German edition, p. 150.

35. The reports of the discussions were published in German by F.H. Reusch. Plummer himself made a translation of the report of 1875, preceded by a foreword by H.P. Liddon (see S. LÖSCH, *Döllinger und Frankreich*, p. 554). The history of the origin of the Conferences has been dealt with in an unpublished dissertation of Chr. OEYEN, *Die Entstehung der Bonner Unions-Konferenzen im Jahr 1874*, Bern, 1971. Oeyen is preparing an extensive study on the Conferences. Further, see especially P. NEUNER, *Döllinger als Theologe der Ökumene* (Beiträge zur ökumenischen Theologie, 19), Paderborn/Munich/Vienna/Zurich, 1979, pp. 171-219.

Some may have had the impression that Döllinger showed an aloof resignation and that he did not suffer from the isolation. Nothing could be less true,[36] although one can only with difficulty deny that his critical orientation and his conviction that the declaration of papal infallibility was historically unjustifiable can arouse this impression. His sharply carved profile and his angular facial features increased the aura of gravity which surrounded him, at least when he appeared in public. But he also radiated something fascinating allowing him to enjoy, to the end of his life, the interest of numerous friends. His correspondence was enormous, and his home remained open for many.

Döllinger's illness was not long. He died on January 10, 1890, after catching what appeared to be a harmless cold. It was the Old Catholic Friedrich who administered the Last Anointing, but the meaning of his life will forever remain God's secret.[37] As historian, theologian and churchman, he was one of the most eminent figures of the Catholic restoration in 19th-century Germany. The limits and risks of this restoration movement were visible in his life.

II

ALFRED PLUMMER AND HIS CONVERSATIONS WITH DR. DÖLLINGER

Alfred Plummer was born in Heworth, near Gateshead, England, on February 17, 1841, the third son of an Anglican priest. He was educated at Lancing College and then continued his studies at Exeter College, at the University of Oxford, where he graduated in 1863. From 1865 to 1875 he was a fellow of Trinity College where he was dean from 1867 to 1874. From 1874 to 1902 he was master of University College, Durham. He was ordained deacon in 1866 by Bishop Samuel Wilberforce, but never applied to be ordained priest. In 1874 he married Bertha Everest, daughter of a canon of the Anglican cathedral of Truro. He died in Bideford, Devon, on April 17, 1926.

Plummer's greatest claim to fame without doubt lies in the field of exegesis. This aspect of his work is treated extensively in Dr. John Muddiman's contribution on pp. XXXVII-XLVI. It is less well known that throughout his entire academic career Plummer was also occupied with subjects in the field of Church history. In 1887 he published a widely read work on *The Church of the Early Fathers*. In the years

36. See S. MERKLE, *Döllinger als Mensch*, in *Hochland* 15/2 (1918) 628-639. On his friendship with Charlotte Lady Blennerhassett, see V. CONZEMIUS, *Charlotte Lady Blennerhassett. Die Bildungsjahre einer liberalen Katholikin*, in *Zeitschrift für bayerische Landesgeschichte* 44 (1981) 723-788, esp. pp. 728-736.

37. More details on his death in V. CONZEMIUS, *Der Tod Ignaz v. Döllingers in den Briefen der Freunde*, in *Kurtrierisches Jahrbuch* 8 (1968) 300-316.

1904-1906, in connexion with the Exeter Diocesan Church Reading Society, he gave three series of lectures which were later collected under the title, *English Church History*. They treated of a critical period, namely the time of the Reformation. In these lectures Plummer discussed the continuity of the Church of England throughout the various experiments which it underwent. In the introduction to the second series he strongly contended that the continuity of the Church of England was not broken and that the English Church of Archbishop Parker and Elizabeth was the same Church as that of Archbishop Warham and Henry VIII.[38] Plummer analysed the notion 'continuity' and made a distinction between continuity in the use of the sacraments, in Church organization, and in doctrine. Only in this last form of continuity could a problem arise, but he still came to the conclusion that it was impossible to prove that, at the Reformation, the Church of England abandoned anything that was essential to the Christian faith and that, consequently, there was any real breach.

In 1910 *The Church in England in the Eighteenth Century* appeared. In it Plummer treated of the Church's further fortunes and its continuing fidelity to the primitive Church. In the same period (April 1910-August 1911), he published articles in *The Churchman* under the title, *Some Chapters in the History of the Early Church*. They were collected in *The Churches in Britain before A.D. 1000*. Perhaps the most important point is his endeavour, in the tradition of Anglo-Catholicism, to point out the difference between the 'British Church' and the 'English Church'. The 'British Church' is several centuries older than the 'English Church'. The 'English Church' was founded by missionaries from Rome, although Christianity was present in Britain before that. He also opposed the presupposition that the 'English Church' was at some time founded by the English State and that therefore the State has the rights of a founder over that which it had once created. He called this "a strange inversion of historical truth", since the English Church existed long before the English State.[39]

In July 1911 Plummer gave four lectures in Oxford which also appeared in abbreviated form in *The Churchman* (October 1911-May 1912). In these he expanded his view of the Reformation, as can be seen in the revised text which appeared in book form in 1912, *The Continental Reformation in Germany, France and Switzerland, from the Birth of Luther to the Death of Calvin*. The book had grown out of his anxiety about the threat of the ever increasing divisions and antagonisms within Christendom. He, therefore, tried to ascertain the causes which produced and deepened the divisions. He took as his

38. *English Church History*, vol. I, 1905, p. vii (see Plummer bibliography, p. XLIX).
39. *The Churches in Britain before A.D. 1000*, vol. I, 1911, p. x.

starting point the idea that prejudice is born of "ignorance of the faults of our own side and ignorance of the just claims which can be made by those who differ from us".[40] It was an attempt to reach a correct appreciation of the impact of the Reformation.

More important, perhaps, than his own historical publications were Plummer's translations of three of Döllinger's works. Most probably one of the reasons for Plummer's first visit to the scholar of Munich in 1870 was his plan to translate one of Döllinger's books. During a walk on August 2, they decided that the *Papstfabeln* were best suited for translation. The translation appeared in 1871 under the title, *Fables respecting the Popes in the Middle Ages*. Two years later *Prophecies and the Prophetic Spirit in the Christian Era* appeared. This was a translation of Döllinger's article, *Der Weissagungsglaube und das Prophetentum in der christlichen Zeit*, that had been published in 1871 in the *Historisches Taschenbuch*. Finally, in 1876, the translation of *Hyppolytus und Callistus* appeared, one of Döllinger's most important historical works. All these translations were of an exceptionally high quality. Plummer not only provided them with extensive introductions, but he also added numerous explanatory notes, margin titles, and detailed tables of contents. Moreover, he enhanced every book with various appendices in which he offered additional information or himself expanded the discussion on the topic treated.

Even though in earlier years several of Döllinger's works had already been translated into English, Plummer's translations made a decisive contribution to the wide-ranging familiarity Döllinger's historical works achieved in England, and this precisely during the crucial period of his conflict with Rome. Newman, who knew no German, came in contact with his work via these translations. But particularly among Anglicans there was a growing appreciation of Döllinger. Gladstone, who visited Döllinger in 1845, 1874 and 1886 in Munich, spoke of him in 1874 as "a most remarkable man" and wrote to his wife: "I know no one with whose mode of viewing and handling religious matters I more cordially agree".[41] Gladstone had words of praise for the book on *The Infallibility of the Church*, written by the Irish theologian George Salmon, but had to recognize that the author "touches much ground trodden by Dr. Döllinger; almost invariably agreeing with him".[42] Salmon himself had written of *Hippolytus and Callistus* that he knew of no more interesting and informative work on Early Church history.[43] Arthur Penrhyn Stanley, Dean of

---

40. *The Continental Reformation*, 1912, p. viii.

41. Quoted in J. MORLEY, *The Life of William Ewart Gladstone*, vol. II, London/New York, 1903, p. 513 (letter of Sept. 1874).

42. *Ibid.*, vol. III, p. 417 (letter to Acton, dated April 28, 1889).

43. G. SALMON, *The Infallibility of the Church. A Course of Lectures Delivered in the Divinity School of the University of Dublin*, London, ²1890, p. 392.

Westminster, kept in mind Döllinger's judgment that theology had as task to "transform her mission from a mission of polemics into a mission of irenics".[44] It was perhaps Dean Church who best represented Döllinger's influence in England when, after Döllinger's death, he wrote to Gladstone: "What a place he filled in Christendom, and how great is the emptiness now that he is gone. I hardly know anything in Church history like his position: so inflexible in his faithfulness, and so utterly free from the taint of self-will or self-assertion. It is worth many martyrdoms".[45]

The German Church historian, who against his will became the central figure in the schism in his own Church, was viewed in the Church of England as a promotor of the reunification of Churches. Plummer himself adopted the conviction of his teacher Döllinger that a clear and unembarassed view of the Church's history can eliminate many prejudices. As late as 1915 he wrote in *The Expository Times* a plea in favour of *Christian Agnosticism*. By agnosticism he meant a philosophy which was the opposite of a dogmatizing tendency to make revealed truths of theological opinions. "What *is* urged is, that in all cases in which certainty is unattainable, it is our duty to abstain from condemning other Christians for not thinking as we do respecting them".[46] Plummer illustrated this view with references to the discussions during the Bonn Reunion Conferences 40 years earlier. A reading of the *Conversations* makes clear that he received this conviction from Döllinger himself.

Plummer's manuscript of the *Conversations with Dr. Döllinger* consists of four notebooks each of approximately 120 pages measuring 18 × 23 cm. This text formed the basis for the *Recollections of Dr. Döllinger*, an extensive article that Plummer published in 1890 in *The Expositor*. In this article Plummer wrote that his recollections were no mere reminiscences but a compilation from memoranda which had been written for the most part within a few hours of his discussions with Döllinger. The transcription of the loose notes in the notebooks took place most likely in the years 1890-1891, thus almost contemporaneously with the *Expositor* article.[47]

---

44. Quoted in R.E. PROTHERO and G.G. BRADLEY, *The Life and Correspondence of Arthur Penrhyn Stanley, D.D., Late Dean of Westminster*, vol. II, London, ³1894, p. 243.

45. Quoted in B.A. SMITH, *Dean Church. The Anglican Response to Newman*, London/New York/Toronto, 1958, p. 301 (letter dated Jan. 26, 1890).

46. *Christian Agnosticism*, in *ExpT* 27 (1915-16) 198-204, p. 204.

47. Two printed text are glued at the beginning of vol. I, unmistakably proof-sheets of the *Expositor* article. Since at the end of vol. IV references are made to events occurring in 1890, it is obvious that a considerable share of this part was written after the above mentioned article appeared.

The greater part of the *Expositor* article is a nearly literal copy of the manuscript. However, minor changes have been made: words were nuanced, some sentences were altered for stylistic reasons, persons whose names are mentioned in the manuscript were omitted or referred to via the letter X—apparently out of discretion since most were Englishmen (Acton, Liddon...)—, data were added for purposes of clarification.

Whereas the *Conversations* present the discussions in a purely chronological order, in *The Expositor* the material is organised thematically under five subject headings: 1. The Vatican Council, 2. Roman Difficulties, 3. English Topics, 4. Continental Topics, 5. Biographical. This method obviously made possible a synthetic overview of the themes treated. Moreover, Plummer also used his publication to include complementary information. In this way it provided explanations of Bishop Clifford, of Hefele's view of papal infallibility, of Döllinger's work method, etc.[48]

On the other hand, such thematic treatment had the great disadvantage that material which did not fall under one of the above mentioned headings was omitted in *The Expositor*. The chief omissions are undoubtedly the reflections on the Old Catholics and on the Bonn Reunion Conferences of 1874 and 1875, important subjects extensively treated in the manuscript. Also missing are the numerous references to time and place, some of which concern Loyson, Theiner and the Vatican Archives, Frohschammer, Döllinger's works and planned translations, the international situation, certain exegetical and historical questions, a number of letters and reports about Döllinger's last activities and death, as well as a few letters which Döllinger himself wrote to Plummer.

As far as the contents of the manuscript are concerned, Plummer noted with extreme care numerous data which evoke the spirit of the period in Bavaria. There are comments regarding the existing tendency toward Bavarian independence and the opposition to the German Empire. Views are exchanged on such topics as the concordat with Austria, the Bavarian Church-State relationship, clerical influence on elections, the Franco-Prussian War, etc. We learn of Döllinger's opinion of the Bavarian government's position on the question of mixed marriages and on the policy pursued by the various kings.[49] In

---

48. The most important additions are included in our notes to the text of the *Conversations*.

49. In the period which preceded the declaration of the dogma of papal infallibility, the Bavarian authorities were attentive to Döllinger's opinion. For additional data, see D. ALBRECHT, *Döllinger, die bayerische Regierung und das erste Vatikanische Konzil*, in K. REPGEN and S. SKALWEIT (eds.), *Spiegel der Geschichte. Festgabe für Max Braubach zum 10. April 1964*, Münster, 1964, pp. 795-815.

addition to data on political life, much information about the University of Munich can be found in Plummer's notes.

Of course, the *Conversations* also provide rich data about Döllinger himself. Scattered throughout the 400 page long text we meet noteworthy details which present us with a picture of the life-style and views of the professor of Munich as Plummer experienced him.

Döllinger led a disciplined life. His study required him to spend many hours behind his desk reading, taking notes, composing texts. Yet he maintained the custom of taking a walk every evening, regardless of the weather. When Plummer — or another — was his guest, it was during such walks that views were exchanged on the most diversified of subjects. Döllinger demonstrated a lively interest in ecclesiastical and political life, not only in his own surroundings, but also in England, as was the case with the question of auricular confession which was much discussed among Anglicans at that time. He also had a deep concern for the Eastern Churches. In such discussions he continually returned to the need for a thorough knowledge of the history of the ancient Church and a feeling for the evolution of this history in order to understand better the relative way in which certain situations had arisen.

At home he lived a very simple life. He wandered about or sat in his library wearing slippers and a little jacket. His books were his great treasure. With pride he led his visitors through his library which in fact consisted of a series of small rooms opening into one another. Plummer refers several times to Döllinger's great ability to assimilate and to the lively interest he maintained until shortly before his death. He continued to follow the progress of historical studies as well as the state of scientific research concerning much discussed questions. After his death three cupboards were found full of notebooks and folders containing loose notes which he had collected. Professor Reusch, who examined all the contents, came to the conclusion that nothing of all that was there was ready for publication.

The contacts which Plummer maintained with Döllinger belong to the period when the scholar of Munich had been ostracized by the Church. That he did not submit was the consequence of the inner evolution he had undergone. He had become convinced that a scientific approach was totally lacking in Church disciplines and thus, to the scientists' great agitation, anomalous travesties were maintained with unbelievable naivety. In his discussions with Plummer he repeatedly referred to his disappointing visit to Rome in 1857. The people in the curia did not show the least interest in Church affairs or theological questions. It seemed impossible to have any serious discussion with them. When he mentioned the need for a critical edition of the acts from the Council of Trent, no one bothered to react. The Italian character did not agree with him. It was too exterior, too superficial, too vague. The curia was dominated by a climate of mistrust and suspicion.

Döllinger's experience during this stay in Rome was extremely negative and continued to find an echo in his conversations with Plummer. This negative attitude to a certain extent appears one-sided. Thus the role which he attributes to the Jesuits results from an over-simplification of the facts. An incorrect interpretation of papal infalli-bility is given when he says: "Now at one stroke all the persecuting bulls were made infallible" (1875, p. 132). The internal tensions and conflicts in the Roman Catholic Church are emphasized, and in some cases rumour forms the only basis for such emphasis. An example of such is the reference to the Irish bishop MacHale who, as Plummer says, "makes no secret of the fact that he does not accept the dogma and that his conviction of its untruth remains quite unshaken" (p. 84). In fact we know MacHale himself declared that he did not dispute the truth of the dogma but the opportuneness of its declaration.

From Plummer's manuscript we can see Döllinger's growing dislike of Pius IX. This dislike runs through his notes like a coloured thread. We learn how Döllinger was disturbed by the rash manner in which the Pope declared canonizations, favoured popular devotions which, in Döllinger's eyes, had no adequate theological foundation, and how especially he reproached him for his ignorance of history. Döllinger believed that the Pope's influence on Church life hindered the freedom of scientific research. By proclaiming Alphonsus Liguori *Doctor Eccle-siae* in 1871, the Pope had bound the Church to a particular theological school. Döllinger found the manner in which philosophy was taught a disgrace and rejected the identification of theology with scholasticism.

Plummer's notes clearly show that it was a continuing annoyance for Döllinger to see how the curia consisted for the most part of poorly educated men who played up to the Pope in order to enjoy his good graces or to further their careers. He was allergic to the Vatican world where fear of science reigned. Rather, he favoured thorough German scholarship as opposed to this southern mentality of superficiality.

In all this, Plummer reflects faithfully the ideas of his German friend, never really takes a critical position, and gives the impression that he always agrees with him. In comparison with Plummer, the judgment Lord Acton wrote of Döllinger is more thorough and above all more nuanced. Still, in Plummer's favour it must also be said that he included a summary of Acton's article in *The English Historical Review* at the end of his manuscript (pp. 247-263).

In this regard one can pose the question as to how far Plummer's *Conversations* agree with our opinion concerning Döllinger's member-

ship of the Old Catholic Church. Nowhere in his conversations with
Plummer did Döllinger ever express himself explicitly on this issue
in one sense or another. Judging from comments made over a period
of time, several points can be stated with relative certainty. Firstly,
Döllinger never seemed to have any intention of abondoning Catholicism. He considered the Old Catholic Church in Holland completely orthodox and its priests validly ordained, but Plummer received the
impression that Döllinger was not pleased to see Archbishop Loos
of Utrecht invited to Germany to administer confirmation to Old Catholic children. He was equally disinclined to participate in the congress
the Old Catholics had planned for September 20-22, 1872, in Cologne.
He feared "a great deal of phrasemaking" (p. 75), which would not
contribute to solving the central question. Even though he had no
principle objection to a married clergy, he found the Old Catholics'
intention to eliminate celibacy a step which would only widen the
divisions among the faithful.

One of the two nieces who cared for Döllinger during the last
years of his life remarked to Plummer, after her uncle's death, how
terrible it was that at his funeral "every confession was represented,
except his own" (p. 238). By this she meant, of course, the Roman
Catholic Church, which at the same time shows that she also continued
to consider him Catholic. Rome had rejected him and he felt "isolated"
precisely because he refused to join the Old Catholics. He even
warned them not to set up a schismatic Church.

A second point complements the first. Döllinger identified himself
with the Old Catholic Church insofar as the latter refused to accept
the infallibility of the Pope as an article of Catholic faith. Even though
he did not go so far as, for example, Friedrich or Reusch and refused
to join the Old Catholic Church, he still mentioned to a friend his
wish that, should something happen to him, Friedrich would administer
the last sacraments. When in 1879 his submission to Rome was
rumoured, he had Nevin publish a letter in England in which he
stated that these rumours were without foundation. Also during the
Reunion Conferences in Bonn he considered himself as a member of
the group of Old Catholics who as such negotiated with the English
and Americans on the one hand, and with the Orientals on the other.

That Döllinger did not want a schism in the Church can perhaps
be most clearly proved from his intention in organizing these Reunion
Conferences. He hoped to be able to prepare the way for a union
of the Old Catholics with the English and Eastern Churches. All three
were opposed to Rome's claims. Perhaps he thought that by finding
a common ground it would also be easier for them to dialogue with
Rome, but he never said this in so many words. Professor Reusch
was the host in Bonn, but Döllinger was really responsible for the

initiative and animation, and despite his age he showed a surprising amount of energy. He presided as chairman, addressed individual groups, and led meetings. The English side was well represented. Plummer mentions, among others, Liddon, Talbot, and Bishop Browne of Winchester. Among the Old Catholics he mentions Bishop Reinkens. The absence of eminent Protestant theologians was regretted. A few representatives of the Eastern Churches came. However, negotiations were very difficult — especially with regard to the *Filioque*. At the end of the first conference, Döllinger was still rather optimistic. Thanks to the Vatican decree on infallibility, the common ground shared by the Churches was taken into account, and it became more clear than ever that closer bonds were desirable.

Plummer's comments on Döllinger's opening lecture at the second conference confirm the observation of this causal connection between the decree on infallibility and the struggle toward reunification on the grounds of common tradition dating from the first centuries. Döllinger explained extensively how the idea of infallibility came into existence and grew in the Church. However, the difficulties increased, and in 1876 it was impossible to organize a third conference. Plummer summarized the reasons for breaking off negotiations : "1. The troubled state of the East, where some of the bishops were taking part in political struggle. 2. The divisions among the Orientals themselves. [...] 3. The mischief done by Overbeck, who has been working to prevent any union of Orientals with Anglicans. 4. The mischief done by Dr. Pusey in the line which he had taken on the *Filioque*" (p. 146). We cannot shake off the impression that Döllinger saw in the end that he was working for a hopeless cause. As a theologian, he stood powerless before this situation of disunity.[50]

The notes which Plummer made day and night after every conversation with Döllinger over a period of twenty years, on the one hand confirm what was already known of the tragedy of Döllinger's life. On the other hand they provide numerous complementary details on the situation of the man who did not feel himself able to submit to the dogma of infallibility.

One could pose a number of questions here. For example, how can it be explained that other known Catholic intellectuals of this period reacted to the dogma in a manner so completely different from Döllinger? This is especially noticeable in Newman's case. Yet both men had much in common. Both stood open to such values as free-

---

50. Döllinger also seems to have spoken to Friedrich along these lines : "Wir Theologen haben das unserige gethan; es kommt jetzt darauf an, wie die kirchlichen Authoritäten sich dazu stellen werden; aber die einen thun nichts aus gewohnter Indolenz, die anderen aus politischen Rücksichten", J. FRIEDRICH, *Ignaz von Döllinger* (see n. 3), vol. III, pp. 649-650.

dom, modern culture, science. They had a feeling for criticism and had had to suffer for their convictions. It is especially thanks to the abundant correspondence between Plummer and Newman that we come to know something of the different attitudes of the two men.[51] Plummer, who had a good relationship with both Döllinger and Newman, served as an intermediary between the two scholars. From his letters, we have the impression that Döllinger let himself be led exclusively by scientific historical thoughts and that history was for him the only measure of all theological questions. Where Döllinger showed signs of a certain bitterness, Newman pointed out to Plummer that one may not turn infallibility into a breaking point and that the decree of 1870 could be relativized: "I marvel that he [Döllinger] should so set his judgment against so very vague a definition as that which passed the Council—In the first place it says that the Pope has the Church's infallibility, but that infallibility has never been defined or explained—then it says that the Pope is infallible, when he speaks ex cathedrâ, but what ex cathedrâ is has never been defined. Nor can it be said that this is special pleading, because the definition would not have passed unless it had been so vague—and it is an acknowledged principle of the Church that 'Odiosa restringenda sunt,' as the wording of a law. The Ultras aimed at far more, and were disappointed because they could not get more. Even Gallicans say that *under certain circumstances* the Pope is infallible. Of course I do not defend the *way* in which it was passed, but other Councils were worse".[52]

Newman further drew upon his theology of the development of Christian doctrine as he had presented it in his essay in 1845. Later Councils could provide interpretations of earlier ones. He admitted that a certain group had succeeded in imposing its opinion on the Council and he regretted this, but he was convinced that later Councils would clarify and complement the matter: "Pius is not the last of the Popes—the fourth Council modified the third, the fifth the fourth.

51. Forty of Newman's letters to Plummer (written between April 22, 1870, and July 1, 1888) were published by F.L. CROSS, *John Henry Newman. With a Set of Unpublished Letters* (The Tractarian Series), London, 1933, pp. 164-182. Since then they appeared in *The Letters and Diaries of John Henry Newman*, vols. XXV-XXXI. A German translation of the fragments relating to Döllinger was published by H. FRIES as an appendix to *Newman und Döllinger*, in *Newman-Studien* 1 (1948) 29-76, pp. 66-76. A comparison of Newman's and Döllinger's views on papal infallibility can be found in W. KLAUSNITZER, *Päpstliche Unfehlbarkeit bei Newman und Döllinger. Ein historisch-systematischer Vergleich* (Innsbrucker theologische Studien, 6), Innsbruck/Vienna/Munich, 1980; see also R. BÄUMER, *John Henry Newman und Ignaz von Döllinger. Der ungleiche Gewissenskonflikt zweier führender Theologen anläßlich der Unfehlbarkeitsdefinition*, in *Newman-Studien* 11 (1980) 32-46.

52. *Letters and Diaries*, vol. XXV, p. 301.

[...] The late definition does not so much need to be undone, as to be completed. [...] I know that a violent reckless party, had it its will, would at this moment define that the Pope's powers need no safeguards, no explanations — but there is a limit to the triumph of the tyrannical — Let us be patient, let us have faith, and a new Pope, and a re-assembled Council may trim the boat".[53]

Newman spoke a prophetic word when he predicted to Plummer that the Old Catholics would go further than Döllinger himself ever approved of and that he would, in the end, feel isolated and less related to those with whom he was obliged to be associated than with those whom he had left. To this he added: "he has taken a wrong course, and has got the Catholic world against him — and whatever be the sins, the intrigues, the cruelties of individuals, Securus judicat orbis terrarum".[54]

The primary accusation which Newman directs against Döllinger seems to have been that he placed himself too exclusively on an historical plane. He wanted to deal with Rome chiefly as historian. According to Newman, the decree on infallibility had become a bogey which obsessed him more than he liked to admit. He saw it as the result of a manipulated Council, something irreconcileable with his stern historical conviction. The collision resulted in an excommunication which Newman regretted, because he also knew that numerous intrigues had played a role in the process of the Council. His letters to Plummer allow no room for doubt in this matter. As early as January 15, he wrote: "the case is quite tragic. [...] I do not deny that the *proceedings* constitute a grave scandal — and that some one will have to answer for it".[55] He spoke of a "cruel trial"[56] and repeated in another letter that Döllinger "has been cruelly dealt with — and a nemesis is likely to come for it".[57] But Newman, who was never a man of extremes, was, more than Döllinger, a theologian who had a wider concept of Church and, moreover, believed that more should be taken into consideration in life than historical criticism. During the Council he had written to Lady Chatterton that he hoped that the promulgation of the dogma would not take place, — it was a superfluous luxury and did not correspond to any necessity, but "If it takes place, I shall say that Providence has ways and purposes for His Church, which at present are hid from our eyes".[58]

It is unmistakable that Newman and Döllinger approached the

53. *Letters and Diaries*, vol. XXV, p. 310.
54. *Ibid.*, vol. XXVI, p. 120.
55. *Ibid.*, vol. XXV, p. 269.
56. *Ibid.*, vol. XXV, p. 308.
57. *Ibid.*, vol. XXVI, p. 120.
58. *Ibid.*, vol. XXV, p. 23.

ecclesiastical problems in totally diverse ways. Döllinger criticized repeatedly Newman's lack of historical knowledge and thought very little of his theory on the development of dogma. He perhaps formulated this criticism most sharply in a letter to Lady Blennerhassett. According to Döllinger, Newman's theory was Darwinism transplanted to religion with one difference: for Darwin the ape evolved to man while for Newman man degenerated to ape.[59] Such extreme expressions are not found in the *Conversations*, but a similar judgment of Newman's vision is presented in a milder form. Döllinger posits that Newman, had he known history better, could not have held the opinion that the Majority at the Council had right on its side (p. 80). And on his theory of development it is suggested that, since the Council, it could be used to make the continuity of the new dogma with earlier tradition acceptable (p. 172). When Plummer notes such negative expressions about Newman in the *Conversations*, it may be assumed that in this he is the mouthpiece of Döllinger.[60]

It is clear that Newman's letters provide a supplement to what Plummer himself wrote in his *Conversations*. They show that Döllinger's standpoint, however much he may have been convinced of his own righteousness, was in the final account perhaps insufficiently nuanced and was, furthermore, the end result of an evolution which had already begun in the 1860's. That, despite an honest generosity, he was to a certain extent bitter at the end of his life, is partly to be explained by the manner in which he had been treated. In Plummer's *Conversations* we find a clear expression of this bitterness and this negative attitude. Döllinger's scientific honesty cannot be doubted. But he seems to have lacked the openness to surmount his historical objections, to view the total event in a broader context, and to interpret it from within a viewpoint grounded in deeper faith.

---

59. "N[ewman] ist ein ungemein geistreicher und dabei tief religiöser Mann, schreibt vortrefflich, aber seine Einsichten in die Kirchengeschichte sind gar zu mangelhaft, und mit seiner theory of development verpflanzt er den Darwinismus in die Religion, nur daß wenn Darwin den Affen bis zum Caucasischen Menschen sich fortbilden läßt, bei Newman umgekehrt der Mensch allmälich zum Affen herabsinkt", I. v. Döllinger-Ch. Lady Blennerhassett, *Briefwechsel 1865-1886*, pp. 597-598 (letter dated Feb. 20, 1875). See also V. Conzemius, *Acton, Döllinger and Gladstone: A Strange Variety of Anti-infallibilists*, in J.D. Bastable (ed.), *Newman and Gladstone. Centennial Essays*, Dublin, 1978, pp. 39-55. For Döllinger's own theory of development, see J. Speigl, *Traditionslehre und Traditionsbeweis in der historischen Theologie Ignaz Döllingers* (Beiträge zur neueren Geschichte der katholischen Theologie, 5), Essen, 1964, pp. 67-117.

60. Plummer himself gave a more balanced typification of Newman's and Döllinger's positions in a review of the *Briefe und Erklärungen*, published in 1890 in *The Critical Review* (reprinted in appendix, pp. 264-267).

ALFRED PLUMMER (1841-1926)

NEW TESTAMENT COMMENTATOR

The bibliography of the works of Alfred Plummer* testifies to his prolific industry as an exegete of the New Testament. He published commentaries on twenty of its twenty seven books. In several instances during his long writing career, he returned more than once to the same text. But even when writing simple guides to scripture for school students, he did not compromise the exacting standards of sober scholarship which he set himself. He was in his own day more widely appreciated for his patriotically Anglican summaries of Church History and his translations of the works of I. von Döllinger, but he was first and foremost a New Testament commentator.

Plummer's most distinguished contribution to the advancement of biblical research was his editorship along with S.R. Driver and C.A. Briggs of the *International Critical Commentary*, and his authorship of three substantial volumes, which with his commentary on Matthew we shall consider in more detail below. One need merely mention the names of some of those whose collaboration was enlisted for the *ICC* to appreciate the enduring significance of the series: Bernard (The Fourth Gospel); Burton (Galatians); Sanday and Headlam (Romans); Moffatt (Hebrews); Ropes (James); Brooke (The Johannine Epistles) and Charles (Revelation). Following the traditions of nineteenth century classical scholarship, it paid particular attention to questions of philology, textual criticism and literary parallels. Within its own limitations, it was difficult to surpass and has indeed outlived many other commentary series, even those which adopted a more radical stance on critical issues than usually was congenial to the contributors to the *ICC*[1].

Nevertheless, Alfred Plummer is a surprisingly neglected figure in the history of New Testament scholarship. He is not mentioned at all in the standard English survey of this field[2] nor in more popular studies[3]. Catholic encyclopedias published in the USA and continental

---

* See pp. XLVII-LI.

1. *Dictionnaire de la Bible, Supplément* 8/42 (1967) 40-41, c. 41: 'Plummer témoigne de toutes les qualités propres à l'*International Critical Commentary*, qui, en raison surtout de ses précieuses notes philologiques, garde encore sa valeur, même si nombre de positions adoptées sont à l'heure actuelle dépassées' (CH. SOUTWOOD).

2. *The Cambridge History of the Bible*. Vol. 3: *The West from the Reformation to the Present Day*, ed. S.L. GREENSLADE, Cambridge, 1963.

3. E.g. S. NEILL, *The Interpretation of the New Testament 1861-1961*, Oxford, 1966.

Europe[4] have begun to afford him belated recognition, but apart from the silent tribute of frequent reference in the footnotes of later exegesis, his work as a whole remains comparatively unknown and unassessed.

Several factors help to account for this neglect. After a short period in Oxford as Fellow and Dean of Trinity College[5] he spent the rest of his working life at the new university of Durham. Founded in 1832, it had yet to achieve the reputation, not least in the field of Theology, which it has subsequently won. Plummer was under no illusion as to the callibre of the students in his charge[6] and yet he remained devoted to Durham and to University College whose Master he was from 1874 till a rather early retirement in 1902, at the age of sixty one. While others, like his exact contemporary William Sanday, used Durham as a stepping stone back to Oxford or Cambridge, Plummer stayed and his academic isolation deprived him of the opportunity to influence the new generation of biblical scholars. During this period also, the University of Durham was overshadowed by the Episcopal establishment which had created it, and in particular by its two most illustrious incumbents, J.B. Lightfoot (1879-89) and B.F. Westcott (1890-1901). In order to fulfil the requirements of his Oxford fellowship, Plummer had become an Anglican deacon in 1866, but he felt no calling to the priesthood and was never ordained. Thus ecclesiastically as well as academically he remained on the margin.

Another factor, related less to the circumstances of Plummer's own career than to the general temper of the period, should be mentioned. The development of higher criticism of the New Testament in Germany, associated above all with the Tübingen school, broke onto the insular English scene in 1860 with the publication of *Essays and Reviews*[7]. Behind the somewhat confused liberalism of that collection, the threat

---

4. See *New Catholic Encyclopedia* 9 (1967) 445 (T.C. CROWLEY) and *Dictionnaire de la Bible* (see above n. 3). Brief articles on Plummer may also be found in *The New Schaff-Herzog Encyclopaedia of Religious Knowledge* 9 (1911) 94; *Enciclopedia Italiana* 27 (1935) 555 and *Enciclopedia Universal Ilustrada* 45 (1921) 883. But, significantly, no article on Plummer is to be found in the British *Dictionary of National Biography* or the *Encyclopaedia Britannica*.

5. One of his pupils during this period, who later distinguished himself as Archbishop of Canterbury, Randall Davidson, records a frank, if rather unflattering, impression of Plummer: 'a pleasant, jovial, round-faced, dark individual with bushy whiskers and considerable ideas of his own dignity. I do not think much of his Bible lectures.' Cf. G. BELL, *Randall Davidson, Archbishop of Canterbury*, London, 1938, vol. i, p. 21.

6. Plummer prefaced one of his lectures with these words: 'There are a good many men who come up here from time to time with considerable industry but very little brains, and we are all very sorry, of course, but they are ploughed. There are also a large number who come up with very fair ability, but they won't work. Unfortunately there is a third class of men who for some reason or other make Durham their Alma Mater, who have no brains and won't work either.' Quoted by C.E. WHITING, *The University of Durham 1832-1932*, London, 1932, p. 158.

7. See S. NEILL, *op. cit.*, pp. 29-32.

of destructive historical criticism was sharply perceived. In the following thirty years, a rational defence of traditional claims concerning Christian origins and the dating and authorship of the New Testament writings, began to emerge through the work of three Cambridge academics in particular. Lightfoot and Westcott, later to be elevated to the episcopate as we have seen, and, perhaps the most original scholar of the three, F.J.A. Hort. The tenor of the Cambridge School was intelligent conservatism, and Plummer was very much of the same cast of mind. But he came a generation too late! By the time his major works were appearing the situation had changed. His conservatism now appeared timid and old-fashioned. Whereas the Cambridge trio were celebrated as champions of orthodoxy and sound learning, Plummer, their inferior in neither respect, was passed over and eclipsed. Arguably, he lacked Lightfoot's powers of historical synthesis, Westcott's spiritual sensitivity and systematic breadth and Hort's philosophical depth, but as a practitioner of the art of scholarly exegesis he was their worthy successor.

The Commentary on Luke

Plummer's commentary on St Luke's Gospel of 1896 was the fruit of many years reflection and lonely research. It first took shape in the form of lectures delivered at Durham, which proceeded at a snail's pace, covering about two chapters of the Gospel a year, and, it is reported, trying the patience of his audience[8]. The resulting mass of material was severely pruned by the author himself, acting in his capacity as editor of the series and conscious of the conflict between his two roles (p. ii). He also laments the lack of a second pair of eyes to help with the proof-reading, and the first edition, as he feared, was marred by a large number of minor typographical errors[9].

In his *Preface* Plummer disclaims pretensions to originality. But it would be unjust to take his modesty at its face value, and underestimate the innovative aspect of the Luke commentary. Comparison with the contemporary *ICC* volume on Mark[10] shows clearly that minutely detailed exegesis of the Greek text was not yet to be expected from English scholars working on the Synoptics. Despite the precedents set by Westcott's commentaries on the Fourth Gospel (1881) and Hebrews (1889) there was still resistance to the method's being applied to a gospel like Luke's. It arose perhaps from an unspoken assumption

---

8. See C.E. WHITING, *op. cit.*, p. 158: 'To the man who wished to get through an examination and nothing else, these lectures were a subject of grumbling; but the men who were really keen learned something of scholarly method in his meticulous examination of every word of Holy Writ.'

9. See the review article in the *Church Quarterly Review* 45 (1897-8) 409-427, p.419.

10. E.P. GOULD, *The Gospel according to St. Mark* (ICC), Edinburgh, 1896.

that, while an element of personal style and theological perspective could safely be admitted in the case of John or the writer to the Hebrews, the Synoptic tradition was exempt from any such idiosyncracies. Continental scholars, like Meyer and Godet, had pioneered a more exacting linguistic approach, and English translations of their work had recently appeared[11] but Plummer's *Luke* indigenized and extended it.

The little merit which Plummer did claim for his commentary, he summarised as follows (p. iii):

> If the commentary has any special features, they will perhaps be found in the illustrations taken from Jewish writings, in the abundance of references to the Septuagint and to Acts and other books of the NT, in the frequent quotations of renderings in the Latin versions, and in the attention which has been paid, both in the Introduction and throughout the Notes, to the marks of St Luke's style.

It may be convenient to comment briefly on these features, and on three other aspects of the *Luke* commentary, which he does not mention, textual criticism, source-criticism, and the relation between the exegesis of Scripture and Christian doctrine.

(i) As Plummer was quick to perceive, the discovery and publication of Jewish pseudepigrapha[12] was the most important new development in Gospel research of his day. These documents are 'now among the most promising helps towards understanding the New Testament,' he wrote (p. iii). No expert himself in paleography or near eastern languages, he was naturally drawn to the more accessible Greek texts like the Testament of the XII Patriarchs. Observing the many literary parallels between this work and the Synoptic Gospels, he explained them by common use of the Old Testament, or the dependence of the pseudepigraphical texts upon the canonical[13]. Nevertheless, he recognised the relevance of the material for understanding the language and thought-world of the Gospel tradition, and in this respect he was, without perhaps being fully aware of all its ramifications, prophetic of a movement in biblical research which was to gather pace in the twentieth century.

(ii) The frequency of reference in the *Luke* commentary to the LXX, Acts and the other writings of the NT, has a double function. It serves

---

11. H.A.W. MEYER, *Kritisch-exegetischer Kommentar über das Neue Testament. Markus und Lukas*, Göttingen, 1846, E. Tr., Edinburgh, 1880. (Plummer recommends the revisions of Meyer by B. and J. Weiss, 1885, etc.); F. GODET, *Commentaire sur l'Evangile de S. Luc*, Neuchâtel, 1871, E. Tr., Edinburgh, 1879.

12. With its (eventual) result in the Oxford edition of 1913, *Apocrypha and Pseudepigrapha of the Old Testament*, vol. II, ed. R.H. CHARLES.

13. Plummer developed this argument against the opposite view held by Charles, in a disproportionately lengthy section of his *Introduction to Matthew*, pp. xxxiv-xlvi.

to establish the common stock of linguistic data, both lexical and syntactic, to which Luke's Greek belongs; and it forms the basis of comparison and differentiation for detecting the peculiarities of Luke's own style. Plummer was conscious of the risk in exegesis of too much subtlety in grammatical analysis. 'Grammar' as he alleged of Meyer's Kommentar could 'sometimes be ridden to death' (p.lxxxiv), and the same accusation was levelled at him by the reviewer in the *Church Quarterly Review* [14]. But whatever may be the merits of the fine distinctions Plummer occasionally draws between near synonyms, or of his discussion of notorious *cruces* such as Lk i, 35 or vii, 47, his method was the correct one, attending to usage in context and placing it against comparative study of usage in the same linguistic tradition. It is in this connection, we note, that Plummer emphasises the value of renderings in the Latin versions: 'the best commentary on the NT is the Vulgate' (p. iii). Perhaps his emphasis here is excessive, a reflection of his own early training in Classical Studies, and of the prestigious edition of the Vulgate by Wordsworth and White then in process of completion. But more often than not, it pays the expected dividend, for example Plummer's fine comment on 'soldiers' at Lk iii, 14 ('militantes' not 'milites').

   (iii) The most distinctive feature of Plummer's *Luke*, and the one which secured its continuing usefulness to a later generation of source-critics and redaction-critics of the Third Gospel, is its preoccupation with questions of style. Rather unguardedly in the preface (p. iv) he expressed the hope that his work might 'render those who use this commentary to a large extent independent of a concordance.' It would be wrong to interpret that remark to mean that word-statistics abstracted from a concordance can ever replace consideration of parallels in context and with proper regard for textual variants. But when Plummer's famous fractions of incidence (p. liv) are used in conjunction with the actual references he gives that danger is avoided. It is certainly the task of a commentator to activate the dormant information available in the concordance and evaluate it. Plummer retained in all this a firm grip on common sense. Although, for example, he held a conservative view of Lukan authorship by Paul's companion, 'the beloved physician', he did not entirely endorse the alluring theory of Hobart concerning Luke's medical language [15]. He pointed out with reason that 80% of the evidence quoted was to be found in the LXX, which is much more likely to be the Evangelist's source (p. lxiv). Or again, on the issue of Lukan semitisms, he was judicious. 'We are struck' he wrote (p. xlix) 'by two apparently opposite features, Luke's great command of Greek and his very un-Greek use of Hebrew phrases and constructions' — many of

14. Cf. above, n. 9, p. 418.
15. W. HOBART, *The Medical Language of St Luke*, Dublin, 1882.

which Plummer was the first to catalogue in detail (cf. e.g. p.45). He admitted the possibility, even probability, that Luke's sources have influenced him in the more semitically coloured passages, but he adds 'it may also be true that Luke has *allowed* his style to be Hebraistic, because he felt that such a style was appropriate to the subject matter.' The new avenue of enquiry which he here opened up, was explored by J.C. Hawkins in his *Horae Synopticae*, with due acknowledgement of his debt to Plummer[16], and through him has greatly influenced subsequent discussions of the Synoptic Problem.

(iv) Plummer's *Luke* contains a wealth of text critical information derived from the increasing resources then available, and his own, often convincing, judgments on variant readings. The Westcott and Hort edition of 1881 is used with respect, but not taken as the final word. The question of 'western non-interpolations', for instance, discussed *ad locos* and in an appendix (pp. 566-9) 'cannot be regarded as settled' (p.567). Plummer saw the importance of the recently discovered Sinaitic Syriac, which along with the old Latin, allows us to penetrate to a period earlier than that of the great uncials. The papyrus discoveries of the twentieth century have confirmed Plummer's estimate of the value of the early versions. He also began mutedly to doubt Westcott and Hort's view that conflate readings were invariably late (p.lxxiii). This doubt was to grow and lead eventually to the hypothesis of an early 'Caesarean' text type[17].

(v) The original plan was for the *ICC* to include a separate commentary on the Synopsis of the Four Gospels, entrusted to W. Sanday and W.C. Allen. For this reason, Plummer avoided detailed comment on the Synoptic Problem in his *Luke*. We can deduce from scattered remarks that he was aware of its great complexity, at the same time as lending qualified support to a form of Two Source theory. He was in particular uncertain whether Luke used the text of the Second Gospel in its present form, and whether the Sayings Source was one or more documents. Plummer noted percipiently that the degree of similarity in wording between Matthew and Luke is higher in the sayings themselves than in the surrounding narrative (p.xxvi) and he allowed the possibility that the same saying could have been spoken by Jesus on different occasions (p.316) but he judged that it was a rather 'violent hypothesis' (p.351) to use this as the sole explanation of the Q phenomenon. His inherent caution made him highly sceptical of our ability

---

16. Oxford, ²1909, p. viii, '... to Dr. Plummer's *Commentary on St. Luke*, which enabled me to add about fifteen entries to the list of 'words and phrases characteristic of' that Gospel' (Preface to the first edition, 1898). Whereas Hawkins' contribution is still celebrated, Plummer's is often entirely overlooked, cf. e.g. J. FITZMYER, *The Gospel According to Luke I-IX* (Anchor Bible), New York, 1981, pp.106-127.

17. Cf. B.H. STREETER, *The Four Gospels, a Study of Origins*, London, 1924, c.IV.

to reconstruct the Q source in detail. Plummer also drew attention in his commentary to the close similarity between Luke and John, but did not attempt to offer a literary explanation of it.

(vi) Finally, and more generally, we return again to the question of Plummer's conservatism. This was a scholarly rather than dogmatic prejudice. In an earlier article published in 1891 and anticipating developments in doctrinal studies represented by the Kenotic theory of Charles Gore, he wrote : [18]

> It is scarcely too much to say that misconceived reverence has been one of the chief impediments in the way of true ideas respecting both scripture and the Christ, and therefore of the God whom both of them reveal.

And again : 'In the whole history of human thought, it has never happened, and it never will happen that a question once raised has been settled or silenced *by authority*' (his emphasis). In the *Luke* commentary, he applies this principle consistently, even if he usually manages to reach reassuringly conservative conclusions. His objections to the opinions of those like Strauss and Renan whom he quotes is not that they are 'critical' but that their criticism is hasty and intemperate [19]. On the issue of whether we are obliged to believe in the Davidic authorship of Psalm cx, on the basis of Dominical authority (Lk xx, 42) he wrote revealingly (p. 472) :

> The authorship of the Psalm is a question of *criticism*; and nothing in the method of Christ's teaching or in the contents of Scripture generally, warrants us in believing that He here frees us from the duty of investigating a problem which is capable of being solved by our own industry and acuteness. We have no right to expect that Scripture will save us from the discipline of patient research by supplying us with infallible answers to questions of history, chronology, geology and the like.

In a sense the third Evangelist himself became Plummer's own model. Commenting on the Prologue (p. 5) he notes that here 'we have an inspired historian telling us in his inspired writings that he is giving us the results of careful investigation. From this it seems to follow that an inspired historian may fail in accuracy if his investigation is defective.' It would of course be easy to quote instances where piety and critical study sit uneasily together for Plummer, for example when trying to reconcile his belief in a personal and invisible devil, with the Gerasene incident (p. 228), but the spirit of the *Luke* commentary is one disinterested inquiry free of dogmatic prejudice [20].

18. *The Advance of Christ in* Σοφία, in *Expositor* 4th ser. 4 (1891) 1-14, p. 12f.

19. See Plummer's *Intemperate Criticism, some remarks*, Durham, 1877.

20. At Lk xxii,38 both Boniface VIII and Luther are reprimanded (even-handedly!) for their doctrines of the Two Swords. Cf. also the reference to Döllinger (p. 188) on the harmful effect of misinterpreting Lk vi, 35 as forbidding usury.

The obituary notice in the London *Times*[21] recorded that Plummer 'will be most widely remembered by the sound and scholarly commentaries that he wrote on many New Testament books, that on St Luke being the most outstanding.' Given the place of the *Luke* commentary in the history of English biblical scholarship, I take that to be a just estimate. But the obituarist allowed himself the licence of eulogy. By 1926, Plummer had been almost forgotten. The article continued : 'While widely read in the literature of New Testament criticism and a painstaking and accurate Greek student, he occupied a strongly conservative standpoint. But those who might differ from his conclusions had to admit that his intense human sympathy gave him an insight and interpretative power in handling the problems of the Gospels and Epistles sometimes lacking in more stringent critics.'

The Commentary on Matthew

The commentary on Matthew of 1909 was not part of the *ICC*, but a supplement to W. C. Allen's work published in that series two years before. This unusual circumstance might seem to imply a negative estimate of the work of his predecessor, and *ICC* appointee. But that is not the case. Plummer explains (p. vii) that the scope of Allen's work had been restricted to literary and source-critical matters, in the nomenclature of the period 'critical' rather than 'exegetical' questions. What he does not mention is that this was due to the fact, noted above, that Allen had originally been invited with Professor Sanday to prepare a commentary on the Synopsis for the *ICC*. When this plan was abandoned, Allen naturally used the material extensively in his *ICC* on Matthew. Thus Plummer undertook in an extra volume to cover other issues which had not received full treatment.

One unfortunate result of this was that Plummer did not feel entitled to include a full analysis of Matthean style comparable to his work on Luke's, though there are many valuable notes scattered through the volume. He detects for example the thoroughly Matthean character of xxviii,9-10 (p. 422), and in the Introduction (p. xxi) refers to Matthew's affinity for triplets[22], even apparently envisaging the possibility that Luke derived some of them from Matthew! But deference to Allen (p. xii) on these questions inhibited him from pursuing them further.

The scholarship and attention to detail in the *Matthew* commentary are the equal of that in *Luke*, particularly in the fields of philology and textual criticism, but it is not unfair to criticise Plummer for being somewhat out of touch with the way Synoptic research was developing.

---

21. *Times*, 20 April 1926, p. 18.
22. See M.D. GOULDER, *Midrash and Lection in Matthew*, London, 1974, p. 26, but without reference here or elsewhere to Plummer.

He refers once to J. Weiss and often to Wellhausen for minor points, but not in connection with the vital issues of the eschatology of the historical Jesus or the nature of the early Synoptic tradition. However, it *is* unfair to say that the *Matthew* commentary was more conservative than that on Luke[23]. Plummer did not defend apostolic authorship in the case of Matthew; the most he was willing to say was that the Apostle may have composed the Logia in Hebrew referred to by Papias (p.viii). In his discussion of problematic incidents like the Coin in the Fish's mouth (pp.224ff) or the Resurrection of the Saints at the Crucifixion (pp.402ff) he adopts his normal stance, cautious, perfectly reverent but ultimately undogmatic.

Plummer's *Matthew*, *extra ordinem* as it was to the *ICC*, perhaps suffered most of all his major works from the lack of recognition afforded to its author.

The Commentaries on I and II Corinthians

Plummer's authorship of two further volumes of the *ICC* was another accident. Archibald Robertson[24], a pupil of Plummer's at Trinity and a colleague in Durham later, had been commissioned to comment on the Corinthian epistles, but he was prevented by his elevation to the See of Exeter in 1903 from carrying out the work single-handed. Plummer composed much of the first volume (1911) and all of the second (1915). The historical issues of Pauline chronology, the literary problem of integrity especially of II Corinthians, and above all the analysis of language and style are taken up with characteristic thoroughness. On the background of Paul's opponents and the current controversy about parallels with the Mystery Religions, Plummer has little to say. He had read Cumont and Reitzenstein, of course, and the others, but he refused to indulge in idle speculation.

The great strength of the *ICC* on Corinthians is not its originality. As Plummer says (II Cor. p.viii) the author 'has no new solutions to offer for any of the numerous problems which this Epistle presents. But he has endeavoured to show that in some cases there is one solution which is so reasonable in itself and so much more probable than any other, that students who have no time to investigate every point for themselves, may be allowed, without discussion, to assume this solution as the right one.' A good example of this might be Plummer's discussion of the relation of II Cor x-xiii to the preceding chapters (pp.xxvii-xxxvi). Nor is the *ICC* on Corinthians especially notable for its theological insight. Too often the agenda for theological comment is set in advance by the concerns of later Christian dogmatics. The strength of the volumes

23. *Dictionnaire de la Bible, Supplément* 8/42 (1967) c. 41, on the *Matthew* commentary: 'Ce travail, marqué d'un esprit assez conservateur, est peut-être moins réussi.'
24. See *Dictionary of National Biography, 1931-1940* (1949) 734-735 (C. JENKINS).

is above all their detailed analysis of the meaning of each word in the text.

Plummer continued to be active as a commentator long into his retirement, publishing works on the Greek text of Mark (1914), I and II Thessalonians (1918), and finally at the age of 78, his last commentary on Philippians (1919). He died seven years later having outlived his own generation of careful and meticulous New Testament scholars, that happy band for whom godliness and sound learning were never incompatible. He had survived into a very different age in which New Testament research was to be thrown into a state of almost continuous turmoil.

Plummer's monument, and his compensation for the lack of recognition he was given in his day, is that, whereas many more sparkling works of the same period have been relegated to the dusty stacks of theological libraries, his often remain on the open shelves, and are consulted with profit by those who want to know simply what the Greek of the New Testament authors signifies. Perhaps he was naive in this, but he evidently believed that this was the paramount task of the New Testament commentator and indeed of the Christian theologian.

University of Nottingham   Dr. John Muddiman
University Park
Nottingham
NG7 2RD

WORKS OF ALFRED PLUMMER

I. Biblical Works

1. Commentaries

Ch. J. Ellicott (ed.), *A New Testament Commentary for English Readers.*
Vol. III: *Ephesians-Revelation*, London, 1879 [Plummer on 2 Peter
(pp. 437-463) and Jude (pp. 508-519)].

The Gospel according to St. John. With maps, notes and introduction
(The Cambridge Bible for Schools and Colleges), Cambridge, 1881.

The Gospel according to S. John. With maps, notes and introduction (The
Cambridge Greek Testament for Schools and Colleges), Cambridge,
1882; reprint (Thornapple Commentaries), Grand Rapids, Mich.,
1981.

The Epistles of S. John. With notes, introduction and appendices (The
Cambridge Bible for Schools and Colleges), Cambridge, 1883.

The Epistles of S. John. With notes, introduction and appendices (The
Cambridge Greek Testament for Schools and Colleges), Cambridge,
1886; reprint (Thornapple Commentaries), Grand Rapids, Mich.,
1980.

*I. John. II. John. III. John. Exposition by A. PLUMMER. Homiletics by
C. CLEMANCE. Homilies by various authors* (The Pulpit Commentary),
London, 1889.

The Pastoral Epistles (The Expositor's Bible), London, 1889, ⁶1900.

*Revelation. Exposition by A. PLUMMER. Introduction by T. RANDELL.
Homiletics by C. CLEMANCE. Homilies by various authors* (The Pulpit
Commentary), London, 1890.

The General Epistles of St. James and St. Jude (The Expositor's Bible),
London, 1891, ³1899.

A Critical and Exegetical Commentary on the Gospel according to S. Luke
(The International Critical Commentary), Edinburgh, 1896, ⁵1922.

The Second Epistle of Paul the Apostle to the Corinthians (The Cambridge
Greek Testament for Schools and Colleges), Cambridge, 1903.

The Second Epistle of Paul the Apostle to the Corinthians (The Cambridge
Bible for Schools and Colleges), Cambridge, 1903.

An Exegetical Commentary on the Gospel according to S. Matthew,
London, 1909.

A.T. ROBERTSON - A. PLUMMER, *A Critical and Exegetical Commentary
on the First Epistle of St. Paul to the Corinthians* (The International
Critical Commentary), Edinburgh, 1911, ²1914.

The Gospel according to St. Mark. With maps, notes and introduction
(The Cambridge Greek Testament for Schools and Colleges),
Cambridge, 1914; reprint (Thornapple Commentaries), Grand
Rapids, Mich., 1982.

The Gospel according to St. Mark. With maps, notes and introduction
(The Cambridge Bible for Schools and Colleges), Cambridge, 1915.

*A Critical and Exegetical Commentary on the Second Epistle of St. Paul
to the Corinthians* (The International Critical Commentary), Edinburgh, 1915.

A Commentary on St. Paul's First Epistle to the Thessalonians, London,
1916, ²1918.

A Commentary on St. Paul's Second Epistle to the Thessalonians, London,
1916, ²1918.

A Commentary on St. Paul's Epistle to the Philippians, London, 1919.

2. Articles

This Do in Remembrance of Me. Luke xxii. 19; 1 Cor. xi. 24, in *Exp* 3/7
(1888) 441-449.

St. Mark xiv. 14,15; St. Luke xxii, 11,12, in *ExpT* 2 (1890-91) 81-82.

The Advance of Christ in Σοφία, in *Exp* 4/4 (1891) 1-14.

The Parable of the Demon's Return, in *ExpT* 3 (1891-92) 349-351.

The Inspiration of Waiting, in *ExpT* 5 (1893-94) 492-494.

Luke xvii. 5-10 (Requests and Replies), in *ExpT* 7 (1895-96) 460.

Luke v. 6 (Requests and Replies), in *ExpT* 8 (1896-97) 304.

Dr. Swete's St. Mark, in *JTS* 1 (1900) 613-619.

The Witness of the Four Gospels to the Doctrine of a Future State, in
ExpT 22 (1910-11) 54-61.

'Danaïds and Dirces' in the Epistle of Clement to Corinth, in *ExpT* 26
(1914-15) 560-562.

The Woman that was a Sinner, in *ExpT* 27 (1915-16) 42-43.

William Sanday and his Work, in *ExpT* 32 (1920-21) 151-155, 199-203,
247-252.

The Apocryphal Gospels, in *ExpT* 34 (1922-23) 373-376, 473-474.

3. Contributions to Dictionaries

J. HASTINGS (ed.), *A Dictionary of the Bible, dealing with its language,
literature, and contents, including the biblical theology*, 5 vols.,
Edinburgh, 1898-1904.

Vol. I :   Baptism (238-245), Baptism for the Dead (245), Barabbas (245), Beati-
tude (261-262), Bride (326-327), Bridegroom (327), Bridegroom's Friend
(327-328), Cremation (518-519).

Vol. II :   Hypocrite (441), Judas Iscariot (796-799).

Vol. III : Lazarus of Bethany (85-88), Lazarus and Dives (88), Lord's Prayer
(141-144), Lord's Supper (144-150), Parable (in NT) (662-665).

Vol. IV: Quirinius, Census of (183), Sacraments (327-329), Transfiguration, the (807-808).

J. Hastings (ed.), *A Dictionary of Christ and the Gospels*, 2 vols., Edinburgh, 1906-08.

Vol. I: Annunciation, the (74-78), Bartholomew (172-173).
Vol. II: Nathanael (227-229), Prayer (390-393).

J. Hastings (ed.), *Dictionary of the Apostolic Church*, 2 vols., Edinburgh, 1915-18.

Vol. I: Apostle (82-84), Bishop, Elder, Presbyter (149-150), Church (203-209), Church Government (209-211), Deacon, Deaconess (284-285), Disciple (302-303), Elder (325), Evangelist (379), Governments (507), Helps (560).
Vol. II: Minister, Ministry (37-39), Ministration (39), Pastor (135), Teacher (550).

II. Historical Works

The Church of the Early Fathers. External History (Epochs of Church History), London, 1887, ⁹1901.

The Continuity of the English Church during the Medieval and Reformation Periods. A paper read at the Durham Diocesan Conference, October 20th, 1887, Durham, 1887.

English Church History,

[vol. I:] *From the Death of King Henry VII. to the Death of Archbischop Parker. Four Lectures*, Edinburgh, 1905, ²1914.

[vol. II:] *From the Death of Archbishop Parker to the Death of King Charles I. Four Lectures*, Edinburgh, 1904.

[vol. III:] *From the Death of Charles I. to the Death of William III. Four Lectures*, Edinburgh, 1907.

The Church of England in the Eighteenth Century (Handbooks of English Church History), London, 1910.

The Churches in Britain before A.D. 1000 (Library of Historic Theology), 2 vols., London, 1911-12.

The Continental Reformation in Germany, France and Switzerland, from the Birth of Luther to the Death of Calvin, London, 1912.

III. Döllinger Studies

John J. Ign. v. Döllinger, *Fables respecting the Popes of the Middle Ages. A Contribution to Ecclesiastical History. Translated, with Introduction and Appendices, by Alfred Plummer*, London/Oxford/Cambridge, 1871.

Introduction (pp. ix-liv); Appendix A (pp. 273-279); Appendix B (pp. 280-282); Appendix C (pp. 283-288); Appendix D: Pope Hadrian's Letter to Henry II., King of England, A.D. 1154 (pp. 289-291); Appendix E: Decisions "ex Cathedrâ." (pp. 294-297); Appendix F: The latest Defenders of Honorius (pp. 298-302).

John J. Ign. v. DÖLLINGER, *Prophecies and the Prophetic Spirit in the Christian Era. An Historical Essay. Translated with Introduction, Notes, and Appendices by Alfred* PLUMMER, London/Oxford/Cambridge, 1873.

Introduction (pp. vii-xx); Translator's Preface (pp. xxiii-xxiv); Appendix A : The Prophecy of Hermann of Lehnin (pp. 171-212); Appendix B : Instances of persons prophetically summoned to appear before the tribunal of God (pp. 213-217); Appendix C : Theories respecting Antichrist (pp. 218-220); Appendix D : Merlin (pp. 221-226).

John J. Ign. v. DÖLLINGER, *Hippolytus and Callistus; or, The Church of Rome in the First Half of the Third Century. With special reference to the writings of Bunsen, Wordsworth, Baur, and Gieseler. Translated, with Introduction, Notes, and Appendices, by Alfred* PLUMMER, Edinburgh, 1876.

Translator's Preface (pp. vii-x); Appendix A : Dr. Salmon on the chronology of Hippolytus (pp. 333-340); Appendix B : Dr. Newman on the author of the Philosophumena (pp. 340-344); Appendix C : The poem of Prudentius on the Martyrdom of Hippolytus (pp. 344-352); Appendix D : One more theory about the Bishopric of Hippolytus (pp. 352-353); Appendix E : One more theory about the authorship of the Philosophumena (pp. 354-355); Appendix F : Professor Caspari's contributions to the subject (pp. 355-360).

Intemperate Criticism. Some remarks on an article in the Saturday Review [for Aug. 1877] on Mr. Plummer's edition of Dr. Döllinger's Hippolytus and Callistus, Durham, 1877.

Dr. Döllinger on Madame de Maintenon, in *The Churchman* n.s. 1 (1886-87) 293-306.

Dr. Döllinger and Dr. Reusch on Cardinal Bellarmine, in *The Churchman* n.s. 1 (1886-87) 409-419.

The Jesuits and Casuistical Morality - Probabilism, in *The Churchman* n.s. 3 (1888-89) 372-390.

Dr. Döllinger on the Medieval Sects, in *The Churchman* n.s. 4 (1889-90) 281-290.

Recollections of Dr. Döllinger, in *Exp* 4/1 (1890) 212-225, 270-284, 422-435; 4/2 (1890) 116-130, 455-472.

Döllinger's Letters, in *ExpT* 2 (1890-91) 179.

Dr. Döllinger on the Infallibility of the Pope, in *The Churchman* n.s. 5 (1890-91) 289-294.

Review of *Briefe und Erklärungen,* in *The Critical Review* 1 (1891) 21-28.

IV. VARIOUS

[Ed.] *Historical Essays by the late J.B.* LIGHTFOOT, London/New York, 1895.

Prayers for the Dead. III, in *ExpT* 10 (1898-99) 237.

The Humanity of Christ, and other Sermons, London, 1913.
Christian Agnosticism, in *ExpT* 27 (1915-16) 198-204.
The Submerged City of Is, in *ExpT* 27 (1915-16) 429-430.
Some Conditions of Victory in War. A sermon, preached in Salisbury cathedral the first Sunday in Advent, 1915, London, [1915?].
Consolation in Bereavement through Prayers for the Departed, London, 1916.
'There was War in Heaven', in *ExpT* 30 (1918-19) 59-62.

WORKS OF IGNAZ VON DÖLLINGER*

Die Lehre von der Eucharistie in den drei ersten Jahrhunderten. Historisch-theologische Abhandlung, Mainz, 1826.

J.N. HORTIG, *Handbuch der christlichen Kirchengeschichte*, Band II, 2. Abtheilung, fortgesetzt und beendigt von Joh. Jos. Ign. DÖLLINGER, Landshut, 1828.

Geschichte der christlichen Kirche. Band I, 1.-2. Abtheilung, 2 vols., Landshut, 1833-35.

English translation: *A History of the Church*, translated by E. COX, 4 vols., London, 1840-42.

Lehrbuch der Kirchengeschichte, 2 vols., Ratisbon/Landshut, 1836-38, ²1843.

Muhammed's Religion nach ihrer inneren Entwicklung und ihrem Einfluße auf das Leben der Völker, Ratisbon, 1838.

Die Reformation, ihre innere Entwicklung und ihre Wirkungen im Umfange des Lutherischen Bekenntnisses, 3 vols., Ratisbon, 1846-48; reprint, 1962.

Luther. Eine Skizze, Freiburg i/Br., 1851; reprint, 1890.

English translation: *Luther: A Succinct View of his Life and Writings*, London, 1853.

Hippolytus und Kallistus; oder die Römische Kirche in der ersten Hälfte des dritten Jahrhunderts. Mit Rücksicht auf die Schriften und Abhandlungen der hh. Bunsen, Wordsworth, Baur und Gieseler, Ratisbon, 1853.

English translation: *Hippolytus and Callistus; or, The Church of Rome in the First Half of the Third Century. With special reference to the writings of Bunsen, Wordsworth, Baur and Gieseler*, translated by A. PLUMMER, Edinburgh, 1876.

Heidenthum und Judenthum. Vorhalle zur Geschichte des Christenthums, Ratisbon, 1857.

English translation: *The Gentile and the Jew in the Courts of the Temple of Christ: An Introduction to the History of Christianity*, translated by N. DARNELL, 2 vols., London, 1862, ²1906.

Christenthum und Kirche in der Zeit der Grundlegung, Ratisbon, 1860; 2nd improved ed., 1868.

English translation: *The First Age of Christianity and the Church*, translated by H.N. OXENHAM, 2 vols., London, 1866, ⁴1906.

---

* An extensive bibliography is provided by S. LÖSCH, *Döllinger und Frankreich*, Munich, 1955, pp. 499-556: "Döllinger-Bibliographie. Werke und Abhandlungen, akademische und parlamentarische Reden, Vorträge und religiöse Ansprachen, Recensionen, Kritiken und kleinere Berichte 1826-1892 in zeitlicher Folge".

Kirche und Kirchen, Papstthum und Kirchenstaat. Historisch-politische Betrachtungen, Munich, 1861, ²1861.
English translation : *The Church and the Churches; or, The Papacy and the Temporal Power. An Historical and Political Review*, translated by W.B. MAC CABE, London, 1862.

Beiträge zur politischen, kirchlichen und Cultur-Geschichte der sechs letzten Jahrhunderte. Herausgegeben unter der Leitung von Joh. Jos. Ign. v. DÖLLINGER, vols. I-II, Ratisbon, 1862-63; vol. III, Vienna, 1882.

Die Papst-Fabeln des Mittelalters. Ein Beitrag zur Kirchengeschichte, Munich, 1863; 2nd ed., with additional notes by J. FRIEDRICH, Stuttgart, 1890; reprint, Darmstadt, 1970.
English translation : *Fables respecting the Popes of the Middle Ages. A Contribution to Ecclesiastical History*, translated by A. PLUMMER, London/Oxford/Cambridge, 1871.

Der Papst und das Concil von JANUS. Eine weiter ausgeführte und mit dem Quellennachweis versehene Neubearbeitung der in der Augsburger Allgemeinen Zeitung erschienenen Artikel : Das Concil und die Civiltà, Leipzig, 1869; reprint, Frankfurt, 1968.
English translation : *The Pope and the Council by JANUS*, London/ Edinburgh, 1869; 3rd, rev. ed., London, 1870.

Das Papstthum von I. von Döllinger. Neubearbeitung von Janus "Der Papst und das Concil" im Auftrag des inzwischen heimgegangenen Verfassers von J. FRIEDRICH, Munich, 1892; reprint, Darmstadt, 1969.

Römische Briefe vom Concil von QUIRINUS, Munich, 1870; reprint, Frankfurt, 1968.
English translation : *Letters from Rome on the Council by QUIRINUS*, 2 vols., London/Oxford/Cambridge, 1870.

Der Weissagungsglaube und das Prophetentum in der christlichen Zeit, in *Historisches Taschenbuch* 5/1 (1871) 257-370 [reprinted in *Kleinere Schriften*, pp. 451-557].
English translation : *Prophecies and the Prophetic Spirit in the Christian Era. An Historical Essay*, translated by A. PLUMMER, London/Oxford/Cambridge, 1873.

Ungedruckte Berichte und Tagebücher zur Geschichte des Concils von Trient, 1.-2. Abtheilung, 2 vols., Nördlingen, 1876.

Die Selbstbiographie des Cardinals Bellarmin lateinisch und deutsch. Mit geschichtlichen Erläuterungen herausgegeben von Joh. Jos. Ign. v. DÖLLINGER und Fr. Heinrich REUSCH, Bonn, 1887.

Über die Wiedervereinigung der christlichen Kirchen. Sieben Vorträge gehalten zu München im Jahre 1872, Nördlingen, 1888.
English translation : *Lectures on the Reunion of the Churches*, translated by H.N. OXENHAM, London/Oxford/Cambridge, 1872.

Akademische Vorträge, vols. I-II, Nördlingen, 1888-89; vol. III, ed.
M. Lossen, Munich, 1891.
English translation :
*Studies in European History, Being Academical Addresses Delivered
by John Ignatius Döllinger*, translated by Margaret Warre, Lon-
don, 1890 [translation of vol. I].
*Addresses on Historical and Literary Subjects [in Continuation of
'Studies in European History']*, translated by Margaret Warre,
London, 1894 [translation of parts of vols. II-III].
*Geschichte der Moralstreitigkeiten in der römisch-katholischen Kirche
seit dem sechzehnten Jahrhundert, mit Beiträgen zur Geschichte und
Charakteristik des Jesuitenordens. Auf Grund ungedruckter Akten-
stücke bearbeitet und herausgegeben von Ignaz v. Döllinger und Fr.
Heinrich Reusch*, 2 vols., Nördlingen, 1889.
*Beiträge zur Sektengeschichte des Mittelalters. 1. Theil : Geschichte der
gnostisch-manichäischen Sekten im früheren Mittelalter; 2. Theil :
Dokumente vornehmlich zur Geschichte der Valdesier und Katharer*,
2 vols., Munich, 1890; reprint, Darmstadt, 1968.
*Briefe und Erklärungen von Ignaz von Döllinger über die Vaticanischen
Decrete 1869-1887*, ed. F.H. Reusch, Munich, 1890; reprint,
Darmstadt, 1968.
English translation : *Declarations and Letters on the Vatican Decrees
1869-1887*, Edinburgh, 1891.
*Kleinere ·Schriften, gedruckte und ungedruckte, von Joh. Jos. Ign. v.
Döllinger*, ed. F.H. Reusch, Stuttgart, 1890.
Ignaz Döllingers Briefe an eine junge Freundin, ed. H. Schrörs, Kempten/
Munich, 1914.
Briefwechsel 1820-1890, ed. V. Conzemius,
vols. I-III : Ignaz von Döllinger - Lord Acton, *Briefwechsel
1859-1890*, Munich, 1963-71;
vol. IV : Ignaz von Döllinger - Charlotte Lady Blennerhassett,
Briefwechsel 1865-1886, Munich, 1981.

A NOTE ON THE TEXT

The additions which Plummer himself made in the margins or on the facing pages of his text have been placed in footnotes below. To make the reading easier, obvious abbreviations have been written in full and evident writing errors corrected. Plummer's use of capitals has been systematized, as has his punctuation, which in some cases has been adapted to the currently accepted norms. Our own additions to the text are placed within square brackets. Our explanatory notes are located at the end of the book and are indicated by a figure in the margin. Biographical information on the main personages is given in the index of persons. Plummer's concise indices and his margin titles in the text formed the basis for our expanded index of subjects.

CONVERSATIONS WITH DR. DÖLLINGER

Volume I

1870

Monday, July 4th. After breakfast I took the letter of introduction from Dr. Pusey and went to call on the great Munich theologian, Dr. von Döllinger. I felt a little nervous at going to see the man on whom the eyes of all those in Europe, or indeed in the world, who take any interest in the Vatican Council, have been so long fixed, especially since his signed article in the *Allgemeine Zeitung* last March. Frühlings *1* Strasse 11/1 was his address, and I found him at home. He came to me in a few minutes, and began speaking English quite fluently. He soon showed me that he was not at all a person to frighten any one. Indeed he was extremely courteous, not to say very friendly, but with a quiet dignity which was very pleasing. He looked old, but his hair was not nearly so gray as one would have expected in a man of seventy-one. He said that I might certainly come to his lectures, if I liked, but he feared that the hour would be inconvenient, viz. 7 a.m. He was lecturing on the third and fourth centuries of Church history, mainly the history of doctrine. He had written on the subject some twenty or thirty years ago, but further study had induced him to alter a good many of his views. We soon got on the subject of the Council. He had read — perhaps written in part — the long and important 'letter from Rome' in yesterday's *Allgemeine Zeitung*, which I had been reading just *2* before I came to him. He thought we should have something definite soon, for about eighty speakers who had given in their names had since renounced their right to address the Council. I asked what he thought the conclusion would be. "The dogma will be proclaimed." "Might they not take refuge in an ambiguous formula?" "No, for there was no middle ground on which both parties could stand. The *absolute* and *personal* infallibility — nothing less would satisfy the majority; and this the minority could not accept." "And if the dogma is defined, what will happen?" "What the bishops of the minority will do, one cannot say. Probably the question will be raised as to whether this Council has authority, whether it fulfils the indispensable conditions, whether discussion and voting have been free, and so forth. And this I believe that many will answer in the negative. No doubt it may be a terrible thing for the Church for a time. But it may be God's will to bring good out of it, and this I believe will be the case. There are many now nominally in the Church, who are scarcely believers; and it will be a good thing for an *Ausscheidung* (you understand that word?), for a distinction to be made. This, I think, will be necessary before we can look for that Union of Christendom, to which we may be tending. And this the definition may bring about. But meanwhile it will cause great trouble." "Is it not strange that any one should believe in his *own* infallibility? And one must suppose that the Pope does so." "Yes, he does; but that is not so wonderful in a man of the Pope's temperament. He believes himself to be inspired[1]. I have this from persons who know him far better than I do. For instance, in appointing men, not merely to ecclesiastical posts, but to offices in his temporal government, he will wait till he gets what he thinks is an inspiration, and then he nominates. Now a man who is of that turn of mind—" and the Professor raised his shoulders. "He is not, I believe, a learned man." "Quite the contrary, quite the contrary. He was ordained priest only as a special favour, his ignorance of the ordinary theological subjects being so great. He is the younger brother of a house of rank."

We talked of Dr. Newman's celebrated letter about the "insolent aggressive faction" which was driving all things to extremes in the Roman Church[2]. This letter, written to Bishop Ullathorne of Birmingham, was (it was said) shown by him to Bishop Clifford of Clifton, and by him sent to England, where it appeared in the *Standard*. Dr. Döllinger did not seem to think that Newman had been badly treated, and certainly did not appear to condemn those who had published the letter. "The letter was no doubt a private one," said Dr. Döllinger, "but the respect in which Dr. Newman is held by all persons, both Catholics and members of the English Church, is so great, that it was scarcely

3   1. Pius IX. is firmly convinced of two things: 1. that he, like his predecessors, is infallible; 2. that over and above this he is under the special guidance and protection of the Virgin Mary. He has a personal illumination in addition to his official infallibility. In 1866 he said to a crowd of admiring pilgrims, "*Seul, j'ai la mission de conduire et de diriger la barque de Pierre. Je suis la voie, la vérité, et la vie.*" *Monde*, Apr.i.1866; also in *Union* and *Observateur Catholique* of that date.
   A witty member of the Italian nobility said of him, "The other Popes believed that they were Christ's Vicars on earth, but this Pope believes that Christ is *his* Vicar in heaven"— *Ma questo Papa crede che nostro Signore sia il suo Vicario in cielo.*
   April 20, 1870, Rome was illuminated in commemoration of the return from Gaëta. One of the illuminations leading to S. Peter's proclaimed Pius as "the corner-stone of the Church"— *Esso è la pietra angolare della mia chiesa.* This of the most ignorant Pope since Innocent VIII. and Julius II.

4   2. The letter in question contained the following: "I cannot help suffering with the many souls who are suffering; and I look with anxiety at the prospect of having to defend decisions which may not be difficult to my own private judgment, but may be most difficult to maintain logically in the face of historical facts. What have we done to be treated as the faithful never were treated before? When has a definition *de fide* been a luxury of devotion and not a stern, painful necessity? Why should an aggressive, insolent faction be allowed 'to make the heart of the just sad, whom the Lord hath not made sorrowful'?... With these thoughts ever before me, *I am continually asking myself whether I ought not to make my feelings public*; but all I do is to pray those early doctors of the Church whose intercession would decide the matter—Augustine, Ambrose, and Jerome, Athanasius, Chrysostom, and Basil—to avert the great calamity."

possible for him to remain silent. I felt so in my own case. I felt that, holding the views which I do on this subject, it was my duty to make them known. I think that hereafter Dr. Newman will be glad that his opinion has become known, although at present the circumstances may be painful to him." When I rose to go, he said, "If any time you care to repeat your visit, I shall be quite at your service." He also promised to put down my name next day at the Royal Library, so that I could get out any books that I wanted.

Tuesday, July 5 th. Dr. Döllinger lectured in No. 12 Hörsaal. At 7 a.m. the room was still empty, but people soon began to arrive, chiefly (I thought) theological students; also some Benedictines from S. Boniface. The fanatical Bishop Senestrey of Ratisbon had recently forbidden his theological students to attend Döllinger's lectures. Evidently other 5 bishops had not as yet imitated him, and perhaps his authority in such a matter had been questioned. I got a front place, and to my delight found that I understood well. It was my first attendance at a lecture in German. Dr. Döllinger lectured quietly and slowly, often referring to a manuscript which he had before him. He was very clear in his statements, and spoke as one *who had made up his own mind, but had no wish to make up yours.* "Such are the facts; judge for yourselves" was the attitude throughout. He was at the beginning of the fourth century, — the last days of S. Chrysostom. He went on till passed eight, bowed and went out. His audience rose as he entered and as he left. All was very quiet and orderly. Altogether I was much charmed with my first experience of a German Professor's lectures. I continued to attend them, and began reading Döllinger's *Kirche und Kirchen* in the original.

Friday, July 8th. Dr. Döllinger was now treating of the Nestorian controversy, and one could not help feeling that some of his remarks had reference to current events. He said that one gathered a different account of Nestorius' position from his own statements, from that which one would gather, if one had only Cyril as an authority. As so often happens, both parties in this controversy attributed to their opponent *conclusions* drawn from his statements, which he himself would not have admitted. This is very much what has been done in Döllinger's own case. Again he remarked that the only condition on which an Œcumenical Council could meet to settle the question was that the Emperor should summon one and declare *when* it was to meet. Which perhaps meant that the Vatican Council had been summoned by the Pope, who had fixed an unfair time for this deliberations, and that therefore it was not œcumenical. When he pointed out that at Pentecost, when the Council of Ephesus met, *the heat was so great* that many of the bishops were unwilling to remain on account of their health, there was something like a titter throughout the room. It is believed to be the tactics of the ultramontane party to prolong the Council during these summer months; for now Rome is scarcely bearable to any excepting Italians and Spaniards, who are nearly all infallibilists. The anti-infallibilists for the most part come from northern countries, and they are either obliged to leave Rome or are too unwell to do much.

It was probably no mere coincidence that the Roman Letter in the *Allgemeine Zeitung* (which had passed through Dr. Döllinger's hands)
6 began to-day in this style:

"In the Middle Ages ecclesiastical controversies were decided by the ordeal of the cross. Representatives of the two parties placed themselves with their arms outstretched in front of a large cross. Whoever first let his arms drop or (as sometimes happened) fainted away, lost his cause. The heat, and the fever caused by it, have at the present time taken the place of this ordeal at Rome. ... How clearly the inestimable value of this new ally, Heat and Fever, is recognised by the authorities, is shown by the papal pet journalist Veuillot, in his laconic but significant words, '*Et si la définition ne peut mûrir qu'au soleil, eh bien, on grillera*' (in his 125th 'Letter on the Council')."

In the previous Roman Letter in the *Allgemeine Zeitung* it was stated that Rome was like an episcopal hospital, so great was the number of the prelates who were laid up or seriously unwell. When this was reported to the Pope, and he was told that the lives of some of the bishops were in danger, he is said to have made a reply so brutal that
7 the *Allgemeine Zeitung* would consider it 'a sin' to repeat it.

Friday, July 15th. News that war had been declared between France and Prussia. But not until *Monday, July 18th* did the formal declaration take place. On this day the final voting on the Infallibility dogma took place, and the Pope was voted infallible by 547 to 2. A minority of 115 left Rome beforehand leaving written 'non placets' behind them.

Wednesday, July 20th. Dr. Döllinger began the Honorius question. One knew his view beforehand; but it was most interesting to have it from his own lips and at this crisis. The war has greatly reduced the number of his audience.

Thursday, July 21st. Dr. Döllinger was, as on other occasions, very strong upon the folly of attempting—"what in the whole history of the human mind never has happened, and never will,"—to *silence* the discussion of an important question *by law*. Free discussion is the only way of finding an end to controversy. Will the ultramontanes succeed in silencing the discussion of the Pope's infallibility, or any other question which he may infallibly decide for us?

Thursday, July 28 th. Dr. Döllinger brought his lectures to a close this morning. I waited while he signed the certificates of the students and then walked home with him. He was again very ready to talk about the Council. He told me that Archbishop Scherr of Munich was one of the 115 who left 'non placet' in writing and retired before the dogma was proclaimed. "These bishops," said Dr. Döllinger, "find themselves in a very novel and very uncomfortable position : they are so accustomed in all things to submit entirely to Rome. And the French bishops are worse off than the German, for they have the inferior clergy and the mass of the religious people against them. A schism of the Oriental bishops, which is talked of, is not impossible. But at the Council of Trent the decrees were not supposed to come into operation until the Council had broken up and been formally closed, so that these anti-infallibilist bishops *may* have a respite in which to consider their position. For the Vatican Council is still sitting. A good many Italian bishops with some Spaniards and South Americans are still in Rome to keep up the name of a Council. It is to reassemble in reality in November. Until it has finally broken up these decrees may be considered as not yet in force. Meanwhile the war is withdrawing attention and causing a diversion; not so much, however, in Austria, where the proclamation is considered as a fact of pressing importance."

I asked him what the revocation of the Concordat, which is seriously talked of, would amount to in Austria. "It would transfer a great deal of power from the Church to the State." "In the making of ecclesiastical appointments?" "No, those are in the hands of the Crown already, with the exception of about two bishoprics, one of them being Salzburg, where the chapter retains the old right of electing the archbishop. No, the revocation of the Concordat would restore the old state of things under the *Placetum Regium*, in which state the Church has little or no power of legislation, for nothing is valid without receiving the assent of the State. Here in Bavaria the *Placetum Regium* is still in force, although we have a Concordat. Our Concordat leaves the *Placetum Regium* unmentioned and therefore in force. In Austria it was expressly surrendered by the Crown." Dr. Döllinger was amused at my supposing that the lectures which he had just been delivering would be published. As they corrected some of his published works, I thought this might be the case. "Oh no," he said, "I am writing, it is true, more than one work; but on the constitution of the Church. That is the subject which interests me most at present, and it is the question which most presses." We parted to meet again at 2 p.m.

At 1.30p.m. I called for Liddon, as agreed with him the evening before, and we went to Dr. Döllinger's together. Places were laid for four, the fourth being Sir Rowland Blennerhasset, an Irish baronet, and a Ch[rist] Ch[urch] man, just returned from Rome. He was a strong anti-infallibilist and very agreeable. Conversation flowed very freely, and was most interesting. Our host was extremely entertaining. He corrected Sir Rowland for saying that the Council had broken up. "Oh, no, there are a certain number of bishops still remaining who are nominally the Council,—just to make it possible to say that the Council is still sitting. That is a very old trick. At that 'miserable synod',[3] the Fifth Lateran, a handful of Italian bishops were kept together, just for the name of the thing, for years. They did nothing, literally nothing. There are two or three years in which not a single act of the Council is recorded. But the Pope, Leo X., wished to be able to say that the Council was still sitting. At the Council of Florence again, some bishops, chiefly Italian, were kept together, merely as a set off to the reforming Council of Basel, long after the Greeks had gone away. But they did nothing."

Dr. Döllinger gave us some of his own Roman experiences. He had been in Rome in 1857, but neither before nor since. He was greatly struck by the apathy and indifference of the ecclesiastics. There was no interest whatever in Church matters. "Everywhere else where I travelled I was asked questions; but not there, not a word. No one seemed to care how ecclesiastical affairs were going on in Germany, what the state of religion was in Germany, or anything of the kind. And this was in 1857, before I was a suspected man. I was not distrusted by all of them then. *Now* I should not be surprised at not being questioned. I was presented to a cardinal as a German theologian of some repute (or something of that sort) who had written a great deal. '*Bravo, Signor*' was all he had to say to me; a bow, and then the interview ended;—not a word more. A friend asked me if [I] should care to be introduced to any one in particular : he would ask some people to meet me. What sort would I like? I said that as theology was my study I should be glad to meet one or two theologians. He was a little taken aback at this, said that they were not so easy to find, but he would try. Well, they came. I raised one subject after another, but could not get them to talk. Nothing seemed to interest them. I speak Italian, so that it was not the language which was the obstacle. If I asked a question, it was '*Si, Signor*,' or '*No, Signor*,' and then the matter dropped. At last in despair I gave up theology and began to talk of the weather. Then they began to talk also."

3. Dr. Döllinger was perhaps quoting Jerome, who calls the Council of Diospolis, which acquitted Pelagius, *miserabilis synodus*, as Dr. Döllinger had told us that very morning in lecture.

The fact that Dean Stanley had admitted a Unitarian to holy communion at the gathering of the Committee for the Revision of the Bible became a topic of conversation. Liddon remarked that one 9 apology which had been made for this act of the Dean's was that the person was not really a Unitarian, but only an Arian, in his opinions. He did not think that this made so very much difference. "Ah, they just cut off the *Unit*, then," said Döllinger, "and made him an Arian;" and he laughed heartily at the joke, but he gave no opinion as to the Dean's conduct.

On the subject of the *war* he thought it quite possible that united Germany could bring a million of men (people do say 1,200,000) into the field, if necessary. He did not expect that it would be a short war. A few defeats on either side, especially the French side, would only excite to greater efforts. I suggested that there was a fairly strong peace party in France, which would have a chance of being heard, if the French were severely defeated; but Dr. Döllinger did not think that there was much evidence of a peace party of any considerable strength.

As to the feeling in Munich about the new dogma, he said that there were about 220 priests in the city, and that out of these only 8 or 9 were infallibilists. Hence the archbishop's position was a very strong one. The king and government with him, the University with him, and the bulk of the clergy—including Döllinger. But then the archbishop himself is not a strong man. Dr. Döllinger had told me in the morning that the archbishop was very undecided how to act, and that the separation of the bishops of the minority may have a very weakening effect. They may succumb one by one before they meet again in November. He added now that the number of infallibilist priests in Munich may have increased greatly since the dogma has been proclaimed. "And this is one of its most deplorable effects. People who are known to have held it to be false, now turn round and profess to believe that it is true, merely on the strength of authority, without their reason being convinced in the least[4]. And then of course this is used as a lever to overthrow all positive truth. 'Now we know how dogmas are made!' is the cry. 'You profess to believe all these things, and try to make us do so also, not because you are convinced of their truth, but because some authority which you choose to obey tells you that they must be true. Now we see how Councils are worked! Assemblies packed, discussion suppressed, and the result a dogma which every one must accept or perish.'"   10

Dr. Döllinger thought it extraordinary that Manning should be so

4. A Roman cardinal declared of some of the bishops of the majority, "If the Pope 11 ordered them to believe and teach that there are four Persons in the Trinity, they would obey."

ignorant of the state of men's minds as to declare (as Sir Rowland assured us that Manning had told the Pope), that thousands of people in England would join the Church of Rome, if the dogma were only proclaimed. Dr. Döllinger supposed that Manning's experience was confined to a few ladies in high position, who thought that an oracle on earth would be a very comfortable thing; and that he drew a large conclusion from a few instances. Manning, he thought, was sure of a cardinal's hat, of which a good many were vacant just then. The position of Bishop Clifford of Clifton was noticed as peculiar : so many of his antecedents would have tended to make him an infallibilist;—brought up in Rome and consecrated by the Pope himself. His enemies said that he had turned against the Pope out of pique, because Manning had been put over his head as Archbishop of Westminster. Liddon remarked that no one who knew Bishop Clifford would
12 be ready to believe that; and he gave some striking instances of his continued tenderness and attention to some man in a very humble position.

Dr. Döllinger had not seen a strong article in the extra supplement of the *Allgemeine Zeitung* of Tuesday blaming England for not stopping the war by being more explicit. The writer said that it would go down to history that England under Gladstone might have prevented this scandalous war, and did not do so. Dr. Döllinger thought this unjust. Whatever England might do, it could not stop the war : things had gone much too far for that. The writer of course meant that England ought to have said, 'If you declare war, we shall fight for Prussia,' and that then France would have given way. It was at least doubtful whether France would have given way under such circumstances.

Liddon expressed a hope that some future Council, still more largely attended,—without exactly contradicting the decrees of this one,—might put things on a more tolerable footing. Dr. Döllinger said that this would be very difficult to accomplish. Care had been taken to stop every loophole. There was no chance of escape. *Romani Pontificis definitiones esse ex sese*, NON AUTEM EX CONSENSU ECCLESIAE, *irreformabiles*. There was no getting out of that. Sir Rowland had heard that some bishops had declared that they would never promulgate the dogma in their dioceses. But if excommunication was the inevitable consequence of rejecting the dogma, a refusal to promulgate would amount to a schism.

It was past four o'clock when the servant announced a visitor. It was Professor (?) Gregorovius, whom Dr. Döllinger introduced to us as
13 the author of a well-known History of the City of Rome, about the best in the German language. This was a signal for us to move. I whispered to Liddon not to forget the photographs (He and I had each got photographs of Dr. Döllinger with a view to getting his

signature). "Do you think we can venture, now that this stranger has come?" "Oh, yes: *do* try." At this moment Dr. Döllinger came into his study, where we were, leaving Dr. Gregorovius with Sir Rowland. So we pounced upon him and got him to write his name under our photographs, and departed, much delighted. Sir Rowland came with us. We all three strolled up the Brienner Strasse together, talking chiefly of Rome and the Council, of which Sir Rowland, who had just been there, had much to tell. He spoke of Manning's audacious dictum that the dogma must override history, and also of his astounding statements, publicly made, respecting the Council. Some of these Sir Rowland heard himself, — to this effect. "There was much talk in the newspapers and elsewhere respecting divisions in the Council, violently opposed parties, factions proceedings, and the like. Such statements were simply untrue. His audience were not to put any faith in them. How should journalists know anything about it? He was *in* the Council, and they might believe him when he assured them that the bishops were *perfectly unanimous. There was no dissension whatever.*"

Sir Rowland said that the Pope had lost immensely in public estimation since the opening of the Council. His conduct on some occasions had been so outrageous. Till lately he had been beloved as a kind-hearted well-meaning man; but he had proved himself capable of the greatest harshness: e.g. his bullying of the poor old Chaldean Patriarch and making him sign away not only his own rights but the hereditary rights and privileges of his Church, was little less than brutal. The *14* Patriarch was infirm and alone. The Pope was not alone, and is hale and strong[5]. I asked Sir Rowland what it was that the Pope had said about the heat. (Some of the prelates had petitioned the Pope to adjourn the Council, because the extraordinary heat was making many of the Northern bishops seriously ill, indeed was killing some of them. The correspondent of the *Allgemeine Zeitung* said that he should consider it a sin (*für Sünde*), which I do not, to repeat the Pope's reply, which was then in every one's mouth in Rome.) Sir Rowland replied that what the Pope is reported to have said is *"Crepino"*, for which the English equivalent would be 'Let them die and rot like sheep'. The German word would be *crepiren*: 'to die the death of

5. He rated Cardinal Guidi soundly in June 1870 for his speech in the Council, in which he said that the personal infallibility of the Pope had been unknown to the Church for the first fourteen centuries. Guidi replied that he had merely held fast to the doctrine of tradition; to which Pius made the famous and characteristic rejoinder, '*La tradizione son'io.*' Since Boniface VIII. said that "the Pope holds all rights locked up in his breast" nothing more significant of the papal system has been uttered.

The Duke of Sermoneta [M. Caetani] said that the bishops went into the Council like shepherds and came out of it like sheep.

a brute, to perish miserably'. This report *may* be a slander invented by the Pope's enemies; but that it was so readily believed in Rome shows how low he has fallen in public estimation. One thing is certain, — that he did not grant the request for an adjournment. After 5 p.m. Sir Rowland left us.

Tuesday, August 2nd. In accordance with a note which I had received from him I went to Dr. Döllinger's at 6 p.m. for a walk;—as usual, in the English Garden. News from Italy was important. The French troops were leaving; the only question was whether others, which must be mere recruits, would take their place. The government in Florence was confident that no others would be sent; and so was Antonelli. Dr. Döllinger seemed to be surprised that the English government should offer the Pope a refuge.

It was said that the submission of those bishops who had left Rome protesting against the dogma would be demanded. Dr. Döllinger thought that this would certainly be done. It was still possible for them to correspond and combine; but more difficult now that they were separated. If only fifty of them would hold out, nothing more would be said about compelling them to submit. There was no security that the Pope would wait for the formal conclusion of the Council before proceeding to try compulsion. Precedents and principles had been so utterly disregarded during the Council, that it was impossible to say what would be done. "We are in a state of license and anarchy," said Dr. Döllinger. "We have gone back to absolutism. All depends upon the will of one man."[6]

He was very decided in his opinion, which I asked, as to the position of the laity in the early Councils. With the exception of the Emperor, or Emperor's legate, who had very *great* influence, the laity had no voice whatever. In provincial synods, sometimes, when a question which concerned the laity was discussed, no canon was passed until the wishes of the laity were known. But they were *never* consulted at all on questions of doctrine. As to papal legates at early Councils, he said that they usually had the seat of honour, if they were present. At the Third Council (Ephesus) there were none. Roman writers say that Cyril was papal legate; "but this," said Dr. Döllinger, "was not the case. *Before* the Council the Pope entrusted Cyril with his judgment respecting Nestorius, just as (I think) the Bishop of Carthage did. *At* the Council Cyril had no commission from the Pope, and presided quite independently of him. At the Fourth Council (Chalcedon) the papal legates were present and presided. At the Fifth (Constantinople) there were

---

6. "It really seems sometimes as if the object was to turn the Church upside down and delight in doing exactly the opposite of what the Church of earlier times used to do." Quirinus, 1st letter, Dec. 1869.

of course none. The Pope himself (Vigilius) was in the city and declined to be present. At the Sixth (Constantinople) the legates presided again." I asked what this presiding amounted to? Was their vote more important than that of other bishops? "Oh, no. But at the early Councils there was no voting strictly speaking. The question was discussed, and then the whole assembly passed, or did not pass, the proposed measure. There was no taking each man's vote one by one."

As to the war, he did not think that the mere want of money would keep Italy neutral. France had offered a large sum if Italy would send 50,000 men to the Rhine. But popular feeling was so strong against war with Prussia, that the government would not dare to decide for it. Such a decision would probably cause an insurrection. Austria had defeated the Italians, and Prussia had defeated the Austrians in 1866, so that Italy would not be very eager to go to war with Prussia. And the Italian government had no great reason to feel gratitude to France for the campaign of 1859. The loss of Nice and Savoy was a high price to pay for what France did for them. Dr. Döllinger did not believe that Russia would join in the war. Its policy was to push for Constantinople while France had its hands full. In the East it had no one to stop it but England, which could not do much. It was said that Denmark had been asked by France to join, but Russia would not allow that. I asked him if he had noticed Gladstone's remarkable admission that it was very difficult for England to remain neutral. Dr. Döllinger supposed that this referred to the difficulty of keeping Belgium neutral.

I asked about the way in which the liturgy in Rome changed from Greek to Latin. "The first Christians in Rome were chiefly people who came from the East and spoke Greek. The founding of Constantinople naturally drew such people thither rather than to Rome, and then Christianity at Rome began to spread among the Roman population, so that at last the bulk of the Christian population in Rome spoke Latin. Hence the change in the language of the liturgy." "But such a change must have been made once for all; and is there any record of that?" "No," said Dr. Döllinger, "it need not: I fancy the change was made gradually. The liturgy was said in Latin first in one church and then in more, until the Greek liturgy was driven out, and the clergy ceased to know Greek. About 415 or 420 we find a Pope saying that he is unable to answer a letter from some Eastern bishops, because he has no one who could write Greek. Yet there was a Greek convent in which the monks for a long time kept up the use of the Greek language. Not till Novatian the heretic do we get Latin Christian writings; but the real birth of ecclesiastical Latin is in Africa with Tertullian."

But what work of Dr. Döllinger's was I to translate? That was the

main subject before us. There was a work on *Mahometanism*, written
a long time ago, which would need, he said, not so much recasting as
large additions : so much oriental literature had come to light since he
wrote it. Then there was a voluminous work in three volumes on the rise
of the *Reformation in Germany*. That would hardly admit of translation.
It contains large quotations from the writers of the time in their own
language. It was a *very one-sided book*, written with the definite object
of disproving the theory that the German Reformers in their presbytery
revived pure Apostolic Christianity. A whole volume was devoted to
the development of the doctrine of justification by faith alone. The
work, if translated, would interest only a very limited number of theologians. He thought that his work on *Hippolytus and Callistus* was open
to this last objection : it was a special subject, of interest to only a
few. He had for some time been at work on a treatise, which would
be of more general interest, but he was unable to complete it, owing
15 to the distraction caused by other matters. This was a work on *Dante*.
He thought that Dante had never been properly considered in the
character which he assumes in his great poem, viz. as a *prophet*, —
and that in both senses of the word, as an inspired person with a
commission from God to declare His judgments to the people, and
as one who foretells future events. Such a work was needed, and there
was plenty of material for it. He believed that Dante was much more
read in England than thirty years ago, especially in Longfellow's translation. English works on the subject with notes and illustrations were
more common. He condemned Barlow's as constantly misinterpreting
Dante. I suggested that until his own treatise on Dante was ready,
I might collect and translate articles written by him in periodicals.
He said that there were not very many of such things, and he himself
would be puzzled to know where to find them; and the subject dropped
for a while.

"You are happy in your insular position," he said; "no foreign war
in the country for centuries and centuries." "Yes, but we pay rather
dearly for that intellectually. Ideas penetrate with almost as much difficulty as invading armies." He laughed. "But things are better now
in that respect. The average of learned men is possibly not so great as
in Germany, but you have a fair number. And you have a great many
earnest-minded men, men with a purpose, and perseverance in carrying
it out." He was much interested in schemes for the extension of universities in England, and seemed to approve the system of unattached
students. "Is Dr. Pusey's power great?" "Yes, especially among non-
residents; but it is not what it was." "And what is the reason?" "Partly
the High Church party is less powerful, and partly Dr. Pusey has lost
influence in the High Church party by holding fast to Gladstone in the
last contest." This appeared to surprise Dr. Döllinger greatly. "But how

has Gladstone offended the High Church party? By disestablishing the Irish Church?" "Yes; but before the election it was chiefly the Burials Bill that offended them;" and I explained what that was. "But that is *16* astounding. Among ourselves there would not be two opinions about it. We would far rather give up the churchyards to dissenters than have to use the Church liturgy for them." "Another of his crimes is the University Test Bill." "Ah, but that has not passed yet." "No, but the *17* Tories know that it is only a question of time." Dr. Döllinger expressed surprise that the disabilities of dissenters at the universities should have survived so long after they had ceased in reference to political privileges. "And yet, in spite of all this, Gladstone remains one of your most popular men." "Yes: what are crimes in the eyes of some are right actions in the eyes of others. Some even of the High Church thought that the disestablishment of the Irish Church was quite right." "Yes," said Dr. Döllinger, "the Bishop of Brechin [A.P. Forbes] told me that he thought so. But I suppose there are many who regard Gladstone as an apostate." As regards tests, Dr. Döllinger agreed that they keep out just those dissenters whom one would prefer to admit, viz. those who are too conscientious to subscribe a formula of which they believe only a small portion or none at all. "Another advantage which you English have is that you are a very growing nation. The Anglo-Saxon race is spreading very fast over the globe. And you amalgamate very readily with others, — at least with us. In North America English and Germans are fast becoming fused. Not so the French. They neither increase nor amalgamate. Although there is no emigration the population of France remains stationary; and the line between them and the Anglo-Saxon races in North America is as sharp now as it was a century ago." "And I believe it was the opinion of Grimm that the Anglo-Saxon speech was to be the language of the future; if that proves correct, the fact will have a great influence on the history of the Church." "Yes," said Dr. Döllinger, "the time is coming when Latin will cease to be the language of Catholicism; and with the cessation of Latin much of the power of Rome will go."

I asked him about the story of the woman-pope. How far back could it be traced? "I have written on that subject," he said, "in the Fables of the Popes of the Middle Ages. Ah! that was a book which I had forgotten, and which might be translated with some chance of success." "The *Papstfabeln* had occurred to *me*," I said, "but I did not feel sure about it;" and after some more discussion that was agreed upon as the work on which I was to try my hand.

Dr. Döllinger told me of an absurd mistranslation in some English version of *Faust*: where Gretchen hears "*angelic* voices", the English translator makes her hear "*English* voices"! And where Gretchen is about to swoon away in church and asks her neighbour for her smelling bottle—"Nachbarin, Ihr Fläschen"—the translation has "Neighbour, your *dram*-bottle".

He had been talking of the American Episcopal Church, and I remarked that the subject was specially interesting to us, as we expected to be in the same condition before long. "You mean that you will be disestablished. Well, an Establishment among other things has this great advantage : it gives you the right to appeal to all those numbers of merely nominal Christians who have not declared themselves dissenters. If they are Christians and not avowed dissenters, you have a right to assume that they belong to the National Church. But if there is no Established Church, then you have no right to interfere with any but those who declare themselves to be Churchmen.[7] The Episcopal Church

7. "It is generally known that Dr. Döllinger conceived a very great admiration for the Church of England, and held that she was the only possible medium for effecting the unity of Christendom. Some of his language about her may fitly and usefully be gathered together here, now while his memory is green.

The first passage is from his *Lectures on the Reunion of the Churches,* quoted by Mr. Gladstone, in the House of Commons, in his speech on Mr. Miall's Motion, in May, 1873 : —

It may still be said with truth that no Church is so national, so deeply rooted in popular affection, so bound up with the institutions and manners of the country, or so powerful in its influence on national character. During the last forty years it has extended its range, besides strengthening itself internally, by the foundation of numerous colonial bishoprics in all parts of the globe. It possesses a rich theological literature, inferior only to the German in extent and depth, and an excellent translation of the Bible, a masterpiece of style and more accurate than the Lutheran. ... But what I should estimate most highly is the fact that the cold, dull indifferentism, which on the Continent has spread like a deadly mildew over all degrees of society, has no place in the British Isles. To whatever extent scepticism may have advanced among the younger generation, on the whole the Englishman takes an active part in Church interests and questions, and that unnatural hostility and division between laity and clergy produced by Ultramontanism in Catholic countries is quite unknown there. ... What has been accomplished during the last thirty years by the energy and generosity of religious Englishmen, set in motion and guided by the Church, in the way of popular education and Church building, far exceeds what has been done in any other country.

The second utterance is incorporated in a letter from Canon Liddon to the *Times,* in October, 1885 : —

When Mr. Gladstone's manifesto to the electors of Mid-Lothian appeared, I was with Dr. Döllinger at Tegernsee, in Bavaria. The Manifesto, of course, was much commented on in the German papers, and it was a natural topic of conversation. On the paragraph relating to Disestablishment, Dr. Döllinger said:—'For my part I think that any such measure should be firmly resisted. It would be a blow to Christianity, not only in England, but throughout Europe.' Thinking that I might have partly misunderstood him, I begged him to repeat his words. He did so, with increased emphasis. Without maintaining that intimate association with the civil power had always been an advantage to religion, or that the existing relations of Church and State in England are of an ideal description, or that, if disestablished and disendowed, the Church of England would perish as a religious body, or that she might not, after an interval, enjoy a more vigorous life than now—at least, in some respects—he yet held that the broadest and most serious aspect of such a 'catastrophe' would be that of a 'blow' to the cause of religion throughout Christendom. If such a measure were adopted by the Legislature

of America is gaining from the Unitarians, because the latter find themselves on an inclined plane, on which there is no standing point. They
must go on and on, down to the abyss." He quite agreed that the
Unitarians were the most intellectual of all dissenting bodies, and the only
one which had anything worth calling a literature.

There were long pauses at times in our conversation, and at first
I felt rather uneasy during these gaps; but after a time they seemed to
be quite natural and pleasant. During them he walked along at one's side,
generally with his hat off, his waistcoat half unbuttoned, and one hand
thrust up under it. Sometimes he whistled in a very low tone, too low
for any tune to be discernible; or he thought, and almost talked, to
himself, every now and then clenching his train of thought with a 'ja'
or a 'yes' said out loud. We did not walk fast, and constantly, when
he was specially interested in the conversation, he would halt and finish
what he had to say standing still. We started a few minutes after six
and got back exactly at nine. It was our last conversation that year.

of a country with a history like that of England, there could be no mistake as to its
significance. It would be well understood alike by the friends and the foes of Christianity — in Germany, in France, throughout the civilised world."

1871

The Archbishop of Munich called upon Döllinger and Friedrich to
21 submit to the new dogma by March 15th. On that day Friedrich sent
his answer, denying the authority of the Vatican Council and the truth
of the dogma. Döllinger asked for an extension of time, and another
fortnight was granted. The explanation of the delay will be given
hereafter. March 28th the famous declaration, in which he replied to
the archbishop's summons was published. In it he declared that neither
as a *Christian*, because it contradicts the plain words of Christ and the
Apostles, nor as a *theologian*, because it contradicts the whole of the
true tradition of the Church, nor as a *student of history*, because the
contention for it has cost Europe rivers of blood, degraded nations,
and corrupted Churches, nor as a *citizen*, because it will lead to ruinous
disputes between Church and State, could he accept the doctrine of
papal supremacy and infallibility[8]. On April 23rd both Döllinger and
22 Friedrich were formally excommunicated by the archbishop[9].

23   8. April 3, 1871, Dr. Newman wrote to me from the Oratory, Birmingham :
"You are not wrong in thinking that my heart goes along with Dr. Döllinger with
extreme sympathy in this his cruel trial — and it was most interesting to me to receive
your letter about him. Nay more, I will say I can hardly restrain my indignation at
the reckless hardheartedness with which he and so many others have been treated by
those who should have been their true brethren, and of whom the least that can be
said is that they know not what they do. If indeed there be those who have a divine
call, like Abraham, to slay their son, such persons have an intelligible justification;
and this thought suggests to me that there must be a measure in one's grief, but surely
some great motive is required for causing such suffering, such undoing, as has followed
on the mooting of the question which is the subject of your letter.
   While I say all this, and feel more than I say, I must say on the other hand I neither
can take Dr. Döllinger's view of it, nor do I enter into the reasons which are contained,
as you report them, in his Reply. You will easily enter into my side of the controversy.
I never should have been a Catholic, had I not received the doctrine of the development
of dogmas — and, as to the present instance, I think I have said 26 years ago in my
Essay on the subject, that, as the promises to Judah made by dying Jacob were not
fulfilled for many centuries, during which that tribe was almost as little in Israel, as
David was, before he was chosen to carry them out in his own person, so the promise
'Thou art Peter etc.' might belong to Peter and his successors, though there were few
indications of divine performance of it till the fourth or fifth century, or till the
middle ages."
   [Plummer further adds a transcription of an undated letter addressed to him :]
   "Among your collection of 'Döllinger' remains you have most likely his 'Erklärung'
to the Archbishop of March 28, 1871. But you may not have the counter 'Erklärung'
24 of the 9 Parish Priests of Munich to their flocks, dated 13th April 1871, which contains
the most exquisite bit of impudence I ever saw. Among other arguments by which they
try to convince their people that the Council was right and Döllinger wrong, they
say 'Wo der Papst und die Bischöfe sind — da ist die Kirche.' And then after a few
lines enlarging on this thesis, they add the following, in which please observe that the

June 6th the University of Oxford conferred upon Dr. Döllinger the degree of D.C.L. by diploma; and to my great delight the document was committed to my charge to present to him in person. I left England Saturday, June 10th, and next day in Cologne Cathedral heard the letter of the German bishops (minus Hefele) read from the pulpit. *25*

Tuesday, June 13th. I called at an early hour on Dr. Döllinger to know when I might bring the diploma. He came out to me at once and welcomed me almost like an old friend. "We are very old acquaintances," he said, "but it is some time since we met." And he took me into his inner room, placed me on the sofa, and sat down beside me. I explained to him, as I had previously done to the *Allgemeine Zeitung*, that the degree was by no means merely honorary, like that conferred recently on M. Taine. It was a full degree of D.C.L. with full rights. Moreover, a degree by diploma was a very rare honour; hitherto seldom given, so far as I knew, to any excepting princes. He spoke of the opposition to the degree in Convocation. I told him that Max Müller thought that the opposition was a good thing, as it showed that the significance and importance of the degree was appreciated. Dr. Döllinger had read R.F. Clarke's fly-sheet, urging people to vote against the degree: probably Clarke had sent it himself. Dr. Döllinger spoke very generously of it, and said that he thought that the grounds urged were very reasonable.

We soon got on the topic of the present state of things in the Church. He thought that doubtless good would come out of all the evil. Present difficulties both within the Church from abuses, and without it from the attacks of infidelity, would compel all parties to reconsider the grounds of their separations, and this would tend to bring Churches

inverted commas are in the original. 'Und wenn auch ein Engel vom Himmel ein Evangelium verkünden würde wider das welches *die Kirche verkündet*' (Gal. I. 8), wir stehen zur Kirche. This precious document was exposed in *some* of the shop windows, and in all the churches of Munich, where I happened to be for a week at the time. Noticing the false quotation I watched to see whether it would be corrected. But no, there it was during the whole week; and I have a copy which I got from one of the sacristans.

I had thought it might be from some R.C. translation; and I asked the head waiter of our hotel to get me a Bible (R.C. German). After 2 days he told me *he could not find any one that had one*!! However, I found two big folio translations in the Royal Library, where the passage was rightly rendered.

So I suppose these 9 Parish Priests, or some one who wrote the letter for them, thought no one would detect the misquotation — as in fact was the case with several Germans to whom I shewed it!!!!

Believe me

Yours very truly

[signature illegible]"

(Friedrich in his Life of Döllinger, III. p. 577, gives *14* April as the date of the Erklärung of the Stadtpfarrers, but quotes very little of it, and does not notice the misquotation.)

9. Döllinger was ordained priest Apr. 22nd, 1822.

and sects together. "Might not this reconsideration tend to deepen and widen differences?" "It might," he said, "in some cases; but on the whole not. For instance, I do not think that the question of the Procession of the Spirit can long continue to be a barrier between the East and the West." The Greek and Anglican Churches, he thought, were drawing closer together. The Greek clergy were becoming better instructed; and an increased knowledge of theology and history would lead them to take a different view of the disputed points. On the other hand a tremendous and irreconcilable split in the Roman Church

26 was inevitable. The Infallibility dogma was a rock of offence impossible to get over. There were many who simply *could* not accept it. "But," I said, "when men of Bishop Hefele's learning and ability submit, what is one to expect?" "His submission," replied Dr. Döllinger, "is the result of great debility of character. He is, I know, at the present moment very unhappy in his mind. He has not the courage to state the plain truth and take the consequences." Dr. Döllinger seemed to

27 agree in thinking that Bishop Hefele's letter to his clergy was a quibble. He said that they had a case in Munich very similar to Hefele's in Haneberg, the Abbot of S. Boniface, a learned man and a scholar, who like the Bishop of Rottenburg preferred unity to truth. "Yes, it was true that some were deprived of the sacraments for not accepting the dogma. But in the towns there was no great difficulty : there were always some clergy, who, although giving outward submission by publishing the dogma, did not believe it, and would give the sacraments to those who were known to reject it." The course adopted by bishops towards their clergy and by clergy towards the laity differed much in different places. There was no unity of action. Some bishops published the dogma, and forced their clergy on pain of suspension to accept it. Others, like Cardinal Schwarzenberg, published it as an official document, for which they were not responsible, and left their clergy free. Even in the same diocese there was a difference. The clergy under him as Provost of the Royal Churches had not been questioned as to their acceptance of the dogma. So also with the clergy. Some made the dogma a test : others left their flock to settle the matter with their own consciences. Dr. Döllinger had heard that Bishop Strossmayer was resolved to hold out to the last. As an instance of episcopal caprice he mentioned the conduct, now notorious, of the Bishop of Passau [H. v. Hofstätter] on the festival of Corpus Christi. In Passau there has been a good deal of opposition to the dogma, so the bishop absented himself from the procession. In order still further to express his displeasure he hung out *six black flags* from his palace, flanking them on each side with the Bavarian flag, in order to save himself from the charge of disloyalty.

Dr. Döllinger spoke of the marked changes in phases of thought, new questions perpetually rising to the surface, like waves on the sea, and *requiring new treatment*. This, as I afterwards noticed, was an echo of the declaration signed by him and many others, which was to appear *28* in print that very day, in which the remonstrants speak of the increasing incapacity of the hierarchy; which attempts to direct or oppose the huge intellectual movement with the *Schellengeklingel* of obsolete formulas and powerless anathemas.

I asked if there was any chance of hearing him lecture. Not at present : it was impossible to lecture on ecclesiastical history at the present crisis. Besides he would scarcely get an audience : at least no theological students would be allowed to attend. He thought of giving some lectures in the winter on general history, with special treatment of the religious side of it. He asked me to come back at one o'clock with the diploma, and then dine with him. I noticed two new photographs in his outer room, large portraits, one of the king, and one of himself : probably presents. I succeeded in getting a reduced copy of the photograph of Dr. Döllinger.

When I went back to him at 1 p.m. I found Mr. Macnamara, a friend of Bishop Forbes of Brechin, there before me. I had not quite undone the diploma, when Dr. Döllinger joined us. He was very pleased with it, and admired the old seal and the silver gilt box which protected it much. He read a little of it, and then laid it on one side, not caring to peruse his own praises in our presence. At dinner he seemed to avoid Church matters, and to prefer university topics, whether of Oxford or Munich. The governing body there is the professors, who elect the Rector, who is absolute, and holds office for a year. I was glad to find that he was inclined to the belief that the library at Strasburg has not been destroyed : the most ordinary care would have saved it. He praised the Clarendon Press for its liberality and good work in printing sterling books. He enquired after Meyrick, saying that he had done good service in exposing the immoral teaching of Liguori. *29* Liguori was an ignorant enthusiast. His works, for which he had just been made a Doctor of the Church, were full of quotations from false documents; and there was no doubt that his teaching had given great countenance to downright intentional lying. Dr. Döllinger spoke in terms of high praise of the French theologian Bailly, whose works, once text-books of great advantage to the clergy, had now been put on the Index! The fact was that Bailly taught the truth on some points *30* far too plainly. *Tractatus Theologiae ad usum Seminariorum*, to be had of the bookseller Taranne, ci-devant Toulouse, at Paris.

At the procession on Corpus Christi day in Munich, never had there been such a poor show as this year. Neither king nor court was there; excepting the ministers Bray and Von Lutz, the government was not there; excepting one legal and a few theological professors, the University was not there. Of course this meant indignation against Archbishop Scherr and sympathy with Döllinger, although the latter did not give this explanation. Mr. Macnamara asked about the king's character, and I about his constitutional power. Dr. Döllinger said that the king was a man of peculiar tastes and tone of mind. Music and poetry, especially mediaeval poetry, were his delight. His education had been not so much neglected as conducted in a monstrously pedantic way. He abhorred state business, and left all that he could to his ministers. Yet constitutionally his power was very great : e.g. all appointments in the Church were absolutely in his hand. If he liked to take a decided line, he might have an enormous influence at the present crisis. "Are the decisions of the Cultusminister really the king's or the minister's own?" "The latter."

31   The divisions in the Scotch Kirk, of which Macnamara could speak, interested Dr. Döllinger. It seemed so strange that persons who were entirely agreed about doctrine should be such bitter foes on a question of state patronage. Strange that, while Catholics in many cases prefer unity to truth, Scotch Calvinists will sacrifice unity for a detail of discipline.

I mentioned that I was going on to Rome to stay as long as the heat would allow me; on which Dr. Döllinger mentioned that in 1857 he had been glad to get away in May. The next year he went to Oxford for a second visit : the first was in 1851. To my great delight he said that he had something to send to Père Hyacinthe, who was in Rome : would I call for it at eight that evening? Soon after 3 p.m. Macnamara and I took leave of him.

I went direct from the Jesuit church, where there was to be a great function, to Dr. Döllinger's in the evening. I found him completely 'at home', in slippers and in a little jacket which I afterwards got to know very well. Not even so did he look otherwise than a dignified theologian. He left his work and took his seat beside me on the sofa

32 once more. He had just received a letter from Bishop Hefele, but he had not yet had time to read it. I own that I *did* rather long to know the contents. I told him that I had heard the letter of the German bishops read from the Cathedral pulpit at Cologne the previous Sunday, and remarked that Hefele had not signed it. He said, "No, Hefele could hardly sign a document which contained such an attack upon German learning and science." He spoke again of his visits to Oxford and of those whom he had seen there : Dr. Pusey, of course, Church of Oriel, and (he thought) James Mozley. Dr. Döllinger told me to "be sure and tell Mr. Mozley how glad he was to hear of his promotion" to be Regius Professor of Divinity. He enquired about my own life in Oxford, and said that it seemed to him when he was there that a fellowship was a very enviable position. Why was I a tutor,

if a tutorship was such a hindrance to reading on one's own account? Was I obliged to be one?

I believed that he always saw the *Spectator*, which contained an article hostile to the Oxford diploma of D.C.L., so I gave him the *Daily News*, which said that Oxford had honoured both itself and Dr. Döllinger in conferring the degree. I also gave him the *Battle of Dorking* to amuse him in a spare quarter of an hour. He asked if I should return through Munich from Italy. I said that I would make a point of doing so, if I could be of any service to him. But he would not hear of that : I must make my travels as instructive as possible, without thinking of him. He hoped that I would write from Rome, if I heard anything of importance. Père Hyacinthe wrote but seldom, and then very briefly. We took leave of each other warmly, he with many thanks for what I had done and undertaken. "Ah! no," I said, "it is all the other way. I think that you little know, Sir, how grateful many of us are in England for what you have done — for our Church as well as your own." "I hope that good will come of it," he said quietly. "Some of us thought much of you before the Ides of March," I added. "Thank you; Goodbye." And we parted. An hour or two later I was on my way to Rome[10].

He had mentioned his last publication, the essay on *Weissagungsglaube und Prophetenthum*, and was surprised that I had already read it. "I did not think that it was yet known in England. How did you hear of it?" "I saw in the *Allgemeine Zeitung*—" "Ah! if you read that you would know—" "that the king had written to congratulate

10. Later in the year I received the following letter from him.

"Geehrtester Herr und Freund!

Sie haben mich durch Ihre Uebersendung der Papstfabeln mit einer sehr angenehmen Gabe überrascht; ich war fast erstaunt, als ich statt des dünnleibigen Deutschen Büchleins einen so stattlichen Englischen Band vor mich sah und darin eine für mich so wohlwollende Einleitung, für die ich Ihnen noch ganz speciell von ganzem Herzen danke. In den Eigennamen finden sich wohl hie und da Druckfehler, aber die Uebersetzung ist, so viel ich bemerkt hatte, correct und fliessend. Sie wollen von mir vernehmen, welche von meinen Schriften ich sonst noch zur Uebersetzung empfehle. Ausser dem Buche über Hippolytus und Callistus weiss ich nur noch die Ihnen bekannte jüngste über die Weissagungen anzugeben. Es war freilich meine Absicht, noch eine Abtheilung oder Fortsetzung nachfolgen zu lassen, Dante und die 3 letzten Jahrhunderte umfassend. Allein, ich habe jetzt keine Aussicht, in den nächsten Jahren dazu zu kommen, da ich so viele wichtigere und dringendere Arbeiten fertig machen muss. Und das Gedruckte ist ein Ganzes für sich. Von meinen früheren Werken eignet sich keines zur Uebersetzung.

Aus den Zeitungen (hält man in Oxford den 'Rheinischen Merkur'?) werden Sie erkennen, dass die altkatholische Bewegung in steten Wachstum bei uns in Deutschland begriffen ist. Mein trostvoller Grundgedanke ist dabei : Es ist da in Gottes Hand ein Weg, auf welchem, — ein Mittel durch welches, eine grosse Wiedervereinigung getrennter Christen vorbereitet und endlich wird erreicht werden. — Vergessen Sie nicht, dass jeder Ihrer Briefe mir ein grosses Vergnügen macht.

München 29 Novb. 71　　　　　　　　　　Totus tuus　　　　J. Doellinger"

you and thank you for the essay," and he did not deny that this was the case. He added that the essay on Dante would be a sequel to *33* the one just published; but his work on the constitution of the Church must take precedence of everything.

1872

Wednesday, June 26. After spending several days in Paris with Père Hyacinthe (June 21-24) I arrived in Munich, and almost immediately went to call on Dr. Döllinger. I found that his street had changed its name from Frühlingsstrasse to Von der Tann Strasse, in honour of the general who lives in it and who had so distinguished himself in the Franco-Prussian war. The housekeeper, without asking my name, ushered me in at once, and Dr. Dollinger and I were very soon sitting side by side, as on one or two other occasions, which I am not likely to forget, and were talking of the subject which has contributed so much towards bringing me into contact with him. He was looking well, and said that he had been well continuously since I saw him last; but I thought that he seemed just a shade more worn than before. He had his old spirits, however, and was quite able to laugh heartily over the ludicrous side of this great trouble, in which amid the great "bankruptcy" (as he called it) of morality and honesty, people professed submission to what they did not believe. I told him that I had heard the previous week from Dr. Newman, who had sent kind messages to him, but of course thought that he was entirely in the wrong[11]. "I don't think Dr. Newman can be very satisfied with his position," he said : "he cannot like the state of things in which he finds himself. He must find it difficult to reconcile himself to accepting the dogma." "He is

11. June 17th, 1872, Dr. Newman wrote to me from the Oratory, Birmingham:

"Of course you may say everything which is kind and sympathetic from me to Dollinger and Fr. Hyacinthe. The former at least of them has been cruelly dealt with—and a nemesis is likely to come for it. But I should not be honest, if I implied that anything but evil would come of their present position. Their associates are not like them, and they will either find themselves alone or with those from whom they will dissent more than from those whom they have left.

You will say that Dollinger is an historian and has a right to go by facts. But more than an historian is necessary in this case—he is not (speaking under correction) a philosophical historian. I was struck with this especially in the work of his which Oxenham translated. He does not throw himself into the state of things which he reads about—he does not enter into the position of Honorius, or of the Council 40 years afterwards. He ties you down like Shylock to the letter of the bond, instead of realizing what took place as a scene. How he can defend the 3rd General Council and yet quarrel with the Vatican, I cannot make out. But perhaps by this time the very force of logic, to say nothing of philosophy, has obliged him to give up Councils altogether. Certainly if their Acta are to be the measure of their authority, they are, with few exceptions, a dreary, unlovely phenomenon in the Church.

However, I have said all this only for yourself, to explain how it is that, though I am sincerely afflicted that so great a man should be lost us, though I feel the scandal and the reproach which it is to us, and though I am indignant at the way in which he has been treated and am much distressed at his distress, still I think he has taken a wrong course, and has got the Catholic world against him—"

able to accept it by making it mean as little as possible; and he thinks that you are making a great mistake in making it mean so much. You are playing, he says, into the hands of the Jesuits, in contending that their interpretation of the dogma is the right one. The true course is to consider that the dogma means next to nothing." "But the world will never believe that. Future generations will never believe that a dogma of the Church means nothing. It will not do to let the dogma pass with the expectation that people will understand nothing by it : things have gone too far for that. But that is the way in which many people in Germany have brought themselves to accept the dogma, and are not very comfortable in consequence." "Bishop Hefele among the number." "Yes; and what is more, he does not believe in his own interpretation of the dogma." I asked Dr. Döllinger what he thought would come of the movement. "It is impossible to say. There is a great disease in the Church, and if you ask a physician what will come of a disease, in some cases he will be unable to tell you. I hope that good will come of it in the end; — that it will be the means of clearing the body of the Church of many evil humours. But I do not look for any great results at present : the struggle will last far beyond my day."

He said that he was lecturing on Tuesday and Friday afternoons on general history. Of course I could come if I wished to do so. A visitor, some professor from Zurich I fancy, interrupted our conversation, which had then to become general. Dr. Döllinger turned it on Oxford, especially its great strength in historians, — Stubbs, Freeman, Bright, Bryce, — "a strength such as it has had at no other time." He spoke with great admiration of Stubbs' introductions in some of the Master of the Rolls series, "which are known and appreciated even in Germany." Bryce he had known personally some years ago. I rose to take my leave for the present. "Any day at two o'clock you will find me disengaged, just after my dinner," he said at parting.

Friday, June 28th. I went to Dr. Döllinger's lecture, which was not in the same room as before, but one as like it as a twin brother. There was a good audience, but of course there were no theological students present. Certainly summer afternoons are not as good as early mornings for lectures. Dr. Döllinger seemed to be less lively in his delivery, and perhaps to have less interest in his subject, which was the French Revolution, especially the condition of the French Church at that period. Certainly I found it less easy to keep my attention than in 1870. But one must not judge from a single lecture. The remark with which he concluded his lecture respecting the year 1790 might very well have been made respecting 1870. "France now stood on the brink of a Republic; yet there was no country in the whole of Europe at that time which was less ripe for a Republic than was France."

Monday, July 1st. After taking up my abode at Von der Tann Strasse 23/3, I went to call again on Dr. Döllinger. I had asked him on Wednesday about the reported appointment by the Bavarian government of two additional professors to lecture to the theological students who could not attend the lectures of Döllinger and Friedrich, a report which had given Hyacinthe very much concern. Dr. Döllinger told me that the matter had been misunderstood even in Bavaria, and therefore all the more so elsewhere. *No new professors had been appointed.* The government had by no means given in to the infallibilists. It had done the very least that could be done under the circumstances. He quite approved of what had been done; — indeed the Minister had come and consulted with him before acting. What had been done was this. The salaries of two of the existing professors had been raised, that they might deliver lectures on ecclesiastical history and philosophy in addition to their own, these lectures being for the theological students forbidden to attend Döllinger's and Friedrich's lectures in these subjects. Silbernagel, one of the two selected, had already been delivering lectures on ecclesiastical history on his own responsibility, before receiving the extra pay. Had government refused to pay for these extra lectures, the archbishop would have removed all the theological students of his diocese to his theological college at Freising; other bishops would have done the same; the University would have lost all its theological students; and the theological faculty would have been ruined. The present arrangement is temporary, and may easily be changed when times are better. To have got back the students, after they had been firmly established elsewhere, would have been no easy matter. Silbernagel's own subject is (I think) Civil Law. He has submitted to the *37* dogma and therefore is acceptable to the bishops[12].

12. "The *ordentlicher* professor is responsible for his department, and is anxious that *38* the fundamental and most important subjects in his branch be regularly taught. Under the German system, or lack of system, the professor in charge of a department cannot direct that any of this work be done by the *ausserordentlicher* professor or by a *Privatdocent*, and consequently he must do it himself. Still, in most cases he prefers to do so, for he desires to give the stamp to the instruction of the institution he represents. The courses we have in mind are encyclopædic rather than compendious, occupying four or five hours a week, and are by no means to be confounded with elementary work.

Still, though a professor cannot tell a *Privatdocent* what to teach, he can, practically, tell him what not to. It is common in this country to picture the bright young German *Privatdocent* as lecturing on the same subject as the professor, and drawing a full house, to the great discomfiture of his antiquated superior. Nothing could be more false. A *Privatdocent* knows well enough that it would be very poor policy on his part to openly set up a rivalry with the professor. He almost always carefully avoids the courses the latter is in the habit of reading, and is consequently, for the most part, restricted to special courses. If he does lecture on the professor's favorite subjects, he takes pains to do so some other semester. Years ago a now famous German professor was *Privatdocent* at one of the larger universities, and had announced a course of lectures for the following

The visitor from Zurich had interrupted me on Wednesday in telling Dr. Döllinger all that Dr. Newman had said of him and of the treatment which he had received. "He thinks," I now continued, "that you have been cruelly treated, and that a nemesis will come. Those who did it had perhaps the right to do it; but still cruelty is cruelty. It did not, I believe, come immediately from Rome." "*That*," said Dr. Döllinger, "*was never known with certainty*. How far the archbishop acted on his own responsibility, how far under directions, whether definitely expressed or otherwise conveyed to him from Rome, I cannot tell. They succeeded in keeping that point quite secret." "Dr. Newman says he cannot understand how you can accept the Third Council and yet reject the Council of the Vatican." Dr. Döllinger did not seem quite to see the point of the argument. "Dr. Newman means, I suppose, that at Ephesus there was all the intrigue and violence which disfigures the Vatican Council, and yet the Council of Ephesus is allowed to be œcumenical." "The cases are not parallel," replied Dr. Döllinger. "It is quite true that Cyril and others behaved badly, and that the proceedings were irregular; but the Council of Ephesus imposed nothing on the Church. It merely condemned the doctrine of Nestorius, which had already been rejected by the greater part of Christendom. It never altered the existing state of things one iota; it merely confirmed what existed already. The result would have been the same if the proceedings had been perfectly regular : Nestorius would have been condemned. But the Vatican Council has altogether changed things, and has imposed a great deal upon the Church; and had the proceedings been regular, the result would have been altogether different. The numerous bishops who were opposed to the dogma would have been able to make their voices heard, and the dogma would never have been passed."

He asked me about some meeting, which he supposed had been held about the re-union of Christendom. In explanation he brought me a cutting from an English newspaper, saying, "There is some friend, or enemy, of mine in England (I don't know who it is), who, whenever there is anything against me in the *Tablet*, or *Weekly Register*, or elsewhere, cuts it out and sends it to me." The cutting which he handed me was a review of a pamphlet entitled *The Westminster Synod*. I know nothing of it, but from the review imagine it to be a sketch of a synod to be held in the future, in which one of the speakers is to

semester. But before the semester opened, a new *ausserordentlicher* professor was appointed, who wished to make his début with a course on the same subject. At his request the *ordentlicher* professor asked the *Privatdocent* not to lecture on that subject. As the latter had already made his announcement, he declined to yield to the request, and a struggle ensued, which ultimately resulted in his favor; but his persistence brought upon him the lasting hostility of not only the *ordentlicher* and the *ausserordentliche* professors, but also the whole 'school' to which they belong—a hostility that makes itself felt whenever his name is proposed for a better position than the one he now holds."

say that the Old Catholic movement has ended in atheism and materialism; and this was the end of the cause for which "the unfortunate Döllinger" had suffered so much. Döllinger can afford to laugh, and does laugh, at such insinuations; but still I think that they pain him.

The insinuation reminded me of Dr. Newman's remark that Döllinger might end in finding himself united with those who would be far more distasteful to him than ultramontanes. "Not *united* with them," said Dr. Döllinger. "Say *working for the same ends*, and then what Dr. Newman says is true. We and the distasteful people have common objects, but for quite different reasons. The same thing happens in England. Roman Catholics find themselves working with ultraradicals and atheists to overthrow the English Church. Dr. Newman attacks the English Church. So do the atheists. The one wishes to clear the ground for his own religion, the others to clear away religion altogether. Such is the case with the Old Catholics in Germany." From Dr. Döllinger's manner when I spoke of the Archbishop of Utrecht [H. Loos] coming to confirm here for the Old Catholics, I gathered that he did not approve of the step; but I am not at all sure of this. I did not continue the subject.

He does not think that the Vatican Council, which has never been formally closed, will ever assemble again. Nor does he expect that any Council can do much to heal the divisions in the Church for some time to come. He has never looked to a Council as the means of uniting Christendom. Very much must first be done in other ways. *Theology must become conciliatory instead of polemical*; be made a means of making peace, not an arsenal from which to draw weapons of war. Christians must learn to make more of the points they hold in common, less of those about which they differ. As the education of the clergy and people progresses it will become impossible for differences on subjects too mysterious for anyone to *know* anything, one way or the other, to separate Christians, e.g. the subject of the double Procession. Much may be done by individuals ignoring differences, and (so far as it can be done without sacrifice of principle) joining with those of another communion, as if the separation did not exist. And perhaps that is the way in which the union will come about at last. *Then*, perhaps, when differences are thought less of, a Council may do something; but we are not ready for it yet.

Dr. Döllinger did not think that the *Council of Trent* could be made the basis of any union. Some of its decrees were excellent, and many Protestants would readily accept them; but others were of such a nature, that, either they had to be explained in a sense which was evidently not that of the framers, or else the Council had to be abandoned, because some of its decrees are heterodox. In the decree about *transubstantiation*, for instance, no definition of substance can be given which will not involve you in a contradiction when you come to contrast it with species[13].

He promised to introduce me at the Royal Library again, so as to enable me to take out books. And then he took me into his own library (I had never been there before), and told me that I might have the run of it. It is a series of small rooms opening one into another, all lined from top to bottom—in some places *doubly* lined—with books. "Put down your hat and umbrella, and stay as long as you like. If you want history, you will find it chiefly there; general literature is in this room; and what I have of dogmatic theology I keep in there. Take anything you like. I shall be going for a walk at half past six or seven, if you care to come." Of course I jumped at this. "Very well then, come at seven o'clock." Left alone in the library, I dipped into this and that and feasted my eyes on the well filled shelves. Many of the books were filled with narrow slips of thin paper as references to special passages, which were sometimes marked also in the margin. Many such slips were lying in the library ready for use, and Dr. Döllinger always read with a small sheaf of them by his side. I left at 40 last carrying with me two volumes of Von Sybel's *Revolutionszeit* to accompany Dr. Döllinger's lectures, and Rosmini's *Cinque Piaghe della* 41 *Santa Chiesa*, a book of which one had heard much, but which had never come in my way before. It is of special interest just now, and I began to read it before returning to walk at seven.

The walk was for more than two hours, and as usual in the English Garden. We had a great deal of bowing to do, so many persons took off their hats to Dr. Döllinger. We met the theological seminary walking two and two, and I was pleased to see that all the students took off their hats to the arch-heretic. This involved our standing bareheaded until the procession had passed.

Dr. Döllinger thinks that the Athanasian Creed is of the sixth century, about 580 or 590, soon after the conversion of King Reccared in Spain. In Germany such a commotion as we have had about the creed would be scarcely possible. Few people here would insist on orthodoxy on a matter of such inscrutable mystery as the Trinity. It is impossible to

13. See an article on "The Council of Trent in its relation to the Present Time" in the *Contemporary Review*, Dec. 1870, by Dr. Pichler, who was formerly under Dr. Döllinger as Vicar of S. Cajetan, one of the Royal Churches of which Dr. Döllinger is Provost. Pichler was also a Teacher of Theology in the University. The ultramontanes got all his writings put on the Index, and he left Munich and became Librarian of the Imperial Library at St. Petersburg. "Dr. Döllinger, my much-esteemed master, during his visit to Rome pointed out publicly the necessity of publishing the original documents concerning the Council of Trent. But who is Döllinger compared with the gentlemen of the Curia? His pamphlet went direct to the waste-paper basket. Regard for the religious conscience or for truth does not affect them. They simply want to rule; whatever opposes this will be suppressed, falsified, or destroyed."

know the meaning of the terms used. The most subtle theologian cannot explain the difference between the "Generation" of the Son and the "Procession" of the Spirit. "That," I said, "is what gives offence : the attaching of such tremendous anathemas to disbelief in statements of which one cannot understand the meaning." "When the creed was composed," said Dr. Döllinger, "Arianism was abroad. Whole nations were converted to Arianism. Every one was keenly alive to the doctrine of the Trinity. The questions which *we* have to settle are very different. The Reformers made a great mistake in putting the creed into the public service. It should never have been there. With us it is recited only in the choir service on Sunday, a service at which few if any lay persons are present; and if they are present, they are not likely to be offended by the creed, for it is said in Latin, and so fast that no one but the clergy knows what is being said."

Haneberg, the Abbot of S. Boniface, has been nominated to a bishopric, but has not yet been consecrated, not having been proclaimed in the consistory at Rome. He is a professor in the University, an accomplished scholar and a theologian. Like Hefele, he has submitted to what he does not believe. To his discomfiture a private letter of his, written since the Council and (I think) since his submission, has 42 been printed, in which he says, "The doctrine, it must be owned, is a new one. It was not taught in the first eight centuries of the Church. On the contrary, the opposite doctrine was taught." He is lecturing 43 on the Old Testament.

Dr. Döllinger certainly walks with less vigour than he did two years ago. He still likes to *stop* to finish the discussion of a point, and falls into a low whistle very often when he is not talking. He laughed very wickedly when I told him of the changes which were being made with regard to celibacy at Oxford, almost as if he suspected me of being among the agitators for the change, which would be very wide of the truth. "Come again to-morrow evening, if you care to," he said, as we shook hands at his door a good deal past nine o'clock; "at the same hour. Good-night."

Tuesday, July 2nd. Dr. Döllinger was more like his old self this afternoon at lecture. But the afternoon was close, and the lecture-room very full. Two windows, opened by a courageous Englishman, were promptly shut by two Germans, and I soon had to struggle with drowsiness. Moreover, though I had my note-book, I had left my pencil at home.

At 7 p.m. I called for Dr. Döllinger, and we went across the bridge at Brunnthal and walked on the other side of the Isar. Like myself, he seems to be fond of the view from the bridge. I asked him what the purpose of the Maximilianeum was — an immense building close to the river, now nearly finished. He laughed, and said that it was a fancy of the late king's (Maximilian II.). "He intended it as a place of higher education for those who are to occupy high positions and fill important offices. It was quite useless to point out to him that you cannot tell beforehand who will occupy the high positions; that men must begin low down and show their fitness in less important spheres; that you cannot take a young man and inspire him with the idea that he is to hold high office, and that he must educate himself specially for it. The king was not to be moved, and *would* have his way. I don't suppose that the Maximilianeum contains more than a dozen young men, and they are educated at the University with the rest of the students. "The cost of attending lectures at the University is very small; about 15 shillings for a course which lasts half a year. Few students attend more than four courses, which would be only £3 for the half year. But very many of them bring certificates of poverty, and they get their lectures free, or almost free. There are about 1250 or 1260 students at the present time. The coloured ribbons which they wear distinguish the clubs which they have among themselves, and I believe there are from 15 to 18 such clubs. They have nothing to do with the different faculties. The students are free to live just as they please. If they do not attend lectures, no notice is taken. We want the College system, as you have it at Oxford. I have often said that a mixture of the College system with the professorial is the right thing[14]."

About the marriage law he said, "We have no civil marriage in Bavaria, excepting for rare cases, when neither of the parties is of a religion recognized by the State. In ordinary cases the religious ceremony constitutes a valid marriage. But soon we shall have the civil marriage for the whole of Germany."

44

The Franciscan convent suggested the question of the stigmata of S. Francis. "It is a thing," said Dr. Döllinger, "about which there is a good deal of doubt as to the fact, and also (if it was a fact) as to the cause. Instances of the stigmatization of women are common enough; but that of S. Francis is the only case of stigmatization of a man." I asked what he meant by saying that it was frequent in the case of women. "It is recorded of many female saints, and it is *known* to have taken place in some cases. I saw one instance of it myself in the Tyrol. The woman had a reputation for great sanctity, and pil-

---

14. About a fortnight later he was talking of the College system again, as a thing that ought to be introduced in Germany, and I asked him whether that view was gaining ground. "Humbolt says," he replied, "that it requires a century for a good idea to be recognized in Germany *as* a good idea; and that then it takes another century to get it carried out." "And you have not been recognized yet." He laughed, and said, "No, I am afraid not."

grimages were made to see her. She may be living yet. I was living close by and saw her several times and observed her. She was constantly in a state of ecstasy, quite unconscious. I remarked that flies walked about over her eye-balls, without her taking any notice. She was an invalid and confined to her bed. But every Thursday evening and Friday she gave herself up to the contemplation of the Passion, kneeling up in bed in quite an ecstatic condition. When she returned to consciousness, she did not speak, but made signs of recognition. The stigmata were rosy-coloured spots on her hands; and she was believed to have the same on her feet. The latter of course I did not see. How they were produced I do not pretend to say. It is not yet sufficiently known how far such things may be the result of natural causes, e.g. of a very violently excited imagination. At the beginning of this century breaking on the wheel was still in use as a punishment in Prussia. A woman with child was greatly excited at witnessing such an execution; and when the child was born it had marks on its body similar to the bruises produced by breaking on the wheel. On the other hand, some women have such an intense passion for being considered peculiarly saintly or endued with special spiritual gifts, that they will do the most extraordinary things to obtain such a reputation. Some of these cases of stigmata may be mere trickery. In a correspondence still extant between Spanish Jesuits of the seventeenth century they inform one another of the state of religion etc. in their respective localities. In Spain women who profess to devote themselves to a life of great asceticism and peculiar sanctity are called ... [15] In one of these letters the writer says, "All our ... here want to have the stigmata." Now if that was trickery, it was dangerous work in Spain. Had they been found out, they would have been handed over to the Inquisition. The stigmata was a cause of dispute between the Franciscans and Dominicans. The Franciscans wanted to have a monopoly of the stigmata, while the Dominicans claimed the honour for S. Catharine of Siena.

"You will come again to-morrow? Good night."

Wednesday, July 3rd. When I called for Dr. Döllinger at 7 p.m. he was just sending off a letter to Lord Acton, who is said to be about to publish a new and enlarged edition of his account of the Council. "With some things altered," I said. "No, not that I am aware of: he has nothing to alter." "Oh! I fancied that he had somewhat changed his position." "No, not at all," said Dr. Döllinger; "he still thinks the same that he did before." He went on to tell me that there is a prophecy current here, that some time in August there will be a great

15. I did not catch the word used.

and praeternatural darkness, lasting perhaps for days. The prophecy is not attributed to any one in particular, but it is very generally believed in some parts; and at the great Bavarian place of pilgrimage, Alt-Oettingen, they are now selling black wax tapers, which have been specially blessed, for the purpose of illuminating this darkness. A similar notion prevails in South America, and there it is said that the darkness will be a punishment for the sins of the Old Catholics, especially for a well-known leader, one Döllinger!

Alt-Oettingen suggested La Salette, the French place of pilgrimage, respecting which Dr. Döllinger gave me the following particulars, most of which were told him by a cardinal. At the time when the appearance of the Virgin is said to have taken place one of the Vicars-General of the diocese of Grenoble, knowing that the whole thing was an imposture, went to Rome to warn the Pope against believing it. It would cause great scandal if the fiction received sanction. The Pope received him well, and seemed quite to agree with him. Meanwhile others got the ear of the Pope and brought the pretended miracle into connexion with his pet idea. The Virgin was represented as having told the boy and girl that the Pope was to be declared infallible. The boy in writing down the tale which was put into his mouth had to ask how to spell infallible. The woman who really did appear to the children was a person of extravagant habits and was known to have bought the very brilliant attire, in which she appeared to the children, in Grenoble a short time before. The Vicar-General was much surprised to find, when he next visited the Pope, that he was received with great bitterness, and told that the miracle had certainly taken place, and that he was doing very wrong in trying to throw discredit on it. Whether the woman acted spontaneously for a freak, or was inspired by others who were interested in such a miracle taking place, was never clearly made out.

But the darkness prophecy had a more innocent origin. It was the result of a bet, as to whether or no people could be made to believe that a certain astronomer, who was named, had calculated that some time in August a great comet would come in contact with the sun, and the result would [be] a great and prolonged darkness. This statement was published. Forthwith the astronomer named wrote to the papers to say that he was being deluged with letters, asking questions which he was quite unable to answer, and that he did not know who had been amusing themselves at his expense. Meanwhile the joke is an excellent thing for those who sell the holy black tapers.

Dr. Döllinger thinks that the Clarendon Press ought to publish a good edition of the Greek Fathers. "That is a thing still wanted. Dr. Pusey made a good beginning with S. Chrysostomos, but it has not been *46* gone on with. If I had large sums of money to dispose of, the first thing I would do would be to publish a new and entirely revised text of the General Councils, the Greek ones I mean of course, especially the third, fourth, fifth, and sixth, above all the one at Constantinople at the time of Photius. A text was published at Rome in the seventeenth century, when Baronius and Bellarmine were still living, and that [text] is very uncertain and suspicious. I believe that all our existing texts are mere copies from that. They want revising with the manuscripts which exist at Paris, Vienna, here, and elsewhere. You may have some at Oxford. Some society ought to undertake the work, and of course it would require the united labour of many persons to carry it out. It was talked of in Paris not long ago, and I was consulted on the subject; but the war intervened, and I have heard no more about it.

"Père Hyacinthe will not be able to do much in Paris. Not only, as you say, is the ground occupied by politics, but in all the Latin races the population is divided into two great sections,—those who accept everything, however absurd and superstitious, and those who reject everything, and are practically infidels. Between these two is a deep abyss, which you cannot bridge. Such is the case in France, and such is the case in Italy; perhaps in Spain also, but we know too little of the state of religious feeling in Spain. There, however, there is an immense difference between the town and the rural population; in no country more. In the villages they are strongly attached to the old religion and the old Spanish monarchy; in the towns they care little about religion, and there, what republicans there are, are to be found."

In connexion with the darkness wager I told Dr. Döllinger one or two stories about English betting over which he laughed heartily, and he was much amused at the idea of ladies betting gloves. As we parted, "Good-night: to-morrow."

Thursday, July 4th. "We have had a meeting of the Senate of the University to-day," said Dr. Döllinger in his study as he prepared for a wet walk, "and we have decided to ask Oxford, Cambridge, and Edinburgh to send [a] representative to our University celebration. All universities of Teutonic races have been or will be invited." I told Dr. Döllinger that an Oxford professor, when asked last summer whether he was going to Munich in the vacation, is said to have answered, 'No, I can't go there; I'm afraid that I could not keep myself from breaking the archbishop's windows." The archbishop, Dr. Döllinger told me, is a man quite in his wrong element, placed here apparently by a freak, or certainly a mistake, of the late king. The Crown in Bavaria, owing to the *Placetum Regium*, has the absolute appointment of bishops, subject only to the veto of Rome, a veto which could scarcely be exercised, unless canonical objections could be urged against the king's nominee. Archbishop Scherr was abbot of a monastery near Ratisbon, where he seems to have shown some ability as a manager, establishing

a brewery in connexion with the monastery, which was rather a success.
The then Bishop of Ratisbon [V. Riedel] was a pious man of much
influence, author of several devotional works, which are much valued.
The king wished to have him as Archbishop of Munich. Reisach was
at that time archbishop, and perhaps did not hit it off well with the
king. He had been brought up in Rome and was a thorough Italian
in all his tastes and opinions, completely ungermanized. Yet, when
by an arrangement between the Pope and the king Reisach was made
cardinal and sent back to Rome, he was most unwilling to go. "When
we went to take leave of him," said Dr. Döllinger, "we found him
in tears." He died[16] just after the opening of the Vatican Council,
in which he had been much interested : he took an active part in
promoting it and the promulgation of the dogma. But King Max after
all did not get the good Bishop of Ratisbon to Munich, for he died
before he could be promoted. The king mentioned his intentions to
Abbot Scherr, who expressed himself as holding the same views as
the late bishop; 'he constantly used his books,' and so forth. To the
astonishment of many, if not all, the successful monastery manager
was made Archbishop of Munich. Such is the story of the promotion
of the man who excommunicated Döllinger.

As we walked up the Brienner Strasse I asked the meaning of '*Dult*'.
A fair is often called a Dult in Germany, and there is a great fair
once a year at Munich called the Jacobidult, being held on and after
S. James' day. "*Dult*," said Dr. Döllinger, "is a corruption of *Indult*, i.e.
'indulgence'. With most German fairs a religious festival used to be
connected, and at this festival 'indulgences' were granted." Then at
my request he gave me an explanation of the theory of indulgences,
which I never clearly understood before. "Indulgences were originally
remissions of a part or the whole of the period of canonical penance.
The crusades greatly changed the use of them, for Popes granted them
wholesale to those who joined a crusade : they gave 'plenary indulgences', i.e. remission of all penance for life. When canonical penance
went out of use, the scholastic theory remained that, though no longer
publicly imposed, penance was still obligatory, whether enjoined by
a confessor or not. Therefore there was still room for indulgences.
If you neither performed the penance which was due, nor got an indulgence, there was a debt standing against you to be answered for hereafter. Pius V. made a further and last development of the original
theory by attaching indulgences to rosaries, medals, etc. But the Jesuits
have made a new theory altogether, by transferring the system to
another world and connecting it with the doctrine of purgatory. Debts

16. Dec. 26, 1869, in Savoy. It is said that he had almost forgotten the German language, and that he gave the Pope very unfavourable impressions respecting the state
of Germany.

of penance are wiped out, or rather burnt out, in the purgatorial fires. But if you have the debt cancelled in this world by an indulgence, you are saved a portion, or possibly all, of the time that you would otherwise have spent in purgatory. Plenary indulgences are now to be had with the greatest ease, and in any numbers; almost more easily than a limited indulgence. Thus the whole spirit of the original theory is lost, and of the original system not a shade remains. As now worked, the system does a great deal of harm. Religion is made quite mechanical, and in the calculation of penances and indulgences its spirit evaporates. There is very little Christianity left." Some talk on the state of philosophical study in Germany at the present day, and on certain Church revenues, filled up most of the remaining time. "To-morrow".

Friday, July 5. At Dr. Döllinger's lecture I had both note-book and pencil and had not to struggle against sleepiness. His contrast between Louis XVI. as king and as prisoner was very striking, also his contrast between the execution of Louis XVI. and that of Charles I. As we were starting for our evening walk he said, "I have had one of the ex-ministers of the Italian government (Minghetti) with me to-day, and he says that neither in Florence nor in Rome is it known whether there is or is not any such bull as is reported to exist respecting the election of the next Pope, dispensing with the usual interval between the death and the election, and directing that the election take place *praesente cadavere* of Pius IX. I told him that even if such a bull exists, it must 47 rest entirely with the cardinals whether they choose to be bound by it or not. A Pope cannot enforce an enactment of that kind. After his death the cardinals can always, if they please, fall back upon the old regulations. But it would be impossible to find a man among the cardinals who would be desirable as Pope. They are all such nonentities, men of no power or force of character. I don't suppose that such a state of things was ever known before. They are not likely to go out of Italy for a Pope, though at one time it was said that some parties wished for a French Pope. The Archbishops of Rouen and Bordeaux are both of them cardinals. Manning expected to be made 48 one, but has not been yet[17]. When he was with the late Archbishop of Paris (Darboy) before the Council, Manning urged him to preach up the infallibility and do all that he could to promote the doctrine, hinting that there might be a cardinal's hat for each of them, 'for it would be a beautiful thing for the two great cities of the West (London and Paris) to have cardinals as archbishops.' He really gave that as a reason. The Archbishop of Paris told Lord Acton, who told me[18].

17. It was said in Rome during the Vatican Council that the fifteen vacant cardinals' hats were able to work miracles.
18. Darboy said, "Je n'ai point de rhume de cerveau; je n'ai pas besoin de chapeau." 49

"I have seen Manning twice; I think in 1851 and 1858. The first time was soon after he came over to the Church of Rome, and I was favourably impressed by him. He told me that I had indirectly contributed to his conversion. He had once thought that it was impossible for a Roman Catholic to treat history fairly and openly, and that a Roman Catholic historian could not be honest. My work on ecclesias-
50 tical history had proved to him the contrary, and had removed a great stumbling block out of his way. The second time Lord Acton took me to see him. We both came away with the impression that he had changed, and for the worse. He was cold and stiff and formal; evidently spoke with reserve weighing his words. Whether he had already begun to look on me with suspicion, I don't know. I read a volume of his sermons once, written when he was still a member of your Church, and liked them. There was warmth and depth of true religious feeling in them. All that is gone now. There is nothing of it in the things which he has written since he became a Roman Catholic. All his later writings are inferior. I know of only one writer who is quite equal now to what he was before his conversion" — and we both together said — "Newman."

I told Dr. Döllinger that Liberals in England found it difficult to
51 approve of the recent legislation against the Jesuits. Although the Jesuits were allowed to be pernicious, the law looked too like persecution to be in harmony with Liberal principles. "Oh, there will not be much persecution," said Dr. Döllinger, "the main object is to restrain their influence in the schools. But I confess myself that I should have preferred to have had an oath administered to them; and I should like to have had the commission of drawing up that oath. I think I could draw up one which they would refuse to take, and yet which public opinion would approve as natural and fair." "An oath of allegiance to the Empire?" "Yes, and of renunciation of certain doctrines, e.g. that when a civil law runs counter to an ecclesiastical law, it is right to disobey the civil law. The law against the Jesuits affects only Prussia and Bavaria. There are no Jesuits in any of the smaller states. In Prussia they are very numerous; in Bavaria there is one small community at Ratisbon. They came there in rather an odd way, occupying the Scotch monastery[19]. The Scotch for some time had a monastery there, but it did not flourish. The young Scotchmen who came out to it could never become acclimatized. They fell sick and had to go home; or if they stayed died. It was obvious that the supply could not be kept up. The Scotch bishops wished to have the revenues of the monastery transferred to Scotland, but of course that could not be. After some discussion it was agreed that a certain sum[20] was to be

19. The original foundation was A.D. 1111.
20. 120,000 florins; but in spite of the protest of the Archbishop of Glasgow, it was paid, not to the Scotch Church, but to the Propaganda!

paid to the Scotch Church, and the monastery given up to another religious society. *Rome stipulated that these should be Jesuits.* We here have an instance of what great changes may be caused simply by a name. The *Scotae*, as you know, in the eighth and ninth centuries mean the Irish. Much of Germany, e.g. my own native place (Bamberg), was converted by Irish missionaries, S. Kilian and others (c. A.D. 680-689). In gratitude for this benefit *monasteria Scotarum* were founded in various places, — Würzburg, Erdfurt, Cologne, and Ratisbon. Somehow or other, one does not know how, *Scotae* came to be confined to the people in North Britain, while the Irish were called *Hiberni*; and about the twelfth century these monasteries appear as belonging to Scotchmen. How the transfer from Irish to Scotch came about, is lost in obscurity. I myself learnt the first rudiments of English from an old Scotch Benedictine, — one of the last of them, — at Würzburg."

As we passed S. Ludwig's he told me that only one of the two houses attached to the church is a clergy-house: the other is private property. "I met one of the clergy at Rome last year, at the Jubilee; his name was Geiger." "No," said Dr. Döllinger, "he is not one of the parish clergy, and does not live there; he is the preacher, and has lodgings of his own. In Bavaria it is common to have preachers besides the parish clergy. In Munich this is generally the case, so that some parish priests never preach at all. After a man has not preached for several years, he is rather shy about attempting it again. And then natural indolence comes in. The preachers are paid by special endowments, — money that has been left for this purpose, and so forth. The preacher at S. Ludwig's is a strong ultramontane, one of the bitterest in Munich. It is the usual thing for the parish priest and his assistants to live together, especially in country parishes. As they must all live a celibate life, it saves a great deal of trouble. Goodnight : tomorrow."

Saturday, July 6th. The *Norddeutsche Allgemeine Zeitung* says that it has been waiting for some time for the *Germania* to answer the question, If the infallibility of the Pope has always been the doctrine of the Church, how was it that 27 archbishops and bishops in Ireland declared in 1826 that it is a falsehood to maintain that the Catholic Church teaches that the Pope is infallible? The *Germania* at last answers that 52 in 1826 these prelates declared the infallibility to be an open question; now it is decided. But (1) how can what has always been the doctrine of the Church be an open question? and (2) these prelates say nothing about an open question : they say that the Church teaches no such doctrine[21]. Dr. Döllinger told me during our walk that one of the

21. Their words in the joint pastoral of 1826 were, "They declare on oath their belief that it is not an article of the Catholic faith, neither are they thereby required to believe, that the Pope is infallible."

English bishops has been saying in his pastoral, that the infallibility
53 of the Pope is as certain as the existence of God. "The consequence
of which is," said I, "that when the foundations of a man's belief
in the infallibility give way, the rest goes with it." "Yes," said Dr.
Döllinger, "*we have had many instances of that in this neighbourhood.*"
He had seen one of the Benedictines of S. Boniface to-day and asked
him when their new abbot was to be consecrated. But he could not
say; they expected to have a good deal of trouble about the election.
The position is one of importance, although it is not worth much
pecuniarily. The present abbot gets a good income, because he chances
to be a professor in the University; but that is an accident.

Dr. Döllinger lent me a pamphlet — *Was wir von Frankreich lernen*
54 *können* by Von Sybel. It had just been sent him — probably by the
author. The first of all lessons that Germany has to learn from France
is the causes which bring a powerful Empire to ruin. Another lesson
is to beware of phrases. Epigrams are apt to contain fallacies. Again.
Care more about liberty and less about equality. To sow oppression
in State or Church is to reap revolution.

Sunday, 6th after Trinity, July 7th. I was at the beautiful chapel of
the Residenz (one of the churches in Dr. Döllinger's charge as Stifts-
probst) before breakfast. Afterward I went over to the little church
on the Gasteig, which has been granted to the Old Catholics, where
the Archbishop of Utrecht (Henri Loos) was to hold a confirmation.
He arrived soon after I did, giving his blessing as he moved along.
An acolyth offered him a brush with holy water to sprinkle the people.
Apparently he did not know what it was for : he did not take it.

Dr. Döllinger had a photograph to show me when I went in the
evening. I had seen many like it in Rome the year before, and had quite
meant to bring one away with me. It is an ultramontane publication,
but so extravagant, that it might well be thought a satire by the opposite party. The Pope on a magnificent throne forms the centre of
the picture. Below are four allegorical figures of the four continents
bowing down in adoration before him. Above is heaven revealing the
Trinity, the Virgin, and S. Peter; and the sacred Dove pours a stream
of inspiration upon the Pope. Christ, as Dr. Döllinger remarked, is
in quite an insignificant position; and S. Peter is on bended knee
towards the Virgin. It is ultramontanism to the nth. The Pope is the
centre of everything in heaven and earth, the recipient of all grace
from above and of all worship from below, the focus of Christianity
and of the Universe. Dr. Döllinger was, I think, not a little shocked,
but at the same time immensely amused. Pantaleoni, the well known
author and a member of the Chamber, had brought it with him from
Rome. He seems to give a gloomy account of affairs. Between the

extremes of gross superstition and blank infidelity, there is little material in which Protestantism or reformed Catholicism could take root. What is a weak and hesitating party of moderates to do between infidel socialism and jesuitical despotism, between the red International and the black?

During our walk we talked of English sympathies during the war, first with Germany, and then very decidedly with France. Happily I was able to talk as having been very German throughout, even to thinking the taking of Elsass and Lothringen quite justifiable. Dr. Döllinger quite agreed that a war of revenge on the part of France would have been quite as inevitable, even if the two provinces had not been annexed. In taking them Germany was only taking reasonable precautions against such a war.

It is quite untrue, Dr. Döllinger said, that the Emperor does not live on good terms with his wife, or does not live with her at all. They live happily enough together. But she has no influence over him. She favours the ultramontanes! We had a long walk; not home till 9.30.

Monday, July 8th. Dr. Döllinger told me that he had had a letter from Lord Acton, asking whether it would not be possible to give an honorary degree to Dr. Pusey at the approaching centenary. But the 55 theological faculty have resolved to give no honorary degrees. An obviously wise decision. They are divided among themselves into infallibilists and anti-infallibilists, and would have great difficulty in finding any one whom all would desire to honour. The faculty of philosophy is the only one which *could* give Dr. Pusey a degree, and it would not. So that it would be useless to propose it. A doctor's degree in any faculty is so much more easily taken in Germany that it is less common there to give honorary degrees than with us. Doctor is the only degree: there is nothing analogous to B.A. or M.A. Many, perhaps most, students stay at a German university as long as they or their friends think fit, and then go away without taking any degree at all. Excepting in medicine. In that faculty, until lately, students were obliged to take the M.D. Now it is no longer obligatory, but nearly everyone does it. Ordinary students in philosophy and theology have an examination at the end of each half year, like our Collections, but that is all the testing which they receive from the university, unless they take a degree. Each bishop examines candidates for orders, but with that examination the university has nothing to do. Students in *law* are treated somewhat differently. Besides the ordinary examinations at the end of each half year they undergo two *general* examinations. The first of these is purely a university matter. In the second the State takes a part, some of the examiners being appointed by government. This is preliminary to the candidate's practising as an advocate. (Note that an advocate in Bavaria rarely speaks in court : he sends a statement of the case in writing.) Most bishops have a theological college of their own. This is connected with a Lyceum, and the professors at the Lyceums are appointed by the State. There is one notable exception, — Eichstadt. There the bishop has got the appointment of the professors into his own hands. This was the result of an arrangement between a certain cardinal and a Bavarian minister (both are dead now), and was perhaps not a very creditable affair : by it the government was done out of its privilege. At Würzburg there is no Lyceum : the University renders it unnecessary. This archbishop's title is "of Munich and Freising". Here there is the University : at Freising, where he has a theological college, there is a Lyceum.

In the state schools (*Gymnasien*) in Bavaria, the teaching of history has hitherto been denominational (*confessionell*) : one teacher for Catholics, and another for Protestants; — a manifestly evil arrangement. The common practice was that the priest who gave the religious instruction should give the historical instruction also, and the way in which history was treated under these conditions has caused great dissatisfaction. The Cultus-minister has just declared that henceforth the teach-
56 ing of history shall cease to be denominational. The ultramontanes regard this decision of Von Lutz as a heavy blow. That the State should appoint one and the same man to teach history to Catholics, "Protestants, Jews and free-masons", seems to them intolerable. It is doubtful whether the minister intended to deal them a blow; but it is one. It by no means follows that the state teacher will always be an unprejudiced person. But with a mixed audience he will have to try to be decently honest and fair; and history honestly taught is always disastrous to ultramontanes.

In Bavaria and Germany generally the bishops are very well off, but they are not rolling in wealth like some of the Austrian and Hungarian prelates[22]. This archbishop gets 20,000 florins a year. The bishops have from 8000 to 10,000 florins; and they could live comfortably and do all that is expected of them on 6000 florins (about £ 500). Living here is still *very* much cheaper than in England; but Dr. Döllinger says that fourty years ago he could live *more* comfortably on *half* the sum that he spends now.

Today he had to submit to an infliction. Two American ladies, daughters of Protestant pastors in the "great country" came to visit him. They frankly owned that they had come out of pure curiosity, and to be able to say when they got home that they had seen him. "They were discreet enough not to stop long." Another of the penalties

57   22. Some of the bishops of the majority at the Vatican Council, when asked why they did not support the German bishops in opposing the dogma, said, "Ah, they can afford to say what they think; they are rich. It is very different with us."

of being a great man is that the brim of your hat suffers, if you walk in frequented parts.

But it is a beautiful sight to see little children come up to him, and look up at him or touch his hand. They are probably attracted by his kindly look. He is very fond of children and is always very gentle with these little intruders; sometimes stops and talks to them and gives them a small coin, "Da hast Du was." How many of them would be glad to remember it in after life, if they only knew who he is, and what he has done. What does the sadness which sometimes steals over his face, as he looks at them, mean? The possibilities of their future? Or the contrast between them and some of their elders in their treatment of him?

Tuesday, July 9th. Dr. Döllinger took me in quite another direction this evening : out to 'Bavaria', to see some new grounds which have just been thrown open to the public. He had not been there for a year. We went through one street, which I knew fairly well, but which he had never entered in his life before. He remembers when the whole of Schwanthaler Strasse was meadow. He told me that the University authorities (and he as Rector Magnificus, of course, most particularly) are in a difficulty. The Crown Prince of Prussia is coming to Berchtesgaden, and is likely to be there at the time of the centenary. He is Rector of the University of Königsberg, so that it would be almost uncivil not to invite him to the jubilation. On the other hand he is Crown Prince of Prussia, and it would not be etiquette to ask him without consulting the Bavarian government. To ask the government would place the ministers in a fix. If they consented, the Prince would probably come, be (as usual) very affable and pleasant, and consequently very popular; whereas King Ludwig II. "*might* be very popular, if he took the trouble," as Dr. Döllinger put it. He believes that the king does not mean to take any great part in the jubilee; perhaps will only be present at "Lohengrin" in the Hof-Theater. And for the Crown Prince to be at everything and be the centre of attraction, while the king shuts himself up, would not do. On the other hand, if the ministers were to say to the University, "Better not invite him," the Prince would be almost certain to hear of it, and that would not make things pleasant between Prussia and Bavaria.

I asked Dr. Döllinger whether he thought that the retaining or abolishing of the Athanasian Creed by the English Church would have any effect with regard to a future union between the English Church, the Old Catholics, and the Orientals. He laughed and said, "Not the least, whichever you do. The Old Catholics are not so fond of the Athanasian Creed, least of all the damnatory clauses. Of course they believe the main body of doctrine contained in it; but they have no special affection for the creed as it stands. But you will not abolish it: you will retain it and make the use of it optional.". "That is quite what I should like; but we are sometimes told, that if we give it up, there is an end of all chance of union with the Old Catholics." "Oh, no," he said, "it would make no difference."

He has to-day received an invitation from a German Professor in America (Dr. Schaff, I think) to attend a great congress of the Evangelical Alliance to be held next year in America. All his expenses to be paid by the Alliance. Of course he declined. At his time of life (73) such a journey is scarcely to be thought of, even if he were not imperatively wanted at home, and even if there was the remotest chance of an agreement between him and the Evangelical Alliance. "Whereas I imagine," he remarked, "that the lowest of the Low Church party in the English Church would be far too high for the Alliance."

On our way back he talked of the marvellous changes which have taken place in the population of Rome. As we passed the obelisk erected by Ludwig I. to the memory of the 30,000 Bavarians who fell in Napoleon's Russian campaign, Dr. Döllinger remarked, "There is a monument erected to the shame of Germany." "Yes," I said, "the inscription[23] has often puzzled me. In what sense is it true? Does it mean that they died to save Germany from being made Muscovite?" "No, no; not quite so strong as that. There was not the least chance of Russia's overrunning Germany at the time of Napoleon's march into Russia. No, I believe that the connexion of ideas in the king's mind was something of this sort: — that in order that Germany might be made free, it was necessary for some such monstrous outrage to be perpetrated as the carrying off of these 30,000 Bavarians by Napoleon to serve in his army. Such tyrannical acts lead to the overthrow of tyranny."

Wednesday, July 10th. I asked Dr. Döllinger whether he thought that a change would ever be made in the Church of Rome as to the celibacy of the clergy. "Yes," said he, "if other changes come; otherwise not. It will never come as a solitary change. We want both married and unmarried clergy. If the work of the Church is to be done properly, some of the clergy must remain unmarried. Others no doubt would do much better as married men. The difficulty is to know how to combine the two systems." "Are they not combined in the Greek Church?" "Yes, but not in a way that works well. The monks of course are unmarried, and so are the bishops. The rest of the clergy *must* marry: they are not ordained until they have married. Marriage after ordination is not allowed; and ordination after marriage is not allowed, excepting

---

23. Auch ₁sie starben für des Vaterlandes Befreiung.

of course to monks. This implies that the bishops are always monks, who know nothing of the clergy under them and have no sympathy with them. Of the life of a parish priest they know nothing. Bishops and clergy are separated from one another by a gulf and a very wide gulf, and that is a great inconvenience[24]. Here in Bavaria the enforced celibacy works very badly, much worse than in North Germany. Violations of it are common, especially in the country. It is known in the neighbourhood where the violation takes place; but the country people are very indulgent. They think it so hard that the priest is not allowed to marry. The one sin which they do not pardon in a cleric is avarice : a grasping priest is hated. The bishops also are commonly aware of these scandals. But it is very difficult to proceed in such cases; and the frequency of them makes it still more difficult." One thought of the point which Dr. Döllinger had urged in his Declaration, that for 58 holding to what the archbishop himself had just been holding he was threatened with a severe penalty generally reserved for clergy who are guilty of gross immorality, and seldom inflicted even on them; but I kept my thoughts to myself. He told me, to my surprise, that there is a great want of clergy in Bavaria, especially in this diocese. It is sometimes very difficult to get men for the work. Parents often send their sons to the university to study theology, simply in order to provide for them, and not because the sons wish to take orders. If the young man is once in a seminary, he is at least secure of bread and cheese for life. But then he must give up marriage, and perhaps he is already in love, if not engaged. Some are wise enough to give up a life for which they have no calling and leave theology for one of the other faculties. Others go on in desperation, under pressure of poverty, and of course do not make good priests.

Thursday, July 11th. Dr. Döllinger has just lent me Friedrich's *Offener Brief* to the Jesuit P. Rudolf Cornely, who had attacked Friedrich's *Tagebuch während des Vaticanischen Concils.* The letter is crushing, 59 and Cornely probably wishes that he had let the *Tagebuch* alone or handled it differently. Dr. Döllinger was at work looking out passages respecting the Jesuits when I called for him this evening. He said that he had come upon some terrible things. We talked a good deal about the Society during our walk across to Brunnthal and back by Zweibrücken. Among the many things which the world may hope to receive from him if he lives is a very curious passage in the history of the Jesuits[25]. He alone is in a position to write it; for although

24. "Inconvenience" with Dr. Döllinger was a word of strong meaning.
25. This appeared about a year before his death. *Geschichte der Moralstreitigkeiten in der römisch-katholischen Kirche etc.* Nördlingen, 1889. See the *Churchman* for April, 1889.

some of the necessary documents have been published, others have not been, and the originals are in his hands. They relate to *Gonzalez* who was General of the Society under Innocent XI., Alexander VIII., and Innocent XII. (from 1687 to 1705). He was forced upon the Society by Innocent XI. That Pope had a special aversion to the pernicious doctrine of probabilism, which is a pet doctrine with the Jesuits. He had heard that there was a Jesuit professor in Spain who dared to combat probabilism[26]; and when the General of the Jesuits died (Noyelle† Dec. 1686), Innocent got Gonzalez elected (by a narrow majority, July 1687). A few Jesuits were of Gonzalez' way of thinking, and thus for a long time there was open war in the Order. The rules of the Society prescribe that if there is sufficient reason, an extraordinary Assembly of the Company may be summoned, and such an assembly has power to depose the General. Gonzalez' friends had sufficient influence to prevent an extraordinary Assembly or General Convocation of the Society from being called, and Gonzalez remained General until his death. He had written a book against probabilism; but such was the power of the Company that he could not get it printed, in spite of the approbation and protection of Innocent XI. No printer in Rome would undertake it. At last he got the work printed at Dillingen in 60 Bavaria.

Innocent XI. is the only Pope in the last three centuries that there has been any thought of canonizing. Pius V. (1566) was the last that was canonized. The 'Acts' for the canonization of Innocent XI. were drawn up and are still in existence, printed. Gonzalez' narration of his intercourse with Innocent is among the evidence. But the Jesuits have done their utmost to prevent a man, who was so opposed to their Society, from being declared a saint. And they have succeeded. The suppression of the Jesuits by Clement XIV. in 1773 was no voluntary act on his part. He was driven on to do it by the Spanish ambassador and others, who threatened him with the exposure of certain awkward facts if he did not comply. The Bull gives full directions for the manner in which the suppression is to be carried out, and some of the measures are very harsh. The General [L. Ricci], who seems to have been a harmless man, was imprisoned in the Castle of S. Angelo, where he died. Clement XIV. died of terror at his own act. He lived in perpetual fear of being poisoned by the Jesuits, and at last killed himself with the antidotes which he was perpetually taking. Up to 1773 Munich was quite a paradise for the Jesuits. They were the lords of the situation. The 'Latin Congregation' and 'German Congregation' owe their origin to them. But when Pius VII. in an evil hour (1814) allowed the reinstitution of the Society, they were not allowed to return to Munich. Under the

26. As professor he had taught it, but afterwards (1665-1676) as mission preacher he saw the harm that it did and wrote against it.

late King Max they made one astounding effort to get back. King Maximilian was often unwell and suffered dreadfully from headache. Some Jesuits asked for an audience. They said that they were in possession of a secret remedy, which would cure the king, and they would tell him of it, if he would allow the Society to reestablish itself in Munich. King Max would not even see them, much less listen to such proposals.

I reckoned up the immense amount of work which Dr. Döllinger has on his hands at the present time. He assented to it, saying that it was "too much, too much." And the list which I told off at the moment as we walked along was by no means complete. There was much of which I knew nothing, besides one or two items which I forgot. 1. A complete edition of the lectures on the Reunion of Christendom 61 delivered in Munich last winter.   2. Historical letters to the German bishops touching the Vatican decrees and Alfonso de' Liguori as a Doctor of the Church.   3. An essay on Dante as a prophet.   4. An essay on the Lehninische Weissagung.   5. A vindication of the Knights Templar. He expects to be able to demonstrate their innocence. "It is very pleasant work," he remarked, "clearing the character of a much wronged body of men. The suppression of the Order was the most iniquitous act of that age of monstrous crimes."   6. A discussion of the authorship of the False Decretals. "It is commonly said that this is an unanswerable question; but I feel confident that I can prove when, and by whom, and with what object the forgery was committed." This brought us to his door. We stood there for a moment or two without speaking. There was a thought which must have been present to both of us after this summing up of the immense amount of work which this brave old man not only calmly sets before himself, but calmly labours at day by day. Would he ever live to finish it? I was struggling to find words that would not seem commonplace and heartless, in which to express a wish that his life might be spared until all was done. I had begun with "We must hope," when he too broke silence. With a sadder look than he often wears he said his usual parting words, "Good-night : to-morrow," and went in.

Friday, July 12th. An excellent lecture from Dr. Döllinger this afternoon on the period of Robespierre's greatest power. He has not the smallest sympathy with Louis Blanc's view that Robespierre was the hero of the Revolution. Rather he was a creature "without an idea in his head 62 or a feeling in his breast." When I called for him in the evening it was beginning to rain; but we would both of us rather get wet than not go out. We stayed out till 8.30, although at times the rain came down rather smartly.

The Jesuits were the chief subject of our conversation. "There was a time when I admired the Jesuits," said Dr. Döllinger; "but that was before I knew so much about them as I do now." "The corruption in the Order must have begun very soon." "Yes; there is a little book written by a well known Spanish Jesuit, Mariana,—perhaps the ablest man the Jesuits ever had,—in which he speaks of the diseases already existing in the Society[27]. It was written in Spanish and afterwards translated into Latin. It has since been published in Spanish again. The Jesuits declare that it is not Mariana's, and have had it put on the Index; but there is no doubt of its authenticity. Indeed they some-times admit it among themselves. I have myself seen a correspondence between a General of the Order and a member, in which the genuineness is admitted, but is nevertheless to be denied; and the book is to be carefully kept from members of the Order. To no country have the Jesuits done more harm than to *Poland*. It has not yet been sufficiently recognized how largely the ruin of Poland was due to them. They had the bringing up of the Polish nobility, and they instituted that system of oppression and persecution of all other religious communities, espe-cially the independent Greek Church. A country thus divided against itself could not stand. To *Spain* also they have done infinite harm. Hence the anxiety of the Spanish ambassador for the suppression of the Order. And I don't think that English Roman Catholics know how much better their position would have been in the old days of oppres-sion, had it not been for the Jesuits. I want to bring that out in my lectures on reunion."

Canonization was another topic. "No Pope has canonized so many people as the present one, and he has taken all sorts. Any one can be canonized now-a-days. Several whom other Popes have refused to accept, have been made saints by Pius IX. A Spanish inquisitor (Arbuez, the subject of Kaulbach's famous picture); a Polish persecutor, killed by an enfuriated mob; a crazy French nun (Maria Alacoque), who under the inspiration of a Jesuit (Colombière) invented the new devotion of 63 the heart of Jesus; etc., etc. And yet the bishops say nothing : not a word of protest. The beatification of the Spanish inquisitor seems to have passed almost unnoticed in the rest of Europe. In Germany it caused the greatest indignation, and evoked some very good articles in the *Allgemeine Zeitung* on the Inquisition generally. Kaulbach painted 64 the inquisitor at his work and exhibited the picture here in Munich,

---

27. *De las enfermedadas de la Compañia de Jesús.* The manuscript got into the hands of a French bookseller, who printed it in Spanish, French, Italian, and Latin, Bordeaux, 1625. It prophesies the downfall of the Company, if it does not mend its ways. It points out the divergence of the Company from the old monastic Orders, and condemns the despotic power of the General, who, with two or three subordinates in the provinces, controls everything. The number of regulations is so great that to keep them is scarcely possible; and the provinces get very little consideration from the central authority in Rome.

until the ultramontanes declared that it was creating quite a scandal and begged him to withdraw it, which he did. But other towns asked to see it, and I believe that it is still making a tour in Germany and Austria.

"It is surprising what one man can sometimes do. Baronius was charged with revising the *martyrology* and bringing out a new edition. In the *65* new one he made all the Popes of the first three centuries saints, and they have remained so ever since. In the martyrologies previous to Baronius only one or two here and there are called saints, and only one or two had been considered to be such. He canonized the whole list, entirely on his own authority. He did not know much Greek. He did not know that συνωρίς means 'a pair', and finding the word in the calendar with a pair of names after it, he thought they were three names of saints; and accordingly he enriched the calendar with a S. Synoris. His mistake was pointed out to him; but his first edition was out, and the mistake could not be corrected until the second. The formal ceremony of canonization is not older than the tenth century (Udalric, Bishop of Augsburg, by John XV., A.D. 993, a doubtful instance); but Alexander III. († 1181) was the first to claim it as a special privilege of the Pope. The present Pope (Pius IX.) has, under the direction of the Jesuits, made a very free use of his privilege [28]. Of course every Jesuit who is canonized is a proof of the excellence of the Order and a gratification of Jesuit pride. The last historian of the Order (*Cordara*), the one who brought down their own history of themselves to about 1625, since when it has not been continued, lived to see the suppression of the Order in 1773. He has left us his opinion *66* as to *why* they were put down, why the Almighty allowed so useful a society to be extinguished; and he comes to the conclusion that it is on account of their pride. 'We have been inordinately proud,' he confesses; 'we have set ourselves above everything, every office, and every institution. We have assumed our own superiority, and have treated all other Orders and Societies with contempt. Pride has been the cause of our fall'."

Saturday, July 13th. The Vienna *Presse* has a short history of the Jesuits at Innsbruck, scarcely an edifying one. Austria is being flooded with them, from Germany, Italy, Poland. Everywhere where a storm seems to be brewing against them, the Jesuits fly to Austria as to a promised

---

28. It was Alexander III. who canonized S. Bernard; and it was he who first used the formula (in the Third Lateran, 1079) *Nos*, SACRO APPROBANTE CONCILIO, *illa ita decernimus*. Pius IX. is specially in the hands of the Jesuit Piccirillo of the *Civiltà*. Care is taken that he does not hear much of the actual condition of modern society or of the real needs of the Church.

land. The papers are beginning to ask whether the government is going to take any steps in consequence.

A tremendous storm with such rain as one seldom sees prevented my going across to Dr. Döllinger until long after the usual time, and he had then given up all thought of a walk and was hard at work. Prince Hohenlohe had been to see him, having just come from Berlin. He says that one great cause of the government's proceedings against the Jesuits is fear of the influence which they exercise upon the troops, making the Roman Catholic soldiers disaffected, and unwilling to fight for a Protestant Empire. It was said in Italy that the clergy there tried to sow disaffection in the army, but without much success. In Germany, however, religion has a far more real hold upon the people than in Italy. Dr. Döllinger had just received from England a large octavo

67 volume on the doctrine of the Eucharist, by Dr. Vogan, Canon of Chichester. Neither of us had ever heard of him before. I only stayed a few minutes.

I take the opportunity of jotting down one or two things which Dr. Döllinger has told me at other times. The talkative old Pope has been

68 making some queer speeches lately. He was granting an audience to some charitable society, which gives relief to poor women in childbirth; and in his address to them he remarked that in these wicked times it might be just as well if women did *not* bear children. *Beata sterilis, quae non parit.* But then of course the world would come to an end; and that must be left in the hands of God.

A little while ago he raised a storm by talking about a challenge to Bismarck to answer a question, which had never been answered. The truth being that the challenge had never been sent and the question never asked. The commotion excited in Germany by this foolish speech and that about the Colossus which a small stone is soon to shatter, has not yet subsided. But now, after this unhappy attempt at political prophecy, he has been getting into a mess with his biblical history. Wishing to warn the Italians that they would probably find Victor Emmanuel's rule far worse than his own, he reminded them of the change in Israel from Samuel's rule to that of Saul. *Samuel* may have chastised them with whips, but *Saul* chastised them with scorpions. His own organ, the *Voce della Verità*, printed the speech without noticing the blunder, and then seems to have made matters worse by correcting it. But the Pope's ignorance is quite astounding. Not until the time of the Vatican Council did he know that the case of Honorius was a difficulty in the way of the dogma. When some one explained that the Sixth Council had condemned Pope Honorius for heresy, he said, "It is impossible. I order that the Papal Archives be searched, and it will then be discovered that the whole story is a lie." The possessor did not know that his archives only go back to Innocent III., some 550 years later than Honorius!

Sunday, 7th after Trinity, July 14th. In the evening Dr. Döllinger and I walked to Ober-Föhring, turning back before we quite reached the village. The dancing which was going on in the Paradies-Garten turned the conversation on to English and Scotch Sabbatarianism. He did not think that there was any truth in the view that strict Sabbatarianism comes from the Schoolmen. The scholastic theologians do *not* transfer the Jewish sabbath to the Lord's Day.

His opinion of Mommsen, the Macaulay of Roman History, is not a high one; he thinks him brilliant, but going far beyond what the evidence warrants. A much more solid writer is Drumann, Professor of History in the University of Königsberg. He has written the history of the later days of the Republic in a series of biographies—Pompeius, Caesar, Cicero, etc. Not such pleasant reading as Mommsen, but a *69* much more valuable work. Authorities are exactly quoted, whereas Mommsen gives you none. You are left to find out as best you may what is history and what is Mommsen. Drumann has also written a life of Boniface VIII., which, although by no means bad, is by no means *70* such solid work as his Roman History : original authorities have not been so thoroughly investigated. "I can lend you Drumann, if you like, any time to-morrow; and I will give you an introduction to the periodical room at the Royal Library. There is a first rate collection—some 200 different periodicals. I'll give you a note to the director, and then you can go there any morning you like. If I should go out, I will leave all ready for you."

Monday, July 15. This morning Dr. Döllinger *was* out, but Drumann and a note to Dr. Halm were waiting for me. I went into Dr. Döllinger's library to change some books and then went to the Royal Library. The periodical room is certainly well supplied with literature, but is most forbidding in appearance. Only the barest amount of furniture of a very comfortless type, while round the walls are tiers of cardboard boxes, in which are placed the back numbers of the periodicals. I was glad to find the other day that Dr. Döllinger was quite of the opinion that every large library ought to have a *burning committee*, a board who should be empowered to destroy literature which was likely to remain mere lumber, filling up valuable space. Of course such a committee would sometimes make mistakes and destroy things of real value, but the gain would be immense on the whole. There would not only be the saving of space, but saving of precious time to unfortunate authors hereafter. The amount of all but useless material that a "researcher" will have to wade through hereafter, is something awful to contemplate. I was delighted to find that Dr. Döllinger quite agreed with this idea.

Tuesday, July 16. The wet S. Swithin holds good thus far. I asked Dr. Döllinger whether S. Swithin's forty days were believed in in Germany.

He said, "No, for S. Swithin is not known. But there are three saints whose names end in -atius, S. Pankratius, S. Servatius, and — I forget the third[29], but they come close to one another in the calendar; and those are the saints who are supposed to control the weather." À propos of the Pope's biblical slip respecting Samuel and Saul for Solomon and Rehoboam, he told me of an absurd mistake made by the Archbishop of Munich. In one of his Lenten pastorals he gave as a reason for observing the season as a fast the text (!) that 'the flesh is strong, but the spirit is weak.' What made the slip all the more ludicrous was the fact that the archbishop is a large full-bodied man, who looks as if he lived well, and the supposed 'text' seemed to be the outcome of his own experience.

The Church of *Ara Coeli* on the Capitol at Rome was mentioned, and I remarked that I had never seen the famous *Bambino* there, — the doll which is dressed to represent the Infant Christ, and is supposed to have miraculous powers of healing. It is constantly taken out by the monks to work cures on sick people; but evidently its visits do not exclude the services of a doctor. Dr. Pantaleoni, who was here the other day, told Dr. Döllinger that he was once attending a patient in Rome, and the Bambino arrived at the same time that he did! It would have been awkward, if both had been doctors, or both had been wonder-working dolls. As it was, things passed off quite happily, and *both received fees*, the Bambino receiving exactly the same fee as the physician! In the event of a cure, which would get the credit?

Wednesday, July 17th. I asked Dr. Döllinger his opinion of the value of Brockhaus' *Conversations-Lexicon*. He spoke very highly of it, and said that Germans found it quite indispensable. He told me of a laughable mistake which appeared in the first edition in the article on Anaxagoras. The compiler of the article apparently knew no Greek, and gathered most of his information from the *Biographie Universelle*. It states there of course that the central idea of Anaxagoras' philosophy was νοῦς; νοῦς was his principle. But the word was printed in Latin characters, not in Greek; *nous*, not νοῦς. The compiler mistook the Greek *nous* for the French *nous*, and translated accordingly. The new principle which Anaxagoras introduced into philosophy was 'das *wir*'. Thus the 'we', and not 'mind', was made to be the principle of Anaxagoras. An amazing slip in a German encyclopedia! This led on to the mention of other translations, especially of the Bible. I was surprised to find that German Roman Catholics have no authorized translation. In every Church there is a translation of the Epistles and Gospels; but these are very various. Protestants for the most part used a corrected Luther. Dr. Döllinger told me that Newman had once been asked by

29. S. Bonifazius, May 12, 13, and 14.

the Pope to edit an English Bible for the use of Roman Catholics. The idea was believed to have emanated from Cardinal Wiseman, and the object of it to be, to give Newman harmless occupation for the rest of his life, so as to keep his mind, or at any rate his pen, from working in a way that persons in high quarters might not like. But Newman was not to be caught in such a snare, and English literature is so much the richer in consequence.   71

This was interesting, but what followed was still more so. Cardinal Wiseman once wrote to Dr. Döllinger (he believes that he has the letter still) claiming the credit of Newman's conversion. An article in the *Dublin Review* was supposed to have convinced Newman that his position in the Church of England was untenable. When Newman and Wiseman 72 at last met, the latter discovered that his supposed convert was a *far* more able man than himself and not very likely to have been influenced by his arguments. He never quite got over it; and his endeavour to silence Newman by giving him a translation of the Bible to play with was the result of the impression which Newman's intellect made upon him.

Dr. Döllinger also told me a good deal about the visions and revelations of the ecstatic nun Anna Katharina von Emmerich. Brentano had heard of this celebrated Westphalian nun, and had gone to observe her and converse with her, and in fact had supplied her with the materials for her revelations; i.e. he used to tell her things which she had never heard before, and these used to come back to him again in the form of visions and so forth, which he took down and afterwards published. These chiefly had reference to the Passion of Christ, going into minute details, such as are not found anywhere but in legends. The book was published both in French and German, and created a great sensation in both countries. Brentano[30] was son of a Frankfort merchant, and when he was in Munich Dr. Döllinger saw him pretty often and used to walk with him. Of course he heard a good deal from him about this nun. Brentano apparently did not see that what she told him was merely what he had told her, transformed into a so-called vision by a very excitable temperament, a very active imagination, and perhaps something of deceit. I asked Dr. Döllinger whether he thought that in such cases the woman was generally honest. "Only half, only half. The temptation to be 'interesting' is to most women almost irresistible. They will practise deception involving the most painful privations and sufferings in order to be thought specially

---

30. Clemens Brentano, born 1777 or 1778, died 1842 at Aschaffenburg; 1822 he became secretary to the Propaganda at Rome and afterwards lived in Ratisbon and Munich. His *Leben der heil. Jungfrau Maria. Nach der Anna K. Emmerich Betrachtungen*, München, 1852, was published after his death. His sister, Bettina v. Arnim, and his wife "Seraphine" were authoresses. Another sister married Savigny.

gifted with spiritual graces. Another very famous case was that of a Spanish nun at the end of the sixteenth century, Maria D'Agreda[31], authoress of *The Mystic City of God*[32]. It created an immense amount of controversy. Bossuet and other French prelates urged Rome to condemn it. The whole Franciscan Order defended it, for the nun was a Franciscan. Meanwhile the book was translated into all languages and circulated everywhere. It makes the Blessed Virgin a kind of second Saviour, and has been one of the main causes of the modern extravagant cultus of the Blessed Virgin. An attempt was made to get the nun canonized, but the Pope refused. Pio IX., however, is only too likely to do it, if he is pressed. Brentano told *his* nun about the Spanish nun, of whom she had not previously heard. A few days afterwards she had had a vision. She had seen a church with an open door, and a nun in the Franciscan habit on the door-step. Two monks, one on each side of her, were endeavouring to push her into the church. All of no avail. The Franciscan nun was too *stout*, and could not be made to go through the door-way! This was Anna Katharina's reproduction of what Brentano had told her; with the implication that the Spanish nun ought not to be canonized, and that *The Mystic City of God* was all nonsense." This was Brentano's own opinion of the book, as he told Dr. Döllinger. He never seemed to see the similarity between his own nun and the Franciscan nun.

Bossuet's nephew, who went to Rome to influence the Pope and Curia in favour of his uncle against Fénelon, gives an account of a curious case of deception, which was discovered while he was in Rome. The chief actor in it had obtained such a reputation for a sanctity that people used to visit his room as if it were a holy place. The nephew's letters are in the complete edition of Bossuet's works, and there the whole story may be found. The letters take one behind the scenes into a maze of intrigue, and one learns something of the means taken to

73   31. "Sister Maria d'Agreda was born 1602, and at 17, entered the Convent of the Immaculate Conception at Agreda, during the early years of her profession she had frequent commands in a Vision to write the life of the B. Virgin, but did not commence her work until 1637. She died in May, 1675. There has been much controversy in regard to these Revelations."

32. *Mystica Civitas Dei* of Maria d'Agreda, commonly called Sister Mary of Jesus, of Agreda in Burgos. It exists in Spanish, Italian, Latin, and German. The second title of the book is *Vita Virginis Matris Dei, Reginae et Dominae nostrae SS. Mariae*. The authoress wrote it twice. After she had written it the first time she changed her confessor, and the new one told her to burn it : he did not approve of women writing books. Her biographer suggests that he was under the influence of evil spirits. As specimens of its contents it may suffice to mention that there is a chapter on what the B. Virgin was doing before she was born (quae Maria intra materna viscera operata est) and that it contains a long prayer which she offered during that period (lib. I. xx), that she ascends with Christ (VI. xxix), and then descends to earth to become *Ecclesiae Patrona et magistra* (VII. i). She instructs the Apostles, sends S. James to Spain, etc. etc.

ensure Fénelon's condemnation, not at all connected with the goodness or badness of the cause. Fénelon's submission, Dr. Döllinger holds, was very much like many of the submissions to the new dogma; submission, for the sake of peace and unity, without internal assent; an agreement to use the same words and mean something totally different by them. There are letters of Fénelon's in existence, written after his submission, which show that he still believed in the truth of his original position. He knew no doubt *how* his condemnation had been procured, and that rash or heretical statements in Bossuet's works had been spared in order to serve political and other purposes.

I mentioned that I had just heard from England that experts had been examining the Utrecht manuscript containing the Athanasian Creed, and had pronounced it to be of the sixth century, and the latter of it. He shook his head very doubtfully. "That is very difficult to affirm. It is almost impossible to distinguish between manuscripts of that date and those of the seventh or beginning of the eighth century. There is no difference in the writing, nothing by which you can decide, unless there is internal evidence in the matter of the manuscript." He went on presently to say, "I suppose that no one now defends the verse in S. John about the three Heavenly Witnesses; *that* must be given up." "No critics, I imagine; but there are a few persons who do so;" and I told him of Dr. Tatham's celebrated sermon. "Cardinal Wiseman," 74 said Dr. Döllinger, "once wrote a pamphlet to try and show that the verse was in the old African Version which preceded the Vulgate. 75 But the passage is not in a single Greek manuscript. It caused years of delay in the bringing out of Cardinal Mai's edition of the Vatican manuscript (B), so that it was not published until after his death. Some 76 persons in Rome would not hear of the edition being printed without the passage, and Mai could not bring himself to consent to its being inserted. Unfortunately the work was so carelessly done in other respects that it is almost worthless. Tischendorf's edition, which costs only a few shillings, is quite trustworthy, and is all that one needs." About 77 the last verses of S. Mark he seemed to have no decided view.

Thursday, July 18th. Dies Alliensis. Anniversary of the formal declaration of war between France and Prussia, and of the passing of the dogma at Rome, in 1870. I spent a good part of the afternoon in Dr. Döllinger's library, overhauling the *Historisches Taschenbuch* and the *Relazioni degli Ambasciatori Veneti al Senato.* In the latter I found something like a parallel to Disraeli's sarcasm "The worst of Mr. Gladstone is, that he has no redeeming vices." Marino Cavalli, ambassador at the court of Charles V., in writing to the Senate, gives a description of the Emperor; how eminently proper, respectable, polite, and pious he was; adding *"non ha imperfezione alcuna, che s'astiene da tutti i vizj,"* which, how- 78 ever, has by no means the point of Dizzy's remark. Huber was also at work in the library at the same time on the Jesuits and their tendencies. It is reported that the Jesuits are urging the Pope to leave Rome and are leaving it themselves. On which Dr. Döllinger remarked, as we crossed the Isar afterwards, "*Now* perhaps we shall be able to get at the Papal Archives;" and, after a pause, "*You* may live to see *very* wonderful changes." I told him of Cavalli's remark about Charles V. "Not that it's true," he said : "Charles V. had several mistresses and illegitimate children. But he is admirable compared with his son. One might say just the reverse of him — that he had not a single virtue. I don't think that there is any character in history that I hate so much as Philip II." "Our King John would run him hard for badness; and he was so mean with it all." "Still I don't think that he was as bad as Philip II."

79   In the *Historisches Taschenbuch* for 1843 I had found an essay by Kurtzel on "the Jesuit Girard and his saint". This was Catharine Cadière; another case of visions used for a purpose, like Maria Alacoque under the influence of the Jesuit Colombière, who invented the devotion of the heart of Jesus. "With the Jesuits," said Dr. Döllinger, "the purpose of such impostures has generally been to invent some new doctrine or devotion, to be used as an instrument for working on the minds and feelings of men. The history of the doctrine of the Immaculate Conception of the Blessed Virgin illustrates this. The Franciscans were jealous of the Dominicans, who had quite thrown them into the shade, and had got possession of all the high places, — the Inquisition, the Index, the chief theological chairs, and the office of *Magister Palatii*, once a *very* important office in Rome. The Franciscans found the doctrine of the Immaculate Conception given as 'probable' in their great doctor Duns Scotus. Thomas Aquinas rejects the doctrine; so of course the Dominicans were bound to reject it. Here then was an engine which might be worked against the Dominicans. Then came the Carmelites, devoted to the culture of the Blessed Virgin, and of course they sided with the Franciscans. Lastly we have the Jesuits. They were already opposed to the Dominicans on the questions of grace and free will, and therefore naturally opposed them in this other doctrine also. Besides they wanted the doctrine of the Immaculate Conception as a new machine for winning influence. There must from time to time be some novelty introduced; old dogmas and forms of cultus lose their power. It is remarkable that the Dominicans stood out so long against the combined attack of three Orders. They did not succumb until the present Pope made the doctrine an article of faith in 1854. Now they have much fallen in numbers and influence. The Pope finished them by giving them a General who

80   is entirely the creature of the Jesuits. There are a few Dominican convents in Germany. Lacordaire tried to revive the Order in France. But the new monasteries have not thriven; and since Lacordaire they have not produced a single man of note."

I have lately seen a sketch of the interview between the old Napoleon and the cardinals, in which Napoleon became abusive and received a good answer. "*Siete birboni*," said the little man, "*tutti quanti.*" "*Non tutti quanti*," was the reply, "*ma* BUONA PARTE." This anecdote drew the following from Dr. Döllinger. "When Lamennais was here in Munich after his return from Rome[33], I saw something of him, and used to walk with him. He told me that he was talking to one of the cardinals, who was lamenting the deplorable state of the Sacred College. 'In most societies,' said this cardinal, 'you will find one, or two, or perhaps even three able men; but in our College we are *every one of us* block-heads'." Bishop Dupanloup told Dr. Döllinger another story which illustrates the ignorance and isolation of the Roman *prelati*. Some French bishop was telling a Roman cardinal of the trouble they had in France with the marriage question. Many people simply went to the *Maire* and obtained the civil marriage without ever coming to church for the ecclesiastical rite; which caused much scandal and difficulty. "Difficulty! you call that a difficulty? *dunque perchè avete i vostri carceri?*" The worthy Italian prelate did not know that French bishops have no prisons, nor that putting people in prison would not solve all difficulties. "In Italy," Dr. Döllinger added, "things are just the reverse at present : the difficulty is all the other way. The clergy urge the lower orders to come and be married in church, which is very right and proper. But they also urge them *not* to go and obtain the civil marriage, which is the *only* marriage recognized by the State. The consequence is that a large number of children are in the eyes of the law illegitimate, and consequently cannot inherit property. The amount of difficulty and distress which is thus being laid up in store for many of these unfortunate people will soon call for some strong measures on the part of the government. People are losing their birthrights."

The *Spectator*, or some correspondent, has been wondering with what face Dr. Döllinger could receive the Jansenist, i.e. heretical, Archbishop of Utrecht. "What I should say in answer to such a question," said Dr. Döllinger, "would be just this : — that I agree with Pope Benedict XIV. in thinking the so-called 'Jansenist heresy' a piece of humbug got up by the Jesuits to suit their own purposes; that I regard the Church of Utrecht as orthodox and the excommunication of its members invalid; and that therefore I have a perfect liberty to hold communion with the archbishop or any one else." He went on to say that the archbishop is chosen by the whole community, and due notice is always sent to Rome. Rome always answers by excommunicating him, and he reads his own excommunication from the pulpit. Then all goes on as before. There are two bishops as well [as] the archbishop, so that the succession is always kept up.

33. viz. in 1832 after the *Avenir* had been stopped.

Friday, July 19th. The *Norddeutsche Allgemeine Zeitung* returns to the charge against the *Germania* about the 27 Irish bishops who in 1826 declared that the Infallibility of the Pope was no part of the Catholic faith[34]. Of three things one must be true. *Either* the Catholic faith has been changed; *or* the bishops did not know the Catholic faith; *or* they knew it and told a lie. The *Norddeutsche Allgemeine Zeitung* would hardly have mentioned the third possibility, had not a French ultra-montane given it as the true one. He says that the bishops, bent on winning from the English government that liberty for the Church which was due, made such statements as they thought best calculated to induce the government to make the desired concessions! The letter is quoted *81* in Pressensé's recent book on the Vatican Council. But it is certain that Bailly's work on dogmatic theology was still the text-book in the seminaries in Ireland in 1826; and it has now been placed on the *82* Index (1852) while the infallibilist Denz has been made the text-book in dogmatic theology, and the infallibilist and probabilist Liguori has been made the text-book in moral theology. "That is another thing that I want to write," said Dr. Döllinger, as we walked out to Biederstein in the evening talking of these things. "The story of how the way was prepared for the Vatican Council has not yet been told; and I mean to tell it. The putting Bailly's book on the Index was one step, and the introduction of Liguori was another ... I have often wondered, and I have never been able to satisfy myself about the matter, why it is that the Jesuits have never made any way in Ireland. They never seem to have done so. In the seventeenth and eighteenth centuries one hears little or nothing of them there, and I fancy that their influence there now is very small. I think there must be something in the Irish character, which makes it not good material for Jesuit influence. One would have thought, however, that the English character was still more alien from the Jesuit system with its espionage and the like. And yet when I was at Stonyhurst (in 1858?) there were about a dozen Oxford men, converts, being trained as Jesuits. The same thing is seen among the Irish Catholics in the United States; the Jesuits get very few recruits from them. I don't know what the reason is."

Saturday, July 20. There is important news to-day. It is stated that the Chaldean Patriarch has declared himself and his Church to be separated *83* from Rome. "But Rome is past teaching," I remarked, as we talked the matter over during our walk : "No amount of secessions would induce her to change." "No, not so long as there are Jesuits," said

34. At the Vatican Council Cardinal Cullen, Archbishop of Dublin, appealed to Archbishop Mac Hale of Tuam to witness that Ireland had always been infallibilist. The aged Mac Hale, who had been Archbishop for 35 years, at once rose and said that *84* neither he nor Ireland had believed the doctrine.

Dr. Döllinger. "And the system has become too rigid, too stereotyped, to be changed." "Not even the secession of all the German bishops, which certainly seemed to be a possibility *before* the Council, would have had the effect." With characteristic generosity he made a diversion to defend the men who had so cruelly deserted him in the hour of trial. "There would have been a schism in every diocese," he said. "Every bishop would have had a large number of his clergy and of the laity also up in arms against him. Those opposed to him would of course have Rome on their side. And among those opposed to him would be all the religious orders and all the old women; and those are two hosts in themselves. The state of things would have been intolerable; it would have been impossible to go on." "And now, instead of a schism in every diocese, you have a schism in every individual conscience. I am not sure that that is not worse." He gave no answer. After a pause he said, "Had I been a bishop in the circumstances, what I should have done would have been this. As soon as I returned from Rome I should have called a diocesan council, — as many of the clergy as I could get and a certain number of the laity, — and I would have said to them, 'I cannot accept this new doctrine : it is not the doctrine of the Church. If you cannot accept it either, — good : we will stand by one another. You must support me, and I will support you.' But if a large majority had said, 'We submit; we accept the dogma,' then I should have resigned my bishopric. This is what our bishops might have done; but they were not men of character enough for that." "What would have been the result here in Munich? Would the archbishop have been supported by his clergy?" "Yes, he would." "I knew that the city clergy would have done so; I did not know what the case would have been with the country clergy." "About the country clergy it is difficult to speak. They are usually under the influence of a newspaper and the newspaper they take in is commonly an ultramontane one."

We talked much of schools, English, French, and German. The German *gymnasien* are all day schools, no boarders. But in some places, as here, there is also a 'college', in which boys are boarded while they attend the *gymnasium*. There are seldom, if ever, any places in which boys are both boarded and taught. Both boys and parents like the 'college' system; the parents get rid of the boys, and the boys are more with other boys. In Munich, besides four *gymnasien* and a 'college', there is also a *pagerie*. The *pagerie* is a college for the sons of noblemen; but they are merely housed there. They go out for their education, which as a rule is very superficial, because they attempt to learn such a number of subjects. The result is a mere smattering.

Sunday, 8th after Trinity, July 21st. As we walked home in the evening, I asked Dr. Döllinger what had been the meaning of the great discussion respecting the *colours* of the Empire, i.e. what combination it

ought to have in its flag. He said that it was a matter of doubt what the right colours were. The Empire had been so long in the House of Austria, that the Austrian colours (yellow and black) had been the colours of the German Empire. The question was, had the Empire any colours other than those of Austria, and if so what? Many people contended for red, black, and gold, which had been the colours used in 1815 and again in 1849. But it is now pretty generally agreed that the right colours are red, white, and black, colours which are much older than 1815; and these prevail. "I remember," I said, "that the Bishop of Passau last year invented new colours for Bavaria; i.e. he hung out black flags along with the Bavarian blue and white on Corpus Christi." "Yes," said Dr. Döllinger, "to express his grief at the wickedness of the world in general and of Bavaria in particular. He is a strange man, the Bishop of Passau. He was the last of the German bishops
85 to give in his adhesion to the Vatican Council; only at Easter last year. He wrote to the Archbishop of Munich to say that he had been meditating much during Holy Week on the Passion of our Lord, especially upon the Bloody Sweat; and that he himself had been well nigh in the same condition in considering what was to be done respecting the decrees of the Council. He had a great deal more trouble than I had. It did not take me two minutes to decide what I ought to do. I very soon made up my mind about that." "Although the archbishop *did* give you two or three extra weeks, after the 15th of March[35], in order to think it over." "Yes, I had been told to declare myself by that time. But I wrote and told the archbishop, in a letter which I mean to publish some day, that I was not ready with my statement; that I should require some weeks before I could finish, but that as soon as it was completed he should have it. The fact was I had not quite made up my mind what points I would bring forward most prominently and what I would leave out altogether. The archbishop wrote back and

86   35. March 15th, 1890.
"THE BAVARIAN OLD CATHOLICS. Munich, March 15.
Baron von Luetz, the Prime Minister and Minister of Public Worship, made a statement to-day in the Bavarian Diet defining the position of the Bavarian Government towards the Old Catholics. The statement was made on the discussion of a resolution brought forward by Dr. Rampf, Sub-Dean of Munich, accusing the Old Catholics of denying the Papal infallibility and repudiating the decrees of the Council of Florence regarding the honours and primacy of jurisdiction of the Pope. The Premier acknowledged that the Old Catholics had rejected the *vaticanum* and other doctrines of the Church. The Bavarian Government had not, it was true, formally notified by *placetum regium* its acceptance of the Vatican decrees, but it had done so by implication, by its actions and decisions. The Government had therefore informed the community of Old Catholics in Bavaria that the Old Catholics of the Munich diocese could no longer be recognised as members of the Catholic Church."
Döllinger died Jan. 10th, 1890. Von Lutz did not save himself by throwing over the Old Catholics. He had to resign, on a plea of ill health, at the end of May.

said that I could have two more weeks. I sent him my declaration within the time, telling him that it would be published in the *Allgemeine Zeitung* the same day." "It was said at the time (although I knew that it could not be the right explanation) that there were certain services during Holy Week in the Royal Chapel in which, in the ordinary course, you would take a prominent part; and therefore, if you made your declaration on the 15th, there would be the difficulty, either of your being absent because of the excommunication, or of your being present in spite of it. The three extra weeks were to tide over the difficulty." "Oh no, not at all that. It was merely that my declaration was not ready."

After a pause he went on, "In the fifteenth century it was the German universities which stood up for the liberties of the Church against the Pope, and which contended for the principle of the Council of Constance, — the superiority of Councils to Popes. It was that wretched Frederick III., the worst Emperor in the whole succession of Emperors, that made a bargain with the Pope, and for a large sum of money and absolution from all his sins sold to Eugenius IV. the liberties of the German Church. He forced the universities to give way. Vienna held out longest; it still held to the Council of Basel. But at last it gave way also. The faculty of theology held out longest." "Things are just reversed in that respect now-a-days." "Yes. *Janus* exposes that transaction between Frederick III. and the Pope[36]. It was not so well known before that. People have remarked a likeness between *Janus* and *Quirinus*; but whether they are cousins, or brothers, or what, is still discussed. *It was a bishop who supplied most of the material for* 87 *Quirinus' letters from Rome. Ce qui se passe au Concile* was written 88 by a Parisian, Jules Galliard; but he had good materials to work from." 89

Monday, July 22nd. There has been some discussion as to how far Bismarck is responsible for the law against the Jesuits. Dr. Döllinger seems to have no doubt that he is the originator of the law : indeed he speaks as if he knew this. He told me of a ministerial council held before the debate in the Reichstag, in which Bismarck made his famous speech, "We are not going to Canossa either in the body or in the spirit[37]." At the council of ministers discussion had gone on for some 90 time and Bismarck had not yet spoken. At last he said, "It is my opinion that the Jesuits should be excommunicated from the German Empire. They must be put under the ban of the Empire. *Hinaus mit ihnen.*"

During our walk we talked of the Bavarian Lakes, Theatines, and short sight; but Dr. Döllinger was not inclined to talk much. During his visits to England one of the things which struck him was the com-

---

36. §XXVI, p. 352.
37. "Wir gehen nicht nach Canossa weder körperlich noch geistlich."

paratively few people who wear spectacles. Here short sight is very common among the upper classes, not among the peasantry. He attributes it partly to want of exercise in the boys' schools and partly to the badly printed books of 100 or 150 years ago. Before 100 or 150 years ago there is not much trace of the disease being prevalent; but now it is perhaps in some cases hereditary. He evidently did not think much of my view that young men sometimes think it fine or interesting or becoming, to have a pair of glasses to dangle and to stick occasionally on the bridge of their noses. The habit of using them would weaken the sight.

Dr. Döllinger is not fond of dogs. A dog is the only animal that makes a noise for the mere sake of making it. No animal is so shamelessly obscene. Having dogs for pets is a modern and western invention. Neither the old Greeks nor the old Romans made pets or companions of them; nor do Orientals at the present day.

Tuesday, July 23. The Protestants in Munich have at last begun to build a second church; — not before it was wanted. Dr. Döllinger told me as we walked that there are now nearly 20,000 Protestants in Munich; and in 1800 there was not one. The Queen's preacher was the first, and no one would give him a lodging! The king had to let him have rooms in the Residenz. A wine-merchant from the Palatinate was the first Protestant citizen, about 1803. Augsburg on the contrary was once entirely Protestant; but the Catholics gained admission, and are now two thirds of the population. In the sixteenth and seventeenth centuries it was·not uncommon in Germany for one party to turn the other bodily out of the town; but, excepting in the early days of the Reformation, persecution in Germany did not take the form of bloodshed. By the peace of Westphalia it was agreed that all parties should be as they were in 1624. All persons, whether Catholics or Protestants, who had been driven out or dispossessed for their religion, should be reinstated. In 1624 the Catholic reaction had scarcely begun; a later year would have been disadvantageous to the Protestants. This agreement applied only to the Empire; the kingdom of Austria would not accept it. Hence the Protestants in Bohemia and Moravia were very badly treated; and in Silesia the Jesuits preached persecution with fire and sword.

We talked also of the evil effects of seminaries, i.e. special schools and colleges for boys and young men who are intended for Holy Orders. The system was ordered by the Council of Trent, but until the last thirty years or so it was but little known in Germany. It has its advantages, as Dr. Döllinger allowed, but he was strong as to its enormous disadvantages, and he said that the marked inferiority of the younger clergy, who had been brought up under this system, to the older, who have not, is everywhere admitted. By the seminaries boys and young men are, so to say, *cheated* into taking Orders. They are taken from their families before they know anything of the world, or what their own tastes are likely to be; and they do not return into the world until the irrevocable step is taken. They know nothing of women, young or old; and at four and twenty they are in the confessional hearing confessions from girls and women of all ages and all classes, with nothing to guide them but the coarse books of casuistry on which they have been trained in the seminary. With some brutal question they rush in indiscreetly and ruin a young girl's delicacy for ever. The very best seminaries involve these "inconveniences";—a fatal isolation from the world which these young men are hereafter to guide and teach, and a fatal destruction of sympathy in preparation for an office in which sympathy is the indispensable quality. And of course there are many seminaries which are very far from being the very best.

Dr. Döllinger thinks that the confessional is almost a necessity in schools. Without it giant evils may exist without your knowing anything of them, or, if you do know, without your being able to get at them. He admitted that confession was neither prevention nor cure; but at least it lessened the evil and acted as a check on its growth.

"One thing which a German is struck with in England," said he, "is the silence of church-bells. During the whole six work-days he never hears them; and his ear is so accustomed to the sound, that the absence of it at once makes itself felt. Only on Sunday does he hear it." "Daily service, however, has become much more common : it has spread enormously during the last thirty years." I might have added that in Germany they often have bells without any service; but yet the bells remind people of the hour of prayer. It was probably the 9 p.m. bell which prompted his remark. "Still," he replied, "the lower orders in England—I am speaking of Protestants—hardly know what prayer is; they have never been brought up to it. Now the poor with us, especially the women, when they are in trouble, go instinctively to church and pray, and come away refreshed, soothed, and comforted. English poor read their bibles, but they don't pray much. Much the same may be said of our Protestants; but they have their hymns, their religious songs, their *Lieder*, and many of these are prayers and are a great help to them. They know them by heart; for owing to rhyme and rhythm they are easily remembered, so as to be ready when wanted. In England you have not this. You have not the word to express it even, not having the thing. *Das Lied*—'Song' will not do; a *Lied* is not exactly a song." I told him that a great advance had been made in England in the way of hymns during the last ten years. He had never heard of *Hymns Ancient and Modern*. The *Christian Year* of course 91 he knew, and asked if it was sung in churches. I said that a few pieces were, but not many. "We all of us," he said, "have a great deal to learn from one another. All the great Christian communities must try to learn the others' good points. That is one of the ways in which reunion must come about. We must break through the walls of partition more and more." "They have begun to crumble away somewhat already." "Yes, another such Pope as Pius IX. will help forward the work greatly." "You mean that he will cause the barriers to burst; the constraint will be felt to be intolerable." He nodded assent and added, "I only hope we may have a Pope who will make two more new dogmas. I could wish for nothing better." "Have you any idea what they would be?" "Oh, impossible to say; — the immaculate conception of Joseph perhaps, or of the legendary grandmother, S. Anna." "Or the assumption." "Yes, it is quite possible that they might make the bodily assumption of the Virgin into a dogma." "Do not some now teach the assumption of S. Mary Magdalen?" "I never heard of that; but it is quite possible that some teach it." It was then agreed that I should not call for him next evening, as there was a meeting of the Senate to elect the next Rector of the University.

No lecture to-day. Dr. Döllinger's lectures ended last week [38].

92 *Wednesday, July 24th.* A letter from Dr. Newman at Abbotsford:

"Give my best love to Dr. Döllinger and tell him, not that I was surprised, but sorry that he was separated from me, and that he has no cause for being more than sorry, not surprised, that I should be separated from him. His message about being surprised at me is not — "Tu quoque", because *I* was not surprised at *him* — but it is a proof that the most excursive of readers and the most accurate of memories are sometimes at fault.

I have for these 25 years spoken *in behalf* of the Pope's Infallibility. The other day a review (I forget what) observed with surprise that even in my article on la Mennais in 1838 I had tacitly accepted the Pope's Infallibility. I think I have spoken *for* it in my Essay on Development of doctrine in 1845. In 1851 I have introduced the Pope's Infal-
93 libility several times into my lectures at the Birmingham Corn Exchange. In 1852 I introduced it most emphatically and dogmatically into my lectures delivered at the Rotondo at Dublin. In 1856 I spoke of it in a new Preface I prefixed to the new edition of my Church of the Fathers, and in 1868 I reprinted the passage from my Dublin Lectures in a collection of passages made by a Roman Jesuit Father on the dogma in an Italian translation.

This is quite consistent, in my way of viewing it, with my being most energetic against the *definition*. Many things are true which are not points of faith, and I thought the definition of this doctrine *most*

---

38. He never delivered any more.

inexpedient. And, as St. Paul, though inspired, doubted whether his words might not do harm to his Corinthian converts, so do I now fear much lest the infallible voice of the Council may not do harm to the cause of the Church in Germany, England, and elsewhere.

What I said in the private letter to my Bishop, to which Dr. Döllinger alludes, was that the definition *would unsettle men's minds*. This anticipation has been abundantly fulfilled. I said moreover expressly that it would be *no* difficulty to *me*, but that it was making the defence of Catholicism more *difficult*. As a proof that all this is the true view of my position, I have *never been called* on, as Gratry was, publicly to accept the doctrine — *because* I had never denied it."

Thursday, S. James' Day. It is the turn for Medicine to have the Rector for the coming University year. Professor Dr. Plank was elected last night by 60 votes against 7. The senators elected were Friedrich, Brinz, Seuffert, Pözl, Seidd, Lindwurm, and Christ. I said to Dr. Döllinger that I hoped the elections had gone as he wished. "Oh, yes; the ultramontanes are powerless in this University. Once it was all the other way. Now they are not even a party, — only the wrecks of one. Gladstone, Lord Shaftesbury, and Lord Acton are to have honorary degrees, with some others whose names I have forgotten. It is said that Max Müller has been commissioned to represent Oxford; but there has been no formal answer yet.

"I have had a call from Graf Tauffkirchen, the Bavarian ambassador at Rome, to-day. He says that the Pope is well in health, but there are signs of his mind giving way. Antonelli also is breaking up and looks very much older than his years. It is said that the editor of a radical paper in Rome has got possession of some letters of Antonelli's to a lady, which compromise Antonelli very much, and they are being used as an engine to extort money. Graf Tauffkirchen says that he saw no signs of the Jesuits leaving Rome. The question of the Pope's leaving Rome, and of the next conclave being held out of Rome (in France, no doubt), is hotly debated. Antonelli is said to be very strong against the conclave being held in Rome." I asked Dr. Döllinger if there was any instance of a Pope going out of his mind, and he said, "No, none. It is reported sometimes that Boniface VIII. died in a state of frenzy, tearing the flesh off his arms with his teeth, at the treatment which he received from Nogaret and Sciarra Colonna at Anagni and the Orsini in Rome. But those who would be most likely to know say nothing about it. By the way, Cardinal Wiseman once wrote an apology for Boniface VIII. in the *Dublin*; and I have several times been told that 94 he wrote it by *my* advice; that he had asked me what I thought would be a good point to elucidate in the history of the Papacy, and that I had recommended a defence of Boniface VIII. I cannot remember having said anything of the kind. Anyhow the apology was a complete failure. He defended Boniface by the simple expedient of ignoring all that tells against him. The case against Boniface has become much stronger of late since the discovery and publication of documents which place a good deal of the wickedness with which Boniface was charged, beyond a doubt. You might defend Alexander VI. by Cardinal Wiseman's method; indeed it has been done by a Frenchman, — quite a worthless book. Clement XIV. is also sometimes said to have gone mad. Pius VII., after having been tormented into signing, what he believed he ought never to have signed, by Napoleon, and being much stricken in conscience afterwards, is reported to have exclaimed, 'I shall go mad, like Clement XIV.' But Clement never went mad. What *is* true of him is that he lived in perpetual terror of being poisoned by Jesuits for having suppressed their Order, and that he killed himself at last by antidotes."

Mr. Hind the astronomer has been writing to the *Times* about the various occasions on which there has been great darkness over the earth. The last total eclipse of the sun was in 1742; the next will be in 1999. I was telling this to Dr. Döllinger when he exclaimed, "In 1999! Poor man, he does not know about the great darkness which is to come in August! And there is something more to tell about that. The black tapers which are being sold have given rise to a further question : — *How are the tapers to be lighted*? So now they are selling consecrated matches to light the consecrated tapers!" I simply roared and stamped with laughter. Happily no one was by. "Yes," he went on, "it might seem impossible, but for all that it is a fact. There is a priest here who goes about with a mysterious look. He has written upon asceticism; among other things he has written a translation of *The Mystic City of God* by that Spanish nun. Well, he is now selling consecrated matches to light the black tapers!"

Of course I told Dr. Döllinger of Dr. Newman's letter; indeed read most of it to him. "It is very strange," he said, "that a man who has written a history of the Arians should believe in the Pope's infallibility. No one asked a Pope to give an infallible judgment on that great question. And it is all very well saying that we must wait till theologians have debated on the dogma and settled exactly what it means and does not mean. Meanwhile the world has quite made up its mind what the dogma means. The Pope has condemned certain things in the Austrian constitution; — toleration of other religions, free schools, etc. — principles admitted by all governments. The Tyrolese believe this to be an infallible decision, and consequently that the laws under which they live are in these respects iniquitous. Will it help the Austrian government or convince the Tyrolese, if a handful of theologians at last decide that this is not an infallible judgment? Fifty Newmans living all at once, and all working to explain and pare down the dogma, would not have any appreciable effect on the working of the dogma. I suspect that Newman would have been a very different man, if he had been well read in mediaeval history. But that, I fancy, is a field of which he has not even touched the precincts." "Like Lamennais, he went to Rome 96 believing in the infallibility of the Pope; unlike Lamennais he came away still believing in it." "Lamennais," Dr. Döllinger had remarked on another occasion, "made the whole of Christianity depend on the Pope's infallibility : that was the centre of his system. His visit to Rome convinced him that the Pope was not infallible; and with his belief in that went his belief in Christianity[39]." Dr. Newman in his essay on him in 1838 seems to forebode some such end, and Copeland regarded 97 this as a striking instance of Newman's insight into the tendency of a theory. As we came home we saw coloured lamps, Bengal lights, and rockets. Dr. Döllinger thought that these were probably in honour of S. Anna, the reputed mother of the Blessed Virgin. Tomorrow is her festival in the Roman calendar as well as in ours.

39. Lamennais wrote to a friend after his long stay in Rome had opened his eyes, "*Restait Rome : j'y suis allé et j'ai vu là le plus infame cloaque qui ait jamais souillé les regards humains.*" *Correspondance*, 1. 247.   98

CONVERSATIONS WITH DR. DÖLLINGER

Volume II

1872, continued

Saturday, July 27th. Dr. Döllinger has to-day had a letter from that strange man the King of Bavaria who writes to "Mein lieber Rector Magnificus Dr. von Döllinger" to express his congratulations and wishes respecting the celebration of the 400th anniversary of the founding of the University. He will receive a deputation from the University at the Jubilee festival. So far good; but he goes on to say *whom* he will receive. Any other sovereign in Europe would have left that to the University to settle. He will see only three members : the Rector, the Pro-Rector, and one of the Senior Doctors, von Pözl. "He didn't tell you at the same time how long you were to stop," I asked. "That he has entirely in his own hands : he can dismiss us when he pleases." The king lives entirely alone, hates society, and abominates state ceremonies. Moreover, he has left it entirely open, whether he will be at the performance of *Lohengrin* in the Hof-Theater. "Which is very inconvenient," said Dr. Döllinger; "for, if he is present, the professors ought to go in court-dress, which would be rather serious for them. Many of them have no court-dress, and others (he described a semicircle at a distance from his own spare figure) have outgrown them." That is not the worst of the letter. "He has told me that the torchlight procession must be addressed to *me* (the Rector) and not to him (Ich werde sowohl bei dem Festzuge als bei dem Fackelzuge, welchen Ich Ihnen als dem derzeitigen Vertreter der Alma Mater dargebracht wissen will, anwesend sein). That *one* word will cost me £50. Of course if I am to receive the Fackelzug I must do it at the University. Our little street is not large enough. Moreover, I must entertain those who take part in the ceremony, give a supper and have champagne, etc. I have been calculating (at least others have for me) that it will cost me about £50." I did not say so, but it seems to me that the University ought to pay. The king really might be more considerate. Now that his brother has ceased to live with him, owing to disease both of body and mind, he has no one to suggest to him the right thing to do when something else than mediaeval poetry, horses, or Wagner's music has to be considered. So far as I have observed, his subjects speak of him with neither affection nor aversion, but regret. As Dr. Döllinger aptly put it the other day, "He *might* be popular, if he liked." The Rector is dreading next week, as well he may. The mere physical exertion will be tremendous, to say nothing of having his mind on the stretch for so long. If several sovereigns were to be present, Dr. Döllinger would still be *the* centre of attraction and attention. The Rector Magnificus of the University which celebrates its 400th year, the first Ecclesiastical Historian in the world, and the excommunicated leader of the Old Catholic movement. He will have speeches to make in which he must accept his position without saying too much, cheer his friends without giving a handle to his enemies, and steer his way dexterously among the ecclesiastical and academical questions with which German politics now teem. Then again he will have guests from fifty different universities and some dozen nationalities to receive, and "the right thing" must be said to each of them. The mere drudgery of giving orders is no slight matter. He will be very glad when this day week comes.

The *Deutscher Merkur* of to-day says that it has reason to believe that the articles which have rather frequently appeared in the German press, admiring and praising Prof. Frohschammer, and which have also spread to England in the *Contemporary Review*, are written by Prof. Frohschammer himself! I was talking of this to Dr. Döllinger, and he said that he knows that the long article in the *Contemporary* signed *1* 'Clericus Bavaricus' is by Frohschammer. "I never pay much attention now to what he writes. I know so thoroughly all that he has to say, that I feel sure that there will be nothing new to me, before I begin to read. Moreover, everything with him takes such a personal form, that it is not pleasing to be concerned with it. He is always harping upon the theme that his merits have not been recognized. He wishes to be the leader of a movement for Church reform; and as that has not come to pass, he has retired very much from society, and lives to a great extent by himself. The other professors see very little of *2* him. He wrote a good pamphlet on the Council, in which there were some telling statements very well put." One may read him at times in the *Allgemeine Zeitung*, the *Neue Freie Presse*, the *Gegenwart*, and Schenkel's *Kirchliche Zeitschrift*. His idea of Church reform is a going back (?) to the simplicity of a supposed primitive Christianity, a something so simple, that it is difficult to know what is left beyond a general obligation to benevolence. "I have so much business that I must stay at home to-morrow," said Dr. Döllinger as we parted; "but come on Monday."

Monday, July 29th. It was evidently 'packing up' for rain when I went for Dr. Döllinger. However, he is not easily daunted. So we started under a threatening sky, which with the sunset lights gave some beautiful effects. Some articles in the *Allgemeine Zeitung* on student life in Munich University led the conversation to Lola Montez and the wonderful time of her reign in Munich. Strange that, although I never was in Munich until 1869, when Lola Montez was already in her grave (she died in comparative poverty in a hospital in New York, June 30th, *3* 1861), I should have seen the famous ballet girl, and that Dr. Döllinger has not[1]. Like most public men, and many private ones, he suffered from her influence at the time of her ascendancy (1846-1848) in Munich; indeed he lost his professorship for a while through her intrigues; but he never saw her. I heard her lecture once, years ago, at Newcastle. Her subject was *Fashion*, which she treated with much vivacity and humour, hitting herself rather hard at times, and perhaps intentionally. While in Munich she tried to gain over some of the student clubs to her coterie, and quite without success; but she took captive various individual students and made them into a club of her own. When no Gasthaus in the city would allow her club, which she called the Alemannia, to make its premises their rendez-vous, she had an elegant Kneip-zimmer filled up at the back of the charming house in the Barerstrasse, which old King Ludwig had given her. Here the charmer would not unfrequently appear in student's dress, booted and spurred, to the enchantment of her worshippers. Red, blue, and gold were the colours of the Alemannia, which sometimes had great collisions with the other student clubs. Will many of its members be present at the Jubilee this week? If so, they will hardly venture to show their old colours, and perhaps few of them would wish to remember their youthful folly.

When we had got well over on the other side of the river, the rain began to come down, and before long in torrents. The way in which Dr. Döllinger continued to talk through it all, — of Cathari, Paulicians, Bulgarians, Albigenses, Patarini, and other strange mediaeval sects[2], — sometimes even standing still in his usual way to finish a sentence, as if drenching rain were a matter of no importance whatever, — was as marvellous as it was delightful. His memory is really prodigious, and the way in which he has all his learning at command is astonishing. The origin, and the tenets, and the vicissitudes of these eccentric and sometimes obscure sects, were all in his mind, and all in logical and chronological order. Not until he had finished illustrating his main subject did he cease, and then we plodged home in silence.

Tuesday, July 30th. It was our last walk together that year. It was

1. Lola Montez was the natural daughter of a Scotch officer, named Gilbert, and a Creole. Her mother afterwards married, and Lola was educated in a school at Bath. She married a young officer named James, went to India with him, and then ran away from him. After adventures in England, Paris and Brussels, she came to Munich in 1846 as a Spanish dancer, and there captivated Ludwig I. She caused the overthrow of the ultramontane ministry of Abel, which opposed the king's desire to ennoble her. Under the ministry of Wallerstein, this was accomplished and she was made Gräfin Landsfeld. Her insolence, and that of her club, led to the closing of the University for several weeks, Feb. and March, 1848. Then came popular disturbances which forced her to retire to the Lake of Constance and thence to England. She never returned to Munich.

2. Two volumes on Mediaeval Sects were the last that he published, in the autumn of 1889.

more than likely that he would not be able to walk this evening; and when I went to his library late in the afternoon, he looked in for a minute to say so, and to tell me that he would try to get me a ticket for the great celebration on Thursday. Munich is beginning to fill.

Wednesday, July 31st. My landlord, Herr Oberförster Wacker, had just given me a ticket for Lessing's Minna von Barnhelm, the Jubilee piece in the Residenz-Theater, when there came a ring at the bell and two tickets from Dr. Döllinger, one for *Lohengrin*, the opera in the Hof-Theater, and the other for the banquet in the Odeum to-morrow. As the ticket for *Lohengrin* was the Rector's own, I had a magnificent place in the very centre of the Galerie Noble, in the midst of any number of dignities, court and military, brilliant in scarlet, blue, silver, and gold. Close in front was Max Müller, the representative of Oxford. The opera in execution, dresses, and scenery was quite magnificent. Wagner is the Munich favourite, and on such an occasion as this every effort was made to secure a triumph.

Thursday, August 1st. The grand day of the Centenary Festival. I took up my position to see the Festal Procession first of all by the Residenz, where the king appeared in uniform to receive the 'Hochs' of the different corps of students. About the middle of the procession came the Rector Magnificus, Dr. von Döllinger; and truly magnificent in the best senses of the word he was. Seldom, if ever, have I seen a man look so really *grand*, and yet at the same time so perfectly natural and easy[3]. He seemed to be thoroughly at home as he walked along talking gaily with his companion, who I suppose was the Pro-Rector, Dr. Giesebrecht. Dr. Döllinger wore a black gown, with a very handsome gold collar or chain thrown round the neck, like a badge of the Order of the Garter. Both walked bareheaded, and two maces were carried in front of them. Then followed doctors in law in scarlet, political economy in crimson, medicine in green, and philosophy in blue. When the Rector arrived at the Platz in front of the University he was loudly cheered by the students already assembled there, who had formed the first half of the procession. There I left them. At the banquet there was no 'high-table', no table on a dais above the rest; and it was not until the Rector rose to propose the king's health that I found out where he was sitting. I left long before the banquet was over to hear *Wilhelm Tell*, after the third act of which there was a pause, enabling the audience to go out and see the torch-light procession of students. It was a fine sight and a strange one. The king left his box in the theatre like the rest

3. Döllinger was not fond of processions. The ecclesiastical one on Corpus Christi Day was a sore trial to him. There was hardly any duty in the whole year that he disliked so much.

of us, and went to a window in the Residenz to receive the procession of torches, which afterwards went on to the University to do honour to the Rector and his champagne. He told me afterwards that one of the waitresses had said that the rate at which the bottles were emptied was quite astonishing. Not at all to me : students don't get good champagne every night, and they were tired and had their mouths full of the smoke of the torches.

Friday, August 2nd. It had come at last,—the day on which I was once more to bid farewell to Dr. Döllinger. Happily I found him alone; much tired by his last few days of trying work, but wonderful as ever, and very thankful that all was over, and well over. We talked awhile as to what each of us was going to do during the next few weeks, and what chance there was of our meeting again in September. He did not expect to be present at the Alt-Katholik Congress in Cologne, September 20-22. He had no wish to go, for he did not like such things, and he doubted whether they did much good. There was always a good deal of phrase-making, a thing for which he has a special abhorrence. "You make phrases in England sometimes, do you not?" "Oh yes; but we don't equal the French." "Yes, the French and the Italians; —they are unrivalled in phrase-making. *La phrase et la pose*—those are the two essentials for a Frenchman. But there is a French writer who has just been saying that *la phrase et la pose* have been their ruin; that it was these things which brought them to destruction in the late war."

Honorary degrees had been conferred the previous day on Gladstone, Lord Shaftesbury, and J.S. Mill in absence, and on Lord Acton in person. On the other hand Dr. Döllinger had received one from Edin- 4 burgh; also an additional distinction from the King of Bavaria, one of the chief, if not *the* chief Order in the kingdom. I saw a blue and white ribbon with a badge attached to it lying on Dr. Döllinger's writing table, and asked if that was his new Order. "Yes," he said; "but you must see the star; that is something to see!" And he went and got a coat, which he had lately taken off, on the breast of which the star was fastened; and a very brilliant decoration it was. "There now," said he playfully, "isn't that magnificent? Don't you think it a grand thing to wear such a star as that?" And as he laid the coat on one side he continued, "*Vanitas vanitatum, vanitas vanitas vanitatum; omnia vanitas.*" "Yes, but such things weight : other people think a good deal of them." "No doubt; especially in Germany. A thing like that is thought as much of here as the Order of the Garter is in England." I prepared to go, thanking him for all his great kindness : "It is a time in my life which I shall never forget." "You are very kind to say so. You will come and see me on your way back. If that is late in September, I shall probably be here; if earlier, I might be in the country. But I never like to be very long away from my books. If one takes books with one, one finds that just those which are wanted most have been left behind." "But you are going to take a complete holiday, I hope, when you do get away. I am sure you need one." "Yes, I need a holiday," he said; "Good-bye." And we parted, I wondering when I should see him again. 'The young *may* die, and the old *must*'; and he is past three score and ten!

The next day was miserably wet, and most of it was spent in writing letters and packing. In the evening I started for Salzburg, Vienna, and Constantinople.

1873

Monday, July 7th. It was a lovely morning that greeted me in Bavaria after travelling two nights and a day from London. Breakfast over in the dear old Hofgarten at what was once Tambosi's, I went on to call on Dr. Döllinger, with just the faint shadow of a dread that there might be *some* element of truth in a report which had got into the English papers, and which I had derided at the time, that he had gone to the East to visit the plains of Troy[4]! He was at home, however, and gave me the warmest, heartiest welcome and embrace, and took me in to have a chat with him on the familiar sofa in his inner room. He was looking wonderfully well, and his looks, he said, told the truth. He really seemed to be younger than ever and very glad to see me. He had expected me a day or two sooner; for I had not written to him about my enforced change of plans, owing to my having to be in Oxford for the Congregation on the 5th. He was full of interest as usual in all that is going on in the English Church, especially the controversy about auricular confession. It seemed to him that a culpable 5 amount of ignorance had been exhibited in the controversy : writers evidently did not at all know what had been the custom of the primitive Church, or how the present system, which is not primitive, had been developed. I did not stay long, knowing how precious his time was,

---

4. Early in the year I received the following letter from him :
"Lieber Freund! München 5 Febr. 73
   Ihr letzter Brief und die Tags darauf von der Bank eingelaufene Weisung, die bewusste Summe in Empfang zu nehmen, waren eine grosse Ueberraschung für mich. Ich hatte an so etwas nicht gedacht, denn obgleich ich häufig in's Französische, Englische, Italienische übersetzt worden bin, so habe ich doch niemals ein Honorar von den Uebersetzern oder ihren Verlegern empfangen, auch nie eines begehrt. Diess ist das erste Mal. Da nun diese Gabe so ganz unerwartet gekommen ist, so kann ich nichts thun als Ihnen herzlich dafür zu danken.
   Haben Sie the Charge of the Bishop of S. Davids gelesen? Er hat die einschneidende 6 Bedeutung der durch die Vaticanischen Decrete vollbrachten Veränderung in der Stellung der Römischen Kirche gut begriffen und richtig angegeben; es wird sich nun bei der Irish Education-question zeigen, ob auch sein den Englischen Staatsmännern gegebener Wink beachtet wird.
   In Deutschland und der Schweiz nimmt der durch hierarchischen Uebermuth herauf beschworene Kampf immer grössere Dimensionen an. Bei Ihnen wird man ohne Zweifel Weherufe [hören?] über den masslose 'Erastianism' der Preussischen Regierung—aber sie kann zu ihren Gunsten geltend machen, dass sie sich im Stande der Nothwehr befindet, und ihr keine Wahl gelassen ist.
   Schreiben Sie mir bald wieder, ich freue mich immer, wenn ein Brief von Ihnen einläuft, obgleich ich freilich die Reciprocität wenig einzuhalten pflege—aber Sie kennen ja meine Lage, und wie spärlich die Zeit dafür mir zugemessen ist.
   Totus tuus J. Döllinger"

although he seemed to be quite willing to chat. He gave me the run of his magnificent library again, arranged a walk for the evening at the old hour, and asked me to dine with him on Thursday to meet Lord Acton, who comes from Reichenhall on Wednesday to stay with Dr. Döllinger.

At 7 p.m. I was with him again, and we were soon strolling through our old haunt, the English Garden. He at once began questioning me about my oriental experiences the previous year, and was much interested in what I had to tell. A colleague of his had lately been visiting the same scenes, and had come back as enchanted as I was. Had I published an account of my travels? His own book, on which he and Lord Acton
7 have been at work so long, is not out yet. Lord Acton is correcting the proof sheets now; so we may hope to see it before long. Prof. Huber
8 has just brought out his work on the Jesuits. I met him at work on it in Dr. Döllinger's library last year. I asked about Strauss's last work,
9 *Der alte und der neue Glaube*. Dr. Döllinger said that it had made a good deal of noise in Germany, but the general opinion was that it was quite unworthy of Strauss. Something much more able might have been expected of him than such meagre atheism and materialism. The book was practically the same as that published a century ago in
10 Paris by Baron Holbach. It had provoked various answers; one quite
11 recently by an Old Catholic here.

Dr. Döllinger asked what the opinion in Oxford had been with regard
12 to Gladstone's Irish University Bill. I said much the same as in England at large;—general approval at first, followed by criticism of details, and ending in very strong hostility. Dr. Döllinger had heard from Gladstone after the latter's defeat. The Premier explained the drift of the Bill and ended in a somewhat despirited tone by expressing a wish of not remaining in office much longer but retiring into the quiet of a private life. Dr. Döllinger quite understood ultramontane opposition to the Bill. If the University was made such as to attract Catholic laymen and bring them into contact with sound education and with the better class of Protestants, the Catholic laity would soon be emancipated from the power of the priests. At the same time he thought that the Bill offered advantages to Catholics which were not likely to be offered to them again; and hence the opposition of the Protestants to it. He did not think that the having two professors in the same faculty preaching diametrically opposite doctrine was the objection to concurrent endowment : they had had Catholic and Protestant professors in theology and other subjects for years at Bonn, Tübingen, and elsewhere, and no difficulty had arisen on that score. *The* objection was, that directly you appoint a Catholic professor as such, you put the whole faculty at once in the power of the bishops, i.e. of Rome. Dr. Döllinger spoke with admiration of Fawcett's ability. I said many people thought

that the Irish ultramontanes had overreached themselves. They wanted
to grumble at the Bill but get it passed. They had grumbled a little
too much and lost it. But from a letter which I had received from
Dr. Newman at the time I gathered that Cardinal Cullen's opposition
to the Bill had been quite *bona fide*. Dr. Döllinger was inclined to   *13*
believe that this was the case. In spite of its concessions to Catholics,
the Bill was too much against ultramontane interests to be acceptable.

À propos of the University Press the Oxford translation of Ranke's
History of England was mentioned. Dr. Döllinger wondered how it   *14*
would be received in England, when completed : Ranke was so different
from Macaulay. He spoke with great admiration of Ranke's thoroughness and prodigious powers of production. No one like him even in
Germany. He admired especially the Histories of England, of the Reformation in Germany, and of Wallenstein. These formed complete   *15*
wholes and were the outcome of good work in Ranke's maturer days.
The History of the Popes was an earlier work and very deficient in   *16*
many respects. Changes of policy in the Popes were not noticed; the
whole Jansenist controversy was very inadequately treated and apparently not understood.

Dr. Döllinger supposed that English sympathy with France was now
not quite so strong as it had been. I said that I thought not; I had
never shared it. He spoke with strong disapprobation of the present
spasmodic efforts at religious revivals in France; gigantic pilgrimages
and similar theatrical displays; more especially the late pilgrimage to
Paray-le-Monial (where once stood the convent in which the visionary
Maria Alacoque lived), with deputies from the National Assembly,
generals, bishops, and banners of white bearing a red heart and the
words, "Arrête, le cœur de Jésus est là!" God was prayed to save
France in the name of the Sacred Heart; a petition which Dr. Döllinger
said reminded him of what he once saw put up in a village church,
viz. a representation of the Trinity, and under it the words, "Holy
Trinity, *pray* for us." All this sentimental dramatizing of religion is
thoroughly French.

I asked Dr. Döllinger what had taken place here on Corpus Christi
Day. He said that there had been a good deal of controversy. At first
the troops were not to be present. Then came an order from the king
that they were to be so. After much discussion in the newspapers almost all the corporations and public bodies abstained from taking any
part in the procession, which the clergy then tried to make as imposing
as possible by beating up individuals. The procession on this day is
always regarded rather as a show of strength on the part of the priests.

By this time we had reached No. 11, after a walk of 2 1/2 hours.
"Now go and have a good night's rest after your fatigues, and don't
get up early to-morrow," said Dr. Döllinger, as we parted on the
door-step. "To-morrow we meet again at the same hour."

Tuesday, July 8th. I began the translation of Dr. Döllinger's *Hippolytus und Kallistus* in the afternoon. About seven we started for our walk, making to the Isar through the English Garden. I read to him Dr.
17 Newman's message to him in a letter to me written June 16th.

"When you see Dr. Döllinger, say everything that is kindest to him from me. Of course I cannot overcome the sad feeling that he should have felt it right to place himself in such antagonism to men, who, though his inferiors in moral worth and unscrupulous in their proceedings, have, as I think, the right on their side."

At the words "unscrupulous in their proceedings" Dr. Döllinger laughed assent. Then after a pause he said, "If Newman knew the history of the fifth and sixth centuries and also modern Church history better, he would not think it possible that those men can have the right on their side. I suppose that he has not been in the way of studying all the falsifications and frauds of those times. The matter has scarcely been sufficiently investigated and exposed yet, and cannot be studied in convenient books, as it deserves to be."

Later on he spoke of his conversations with the Bishop of Lincoln (Wordsworth) at the time of the Cologne Congress last September. I told him how indignant many in England had been at the Bishop's singular want of good taste, and how they had deplored the dictatorial
18 tone which he had thought it right to assume; also how much the forbearance and courtesy of the Congress towards him had been admired. "Yes," said Dr. Döllinger, "when we ventured to tell him with all possible politeness, that the Old Catholics were not prepared at once to accept all the doctrines of the Church of England, he began to complain, and said that it was very hard, after he had come all that way at considerable sacrifice of time, money, convenience, and so forth, that his suggestions should not be accepted. The Bishop of Ely [E.H. Browne] was altogether different. But I had no conversation with him. He did not come to Bonn, where I remained most of the time, as Bishop Wordsworth did."

Dr. Döllinger hears that the Bishop of Marseilles[5] has not accepted
19 the new dogma. It is also said that some of the other French bishops are about to make an official declaration on the subject. Michaud
20 cannot do much in France at present. The Old Catholic movement is looked upon as essentially German, and everything German is an abomination. One of the first of living Portuguese writers, Herculano, author of a History of Portugal and of the best work on the Portuguese
21 Inquisition, has just declared himself publicly as an Old Catholic. "It will be interesting to see how he can maintain such a position single-
22 handed in Portugal. A little while ago he sent me a book of his,

---

5. Bishop Place; he voted 'non placet' on the Infallibility dogma.

collected articles and so forth, with the dedication 'Doctori von Doellinger, antiquae fidei defensori, etc.' So I knew what his views were."

I asked whether 'civil funerals', i.e. without religious rites, about which there has been so much commotion in France, ever took place in Germany. Dr. Döllinger said, "No, except in the case of suicide. Then it is left to the discretion of the priest. If he thinks that there is a doubt about the fact of suicide, or about the man's sanity, he will probably perform the service; otherwise not, and the law would not interfere to compel him. There is no jury to decide the question of suicide. A request by a dying man to be buried without religious rites would be disregarded by the family. Civil marriages are very uncommon, confined chiefly to those cases in which the parties belong to a religious body which is not recognized by the State. But such marriages will in time become general by law. The chief opponents of this measure are the Protestant clergy, who fear that their flocks will then very often dispense with the religious ceremony altogether. Catholics have little to fear. The bride at any rate is sure to insist on being married by a priest. Mixed marriages are allowed by the Church, if both parties are baptized Christians, and *if they engage to bring up their children as Catholics*. Unless this promise is given, the priest refuses to marry a Catholic to a Protestant; and these are the cases in which the marriage is performed by the Protestant minister only, and not (as is usual in mixed marriages) by both the Catholic and the Protestant minister. There is much dispute about the legality of such marriages. The Council of Trent rules that a marriage must be performed *a proprio parocho*. Can a Protestant minister be regarded as the *proprius parochus* of a Catholic? Or indeed of any one? The marriage of a Catholic with a Jew or a Quaker would under any circumstances be invalid. So also in the case of divorced persons. The priest would refuse to marry and the law would not interfere to compel him to perform the ceremony."

Yesterday evening we passed the youths of the theological seminary walking out two and two in their cassocks. I noticed that the number of them seemed to be smaller than usual, and asked Dr. Döllinger how the theological faculty was flourishing. "Not at all; numbers are diminishing; few enter who can help it. At the present time in Germany *desperatio facit presbyterum* : the times are against the study of theology." Tonight he told me that not a single degree in theology has been taken in this University for several years. Previously there used to be two or three every year.

Prinz Karl, brother of the late King Ludwig I., celebrates his birthday to-day. His palace at the end of the street in which Dr. Döllinger lives has been empty since 1866. Some Munich papers spoke rather strongly about his want of ability in that war, and he has avoided the place ever 23 since. He and the rest of the royal family are strongly opposed to the German Empire, which they regard as fatal to Bavarian independence. The Prince is said to be always urging the king to withhold from performing those acts which from time to time are necessary to complete the consolidation of the kingdom with the Empire. The king's cousins and cousins' sons, who are likely to succeed, for the king is unmarried and his brother is an imbecile, are of this way of thinking also.

Dr. Döllinger has lately seen reviews in the *Guardian* and *Church Times* 24 of Sir William Estcourt's work on Ordination. On the question as to the validity of Orders Dr. Döllinger said that he believed, that the more the subject was investigated, the more it would be seen that a better case can be made out for English Orders than for Roman. At the time of the Council of Florence Pope Eugenius IV. published a decree in which the matter and form of the sacraments were defined, and in the case of ordination the matter essential to validity was ruled to be, *not the imposition of hands*, but the giving of the paten and chalice into the hands of the person ordained. Ordinations in which the customary tradition of the paten and chalice had been omitted were declared invalid. On the other hand, the imposition of hands was treated as a mere symbolical act, a usual accompaniment of the ceremony, but not essential. So that in numberless ordinations in the Roman Church, since the decree of Eugenius IV., there is at least a possibility that the imposition of hands was omitted. The decree was framed by the famous Turrecremata (Torquemada), and is one more instance of the astounding ignorance of scholastic theologians as to the doctrine and discipline of the primitive Church. Here we have one of them inducing a Pope to decree as of Apostolic authority what (as Dr. Döllinger said) is known to be no earlier than the twelfth, or latter part of the eleventh, century. It was about then that the *porrectio instrumentorum*, the custom of presenting the candidate for ordination with the cups and paten, was introduced. This fact, Dr. Döllinger remarked, if thoroughly investigated and treated with ability, might be made a formidable weapon in con- 25 troversy and help to put an end to unjust attacks upon Anglican Orders.

Thursday, July 10th. At one I went to Dr. Döllinger's in accordance with his invitation on Monday, and was rejoiced to find that no one else was there excepting Lord Acton. After the first few minutes conversation flowed freely and was interesting enough. I was glad to have both Dr. Döllinger and Lord Acton on my side in a controversy which is now occupying many of us in Oxford, as to the propriety of allowing books to be *taken out* of the Bodleian Library. At present those who wish for some relaxation of the rigid confinement of books to the Library are in a minority; but I hope that we may yet win. Lord Acton, as having one of the finest private libraries in the world, and as being in an official position at the British Museum, is an authority on such a question. Dr. Döllinger went so far as to say that if the restrictions enforced at the Bodleian prevailed in the public libraries in Germany, the literature of the country would be diminished by half. "That would not so much matter," said Lord Acton, "if one might choose the half." "True," said Dr. Döllinger, "but it would be precisely the more solid and valuable half that would be sacrificed." Lord Acton told us that an emissary from the British Museum (Stephenson) has actually obtained admission to the Archives at Rome, and has been at work there since October. This seemed to be news to Dr. Döllinger as well as to myself. 26 Mr. Stephenson appears to have succeeded beyond every one's hopes in obtaining permission from the Pope and the assistance of papal officials. No doubt his being a convert to the Roman Church, and therefore presumably a 'safe' person, has had something to do with his success. The reign of Henry VIII. is the period on which he is at work. Lord Acton thought that if ever the Pope and cardinals left Rome, the Italian government would seize on the Archives. Whenever that store of documents *is* thrown open to the world, much history will have to be rewritten.

The news which I chanced to be the first to tell Dr. Döllinger on Monday, that Minghetti has at last succeeded in forming a ministry, is confirmed; but Minghetti cannot get the man he wants to take the portfolio of Minister of Finance. In the present state of Italian finance, which is perhaps worse than that of any other country except Spain and Turkey, it is not surprising that any one should decline such a post. A relation of Lord Acton's, who is also a relation of Minghetti, is a member of the new government. A little after 3 p.m. Lord Acton retired, 27 and I soon followed, with the promise of a walk with Dr. Döllinger to-morrow. For the moment I took refuge in his library.

Friday, July 11th. In the evening I called for Dr. Döllinger. He went into the adjoining room to see if Lord Acton would join us; and in a few minutes we all three set out. It had been an oppressive afternoon and thunder clouds still threatened, so we kept to the walks near home. The atmosphere seemed to tell upon us, for conversation flagged at times. The appointment of professors turned up as a subject; and we all seemed to be agreed that appointment by the whole body of the university, as when Professors of Sanskrit or Political Economy are elected by Convocation at Oxford, is about the very worst method of all those in use. "That ought to be altered at the earliest opportunity," said Dr. Döllinger. And, on the whole, appointment by the Crown ("an intelligent despotism," as Lord Acton called it) was thought to be the best, or one of the best. Here the king used to be almost absolute in making such appointments; but now the Senate have it nearly in their own hands. The faculty, in which the vacant chair is, nominate a candidate; and if he is approved by the Senate, he is pretty sure of the post. The minister has a veto, but it is rarely exercised. The Senate consists of two professors from each of the six faculties together with one or two officials, such as the Rector and Prorector. The result of this method of appointment is occasional, or even frequent, nepotism. Sons of existing professors have too good a chance; and their relations and friends generally have a decided advantage. In the Irish University of the future nothing but Crown appointments would be feasible in all probability. And yet, as Lord Acton remarked, the Irish mistrust Crown patronage to such an extent, — always suspecting a job, — that it is almost impossible to get an Irishman to tolerate the notion of such a method of appointing professors.

It is said, by the way, that one of the Irish bishops makes no secret of the fact that he does not accept the dogma, and that his conviction 28 of its untruth remains quite unshaken. "Not peace, but a sword" might be the motto for that unhappy decree. It is causing terrible divisions in families in Germany, when some members accept and others reject it. Dr. Döllinger told us of a remarkable division in a well known family on a broader question. The great Savigny and his wife, who was a sister of Brentano and of Bettina von Arnim, agreed to bring up their children with nothing more of religious teaching than is common to Catholics and Protestants, in order that the children, when they came to years of discretion, might choose for themselves. Savigny was a Protestant and his wife a Catholic; and the result of the compact was that the sons became Catholics and the daughters Protestants.

29   The great Sydow case was also a topic of conversation. It seems at last to have come to a conclusion, and one which gives satisfaction to few, as is commonly the case with a compromise, which this seems to be. I asked Dr. Döllinger for some information on the case, the main facts of which appear to be these. Dr. Sydow is a Protestant pastor in Brandenburg, who some months ago preached a sermon, in which he denied the miraculous birth of Christ, and assumed that He was the actual son of Joseph and Mary. This created a commotion, which for the time ended in the Consistorium of Brandenburg ejecting Dr. Sydow from his office. Dr. Sydow has personal friends and admirers besides those who agree with him in doctrine. There was an appeal to the Oberkirchenrath at Berlin; and this body has found the question a very thorny one indeed. Dr. Döllinger seems to think that they were at first inclined to confirm the sentence of the Consistorium. But there was a very strong feeling against this. It was argued, as in England 30 with reference to *the Sling and the Stone*, that Dr. Sydow was only teaching openly what many clergy and thousands of laity believe in their hearts. There was also talk of a loophole in the law, which would

prevent the original sentence from being confirmed. Anyhow it has not been confirmed. Dr. Sydow returns to his cure, not exactly in triumph, for he has received a severe censure (a *verschärfter Verweis* in spite of the *Lücke im Gesetz*), but on the whole a victor. Those who esteem him as a pastor will put up with the censure for the sake of having him back; but those who prosecuted him will hardly be satisfied with a mere censure; while those who sympathize with his views, or at any rate think that Protestant liberty of private judgment gives a man a right to preach such views, openly protest against the censure as unjust. Thus the decision of the Oberkirchenrath is in one respect similar to that in the Bennett case : it is likely to make prosecutions *31* for extreme views less frequent. Dr. Döllinger remarked that it was unfortunate that such a case had to come before the Oberkirchenrath of Berlin. Berlin, with its 930,000 inhabitants, of whom only 50,000 go to church, is not quite the place in which a case of this kind is likely to be treated in a satisfactory manner. "And I am told," added Dr. Döllinger, "that in the matter of church attendance the Catholics of Berlin are no better than the Protestants." He thought Berlin the most godless city in Europe[6]. I was much struck a few years before by the emptiness of churches and fulness of theatres on Sunday, as also by the scarcely disguised Sunday trading.

At a dinner party at Worcester College last week the question was raised whether the influence of Hungary on Austrian affairs was increasing, and most present were inclined to think that it was. Dr. Döllinger and Lord Acton were very strongly of opinion that it was not. Hungary has 'home rule'. The line of demarcation between the two governments is as rigid as possible under the circumstances. This of itself almost cuts off Hungarians from any chance of leavening Austrian politics. In this they are very unlike the Bohemians. The Czechs mix very much more freely with the other elements of the Empire, and consequently both exercise, and are subject to, much more influence than the exclusive Hungarians. The almost puerile separatist

6. After the Prussians' decisive victories at Sadowa and elsewhere in July 1866, Döllinger wrote that in Munich all were in excitement and anxiety, for they saw plainly that the Bavarian army was not in a condition that could withstand the Prussian army in its march on Munich; and people have a very unfavourable opinion of the rapacity and predatory practices of the Prussians. In the Palace, the Picture Galleries, Museums, and Royal Library, a good deal is already packed up, so that, if the danger comes much nearer, the treasures may be sent into a neutral country.

Much the same was done in 1870, when it was feared at the beginning of the war the French might march in.

In July 1867 Döllinger wrote that the political outlook in Munich was very gloomy; a weak government, general discontent, a very large and influential party striving to get Bavaria incorporated with Prussia, a thing for which genuine old Bavarians have a deadly detestation, and, at the head of everything, a romantic young man (Ludwig II.).

spirit of the Magyars is one of the things which strikes even the ordinary traveller in Hungary. I think I made some remarks on it at Pesth in my journal of last year.

Sunday, 5th after Trinity, July 13th. In the evening Dr. Döllinger and I went for a stroll round the little lake at Kleinhesselohe. We talked of the reservation of some sins for the absolution of the Pope and the kindred subject of *excommunicatio latae sententiae*, i.e. where the sinner is excommunicate *ipso facto* by the mere commission of the sin, without any sentence being pronounced against him personally, — a great abuse of the discipline of excommunication. The first sin reserved in this way was personal violence to priests. Dr. Döllinger did not remember under which Pope the reservation was made, but I think about the eleventh century. Then partly through a laudable wish to mark certain crimes as specially heinous, partly through the ambition of the Popes, who wished thereby to increase their power, the number of reserved sins became very much enlarged. Confessors sometimes refused absolution to great criminals and sent them to Rome on a penitential pilgrimage; and then the crime easily became a case to be always reserved to Rome. Moreover, the system did and does involve the paying *fees*; and this fact may well have contributed to the continuance and growth of the system. The list of reserved sins at last reached the appalling number of between 200 and 300! Who but a professed and deeply read canonist could be expected to know more than a fraction of them? This has become a great stumbling-block to confessors. Moreover, other practical difficulties arose and became insuperable. So many individual applications to Rome rendered answers impossible. Hence the 'quinquennial faculties' granted to bishops; i.e. they have leave given them by the Pope for periods of five years at a time to grant absolution for most of these reserved sins, to grant dispensations, and the like. But they perform these functions, not as priests, or even as bishops, but simply as the Pope's deputy. This is one more strong fetter to bind them to Rome, for if Rome were to refuse to renew these faculties, it would be scarcely possible for them to govern their dioceses. Hence there is a very strong wish in some quarters that these faculties should be granted for life. Besides sins reserved for papal absolution, there are others reserved for episcopal absolution. These vary in different dioceses. In some, for instance, incendiarism is reserved, in others not. But the whole system is quite sterile of any good results. So far from these reservations deterring people by impressing them with the heinousness of the crime, the criminal in almost every case is quite ignorant of the reservation until he goes to confession. Then the priest tells him that he has no power to absolve. The case is sent to the bishop under fictitious names, and he either grants leave to absolve or sends it on to Rome. The chief persons benefited appear to be the secretaries who get the fees. The opportunities of abuse of such a radically mistaken system are immense, and the total abolition of it is one of the many reforms for which numbers of earnest persons in the Roman Church are yearning. But *quis custodit ipsos custodes*? What is to be done when the bishops themselves are the slaves, and often the willing slaves, of Rome? This is true to a terrible extent everywhere, and specially so in Italy. Thanks to the very short-sighted policy of the Italian government, all the Italian bishops are completely in the power of the Pope. He has the absolute appointment of them, the Crown having surrendered all its rights. Moreover, *32* he retains the right of paying them; a relief to a bankrupt exchequer, but a very dear relief. The sole duty of the bishops to the government is to give notice of their appointment to the see. This done, the State would pay them, but the Pope will not allow them to make what might seem to be an acknowledgment of the legality of the present Italian constitution. He prefers to pay them himself, and thus not only fill the Italian sees with creatures of his own, but secure their absolute subjection for ever, for they are dependent upon him for their daily bread. The country is thus honeycombed with influential persons, who probably by conviction, and certainly by interest, are the sworn enemies of the government. A man's best road to ecclesiastical promotion lies in exhibiting ceaseless hostility to the civil power. Dr. Döllinger left me at the Sieges Thor to make a call in the Schwabinger Strasse. So I returned alone.

Monday, July 14th. Dr. Döllinger had promised to send me the University Calendar for this semester, and it arrived this afternoon. In return I took him the first number of the excellent *Hermathena*, with a first rate article by Dr. Salmon on the chronology of Hippolytus. Some *33* of the statistics from the University Calendar are worth quoting. Total number of students — 1128, of whom 903 are Bavarians, 100 Prussians, 47 from other parts of Germany, and 78 foreigners. Among the last are 17 Greeks, 11 Russians, and 2 Englishmen. Theology has 72 students, of whom 2 are not Bavarian; Law 253 (55 not Bavarian); Medicine 253 (81 not Bavarian); Philosophy 278 (67 not Bavarian). 69 students of various sorts make up the total of 1128. The miserable state of the theological faculty is manifest. When the best teachers are silenced, who can wonder. As Dr. Döllinger says, the times are against the study of theology. Truth may not be taught as such; what has to be taught is what will be useful in controversy; its truth is not of the first importance. The faculty of law has also diminished; not many years ago there were 500 Juristen here. The causes of this lie outside the University. Great changes in the administration of justice have made the law a less desirable profession. There are far fewer openings.

Tuesday, July 15th. Tzetzes, a Greek student, whose acquaintance I had made in Oxford before Easter, returned my call. He is in the philological faculty and does not think much of the theologians. He says that it is quite common for a lad to be sent here to study theology and then to enter one of the other faculties instead. When I went out with Dr. Döllinger we began discussing what is now the talk of all Munich, the *cause célèbre* of Adele Spitzeder, a clever woman who about two years ago founded a sham bank, which she carried on with immense success by the simple expedient of paying enormous interest out of capital deposited. When the crash came, her liabilities were ten millions, and her assets two millions, of florins. The chief depositors were poor and ignorant people who did not know that such attractive interest could not be safe. She bribed right and left, bribed newspapers to puff her, started one of her own, kept open house, was godmother to numerous children and gave handsome presents, spent considerable sums on charitable objects and got the clergy to recommend her, was an ultramontane, wore a cross, put 'Do what is right and fear no man' on her note-paper, and made herself quite the rage. The poor almost fought for a turn to deposit their savings with her. When some newspapers raised a warning voice, it was put down to malice, or the utterance of rival banks who were losing custom. She and her confederates are now being tried; and the number of witnesses to be examined is so large, that the trial is likely to be a protracted one.

We also talked about the new law respecting the education of the clergy. Is it to be made retrospective? The *Allgemeine Zeitung* seems to think that it ought to be. Dr. Döllinger says that that would be unjust; and most reasonable people would agree with him. But the question is about to be brought to a practical issue. A member of the Chapter (I think) of Fulda has just been presented to a living. According to the new law he is not qualified to hold one, not having been through the required courses of instruction. But is he to be debarred from preferment for not complying with conditions which were not imposed at the time when he might have fulfilled them, if he could have foreseen them? Surely the law ought to apply only to those who are now being educated as clergy. Church patronage in Bavaria is curiously distributed. The Crown has the absolute appointment of the bishops. Deaneries, canonries, and other cathedral preferment, which fall vacant during the *odd* months in the year, January, March, May, etc. belong to the Crown; those which fall in the even months, February, April, etc. are divided between the bishops and the chapters. Ordinary livings, as with us, are in the gift—some of the Crown (e.g. all that once belonged to monasteries), some of the bishops, others again of the universities, while some are in private patronage. Curates (*Hilfsclerisei, Coadjutoren, Kapläne*) are appointed absolutely by the bishops, who remove them at pleasure. The parish priest has no voice either in the appointment or the removal. He can petition of course; but, unless the bishop is willing to grant him a favóur, he can neither have, nor refuse to have, any particular man as curate. As curates almost invariably have to live at the parsonage, at any rate in country parishes, both parsons and curates have a good deal to endure sometimes.

The attack on the Austrian minister Stremayr was another topic. Last year there was a dispute in the University of Innsbruck about the Rectorship, and Stremayr decided against the Jesuits; this year there has been another dispute, and he has decided in their favour. Both sides seem to regard the recent decision a reversal of the former one. The four faculties took turns in nominating the Rector. Last year it was the turn of the theological faculty, which in Innsbruck is dominated by the Jesuits; and they were about to nominate a Jesuit. The other three faculties protested, saying that it was a monstrous thing to have a Jesuit at the head of the University. They appealed to the Cultus-minister, and Stremayr, perhaps on some technical ground, decided against the Jesuits, and the theological faculty was ignored as regards the nomination of the Rector. This year the three secular faculties have applied to Stremayr to deprive the theological faculty of its right in taking part in the election of [the] Rector, and he has declined to do so. The liberal newspapers are consequently abusing him for this. Dr. Döllinger said that the decision seemed to have more significance than it really possessed. It made no practical difference whether the Jesuits had or had not a vote; it was quite impossible for them to get their candidate elected. It was an empty compliment which Stremayr had paid them; perhaps in order to please some ultramontanes in the imperial family of Austria. His decision of last year meant a great deal : it deprived the Jesuits of the Rectorship. But the mode of electing the Rector has now been changed. The faculties no longer nominate in turn. The whole University now elects on each occasion; and the Jesuits will always be hopelessly outvoted. Ultramontanism, although still powerful, is on the wane at the Austrian court. Its influence tells chiefly through the ladies, whose confessors urge them to do what they can in influencing the politics of the day. But the almost simultaneous deaths of the Emperor's mother and grandmother have been a great blow to the papal party. Stremayr is not at all of that way of thinking. He is an Old Catholic, but has to be cautious about exhibiting his convictions.

Thursday, July 17th. We have had two cases of suicide this week, and Dr. Döllinger tells me that they are by no means uncommon here. The euthanasia controversy does not seem to have attracted much notice in Germany. Tzetzes had been telling me that dancing still exists as

part of the ceremonial of the Greek Church. It takes place at marriages and also at the ordination of priests! The movements are slow,
defined, and accompanied by music, which of course is only vocal.
Greek music is a special study with Tzetzes; it was to see what there
was in the Bodleian on the subject that he came to Oxford. The movement
in these liturgical dances is circular, those who take part in them joining
hands. I asked Dr. Döllinger about it in the evening, but the subject
seemed to be as new to him as it was to me.

He thinks that Manning's promotion to be a cardinal, of which
the newspapers are talking, is probable, but not likely to take place
just at present. The Pope has to keep up the appearance of being a
prisoner, and is not in a position to think of anything so bright as
cardinals' hats. Earthquakes, floods, and epidemics are much more
suitable topics than the distribution of honours. He has just been account-
ing for the present mortality among children at Rome by supposing
that a merciful Providence is taking these innocents away from the
shame, and misery, and liability to sin, which is inseparable from the
35 new kingdom of Italy. Riario Sforza is often talked of as likely to
be his successor; but not even the cardinals can know that. Dr. Döllinger
says that there is no instance on record, ever since the election of [the]
Pope has been confined to the College of Cardinals, of the next Pope
being known as such during the existing Pope's lifetime. The conclave
meets without anyone knowing what the result will be. Mistrust and
suspicion are natural to the Italian character, and are intensified in the
case of ecclesiastics in high places. This is fatal to anything like a
coalition before the time. The intrigue begins in the conclave. Each
cardinal is accompanied by a priest as *conclavista*, and he is commonly
the go-between in carrying on intrigues during the session. A book
has been written, but never published, on the duties of a *conclavista*,
by one who acted in that capacity several times (Liotti?). For centuries
no one but an Italian has had any chance of being elected; and there
is less chance than ever for a foreigner now.

The question of mixed marriages is constantly coming to the front.
Provost Hoppe of Elbing has been trying to make a 'mixed' couple
promise, not merely to bring up their children as Catholics, but to
take care that their children *marry* Catholics! That is, they are to teach
their children what a foolish thing they themselves have done. Other
parish priests have been doing the like, so that they are probably acting
under instructions from higher quarters. The marriage of an Old Catholic
with a New is of course regarded by the latter as a mixed marriage.
Dr. Döllinger told me of another case of which he had lately heard
from an ex-ambassador at the court of Baden. A mixed marriage was
planned between two young persons of distinguished family in England.
The Roman priest referred them to Manning. The archbishop said

that a special dispensation from Rome would be necessary, and the parties must promise to be content with the marriage by the Roman priest and not have an Anglican marriage also. This was intolerable to the non-Catholic party; and it was decided to see whether the marriage could not be performed in the usual way, i.e. according to *both* rites, in Germany. This they discovered was possible; and accordingly they wrote to the archbishop and told him that they would not trouble him any further in the matter. Manning then turned round, said that he would not press his objections, in fact would be very happy to marry them himself on the usual conditions. Which was accepted, and the Pope sent his special benediction to the happy pair.

Austria is admiring English party government as compared with her own. An Austrian minister, when compelled to resign, does not go into the Opposition, with the hope of returning to office : he retires absolutely. There are at the present moment some eighty ex-ministers in Austria, all receiving pay! No wonder that Austrian finances are not in a flourishing condition.

Before we started for our walk Dr. Döllinger asked me if I was a friend of Biblical commentaries. "Meyer's is the one which I prefer 36 myself on the whole." And he forthwith presented me with several volumes of it. Of Olshausen he said, "It is very fair; but Meyer is a 37 stronger man, and besides has the advantage of coming after Olshausen."

Friday, July 18th. The five volumes of Meyer arrived in the morning, marked here and there with pencil in the margin, no doubt by Dr. Döllinger himself, which is no small augmentation of their value. The man who brought them said they came from 'Herr *Reichsrath* Döllinger', not 'der Herr Stiftspropst', which may have been accidental, but may also have been in imitation of ultramontane newspapers. They call him Reichsrath, which is a civil distinction, and not Stiftspropst, probably to insinuate that as an excommunicated priest he can no longer be considered as Provost of the Royal Chapter. But such he is certainly likely to remain, as long as the present king lives. And here we have the third anniversary of the fatal day, on which the lying dogma, which has caused all this misery, was sent forth to the world as an eternal truth. If ever Carlyle's saying that 'eternal truth' is frequently only another name for 'infernal lie' held good, it is of this dogma of July 18th, 1870. The *Allgemeine Zeitung* devotes an article to the anniversary in its Hauptblatt, and in the Beilage begins a review of Prof. Huber's new work on the Jesuits.

Tzetzes met me in the Hofgarten, and we talked a good deal about the Greek Church. He has no love either for ecclesiastical ceremonies or dogmas, and asked me what sort of impression the elaborate ceremonial which I had seen at Athens had made on me. I said, "not a favourable one : to me it was simply distracting instead of helping one to pray." "Pray!" said he; "one can pray anywhere. When I go to church, it's to *look on!*" No doubt that is the case with many. Only last night Dr. Döllinger and I were talking of the distracting character of very ornate ritual both in the Greek and in the Roman Church. At a full choral celebration, in which several clergy are taking part, the attention is chiefly taken up with seeing that the ritual is observed. At pontifical high mass the celebrant's mind is on the stretch the whole time, to make certain that he does not get wrong and put the elaborate sequence of details out. Any other form of devotion is impossible. And as a matter of personal taste, as distinct from principle, Dr. Döllinger finds music anything but a help to devotion in the eucharist. He is extremely fond of music, and said that when celebrating at high mass in the Royal Churches, "where the music of course is exquisite," he found it simply impossible to attend to the service. The music carried him quite away; and he found himself anticipating how some beautiful passage would work itself out, instead of worshiping. He is certainly not alone in finding music no help.

Monday, July 21st. The 100th anniversary of the suppression of the Jesuits by Clement XIV. They were reinstated by Pius VII. August 7th, 1814. What is to be the date of their second suppression? A liberal Verein celebrates to-day at Linz. "At Linz!" exclaimed Dr. Döllinger when I told him of this some days ago, half surprised and half amused that at Linz of all places in the world the suppression of the Jesuits should be celebrated; for at Linz the hierarchy are very ultramontane indeed. The *Allgemeine Zeitung* has suggested that to-day lectures and addresses should be abundantly given to call attention to the pernicious activity of the Jesuits in the past and in the present, and calls upon Protestants to help in the celebrating the day on which the then infallible head of the Church declared in the bull *Dominus et Redemptor noster* that the Society of the Jesuits is an intolerable evil. In all schools and seminaries, even down to the Volksschulen, the children ought to be told something of what happened on this memorable day. I celebrated the day by renewing my acquaintance with the University of Munich and went to two lectures, an excellent one on Staatsrecht by Prof. Riehl, and a tolerable one on Aristotle by Sprengel. The latter is one of the oldest of the professors. He made much play with a door-key, flourishing it in the air and beating the desk with it. I was told that one of the desks at which he often lectures has a hole in it made by repeated raps with the key to his philosophy. He also lectures on Demosthenes.

Tuesday, July 22nd. Another excellent lecture from Riehl on diplomacy.

A canard has been going the round of the papers stating that the Archbishop of Cologne [P. Melchers] has had a long audience with the Emperor at Ems in order to propound a scheme for the reconciliation of Church and State. Dr. Döllinger does not credit it. The Emperor leaves such things to his ministers; and the audience, if it ever began, woud not last long. The imperial scheme would be a very simple one, and might be stated in the one word 'Obey'. The answer to the protest of the Bishop of Ermland shows how such things are to go in future. The *39* State holds the purse-strings and will not pay men to preach insubordination[7].

Thursday, July 24th. After Prof. Riehl's lecture I went to the Journal Room of the Royal Library,—one of the best supplied in Europe,— and there learnt the tragic news of Bishop Wilberforce's death, on the same day and apparently almost at the same hour as his old opponent Lord Westbury. I was in Dr. Döllinger's library in the afternoon, and he came in and asked me if I had heard the news. "A great place for Gladstone to give away," he remarked. "Yes, some other bishop will probably be promoted, and the vacancy will be lower down." "Lord Acton thinks that Church will have a good chance." "He is no doubt a likely man to have the offer, but it is doubtful whether he would accept it : he went very unwillingly to S. Paul's." After making sure *40* that I had got all the books that I wanted and arranging a walk for the next evening, he went back to his work. I finished my work there and then went back to my own quarters to continue the translation of his *Hippolytus*.

Friday, July 25th, S. James. Prof. Riehl gave us an interesting lecture on the parliamentary system generally, promising a discussion of the question between two chambers and one next time. After this I went to the Academy and heard Dr. Döllinger's *Inaugural Address* as President of the Academy. He had told me the day before that I might come. *41* About half the room was filled with members of the Academy, many of whom looked very magnificent in uniform and other decorations. Dr. Döllinger looked dignity itself. He was in plain black, but wore

7. Earlier in the year Dr. Döllinger had written to me, "Have you read the Charge *42* of the Bishop of S. Davids? He has well grasped and correctly stated the penetrating significance (*einschneidende Bedeutung*) of the change in the position of the Roman Church which has been effected by the Vatican decrees. It remains to be seen whether in the Irish Education question English statesmen will avail themselves of the hint which he has given them. In Germany and Switzerland the contest provoked by hierarchical arrogance constantly increased in dimensions. In England people will doubtless bewail the boundless 'Erastianism' of the Prussian government; but you may be satisfied with the plea which it can establish, that it is driven to defend its own existence, and has no choice left."

several orders; on his left breast hung the star which he received last year from the king at the Jubilee, and which he showed me as I took leave of him, saying "*Vanitas vanitatum, omnia vanitas.*"

He began his address with a tribute to Baron Liebig, his immediate predecessor as President, of whom he spoke with enthusiastic admiration, not merely as a man of true scientific spirit with a genius for discovery, but still more as a noble character, whose influence was manifold and for good. "I never left him without feeling myself instructed, stimulated, and inwardly quickened." He then glanced at earlier Presidents, Jacobi the first of all, Schelling, Freyberg, and Thiersch. He passed on to the other and *non*-German Academy, viz. the French one, on which he did not bestow high praise. The cultivation of style, *le grand art de bien dire*, is neither a lofty nor a useful object for an Academy to set before itself. But, as De Tocqueville has said, it is the one corporation in the whole of France which still maintains its independence, the one surviving guardian of national traditions. In contrast with this, how strange it is that England with its wealth, its high average of education, its abundance of scientific material, its unrivalled museums, collections and libraries, should nevertheless have no Academy to make use of all these good things. Probably the two great universities absorb the talent which is required for such an institution, and yet each is too one-sided to supply the necessary men. He spoke also of the amazement with which the world had seen a great and gifted nation,— the possessor of the garden of Europe, full of self-confidence and belief in its invincibility,— suddenly thrown down from its high position, and by its own rather than by strangers' hands made to suffer a humiliation such as it had never experienced before. The best men in France were unanimous as to the cause of her overthrow, which is a moral one. The nation has become so arrogant as to be indifferent to truth; it has chosen to be deceived with vainglorious lies. He went on to point out how enormous the work of scientific men has become, how much has been attained revealing the immense amount which still remains to be attained, and which can only be won by minute sub-division of labour and intense self-devotion of individuals. He warned us of the dangers attending the necessary sub-division, in that sciences may become isolated and cease to understand one another. He also warned us of the dangers of rapid scientific progress. Young men seeing old conclusions frequently disproved think that all that is old is probably false and that nothing can ever be certain. Renan is right in saying that Germany in particular is cursed with a feverish desire to be the first to announce new results and to surpass previous teachers; hence a deluge of paradoxical hypotheses. In conclusion he returned for a moment to his predecessor's death. The history of the sciences is like the torch-race in Lucretius : *quasi cursores vitai lampada*

tradunt. Each hands on the torch to his successor. The bearers of the *44*
light vanish one by one; but the light remains — "das Licht aber bleibt."

I was only a few yards from him and could hear him distinctly and
perfectly; and I thought myself very fortunate in being present upon
such an occasion. One may safely predict that the presidency of Döllinger
will be an epoch in the history of the Bavarian Academy, which is
now somewhat over a century old. He is the one man in Bavaria
whose name is likely to be better known to posterity than even Schelling
or Liebig. After the address the names of newly elected members were
read out, among them John Mair of Edinburgh and Gutbrandus
Vigfusson of Oxford. In the evening papers the latter had the magnificent
title '*Magister Urbium*'! But there was no report of either Dr. Döllinger's
address nor of the lecture on electricity by Dr. Beetz which followed it. *45*
The lecturer told of the time when lightning conductors were considered
impious as an interference with God's judgments, and when the Academy
gave a reward to the first private individual who put up a conductor.
Bavaria has made up for lost time in that respect. I know of no
country in which they are so common. Munich and Würzburg, in which
violent storms are very frequent, bristle with lightning conductors.

When I called for Dr. Döllinger in the evening, he was not quite
ready; so I read the *Kölnische Zeitung* while he finished his letter.
A scrap of news, which I read there, I communicated to him during
our walk. "They seem to have had a large meeting the other day at
Linz to celebrate the 100th anniversary of the suppression of the Jesuits.
I suppose Linz is one of the chief strongholds of the Jesuits in Austria."
"Oh no," said Dr. Döllinger; "there are no Jesuits in Linz." "Oh, yes,
Sir, there are : they have the Castle there. It was given them." "You
are quite right," he replied : "it was given to them." "And a charming
place it is too. Is Linz a bishopric or an archbishopric?" "Only a
bishopric, and not a very old one; created by the Emperor Joseph.
Linz formerly belonged to Passau. But the Emperor Joseph found it
disadvantageous to have part of his dominions under an outsider in
the diocese of an outsider; and so Passau is now confined entirely to
Bavaria. Originally Passau must have been almost the largest diocese
in the world. Three bishoprics have been cut out from it : — Vienna,
S. Pellau, and Linz. Vienna was separated some centuries ago, the other *46*
two in the last century. S. Pellau is one of the numerous corruptions
of S. Hippolytus." "Yes, it is almost further from the original than
Abulides" (the Coptic corruption of the name). "Is it not extraordinary,"
Dr.Döllinger continued, "that in the West Hippolytus, Bishop of Rome,
was quite unknown for centuries[8]? Only the Greeks and Orientals

8. Dr. Döllinger begged me in translating his work on *Hippolytus und Kallistus* to
soften down the criticisms on Wordsworth's book on the same subject. "The book *47*
came out at the time when I was writing and it made me *very* angry. There is no need
to reproduce now the severe things that I was moved to say then. Please make them a
little more gentle in your translation."

knew of him." "I suppose the Westerns could not read him, no one knowing Greek." "Oh, I don't suppose that a copy of his works existed in the West. As to a knowledge of Greek,—no one throughout the middle ages read the New Testament in Greek in the West, not one. And yet there are passages in the Vulgate which are scarcely intelligible unless one knows the Greek. One would have thought that a theologian's first idea would have been, when he found a difficulty, 'let us see what this is in the Greek.' There is no trace of anything of the kind. No instance of any one in the West sending to the East for a Greek manuscript. There were always Greeks at Grotta Ferrata. *They may* have had the New Testament in Greek. But even if they had, and even if they read it themselves, there is no sign that any one else ever asked them for it."

We walked down the river to Ober-Föhring, where there was a most delicious air; but in the underwood the gnats were rather troublesome. It was past half past nine and bright starlight when we got home. "There, we have had a good long walk!"; which was certainly true. I hoped that it had not tried him, especially after his speech in the morning. He laughed, and said, "Oh, a walk never tries me." And it certainly seems like it. He walks for 2 1/2 or 3 hours without ever sitting down, and never seems to be tired. "Tomorrow and Sunday I am quite full and shall have no time for a walk; but on Monday, if you like, we may have another."

Saturday, July 26th. Today the University elects its Rector Magnificus for the coming year. Dr. Döllinger tells me that Professor Riehl, whose lectures I have been attending this week, is sure to be elected. It is the turn for the faculty of Staatsrechtswissenschaft, of which faculty he is professor.

Monday, July 28th. It looked rather black when I called for Dr. Döllinger. "I think we may risk it," he said; and into the English Garden we went. In front all was tolerably bright; the heavy clouds were over the city behind. "It has all blown over," said Dr. Döllinger. And we left off thinking of the atmospheric storm to talk of the political storm 48 in Spain."There appears to be no moral power in the nation," I remarked. "The party of order is helpless, and there seems to be no hope left but a military despotism." "But," he said, "the army is demoralized as well as the people. A military despot must have troops on whom he can rely. The materials for such a despotism don't exist in Spain even if they could find the man." I asked him what he thought were the main causes of the steady decline of Spain during the last few centuries. "First of all," he said, "*idleness*. The Spaniard for generations has been taught as a duty to do nothing. Large monasteries existed throughout the length and breadth of the land. The monks abjured manual labour and gloried in so doing; and the people followed their example. Physical exertion was looked upon as useless and degrading, and it became a point of national honour not to work. Every Spaniard is born a gentleman, a Cavalliero; and a gentleman does not work. Secondly, *cruelty*. The Inquisition made the nation cruel. Accustomed to burn and torture people as a work of Christian charity, and to see this done publicly as one of the best ways of serving God, the nation grew careless about inflicting pain and death, and even delighted in it. This made their warfare, and especially their civil warfare, bloody and internecine. Thirdly *ignorance*. The Index stifled literature. The Spaniards after a while had no literature of their own. None was produced at home, and the very means of production were wanting. Those Spaniards who read went to their neighbour France for books. This was their mental food, — French literature, and French literature of the eighteenth century. One of their late historians, after deploring the condition of his country, says, 'What we want is something of our own, a literature of our own, opinions of our own, something not French.' Then, the machinery of education was worn out and useless. They had their old universities in abundance; but there were no teachers, and the students were beggars — literally. It was a common thing for university students to beg for alms in the streets. Schools for the lower orders, national schools, did not exist. The children never went to school, because there was no school to go to; and there was no school, because the parents never cared to have one. The peasantry were dependent for instruction on the parish priests, who were nearly as ignorant as themselves. Country gentlemen there were none : the Spaniard lives in town."

By this time it became evident that the storm had *not* passed over. The sky was darkened everywhere and a tremendous wind had suddenly arisen. The Garten was filled with clouds of dust, apparently brought from the city, so thick that it was advisable not to open one's mouth. The tops of the trees were twisted like wisps of straw. Large branches were wrenched off and fell with a crash. One came rattling down behind us just after we had passed. I really became a little apprehensive for Dr. Döllinger and kept à look out over head. He only put his handkerchief to his mouth and seemed to be rather amused than otherwise. Five minutes before we reached home down came the rain in torrents. We parted somewhat in haste at his door. I knew that it was likely to be our last walk together that year, for he had told me that on Thursday he was going to Reichenhall. Oddly enough it was during our last walk last year, and on the last Monday in July, that we got caught in a storm and were drenched together.

Wednesday, July 30th. I went to take leave of Dr. Döllinger, for I was to leave Munich and so also was he. His housekeeper looked at me in a melancholy, enquiring sort of way. "Yes, he goes to-morrow," I said. "He's *gone*," said she, "already, early this morning." "He told me he was not going till Thursday." "So he told me; but Lord Acton came, and they went off together at 9.30. I had everything to pack all in a hurry." And then she went on to commiserate us for having been caught in the storm on Monday. "He always goes out in a storm." "Yes," I said, "it was the same last year, the last time." And I retired into the library. It was rather a blow;—to have parted from him without ever saying farewell or thanking him for all his kindness. One can write; but that is not at all the same thing. I did not think that the hasty 'good-night', as we both arrived dripping at his door the other evening, was to be my last word with him. But it is no one's fault, and that is some comfort. I went home, did some work, and then consoled myself with the Residenz-Theater, where Fräulein Meyer's acting is always a delight.

1874

Saturday, September 12th. My books and furniture having all been sent off to Durham from my dear old rooms at Trinity, at noon I left Oxford for London, lunched with Aunt Sophie in Somerset Street, dined with Arthur Hopkins and his wife in Kensington Crescent, and then set off on my journey to Bonn to attend the Conference summoned by Dr. Döllinger[9] with a view to preparing the way for a union of the Old Catholics with the English and Greek Churches. The journey and absence from England were singularly inconvenient, coming just in the midst of my removal from Oxford to Durham. But the Conference

9. In the Spring of 1874 the following letter prepared me for the Conference:
"Lieber, verehrter Freund!   München 2 April 74
   Es ist hohe Zeit, dass ich Ihnen ein Lebenszeichen gebe, und Ihnen für Ihre Briefe danke, die mir immer höchst willkommen sind, und mir wahren Genuss gewähren. Durch Sie bleibe ich in Berührung mit Englischen Dingen, und bitte ich Sie, wenn im theologischen und historischen Gebiete etwas Beachtenswerthes bei Ihnen erscheint, mich darauf aufmerksam zu machen. Flüchtig durchlaufe ich wohl den Guardian und die Church Times, und im Ganzen glaube ich die Strömung des Geistes und die Meinungen in der Englischen Kirche doch ziemlich richtig zu erkennen. Einiges ist mir durch die in den letzten Tagen mit Malcolm MacColl (der hier durchkam) gepflogenen Gespräche noch deutlicher geworden. Im Ganzen scheint mir die Stimmung im Englischen Klerus den Tendenzen zu einer kirchlichen Annäherung und allmäligen Einigung überwiegend günstig zu sein, und diess gibt mir Hoffnung und Muth, und ich denke ernstlich daran, im Spätsommer oder Herbst zu einer Conferenz in einer Rheinischen Stadt den Impuls zu geben, damit ein ernser Versuch gemacht werde, ob die Schwierigkeit der Sprachen-Differenz zu heben und eine regelrechte Discussion auf solchem mündlichen Wege möglich sei. Ich denke, dass Deputirte aus Russland wohl Theil nehmen würden. Ich hoffe, dass Sie dann auch sich betheiligen. Die Schwierigkeit, oder eine der Schwierigkeiten würde aber sein, Leute von dem Gepräge des Bischofs von Lincoln ferne zu halten oder unschädlich zu machen, welche für die Altkatholischen nur den einen Trost haben: sign the 39 articles, adopt the English prayer book, and then all will be well. Dass dann jede Verbindung mit der anatolischen Kirche rettungslos abgeschnitten wäre, ficht sie nicht an.
   Bezüglich der Äusserung Newman's haben Sie ganz Recht. Die Altkatholischen trennen [49] sich nicht von der R.K. Kirche, verdammen nicht ihre Mitglieder, üben aber das unveräusserliche Recht der Noth- und Selbsthülfe, wie es in der alten Kirche der ersten Jahrhunderte auch geschah.
   Nun eine Bitte. Ich besitze von William *Palmer*: A fifth letter to Dr. Wiseman, Oxford 1841. Es wäre mir wichtig, die vier ersten Briefe zu erhalten, vielleicht konnte [50] ich sie durch Ihre Güte erhalten. Kürzlich habe ich Ihnen eine Schrift betitelt: Hus redivivus, über die Zukunft der Kirche, geschickt. Ich kenne den Verfasser nicht, finde [51] aber, dass sie sehr gute und richtige Bemerkungen enthält. Solche signa temporis sollten in den kirchlichen Zeitschriften Englands mehr beachtet werden, als es bis jetzt der Fall ist.
   Nochmals herzlichen Dank für Ihre Briefe, und Bitte um deren Fortsetzung. Mit herzlicher Freundschaft
                                                              Ihr J. Döllinger"

might prove to be of importance, and one would be glad in after life to have been present. Above all, Dr. Döllinger had so pressed one to come, that little short of necessity could have kept me away. I reached Bonn rather late on Sunday evening, found that at the Hotel du Nord none of my friends were staying and went somewhat early to bed.

Monday, September 14th. Immediately after breakfast I went out and had the good luck to stumble upon Liddon. We went together to the University, picking up Talbot of Keble on our way, and were just in time for the opening of the Conference. Dr. Döllinger seemed to be so very glad to see me — as if it had been almost a relief to him to find that I *had* turned up at the last moment, — and received me with such kindness, that I felt at once more than repaid for the inconvenience of coming. "I want you," he said, "to come to the house of Bishop Reinkens between two and three to prepare some subjects for discussion, with a view to avoiding questions which might cause unnecessary difficulty." Of course I was delighted to be of use.

Prof. Reusch of the University of Bonn opened the proceedings by stating what the wishes of the Germans, who had taken the initiative in the matter, were. 1. The Conference was not a *public* one, although the invitation to it had been very general. It was not intended that detailed reports should be published; and it would be well if reports sent to newspapers were brief and couched in general terms. 2. No one was present in any *official* capacity. Each member was to be understood as stating only his own personal convictions, not anything which could bind others. We were there to suggest, and discuss, and prepare the way for agreement, not to determine the exact terms. He concluded by proposing 3. that Dr. Döllinger be asked to preside; which was carried of course unanimously.

Dr. Döllinger spoke sometimes in German and sometimes in English. He appeared to be much gratified by the number of members of the English Church who were present. He was interrupted twice, once by the entrance of the Bishop of Winchester (Harold Browne), and again by that of the Bishop of Pittsburgh U.S.A. [J.B. Kerfoot]. Dr. Döllinger proposed that the proceedings which chiefly concerned the relations between Old Catholics and the English Church should commence at 5 p.m. The Bishop of Winchester begged for 3 instead of 5: his brother was dying, and he must leave Bonn by an evening train. This was at once agreed to. The Orientals then asked for 6 p.m. as the hour for discussion with them. Dr. Döllinger seemed to be a little taken aback at their proposing to come forward to-day; but he granted the request at once. He went on to say that he had received communications from Mr. Meyrick, secretary of the Anglo-Continental Society, with suggestions as to the limits of the discussion, viz. to the doctrine and usages of the undivided Church of the first six centuries; also with some statements respecting points of difference between the three communions represented at the Conference. Mr. Hogg came forward to explain Meyrick's letter; soon after which the preliminary meeting came to an end.

Directly it was over Dr. Döllinger said to me, "The Bishop of Winchester has changed all our plans; I shall want you at once." After exchanging a few words with Michaud, who seems to have grown younger since I saw him in Oxford and Paris, I went off with Dr. Döllinger. A third person was with us, whom I did not know. After a minute or two I asked Dr. Döllinger whether Bishop Reinkens was there. He smiled, touched his companion and made a gesture of introduction between him and me. The third person was the Old Catholic bishop. They both appeared to be disappointed at the non-appearance of distinguished *Protestant* theologians. I asked the reason of their non-appearance. "Oh, they are various," said the bishop. "In some cases prejudice keeps them away. Some of the so-called orthodox Lutherans are as fast bound by the wording of their formularies as any ultramontane can be by utterances of the Pope. Then again they are so divided among themselves. To take a single instance. Here in Bonn we have some five or six theological professors, and among them there are at least three entirely distinct schools of thought, schools utterly at variance with each other. That in a single faculty in a single university!" "And moreover," added Dr. Döllinger, "the points of difference are the most fundamental; those on which all the rest depend." The bishop told us of an Old Catholic funeral which had lately taken place, and said that it was not uncommon for such funerals to be followed by several persons openly joining the Old Catholics. "The reason is this. Waverers who still remain openly united with those who have submitted to the Vatican decrees cannot come to Old Catholic services in *churches* without incurring censure. But the church*yard* is a sort of neutral ground. They venture thither and listen to the address at the grave; and if the Old Catholic priest makes a good use of his opportunity, it ends in some of the waverers coming forward and confessing themselves publicly as Old Catholics."

When we reached Bishop Reinkens' house he disappeared, and Dr. Döllinger and I together with Nevin, an American cleric who has a cure in Rome, set to work to draw up in English a series of propositions for discussion in the afternoon. The propositions had already been prepared by Dr. Döllinger and his colleagues in German, and some of them were rather lengthy. The thing required was to condense them and to put them into such a form in English as would be most likely to win assent, or at least avoid undesirable consequences. This kept us well at work until dinner-time, and it was not until some time after

2 p.m. that my new acquaintance, Nevin, and I sat down to refresh ourselves at his hotel. We had to go direct from table to the afternoon discussion of our work.

Dr. Döllinger thought it best to begin with the *Filioque* question. We must come to some understanding about that before meeting the members of the Greek Church at six o'clock. He briefly stated the history of the controversy. All parties, he believed, would now agree that the *Filioque* was introduced into the Nicene Creed in an unlawful manner. The creed drawn up at Nicaea, completed and confirmed at other Councils, ought never to have been changed. No such addition as the *Filioque* could be rightly made except by a General Council. Pope Leo III. had pointedly refused to consent to the addition, when requested to do so by Charles the Great. The Bishop of Rome, Leo said, had no power to change anything in the creed or to add anything to it. (In strong contrast, we may remark by the way, said Dr. Döllinger, to the claims of the Pope at the present time.) The words *Filioque* were not introduced into the Western creed generally until the eleventh century (?); and the time of their introduction coincides pretty nearly with the time of separation between the Eastern and Western Churches. They inflicted a wound which has festered ever since; which has never been healed and never will be healed so long as this stumbling-block remains. Orientals said with justice that a creed, to which three Councils had declared that no addition must be made, had been interpolated by one portion of the Church. We ought to endeavour to redress this wrong that the wound might be healed. He proposed : "We agree that the way in which the words *Filioque* were inserted into the Nicene Creed was illegal, and that, with a view to future peace and unity the original form of the creed, as put forth by the General Councils of the undivided Church, ought to be restored."

The Bishop of Winchester pointed out the difficulty of removing the *Filioque*. The Bishop of Pittsburgh, as having sworn to maintain the creed in its Western form, took the same line. He suggested that "*might* be restored" would be better than "ought to be restored". Liddon spoke strongly against the removal of the words. Nevin could not see how any one could admit that the insertion had been illegal without admitting that it ought to be expunged. When the choice lay between eleven centuries of the undivided Church and seven centuries of a portion of the Church, he must abide by the former. Dr. Döllinger said that no question of principle was involved. It was the rectification of a wrong, which all parties acknowledged to be a wrong. If members of the English Church there present were seriously of opinion that the *Filioque* could not now be surrendered, he conceived that the present negociations, so far as they had reference to members of the Greek Church, were at an end. It would be useless to meet them with a view to approximation, if we had already made up our minds that the *Filioque* must in any case be retained. It was called a formal difficulty; but every attempt at reconciling East and West had hitherto failed because of this 'formal' difficulty. Dean Howson was willing to accept the proposition, if these words were added, "such restoration being understood as any abandonment of the doctrine involved in the words *Filioque*". H.N. Oxenham was strongly against the motion, which would not be made much less objectionable by the Dean's addition. Eventually the Bishop of Winchester proposed an amendment which was adopted; that the second half of the motion run thus : "that, with a view to future peace and unity, it is much to be desired that the whole Church[10] should set itself seriously to consider whether the original form of the creed can be restored, without sacrificing the truth of the doctrine embodied in the form now in use in the Western Church (in the Western form)."

We had now less than an hour left for the following propositions. 1. *We agree, that the apocryphal or deuterocanonical books of the Old Testament are not of the same canonicity with the books contained in the Hebrew Canon.* 2. *that no translation of Holy Scripture can claim an authority superior to that of the original text.* 3. *that the reading of Holy Scripture in the vulgar tongue cannot lawfully be forbidden.* 4. *that, in general, it is more fitting and in accordance with the spirit of the Church, that the liturgy should be in the tongue understood by the people.* All these four were passed at once. 5. *that faith working by love, and not faith alone, is the means and condition of man's justification before God.* This was passed easily with the substitution of "and not faith without love" for "and not faith alone", to avoid misconception. 6. *Salvation cannot be merited by 'merit of condignity', because there is no proportion between the infinite good of the salvation promised by God and the finite merit of man's good works.* This was carried with an amendment of the Bishop of Winchester : "the finite *good* of man's works" substituted for "the finite *merit* of man's good works"; a mere verbal change to improve the antithesis. 7. *We agree that the doctrine of 'opera supererogationis' and of a 'thesaurus meritorum sanctorum', i.e. that the overflowing merits of the saints can be transferred to others, either by the rulers of the Church or by the authors of the good works, is untenable.* Carried. 8.α. *We acknowledge that the number of sacraments was fixed at seven first in the twelfth century, and then was received into the general teaching of the Church, not as a tradition coming down from the Apostles or from the earliest times, but as the result of theological speculation.* 8.β. *Catholic theologians (e.g. Bellarmine) acknowledge, and we acknowledge with them, that baptism and the*

10.   ? whole *Western* Church

eucharist are 'principalia, praecipua, eximia salutis nostrae sacramenta'.
Dr. Döllinger remarked that in earlier centuries the Latin term *sacramen-tum* was very vague and undefined in meaning, much as the Greek term μυστήριον was and remains still. 'Sacrament' since the rise of scholastic theology with Peter Lombard has acquired a special and definite signifi-cation unknow to the first ten or eleven centuries, while 'mystery' remains as indefinite as ever. In early Latin writers the Trinity, the Incarnation, and the Procession of the Spirit are *sacramenta* no less than baptism, eucharist, or Orders. The proposition, therefore, in 8.α. is merely a statement of historical fact, not of doctrine; but the fact is of importance in order to remove doctrinal or apparently doctrinal differences. None of the Anglicans objected to 8.α. when taken in conjunction with 8.β.

It was now about 5.45 p.m. and we all went out to get a little fresh air before meeting the Orientals at 6 p.m. I went off to the post office to get a letter.

The next meeting was a more stormy one. The Greeks objected strongly to the amendment by the Bishop of Winchester of the article on the *Filioque*. "Without sacrificing the truth of the doctrine embodied in the form of the creed now in use in the Western Church" was an inadmissible clause. They could not admit that there was any truth in the statement that the Holy Spirit proceeded from all eternity from both the Father and the Son. *Principaliter*, i.e. *ex aeterno* or *in principio* the Holy Spirit proceeded from the Father only. This was reiterated in various ways and with more or less vehemence by successive speakers. Dr. Döllinger rose and said that it was now evident (what he had been convinced of from the first), that the position assumed by all the Anglican speakers in the previous meeting was erroneous, viz. that there was no essential difference of *doctrine* between themselves and the Orientals, that the whole difference was a *formal* one, whether the words *Filioque* could *now* be retained in the creed. It was clear that there was a serious dogmatic difference : the Orientals maintaining that from eternity the Holy Spirit proceeded from the Father only, the Westerns that from eternity He proceeded from both the Father and the Son. We seemed to be at a deadlock, when Bishop Reinkens rose and in a very forcible speech pointed out that on their own principles the Orientals were wrong in condemning the *Filioque* as certainly false. Their own principles compelled them to acknowledge that a point on which the *whole* Church had not spoken was still open, so that neither side ought to condemn the other. The Westerns had admitted the illegal insertion of the *Filioque*. The Orientals had no right to lay an anathema on a proposition, about which the whole Church had not yet spoken. To anathematize the *Filioque* as false was to fetter the Church in the development of doctrine. The proposition before the Conference said nothing as to the truth or falsehood of the *Filioque* : that question was not raised. He begged the Greeks not to go beyond their own principles in dealing with the proposition before them.

The Greeks had at first taken a very high line. The illustration used by Dr. Döllinger of a cleft tree, of which the divided parts were always being bound up and always falling asunder again, did not seem to them to be at all a true representation of themselves in relation to other Churches. They were no part of a cleft tree. Their Church was a mighty stream flowing in one unbroken course from the fountain-head of Christ and His Apostles. After Bishop Reinkens' speech they became more moderate, and at last were disposed to accept the wording of the Bishop of Winchester with one important change. For "without sacrificing the truth of the doctrine which *is* embodied etc." they would read "without ... doctrine which *may be* embodied". Dr. Döllinger said that he accepted this alteration provisionally : it remained to be seen whether the English and American members of the Conference would assent.

He told Nevin and me that there would be more work for us next day at 7 a.m. We had already been hard at work for about eleven hours with but little break. Yet Dr. Döllinger was going to work again with his colleagues.

Tuesday, September 15. I was at Bishop Reinkens' house before 7 a.m. Dr. Döllinger was just preparing for us. He disappeared for a moment with hot water in one hand and his breakfast in the other, remarking that he must shave then, or he would not be able to do so at all. While he was away Nevin arrived. Dr. Döllinger returned shaved; and I imagine that all the breakfast he got was just what he managed to swallow while he was shaving etc. His powers of work are something quite marvellous. Our labours with him lasted till 8.30, and then he went off to have another conference with his German colleagues before 9.0, when we were all to meet. He wanted to lay before them what we had just been drawing up. Nevin went off to do the same before the Bishop of Pittsburgh. I ordered coffee at their hotel, and while I was hurriedly disposing of it, Liddon and Talbot arrived with Michaud; and then, with the addition of Dean Howson, we had a preliminary meeting in the bishop's bedroom. We were all of us, Dr. Döllinger included, very late in arriving at the University, where there was much informal discussion in groups, before the session was formally resumed [11].

11. Before we began the regular programme for the day the *Filioque* had again to be discussed. Almost all the Anglicans dissented from the article as amended by the Greeks the previous evening : "without sacrificing the truth of the doctrine which *may be* embodied" in the Western form of the creed. After various proposals and counter proposals and some rather unpleasant disputation, it became evident that the Greeks were not

The first point was a very important article on tradition.   9.α. *We agree, that the genuine tradition, i.e. the unbroken transmission, partly oral, partly by writing, of the doctrine delivered by Christ and the Apostles, is an authoritative source of teaching for all successive generations of Christians. This tradition is partly to be found in the consensus of the great ecclesiastical bodies standing in historical continuity with the primitive Church, partly to be gathered by scientific method from the written documents of all centuries.* The Orientals at once asked, "Who are meant by 'the great ecclesiastical bodies'?" Dr. Döllinger replied, "Of course the Eastern Church for one, the Latin Church for another;" and this seemed to satisfy them. A Lutheran pastor from Denmark [J.V. Bloch] was not so satisfied with an answer which excluded the Lutherans and Calvinists, especially as Dr. Döllinger had explained that those who had abandoned the Apostolic succession could not possibly be said to stand in historical continuity with the primitive Church. But Bishop Reinkens protested against a discussion of who were, and who were not, in historical continuity with antiquity. An Athenian professor [Z. Rhossis] wished the exact limits of the tradition marked more definitely. It must include nothing since the Seventh General Council. Orientals could not admit that the traditions of particular Churches were binding. Dr. Döllinger said that this was sufficiently marked by the word 'consensus'. The traditions of a particular Church could not be called a "consensus of the great ecclesiastical bodies etc." The Athenian admitted this; but he would have liked something clearer. "It is impossible to find a clearer expression than consensus," said Dr. Döllinger. And the article 9.α. was adopted.

As a sort of rider to the article on tradition was then proposed an article of special interest to members of the English Church.   9.β. *We acknowledge that the Church of England and the Churches derived through it have maintained unbroken the episcopal succession.* Dr. Döllinger said that he himself had not the slightest doubt of the validity of Anglican Orders. If the objections usually urged against them were to be allowed as destroying their validity, then the Roman Church was in a *far far* worse plight than the English. Nothing which could be urged against English Orders was in the least degree to be compared with the confusion which had prevailed in the Latin Church for about three centuries, — from the ninth to the eleventh or twelfth century. Popes and anti-Popes ordained, cancelled ordinations, and reordained, until everybody was thrown into the gravest perplexity as to what ordinations were

---

united among themselves. Some said 'Yes' and some 'No' to the same proposal. At last the following expression was all but unanimously adopted : "without sacrifice of *any* true doctrine *expressed* in the present Western form". There was for a time a debate and some misunderstanding as to whether the word to be used was '*enthaltene*' (contained) or '*ausgedrückte*' (expressed). The latter was finally adopted.

valid and what not. The Orientals were unwilling to vote on this article. They said that they were not well acquainted with the controversy, but they believed that their late Patriarch, Philaret, had serious doubts on the subject. Liddon, who had conversed with Philaret, stated that he knew from his own lips that his doubts were the result of imperfect knowledge. Dr. Döllinger said he was confident that the more the Greeks investigated the question, the less their doubts would become until they disappeared entirely. Bishop Reinkens stated that as a student of history he was thoroughly convinced of the perfect validity of Anglican Orders. The Bishop of Pittsburgh pointed out that even if the consecrations of Parker and Barlow *were* doubtful, the succession would be safe. The succession of Irish bishops was beyond dispute, and through them English bishops could trace their descent. The Orientals could only reply, and with reason, that as yet they knew too little about the question to express an opinion upon it. We then passed on to the next article.

10. *We reject the new Roman doctrine of the Immaculate Conception of the Blessed Virgin Mary as being contrary to the tradition of the first thirteen centuries, according to which Christ alone was conceived without sin.* This was vehemently opposed by H.N. Oxenham, and more moderately by Liddon. Liddon believed that the doctrine in question was false, but we were going too far in declaring it to be false. Even in the first thirteen centuries there were (he thought) traces of its being believed by some. Certainly since the thirteenth century it had been believed by many as a 'pious opinion'. Christian liberty ought to be respected. Pius IX. had curtailed liberty by declaring that Christians *must* believe this doctrine; we ought not to curtail it by saying that they must *not* believe it. Oxenham declared that he had believed the doctrine before 1854. It would be suicidal, with a view to union with other Christians, to pronounce such a belief false. He hoped that Liddon's proposal would be adopted; that we should declare that the doctrine was not *de fide*, and not go beyond that. Nevin thought that the words "*new Roman* doctrine" saved all that Liddon and Oxenham wanted. Dr. Döllinger explained the reasons which had determined the German theologians to condemn the doctrine in this strong form. The doctrine had been to them *fons et origo malorum*. It was well known that this dogma had been made to prepare the way for the later dogma of Papal Infallibility. The dogma of 1854 was not merely a feeler; it virtually included the dogma of 1870. If the Pope, without a Council, could make the Immaculate Conception an article of faith, he was already infallible. Only as infallible could he do so. Those who allowed him to act as infallible in 1854 supplied the premises for the conclusion drawn in 1870. Moreover, the doctrine itself, long before it had been erected into a dogma, had produced most disastrous results

in a long series of abuses and gross superstitions. It was necessary to cut off all occasion of these. If we merely declared the doctrine to be not an article of faith, it would be implied that we thought it might possibly be true. Having regard to the welfare of many thousands of souls, whose condition had already been seriously injured by this doctrine, he and his Old Catholic colleagues could not allow such an implication. They preferred to assert their confident belief that the doctrine is absolutely false. Liddon said that such was quite his own conviction; but he spoke in the interests of liberty. He should have thought that even in the first thirteen centuries there was a faint tradition, — slight, vague, and wavering no doubt, but still amounting to something like evidence, that the doctrine was by some persons thought tenable. Dr. Döllinger shook his head with a confident smile which was much more impressive than words. Liddon continued, that for the sake of the many persons who *since* the thirteenth century had held this as a 'pious opinion' might we not allow it to pass as such, although in no case an article of faith. Dr. Döllinger did not see how an opinion which was contrary to the belief of the first thirteen centuries could be regarded as 'pious'. But as it was near 1 p.m. he adjourned till 4 p.m.

At that hour Liddon had handed in the following amendment : "We maintain, that the new Roman dogma of the Immaculate Conception of the Blessed Virgin Mary, as being contrary to the tradition of thirteen centuries, that Christ alone is born without sin, is not an article of the Christian faith." "From what I hear," said Dr. Döllinger to me before the sitting began, "the amendment will not get many votes." Trinder followed Liddon, but less decidedly, on the same side. The Bishop of Pittsburgh said that he could not conscientiously support the amendment. He believed the doctrine to be heretical. It was doing mischief to many souls, and for their sakes we ought to protest strongly against so pernicious an opinion. Dean Howson was on the same side. We were not making articles of faith. If we believed the doctrine to be false, we had the right to say so. The Orientals had declared at the outset that they very much preferred the rejection of the doctrine as certainly false. This fact and Dr. Döllinger's decided preference for the article as written down with him before breakfast decided my vote. When he called upon those who were in favour of the amendment to stand up, only eight or nine persons rose; and the original article was then carried by a large majority.

11. *We agree, that the practice of confession of sins before the congregation or a priest, together with the exercise of the power of the keys, has come down to us from the primitive Church, and that, purged from abuses and freed from constraint, it should be preserved in the Church.* Johannes Janyschew, Rector of the Spiritual Academy at S. Petersburg, the chief speaker among the Orientals and the most amiable of them,

asked for some explanation of "freed from constraint (*Zwang*)". He seemed to think that this implied that confession was in no case a duty. Bishop Reinkens assured the Rector that nothing of the kind was meant. *Pflicht* (duty) and *Zwang* (constraint) were *opposed* rather than synonymous terms. With this explanation the article was unanimously accepted. No one proposed to abolish confession.

12. *We acknowledge, that 'indulgences' can only refer to penalties actually imposed by the Church herself.* Dr. Döllinger explained that the object of this article was to strike at the root of the abuses which had grown out of the mediaeval theory of indulgences, according to which they could free souls partly or wholly from suffering in purgatory. An indulgence, he maintained, could only be a partial or entire remission of penances imposed by authority *in this life* : it could not reach beyond the grave. To this the Orientals quite agreed. But some of them seemed not to like the expression "by the Church herself". They knew nothing of penalties inflicted by the Church collectively. When a person confessed to a priest, the priest might impose a penance with a remedial object; but such a penalty was imposed by an individual, not by the Church at large. But the objection was not pressed, and the article was adopted as it stood.

13. *We acknowledge, that the practice of the commemoration of the faithful departed, i.e. the calling down of a richer outpouring of Christ's grace upon them, has come down to us from the primitive Church, and is to [be] preserved in the Church.* This article had been slightly modified in consequence of the preliminary conference in the bedroom of the Bishop of Pittsburgh. Before breakfast I had written down for Dr. Döllinger "the practice of praying for the dead". But some preferred the other phrase as seeming to exclude the notion that prayer could help those in torment. When I mentioned the proposed change to Dr. Döllinger and asked him whether he would object to it, he said, "Oh no, not at all. I don't care which expression is used, so long as our explanation of it is retained." Dean Howson announced his intention of not voting on this article. He did not oppose it, and he believed that the statement of historical fact was correct. The practice *was* a practice in the primitive Church; but still he could not see his way to saying that it ought to be preserved. That would be saying that the Church of England had failed in her duty; for she had not preserved it. He hoped that the Conference would not regard as unfriendly what was perhaps only timidity on his part. The Bishop of Pittsburgh supported the article in its present form. The dead no less than the living received grace from Christ and were dependent upon Him for it; it was therefore right to pray that grace might be more richly poured upon them. Liddon said that, in spite of the great reticence of the English Church, there was no doubt as to what her teaching must be.

The one thing on which she relied for what she taught and did was the appeal to antiquity. He would undertake to produce passages out of thirteen or fourteen great English divines quite as strong as the article. The Orientals were not likely to it, except as being an understatement; and it was passed without opposition.

We now came to a very delicate subject as regards the Eastern Churches, the question of the practice of the invocation of saints. 14. *We acknowledge, that the invocation of saints is not commanded as a duty necessary to salvation for every Christian.* Greeks and Russians were unanimous in saying that they could not possibly assent to *that*. Dr. Döllinger pointed out, that it was nowhere commanded in Scripture; that it was not commanded in the canons of the Councils of the Church; that in the first five or six Councils the subject was never even mentioned. Could it then be said to be a *"duty, necessary* to salvation for *every* Christian"? Would a duty of such importance have been passed over in silence for so long? Ricos Rhossis replied that a Council to which they paid unbounded respect had declared the practice to be a whole-
52 some one : they could not, therefore, venture to say that it was not a duty. "Yes," said Bishop Reinkens, "the Council says it is wholesome, but that is a very different thing from saying that it is necessary for the salvation of every one." But the Orientals had the greatest objection to admitting, even in the most qualified form, that the invocation of saints was not of paramount importance for man's spiritual welfare. "I expected this," said Dr. Döllinger to Liddon : "the Orientals attach almost as great importance to the acts of Councils as to the canons, and consider them almost as binding; and certainly in the acts of the Council referred to there is a great deal about the invocation of saints." He then resumed his place as President and said, "I suppose then that we can do no more than leave this article unpassed, as one on which the gentlemen of the English Church agree with us Germans, but in which our brethren from the East find themselves unable to go along with us." And no subsequent appeal moved the Orientals to yield[12].

Wednesday, September 16. Dr. Döllinger had no work for me. There was only one article to be drawn up, and for that he wanted the assistance of the English committee, of which I am not a member. About 10 a.m. people began to assemble. Great care had been taken in drawing up the

---

12. It was probably because Dr. Döllinger expected that the Orientals would reject this article that he kept it until the last on the programme for that day's discussion. In the series of articles which I had drawn up for him in the morning it stood last but one; but in reading the articles out for debate Dr. Döllinger placed it last of all. The Old Catholics and Anglicans assented to it, but the Orientals—for the present at any rate—remained aloof.

article to be submitted to the Conference, and it was hoped that all the Anglicans would accept it. The main doubt was whether the Orientals would not think it too considerable an understatement of the truth.

15. *The eucharistic celebration in the Church is not a continual repetition or renewal of the propitiatory sacrifice offered once for ever by Christ upon the Cross; but its sacrificial character consists in this, — that it is the permanent memorial of it, and the representation and presentation on earth of that one oblation of Christ for the salvation of redeemed mankind, which, according to the Epistle to the Hebrews (IX. 11, 12), is continuously presented in heaven by Christ, Who now appears in the presence of God (Heb. IX. 24) for us. — While this is the character of the eucharist in reference to the sacrifice of Christ, it is also a sacred feast, wherein the faithful, receiving the Body and Blood of our Lord, have communion with one another (1 Cor. X. 17).*

Mr. John Hunt, a writer in the *Contemporary Review*, asked whether the article was intended to assert that we receive Christ in the holy communion in a way different from that in which we receive Him in other ordinances. Dr. Döllinger replied, "Most certainly it is intended to assert that. The view of Calvin, that the reception of Christ in the eucharist is of the same kind as the reception of Him in other means of grace, is entirely excluded by the article." Mr. Hunt asked, because Cranmer had declared that the reception in all cases was the same. Cranmer quoted numerous passages from the Fathers, some of them stating the presence of Christ in [the] eucharist in the strongest terms, and said that he approved them all; and yet says in conclusion that all that has been stated means no more than that Christ is in the holy communion only in the way in which He is present in other ordinances. Dr. Döllinger said that he believed that view would be rejected by almost, if not quite, every one present, whether Oriental, Anglican, Lutheran, or Old Catholic.

The Orientals gave the article much consideration. One, who I think was Arsenius Tatschaloff, Provost of the Russian Church at Wiesbaden, stated their own doctrine, which went a good deal further than the article. They believed that the sacrifice in the eucharist *is identical with* the sacrifice perpetually offered by Christ in heaven. With this explanation of their own belief they could accept the article. This was a matter for great thankfulness, but (as Dr. Döllinger had pointed out) the language of the article had been framed as much as possible in the words of Scripture, and it was difficult to object to language which was biblical.

Dr. Döllinger then announced that certain persons wished to prefix these words to the ninth article, the one respecting tradition : "The Holy Scriptures being recognized as the primary rule of the faith". This was not a happy proposal. If one article already settled might be retouched, why not all? Moreover, this particular article had given the Orientals a great deal of trouble. The whole question of tradition and its relation to Scripture, i.e. whether it was subordinate, coordinate, or supreme, had in their Church (as Janyschew told us then and now) 'eine ganze Geschichte gemacht.' It was a burning question with them. They naturally did not want it thrust upon them again with an addition which touched them in the tenderest part. What did 'primary' mean? Did it mean anything more than first in order of time? Dr. Döllinger explained that 'tradition' had a wider and narrower sense. In its narrower sense it stood side by side with Scripture : in its wider sense it included Scripture. Scripture itself was part of what had been handed down to us. But not only had the Bible come to us by tradition, it was tradition also which gave the right and authoritative interpretation of it. In some sense the Scriptures must be allowed to be 'primary'. But the Orientals were not at all comfortable about the addition. Still they did not wish to seem cantankerous. After some consideration Janyschew said that they would like to state their own view about tradition and Holy Scripture, and that with this explanation he thought that they could accept the addition. Rhossis of Athens had more difficulty in assenting, but at last said that he did so, although with misgivings (*mit Bedenken*). This really was most generous of the Orientals, and their admirable behaviour in this matter more than atoned for their combativeness about the *Filioque*. The enthusiastic little Danish pastor tried to detain us with a speech of broken English and German in which he maintained that Christianity was prior to both Scripture and tradition. He was allowed to gesticulate for some time, when Bishop Reinkens at last rose and asked him where the Greek, which he had been quoting, came from. He seemed much taken aback, but at last said, "Why out of the New Testament." "Precisely so; and the New Testament is Scripture. So you see you have to go to Scripture for your proofs of Christianity." Which silenced the good man's enthusiasm, and we were able to end the sitting. Dr. Döllinger announced that the Conference between Anglicans and Old Catholics was over. He and his German colleagues had still some points to discuss with their Oriental brethren, and these would be taken at 3.30 p.m. He hoped that Anglicans would be present, if they cared to be so. They would probably find much to interest them.

In conducting the final session of the Conference Dr. Döllinger took as a sort of text-book the comparative statement of the doctrine of East and West on certain important points, which had been printed in parallel columns by a society in St. Petersburg — 'The Friends of Spiritual
53 Enlightenment'. This comparative statement had appeared in the *Deutscher Merkur* early in the year and had been translated in the *Guardian*. Meyrick also had published it for the Anglo-Continental Society append-
54 ed to a pamphlet of letters.

The *first* article on the Church and its Primate was shelved for the present. The Old Catholics were not ready yet with their own answers to the questions, Has the Church a Primate on earth? If so, who is he? And in what sense is he styled Primate? The *second* article, on the Procession of the Holy Spirit, had been referred by the Conference to a select committee not yet appointed. The *third* article, on the conception of the Blessed Virgin Mary, had been decided. The *fourth*, on good works, and the *fifth*, on remission of sin, had been settled. Serious discussion began with the *sixth* article, on the life beyond the grave, the intermediate state between death and judgment. It was evident that some of the Orientals held views of their own distinct from the ordinary teaching of their Church. They agreed that there could be no repentance after death, but allowed the possibility of spiritual and perhaps moral progress. Dr. Döllinger said that it was a subject on which very little could be either asserted or denied with certainty. In any case there was no material for a difference which need separate Orientals from Old Catholics. To this the Orientals quite agreed. The *seventh* article, on the Nicene Creed, was reserved, like the *second*, for the committee.

The *eighth*, on baptism, produced some discussion. The Greeks were naturally proud of having preserved the primitive use of immersion. Dr. Döllinger conceded all that was due to them for this. But he said that the Western use was something more than ῥαντισμός, as it was sometimes styled. It was commonly no mere sprinkling, but a pouring of water on the person to be baptized, and for this practice very high antiquity could be claimed; so high that its beginning could not be determined. There was no trace of its ever being regarded as an 'innovation' of questionable propriety. This difference between East and West existed long before the schism, and the East never reproached the West with having erred in the matter. All that Westerns claimed was that their own practice was lawful and often convenient, while fully admitting that in the primitive Church immersion had been the rule. Each Church ought to be free to follow its own traditions in this. The Orientals entirely assented : the difference was not a reason for separation.

The *ninth* article, on confirmation, caused some discussion. In the Eastern Church confirmation is almost part of baptism, and it may be administered by a priest. This difference from Western usage is connected with the fact that the East, ever conservative of what is primitive, has retained the practice of infant communion. Dr. Döllinger once more gave the Orientals all credit for their fidelity to the customs of the ancient Church. Still there was much to be said in favour of deferring so solemn a rite as holy communion and confirmation until the recipient could be conscious of the awfulness of it. Under *very exceptional* circumstances confirmation was administered by a priest even in the Western Church. So that this could not be regarded as an *essential* difference. One of the Orientals, I think the Russian Provost from Wiesbaden, rose and said that he remembered a speech of Prof. Friedrich's at an Old Catholic Congress, in which he said that it was only in order to advance the power and pretensions of the hierarchy *55* that confirmation in the West had been reserved for bishops. Reusch said that he remembered the speech well, but that Friedrich had been misunderstood. Yet it made no matter, except for Friedrich's sake, what he had said; for the opinion quoted as his had no bearing on the present question. The Provost still remained standing, as if he had given a challenge to which no satisfactory reply had been made, and there was rather an awkward pause. At last Dr. Döllinger said, "What does the reverend gentleman require? To what do his remarks tend? The question for our consideration is, whether the difference of usage with regard to confirmation in the Eastern and Western Churches ought to be regarded as a ground for continued separation. Will it not be possible for each branch of the Church to retain the practice which has become authoritative for itself, without condemning the different practice of the other branch? Are we agreed that on this point also we are prepared to recognize each other's liberties?" The Provost then sat down, and the question was answered in the affirmative. This difference respecting confirmation need not separate.

The *tenth* article, on the eucharist, although partly anticipated, raised questions not yet discussed. As to the use of leavened or unleavened bread, Dr. Döllinger pointed out that the difference was purely one of custom. No one on either side would be likely to maintain that the sacrament was null and void, because bread other than that which his own Church prescribed was used. About the words of consecration there was a little more discussion, viz. as to whether the invocation of the Holy Spirit is the most necessary part of the prayer or not. The Eastern Church holds that it is; but no serious difficulty was raised by the Orientals on this point. On a third point Dr. Döllinger fully admitted that the Roman Church had departed from the primitive and normal usage, viz. in administering in one kind only. It was quite true that any one who received either the bread only, or the wine only, received the sacrament in its entirety; but the proper way of receiving was to partake of both. The return to the ancient and right practice was with the Old Catholics only a question of time. In principle they agree with the Oriental and Anglican Churches, but there are difficulties in the way of their realizing this in practice immediately. They are watching for an opportunity of returning to the usage of the whole primitive Church. It was once more agreed that these points of difference were no real ground for continued separation between East and West.

The *eleventh* article, on penance, had already been virtually settled in the previous general discussion of 'indulgences'. There was more debate, and at one time it seemed likely to become warm, about the *twelfth* article, on the marriage of the clergy. The Old Catholics were here in a difficulty similar to that about the Primacy;— they have not yet decided the question for themselves. Other more pressing questions have to be settled first. They are prepared to admit that there are grave objections to enforced celibacy, although at present they think it best to maintain the rule. The Orientals were needlessly forward in insisting on the superiority of their system, which is that bishops must be single, and that parish priests must be married. The Orientals condemned the enforced celibacy of Rome as intolerable slavery. Bishop Reinkens pointed out that their own enforced marriage was anything but freedom. To make a youth of three or four and twenty marry, before he knew his own mind, either about a wife or even about marrying at all, merely in order that he might be better qualified for parochial work, was not liberty. As before, however, it was agreed that the difference was not a sufficient reason for the Churches being apart.

The *thirteenth* and last article was on extreme unction. The main points of difference are these. The Easterns hold that the sacrament of anointing has for its object the healing both of body and soul; that it is to be given to persons who are dangerously, but not hopelessly, ill; that the oil is to be consecrated by the priests who administer the sacrament. The Romans hold that this sacrament has for its object the painless and blessed death of the recipient; that it is to be given to those who are *in extremis*; that the oil is to be consecrated by a bishop. There was not much discussion about these differences, and the same general conclusion as before was reached. These things do not constitute reasons for the Churches remaining apart. With this the separate discussion between Old Catholics [and Orientals] concluded, and with it the Bonn Conference itself came to an end. A formal conclusion was all that remained. Dr. Döllinger warmly thanked us all for having accepted the invitation of himself and his colleagues and having come so far to meet them. He was very thankful for the results. They were so large, so much greater than we had had any reason to expect, that he hoped we might look upon them as evidence that the blessing of heaven was upon our endeavours. He hoped that next year we might meet again there or elsewhere and carry the work still further. Meanwhile the suggestion of the Archpriest Janyschew was a very valuable one;— that the points agreed upon should be embodied in a catechism and submitted to those in authority for approval. Dr. Döllinger's face quite beamed with satisfaction. The very severe work of these three days seemed positively to have refreshed him, so encouraging had been the outcome. Janyschew and Liddon replied on behalf of the members of their own communions, thanking Dr. Döllinger very heartily for his efforts in bringing about and conducting the Conference, and attempting to do some justice to the courtesy, moderation, and exquisite tact, with which he had presided over the debates. An illustration, which he himself had used in the troubled discussions about the *Filioque*, seemed to have been realized. We were there, he said, not to build a house in which we could all live in common, but merely to construct a bridge over the chasm, which dissensions had caused to open, and which centuries of separation had deepened and widened between us. It would be the work of the future, and probably of very many years, to build a common and permanent habitation. The last solemn act of the Conference was some evidence that a bridge, frail possibly and far from secure, had really been thrown across the abyss. We all, Old Catholics, Orientals, and Anglicans stood up together and recited the *Te Deum* and *Pater noster*, Bishop Reinkens leading us; after which he gave us his blessing. It was at least one act of intercommunion, a mark of earnest desire for reunion, and an earnest of more perfect union in the future.

We then broke up into knots and there was much leave-taking. I watched my opportunity of saying farewell to Dr. Döllinger, for I was by no means sure that I should see him on the morrow. The warmth with which he took leave of me was a thing never to be forgotten by me. He told me that I must come to Munich next year and bring some one else with me. (He knew that I was engaged to be married.) "Yes, you must. Tell her I say she *is* to come. She will have a very hearty welcome. *You* know that I shall do *my* part." And with that he gave me first one and then the other side of his face to kiss, and dismissed me.

It was with a very full heart that I went away from that memorable room. The whole proceedings, and especially Dr. Döllinger's affectionate farewell, had raised one's feelings to a very high pitch indeed. Never before had that Musik-Saal produced such harmony. Let us pray earnestly that the echo of that last grand chord may never die away. The harmonious vibrations of so many hearts ought not to end in oblivious silence. At least they ought, to all who experienced them, to make discord more painful in the future. For the rest — *Fiat voluntas Domini.*

1875

Wednesday, July 14th. Early in the morning I was once more in Bavaria, this time with a wife, and in the afternoon we went to visit Dr. Döllinger. He was as kind as ever, looking no older, but a little thinner than when I parted from him at Bonn. We talked of various matters, chiefly ecclesiastical both in England and Germany. He was much interested in the probable working of the Public Worship Act. Gladstone had 56 told him that the repugnance to Ritualism among the lower orders in England was very strong indeed. I replied that I quite believed that : they were not used to it, and did not understand it. "You are aware," said he, "that here in Germany the fight between the government and the ultramontanes is as fierce as ever : no prospect of peace or of arrangement. It is not commonly understood in England what a tremendous power the government here have to contend with; how Vaticanism hangs round the neck of a continental government like a millstone. If the clergy are against the laws, and use their influence to prevent their being carried into effect, what is left for a government to do, but to put every engine in its possession to work to control the clergy? It is ignorance of the enormous difficulties of the German government which causes Dr. Liddon and the *Times* to write as they do about the Falk laws. They cannot appreciate the circumstances which make 57 those laws just." I asked what steps the Bavarian government was likely to take respecting the pastorals which the bishops have issued with a view to influencing the elections. "None," he said : "there are none to 58 be taken." "But surely the bishops have contravened the law by publishing such documents without the royal assent." "No doubt; but the law is without a sanction." "You mean that no punishment can be inflicted." "Exactly," said he : "if the government were to prosecute the bishops, it would gain nothing. It is just the same as the publication of the Vatican decrees. The minister then declared publicly that it was impossible to punish the bishops for the offence which they had committed : such was the state of the law. In Prussia it would be different. There the State could, and no doubt would, proceed against the bishops with effect."

Dr. Döllinger mentioned that he had had a distinguished visitor from Oxford the day before, — Jowett. I said, "You do not expect *him* at Bonn this year, do you?" "No, we carefully kept off all religious topics. We talked of philosophy, the probable future of Hegelianism in Germany, and so forth." Dr. Döllinger ended by asking us to dine with him next day at one o'clock.

Thursday, July 15th. Dr. Döllinger gave us a most hospitable reception, and at his round table placed my wife (whom I henceforth designate as B.) in the arm-chair between himself and me. He was more abstemious than ever, although for years an early dinner has been his *only* meal in the day, with the exception of a little bread and butter and coffee early in the morning. He rarely takes wine. He spoke of how the clergy endeavour to influence the elections (at this very time going on) in every possible way, including the confessional. The schools are closed because of the elections, and before coming to him we had found the Museum closed for the same reason. B. asked him whether Roman Catholics were obliged to go to confession before communicating. Dr. Döllinger replied, "No, but as a rule most religious people, and especially women, would be afraid to go to communion without confessing. All that the Church enjoins is that people should confess once a year *and* as often as they are conscious of having committed a *mortal* sin. Now a mortal sin is a thing of rare occurrence in the life of a good Christian. But still religious women would think that they had committed a sin or something like it, if they received the communion without confessing. What many women, especially in France, desire, is not so much a confessor as a *director, un directeur des âmes.* They do not want a priest to whom to confess their sins, but some one to direct them in every detail of their life, all their home troubles, quarrels with their relations, and so forth. It is the Jesuits who have been active in spreading the notion of the expediency, if not necessity, of frequent confession, — of course to increase their influence by means of the confessional. The Abbé Michaud, who was once a Vicaire at the Madeleine, the church" (said Dr. Döllinger turning to B.) "which is frequented by most of the fashionable ladies in Paris, has told me how he has been troubled by ladies requiring 'direction'. Such ladies might be told, 'Tell me your sins; never mind about anything else.' There are three classes of women in the world. Some make their husband their confidant, consult him in everything, and make him their director. Others are very anxious and timid about their religious life; and they make the priest their director. Others are very fidgetty and timorous about their bodily health; and they make the physician their director. This third class is a very considerable one."

Dr. Döllinger was entirely of the opinion that Pusey and Liddon had made a great mistake in backing up Archdeacon Lee in his attempt

59 to create a schism in the Irish Church. Dr. Döllinger was more surprised at Liddon than at Pusey taking such a line.

We talked also of the recent return of the last remnant of the 'United' Greeks into the bosom of the Greek Church, thus bringing a schism

60 of nearly 300 years to an end. Dr. Döllinger, as usual, was full of information. These 'Uniteds' were kidnapped by the Roman See in the sixteenth century. They were half cajoled and half bullied into submitting to the supremacy of the Pope and rejecting the authority of the Patriarch; being allowed, however, to retain their own rites and ceremonies. In these, therefore, there was no difference between them and the rest of the Greek Church : the main point of difference was submission to the Pope. These 'United' Orientals were chiefly inhabitants of the *old* kingdom of Poland, i.e. Poland together with other provinces, which have long since been purely Russian. The tyrannical bishop[13], who by violent persecution of those who resisted, was greatly instrumental in establishing this schism in the interests of Rome, carried matters to such lengths that he lost his life in the struggle. Some of his exasperated flock murdered him. One of Pius IX.'s many outrageous proceedings was the canonization of this persecutor as a martyr of the Church! This canonization, not much noticed in Western Europe, made a profound sensation in Russia. It preceded by some years the canonization of Arbues the Inquisitor[14], which has since been made so notorious by Kaulbach's famous picture; a picture which Dr. Döllinger had seen at various stages from the time when it was first put on canvass. These 'United' Greeks have of late years been returning in large numbers to the Greek Church. Now the last remnant has returned, and the schism is at an end.

Dr. Döllinger compared the fatal mistake made by Sir Robert Peel in allowing the Roman Catholic hierarchy to be appointed directly by the Roman See, without the English government retaining even a veto, with the no less fatal mistake of the Italian government in recent times in allowing precisely the same thing. I said that I thought the *61* later error the worse of the two; its consequences were much greater and far-reaching. "True," said Dr. Döllinger; "but in one respect the English government was more culpable. An Italian minister when reproached with this error, replied that the ministry could not help themselves. Those Italians who are not ultramontanes are for the most part indifferentists, who care nothing about religion whatever, or else are infidels and think that the surest way of bringing religion to ruin is to allow the Papacy full swing. 'Consequently,' said this minister *62* (Minghetti?), 'if we fought the Papacy, we should have no support from any large section of society; and without that it would be hopeless to fight. So we had no course left but to throw everything over to the Curia.' Now if the English government had determined on taking

13. Josaphat Kunczewicz, Archbishop of Polotzk.
14. Peter Arbues, the heretic-burner, was canonized by Pius IX. in 1867, and the act was recognized as official approbation of the whole policy of the Inquisition, but not until Döllinger had shown the significance of it by his articles on Arbues and the Inquisition in the *Allgemeine Zeitung* and in the *Neue Freie Presse*. Kaulbach's picture was probably *63* inspired by him, and did much towards rousing the public conscience.

a firm line in the matter, they would have been backed very strongly indeed by public opinion."

After coffee Dr. Döllinger proposed a walk in the English Garden either at once or at five; and we decided for five, as I knew that to be more in accordance with his usual custom. At five B. remained behind, and Dr. Döllinger and I started together. We were almost at once passed by a youth with a gash on his face, which looked as if it were the result of a student's duel. I expressed a surprise at this barbarous custom, still so firmly rooted in German universities. "It is a survival," said Dr. Döllinger, "of the mediaeval superstition"—"that God defends the right," I continued. "Yes; and it would be well if our students in acting on that principle would adopt the more gentle mediaeval institution, the Ordeal of the Cross. You know that one very favourite way of settling disputes in the middle ages was to erect two crosses and place the two disputants face to face with their arms extended level with the crosses, but perfectly free. The one who could hold his arms out longest won. The one who let his arms drop below the level of the wooden cross lost. This was specially done in cases of rival claims to property: e.g. if a monastery's title to some of its lands was disputed, the monks would appoint one of their tenant farmers to undergo the Ordeal of the Cross with the claimant. This, I believe, is the origin of the phrase *experimentum crucis*. And, as I have already said elsewhere, the contest between the German government and the Papacy is an Ordeal of the Cross. The one that holds out longest will win.

"Bismarck has been giving himself much trouble to get various governments to join with him in the attempt to exercise an influence on the
64 election of the next Pope. He has tried to get Russia, Austria, and Italy to combine with Germany. In each case he has had no success whatever. None of the governments will help him. Even if they would, it would be of no use. Bismarck is not sufficiently informed in these matters. From his youth he has studied entirely different questions, and he does not know the conditions under which influence could be exercised in this case. The only government outside Italy which could exercise some small amount of influence is France. And France has only got four or five cardinals. In the case of Clement XIV. France determined the election. The Bourbons in France, Spain, and Naples combined to instruct the French, Spanish, and Neapolitan cardinals
65 to prevent the election of everyone but Ganganelli; and as two thirds are required to carry an election, these cardinals were quite numerous enough to accomplish their object. Once in the history of the Papacy the election has been in the hands of one man—the Emperor Philip II. He had two thirds of the cardinals in his pocket. He gave them lucrative bishoprics and other posts in Spain and elsewhere, without compelling

them to reside; and in other ways made it agreeable to them to do as he pleased. The Bourbons could do much to determine an election so long as they held the three thrones. But now no foreign government could do anything by interfering. It is more unlikely than ever that a foreigner should be elected. The Italians, who have a clear majority in the conclave, are more than ever bent on having an Italian. Manning has no chance. Even among the foreigners his chance is not the best. Of the foreigners a French cardinal would be chosen. In the present state of affairs a foreigner would be likely to remove the seat of the Papacy from Italy, and the Italian cardinals would not risk that. Moreover, many of the Italians are quite disposed to come to terms with the Italian government. An Italian naturally looks to the government for promotion, for places for relations and friends, and so forth. While the Papacy maintains its present attitude of implacable hostility to the government, Italian ecclesiastics are entirely cut off from all the advantages which government alone can grant. It is quite possible that the next Pope will concede the temporal power and be reconciled to the king.

"It is sometimes thought that Hadrian VI., the last foreign Pope, owed his election to the influence of his former pupil, the Emperor Charles V. This is quite a mistake. The Emperor never thought of his tutor, and used his influence in quite another direction. Hadrian of Utrecht owed his election to the impossibility of coming to any other arrangement. The Italian cardinals could not agree among themselves as to any one Italian. Each Italian that was tried failed to obtain two thirds of the votes; and at last in despair they accepted a foreigner as a compromise. Nothing of the kind is at all likely to happen now."

I asked Dr. Döllinger whether the modern doctrine of the necessity of a sensible conversion could be traced to any definite source, and whether there was any point before which it was certainly unknown. He believed that it owed its origin to Wesley and Whitfield, and had never been heard of before they preached it. The old Reformers knew nothing of it. Calvin would certainly have most strongly repudiated it. John Knox never preached it. He had no original ideas : he was a mere exponent of Calvin. It is not a doctrine which harmonizes very well with that of justification by faith alone. The doctrine of justification by faith only implies the appropriation by faith of the merits of Christ, necessarily *without experience*. Whereas the doctrine of a sensible conversion necessarily implies experience. You are conscious of the change : experience is a *sine qua non*.

We talked also of the approaching Conference at Bonn. The *Filioque* was to be the great question to be discussed : not, as last year, whether it was to be retained in the formula; that might very well be left an open question, each Church retaining its own use. The doctrine itself is to be discussed this year. I asked him whether he considered the Greek position with regard to the Procession a strong one. Dr. Döllinger said that he believed that, as regards mere *wording*, the Greek position, based upon their own Fathers, was *unattackable*. There can be no doubt that in the passages in which the Greek Fathers treat of the subject they are quite silent about the Procession of the Spirit from the Son. But he believed that if these passages were thoroughly sifted, and the quintessence of thought expressed from them, it would be found possible to bring them into harmony with the belief of the West. He did not think that Pusey in his preface to the commentary of Cyril had done much to help us out of the difficulty. Pusey had merely cited the old well-known passages and said about them what had already been said before. Much more, he thought, might be made of Bishop Wordsworth's suggestion, that ἐκπορεύεται and *procedens* do not cover the same ground but represent different areas of thought, and that, therefore, there is no contradiction involved in the fact that the language which accompanies each of these words does not coincide. Perhaps on the basis of some such explanation as this some agreement will be possible.

"Another very difficult question which will have to be discussed," said Dr. Döllinger, "is the doctrine of the eucharist. I don't yet see my way out of that difficulty. I must think still more as to what will possibly lead to agreement. One thing I am quite clear about, — that the mediaeval doctrine of transubstantiation, as taught by modern Roman theologians, cannot be maintained. It is at variance with the teaching of the primitive Church, it is at variance with science, it is at variance with itself. I have looked at it in all kinds of ways, and sooner or later it lands you in a contradiction. We owe the doctrine to the influence of Aristotelianism on mediaeval religious speculation. What can be made of the difference between 'substance' and 'accidents'? What is the meaning of the accidents remaining the same while the substance is changed? What *is* the substance but the *tout ensemble* of the accidents?" "Do you think," I asked, "that the change which takes place at the consecration *can* be explained scientifically?" "Certainly not : such a mystery as that must be left in the unsearchable counsels of the Almighty." "But will you ever get modern Roman theologians to accept such a view?" "Of course not, so long as they remain Vaticanists. But when the time comes, as it *must* come and *will*, when Vaticanism breaks down, then truer views respecting the eucharist will find acceptance[15]. In the Fathers you will find a wide difference of expression on this question. S. Gregory of Nyssa, for instance, uses very strong language, and goes almost as far as the mediaeval doctrine

---

15. I do not remember ever before to have heard Dr. Döllinger speak with such enthusiastic confidence of the ultimate success of his cause.

of transubstantiation. S. Augustine, on the other hand, in this matter is at one with Calvin. Calvin's statements about the eucharist are identical with those of Augustine; no doubt derived from S. Augustine, like Calvin's views about grace, predestination, and election. Not that Calvin was a mere borrower. He was, I believe, a sincere seeker after truth, and took from the Fathers what commended itself to him as true."

Dr. Döllinger believed that the joint committee of Old Catholics, Orientals, and Anglicans, agreed upon last year at Bonn to discuss certain questions which had been shelved at the Conference, had done nothing. It was almost impossible for a committee to do anything unless the members of it lived together, or at any rate could meet at times. It was just 7.30 when we returned to his door, so our walk had lasted 2 1/2 hours. He charged me to tell B. that she must rest to-morrow afternoon, so as to be able to walk in the evening with him. "Give her my best compliments, and say that I shall hope to see her at six o'clock."

Friday, July 16th. When we went at six, Dr. Döllinger was so absorbed in work, that although the door between his study and the adjoining room, in which we were, was ajar, and although we talked and walked about the room, he evidently was quite unaware that we were there for more than twenty minutes. He led the way to the temporary bridge at Bogenhausen. The permanent one had been swept away by the violence of the Isar since I was here last. At Bogenhausen there is a large building looking like some public institution. "You will not guess what that building is for," said Dr. Döllinger to B. "It is for ladies only, and yet it is not a convent. It is for the daughters of public functionaries, whose fathers have died without leaving provision for them. It was an idea of the late king's; but it has not been a success. Not nearly so many have availed themselves of it as was expected. I believe it is far from being full. It is not liked, although (so far as I know) the quarters are comfortable enough. It is too far from the town for the ladies to take much part in the gaities there, theatres, concerts, and so forth. Moreover," (with a roguish look at B.) "I believe that the inmates are not very well satisfied with having nothing but ladies' society. Women cannot apparently be so content to live by themselves as men can to live by themselves." He said that since he knew Munich first, which was about 1818 or 1819, when he came to the University as a student, the population had increased enormously. Then the stated number was about 60,000; now about 140,000. We walked along the Gasteig round the back of the Maximilianeum and up the Maximilian Strasse. As we passed the National Museum he told us that it had been the creation almost entirely of one man under King Max. He collected funds, travelled about, ransacked old houses, churches, and other buildings, and astonished everyone by the immense number of antiquities and curiosities which he found in Bavaria. It certainly is a very noble collection and admirably arranged. Before we reached the post office Dr. Döllinger left us asking us to call for him again next evening.

Saturday, July 17th. When we returned home in the afternoon we found a note from Dr. Döllinger saying that Liddon had suddenly appeared, and as he was only staying till Monday, Dr. Döllinger had ventured to postpone our walk; but he hoped that we should dine with him next day. In coming away from leaving the reply, I met Liddon and had a few minutes talk with him. It was a wet evening and he and Dr. Döllinger were drenched.

Sunday, 8th after Trinity, July 18th. A wet morning. A little before one we drove to Dr. Döllinger's, where we were the first arrivals. Nevin came next; and then Liddon and his sister Mrs. Ambrose. I hinted to Dr. Döllinger that he was giving a dinner party in honour of the *dies Alliensis*, for this is the fifth anniversary of the proclamation of the Infallibility. Dinner was soon announced, and Dr. Döllinger once more placed B. in the armchair at his side. Liddon sat next to her, I next to him, and Nevin next to me. Mrs. Ambrose was between Dr. Döllinger and Nevin. Conversation was very general and on a great variety of topics. Dr. Döllinger lamented the change of dress among the lower orders here. He could remember when they dressed in a fashion quite different from the gentry, not only in the country but in the city; and the old dress was much more picturesque. He had just received from Gladstone a parcel of books containing his recent
67 article in the *Contemporary*, "Is the English Church worth preserving?", and also the preface to the volume which is to contain his three articles
68 against Vaticanism and Pius IX. Dr. Döllinger told us how some of the Liberal French bishops, Dupanloup[16], Maret, and others, had been among the first to suggest to the Pope the idea of a General Council, wishing by means of it to put some check upon ultramontanism, and get certain reforms. The Pope, who saw in the Council an opportunity for much ceremony and parade, was greatly pleased with the idea. Thereupon stepped in the Jesuits on one side and Manning on the other and turned the Council into an engine for effecting the very reverse of what the French bishops had intended, viz. the proclamation of the Pope's Infallibility. Dr. Döllinger had the best authority for this,

16. In Jan. 1865 Döllinger expressed him[self] very strongly in a letter to Anna Gramich about Dupanloup's brochure on La Convention du 15 septembre et l'Encyclique du 8 décembre, as "a very flimsy, rhetorical, unsubstantial performance. And he is now the
69 oracle of the French Episcopate. That is enough to make Bossuet turn in his grave."

for Maret himself had come to consult him on the matter, and Dr. *70*
Döllinger had then told him that he thought the plan of a General
Council was a very dubious one indeed. When Dr. Döllinger was in
Rome himself, his audience with the Pope made a very unpleasing
impression on him. The adoration paid to the Pope was even then so
offensive, that he said to himself as he left the Vatican, "Of my own
free will I will *never* come here again." He had been carefully instructed
by one of the cardinals as to the proper amount of adoration to show;
"and I was very careful to follow the instructions most obediently,
that I might not omit any essential point. The Pope, I think, watched
me narrowly to see whether I did so. I genuflected as I entered the
room, and then a second time as I reached the centre; and when I
reached the Pope I knelt and kissed his shoe. When I rose the Pope
asked me what languages I spoke. I told him that I understood Italian
and French, and then to my surprise he began to address me in French.
He said, 'Things in Germany would go on very well, if all were obedient
to that supreme power which God has placed upon the earth.' I replied
that I was not aware that there had been any recent want of obedience
shown in Germany. But of course all Germans, and especially German
theologians, are suspected at Rome, and are discountenanced as semi-
eretici. And just about that time a professor in Munich had published
a book on the soul, which had been placed on the Index, and the author
had refused to submit. I think that the Pope rather connected me in *71*
his mind with the unsubmissive professor. However, he called me 'un
grand'uomo' before I left. I was rather puzzled to know what he meant
by that; but I believe he afterwards said something about my having
done good service by my writings in defence of the Pope; and when
I reached Bologna I found a diploma waiting for me conferring upon
me the title of Monsignore. I was in Rome five weeks, and while I
was there I was not asked a single question. No one appeared to wish
for any information about Germany. I said to Father Theiner, who
introduced me to the Pope, 'People here seem to be very well acquainted
with German affairs : no one asks me any question.' He laughed and
said, 'Just the reverse; they know absolutely nothing.' And they did
not care to know. It is the same with the Pope at the present day.
It is all one whether you talk to him about Cologne or some town
in South America. He knows as little about the one as about the other.
There was the strongest contrast at Florence : there the men of distinction whom I met were full of the keenest interest about what was going
on in Germany."

Dr. Döllinger thought that the new law in France with regard to public
education, for which Dupanloup has been fighting with such vehemence,
is not so bad as the Liberals seem to believe. It possibly *may* in the *72*
end prove a better system than the present. It *may* in course of time

do something to prevent the fatal separation of clerical education from lay education which exists now. If these ecclesiastical seminaries granting degrees are to exist at all, they must improve the quality of the education. One of the main sources of the strength of the English Church is that, on the whole, clergy and laity have the same education. In France they have nothing in common but the national vanity. The new law will perhaps do something to modify this; but it is a leap out of a bad state of things into the dark.

Nevin made the not incredible statement that the Jesuits' candidate for the Papacy will be Manning. The Jesuits, he had been told on good authority in Rome, had more confidence in Manning, as likely to carry out their programme, than in any Italian. He had lately been in Louvain, where there is a family of excellent bell-founders, for a carillon for his church in Rome. Dr. Döllinger mentioned that the Jesuits are most jeal-
73 ous of the episcopal seminary in Louvain and do all they can to prevent young men from going to it : not so much as distrusting the education given there, but as wishing to keep education, especially of the clergy, as much as possible, in their own hands. This was apparently their policy with regard to Newman's two attempts to start a college or hall
74 at Oxford.

After dinner the two ladies talked together in one window and the four gentlemen near the other. Dr. Döllinger remarked that the full meaning and consequence of making Liguori a Doctor of the Church were very imperfectly understood. In doing this the Pope had committed the Church to whole of Liguori's teaching. The whole of his moral system, with its bad casuistry and probabilism, was now the doctrine of the Church. It was a masterly stroke of the Jesuits to get this honour conferred upon Liguori. A Doctor was very much more than a Father. By the promotion of one not of their own Order, the Jesuits obtained the stamp of authority for all their teaching, for Liguori's teaching is essentially the same as theirs. This creating him a Doctor of the Church was almost a worse calamity than the Infallibility dogma.

Conversation had been so interesting that it was past 4 p.m. before any one moved to go. We were the first to depart. We wished our host farewell for the present, as we were leaving Munich next day; but we hoped to meet him later on at Bonn.

Wednesday, August 11th. We arrived at Bonn from Worms and went to Hotel Royal, where we got a room with a view over the Rhine to the Seven Mountains. In the evening we met Nevin with a Dr. Potter from New York, a man (Nevin told us) who had immense powers of work, and had been elected to one or two bishoprics, but had refused them. It was rather unfortunate that some one, who did not know this, should remark in Dr. Potter's presence that he believed that in America bishops were elected for their business capacities rather than for learning. The Orientals were already in Bonn, and had been there some days, some of them since Saturday. Liddon had been able to come after all : Gregory had been able to set him free.

[*Thursday, August 12th.*] The Second Bonn Conference met in the same place as the First, in the Musik-Saal of the University, and at the same hour, 9 a.m. When we entered, there was already a good gathering, among whom B. was the only lady, and I soon heard from Prof. Lange that this year ladies were not to be admitted. Last year they had sat and listened in the background. Liddon had told me that there was a Russian lady, who would be glad to have B. to keep her in countenance; but after hearing of the new arrangement we went outside to wait for Dr. Döllinger. We soon saw him with Bishop Reinkens, and went to meet him. B. paired off with Dr. Döllinger, who joked with her about the exclusion of ladies, who had been shut out in deference to the wishes of the Orientals. The Old Catholics had no wishes, one way or the other, on the subject. Bishop Reinkens meanwhile was telling me about the hardness of his own work, especially the amount of travelling and talking which it involved. Sermons at one or two services, followed by public meetings, committees, and so forth. Being bishop to all the Old Catholics throughout the German Empire was of course very laborious work. But it was not unfruitful. In the Grand duchy of Baden the number of professed Old Catholics had doubled within the last year. This brought us back to Music Hall. The arrival of Dr. Döllinger was the signal for order and business.

The great feature of the Conference was the large assemblage of ecclesiastics and professors to represent the Eastern Church. No such gathering of Oriental representatives had appeared in the West since the Council of Florence; twenty-one in all, inclusing an archbishop and two bishops [17]. Two of the Archimandrites were said to be really learned men, well read in the Fathers, one of whom had copied out and annotated all the patristic evidence respecting the Double Procession. The American Church was not numerously represented, and had no bishop present. Anglicans were numerous, but very mixed, the best known being Bishop Sandford of Gibraltar, Howson, Liddon, MacColl, F. Meyrick, Kirkpatrick, Denton, and Lias.

Dr. Döllinger opened the proceedings in German with a speech of con- 75
siderably over an hour. The chief points were these. The mutual estrange-
ment between the Eastern and Western Churches was largely the result of ignorance. Neither side knew much about the other's modes of thought and of life. It was the object of this Conference to remove this ignorance

17. The Archbishop of Syra [A. Lykurgos] was not present until the second day.

and estrangement. The connexion between the dogmatic question about the *Filioque* and the constitutional question about Roman supremacy had not been sufficiently remarked. In the first ages disputes were mainly about doctrine; but these could generally be settled by an appeal to the principle of *quod semper, quod ubique, quod ab omnibus*, for in those days, West as well as East recognized this principle. It was when the question of government and jurisdiction became a burning one that a serious schism began. With the end of the fifth century forgeries in the interest of Rome begin; and then Rome met the East with claims founded upon these forgeries. It was into this constitutional dispute that the dogmatic question about the Procession was dragged. About the sixth, or perhaps as early as the fifth century, the *Filioque* was first added to the formula apparently in Spain. Charles the Great in 809 asked Leo III. to order its general adoption. Pope after Pope refused, and disclaimed the *power*, to do so. But the Emperor Henry II. succeeded in getting Rome to yield in 1014. The question of doctrine at once became a question of authority. Had Popes the power to order an alteration in the creed? The Latin conquest of Constantinople intensified the difference between East and West by forcing a Latin hierarchy and to some extent a Latin liturgy on Greeks, who used their loyalty to the old form of creed as a defence. Against this the Latins had nothing to urge but papal authority, and hence the personal power of the Pope had to be magnified. Early Popes had called themselves "successors and Vice-gerents of Peter". Alexander III. had assumed the title of "Vice-gerent or Vicar of Christ". Innocent III. carried the claim to the uttermost and styled himself "Vice-gerent of the true God": as such he was superior to any Council. The weakness of the Greek Empire made its rulers anxious for reunion with the West. Hence the Second Council of Lyons in 1274 and hence the commission to Thomas Aquinas to prove the validity of the Pope's claim to the right to determine the creed. This he did by means of spurious passages from the Greek Fathers and Councils, prepared by a Dominican, by means of which he was completely duped. Using them in good faith, Aquinas was the first to put forward the theory that the Pope is the source of ecclesiastical jurisdiction and of dogmatic decisions; i.e. he has universal authority and is infallible. He does this with hesitation; but the theory is there. Hence Aquinas was made a sort of theological Dictator by Popes and monks, and hence the connexion between the *Filioque* and the Infallibility. The Council of Lyons failed. The Council of Florence was no genuine effort for reunion. Its objects were mainly political and its results shortlived. Papal claims were still further advanced by the Jesuits and the Dominicans. The Jesuits knew that they could control the Papacy, if only the Papacy could control all else.

The Dominicans were influenced by loyalty to their great theologian Aquinas. And the success of these two Orders was great. The Gallicanism of the French was one notable exception. This noble element in the West was not extinguished till 1870. The gradual process by which it was destroyed would be an interesting chapter in history. The Jansenist controversy was used as an opportunity. Napoleon I. was made a tool. In 1802-1804 the great persecutor of Pius VII. became the chief ally of the Pope in one of his most masterly strokes of policy. The deprivation of all the French bishops was the annihilation of Gallicanism; for all the new bishops had to receive their authority direct from Rome. From this blow Gallicanism never recovered. A remnant of it survived in the express rejection of Papal Infallibility; and this last remnant was destroyed in 1870, when Rome struck its final blow at the Gallican Church and at the same time endeavoured to crush learning and science in Germany. The supremacy of the Jesuits was the end of the Council.

Having shown how the addition of the *Filioque* to the creed by papal authority led to the Vatican decrees, Dr. Döllinger proceeded to discuss the doctrinal question, about which the Orientals and Old Catholics had had much consultation before the Conference opened. He freely admitted that the Greek formula, "from the Father *through* the Son" (διὰ τοῦ Υἱοῦ) expresses the truth better than the Western *ab utroque*, or *a Patre Filioque*, or *a Patre et a Filio*; and it had again and again [been] admitted that these additions ought not to have been made to the symbol. It now remained to be seen how far they could agree about the doctrine. He was hopeful, because he for one, and he believed that he could answer for others, had no *Hintergedanken*. Nothing was being kept behind in the background. This had not always been the case. The Greeks had been inclined to suspect (and were justified in so doing) everything which came to them from the West. For them disputes with the West were fights for existence.

Dr. Döllinger then proceeded to discuss the doctrine of the Procession, pointing out that ἐκπορεύεσθαι and *procedere* were not equivalents, that of the Latin Fathers Jerome and Ambrose keep close to the Greek, and that the *Filioque* is in reality not of Western origin, but a form of expression which Western theologians derived from Greek sources. Augustine's language is more independent and original, but he is speculative rather than dogmatic. It is not until much later that the divergent language of East and West is emphasized as a difference of doctrine.

Professor Ossinin, speaking on behalf of the Orientals in very fluent German (I believe he had lived in Munich), was friendly in tone but his criticisms were not at all encouraging to those who were yearning for agreement. The Orientals would not accept the proposed distinction between ἐκπορεύεσθαι and *procedere*. The one was always used to translate the other and was treated as equivalent. Any difference between them was not such as to affect the present question. Augustine's imperfect knowledge of Greek placed him out of court as an authority. And these were not the only points to which he took exception. Ossinin's comments were not those of a party anxious to make all possible concessions. He was not here last year. Janyschew who was so amiable and conciliatory in 1874 rose after him; but at the same moment Adelberg, a Lutheran pastor from Zell in Bavaria, rose also, and as he evidently was primed with a speech, he was allowed to get rid of it at once. Dr. Döllinger in the course of it moved towards him and said something in a low tone — perhaps a request to be brief. After Adelberg had delivered his truisms about brotherhood and tolerance, and some impracticable suggestions about holding to the Bible and not caring about dogmas, Dr. Döllinger closed the sitting. He would meet the Anglicans and Americans at 4.0 p.m.

At 3 p.m. there was a preliminary meeting in the rooms of the Bishop of Gibraltar. B. came with me to the afternoon session, at which the Orientals were not to be present. Dr. Döllinger had said that the English got their way all the world over, and no doubt if they wished to have ladies present at the sessions devoted to themselves, they would get their way as usual. However, this was not wished. Dr. Döllinger read letters from the Bishop of Winchester and from Gladstone which have been published. After a good deal of discussion Dr. Döllinger remarked on the extreme difficulty of getting the Orientals to assent to propositions taken out of their own Fathers, when these ran counter to the usual Oriental view. A body of quotations had been collected, which he believed to an uninfluenced mind would be irresistible, as abundantly showing that the Greek Fathers themselves spoke of a Procession from both the Father and the Son. But members of the Greek Church, almost from their childhood, are imbued deeply with the notion, that this is the one point on which no concession whatever must be made and that their existence as a Church almost depends on it; so much so that it is extremely hard to get them to look upon the other view as even possibly admissible. We must all of us do what we can to remove this tremendous obstacle. He would be glad to know whether the plan, adopted by himself and his colleagues, of presenting the Orientals with a catena of statements in the exact words of their own Fathers, was approved by the Anglicans present. This was agreed to, not as being calculated to convert the Greeks to the *Filioque*, which was not the object before us, but to show that the *Filioque*, although certainly not œcumenical in authority, was, by the evidence of the Greek Fathers themselves, manifestly orthodox.

Friday, August 13th. Some excitement was caused before we began by the arrival of the Archbishop of Syra with two more theologians. Meyrick presented me to him. I told him that I had been in Oxford when he received his D.D. degree, and also that I had been at Syra[18]. He seemed much surprised and interested by the last statement. He looked wretchedly ill, and was suffering so much in lungs and throat that he could scarcely speak. He wore his special dress, which was very picturesque.

Dr. Döllinger began by pointing out the difference which the Vatican 77 decrees had made in the position of the Eastern Church with regard to the Roman. Before 1870 Eastern Christians were in the eyes of Rome schismatics only. Now they are heretics, and liable to be treated as such as soon as Rome gets the opportunity. Formerly an Oriental who joined the Roman Church had to abjure no errors; he had merely to subscribe the creed of Pius IV. Even the Inquisition never treated Orientals as heretics. Now they have been placed in the same position as Protestants, and if they go over to Rome will need to be formally absolved from heresy. Thus the decrees of 1870 had created new heresies. If Bossuet were living now, he would be condemned not only as a heretic, but as a teacher of heresy, *eretico dogmatisante*. Union with Rome is now hopeless, and if all the 180 millions of Roman Catholics seriously believed the Vatican decrees, then to speak of reunion would be folly.

For fifty years he had always maintained that religious persecution was no part of the doctrine of the Church, and that the Roman Church (whatever may have been her practice in particular cases) was in theory tolerant, and recognized liberty of conscience. Such also had been the teaching of Catholic theologians in Germany, England and elsewhere. In Spain and Italy the teaching had for the most part been otherwise; but still the prevalent teaching had been that religious differences must

18. "*To his Most Reverend Holiness, Alexander, Archbishop of Syros, Tenos, and Melos, 78 the undersigned Priests and Deacons, residing in Oxford, Greeting in the Lord.*

Your Grace's arrival in our city has caused us no ordinary satisfaction. The welcome which we offer you is not only that of persons interested in ancient Greek literature to a Greek, but of Christians to a Christian and a Chief Pastor of the Orthodox Church. For while we look upon you, we call to mind those Bishops and Patriarchs who, a thousand years ago, delivered the doctrine of Christ in the Greek language. Their writings are current among all Christians, and are commended and admired by all. But we who in these days lay claim to the name of Christians, are divided from each other, — unhappily, God knows, and not without sin, — yet not of our own will, not through any preference for party spirit and dissension. Yet it is no work of man to restore the unity of the Church : it rather becomes us all to leave this in the hands of Almighty God, at the same time earnestly making our prayers that, according to His good pleasure, there may be again 'one fold, one Shepherd.' In the meantime, we remember the Apostle's words, 'Nevertheless whereunto we have attained, let us walk by the same rule, let us mind the same thing.' Therefore, my Lord, we greet you with gratitude for your kind acceptance of our kind feelings, and we also entreat for you and all your Clergy and Laity, together with the whole Church of Greece, and all the Orthodox who are in union with the Patriarchal See of Constantinople, all peace and security in the service of Christ our God, and His richest mercy 'always now and ever, and unto ages of ages.'"

be tolerated. Now at one stroke all the persecuting bulls were made infallible, and to maltreat heretics is a duty. The canonizations of the persecuting Archbishop Josaphat Kunczewicz of Polotzk, and the Spanish Inquisitor, Peter Arbues, were part of the same policy, viz. to give the sanction of the Church to the doctrine that dissenters may be put down by force. All these things must be considered in connexion with one another.

But it is impossible that this can last. It is incredible that so many millions of men, including the most cultivated nations in the world, should continue for ever to acknowledge the universal dominion and the infallibility of the Pope. The changes made were nothing less than a revolution. Nothing remotely like it had ever been known in the East; and even in the West it was until 1854 an unheard of thing that new articles of faith should be created. For fifty years he had taught theology and had never taught these doctrines; on the contrary he had contended against them. Yet he had never been reproved by Rome or his own bishop for so doing. Not one word of remonstrance or protest had he ever received. And now what he and hundreds of others had been teaching all their lives was made heresy. The old standard of *Quod semper, quod ubique, quod ab omnibus* was trampled under foot, and the opinion of the Pope of the moment was substituted for it. Once it was a maxim that a new article of faith was impossible : now it [is] openly avowed that dogmas which contradict antiquity can be imposed, and that the appeal to tradition is inadmissible.

He had ventured to detain us with this explanation because it was important to have a clear view of the situation; especially was it necessary that Orientals should recognize Rome's change of attitude towards themselves. All who opposed infallibilism were drawn towards one another by the events of 1870, and what separates them from one another must in the spirit of peace and love be removed. The Archbishop of Syra then moved towards Dr. Döllinger and said something inaudible to us. Dr. Döllinger said that the illness of the archbishop prevented him from speaking, but he had commissioned him to tell the Conference that he entirely assented to the remarks just made. He then went on to discuss the question of the Procession. One general consideration ought to be borne in mind in discussions of this kind : — the inadequacy of language to express such mysteries as these. The most accurate language possible, even if *quite* accurate, must in all cases be inadequate. The expression that the Holy Spirit proceeds from the Father, about which the whole Church is agreed, cannot be a full statement of the truth, for no full statement of such a truth in human language is possible. This consideration ought to make us very tolerant of expressions which seem to differ from those which we have been accustomed to recognize as accurate. To take an instance from theology : the ὁμοούσιον is no more than an approach to the truth; and so inadequate did it once seem that a synod at Antioch formally rejected it as seeming to imply heresy.   79

In the debate which followed the Orientals were more inclined to be conciliatory than Ossinin had showed himself as their spokesman the previous day. In concluding it Dr. Döllinger said that we were now far on the road towards an understanding. He thought that about three quarters of the matter was already peaceably settled. Respecting the remaining quarter it would perhaps be best to appoint a select committee of two or three from each of the three main bodies, Orientals, Anglicans, and Germans, to draw up statements respecting the remaining points of difference, and lay these before the Conference. Rhossis, the Athenian professor, who had been eager to speak before, now jumped up and was determined to have his say. Dr. Döllinger let him relieve himself of some pet ideas of his own respecting the distinctions which *he* drew between the various words used in the controversy. No one seemed to listen, for it appeared to be quite foreign to the matter in hand. Dr. Döllinger stood patiently with his eyes on the ground until Rhossis had finished, and then said quietly, "May I be allowed to return to my proposal? If I hear no dissenting voice, I conclude that it is accepted. At the afternoon sitting, which will again be in English, the Anglicans and Americans will elect two members. The Orientals will do the same at their private meeting. I and my colleagues will also do the same. This committee will sit at 9 a.m. to-morrow and will communicate the results of its deliberations to the Conference at the general sitting at 4 p.m."

Between the session B. had met Dr. Döllinger and he had said that he hoped to see something of us privately, either at dinner or for a walk; but in all this press of business it was difficult to see any one privately. Then we both met him on our way to the Rhine. He was walking alone and was in high spirits. The results so far had greatly exceeded his expectations. I asked him whether he had not been disappointed in the line taken by Ossinin the previous day. "Rather; but I was not much surprised. They like to be critical, and do not much like to admit an error. They must show fight in order to stand well with their fellow-countrymen." I then laughingly referred to Prof. Rhossis' effusion. "Oh, yes, poor man; it could well have been spared. But he would have been unhappy if he had not been allowed to speak. It was best to let him have his say."

When I got back to the Musik-Saal I found that another meeting had been held in Bishop Sandford's rooms, and that *five* members had been provisionally elected to serve on the joint committee. "Don't you think that an outrageous proceeding?" I said to Liddon. "I do indeed; but it was impossible to prevent it." We both agreed that Dr.

Döllinger ought to be told. I watched my opportunity and let him know that the Anglo-Saxons had elected *five* representatives. "Five!" he said, holding out both hands with the fingers distended : "Three are possible, but not more. The Orientals wish to have three. If you think well, I will make that public at once." And he rang his bell and did so. Bishop Sandford, declining to serve himself, proposed Liddon, Meyrick, and Nevin : and these were elected. In the debate on the question I raised my voice against the indecency of the attempt (which was actually made) to force five members into the committee, when the Old Catholics had agreed with the Orientals that each section should have three representatives, and the proposal then dropped. The debate which then followed on the doctrinal question was not edifying, and proved what a mixed multitude the members of the Anglican communion were. We included ultra-Protestants of the Irish Church. Things reached a climax when Dr. Schaff, the Presbyterian secretary of the Evangelical Alliance, came forward and almost insisted upon being heard. "He had come a long way," and had a speech which had evidently been composed with some care. MacColl in vain tried to stop him. Schaff's view was that we should agree in adopting certain statements in S. John's Gospel and S. Paul's Epistles and leave everything else to take care of itself. As soon as he had finished Dr. Döllinger came forward and said, "The last speaker, not being a member of those Churches which have preserved the episcopate, has no claim to be heard at this Conference. But as a matter of courtesy I thought it well to allow him to speak. If his opinions are shared by the other members of the Conference, it follows that we all of us should have done far more wisely if we had remained at home."

I have seldom seen a man so quietly, and at the same time so effectually, snuffed out as Dr. Schaff was by this remark from Dr. Döllinger. B. and I walked with Liddon when it was all over. He was greatly distressed, and thought that little good could come of these mixed gatherings. As we walked along the Rhine we talked of little else excepting the afternoon's proceedings. Liddon apologized to B. for talking such 'shop'; but it was what we all three preferred to talk. Other subjects which we started were very short-lived. We went back with Liddon to the 'Stern', where he was staying, and then returned to our own quarters.

Saturday, August 14th. The joint committee sat the whole morning. When it broke up we became aware that only a partial agreement had been reached. Unexpected difficulties had been started by some of the Greeks, who had pressed five of their number into the committee, and at one time even the patient and resourceful President was almost in despair. However, the Orientals were quite prepared to remain longer and continue the Conference. Consequently it was not to end to-day. There was to be another committee meeting on Sunday and another general one on Monday.

At 4 p.m., before the proceeding formally began, Dr. Döllinger came up to me and said, "Liddon is obliged to leave to-morrow at mid-day; but of course the work of the committee cannot stop on that account. How is his place to be supplied? It seems hardly worth while to call a meeting of the English to elect a substitute." "Could not he be allowed to name his successor?" Dr. Döllinger seemed to be a good deal relieved by the suggestion, and at once went to Liddon to request him to do this. Liddon consented, but said that he was much perplexed. It was so difficult to find a person who knew enough German, and who did not hold theological views which would at once alarm the Orientals. After some deliberation Dr. Döllinger turned to MacColl and myself and said, "Well! I must leave the matter in your hands. I shall trust to you to see that *some* one is appointed to take Liddon's place. It is impossible for me to manage everything." We both assured him that we would see to it, and thus set his mind at rest. The amount that he *does* arrange and manage, and with the utmost tact and success, is quite marvellous. Having provided for this difficulty he returned to the President's place and began what was to have been the final session, but had become merely preparatory to a conclusion.

CONVERSATIONS WITH DR. DÖLLINGER

Volume III

1875

The Bonn Conference, continued.

Saturday, August 14th. Afternoon meeting.

Dr. Döllinger said that at first sight it might seem hopeless to attempt *1* in a Conference of a few days to make any real progress towards putting an end to a controversy which had lasted thousand years and had defied all attempts at a solution. Yet we had all come thither with hopes that something worth doing might be done. On what were our hopes founded? The history of the past was an encouragement to us. Again and again in history strifes which had raged fiercely for long periods had almost suddenly, and just when men were despairing of any conclusion, come to an end. Nor was this hard to explain. The causes of strife cease to exist; men's ideas of and ways of looking at things change; what was once impossible becomes possible. To mention one great example: — the downfall and rapid extinction of Arianism just when it seemed about to triumph.

With regard to the present controversy very great changes have taken place, and on some of these very reasonable hopes may be based. 1. Political fears on the side of the Orientals are at an end. They can no longer dread lest concessions should be followed by attempts to reduce them to subjection either to the Pope or any other power. No such monstrous act of tyranny as the Latin conquest of Constantinople was any longer possible. Not one iota of any Oriental's independence was endangered by his yielding anything in this controversy. Under the mighty Empire of Russia the Eastern Church was secure of its creed, its rites, and its discipline. 2. The contest between faith and atheistic materialism, of which the East as yet knows little as compared with the West, is forcing upon us more and more the necessity of reunion. It is the scandal which prevents the conversion of the heathen, that we Christians cannot agree among ourselves as to what Christianity is. Before the danger which threatens us all, our narrowness and exclusiveness must give way. Woe to the Churches that continue to stickle about mere words and phrases before they will cooperate with one another in repelling infidelity. There have been times when words have been held like pistols at men's breasts with the cry, "Use this word to express your belief, or you are a heretic." The present time is no time for such inflexibility. We cannot afford to be unyielding with regard to the terms in which the truth is expressed. 3. Criticism has made gigantic progress. Its apparatus is now so perfect that in most cases there is no possibility of a dispute. The Council of Florence, with all its display of princes, ecclesiastics, and scholars, spent some three weeks in discussing whether a given quotation from S. Basil was genuine or not, and arrived at no agreement after all. No controversialist now would be likely to quote what is spurious; or, if he did, would be likely to escape conviction. Thus one great source of debate is stopped. It only remains to ascertain the meaning of passages : the question of their authenticity has in almost all cases been settled. These are some of the reasons which, combined with the *wish* for mutual understanding and agreement, render hopes of success not altogether baseless.

It remains to lay before the Conference what has been done by the Committee. They have not come to entire agreement : much still remains to be done before that can be accomplished. Still they have agreed in accepting four articles, and the amount of agreement contained in these four is real and substantial. 1. We accept the œcumenical creeds and the dogmatic decisions of the ancient undivided Church. 2. We admit that the *Filioque* was inserted in the creed in an uncanonical manner. 3. We adhere to the form of the doctrine of the Holy Spirit as it is taught by the Fathers of the ancient undivided Church. 4. We reject every notion and every mode of expression in which in any way the acceptance of two Principles, or ἀρχαί, or αἰτίαι, in the Trinity would be involved. After commenting on these, especially 1 and 2, Dr. Döllinger asked whether he should put them to the Conference at once? Or would any one like to make any remarks respecting them?

Overbeck [1] rose and in a not very pleasing manner asked whether it would not be better to insert in the first article the number of Councils 2 intended to be included under the term œcumenical. Here was a bombshell! Döllinger looked aghast. Agreement between Anglicans and Easterns about the Seventh Council would at this stage be quite hopeless. Dr. Döllinger said that this was opening an entirely new and irrelevant discussion : the question before us was the Procession. Overbeck replied that it was important to know whether the Seventh Council was included or not : it was a critical point. Dr. Döllinger : That Council decided respecting the use of pictures and images, which have nothing to do with the doctrine of the Spirit. Reinkens : The article refers to "dogmatic decisions", decisions on matters of faith. The Seventh Council made no such decisions, and does not come within the scope of the article. If we are to wait till we can agree about such questions as the number of œcumenical Councils we can no more become one Church than one nation. Rhossis justified Overbeck's interference by saying that the article was too vague, and Bishop Gennadios of Bucharest by saying that the number of Councils, though not a dogma, was of great dogmatic

1. Overbeck was first known to the world as a strong ultramontane. Then he became a Lutheran; then a member of the English Church. Finally (if it be finally) he joined the Greek Church; and it was as an Oriental that he appeared at Bonn.

importance. Dr. Döllinger, who was greatly disturbed by Overbeck's disastrous question, was evidently not listening to a speech all about Councils and not about the Procession, and went off to talk to Kiréef, no doubt to get him to help in the crisis. The faces and actions of the Orientals meanwhile were a study. Most of them seemed to be aware that a *faux pas* had been committed and that Gennadios was only making matters worse by his well meant explanation. Some of them pulled his gown as a hint to him to stop. At last, as he saw that Dr. Döllinger was not attending, he said, "It seems not to be the wish of the President that I should continue." Dr. Döllinger replied, "Allow me one observation. We were discussing our subject, the Procession of the Holy Spirit. In a most unexpected way we have thrust upon us the entirely new question of the number of the œcumenical Councils, a subject for the discussion of which we should require a day or two. If it must be discussed, it makes the prospects of success with regard to our main subject very remote. Besides, I know not how many other new questions may await us. If those which are in any degree connected, or can be brought into connexion, with the subject before us, are to be started one after another, we have a discussion before us which is literally endless." Janyschew in a few friendly words endeavoured to show that Overbeck's question was not quite so unreasonable as was assumed. Bryennios [2] came forward and said that he believed that the question of the number of œcumenical Councils was quite distinct from the question of the Procession. It would be best to leave the former entirely on one side and devote our attention to the latter. This proposal was greeted with grateful applause. Dr. Döllinger : "May I then understand that the meeting accepts the four articles already agreed to by the Committee?" There was a general murmur of assent. "And now I will ask your permission to fulfil a promise made to the Anglican members of this Conference, viz. to express to the Orientals my convictions respecting the validity of Anglican Orders." At very considerable length he repeated what he had said in 1874, adding the point about the confusion caused by the decree of Eugenius IV., which made the essential part of ordination to be, not the imposition of hands, but the tradition of the chalice and paten. In spite of this confusion Roman Orders were safe, but Anglican Orders were still more safe.

The sitting closed with Dean Howson's explaining away what he

2. Bryennios was one of the youngest of the Orientals (born 1833) and had done good work in the Committee by promoting harmony and stopping needless objections. He was an Archimandrite and head of the "Great School of the Nation" at Constantinople. He was sent by the Patriarch and Synod to Bonn. While there he received a letter nominating him to the Metropolitan see of Serrae in Macedonia. In 1877 he was translated to Nicomedia. In 1883 he became known to all the world as the discoverer and first editor of the Διδαχή.

had agreed to the year before respecting the eucharist. His explanation, which he said was made for the sake of those at home, ought obviously to have been made in some English newspaper. Liddon explained his view of Anglican doctrine, and then Overbeck came forward and congratulated Howson on his *honesty*; after which he explained to the Orientals what Howson had been saying. So I was told; the result of which was, and perhaps was intended to be, that the Orientals felt very much at sea as to what our doctrine respecting the eucharist is. This I learnt from a conversation with Janyschew, who said that such different views (as Howson's and Liddon's) were not possible in their Church.

Sunday, 12th after Trinity, August 15th. I had been misinformed as to the hour of the Old Catholic service and got there in time to meet the congregation coming out. Knoodt had preached what Liddon thought an exceedingly nice sermon, good both as a sermon and also as a piece of oratory. He alluded to the day as being a festival, but said nothing about the Assumption. The Old Catholic and Anglican members of the Committee met at 7.30 and again after service. The whole Committee at 4 p.m.

Monday, August 16th. Before the morning sitting B̄. and I waited outside the Conference room for Dr. Döllinger, in order that she might be sure of wishing him Goodbye. He said that he was very sorry not to have seen more of us : he had hoped that we might have had a walk together; but in the press of business it had been impossible. "For a whole week I have had no walk; and that, as you know, is a very unusual thing with me." He asked me to make known to the English that there was to be another sitting in German at four o'clock, chiefly for the sake of the Orientals, but he hoped that all who could do so would be present; for he was afraid that, as some people had already begun to leave, the last session might be thin, and give rather a poverty-stricken appearance to the conclusion of the Conference. That determined us to remain until the evening : we had been hoping to be able to leave at mid-day.

3   Dr. Döllinger began by expressing his intense satisfaction at the most unexpected amount of success. The Anglicans and Old Catholics were convinced that no real difference of doctrine existed between them and the East on the subject of the Procession. The Orientals were not yet able to affirm this, until they had consulted the authorities of their Church. All parties had been able to agree on a series of
4   articles based chiefly on the writings of John of Damascus. This Father of the eighth century concludes and sums up ancient Greek theology. He systematized it, reducing the scattered teaching of other Fathers to

a connected whole c. A.D. 750. Hence it seemed probable that his works would supply material for a basis of agreement. The large success which had been attained showed that this selection was a wise one.

He then read out the six articles given in the official report, keeping the third, however, until the last, because he fancied that the Orientals had not accepted it. They were much disquieted at this, and Janyschew and Dr. Döllinger had a short conversation in a low tone. At the end of it Dr. Döllinger apologized for his mistake, and said that this article also had been accepted by all. The Conference as a whole accepted all six articles, and then Dr. Döllinger said that he hoped that they would be accepted by the Eastern Churches at home in the same spirit as they had been accepted here,— in the spirit of peace. When he contrasted the last few days with what had taken place at the Councils of Lyons and of Florence, he could not but think that God's blessing had been on our work. *Here* we had really yearned for peace and tried to understand one another. *There* there was little but intrigue, falsehood, and violence; each party having quite other aims than those which they professed. He hoped for a continuation of these Conferences next year; and that we might have the joy of hearing from the Orientals that their synods had accepted our present agreements.

He then proceeded to explain a point raised by the Orientals, viz. in what sense Anglicans did not consider ordination to be a μυστή-ριον or sacrament. The Reformers, and especially the English Reformers, had unfortunately narrowed the meaning of sacrament to those two ordinances of Christ which are means of grace for *all* Christians. *This* ordination was not, and therefore in the English sense not a sacrament; but Anglican ordination had all the essential points, imposition of hands by a proper minister with the proper words. He then went on to speak of the Romish corruptions and abuses connected with the doctrine of purgatory and indulgences. When he said, "The Eastern Church still has something which might be called indulgences, viz. that the Church can remit or lighten a penance imposed," the Orientals (fancying that he referred to the dead) made signs of dissent. "We only pray for them," said the Archbishop of Syra. Dr. Döllinger explained his meaning more clearly, and they all assented and looked relieved. After further explanation of scandals connected with the Roman doctrine of indulgences he went on to speak of the Infallibility. As a claim made by Popes and for them, it was no doubt a theory which had been maintained for centuries; as an article of faith necessary for salvation it was just five years old. He proceeded to sketch what mischief the papal system had wrought in Germany—the overthrow of the old Catholic Empire; the division of the nation into two hostile camps, which cannot now be reconciled, although the division might easily have been avoided; the preeminence of Protestantism in the whole sphere of intellectual life. With very slight exceptions, all the theologians, historians, poets, men of science, and philosophers of any note have been Protestants. — 'By their fruits ye shall know them.' By this test, the Saviour bids us, test men and things. 'By its fruits' the papal system is judged. They would have been still worse but for the counteracting force of some elements of the German character.

The afternoon meeting was very well attended, and Dr. Döllinger's fears of a poor conclusion were not realized. He continued his sketch of the influence of the papal [system], this time going outside Germany, especially to Poland, France, Spain, Italy and America. In the history of all these nations the effects of papalism have been disastrous. But from history the Roman See has learnt nothing; to Rome history is a book closed and sealed.

In conclusion he begged us to measure ourselves, to measure the Christian world, with that world which is not Christian. We have been at work for nearly 1900 years and how little of the world is converted; how little even of the civilized world is Christian! We must agree among ourselves as to what the Christian faith is, before we can convert many to it. How beautiful to have one Church and one doctrine, or at least Churches united as to the fundamentals of the creed, that we might preach to the heathen in the strength of unity. Let us not grow weary in our work for reunion. "In thus concluding, I tender my heartfelt thanks to my audience for their consideration and attention. Not often does a speaker make such demands upon his hearers' indulgence. I thank you most earnestly for having come here, many from a great distance, and for the patient consideration which you have given to all that has been laid before you. God grant that our labours may in due time bear good fruit."

The Archbishop of Syra, in a hoarse whisper, which was audible to hardly anyone but Dr. Döllinger, Bishop Reinkens, and myself, said a few words of earnest thanks to the President for his marvellous efforts in work of reunion. There would be great joy when they returned home. He hoped that the day would come when we should be once more one flock under our one Shepherd. He earnestly prayed God to continue His blessing. The Bishop of Gibraltar's speech was not pleasing in tone, except when he spoke of the tact, patience, courtesy, learning and wisdom of the President, to which (under God) the large measure of success attained by the Conference was mainly due.

We said the Te Deum and Pater noster together, Bishop Reinkens leading us. He added a short prayer in Latin, and with that the Conference closed. I said farewell to Bishop Reinkens and then to Janyschew. "It will be a good sign," said the latter, "if we come back a third time. We shall meet here again, I hope. If we do not come again to confer with one another, it will look ill for our hopes of reunion. We may fear for reunion then." "I hope to meet you again," I said, "and as for intercommunion—it *must* be possible, for it is a duty." He shook his head doubtfully at the 'must', but when I finished the sentence his face brightened, and I think he murmured assent. I overtook Dr. Döllinger near the Coblenz gate. "You are just going?" said he; "Good-bye. God bless you. You are a good correspondent. Write to me soon." We left Bonn by the next train.

1876

Monday, August 21. My wife and I left the Great St. Bernard in the morning on our way back from Italy and descended to Martigny, where we found a budget of letters; among them one from Dr. Döllinger begging us to come to Munich and make a little excursion with him. I wrote at once that we should start for Munich next day. We reached Munich on the Wednesday evening.

Thursday, August 24th. Soon after breakfast we went to see Dr. Döllinger, whom we found in good health and strength. After general conversation for a time he spoke of the Reunion Conferences, and stated why he thought it would have been useless to have had one this year. 1. The troubled state of the East, where some of the bishops were taking part in the political struggle. 2. The divisions among the Orientals themselves, especially the jealousies and heart-burnings among the Greeks respecting the Slavic populations. 3. The mischief done by Overbeck, who has been working to prevent any union of Orientals with Anglicans. 4. The mischief done by Dr. Pusey in the line which he had taken
5 about the *Filioque*. I told Dr. Döllinger that Père Hyacinthe had told me that Michaud had rather been following in Overbeck's steps, insisting that the Seventh Council ought to be accepted. Dr. Döllinger said he was afraid that Council was going to give trouble. He had had one or two letters from Orientals urging that its claims should be discussed; but of course it was hopeless to expect that Anglicans would admit the authority of the Council. He saw only one way to agreement, viz. to consider the question of image-worship to be one of *discipline* only, not of dogma. The decisions of the Seventh Council might then be regarded as disciplinary rules binding on that part of the Church to which the members of the Council belonged. As a set-off to the discouragement caused by Oriental affairs, he had received two very cordial addresses from America, one signed by more than twenty bishops, the
6 other by enormous numbers of clergy and laity. Dr. Döllinger asked me if Loyson (as he habitually called Père Hyacinthe) had spoken to me of his own position, and what I thought of it. (We had spent a day or two with him and his wife at S. Cergues a few weeks before.) I replied that Loyson seemed to me to be wholly 'unattached', and to have a little community of his own. Dr. Döllinger thought Herzog, the future bishop of the Swiss Old Catholics, a very good man, but amiable to a fault, too pliant and ready to yield to the urgent wishes of others. He had been persuaded against his own desire to accept the office of bishop.

Dr. Döllinger proposed to take us in the afternoon to the German Exhibition in the Glas-Palast, which he said was well worth seeing and admirably arranged. It deserved all his praise and it was delightful seeing it with such a cicerone. He pointed out to me one or two examples of the *fistula eucharistica*, a metal pipe for receiving the wine from the chalice, so as to reduce the possibility of spilling. The prayer-book of S. Henry the Emperor (1002-1024) was one of the curiosities. There was among the pictures one which represented Riccio as a gallant of about thirty, singing to Mary of Scots; "Whereas," said Dr. Döllinger, "he was upwards of sixty, was only the queen's secretary, and perhaps never touched a guitar in his life. Schiller has helped to popularize the myth of the young singer." We were looking at some exquisitely engraved glass, on which he remarked, "What a time it must have taken to execute all that! What a waste of time!" We stayed till it closed. He had taken me aside and said, "There is a portrait of me in one of these rooms : don't tell your wife; we'll see if she recognizes it." However, we never chanced to come upon it.

Friday, August 25th. This morning we went again to the exhibition and saw the picture, the famous one by Lembach. I caught sight of it on entering; and the resemblance, which before has struck me as sometimes flashing out, between Döllinger and Newman, at once occurred to me. B. recognized the portrait at once, as soon as her eyes fell upon it. In Munich people dispute very much as to its merits. We do not think it a success. There is a tragic look about it, as if the artist had in his mind the excommunicated man of intellect. Dr. Döllinger's fate has been tragic enough; but, excepting at rare moments, the tragedy is never seen in his cheerful face. The bright twinkle of his intelligent eyes is quite wanting.

He had asked us to dine at one, and we found Sir Rowland and Lady Blennerhasset there to meet us with their little boy. I had met him there before in 1870. She is a German, very intellectual and pleasant. We talked of the great Wagner celebration at Bayreuth, which is a great success, in spite of some mishaps, such as the machinery men getting drunk and sending the city of Niebelstein *up*, instead of *down*, in the Rhine. The singers are singing for nothing! Could such enthusiasm for any one, living or dead, be found in England or France.

As to the authorship of Pomponio Leto's *Eight months in Rome during the Vatican Council*, Dr. Döllinger said that the matter was very simple. 7 The author had sent the book to Dr. Döllinger begging him not to mention his name until his brother was made cardinal, the author being, as has been commonly supposed, the Marquese Vittelleschi, who was supplied with information on various points of detail by his brother, who was a member of the Council. "If Manning knew this,"

8 said I, "his letter was disingenuous." "Of course he knew," said Dr. Döllinger, "but where the Church's interests are concerned, he holds the casuistical doctrine that it is not necessary to tell the truth, the whole truth, and nothing but the truth. In that notorious marriage case I *know* that the whole matter passed through his hands, and yet, when he was asked about it, he said that he had never heard of any such case." Sir Rowland remarked that Manning generally avoided telling a lie as long as he could, and would try to throw dust in people's eyes instead, but he did not shrink from a downright lie, when he was pressed.

Among other topics we talked of the resting-place of S. Cuthbert's body, Archbishop Thomson of York, the Bravo case, and the chances of Disestablishment, which no one seemed to think would come in the present century[3]. We sat talking until 4 p.m. and then the Blennerhassets rose to go. Dr. Döllinger proposed a walk, so at the door the party divided, the Blennerhassets going homewards and Dr. Döllinger taking us into the English Garden. We crossed the river at Brunnenthal, where the new bridge is still incomplete, and came back by the Maximilianeum, close to which we stopped to examine the excellent monument to King Max, which has been finished since we were here last August. On the way we talked of Dr. Döllinger's present work of publishing documents to illustrate the Council of Trent, and of the possibility of my helping him in the drudgery part of the undertaking. He is now without a secretary. If we lived in Munich, I believe that I could be of real help to him.

He sees no issue for the contest between the Papacy and the government : impossible to predict how the struggle will end. "The ultramontanes hope for a change in their favour, when the Emperor dies;

---

3. Another topic of conversation was the religious crisis in Venezuela, which affords one more proof that the attitude of the Vatican towards the German government is the result of policy and not of religious conviction. What it would be 'impious and sacrilegious' to concede to Prussia, when the concession is inconvenient, can be conceded to other states, when the concession is to the interest of Rome. In Venezuela the government and the Vatican came into collision about the appointment of [the] archbishop, the government refusing to have the Papal Prelate Guevara forced upon them. The Vatican persisted in its absolute right to appoint. Thereupon the President, Guzman Blanco, referred the matter to Congress, which decreed some very drastic ecclesiastical laws, the effect of which would be the disestablishment of the Roman Church in Venezuela. *Then* Rome gave way. The Papal Nuncio Roca Cochia was sent to Caraccas; negociations were reopened; Archbishop Guevara was dismissed; the Senate nominated José Ponte as archbishop; and the Pope ratified the appointment. Nor is this all. Ponte took the oath of allegiance to the constitution and made a speech in which he compared President Guzman Blanco with Augustus, Pericles, and Charles the Great! The President once more communicated with Congress, which cancelled the new ecclesiastical laws as being no longer required. This is one of the most signal abandonments of the *non possumus*
9 attitude of Rome that has been known for a long time.

the liberals hope for something better when the Pope dies. Both parties may easily be mistaken." I asked whether there was any reason for thinking that the Crown Prince was favourably disposed towards the ultramontanes. "None whatever; but still they hope that he will think the present line of action too violent. However, the future may depend more upon the next Chancellor than the next Emperor. Bismarck will not be in office for ever."

A large new Schulhaus suggested the question of religious instruction in schools. Dr. Döllinger said that the matter was by no means settled in Germany, and would again become a subject for legislation. At present the magistrates in each place determine whether the *elementary* schools shall be denominational or not. In Munich they are undenominational, the clergy giving the religious instruction *out of* school-hours. School-hours are devoted to secular subjects. With this arrangement the laity as a rule are satisfied, but the clergy, both Catholic and Protestant, grumble. In the *Gymnasien* or higher schools government keeps the matter in its own hands, appointing both Catholic and Protestant pastors to give the religious instruction *in* school-hours. It has lately reduced the time to be devoted to it from twice to once a week, a reduction which has provoked much murmuring. The Archbishop of Munich has recently expressed himself very strongly on the subject.

We passed a frightful poodle, to which I said, "You ugly dog!" Dr. Döllinger asked me if I ever kept a dog. I said, "No." "Nor have I. I have always been able to live without animals about me. One child is much more interesting to me than the whole of the animal world put together." I knew of old that he disliked dogs: like Dr. Pusey he thinks them such shameless animals. He said that the controversy between Darwinians and Antidarwinians is raging in Germany as fiercely as ever and is producing quite a voluminous literature. To-day is the king's birthday, but Dr. Döllinger says that the notice taken of the day has grown less and less of late years. Very little has been done to-day. The weather continues so cold and dull that there seems to be little chance of our expedition.

Saturday, August 26th. At one o'clock we were once more at Dr. Döllinger's hospitable door, and to-day we had him all to ourselves. Capital punishment turned up as a topic. It is not abolished by law in Bavaria, but under the present king, who has an abhorrence of it, it is very rarely inflicted, indeed is almost obsolete, for he will rarely sign the death-warrant after the prisoner has been sentenced to death; and so the sentence has to be changed to imprisonment for life or a term of years. "He shrinks from the responsibility of shedding blood, and thus unintentionally," said Dr. Döllinger, "does a great deal of harm; for murder and manslaughter are very common, especially in lower Bavaria.

Wives poisoning their husbands is not at all uncommon. Imprisonment is quite insufficient as a deterrent; the prisoner always hopes that a revolution, or an amnesty, or some lucky chance will set him free. About two years ago a very brutal murder was committed, by which two or three persons were killed, and in that case the king did sign the death-warrant. Execution is by means of a guillotine, and is no longer public. The Abschreckungs-theorie is quite exploded. Even when executions were public there was no scandal, no mere coming to see a sight. It was much more of a religious ceremony : all the people prayed. The priest who accompanied the culprit to the place of execution would invite the people to join in prayer for the man, and they would do so. An Englishman who was present at an execution in Bavaria, when they were still public, was very much struck by this."

We found that Dr. Döllinger did not know what a "spelling-Bee" is. When we had explained it, he wondered how any result could ever be obtained; "for surely every one who has been to school can spell any word without difficulty"—from which it would appear that spelling is better taught in Germany than in England.

After dinner he took us into his library, which he wished B. to see, telling her that "not *quite* all his books were uninteresting. Only an unmarried man could have so many books : a husband would not be allowed to have so many. You see I am obliged to make use of all available space. That," pointing to a recess in the wall, "was once a wood-closet." He lent me the third and most important volume of
10 Caspari's *Quellen zur Geschichte des Taufsymbols*, which Caspari had sent him. It was published last year and is already out of print. He recom-
11 mended the *Dogmengeschichte* of Thomasius of Erlangen, which he
12 considers the best on the subject; also Lanfrey's *Life of Napoleon I.* He told us of his seeing Napoleon when he was a boy at Würzburg. He admired him then perhaps almost as much as he detests him now. His mother, however, hated him cordially enough then; for for a whole year the Döllinger family were having three or four soldiers billeted upon them to lodge and feed. "*I* liked it well enough," said Dr. Döllinger, "for I was glad of an opportunity of practising my little knowledge of French with the soldiers, who were always affable enough, and pleased to be understood by me. Moreover, I was scarcely a German then, for in Würzburg we scarcely knew what we were[4]. Napoleon had given

4. "People in those days talked about Austria, Prussia, Bavaria, and so forth; but the idea of Germany was scarcely intelligible to us. Napoleon seemed to me to be superior to Scipio, Hannibal, or Caesar. That this Corsican should have gained the control of the proudest people in the world!—in those days I didn't know the difference between pride and vanity. But, when I was about 17, I read something about Pius VII. and Napoleon's treatment of him, his imprisonment, and his triumphant return to Rome. That made an indescribable impression on me. I have never seen the essay since; but
13 I still remember whole passages of it." See *Döllinger und Platen* p. 77.

us to a Tuscan Duke, who went back to Tuscany again when Napoleon fell. There was not much German sentiment in us then. So as a lad I naturally enough admired Napoleon for his success, and did not care much about anything else. I remember very well hearing that there was to be a review, and that Napoleon would be there. We lads ran off to get as near to him as we could; and I got very near, almost as close as I am to you; and we tried to keep up with him as he went along the line. Of course there was great enthusiasm; every one full of admiration for him. But in his face there was not the slightest response; no emotion whatever; no sympathy with those around him. It was a face of stone, like the statue in *Don Giovanni*. There was nothing human in it. I have never seen anything like it before or since, —never. The turning point of opinion about him in Bavaria was the Russian campaign. When 30,000 Bavarians were left behind dead in the retreat from Moscow, that opened people's eyes. I cannot feel any admiration for him now. I dislike him, if for nothing else, for his heartless conduct to women; and, besides that, his whole policy was utterly selfish." B. asked him how, if that were so, his soldiers came to be so devoted to him. "Because," said Dr. Döllinger, "he gave them plenty of *gloire* and of pillage : a Frenchman is always intoxicated with *gloire*. The Italians, who are not, were not devoted to him : they disliked the whole war and would gladly have gone back to Italy. We had Italian soldiers quartered upon us as well as French." After B. had seen the library we took our departure.

Sunday, 11th after Trinity, August 27. I went to Dr. Döllinger's in the afternoon, and then we called at the Bayrischer Hof for B., after which we all started for Nymphenburg. Almost directly Dr. Döllinger caught sight of Dr. Enzler, Dean of the Royal Chapter, and therefore second to Dr. Döllinger, who is Provost of it. Dr. Döllinger said to us, "I must just go and say a few words to that gentleman." They walked on in front, and we followed behind. When Dr. Döllinger rejoined us, he said, "That is the gentleman we were talking about at dinner the other day—the future Bishop of Speyer. He did not know it until just now. I have been the first to tell him that the king has nominated him to the bishopric." Odd that the bishop elect should know of his promotion 48 hours later than we did[5]! Dr. Döllinger told us of it

5. It did not interest us much at the time, and we paid little attention to it. I watched him as he walked on in front of us, and tried to imagine his feelings at being thus told suddenly in the public streets that he was to be offered a bishopric. He was not, after all, to be bishop. He was too little of a partizan for Rome; and although the Pope could not formally veto the appointment, he could let Dean Enzler know that he must not accept it. Some time after this walk we saw that he had declined it. The same thing happened at Würzburg about the same time. The king nominated Dr. Käs to the see, and, unless he declines it, there will be a serious constitutional difficulty, for Rome has let Dr. Käs know that he is not acceptable.   *14*

on Friday. Dr. Enzler is a moderate man, but not so distinctly anti-ultramontane as to have compromised himself; a man of culture, though not exactly a scholar. "Scholars," said Dr. Döllinger, "are not so common : least of all among candidates for bishoprics."

On our way to Nymphenburg we talked of Père Hyacinthe's marriage, of which of course Dr. Döllinger has always strongly disapproved. He seems to think that he and she were sincere in saying that they married in order to help forward reform in the Church, yet that they were too far entangled to be good judges of their own motives. "If Loyson had joined another communion in which the marriage of the clergy is allowed, it would have been another thing. But it gives people a great handle for reproach, when he holds fast the essentials of the system to which he has belonged and rebels in just the point which suits his own convenience. And again his case is complicated by being not merely the marriage of a priest but the marriage of a monk. He took his vows as a monk at an age when he was quite *compos sui* and able to judge for himself. He has ruined his chance of influence in France. In Germany a married priest would be tolerated, at any rate in the large towns. People would talk a good deal at first, but then all would become quiet again : he would not lose his position in society. But in France this would be impossible. The feeling against a married priest is so strong that it is shared even by the infidel party. Even the Voltairians think the marriage of the clergy indecent. And there is no third party from whom he could gain sympathy. The French people are ground between the two mill-stones of ultramontanism and infidelity."

Nymphenburg has not been a royal palace since the days of the first king—Maximilian I. In one of the adjacent buildings is a convent of the Englische Fräulein, so called because the foundress was an English lady. It is a very common order in Germany. They devote themselves to education and have large schools; but in North Germany they are no longer allowed to teach. Dr. Döllinger's niece, who is one of them in a house at Eichstadt, came to see him the other day and told him that many of the sisters from houses in Prussia were being distributed among other convents in the South. There are no Döllingers in Germany excepting his own family. His father and uncle are well known as authors. In Hungary, he has been told, the name is common.

He has not yet had time to read Pusey's new book—his letter to
15 Liddon on the *Filioque*, but it seems to go over the same ground as Pusey has traversed before. Dr. Döllinger thinks that Pusey catches at every straw, and some of them very weak straws, in order to defend the insertion of the *Filioque*. His argument about the Greek version of the Athanasian Creed having contained the *Filioque* is quite baseless, quite without evidence. "Pusey," said Dr. Döllinger, "has something

of the casuistical spirit and seems to think that in what appears to
tell against the interests of the Church, the whole truth need not be
admitted. He thinks that, *if* it be admitted that the *Filioque* was inserted
in an irregular manner, the symbolum will be unsettled, and Englishmen
will cease to believe in its authority." Dr. Döllinger has sometimes
thought of urging Pusey to come to the Reunion Conferences; but he
fears to do so; for he is by no means sure that Pusey could be induced
to come; and secondly he is by no means sure that, if he were to come,
he would not do more to prevent union than to facilitate it. Dr. Döllinger
walked back with us nearly to the Bayrischer Hof; to the corner of
Pranner Strasse. But, as he said, it seemed to be written in the stars
that we were not to go to Starnberg together. The weather still continued
very uncertain and unpromising.

Monday, August 28th. I went to Dr. Döllinger's library in the morning,
where he had kindly put together some books bearing on Hippolytus
for my use, and while I was at work on them more arrived from the
Royal Library, to which he had sent for some volumes which his library
did not contain. This kept me employed all the morning. In the afternoon we all three had a walk together again. We went through the
Englischer Garten into the Hirschau, where we saw abundance of the
colchicum autumnale, the meadow flower so like a crocus. Dr. Döllinger
told us that it is poisonous, but that in Munich the brewers put the
seeds, which are narcotic, into beer. We heard from him some more
about Max Müller's proposed departure from Oxford, of which enough
is already known in England not to increase Max Müller's reputation
as a man of delicacy and independence. But what follows is not well
known. He wrote some time ago to Dr. Döllinger, telling him that
he wished to return to Germany and that Munich would be especially
agreeable to him as a residence. What prospect was there of an opening
there? Dr. Döllinger consulted other professors and one of the ministers
and wrote back to this effect; that they would feel honoured in having
him among them and would gladly offer him a professorship in the
University with full licence to lecture, but that, as both the philological
chairs were filled (one by Hauch, who has since died, and the other
by Trumpp), the state of the finances did not allow them to offer him
a salary. Max Müller also wrote to some other place as well as to
Munich. Dr. Döllinger said that, now that Ewald is dead, it is not
easy to say who is the best Oriental scholar in Germany. Oriental
scholarship has become so subdivided, that it is difficult for a man
to be great in all the branches. The surviving professor here, Trumpp,
is certainly one of the first. Dr. Döllinger promised to give me an address
recently delivered by Trumpp before the Bavarian Academy. He said *16*
that the school of Baur was on the wane in Germany. Jena represents

it now rather than Tübingen. Berne and Zurich also have leanings that
way. It has not, and never has had, any representative at Munich. Its
ablest living representative is Zeller, of whose History of Philosophy
17 Dr. Döllinger spoke in terms of high praise.

There is no *congé d'élire* in the appointment of bishops in Bavaria
since the Concordat. The Chapter has nothing to do with the matter.
The king nominates, and the Pope almost as a matter of course insti-
tutes the royal nominee. Formerly, when there were Prince-bishops of
Bamberg, Würzburg, Eichstadt, etc., the government made a separate
Concordat with each see.

To-day is Goethe's birthday, and they have *Faust* at Hof-Theater;
not the opera, but the drama. "If Goethe were alive," said Dr. Döllinger,
"he might protest against that. It is evident that he never intended
it to be put on the stage. When it first appeared, he called it on the
title-page a *Puppen-spiel*." I remarked that all the part about the dog
at the opening was rather absurd on the stage. Dr. Döllinger considers
Die natürliche Tochter one of the finest of Goethe's dramas, and supposes
that its incompleteness is what prevents it from being put on the stage.

He said that he had just been reading a very good article on Wagner
in the *Kölnische Zeitung*, in which the writer says that Wagner is a
great master of expression and has enormous resources at his command,
but that all this wealth of power is expended in expressing the more
realistic side of life. He gives us human life, not as it ought to be,
or might be, but as it is, and that in its coarsest features. The high
and the ideal is lost sight of or ignored; the low and the real is made
prominent and exaggerated. Contrast a love-scene as expressed by Mozart with one as expressed by Wagner. In Mozart the passion is refined,
and what is gross is lost in the beauty of the pathos. In Wagner
nothing is refined. All that is expressed, and that in a full-blooded
way, is the animal passion. Music of this kind is likely to produce
a morbid and hysterical effect, especially upon women. Dr. Döllinger
had been told that, as a matter of fact, Wagner's music does have
a bad effect upon women : I think some physician told him so. From
the dramatic point of view also there is danger that scenery and mechanical contrivance will become the masters instead of the servants of the
drama.

Tuesday, August 29th. B. did not feel equal to a long walk, so Dr.
Döllinger and I started without her. Before we went he gave me Professor
Trumpp's Festrede on Nānak the founder of the Sikh religion, and
18 another by Baron Liliencron on Education in the age of Scholasticism,
together with another copy of his own address in memory of the late
19 King John of Saxony. He asked me if I had *La dernière heure du*
20 *Concile*, a copy of which he had put ready for me; and I was rather

sorry to be obliged to say that I had, for I should like to have had
it as his gift. But I had bought it in Munich some years before. I asked
him who was the author. He said that at first it was stated that it had
been written by the Archbishop of Paris himself (i.e. the late archbishop,
Darboy); but afterwards he was told that it was written by someone
under the direction of the archbishop, and he never heard who that
someone was.

We passed two of the theological professors, Schmidt and another.
Dr. Döllinger remarked that such men found themselves in a false
position here. Under the Vatican system it was impossible to teach
theology, — at least in Germany. In France, or Spain, or Italy it was
possible to play at teaching it; i.e. it was possible by mutual understanding to teach something under the name of theology that would
not contradict the Vatican decrees; but in the sunlight of German science
this was impossible. These professors think that the Church is in a
state of transition; that a great change is coming; and they are waiting
for better days. I asked whether he thought that there would ever come
a great crash as regards Vaticanism, or whether people would gradually
and insensibly fall away from it. At Bonn he had expressed a conviction
that so many millions of reasonable beings *could* not go on believing
doctrines so monstrous : how would the change come about? "As regards
that, I suppose that one must distinguish between different nations and
countries. Among the Romance nations there is no interest in the
subject. In Italy, Spain, and Portugal they are *poco curanti*, quite indifferent. In France ultramontanism has this immense advantage, that it
is the only form of religion which exists. The rest of the nation is
infidel or indifferent. And of this the clergy make good capital. They
represent all attacks upon them as attacks upon Christianity. The bishops
are continually doing this. It is never 'Rome', or 'the Vatican', or 'the
Pope', with them, but 'the religion of Jesus Christ'. In Germany ultramontanism has a somewhat similar advantage on account of the Falk
laws. It is always maintained by the clergy, — and the masses to a very
large extent believe them, — that Catholics are persecuted for their
religion by a Protestant and infidel government. And this will continue
for some time longer; but it cannot go on for ever. People will begin
to see that it is not Catholics as such that are interfered with; but
that only the ultramontane system, which is subversive of all government, is severely handled. In time it must become patent to all that Catholics who will obey the laws are as free in Germany as elsewhere. I believe
that if the government remains firm for twenty years, it will win; and
every year makes it more difficult for it to go back. Still, there is no
saying what a new Emperor or a new Chancellor may do. It is in
Germany, therefore, that the battle will be fought out. At the next
conclave for the election of [the] Pope *the* contest will be between those

who think it advisable to come to terms with the Italian government and those who wish to continue the present *non possumus* policy. If a Pope should be elected, who is willing to establish a *modus vivendi* with the kingdom of Italy, ultramontanism and the Jesuit party will receive a great shock, and their moral influence in Europe must suffer accordingly. And if a *modus vivendi* is established between the Papacy and the Italian government, the same is likely sooner or later to follow with regard to the German government. Even now it would be difficult for Rome to answer the question why what is allowed in Austria is forbidden in Germany. The Pope has declared that the laws of Austria are quite as abominable as those of Germany; and yet he orders the Austrian bishops to submit and the German bishops to rebel." I asked the reason of this policy. "Because," said Dr. Döllinger, standing still to give his answer, while a stern look came over his face, such as sometimes comes there, when he is making a statement, of the truth of which he is profoundly convinced; "Because it has always been a principle with Rome to have only one enemy at a time. She never sets all the world at defiance at once. One power is flattered, while another is attacked. But a time may come when Austria will unite with Germany in resisting ultramontanism, and under such pressure Rome may give way."

I asked why it was that the Council had been never formally closed but only prorogued. "The Pope said that he had other canons and dogmas to propound, and that these would have been discussed and promulgated, if the Council had not been violently interrupted. Of course there was no real interruption. The Italian government would have taken care that the bishops were not interfered with, nor the transaction of business impeded." I replied, "The object then was to make it appear as if the Infallibility were not the sole thing for which the Council was summoned." "Well, I believe the Pope really did mean to propose another dogma for discussion with a view to its promulgation — the corporal assumption of the Blessed Virgin[6]. He is said still to have it very much at heart. He thought that he had done a great deal for the Blessed Virgin in proclaiming her Immaculate Conception, and that it would be only decent in her to do a great deal for him in return. Consequently, he wishes to do still more for her (this is no jest), in order to force her, so to speak, to make some return. And so he thinks of proclaiming her corporal assumption. I believe that what lurks in his mind is that, as she is a woman, she cares a good deal about her body, and therefore will be very much pleased if all the world is com-

---

6. A petition was set on foot by the Jesuits, and hawked about Rome and elsewhere with the Pope's approval, praying that the Assumption may be made a dogma, and that all who deny it or point to the notorious fact that the idea is found first in very questionable writings (apocryphal or heretical or both), be anathematized.

manded to believe that her body is in heaven. Did you ever hear the anecdote of an Italian preacher, or rather priest, who on one of the festivals of the Blessed Virgin had to preach the sermon? He had never preached before, and accordingly he prayed to the Madonna that she would inspire him and teach him what to say in her honour, and that the time for her aid would be when he had to address the people; he would wait till then. Accordingly at the proper time he ascended the pulpit and went through the usual preliminaries, and then waited for the inspiration; but nothing came. He waited and waited, but not an idea or word would come. At last, when the people began to be impatient, he threw his handkerchief at a figure of the Blessed Virgin, which chanced to be close to the pulpit, and exclaimed, *Sei donna anche tu!* (Thou art a woman like the rest of them!) I think that there is some such notion in the Pope's mind with regard to the Madonna— *Sei donna anche tu.*

"I suppose that Manning every now and then gets hold of one of your clergy and persuades him to join the Roman Church." "Yes, but one may be quite sure that one hears of every one who is gained by them; whereas one seldom hears of those whom they lose. Those who go over are never people of any learning or culture, but generally some enthusiastic and fanatical ritualist, who has lost his balance." "What an extraordinary thing that is," said Dr. Döllinger, "that enthusiasm about vestments! Growing fanatical about a chasuble! It is a thing that you would find in no other country. And about a *chasuble* of all vestments, which is certainly neither graceful nor convenient. *We* are used to them, and they don't strike us as particularly bad. But I cannot understand why those who care for such things do not go to the Greek Church for their models. The Greek vestments are more dignified." "My father often says much the same; for the Greek Church is nearer to the primitive type." "Of course."   21

I asked him whether any Old Catholic clergy had availed themselves of the concession made at the last synod—that clergy without cure of souls may be married with the rites of the Church. "I have not heard   22 of any instance. Schulte is the great advocate of the marriage of the clergy; but he had only three or four supporters at the synod. The clergy were strongly opposed to it. The effect of the marriage of the clergy would be the dispersion of the congregations. That would follow inevitably. You have no idea how firmly rooted in the minds of our people it is, that a priest is a man who sacrifices himself. Self-abnegation —that is the thing that is looked for. The priest has given up the happiness of having children of his own, in order that all the children in the parish may be his children. His congregation has the first place in his thoughts. They know very well that, if he marries, his wife and children will come first, and the parish second. This is notoriously the case with

the Protestants. They regard their parsons as having not a vocation, but a *Gewerbe* — a means of getting a livelihood. He is a *Gewerbsman*; he has to keep his wife and his family by his work. In large towns, where the population is almost entirely Protestant, it is quite a common thing for funerals to take place without any minister : he has other things to do. This is almost unheard of among Catholics. Again, in Protestant towns, now that the civil marriage has been introduced, large numbers of people are never married by the minister at all. They go without any religious ceremony. Where there is a large proportion of Catholics among the population, this is not the case. The Catholics of course are married by a priest; and the Protestants do not like to be behindhand. Divorce is not so very common now. Formerly in Prussia it used to be very easy to obtain a divorce. There were thirteen causes under the old law, for any one of which it was possible to obtain a divorce; and under one or other of them it would be possible to bring almost any marriage. One of them was 'mutual dislike'. But that has been altered for a good many years. Here in Bavaria divorce on account of change of creed is no longer allowed. — Before I forget it, let me mention that, as far as I know, the collection of documents in illustration of the Council of Trent has been very little noticed in England. I believe that as yet only one short notice of it — by Lord
23 Acton in the *Academy* — is all that has appeared. If the sending of a copy to anyone in England would ensure a notice of it in one of the English papers — the *Guardian* for instance — , I would tell the publisher to send a copy." I promised to see to it.

  Dr. Döllinger appears to be terribly crippled for want of a secretary. He does not like to advertize, and the right kind of man is not easy to get. He must know several languages, and almost necessarily must be a German. He promised to write and let me know whether I could do anything for him at the British Museum. With that we parted at the entrance to the Hof-Garten. We had gone out at the Sieges Thor and across the Marsfeld to the Nymphenburg road. It was starlight when we returned.

Wednesday, August 30th. We both went in the morning to thank him for all his kindness and to wish him 'farewell'. He had said that he would be engaged in the afternoon. We did not stay long. He told us to write to him very soon. The weather had prevented the expedition which he had kindly planned for us, but we had seen a good deal of him, in spite of the weather; and he is more than an expedition! I procured a copy of the *Süddeutsche Presse* containing a most amusing article copied from the *Deutsche Zeitung* on the promotion of Baron Hofmann from the position of Sections-Chef in the Treasury to that of Chancellor of the *Imperial* Exchequer of Austria, which is almost a complete sinecure. Dr. Döllinger told us of it; he said he did not know when he had laughed so much over anything; he hardly knew how to stop. Such an article, he said, would ruin a minister in France, but in Austria such a thing was thought nothing of. It hinted that he had got this nice plum by keeping on good terms with whatever government was 'in', whether Beust, Hohenwart, or Andrassy. Both Austria and Hungary have exchequers, and each has its own minister of finance. But there is a nominal minister of *imperial* finance, who is supposed to manage the combined exchequers. As, however, they are never really combined, and as the work of the two sections is completely done by the special officials, the imperial financier has a *very* easy berth. The article is a mock *obituary* notice of Baron Hofmann, who has been carried off from public life by a violent attack of promotion.

On our way back to England we stayed at Spires, where I procured the funeral sermon in honour of Bishop Haneberg. He had been Abbot of S. Boniface in Munich, and, like Hefele, was a sad instance of one who had every means of knowing that the Infallibility dogma cannot be true, nevertheless submitting to it. He was promoted to Spires, the poorest of the Bavarian bishoprics, soon after the promulgation of the dogma, and he then became rather forward in putting down those who denied its truth. The sermon was full of the most glowing praise of him. I sent it to Dr. Döllinger, who of course had known him well.

1877

Friday, June 29th. We reach Munich a little before 8 a.m. and in the afternoon called on Dr. Döllinger. He looked, if anything, younger than he had done the previous year. Before very long we got on the inevitable
24 Eastern question. Opinion in Germany, he said, was divided very much as in England. The majority are anti-Russian; but a powerful minority is anti-Turk. To the latter of course belong those who look at the question from a religious point of view and sympathize with the Christian population groaning under the Turkish yoke. Dr. Döllinger himself has for years been of opinion that England can never afford to allow Russia to occupy Constantinople permanently. Bismarck would not allow it either. In the two papers which are known to have articles inspired by him, the *Poste* and the *Politische Correspondenz*, he has declared that in this matter the interests of Germany are pretty nearly identical with those of Austria. And this week some articles known to be inspired by Andrassy have appeared, in which it is stated that Austria can never tolerate a united Slavonic power threatening her eastern frontier. It is not stated that it cannot allow Russia to conquer these provinces, but that it cannot allow an antagonistic power to be permanently established there. Another remarkable silence is that not a word is said about Constantinople. The hardest nut is left for others to crack. Dr. Döllinger is disposed to think that Gladstone's "bag and baggage" policy is
25 among the best things possible. He thinks it not out of the range of possibilities that the Turks may be deprived of all rule in Europe, allowed to live where they please in the enjoyment of personal and political freedom, while some Western prince takes in hand the difficult task of governing these discordant elements, Greeks, Roumanians, Mahometans, and Slavs. The Duke of Edinburgh, with his Russian wife, would perhaps be the most likely prince to be tried and to succeed. But the want of a dynasty, with all its endless associations, will be one of the many difficulties to be overcome. A dynasty is a want which is pretty sure to be felt sooner or later in a state. The time may come when even America, tired of perpetual elections which tear the country to pieces, and tired of rapid changes, not merely as to the Head of the State but all his subordinates, may be glad to seek relief in a dynasty.

With the proposal of Lord Harrowby, the Dean of Canterbury, and others to set up Evangelical colleges at the universities as a sort of
26 balance to Keble College, Dr. Döllinger has of course no sympathy. He is wholly in favour of bringing up clergy and laity, and those of very various shades of opinion, all together. There is no need to intensify differences by preparing seminaries of propagandism.

We talked of various other topics, and then it was arranged that we should call for him again at 7 p.m., the time at which he usually takes his walk at this time of year. And this we gladly did. We walked through the English Garden to the new stone bridge over the Isar at Brunnthal, along the Anlagen to the Maximilianeum and the Old Catholic church on the Gasteig; thence back to the Maximilianeum, and so home. The Old Catholics have not succeeded in getting another church here, and are not likely to do so.

Dr. Döllinger agrees with Archbishop Tait and the Liberals about the Burials Bill. The joint use of burial grounds causes no difficulty in Germany, even between ultramontanes and Protestants. I pointed out that the cases of Germany and England were not quite parallel, in as much as the churchyards in England are the property of the Church, i.e. of the incumbents, in Germany of the townships. Dr. Döllinger admitted the difference, but said that even in country villages, where there were so few Protestants that the churchyards practically belonged to the Catholic population, there was no difficulty. A neighbouring Protestant pastor would always be admitted to the burial ground and would have his service in the usual way. Dr. Döllinger had an amusing experience when he was a young curate in a country village in Franconia (Markt-Scheinfeld)[7]. A Protestant had died and a pastor came to bury him. A Protestant funeral being a rare event in the village, the Catholics gathered in numbers to witness the ceremony. The pastor and his congregation were in the churchyard round the grave, while the Catholics crowded round outside the wall, which chanced to be a low one. At Protestant funerals it is usual to sing a hymn, which is given out by the sacristan. The Catholics knew something of the Protestant hymn-book, and knew that there was a hymn beginning with the words, *Ach, Gott, wie ist der Mensch so dumm!* (How foolish, Lord, is man!). Accordingly, before the sacristan could give out the proper hymn, one of the Catholics from the wall gave out this one, to the considerable amusement of the bystanders. The complete equality of Catholics and Protestants established by law makes it easy for both to use the same *church* even. This goes on peaceably all the year round, with the exception of Holy Week, when there is often a tussle for the bells. The Catholics have no bells from Maundy Thursday to Easter Eve, a custom not observed by Protestants. It is not an uncommon thing for some of the Catholic boys to get up into the belfry and tie up the ropes in such a way as to render it impossible to ring the bells for some hours.

7. Döllinger was ordained priest April 15, 1822. At Scheinfeld Platen (afterwards famous as poet) once or twice visited him, and they used to go to Schloss Schwarzenberg together and to a small Franciscan convent close by it, where four monks still held out. Döllinger and Platen had previously been great friends, and read much together. But when Döllinger went to Munich in 1826, Platen went to Italy and they saw little or nothing of one another afterwards.

Dr. Döllinger did not think that the theory started in the *Church Quarterly* (by J.N. Cotterill), that the Epistle to Diognetus is a forgery
27 of Stephanus, is likely to be true. A forger of the sixteenth century would not have written a letter so colourless, that neither Catholics nor Protestants can make any use of it; nor would he have chosen so obscure a name. The method adopted—of showing that the leading words and phrases occur within the compass of a few pages of a few authors, —is a very precarious one, and might be used with strange results against works of which the authenticity is beyond a doubt. Dr. Döllinger did not think the theory that the Epistle to Diognetus is of the sixth century tenable either. No one, he said, (?Gfrörer) had followed Niebuhr in attributing the *Philopatris* of the Pseudo-Lucian to the tenth century (the time of Nicephorus Phokas, 963-969) [8]. It was considered one of Niebuhr's strangest mistakes, and a striking instance of what extraordinary results an erroneous method may produce, however able the man who uses it may be. Niebuhr thought that he could identify events alluded to in this treatise with events which occurred in the tenth century. But who at that time would write an elaborate attack on the doctrine of the Trinity? And where at that time was the literary skill necessary for such a forgery to be found?

The new church at Haidehausen still remains unopened, although it was nearly finished eight years ago. It is still a matter of litigation. The town council, who gave the site and part of the money, claim certain rights, which the archbishop disputes. He claims absolute control over the fabric; but even according to Canon Law the council are in the right. Judgment in the first instance was for the archbishop. Then the council appealed and got the decision reversed; and now the archbishop has appealed again. The want of the church is much felt. As we looked round from the Gasteig upon the towers and spires of Munich, Dr. Döllinger remarked that for a city of 200,000 inhabitants Munich was not very richly supplied with churches. In the last eight years only one new church has been built, viz. a second Protestant church; and that is not yet opened.

The theological faculty here is still in as bad a state as ever. There are only about 75 students, and no prospects of amelioration. The same state of things prevails all over Germany, not only among the Catholics, but among the Protestants also. In the case of the Catholics the impossibility of bringing scientific theology into harmony with the Vatican decrees is one main reason : another is the internecine war between Church and State in reference to the Falk laws. I asked what were the reasons in the case of the Protestants. Dr. Döllinger said, mainly

28   8. See Niebuhr's *Kleine historische und philologische Schriften* II. 73. Wessig has taken
a similar view, but adopts the next reign, Johannes Tzimisces, 969-976, as the date of
29 the composition; *De aetate et auctore Philopatridis*, Confluentiae, 1868.

two. First, the difficulty of living : the stipends of pastors remained unchanged, while the cost of living had more than doubled during the present century. Secondly, scepticism, which begins even in the gymnasien. Before they come to the university at all, young men have their belief in the very fundamentals of Christianity shaken, and of course found it impossible to think of entering the Christian ministry. Those universities which are not considered to be orthodox in their teaching scarcely get any theological students at all. At Heidelberg, with eight or nine 'critical' professors, there are less than twenty theological students. About 9.30 we parted.

At 1 p.m. we went to dine with Dr. Döllinger. He had asked Fräulein Kramer to meet us, a pleasant girl, who spoke English with some difficulty. He told us a story of Theiner, late Keeper of the Archives at the Vatican, which was new to me. Theiner was treated in a very degrading manner by the Curia in his latter days, as is well known. Though nominally left in office, a superior was placed over him to whom he had to surrender his keys, and his private entry into the library was blocked up[9]. By a charming irony the Keeper of the Archives was the one man who found it impossible to have access to them. Dr. Döllinger seems to think that on the whole Theiner deserved his humiliation, not because (as the Curia thought) he had or would publish things from the Archives which would bring discredit upon the Papacy[10], but because (as now appears to be the case) Theiner in publishing abstracts from the Archives altered passages which might cause scandal. Tampering with historical documents is in the eyes of a scholar a crime of the highest magnitude. What was new to me was this. Theiner continued the Annals of Baronius in three volumes. He asked and obtained leave to dedicate his work. He restored the *typographia apostolica*, the beautiful old Roman type, which had fallen into confusion and disuse for many years. The book was handsomely got up in three folio volumes with large margins and a dedication to Pius IX. at the beginning of Vol. I. When all was ready for publication, Theiner went to the Vatican and laid his work at the feet of the Pope. He was

9. This superior was Archbishop Cardoni of Edessa *in partibus*, an enthusiast for the Infallibility, who had much to do with the preparation of material for the Council, author of *Elucubratio de dogmatica Rom. Pontificis Infallibilitate ejusque definibilitate.*

10. Theiner's *Life of Clement XIV*. (1853) was one crime : another was his letting some of the bishops at the Council have some information as to the order of business at Trent. It is said that scholars found it easier to get what they wanted at the Archives under Marini, Theiner's predecessor, than under Theiner. They had to pay a good fee, but they saw their document. Theiner could not be bribed, and was very cautious about letting anything of importance be seen. Hefele had seen the Acts of the Council of Trent in 1869, so that Theiner's disclosure of the order of business did not make much matter. But the Curia was very angry about it. He had begun a History of the Council of Trent, and had printed part of it, but was absolutely forbidden to publish it.

received in the usual manner, was thanked, and went home. Before many hours had passed there came a letter from the Vatican absolutely forbidding the publication of the work with the dedication. Theiner was utterly confounded. Leave to dedicate to the Pope had been readily granted, the volumes had been accepted on presentation, and then the dedication, without any reason being assigned, was suddenly forbidden. Theiner applied to some of the cardinals for an explanation. Antonelli was ready with one which is too characteristic of Pius IX. not to be the true one. *Perchè non ha fatto de' complimenti?* Theiner had not made the dedication complimentary enough, and hence the rejection of it. The volumes were published without it. From people who have lately been in Rome Dr. Döllinger learns that the Pope's health is such that he is not likely to live much longer. Of those likely to succeed him, Cardinal Sforza, Archbishop of Naples, is a comparatively moderate man, who would probably seek a *modus vivendi* with the Italian government, and Cardinal Pecci of Siena, who would carry on the high ultramontane *non possumus* policy of the Jesuits[11].

Dr. Döllinger has additional valuable material for illustrating the Council of Trent; but he is still greatly crippled for want of a secretary to assist him in preparing the documents which are chiefly Italian, for the press. In order to make the documents more intelligible, he means
35 to write a short sketch of the Council, which is much needed. We left about 3.30, after his arranging that we should call for him again at 7 for a walk. But as one of her heels was rather sore B. did not come. Dr. Döllinger took me straight down the left bank of the Isar for two or three miles, then back through the park and the English Garden,— a very pleasant walk; but near the water gnats and midges were troublesome. The work that Dr. Döllinger is chiefly interested in at present is an account of the ecclesiastical and hierarchical fictions and forgeries, which run through the whole of the middle ages. They begin, he says, much earlier than people think. He has traced some as far back as the pontificate of Leo I., about 450. At the beginning of the sixth century there is prodigious activity in this kind of work. It is in most cases difficult to make out how far the Popes were guilty. Evidence is wanting; and the interests of the hierarchy were, as a rule, so intimately connected with those of the Pope, that the test of *cui bono* fails. In some cases the Pope was certainly privy to the fraud, e.g. Pope Nicolas in the case of the Pseudo-Isidorian Decretals. In others he may even have ordered the forgery. In others again he may simply have been duped in the same fashion that Thomas Aquinas was. An edition of the
36 original text of the *Decretum* of Gratian, with notes and various readings,

37   11. Pius IX. has created the existing College of Cardinals; but his successor will be the creation of the College.

is coming out in parts in Germany, and will afford rich material for investigation, for the *Decretum* has from time to time been hugely garbled and interpolated. Fortunately manuscripts almost contemporary with the first publication of the *Decretum* are in existence. Dr. Döllinger is eagerly waiting for the next volume.

He expressed surprise that Protestant controversialists had not made more out of the fact that the Council of Trent decided that by Divine appointment there are three orders of ministers in the Church, and yet in the Roman Church one of them, the diaconate, is practically non-existent. There are no deacons in the Church of Rome, excepting those on the eve of becoming priests : no one remains a deacon. Even those few anomalous members of the Curia, the Cardinal Deacons, are usually only sub-deacons. So that an order, declared by authority to be of Divine appointment in the Church, is not kept up in the Church of Rome. I asked whether a deacon would under any circumstances be allowed to solemnize a marriage. He said, "No, certainly not : a deacon can only be a witness. The scholastic theory of marriage was that the bride and bridegroom mutually conferred the sacrament on one another, and that a couple could be lawfully married without a minister and without witnesses : they are ministers to one another. To this some theologians objected that it was contrary to all analogy for persons to administer a sacrament to themselves : the minister must be another person. Which was a strange over-statement : in the eucharist the priest administers to himself. The Council of Trent decrees that marriages must take place *in the presence of* the parish priest and of *other witnesses*; but there is no need for the priest to open his mouth or move hand or foot. The bride and bridegroom merely express their consent to take one another in marriage. This decree on the whole recognizes the scholastic theory." Dr. Döllinger mentioned the infamous case of Gordon, now made notorious by Gladstone's pamphlet, in 38 which a Scotchman was married at the British embassy by the English chaplain, tired of his wife and lived with another woman, then turned Roman Catholic and discarded his wife on the ground that the marriage was null and void because the Roman priest had not been present at the ceremony. He then married his concubine and probably is living with her still. All this was done with the sanction of his bishop and of Rome. There was a similar case in Munich about ten years ago. Marriages in Germany are not confined to any time of the day and the evening is a very common time.

Friedrich's first volume of his *History of the Vatican Council* will 39 be out in a few weeks. It will contain only the history of the preparations, which, as all the world should know, were very elaborate indeed. Friedrich has rich material. Bismarck has allowed him to take abstracts from the official correspondence of Count Arnim at the time of the Council, and Dr. Döllinger has furnished him with valuable letters sent to him at that time.

The sees of Spires and of Würzburg are still vacant. As already related (p. 151) Dr. Enzler, Dean of the Royal Chapter, was nominated by the Crown to Spires, but declined the offer, when he learnt that he was not a *persona grata* at Rome. Dr. Käs, who was nominated to Würzburg, has accepted the offer and leaves the government to fight it out with the Pope. The number of sees vacant in Germany is now considerable, and that of parishes still more so. Vacant parishes specially abound in Prussia. Many clergy have migrated from Prussia to Bavaria, to avoid the Falk laws; or, having been educated in Prussia, have come to Bavaria to work. In a single diocese there are about seventy parishes without priests. The battle is now to a large extent won by the government. A new Emperor or a new Chancellor may make some concessions; but the clergy will never regain what they have lost, e.g. the inspection of primary schools. This has been taken from them, not merely in reference to religion, but in all branches of instruction; and it will never be given back to them. It is a most serious loss of influence. Formerly, in rural districts, the parish priest as a matter of course had the superintendence of the national schools.

It struck a quarter to ten before we parted at the end of the Englischer Garten. The fire flies had been visible for a long time fitting about under the trees. We agreed to have one more walk the next evening, —the last one; for on Monday we leave Munich.

Sunday, 5th after Trinity, July 1st. In the evening we went to pay our last visit to Dr. Döllinger. B. came merely to say goodbye, not feeling up to a long walk. Dr. Döllinger proposed that we should escort her back to Hotel Leinfelder before going for our walk. On our way he said that he had been reading some articles by Froude on Thomas à Becket, which he thought were good. "He is not very fond of Becket; nor am I. There is too much of the ambitious ecclesiastic about him. It is very odd that, of the two persons whom Englishmen in former times held most in honour, one (S. George) had no existence, and the other was an ambitious priest."

After leaving B. at Leinfelder's we went on from the transformation of the heretic George of Cappadocia into the patron saint of England to talk of the transformation of S. James the Great, the fisherman of Galilee, into a mediaeval knight, the patron of Spain. It was the work of a grasping prelate, who spread the myth about the body of S. James having been brought by his disciples from Jerusalem to Spain, in order to gain for Compostella the reputation of being an Apostolic see[12]. The scallop-shell, which became the sign of a pilgrim, indicated

12. Compostella is a corruption of Giacomo Postolo, *ad Jacobum Apostolum*. The body, it is said, was buried at Iria Flavia, discovered there and moved to Compostella in the

the seashore, where the body of the saint was stated to have landed. Each pilgrim brought away a shell from the beach, and shells became the mark of pilgrims generally, whether to Compostella or other places. The selection of James the Elder for this myth is even more outrageous than that of James the Less would have been. Perhaps there was a wish to avoid the doubt respecting James the Bishop of Jerusalem, which might have involved a doubt as to S. James of Compostella having been an Apostle at all; and this was the main point of the myth. "In my book on the *First Age of the Church*," said Dr. Döllinger, "I have made James the Less identical with James the brother of the Lord. I regard that now as an error. I am perfectly convinced that *41* they are different persons. The first Bishop of Jerusalem was not an Apostle, but was raised to that dignity on account of his relationship to Christ. The confusion of the Apostle with the Lord's brother is owing to the influence of Jerome, which was very great in the West. In the East, where he was not influential, the confusion does not exist. The Eastern Church distinguishes the two. The importance of the distinction between these two is not always recognized. Only two exceptions have been supposed to exist to the rule that the Apostles were never bishops of a particular see, that their work was for the Church at large, not for any one Church. S. James at Jerusalem and S. Peter at Rome are supposed to be exceptions. If, however, as may be regarded as certain, S. James was not an Apostle, then a tremendous presumption arises against S. Peter ever having been Bishop of Rome. S. Peter no doubt was in Rome for a while, but when, and for how long, it is impossible to determine. He was not there when the Epistle to the Romans was written. He probably was not there when the Epistles sent from Rome were written. 'Babylon' is beyond doubt Rome. The hypercritical writers of the Tübingen school even admit that. 'Babylon' is used for Rome in the Jewish Sibylline verses, and therefore would be not only a natural but a familiar expression. The exact relationship of James of Jerusalem to our Lord cannot be proved. It *may* have been that of cousin, or of literal brotherhood. These 'brethren' being found so constantly with the Blessed Virgin points to the latter; and I have always thought the 'until' of Mat. 1.25 very strong in that direction."

I asked him as to the perpetual virginity of the Blessed Virgin having been made a dogma in the Roman Church. He said, "It has not only been made a dogma, but Paul IV. made a law that whoever denied the Trinity, the Divinity of our Lord, or the perpetual virginity of the Blessed Virgin should be condemned as a heretic in the first instance without benefit of recantation; i.e. should be put to death, whether

ninth century. The legend appears in the *Poema de XII. apostolis* of Walafried Strabo about that date.

he recanted or not. And that law has never been repealed, although of course the temporal penalties attached to it cannot now be enforced."

We walked by the old Gottesacker and across the new upper bridge over the Isar to Giesing, where a new church is being built close to the old one, and home by Haidehausen and the Maximilian's Strasse. The lunatic asylum behind Haidehausen suggested the subject of lunacy. "I have been obliged," said Dr. Döllinger, "to give up, or at any rate very much modify, an opinion which I held very strongly in early life with regard to madness. I used always to maintain that purely mental causes were sufficient to cause mental effects, and that without any bodily disease it was possible for people's minds to become unhinged; moreover, that a very common cause of lunacy in the case of men was pride, and in the case of women disappointed affection. But the head of the lunatic asylum here, who is a very high authority, maintains that lunacy is invariably accompanied by disease or defect in the physical organism; and this seems now to be the general opinion of scientific men. So that my theory is no longer tenable; and I suppose we must say that inordinate pride in the case of men, and excessive distress in cases where a woman's affections have been blighted, which are so often the precursors of lunacy in each case, are effects of the diseased or deformed organism rather than causes of lunacy." In the Maximilian Strasse we parted at about 9.30. "I suppose I shall not hear from you before you get back to Durham," said he; "I shall be glad to hear from you then. Thank you beforehand for the *Church Quarterly Review*. Goodbye." I thanked him earnestly for all his hospitality and kindness; and so we parted — once more for a good many months.

A story which he told us was omitted in its proper place and must be recorded here. Strauss is a common name in Germany. There was, perhaps still is, a Protestant divine of this name in Berlin, a Hof-prediger or royal chaplain. Some years ago he visited Munich. While he was there, one of the free-thinkers of the place called upon him, thinking that he was the famous David Strauss, the author of the *Leben Jesu*. The visitor began at once by saying that he had done himself the honour of paying his respects to one of the greatest theologians and philosophers of the age, how rejoiced he was to have this opportunity of meeting such a champion of free thought, and so forth. Before the worthy Lutheran pastor (who being a royal chaplain was probably very orthodox) had recovered from this trying visitor's misapplied enthusiasm, the chamber maid entered, and, dropping a curtsey, said she hoped she might make so bold as to thank the gentleman before he went for all his very pretty *waltzes*! *She* thought he was Eduard Strauss of Vienna, and confused the court preacher with the composer of the
42 *Blaue Donau*!

1878

Tuesday, August 27th, found us once more at Dr. Döllinger's door, and [we] were not surprised to find that he was already in Tegernsee, where he hoped to meet us. He had sent a note from Tegernsee to wait for us in Munich, of which this is a translation. "Dear Friend, It fits in excellently that I have been for the last ten days at Tegernsee, and intend to stay there still longer; and if you and your dear wife come hither, my stay here will be doubly pleasant and refreshing. I am living here, along with Lord Acton, at Villa Arco, which is very easy to find. Totus tuus J. Döllinger." The next evening we reached Tegernsee and found good quarters.

Thursday, August 29th. We went to Villa Arco and found him looking very well. He came out on to the landing to welcome us, and when he had shown us his room, he took B. by both her hands and drew her to the window, saying, "First I must have a look at you to see how you are. Yes, you are looking very well; so that is all right." And then we all sat down to have a chat. He said that we must certainly stay for September 9th, when the golden wedding of Prince Karl (Duke Charles Theodore, who owns the Schloss at Tegernsee) is to be celebrated with great pomp and public ceremony, illuminations on the lake, etc. *He* is going to stay until then, and that fact has more weight with us than the golden wedding. At Villa Arco the present inmates are the Countess Arco, her unmarried daughter and her married daughter, Lady Acton who is on a visit with her husband and five children. Dr. Döllinger said that it was an unusual experience for him to be living in the midst of children, and he found it a very pleasant one. After talking of English affairs for some time, in the course of which he said that he had by no means given up the idea of revisiting England, we passed on to the two great German questions—the compromise between Church and State and Socialism. Dr. Döllinger said that he had no idea what would be the result of the Kissingen interview— between Bismarck and the Nuncio Masella. For his own part he could 43 not see how anything more than an armistice between the German government and the Vatican was possible. The principles of the Curia were now so pronounced and so comprehensive, that it was impossible to retreat or come to terms with the State. The principles of the two parties were irreconcileable. As to the Socialist question, he believed that it was the opinion (and the wish) of most people in Germany that *some* law against Socialism would be passed; but probably the laws now proposed would be a good deal amended in Parliament. The Conservative gains 44 (reckoned now at 40) in the recent elections were not so great as had been anticipated; and the Chancellor was probably disappointed. After we had talked for about half-an-hour he took us down to the drawing room to see Lord Acton, whom I had met in Munich six years before. We soon adjourned to the balcony, which commands a most beautiful view of the Eger end of the lake; and here we talked of the neighbour-hood. When we took our leave, Dr. Döllinger came with us nearly to the Schloss, when a threatening cloud made him turn back. It was agreed that we should meet in the afternoon at a concert — an unusual excitement, for the benefit of the local music-master, and have a walk afterwards, weather permitting. The concert, which was a success, was over by 6.30, and we at once started for a walk.

We talked of the Public Worship Act, which Dr. Döllinger thought to be altogether wrong. I asked him whether the proposed laws against Socialism did not seem to be somewhat of the same character as the Public Worship Act. "I am not so sure of that. Something of the kind is necessary. Things have got to such a pass, that if the law does not interfere soon, it will be too late." "But is it possible to give a *legal* definition of Socialism?" "The proposed law does not attempt to do so. It merely gives discretionary power to magistrates. Of course such power may be abused; but on the other hand it may do a great deal of good. There are thousands of young people at the present time in Germany, who by newspapers, books, and lectures are being systematically taught that the whole organization of society must be destroyed; — property, government, marriage, religion, everything : all are to be overturned. Of course the State cannot prevent such opinions from being held; nor is it necessary that it should do so. But it can prevent them from being taught as innocent. You in England, who have had the fullest liberty for 150 years, are in a very different position from us. No Englishman would jump to the conclusion, that because a thing was not put down by law, therefore it was innocent. Everyone in England knows that many things are wrong, with which, however, the law never interferes. In Germany it is far otherwise. People are so accus-tomed to having everything regulated by law, that what the law allows is commonly considered *morally* lawful. People at the present time can argue that of course the government knows all about this socialistic movement, and that, as it never interferes, these opinions are morally tenable." "But," I urged, "have opinions in past times ever been put down by such means?" "Where in past times have such opinions ever been held and taught? These theories are quite modern. Nothing like them has been known before." "I do not say *these* opinions, but *any* opinions. Have suppressive measures ever been successful in stopping the growth of opinion? Take Protestantism for instance." "I decline," said Dr. Döllinger, "every parallel taken from the sphere of religion.

All the parallels brought forward are religious ones; and their being religious makes them cease to be parallels. The element of religious conviction, of conscience,— the belief that one is a martyr for the truth,— all these things come in in the one case and are quite wanting in the other. There is not much conscience about a general attack on property." "Don't you think that a fanatical young enthusiast may conscientiously believe, that (to adopt their own formula) 'property is theft'?" "I doubt it," said Dr. Döllinger; "the idea of property is so innate in man. And if there be such a person, he must suffer for the sake of society. Terror after all is the mainspring of order, and I for one should shrink from the responsibility of allowing such opinions to be taught unchecked. It is no use saying, 'wait until they are put in practice.' When people begin to be assassinated for holding property, or for being magistrates, it is rather late to be taking measures against the evil. Look at what is happening in Russia. Every official in the secret police has received a secret letter of sentence of death, and several have already been murdered, on the same day, in different parts of Russia. Besides which the organization is becoming so strong throughout Europe that in a little time the government of individual states will find it very difficult to cope with it. In Germany it is specially strong in Saxony, where the population is chiefly artizan, and where there is a good deal of distress. In some parts of Prussia also. Saxony sends Liebknecht, the socialistic leader, to Parliament. The movement makes little progress in Bavaria, where the population is mostly rustic and is pretty well off. You must remember that these laws propose not merely to check the propagation of these opinions, but also to ameliorate the condition of the suffering artizans." "Ah!," I said, "there can be no doubt about the excellence of the latter means of checking Socialism." "But of course," he added, "that cannot be done in a hurry. Benefit clubs don't exist to any considerable extent : wages are too low for men to save. I don't think that the clergy do much in getting up such things. There is very little money to spare. We are still suffering from the effects of war and overproduction." These remarks were in answer to questions. We parted at Villa Arco about eight o'clock. On our return to our quarters we found that Lord Acton had been to call upon us.

Friday, August 30. There was a thunderstorm in the afternoon after which I called for Dr. Döllinger at Villa Arco. Soon after we started he said, "We need not have brought our umbrellas; there will be no more rain." He seemed to know the local signs; at any rate he was right. He said that the Meteorological Society of Berlin had prophesied a bad July and August, which had come true, and a good September, which inspires hope. We soon got on to more serious topics. Dr. Döl-

linger considers that the abolition of compulsory celibacy for the Old Catholic clergy, which had just been carried by the Bonn synod, is
45 fatal. It will be impossible to reconcile German congregations generally to a married clergy. A married priest will not be regarded by them as one who devotes himself for the good of his flock. Moreover, a priest with a family will have to make himself more burdensome to the people, in order to get the means of living. The priesthood will become a profession instead of a vocation. The pressure for this change had come chiefly from Baden. Bishop Reinkens had given way, — chiefly owing to the influence of Schulte, — but he was opposed to the measure himself. Reusch had resigned his offices; whether he had done more than that, i.e. whether he had withdrawn altogether from the Old Catholic body, Dr. Döllinger could not say. Friedrich had not done
46 so. There was no need for any Bavarian Old Catholic to resign or withdraw. The Bavarian Old Catholics had repudiated this resolution of the Bonn synod and had publicly declared that they did so; so that Bavarians remained unaffected. Had they accepted the Bonn resolution, the Bavarian government could not have continued to treat them as Catholics.

The conversation turned on Newman's *Development of Doctrine*. Dr.
47 Döllinger had not seen the new edition. Bishop O'Connor of Pittsburgh in America was opposed to the definition of Papal Infallibility by the Vatican Council; and when he found that it had been made a dogma he owned that at first he was quite dazed, and knew not what to think[13]. But when he read Newman's *Development of Doctrine*, he then understood how the dogma was possible, and was able to reconcile himself to it. When the earlier dogma of the Immaculate Conception was being prepared, the question was raised, on what ground was it to be based. The Jesuits in Rome wanted to base it on the theory of Development, but the French prelates were so strongly opposed to this proposal, that it was abandoned. Newman's theory was wanted more than ever since the Vatican Council : only there was this awkwardness about adopting it to explain the dogma, that the Council had expressly declared that the doctrine had been held from the first in the Church. "Lord Acton tells me," Dr. Döllinger continued, "and I have heard the same from another authority, that when the proposal to hold the Vatican Council was first made in Rome, very few people were in favour of it. The majority were quite taken aback by the proposal and were opposed to the enterprise." "Do you mean by 'the

13. Bishop *Connolly* of Halifax voted *non placet* at the Vatican Council; so also did Bishop *Domenec* of Pittsburgh. Dr. M. O'Connor was the first Bishop of Pittsburgh, consecrated 1843 when the diocese was erected; he resigned May 1860, but he lived
48 till Oct. 18, 1872. *Perhaps* he was at the Council. Domenec resigned 1877 and died 1878; he was succeeded by Twigg.

enterprise' the holding of a Council or the decree of the Infallibility?" "The two were never separated. The Council was summoned to pass the Infallibility. The three powers in favour of this were the Pope, the Jesuits, and the French ultramontane bishops; and these three prevailed over the majority. The present Pope [14] would no doubt never have made the Infallibility a dogma; and in many other particulars he is quite aware of his predecessor's errors. But it is exceedingly difficult for him to go back. Still it is not easy to know exactly what his real opinion is on certain points. He does not commit himself."

I remarked that the dogma of the Immaculate Conception did not seem to be any special honour to the Blessed Virgin; it would seem to honour her parents rather than herself. "Oh!," said Dr. Döllinger, "that was an afterthought. The doctrine was wanted for a particular purpose, and it afterwards occurred to people that it was honourable to the Blessed Virgin. The Franciscans wanted it as a weapon against their more successful rivals the Dominicans, who opposed the doctrine; and it added sharpness to the weapon to be able to call their opponents 'the enemies of the honour of Mary'."

Dr. Döllinger asked who had succeeded Mozley as Regius Professor at Oxford. I said, "Ince; I don't suppose that you know him by name, as he has written nothing." "That would be quite impossible in Germany — to appoint a man to a professorship who was quite unknown to literature." I asked what the usual method was. "The faculty to which the vacant chair belongs select a candidate, and then the Senate of the university considers his claim. If it approves, his name is sent to the government, which almost invariably accepts the recommendation. For a good many years no case has occurred of such a candidate being rejected by the government. But it sometimes happens that the Senate selects a candidate of its own, declining the candidate of the faculty. This happened at Munich two years ago with a theological professorship; and the government took the recommendation of the Senate." We parted at Villa Arco about 7.45. "We cannot settle anything about to-morrow till we see what the weather is," said Dr. Döllinger at parting; "and I must see what arrangements have been made for me indoors." Our walk had been across by ferry to Egern, across the Weissach, and up the valley; back to Egern Church and round the end of the lake home.

Saturday, August 31. A note from Lord Acton awaited us on our return from a morning scramble, saying that his mother-in-law (Countess Arco) hoped that we would dine with them that day at 1.30. Just as Lord Acton was opening the garden gate for us, Dr. Döllinger came

---

14. Pecci was made cardinal 1877 and elected Pope Feb. 20th, 1878.

up in an opposite direction to ourselves from a solitary walk. Dinner conversation was polyglott — a mixture of English, German and French, English prevailing for our benefit; but the fact of there being no language in which every one was at home was rather a hindrance[15]. They were all very pleasant and very kind, especially the old Countess, who was delightful. We adjourned to the garden for coffee, until the rain drove us indoors. Lord Acton then took me off to show me his working room and some of his books, from which he lent me a volume of Taine's *French Revolution* and of the *Historisches Taschen-*
49 *buch*, while B. took *Esmond*. From Lord Acton we learnt that in our morning's ramble we had passed within a few yards of the scene of a suicide. A man had blown his brains out in a hut by which we had passed; but whether the body was found before or after we were there, we do not know. This man came from Munich, and during the few days we were there, there was an attempted suicide. Suicides among visitors at Tegernsee are not uncommon. There have been two or three within the last few years. The rain which drove us in continued and prevented a walk with Dr. Döllinger. Indeed it was so heavy that the Countess sent us home in the carriage.

Tuesday, September 3rd. Dr. Döllinger called for us in the morning, but we were unfortunately out. Between four and five we called at the Villa and found him, Lord Acton, and the children just starting for a drive. Lord Acton insisted on our taking the place of the children and himself. We protested again and again, being very sorry that the children should be disappointed; but Lord Acton was not to be moved. "Kaltenbrunn is a thing you ought to see; we can go for a walk instead." So we drove off with Dr. Döllinger. I asked him whether he had seen the last number of *Kladderadatsch*. He had not. "It has Bismarck and the Nuncio together : the Nuncio has made Bismarck close his mouth and shut one eye, and on the side of the closed eye the Nuncio is holding up the Falk laws." "I understand," said Dr. Döllinger,

---

15. Rather a good story is told of Dr. Steichele, the new Archbishop of Munich. When he was Canon of Augsburg, a curate, who had been suspended for indiscreet language, begged him to intercede with the Ordinary. The curate's indiscretion had been shown in a New Year's sermon, in which he made a summary of the chief events of the preceding year. In speaking of the controversy about the temporal power of the Pope he said that the dispute seemed to him like that of boys fighting in wintertime in defence of their snowman. Perhaps they win and succeed in beating off their opponents. But sooner or later comes spring-time and takes away their snowman after all. "Ah," said the then Canon Steichele, "that's all very true; but you ought not to tell the people that, my good friend." The new archbishop is something of a scholar, and has written a book on some small department of German history — the origin of the Suabian race,
50 or something of that sort : not a very large proof of learning; but a man with any pretensions to scholarship is something new in the see of München-Freising.

"that the negociations between the Curia and the German government have come to stand still. They are not at an end, but they are not making any progress. They remind me of the attempted interview between the anti-Popes at the time of the Great Schism. It was proposed that they should meet and endeavour to come to terms. The French Pope left Avignon and went a few stages towards Italy, and then stopped. The Italian Pope went a few stages towards France, and then stopped. And so they remained, each waiting for the other to advance; the fact being that neither side wanted to meet the other [16]. At the present moment also it is impossible to find a point at which the two sides can meet."

Speaking of the Turkish Convention he said, "I don't see how England 51 can carry out her part of the engagement. The difficulties are enormous. Central Asia Minor is almost as unknown as central Africa : no roads and scarcely any towns. A German who had served in Asia Minor in the service of the Khedive of Egypt told me that they sometimes marched for days without seeing even a village. Then again is England going to try to govern through the Pashas? That will be impossible. Or is she going to sweep them away and put Europeans in their place? That Turkey will not allow."

At Kaltenbrunn we got out and had some coffee *al fresco*. While there reference was made to an anecdote which Dr. Döllinger had told to me and a German lady a few evenings before. When he first came to Munich as a lad, a certain Herr Lange and his sons were painters there. Lange had a good deal to do with arranging the Pinakothek. A visitor once asked him whom he considered to be the first among living artists in Europe. "My *son*," said Lange, "is the *second*: modesty forbids my naming the *first*." I said that a similar story was told of some one in Oxford, who said that Oxford possessed only three theologians, — Pusey, Mozley, and one whom modesty would not allow him to mention. "He was modesty itself compared with Lange," said Dr. Döllinger. "He only put himself third in Oxford : Lange put himself first in Europe. I can tell you another of Lange's feats. He was commissioned to paint an altar-piece for the Studienkirche in Munich — the one on the Karlsplatz. The subject was to be 'Suffer the little children to come unto Me'. Lange had a daughter of about seventeen, who was very coquettish indeed. What did he do but paint this girl, with her coquettish face and manner, as the principal figure among the children brought to Christ! The altar-piece was put up and was the

16. In 1407 it was agreed that the rival Popes should meet at Savona end of Sept. Gregory XII. went from Rome to Viterbo, stayed there two months and then to Siena. Benedict XIII. moved to Porto Venere, and after a while to Spezia. Gregory then moved to Lucca. The year ended without a meeting, and then Gregory broke the compact and the negociations came to an end.

talk of Munich. Every student at the University and most of the boys who went to the church knew perfectly well whose portrait it was over the altar. I saw it there myself. I was a boy in the upper classes just going to the University. But it did not remain there long. It caused such a scandal that after a short time it was removed." I remarked 52 that I had just been reading Huber's Essay on Savonarola, and that he noticed a scandal far exceeding that of Lange and his daughter,— Alexander VI. having the portraits of himself and his mistress Vanozza put up in the Church of S. Maria del popolo; where they remained, reverenced by the people as Joachim and Anna, until Clement XII. had them removed. "Yes," said Dr. Döllinger, "she was the sister of a cardinal, who was made cardinal simply because his sister was the Pope's mistress. This was Cardinal Farnese, afterwards Paul III."

I asked him whether Arco was a German title. "Yes, it is quite a historical family, and its history would be well worth writing, if the materials could be collected. It appears as early as the twelfth century. The original name was Von Bogen. They acquired property in North Italy under the Empire and translated the name Bogen into Arco. A seat on the Lago di Garda is regarded as the original home,— the Stammschloss, as we say. One branch settled in Bavaria; and in the wars between Bavaria and the Tyrolese Count Arco was riding on the left hand of the Elector and noticed that the Tyrolese on the heights around were aiming at the Elector. So he asked the Elector to change places with him, and in a short time was shot down, mortally wounded. The uncle of the late Count Arco, i.e. uncle of our friend's husband who owned the Villa here, was killed in the wars with the Tyrolese at the beginning of the present century. The late Count gave the Villa to the Countess at the time when the last child was born."

We drove off from Kaltenbrunn a little after six, taking the other side of the lake; so that by the time we reached Villa Arco we had made a complete circuit of the lake. And most beautiful it was. It was dusk when we got back, and the moon, half-full, was shining brilliantly over the mountains on to the water. I asked about game and shooting as we drove home. Dr. Döllinger said that he had never fired a gun in his life, and did not know much about the subject. There was no fox-hunting in Germany, and no grouse-shooting: he did not think grouse were found. Partridges were common, pheasants rare. The wild boar was very common in Bavaria.

Wednesday, September 4. It had been agreed the evening before that we should call for Dr. Döllinger about 10.30 for a walk. We went up the 53 Rottach valley. I said that I had been reading Taine's French Revolution : it was surprising to find a republican so severe upon the republican party. "Yes," said Dr. Döllinger, "that is an excellent book. It has made a great sensation in France, and has been the cause of Taine's not being elected a member of the Academy. It gives too unflattering a description of the national character, especially as regards cruelty and carelessness of human life. Mignet, the secretary of the Academy, declared that if Taine were elected, he would never enter the Academy again. The vacancy was caused by the death of Thiers. Mignet said that it would be a scandal if the place of Thiers, who had written a History of the Revolution in sympathy with the republican party, were taken by a man who had so attacked it. But Taine's book is not an attack; it merely states facts. About fifty years ago Mignet and Thiers were very intimate and lived in the same house; and their Histories of the Revolution were written simultaneously; Mignet's a compendium, Thiers' a much larger work[17]. But have you read Taine's *54* introductory volume? That also is a very good work. In it he shows how necessary a revolution was; how impossible it was for France to continue as she then was. In the second volume he shows what mischief the French did in the Revolution. Of Taine's other work his *Voyage en Italie* is one of the best : it is, I think, the best thing of *55* the kind I know. There is another remarkable French work that has recently appeared, by a French priest, the Abbé Duchesne, a critical work, and what is more a very good critical work, on the *Liber Pontificalis*[18]. That a French ultramontane priest should produce such a *56* work, I regard as almost a miracle. He has not ventured to criticize the lives of the particular Popes : that would have carried him too far, and would have been too daring. But he has gone very thoroughly into the history of the various texts and the authenticity of the particular parts."

B. asked Dr. Döllinger what the little boxes like houses on the top of tall poles or on the branches of trees were for. He said they were for a particular kind of bird, which is fond of building in such places and is very useful in destroying insects. He believed the peasants called it Schwarzblättchen; the scientific name he had forgotten.

"Do you know that there is a new edition of Herzog's *Encyklopädie* *57* coming out?" "Oh, yes. I am taking it in," I said. "It is likely to be

17. Mignet and Thiers were fellow-students at Aix (Rhône), where Mignet was born, 1796. Later on they both lived in Paris together. Mignet wrote for the *Courrier Français*, Thiers for the *Constitutionnel*. Thiers' *History of the Revolution* appeared 1823, Mignet's 1824. Mignet was elected to the Academy in 1837 in the place of Raynouard. After the Revolution of 1848 he was suspected of anti-republican sentiments and removed by Lamartine from the post which he had held for many years as Director of the Archives of the Foreign Ministry.

18. Louis Duchesne, born 1843, studied at Paris, Rome, and Mount Athos. His *Etude sur [le] Liber Pontificalis* was published 1877. He has since published an edition of the *Lib. Pontif.*, *Vita S. Polycarpi auctore Pionio*, *Les Origines Chrétiennes*, etc.   *58*

very much improved. They have good men to write for it." "Who is Plitt, Herzog's colleague in the new edition?" I asked. "He is professor, I think, at Erlangen. He is a much younger man than Herzog and
59 has written a very good *History of the Reformation* from the high Lutheran point of view." "I believe there is a new edition of the Roman
60 Catholic *Encyclopedia* also—Weltzer and Wette." "Ah, that won't be worth much," said Dr. Döllinger, "it is to be edited by a Jesuit. Besides which it is not even begun; it is only talked of." By 12.30 we were at Villa Arco once more; there we left him and returned to Gasthof Guggemos.

Saturday, September 7th. We rose late, having ascended the Hirschberg the day before. While we were at breakfast between nine and ten, B., who sat facing the door, cried out, "Oh, Alfred, who's that?" I turned round and saw Dr. Döllinger peering in at the door. Apparently he had been up to our room to look for us. He came in and sat between us until we had finished our coffee and listened with great interest to our account of the ascent of the Hirschberg. Then he said, "Perhaps you are not aware that the same thing is going [on] in Tegernsee to-day as used to go on in Athens many centuries ago, as we learn from Domesthenes. People are being made to furnish ships; and, what is more, illuminated ships, which is a step in advance of Athens. Every house is made to furnish a boat for the illumination on the lake to-morrow. Villa Arco has to contribute a boat and to illuminate itself also." We spoke of the accident on the Thames, the running down of the 'Princess Alice' by the 'Bywell Castle', of which he, from seeing English newspapers, knew more than we did. "It seems to have been caused by much the same kind of thing as the accident to the Prussian man-of-war,—misunderstanding of signals; and one does not see how the possibility of such things is to be prevented."

Breakfast finished, we all went for a walk together. We were talking of the newly coined word 'Jingoism', which I said would puzzle future etymologists. Dr. Döllinger said he believed that 'Jingo' had been found to be the Basque word for 'God', and 'by Jingo' had probably come into England through sailors trading at Basque ports. (But that knowledge won't explain 'Jingoism', without 'We don't want to fight, But Jingo if we do, etc.') "Chauvinism," he said, "is a word of somewhat similar origin. Chauvin is a character in one of Scribe's plays[19]. He was a very favourite writer of French comedy, when I was a boy,

---

19. Augustin Scribe was born at Paris 1791 and died there 1861. From 1816, when he put on the stage *Une nuit de la garde nationale*, *Flore et Zéphire*, and *Le comte Ory*, down to 1842, when he published *Le verre d'eau*, his plays were the rage. But the Revolution of 1830 caused a considerable abatement in the popular interest. In 1838 he was made a member of the Academy.

though he is nearly forgotten now. Chauvin is a fire-eater in one of Scribe's plays who is always wishing for war in order to gain territory and *gloire* for France. He has given rise to a word which bids fair to be universal in its use. It is thoroughly admitted into German. The war with France and creation of the Empire produced a good deal of political poetry, which has been collected into one volume, but there is nothing of much value in it. Germany has no poet of much power at present. Of course we all expect that there will be another war with France. Not that Germany wishes for it, but that France will try to have its revenge. In the early part of the war between Russia and Turkey, when Russia seemed to be in need of help, the French ambassador at S. Petersburg thought that a favourable moment had come for an offensive and defensive alliance between France and Russia, and proposed it to Gortschakoff. He replied, 'I quite see that such an alliance would suit you very well; but it would not suit us at all. We have no wish to be compelled to go to war, whenever it pleases you to attack Germany.'"

I asked him what Germans thought of England's getting Cyprus. "Oh, on the whole it was approved. People knew that such a change could only be for the benefit of the island. At bottom the generality of people in Germany are as strongly anti-Russian as the majority in England. Only, with a war with France always impending, we are obliged to keep on tolerable terms with Russia. If we quarrel with both, we shall be ground between two mill-stones. Russia at the present time is very much what Spain was in the sixteenth century — universally feared and universally detested. It was known to be powerful and believed to be aggressive. A Spaniard was hated all over Europe in the sixteenth century. And it is somewhat the same with Russia now." "But at any rate the Russians have had no Philip II. to make them detested. Such a monarch might make any nation an abomination to the rest of the world." "True," said Dr. Döllinger, "but there again there is a similarity. No matter what their sovereign was, the Spaniards were always enthusiastic in fighting his battles; and a Russian Emperor can always count on the enthusiasm of his people now. A Russian officer attached to the embassy at Munich told me a few years ago that to the Russian people every war undertaken by the Emperor was a *religious* war. No matter whether it was against England, or France, or Turkey, it was a war for their religion, a holy war. The clergy encouraged this view, even in the case of the late Emperor Nicolas, who deprived the Church of such immense revenues. It made no difference : the clergy still preached up his wars. He took away all the revenues of the Church and paid the clergy out of the Treasury instead; and very miserably paid they are. Whether the Church *can* hold property in Russia now, I am not sure. But even if the law allows it, not much is likely to be given or left to the Church. The clergy are so ignorant and so degraded that they inspire no respect. But, though their degradation prevents them from being liked, it seems to create no scandal. Russian peasantry do not seem to be at all shocked at seeing the priest dead drunk on Saturday and celebrating on Sunday."

Dr. Döllinger laughed heartily at the story (Dean Ramsay's?) of the Presbyterian minister whose clerk used to tie him up after a certain hour every Saturday, in order to ensure his being sober on Sunday. We told him we thought of leaving Tegernsee on Tuesday for Achensee and Salzburg, and would come to wish him 'Goodbye' on Monday. "And how do you go home from Salzburg?" "By Munich and Cologne." "Ach! when will you be in Munich?" "About the 18th or 19th." "It is possible that I may be at home then; at any rate you can call."

Monday, September 9. We went to make a farewell call at Villa Arco, the inmates of which had left a sheaf of cards on us the day before. Dr. Döllinger unfortunately was out. Only the old Countess was at home, and she was as delightful as ever. On our way home we met her daughter, but we missed all the rest. The afternoon was thoroughly wet, and we did not get out till six. We went near the Schloss as the dryest walk, and after we had taken a turn or two Dr. Döllinger met us. He had come out, he said, to try to see us again, as there was a chance of our going next day. It delighted us that an old man (he is 79) should come out on a damp evening on our account; but it was just like his kindness. We talked of the spectacle the night before — the torchlight procession and the illuminated fleet on the lake. He said that he had never seen anything like it in his life. Fifty years before, when the old couple were first married, there was something of the same kind, but not at all on the same scale. There were not enough people and not enough purses in Tegernsee to do it. It was then a village of peasants. Old King Max, father of the bride, was very fond of Tegernsee, and so the marriage had taken place there. Dr. Döllinger had been told that there had been 5000 people in Tegernsee the evening before; and of those who remained all night 300 had had to go without beds. He would not let us say 'Goodbye' when we parted at Villa Arco. "If you don't go to-morrow, I shall see you again here; and if you do, I shall hope to see you in Munich."

Monday, September 16. We did not, however, see him in Munich, when we called. We saw his pleasant housekeeper and were able to tell her more about her master than she knew. A day or two later we were back in England.

1879

Saturday, August 2nd. This year I had to travel alone and reached Munich in time to learn that Dr. Döllinger had left for Tegernsee the day before. I went on into the Tyrol determining to take Tegernsee on my way home. I reached it August 15[20].

Saturday, August 16th. I went to Villa Arco to call on Dr. Döllinger and found him and Lord Acton in the new library entertaining Prof. Kraus of Strasburg, who has lately been invited to take a professorship of Ecclesiastical History at Freiburg[21]. He was just then speaking of the tremendous fiasco in which the attempt of Capel and Manning to found a Roman Catholic University in England has ended, and of the immense sum of money which has been sunk in the attempt, — some £80,000 I think he said. And now Capel and Manning are at war. *61* No one well acquainted with English society would hope for success for so exclusive an institution. But Capel and Manning are Roman rather than English in their instincts and do not know how much they are disliked and distrusted by English Roman Catholics who are not [con]verts. Capel's and Manning's names turned the conversation to *Lothaire* and thence to Disraeli. Lord Acton in speaking of the very *62* imperfect harmony which exists between Lord Salisbury and his chief stated that Lord Salisbury had once spoken to him of Disraeli as

20. "MY DEAR NEVIN, — I suppose your influence is sufficiently strong to get a short *63* article or notice inserted in one of the Liberal papers contradicting the lies that have been spread over all Europe respecting my contemplated or consummated submission to the Vatican decrees. I have neither written nor done anything which could have given occasion to such a rumour. The circumstances which are mentioned in some papers are gratuitous inventions. I have only three weeks ago published a lecture (*Allgemeine Zeitung*, April 6, 7, 8), in which I state in so many words that nobody possessing a scientific culture of mind can ever accept the decrees of the Vatican Council. *64* Having devoted during the last nine years my time principally to the renewed study of all the questions connected with the history of the Popes and the councils, and, I may say, gone again over the whole ground of ecclesiastical history, the result is that the proofs of the falsehood of the Vatican decrees amount to a demonstration. When I am told that I must swear to the truth of those doctrines my feeling is just as if I were asked to swear that two and two make five, and not four. Pray, my dear Nevin, let me have some news of what is going on at Rome. Perhaps you can also obtain the reception of a similar notice in one of the American papers. *Totus tuus*, J. DÖLLINGER, Munich, May 4, 1879."

21. Franz X. Kraus, born 1840, became Prof. extraordinary of art, archaeology and history at Strasburg 1872, ord. Prof. of Eccl. Hist. at Freiburg-im-Breisgau 1878. He is a liberal R.C., the author of many works and the editor of a good *Real-Encyklopädie der christlichen Alterthümer* 1880, 1886.

"that beastly Jew." Lord Salisbury would scarcely like to be reminded of the fact at the present time.

After the Professor had taken his departure Lady Acton came in and said that her mother hoped that I would stay to dinner; and as it still wanted an hour to dinner-time, Dr. Döllinger and I went out for a short walk. We talked of the ever increasing want of clergy from which so many, if not all, of the Western Churches are suffering; England not a little, France still worse, and Germany (as Dr. Döllinger remarked) probably worst of all. "Catholics and Protestants alike are in this evil plight. Take the diocese of Freiburg as an instance. Professor Kraus says that the average number of theological students is 40 to 45. As the course is three years, that means that about 13 or 14 are ordained yearly for a diocese in which there are 700 or 800 parishes. The consequence is that 300 parishes are without pastors — more than one third! At Munich the number of theological students remains stationary — between 70 and 80." I asked whether the new archbishop was doing anything to mend the state of things. "Nothing much can be done. There is no possibility of remedy. He is a quiet unoffensive man, who avoids contest, so far as he can do so without compromising his own position; but he cannot do much. Among the Protestants the want of clergy is to a large extent the result of economical causes. Prices have risen, stipends remain low, and a married ministry cannot live with comfort. It is very difficult for a Protestant minister to maintain and educate his family. In the case of the Catholics these economical causes are almost entirely absent. The Church is pretty well endowed, the laity are generous to the clergy, who of course have no families, and who have a source of income which Protestant ministers have not, — fees for saying masses. The upper classes seldom take orders, however. A gentleman who takes orders finds himself, so to speak, in bad company. This has been more especially the case since 1870 (the Infallibility dogma), since when there has been a general flight of the educated classes from the ministry. Consequently the Church has been driven to get its clergy more and more from the lower ranks of society — from the peasantry." With regard to our own troubles in England Dr. Döllinger once more expressed surprise that the Ritualists should care so much about the chasuble. "If we were not so used to it," he said, "we should think it a *shocking* vestment : it is so unbecoming, and such a falling away from the primitive vestments of the Church. The vestments of the Greek Church are so much more dignified."

At dinner I took in Lady Acton and sat between her and the old Countess, who had Dr. Döllinger on her right. Lord Acton took in his cousin Miss Throgmorton, between whom and Lady Acton sat the young Countess. Conversation was mainly in English, with a good deal of French, and some German, and being polyglott did not flow freely.

After dinner we adjourned to the garden for coffee, after which I took my leave.

Sunday, 10th after Trinity, August 17. I called for Dr. Döllinger about 10.30 and we went for a walk of about two hours and a half through Rottach towards the Wallberg, round to Egern, and so home across the lake, which is narrowest there. I asked him whether he thought that the Falk laws were going to become a dead letter. "They cannot become a dead letter. They are worded in such a way that this is impossible; and they are not at all likely to be repealed. The parliament that is to be elected in a few weeks is not likely to be of such a colour as to repeal them; and as long as they remain, all excepting one clause must be carried out. The government has no option excepting with regard to proceeding against ecclesiastics for pronouncing excommunications and other censures. Even where such pronouncements are of an illegal character, the executive need not proceed against the ecclesiastic, if it thinks fit to take no notice. In all other cases the Falk laws must be maintained." "Some of the newspapers, however, are accusing Bismarck of going to Canossa after all." "That remains to be seen," said he : "nothing of the kind has been done yet. I attach no importance whatever to the fact that Falk has resigned, because I know a very simple explanation of it. Falk's policy was antagonistic to the court policy in one particular. He could not or would not change it, and found it so uncomfortable to be in perpetual antagonism to the Emperor in religious politics, that he resigned. The court wishes the orthodox Protestants to be protected and favoured : that is always its line. Falk, either from conviction or circumstances, belongs to the so-called *Protestanten-Verein*, that is Protestant Liberalism with a very strong mixture of infidelity. This party is very strong throughout Germany, especially in the north; and while Falk was in office, this party was constantly victorious, and the orthodox Protestants went to the wall. Puttkammer, Falk's successor, has been put in office for the purpose of supporting the orthodox Protestants; but the Falk laws will still remain. In Parliament on one point, and on one point only, do the orthodox Protestants pull with the ultramontanes against the Falk laws, viz. in trying to get back the elementary national schools to be under the direction of the clergy. The middle class schools, the *gymnasiums*, were not touched by Falk in that particular : they had long since been withdrawn from clerical direction. But Falk withdrew the lowest grade of schools also; and orthodox Protestants and ultramontanes join forces to try to get them back. But in every other particular they are utterly hostile to one another. There is a dispute going on in Munich at the present time about these elementary schools. The town councils have lately made some of these schools, — about half-a-dozen or so, — what we call *Simul-*

tanschulen (undenominational schools); i.e. of such a character that Catholics, Protestants, and Jews can attend them. There is no attendance at mass required of the children, no *Paternoster* and *Ave Maria* before school, no crucifix in the school-room, as in the Catholic schools; no hymns, and no use of the Bible as a reading-book, as in Protestant schools. All that would offend the other sections is excluded. But orthodox Protestants and Catholics are struggling to get these schools made denominational again." "It seems reasonable that in a large city like Munich there should be a few such schools." "Of course. In Munich there are some 25,000 Protestants and some 180,000 Catholics. In such a city it might easily happen that Protestant children would have to walk two miles to a Protestant denominational school, and that in the depth of winter. But where the interests of the clergy are at stake, the interests of the parents and children are lost sight of; and so the clergy are fighting against the establishment of these few undenominational schools. Of the two town councils, according to the last elections, one has a majority of liberals, the other not; and they must act together; so it remains to be seen how the matter will end." I asked how the expenses of these elementary schools were defrayed. "The parents pay a small sum fixed by law; the State pays the master; the parish provides and keeps in repair the building." I remarked that in England we were finding out that secular education without religious instruction will not work. Even Birmingham was making modifications, finding that morality cannot be taught without religion. "That is always the crucial point. In Germany that question has never as yet arisen. No one has ever proposed to abolish religious instruction and have a purely secular education. Where the school is undenominational, the religious instruction is given by the minister of the religion to which the child belongs."

I asked him whether he had had any correspondence with the Orientals of late, in reference to the Reunion Conferences at Bonn. "Not for some ten months or so, so far as I can recollect. They are so completely taken up with political matters that the situation is very unfavourable to any efforts at reunion. The Patriarchate of Constantinople is in a very difficult position. The separation of Bulgaria from it, and the establishment of Bulgarian ecclesiastical independence, was a tremendous blow to the Patriarchate. An immense portion of its revenues came from Bulgaria. It condemned the independence with the severest ecclesiastical censures, excommunicating the whole community. The Patriarch of Jerusalem was deposed by a synod at Jerusalem for supporting it. Russia, on the other hand, favoured the separation of Bulgaria from the Patriarchate of Constantinople. Hence a curious state of affairs. The Russian Church is in communion with the Patriarchate, and also with the Bulgarian Church, which is excommunicated by the Patriarchate. So long as Bulgaria remained part of the Turkish Empire, the Patriarchate had hopes of regaining its hold over the province and recovering the revenues. But now that Bulgaria has been politically as well as ecclesiastically severed from Constantinople[22], the Patriarch must have lost all hope of ever reestablishing his authority over the Bulgarian Church. The evil did not begin or end with Bulgaria. Greece was severed from the Patriarch long before. That was a loss which the Patriarchate could afford to take with complacency. Its hold over Greece had not been very strong, and it drew very little revenue from it. These two precedents are not likely to remain isolated. Macedonia, Thessaly, and Epirus will all be likely to declare their independence when the opportunity comes. As each limb is politically severed from the Turkish Empire, it will be ecclesiastically severed from the Patriarchate of Constantinople. What is the effect of all this with regard to any attempts at reunion? Most disastrous. For these divisions of the Oriental Church are all jealous of one another and mistrust one another. The very fact that one branch entertained proposals from the Western Churches would be enough to make other branches reject them. That is why we have had no answer to the proposals which were made at Bonn. We sent a set of propositions to both the Greek and the Russian Churches, and they have sent no reply; because they cannot agree among themselves. A further difficulty arises from the attitude which the English government has of late years (ever since the Crimean War) adopted in the East as the upholder of the Turk in all things. England is now regarded in the East as the natural enemy of the Christian. That will prove a stumbling block when Oriental Christians are asked to enter into communion with the English Church. That it is any use giving Turkey a chance of reformation and regeneration, I do not at all believe. But it would have been quite possible to give Turkey this chance without leaving Christian populations utterly at the mercy of the Turk. In 1856 not only were the Christians not protected, but what protection they had had up to that time was done away. The Turk knew that from henceforth he could do as he pleased. This has always been the weak place in Gladstone's armour; and, so far as I know, he has never made the only defence that was valid, — that in 1856 he was only a subordinate member of the government and had to follow his superiors." "No," I said, "I don't think he has ever said that. What he says is, that twenty years ago it seemed to be worth while to give Turkey one more chance of reform. Turkey has had the chance, and has grown worse instead of better." "That does not excuse the sacrifice of the Christians," said Dr. Döllinger. We parted at the Villa of the Princess of Mecklenburg, agreeing to have

22. Bulgaria was made an autonomous principality under the suzerainty of the Porte by the Treaty of Berlin, 1878.

another walk together next day. That evening there was an illumination of the lake and the surrounding mountains with illuminated boats and bonfires.

Monday, August 18th. I called early for Dr. Döllinger and found him in the balcony by the front door at Villa Arco. A lady had come from Munich to see him while we were out together the day before, and she was to call again this morning; so we put off our walk until the afternoon. Rain prevented me from calling until past five; and then we got rather a damp walk. But Dr. Döllinger is never afraid of getting wet. "That lady who called to see me this morning from Munich is a person of independent means, who lives a great deal in Rome. She was at Rome during the Council, and at that time became acquainted with Cardinal Haynald, the Hungarian Archbishop (of Calocsa; he voted *non placet*)[23]. He was passing through Munich the other day and called upon her; and he told her the following anecdote. During the Council, while the contest was still very strong between infallibilists and those who opposed the dogma, Bishop Strossmayer of course was one of the leaders of the Opposition;—a formidable one, for he is an eloquent Latin orator, which few of the infallibilists are. They consulted together as to how they could silence him. It was known that he had sometimes met and conversed with a certain actress in Rome; and it was proposed that the Pope should declare that this had given such occasion for scandal, that Strossmayer must be sus-66 pended. Palomba, who was a sort of attaché to the Austrian ministry, was sent to Cardinal Haynald to consult about the matter. The archbishop told him that if the Pope attempted to suspend Strossmayer, he would be infringing the privileges of the Hungarian bishops. The Hungarian bishops (and Strossmayer counts as one) have the privilege of being judged by their peers. Strossmayer, therefore, could only be judged, and if necessary suspended, by a synod of Hungarian bishops. Moreover (Haynald continued), if the prosecution is persisted in, the Hungarian bishops will denounce the scandals of Antonelli's private life. Nothing more was said about the matter." To this day Strossmayer 67 has not submitted to the dogma.

We passed what is a common object in Bavaria and the Tyrol,— a representation of S. Florian in armour pouring water from a bucket on to a blazing house. S. Florian is the patron-saint of fire-brigades. According to the legend, S. Florian was condemned to be burned; but

23. Archbishop Haynald was the last of the Hungarian bishops to submit to the dogma. He held out until late in 1871. Yet in July 1867 he took the lead in presenting to the Pope an address which was so infallibilist in tone that Pius IX. appealed to [it] July 18, 1870. The Jesuits tried to get the Infallibility *expressly* recognized in this 68 address, but this Haynald and the French bischops then in Rome would not allow.

the faggot would not burn, so he was beheaded instead. "Do you know," said Dr. Döllinger, "why S. Barbara is the patron-saint of artillery? Because she was shut up in a tower." "And a tower is round like a cannon?" I asked. "Yes," said he laughing, "that's it. When I was a lad at Würzburg I remember that cannon were always fired on S. Barbara's day. And do you know why S. Catharine is the patron-saint of philosophy?" "Because she silenced the philosophers?" "Exactly. I remember that I was once sent by the government to superintend an examination at Freising. Freising was the first attempt made by the clergy to form a theological college, — started by the Archbishop of Munich and others. The government wanted to know what was going on there, — what was being taught; and I was sent as a commissary. The teacher of philosophy was an old priest, who knew a little scholastic philosophy and had put together a catechism out of the schoolmen, which he dictated to the students, and they learnt the answers by heart. The first question was, *Quid est philosophia?* And the answer was, *Ea scientia cujus patrona est sancta Catharina*! And I was expected to sit by and look serious during such an examination!"

I asked him when the wise men from the East were turned into kings. "I believe it was done when Frederick Barbarossa removed their relics from Milan to Cologne. So long as they were at Milan they were not very famous. But when Barbarossa destroyed Milan and removed the relics of the Magi to Cologne, then a sort of cultus became pretty general. It was then probably that they were made into kings and named. Melchior means 'King of Light'. Balthazar is Belshazzar, borrowed from the Book of Daniel. I don't know the meaning of Caspar." We parted once more at the Villa of the Princess of Mecklenburg, — parted for a year in all probability. His last words were, "Give my love to Lady Bertha and tell her that old as I am I still have some hope of living to see her son. It is just possible. Goodbye." "I am sure I hope it may be so, Sir." And we parted. He is over eighty[24].

I had told him during our walk of rather a good thing which appears in *Kladderadatsch* this week. Bismarck and an ecclesiastic are searching in a large waste-paper basket for a *modus vivendi*. Bismarck has his arms plunged almost to the arm-pits in a mass of contracts and concordats which have become waste paper; but he can't find anything to serve his purpose. The ecclesiastic remarks, "I think that I should have found it much sooner, if you hadn't helped me."

---

24. Harold was then a few weeks old, and it was his birth which prevented B. from accompanying me to Bavaria. Dr. Döllinger lived until Harold was ten and half years old; but alas! he never saw him.

1880

Saturday, July 17th. We reached Munich at 8 a.m. and in the afternoon visited Dr. Döllinger. We found him looking very well and he said that he was both as well and as capable of work as ever. After greeting us his first enquiries were about Harold. He said that the older he grew the more interested he became in children. He took the greatest interest in the many children he met in his daily walks. I said, "I don't know whether you have a similar saying in Germany; — in England we say of children that they are young bears with all their troubles before them." "Yes," said he; "and their *choice* before them also. And the object of education is just that, — to make the choice and the happiness superior to the troubles. I forget whether it was before or after you were at Tegernsee last year that Gladstone and his family came there. After the father, I was most interested in Miss Gladstone. She seemed to me to be so full of intelligence and spirit; much more so than her mother. I think that Gladstone himself greatly underrated the difficulties of the government which preceded him with regard to the Eastern Question; not perhaps that he thought the matter an easy one, but that he did not at all know how singularly difficult it is. He is finding that out now. With his philanthropic and philhellenic sympathies he thought that a generous treatment of Greece, especially with regard to the frontier, and a manifestation of good will towards all, would bring about a speedy settlement. But even within Greece itself, to say nothing of Turkey and Russia, there are so many rival parties and interests, both Christian and Mahometan, and the hatred of each to the others is so intense, that it seems to be quite hopeless to attempt to get anything settled. Germany is interested in the discussion chiefly as being jealous of any increase of power on the side of Russia. Austria would no doubt like to gain some territory, but the occupation of Bosnia has caused her such trouble and expense, that she will not be very eager for more costly acquisitions. For half a century her great difficulty has been the financial one, and the occupation of Bosnia has thrown her back in the struggle with bankruptcy.

"Had you any anticipation of Gladstone's great success at the general election? And to what do you attribute it?" I replied that I thought no one excepting Vernon Harcourt had expected more than a very moderate Liberal gain. He had repeatedly predicted an overwhelming Liberal victory. As to the causes, there were probably several at work. Many Englishmen, especially of the upper middle classes, had come to the conclusion that Beaconsfield's policy was immoral, — a deliberate preference of 'British interests' to justice. The lower classes had a vague idea that the long reign of Conservatism and the long continuance of bad times were somehow or other connected. And when the Liberal success had once begun, people of undecided opinions voted for the winning side. I asked in return whether Bismarck was going to Canossa after all. "Not at all," said Dr. Döllinger, "nor anything in the least degree like it. I don't believe that he has any such intention, and I fancy that he is very well pleased with the result of the struggle thus far. The meaning of the proposed modification of the May Laws I believe *69* to be simply this, — that the proposal was made to please the Emperor. There is to be a great ceremony at Cologne this autumn to celebrate the completion of the Cathedral. The Emperor of course has been invited and wishes to go, and it would be very difficult for him to go, if there were no Archbishop of Cologne there to take the chief part in the ceremony. The main object of the proposed changes in the *70* May Laws, as I believe, was to gain a decent pretext for bringing back the archbishop. But the Chambers have refused to grant the most important of the changes, and the relaxations that have been made are of very little moment. They do not in the least approach to a reconciliation with Rome."

Dr. Döllinger told us that Munich was unusually full just now, not only on account of Ober-Ammergau, but also because a series of model representations is going on at the theatre here. Some of the best actors in Germany have been got together in order to give as excellent a rendering as possible of some of the best plays. Last night *Winter's Tale* had been given, and he had been told that it was very well rendered : an actress from Vienna had created a considerable sensation. *Torquato Tasso* to-night was sure to be good. He insisted on our dining with him next day. To save him trouble I proposed a walk instead. He laughed and said, "We can have both perhaps; at any rate you will come and dine at two o'clock. What he told us about the theatre determined us to go and hear Goethe's *Tasso*, of which the first four acts lasted three hours, by which time we had had enough. The Munich 'artistes' seemed quite to hold their own against the visitors.

Sunday, 8th after Trinity, July 18th. We were rejoiced to find that Dr. Döllinger had asked no one to meet us and that we had him all to ourselves. He told us that the ex-President of one of the English Roman Catholic seminaries had called on him a few days before. He had remained President until the Infallibility dogma. As he could not accept that, he had retired, and had since then had no official or clerical work. He asked Dr. Döllinger whether he thought that there *71* was any hope of the present Pope doing anything for those who were conscientiously unable to accept the dogma, but otherwise wished to remain members of the Church. "I told him," said Dr. Döllinger, "that I was certain that there was not the smallest hope of anything of the kind. The present Pope would have conjured people not to pass the dogma; but now that it has been decreed he must hold to it." I asked, "Don't you think that his making Newman a cardinal was intended to announce that Newman's minimizing of the dogma was henceforth to be an allowable interpretation?" He shook his head. "They do not know at Rome what Newman's theory of the dogma is. It is a cardinal rule there not to understand any English. And they do not *care* what his theory is. Rome does not ask for *faith* : she asks for *obedience*. The question is not, 'Does he believe?', but, 'Has he submitted?' Only submit and you will not be asked about any explanations or reservations. The present Pope has tied his own hands and feet. He saw how much evil resulted from Pius IX. doing everything in an autocratic way, taking advice from a very small clique, and at the beginning of his pontificate he promised the cardinals that he would do nothing of importance without the consent of the College. So there is no chance of much change for the better. Moreover every one that comes from Rome tells me that the general belief there is that Franchi, the Pope's late secretary, was poisoned. The corpse was quite black; and, as Franchi was a great deal too liberal in his views for the majority of the Curia, they would be glad to get him out of the way. This makes others, who are of similar opinions, very shy of displaying them. Among other points, in which Leo XIII. has been obliged to give way, is that of remaining closely at home and keeping up the fiction of the Pope being a prisoner. He wishes to go into the country for change of air, but the cardinals will not allow it. He must be an actor and keep up the part of the prisoner of the Vatican." "How does he manage to keep in good health," asked B., "if he never goes beyond the Vatican." "He doesn't keep in good health," said Dr. Döllinger. "Moreover he overworks himself, sitting up very late till one or two in the morning, working. His brother remonstrated with him about it, and the Pope replied, 'I must work for the Church;' to which his brother rejoined, 'The best thing that you can do for the Church is to take care of yourself and live as long as you can; for when you die things will be still worse.' If I were offered the Popedom, tiara, Vatican, and all, on the condition of never leaving the Vatican, I should say, 'No, thank you; you may keep them all for yourself.' I think that on one condition I *would* accept the Papacy." "What is that?" I asked. "That I might be allowed to make a clean sweep of all the cardinals and all the 600 members of the Curia, and start afresh with a new set who would not be creatures of Pius IX."

We talked also of Caspari, who had paid Dr. Döllinger a visit some weeks before, and of his works, and of Friedrich's and Cecconi's works on the Vatican Council. In both cases so much space is being given to the prelude to the Council that one almost doubts whether the history of the Council itself will ever be written. Cecconi has published three or four volumes and has not reached the Council yet. None of Dr. Döllinger's own works seem to be more than *almost* ready for publication :— his essays on the persecution of the Templars, on the death of Boniface VIII., on Dante, and his documents to illustrate 74 the Council of Trent. He laughed when I reminded him of all these irons in the fire, and said, "There is one very happy thing, however :— that I am still strong and in good health, able to work all day and take pleasure in it. This day all good Bavarians are celebrating with pride the 700th anniversary of the rise of the Wittelsbacher house. That a dynasty should continue for so long a period is a thing perhaps without a parallel in history. On Wednesday week the Academy here has a meeting, and as President I have to deliver an address on the subject. 75 We have elected Stubbs a member of our Academy : it was I who proposed him."

After dinner he took me into his library and showed me some of the books most worthy of notice in theology and history that had come out in Germany during the last few years. It was surprising to see with what ease he went up ladders and handed down books, sometimes half a dozen big ones all at once, from the higher shelves. Most of his shelves are double-shoffed—i.e. contain two rows of books one behind the other. I asked him whether he could remember what books were at the back. He nodded : "Yes, I know what is at the back of every shelf." We left about 4.15, it being agreed that we were to come back for a walk at 7.0. The old woman who let us in when we returned (not Dr. Döllinger's housekeeper, who usually opens the door) grinned with much delight at seeing us. She came up and tapped me on the shoulder and said, "I often think of you and that time when you and the master got such a drenching in the rain, and came in all soaked; and the umbrella broken; and not the first time either;" and she laughed herself out of the room. I remembered it well also, and how Dr. Döllinger talked through the drenching rain just as if it was nothing at all, saying that getting wet never did him any harm. This time we walked, as usual, in the English Garden, round the lake and back, which took us just two hours.

"We Germans have a saying,— I don't know whether you have the same in England,— that what one wishes for much in youth one has in old age in abundance. Goethe has put it as the motto to his autobiography[25]. There are two things which I used to wish for very

---

25. It is the motto to the second part : *Was man in der Jugend wünscht, hat man im Alter die Fülle.* The motto to the first part is ὁ μὴ δαρεὶς ἄνθρωπος οὐ παιδεύεται; to the third, *Es ist dafür gesorgt, dass die Bäume nicht in den Himmel wachsen;* to the fourth, *Nemo contra deum nisi deus ipse.*

much as a young man; and I used to look forward to the day when I should possess them :— a country living and a garden. And I have got neither of them, and am never likely to get them. So that the saying does not hold good in my case. I had them in a sort of way for a very short time. For just one year I was coadjutor—what you would call a curate—to a very old priest. And then I was appointed professor at Aschaffenburg; and so it all came to an end. One thing I used to wish for very much, and that I *have* got, viz. a library."

76 I said that I supposed he had seen what trouble Stanley had got himself into about a monument to the French Prince Imperial in Westminster Abbey. "There never was anything more absurd!" he exclaimed. "It is most extraordinary that a man of Stanley's ability should have made such a blunder. A young man who had no connexion with England, who had done nothing in the world to deserve any special honour, whose name was a standing menace, or at least a threatening difficulty to a government with which England professes to be on good terms,— to give such a lad the distinction of a monument in Westminster Abbey would be almost a challenge to France. Have you ever seen our Westminster Abbey—I mean the Walhalla?" "Oh yes," I replied. "When was the last addition made to it?" "I really can't say," said Dr. Döllinger; "and I don't know who decides now as to what insertions are to be made. I have an idea that one or two additions have been made since King Ludwig's death, but I cannot recall who they are. He was for a time very unwilling that Luther should be admitted; but a monument to him was put up eventually. But there is still no monument to Melanchthon; and no German deserves one more. Of all the Reformers he is the one I admire most."

On the Burials Bill he remarked, as he had done before, that "in Germany no difficulty ever arises from Catholics and Protestants using the same burial grounds simultaneously; and where there is a Catholic mortuary chapel the Protestants never attempt to obtain the use of it. This use of common graveyards has produced a curious influence of Protestantism on the Church. Formerly Catholics never had any address made at the grave;— merely the Church's office for the burial of the dead, but no sermon. Protestants on the other hand always had an address; and now that both use the same burial grounds the Catholics have been induced to have an address also, these addresses being very much liked. And one may add that the Protestant addresses are commonly much better than the Catholic ones. But the whole system is an evil. Of course the dead person has to be mentioned, and much of the address is taken up with the chief points in his life; and for the sake of the friends and relations present the mention is laudatory. In some way or other the deceased is held up as exemplary; and it sometimes happens that the minister at the grave praises up a man whom all the by-standers know to have been utterly godless. I remember the case of a professor, who made no secret of being a sceptic, and told his colleagues that he regarded the Bible as a tissue of fables. When he died, those who attended his funeral were informed by the minister that the deceased was one who in his study of the past ever found God in history! I don't suppose that the word 'God' occurs from the first page to the last of his writings. If some one in England were to lift up a warning voice on this subject, he would be doing good service."

Stanley's second blunder in refusing to believe that Carlyle had signed the protest against the memorial to the Prince was mentioned : — it was soon ascertained that Carlyle had signed, and Stanley had to eat his own words. "Carlyle is a wonderful person," said Dr. Döllinger. "He seems to me to stand quite alone in literature. He is unlike anyone else. *We* certainly have no one like him. He has founded no school, and has had no imitators. Indeed an imitator would be intolerable. Carlyle himself is irritating enough; but it is always worth while puzzling out what he means. One cannot compare him with Victor Hugo : Victor Hugo never wrote anything serious. The only person that seems to me to be at all like him — and he is very unlike — is Ruskin. It is difficult to compare the two : they are so different; and yet one feels that they have something in common." "In the wider sense of the word they both may be called prophets, don't you think?" "But without the gift of prophecy."   *77*

I asked him whether he had seen the discussion in the *Contemporary Review* between Ruskin and the Bishop of Manchester on usury, in *78* which Ruskin maintains that the taking of interest is contrary to the Divine Law of the Bible and the Canon Law of the Church. "In saying that it is against the Canon Law, he is right; that it is against the Divine Law, he is not only wrong, but is upholding a most mischievous error. If he read more deeply into the history of the middle ages he would find that few doctrines have been more disastrous than the theory that taking interest is forbidden by the law of God. It made the Jews both necessary and hated. They were necessary, because they were the only people who could negociate a large loan. Large loans are impossible without interest; and if Christians might not take interest, borrowers must resort to the Jews. And it made the Jews detested, because they allowed themselves considerable profits which were denied to Christians. And hence persecutions and cruel massacres. Of course also the rate of interest was much higher than it need have been if the Canon Law had left the matter alone." "It is precisely the Canon Law that Ruskin approves, and he maintains that it is supported by the Bible." "The Bible gives no support to it," said Dr. Döllinger. "The Jews were forbidden to take interest *from one another*, and the belief that our Lord has laid down a similar rule for Christians rests on a mistranslation." "I suppose that one must admit that the meaning of the Greek is not quite certain,—that μηδὲν ἀπελπίζοντες may be translated in two if not three different ways." "It is quite true that the Greek Fathers have suggested more than one way of understanding the words, but I don't think that there is any real doubt as to the meaning. Not a single passage can be found to justify the rendering, 'hoping for nothing in return'. Taking μηδὲν' for μηδένα is possible, but not very natural. My own belief is that the words mean 'not being at all anxious about your capital', not being afraid that you will never see it again."

I took the opportunity of asking him about 'baptizing for the dead' (Cor. XV. 29), especially whether there was any direct evidence that the first Christians did baptize another person instead of a catechumen who had died unbaptized. "There is no direct evidence," he said; "but I have no doubt that it was done, and that the text refers to such vicarious baptism. The corrupt practice was probably one which crossed over from Judaism into the Church. The Jews baptized their proselytes; and at a time when it was a matter of great ambition, if not of profit, to make a proselyte (Mt. XXIII. 15) it would be likely enough that a deceased Gentile would sometimes be claimed as a proselyte who died before receiving baptism; and then some one else would be baptized in place of the dead. The case is somewhat analogous to that of offerings for the dead, a custom which we find in full bloom in the Book of Maccabees, but of the rise of which we have no trace. So also exorcism, which the Jews certainly practised with more or less success, but of which we have no evidence earlier than the Book of Tobit. I have no doubt that it is to vicarious baptism that St Paul alludes; and I believe that it originated with the Jews."

I asked him whether the common belief that the Prince Imperial of Germany is much more liberal in his opinions than his father was founded on fact. "There is no doubt that in some things the Prince is more liberal than his father; e.g. in matters of religious belief. In religion both Emperor and Empress, especially the latter, are very conservative. The old Empress is very clever in winning golden opinions from the ultramontanes, while she remains a staunch Protestant. She visits convents, and asks the nuns to pray for her and the reigning house; and so forth. Formerly, for many years, she never attempted to influence the Emperor in anything of importance. She had found out from experience that it was no use: he never allowed himself to be guided by her. But since the attempt on his life, which in spite of his recovery has weakened his constitution a good deal, she has begun to have some influence over him; and it is commonly exercised in favour of the orthodox party. I dare say you saw that not long ago the

Princess Imperial took a journey to Italy all alone, remaining there a considerable time. It excited a good deal of sensation in Germany that she should go on such a tour without either her husband or any of her children. The explanation of it is this; and I have it on very good authority. There had been a very serious difference between the Princess and the Empress. The Princess had selected as the spiritual instructor of her daughters one of the more liberal and free-thinking theologians of Berlin. The Empress took her to task about it, and desired that a change should be made; but the Princess would not consent to any further concession than that the Empress might appeal to the Prince and she would abide by her husband's decision. The Prince, as might be expected, confirmed his wife's original choice; and the Empress was so offended at it that it was thought best that the Princess should keep out of sight for a while; so she went for a tour in Italy."

As we got near to Dr. Döllinger's door again I mentioned that the last number of the *Church Quarterly Review* had not yet come when we left England, but that I hoped to send it to him when I got home. "I think," said he, "that on the whole it maintains itself very well, and I like it. There are generally about two articles that are decidedly good. Do you know who writes those articles on S. Peter?" "I fancy Dr. Littledale." "Ah! he sent me the first two editions of his *Reasons* 79 *for not joining the Church of Rome*. It is well done; but I could have 80 told him of a few more things that would have made the book more effective." As we were already past his door it was too late to ask him what these were. Nothing remained but to thank him and say 'Goodbye', — probably for a year at least. Next day we moved onwards towards Ober-Ammergau, B. for the second time, I for the third, both of us probably for the last time.

1882

In 1881 we were in Switzerland and did not come near either Munich or Tegernsee. On S. James' Day 1882 we were once more in Munich and at Dr. Döllinger's. His housekeeper first, and [a] moment or two afterwards he himself, gave us a hearty and warm welcome. He was looking as well as ever, and not at all older than when we saw him last two years ago. After the first questions had been asked and answered, I asked him whether he was going to the Jubilee of the University of Würzburg, which celebrates its 300th anniversary this year. He said, "No, such things are not in my line. Large gatherings, and dinners, and speeches, and all that kind of thing do not suit me now. And therefore, although my father was a professor there and I myself was once a student there, I am not going to the Jubilee." I asked him what was the meaning of the feeling which is said to have been excited by the proposal to confer an honorary degree upon the Cultus Minister, Von Lutz. Dr. Döllinger said that for some time past the ultramontanes have had a majority in the Chamber of Deputies (House of Commons) in Bavaria, and in order to get the necessary sums voted for the promotion of education and science, the ministry made a sort of compact with the ultramontanes to the effect that, if they would be so good as to vote the money, the government would give them two professors, one at Munich and one at Würzburg, to teach that philosophy which the present Pope in one of his earliest encyclicals pronounced to be *the*

81 philosophy for Christians, viz. that of S. Thomas Aquinas. In Germany it is usual for the university to nominate the men whom it would like to have appointed professors; and consequently this compact between the ultramontane majority and the ministry has not given much satisfaction either to Munich or to Würzburg; — least of all when the time came for the Cultus Minister to perform his share of the bargain. As regards Munich, an ultramontane professor has been pitchforked over from

82 Bonn to teach the Thomist philosophy here. "And I am told," continued Dr. Döllinger, "that when the minister indicated the University of Würzburg the kind of person that he would wish to nominate to the Chair of Philosophy there, they wrote back to say that they did not know of any such person in the whole of Germany! This being the state of feeling as regards his compact with the ultramontanes, it is not very surprising that the proposal to give him an honorary degree does not meet with universal approval."

I then asked about the Old Catholics in Munich. They have lately been turned out of the little church on the Gasteig, which was granted to them by the town council ten years ago. The ultramontanes have recently got a majority in the council also; and one of the first things which they did was to turn the Old Catholics out of this building of which the town council has the control. It is not pretended that this little church is wanted for any other purpose: the sole motive is to dislodge the 'heretics'. The poor outcasts, Dr. Döllinger said, had not yet found a resting place. The government is neutral : it has nothing to give and nothing to refuse. At present negociations are going on for sharing the room in the Odeon which for some years has been occupied by the Anglican congregation; but there are considerable difficulties in the way. The English chaplain here derives part of his income from the congregation, and part of it from some Low Church Society in England. He cannot do anything without consulting both bodies; and as the chief members of his congregation are away for the summer, it will be a long time before he can sound them as to their views on the subject.

After some talk about books we got up to go,—it being arranged that I should call for him for a walk at 6.30. He asked us to try to arrange to return from the Tyrol by way of Tegernsee, so as to see him again there. As usual, he spends his holiday at Villa Arco; but this year he expects to be there only about three weeks. He thinks of spending the autumn in Munich and bringing out an enlarged edition of his recent address on the *Policy of Louis XIV*. His essay on the *Persecutions of the Jews* is to be published also. Hitherto nothing but newspaper reports of either have appeared. 83

At 6.30 he took me as almost invariably into the English Garden, and we walked to the lake and round it. He walked slowly and did not seem to know his way about among the multitudinous paths as well as of old. He had just been reading Lavelaye's book, which he said 84 interested him much. "But," he added, "Liberals are very much in the dark as to the internal working of the Roman Curia. They don't come in contact with any one who belongs to it. Gregorovius, who of course lives much in Rome, was talking to me not long ago, and I was asking him some questions about ecclesiastical matters in Rome; but he stopped me saying, 'I don't know anything about it. I know none of that party,—neither cardinal nor prelate.' But I don't suppose that anything is being done in the way of reform. It is doubtful whether the present Pope has any very earnest wish for reform; and, if he has, he finds himself tied hand and foot. Pius IX. was Pope for more than a quarter of a century, and he has filled every place with his own creatures." I suggested that he might strengthen his own hands gradually by appointing cardinals who would be willing to work with him in the direction of reform. "No," said Dr. Döllinger, "even that is scarcely possible. Precedent is so strong, that he has very little choice as to the persons whom he will make cardinals. There are men who have received their first steps of promotion from his predecessor, whom it is hardly possible for him to pass over. He almost *must* make them cardinals when their turn comes. And when by rare exception a foreigner is made cardinal, he is not brought to Rome, and so has no influence there. Hergenröther is an instance the other way; but the experiment has not been a very encouraging one. The Pope wanted a man of learning as Keeper of the Archives, and brought him to Rome. He is an ex-Jesuit, having left the Society, — I suppose, because of some internal quarrel. But he has had a stroke of apoplexy and is now paralysed down one side."

The mention of Hergenröther suggested the case of Theiner to me, and I asked whether anything was being done about the publication of Theiner's papers. To my dismay Dr. Döllinger answered, "They have disappeared. We have at last ascertained that they have got into the hands of the Roman Curia, and we can trace them no further. They were last in the hands of a countryman of the Bishop of Croatia (Why did Dr. Döllinger use this periphrasis?), who had got into disgrace with the Curia, and had been deprived of his ecclesiastical honours. He was one of the *Prelati*, or something of that sort. As a punishment for his offences he was forbidden to wear his red stockings or any other insignia of his rank. But as he had possession of Theiner's papers, he was told that he might be restored to his rank and position if he would give them up; and he consented to this bargain. It is about
85 a year or more since we ascertained this." Dr. Döllinger did not seem to think the loss so calamitous as I did. Possibly he doubted whether Theiner knew what was best worth copying in the Roman Archives, or whether he had *honestly* copied what he had extracted. There was a suspicion that he had garbled the extracts. Theiner's published letters
86 do not exhibit him as a cool-headed scientific scholar.

Along with this bad news Dr. Döllinger gave me some more of a better kind. Bishop Reinkens had been in Munich some weeks before, holding a confirmation, and of course had been with Dr. Döllinger. The bishop seemed to be well satisfied with the condition of things among the Old Catholics. By being sufficiently cautious he gets very good priests to work under him. But he has to be *very* cautious. Sometimes he has to reject five or six in succession of those who wish to join him. He finds out that there is some stain upon their character, and that their desire to become Old Catholics has been preceded by their getting into trouble as Roman Catholics. A new cause has always to guard against disreputable recruits.

Dr. Döllinger asked about the Revised Version, which he had not seen. He expressed surprise at letters in the *Guardian* complaining of the deletion of the text about the Three Heavenly Witnesses; "because, if anything is certain in Biblical criticism, it is certain that that text is spurious." I said that the Editor would have done better if he had refused to insert such letters; but that more scholarly objections had been urged against "Deliver us from the evil *one*". "Ah," said Dr. Döllinger, "that is a change which I should not have made. I believe that as far as the language goes the words mean that; but for various reasons I should not have made the change."

During the latter part of our walk, which lasted about 2 1/4 hours, we talked of the 'anti-Semitic' outrages in Germany and the causes of the outburst. When we parted at his door at 8.45 he would not say more than "Goodbye *for the present*:" he hoped to see us again on our way homewards either at Tegernsee or at Munich; for he expected to be home again before the end of August. But when we returned from the Dolomites August 27th, we found that he had not yet left Tegernsee, and his housekeeper expected that he would now remain there till the beginning of September.

1883

Saturday, August 11th. Dr. Döllinger had told us by letter that he should perhaps have left Munich before we arrived there; but in that case we were to come on to Tegernsee, where Lord Acton would be very glad to see us again. We found his rooms closed and being cleaned, when we called, and we were told by a voice inside that he had gone.

Friday, September 14th. We called again on our return from the Tyrol and this time found him at home. He told us that the party at Villa Arco had been smaller than usual this summer. Neither the old Countess nor Lady Acton was there. Two years ago Lady Acton lost a favourite daughter there of scarlet fever, and since then has not been able to endure the thought of returning to Tegernsee. Lord Acton and the children were there with Dr. Döllinger until the 25th and then went off to Marienbad for his health. Till the end of August Dr. Döllinger had the Villa to himself, and then returned home to his work. He looked exceedingly well, and not at all older than he did a year ago. He does not look at all like eighty-four. His hair is still very far from being entirely white. He told us that we had just missed Père Hyacinthe and his wife, who had been visiting him only a few days before. "He has great journeys in prospect. He proposes making a tour in the United States with a view to gaining sympathy, and also to Constantinople, with a view to promoting the reunion of the Churches. I tried to pour a little water into his wine as regards the latter project. Whatever hopes there may be of awakening a desire for reunion with the West in the Eastern Churches (and to tell the truth I do not think that there is room for very great hopes just at the present time), Hyacinthe is certainly not the man to effect much in that direction. He would have every Oriental prejudice against him. A monk who has broken his vows and married would not gain much of a hearing. And moreover," continued Dr. Döllinger with a twinkle in his eye, "his wife is to accompany him on this errand, and does not for a moment doubt that she will be very useful." I asked him what Hyacinthe thought of his work in Paris. "He is fairly satisfied with it. He has a congregation of 1200 or 1500. But he does not make any secret of the fact that a good many of these come out of mere curiosity and not to worship. The fact is that in France also he is at a disadvantage. French women think it a revolting thing that a priest should be married. Even unbelieving Frenchmen think the marriage of the clergy very indecent." I suggested that this might arise out of the low view of marriage which prevails in France. "Very possibly that has something to do with it. But you will find that, in all countries where the Reformation had made some progress and then was beaten back again, as of course was the case in France, there a very strong prejudice is pretty sure to exist against the marriage of the clergy. A married clergy is an element in the Reformation which has often proved a great stumbling block to people who were otherwise inclined to the teaching of the Reformers." I observed that the Paris correspondent of the *Guardian* (who had been calling on Dr. Döllinger) was very much opposed to Père Hyacinthe. "Yes, he spoke to me about that. He said that he felt it to be his duty to let people know what seemed to be the true state of the case, in order to prevent generous and credulous people in England from giving money and influence to an undertaking which did not seem to have any hope of success."

We did not stay long. It was arranged that I should come back at four o'clock for a walk and that B. should join us at six o'clock for tea. Punctually at four o'clock I was there again. I asked Dr. Döllinger what he thought of the recent letter of the Pope to Cardinals de Luca, Pitra, and Hergenröther, expressing indignation at the way in which history is now taught to the discredit of the Papacy and the temporal power of the Pope, and offering to open the Papal Archives to any earnest searcher after truth, who will there find clear evidence of the benefits which Popes have conferred on the world[26]. Dr. Döllinger said that "it certainly is a very remarkable document. It is something new for the Papacy to appeal to the unadulterated springs of history." On the whole he was inclined to think that the appeal was made at least with a certain amount of good faith. Indeed it might be entirely in good faith. The Professor of Ecclesiastical History at Marburg had 87 recently called on him after a visit to Rome, and he said that he certainly had been treated with a good deal of liberality in the investigation of the Papal Archives, though not in the Library. "In the Archives anything that he asked for he was allowed to have and to keep by him and to make extracts from. So that this looks as if the throwing open of the Archives to scholars was intended to be a reality." I suggested that perhaps the Archives had been previously weeded of all that could compromise the Papacy[27]. "No, I don't believe

26. One passage in the very long letter to the cardinals runs thus : "We have already disposed that, in favour of religion and science, free use may be made of our Archives; and to-day we likewise decree that, for the execution of the above-named studies, the use of the Vatican Library, with all the advantages it may offer, be conceded for that purpose. We do not doubt, beloved sons, that the authority of your office and the fame of your personal merit will gather around you learned men well practised in historic study and the art of writing, to whom, according to their capacity, you might assign their task according to a plan to be submitted to our approval." It is dated Aug. 18th, 1883. 88

27. A correspondent of the *Frankfurter Zeitung* afterwards wrote to say that he had ascertained from a competent source that all documents of a compromising character had disappeared from the Archives. Some had been hidden in secret lockers; some sent out of Rome.

that that has been done; nor did my informant think so either. What he asked for was given him without question. But he *had* to ask for it. He had to know that it was there. There are no catalogues into which you can look to see what is there. But if you know that something which you need is in the Archives and can tell the custodians exactly what it is, they will let you have it to make any reasonable use of. No; I am inclined to believe that the Pope really thinks what he says; really believes that history will be found to support the claims of the Curia and to prove the Papacy to have been all that he asserts it to have been. He knows no history : no Italian ecclesiastic does. They have no opportunity of studying it. History in any comprehensive sense of the term is the last thing that an Italian studies. Until the present generation there was no such thing as an Universal History written by an Italian. The Inquisition made it impossible to possess the materials for writing such a work. Cantu's is the first attempt; and he is still living. So that the Pope, in his ignorance of what history really does tell about the Papacy, may seriously believe that the contents of the Papal Archives will do much to rehabilitate the Popes in the eyes of the world. I don't know whether I ever told you[28] the story of Pius IX. in the early stages of the Vatican Council. It was not until then that he became aware of the difficulty about Pope Honorius. He knew nothing about it. When he was told about it he exclaimed, 'It is untrue; it cannot be true. Send to the Archives and say that I desire that search be made for the original documents. It will then be found that the whole story is false.' The poor man actually did not know that the Archives do not go back further than Innocent III. The series begins with the year 1198; and he was going to appeal to the Archives for evidence about Honorius! The present Pope, without being so naively ignorant as that, may very possibly believe that the Archives will glorify the policy of the Popes. As to the composition of the letter, his brother, whom he sometimes employs in such cases, may have written it; but I believe it to express the Pope's own sentiments. The brother is supposed to be of a liberal turn of mind; and his having left the Order of the Jesuits looks as if there was some truth in the supposition. It is worth noting that the three cardinals are representative of three nations, Italy, France, and Germany. Pitra is French; Hergenröther of course is German. But these two, as Keepers of the Archives and of the Library, *must* have been addressed in a letter of such a character : so the representation of nations may be accidental. At any rate the letter will be a help to scholars who will now be able to put pressure upon the Pope through their Consul or other representative in Rome. A Consul will now be able to write to the Pope and say, 'These gentlemen have come to Rome by the invitation of your

28. In 1872; p. 50.

Holiness to study at the Vatican. They find endless difficulties placed in their way by the librarians, difficulties of which I am sure that your Holiness only needs to be informed in order to ensure their entire removal.'"

We walked round the little lake at Klein-Hessellohe and then turned homewards. Dr. Döllinger said more than once, "We must hasten our steps, or we shall be keeping Mrs. Plummer waiting for us;" but the hastening did not come to much. That is the chief way in which his age seems to tell : he cannot walk otherwise than slowly. We got on to the subject of S. John. Dr. Döllinger does not think that the 2nd and 3rd Epistles are by the Apostle, and considers it very improbable that the Apostle would call himself 'the Elder'. He believes in the existence of the Presbyter John, and thinks that the Eusebian interpretation of the famous passage in Papias is not only the right one, but the only reasonable one; — that the ἕτερος entirely excludes the possibility of the John who is coupled with Aristion being the same as the John who in the previous sentence is joined with Matthew, Thomas, Philip, etc. He considers that the evidence of the Muratorian Canon respecting the authorship of the Fourth Gospel has not been sufficiently attended to, and that (whatever that evidence may be worth) it is very adverse to the Apostolic authorship; for it is highly improbable that the author of the Canon would write 'cohortantibus condiscipulis et episcopis suis' of the Apostle. The writer must mean some other John, and probably the Presbyter[29]. Again, the probability that a Galilean fisherman would acquire sufficient command of Greek to write so completely like a Hellenistic Jew, as does the author of the Fourth Gospel, seems to him to be too hastily assumed. Dr. Döllinger quite admits the *possibility* of his doing so, and allows that in the Revelation we may have an earlier attempt at writing Greek, before the Apostle had mastered the language; but this possibility hardly amounts to a probability. Once more, theologians and painters have too hastily assumed that none but Apostles were present at the Last Supper. We know that disciples who were not Apostles were present at some of the appearances of the Lord after the Resurrection. May they not also have been present at the Last Supper? If so, then the possibility that 'the disciple whom Jesus loved', and 'who leaned back on His breast' at the Supper, may be some other disciple than the Apostle John, becomes considerably increased. May not this unnamed disciple be the Presbyter John? It is worth noting also that some of the earliest witness-

---

29. *Quarti evangeliorum Iohannis ex decipolis cohortantibus condescipulis et eps̄ suis dixit conjejunate me.* etc. Credner thinks that the Canon distinguishes between John a *disciple*, who wrote the Gospel and 1st Epistle, and John an *Apostle*, who wrote Revelation and the 2nd and 3rd Epistles. But *Johannes ex discipulis* may be a phrase to *90* distinguish him from the Baptist.

es, e.g. Irenaeus, do not say in so many words that the John who wrote the Gospel was the Apostle : they speak of him simply as John, or as the disciple who leaned on Jesus' breast, and the like[30]. That by these indications the writer in each case intends to mark the *Apostle* S. John is a meaning which has been assumed : it has been read into the words rather than found there. In short Dr. Döllinger seems to incline to the view that the author of the Fourth Gospel is indeed the beloved disciple, and that his name was John; yet that he was not the Apostle, but some other John, and very possibly the Presbyter. To him, therefore, would have to be assigned the Gospel and the three Epistles, only the Apocalypse being reserved for the Apostle. Dr. Döllinger is not satisfied that the XXIst chapter of the Gospel is by the author of the first XX chapters. No doubt it may be an appendix by the original writer; and Dr. Döllinger can remember the time when he was quite content to accept and give such explanations. But further acquaintance with the shifty devices of ecclesiastics and theologians has made him more 'lynx-eyed' (to use his own expression) respecting such things. I spoke to him of Zahn's desire to abolish the

91 Presbyter John altogether. Dr. Döllinger said that he distrusted Zahn and always read him on the defensive. Zahn always seemed to be writing with a motive : it was not disinterested search for truth that one got from him. "And then his method is so arbitrary. If evidence did not suit him, he dogmatically set it on one side. What could be more arbitrary than his treatment of the Muratorian Canon respecting

92 the Shepherd of Hermas?"

We reached his house somewhat late, B. having been waiting for us over a quarter of an hour; which meant that we had been walking for over two hours, which is a good long time for a man of eighty-four. It was amusing to see Dr. Döllinger's disgust at finding that his housekeeper had filled the table so full of plates, dishes, cups, etc., that there was no room for *books* on it. He wanted to look out the exact words of the passages of Papias and of the Muratorian Fragment, about which we had been talking. He remarked by the way that Ewald's arguments to show that the words of the Fragment are *not* adverse

93 to the Apostolic authorship "would satisfy no reasonable person."

94 He spoke very highly of the *Dictionary of Christian Biography* as far as it goes at present, and assented when I said that I thought it superior to Herzog and Plitt. He said that the stride made in English theological learning during the last half century was gigantic : Germany could show nothing at all equal to it. I told him that my father would be sure to be asking me when his Essay on the Templars was coming out. "Does he take an interest in the subject? I have been all over the Acts

95   30. Theophilus of Antioch : ἐξ ὧν Ἰωάννης λέγει· ἐν ἀρχῇ ἦν ὁ λόγος.

and Processes in the trials of the Templars a second time, and I am
more than ever convinced of their innocence of the charges brought
against them. Of course there were bad men among them; but the
Order as a whole was innocent of the crimes for which it was condemned.
During this second reading I have seen much more clearly than I did
at first how shockingly the Pope behaved in the whole matter. He was
willing to commit any injustice at the dictation of the King of France.
Clement was completely in the hands of Philip, and Philip could make
him do what he pleased. The Templars were most cruelly treated."
Dr. Döllinger went on to say that his publishers had written to him
to tell him that the second edition of the *Papstfabeln des Mittelalters*
was just at an end and that a new one was wanted. "I have accumulated
such a quantity of new material since the last edition came out, that,
if I republish, I shall have practically to write a new book."   96

Before we took leave of him he gave the new edition of Meyer's
Commentary on the Fourth Gospel largely rewritten by B. Weiss, and 97
also Weiss's *Leben Jesu*, which Dr. Döllinger thinks is the best *Life* 98
of Christ in German literature at the present time. He had not only
procured them for me but had had them bound for me in the same
style as he has many of his own books bound. I thanked him heartily
for them and carried them back in triumph to Leinfelder's. Next day
we started for England.

CONVERSATIONS WITH DR. DÖLLINGER

Volume IV

Particulars of his Death

1886

In 1884 and 1885 we did not visit either Munich or Tegernsee and consequently did not see our kind friend. In 1886 I had to travel without my wife, and I went direct to Bavaria.

Monday, July 12th. Dr. Döllinger's housekeeper gave me a hearty welcome, but he himself had gone to Starnberg for the day with Lady Blennerhasset. I met one or two of the trains in the evening, but failed to catch sight of him.

Tuesday, July 13th. After breakfast I found Dr. Döllinger at home, and looking as well preserved as ever. Indeed I think he looks younger than when we saw him last in 1883. He is eighty-seven, and he looks barely seventy. He has all his faculties, but is growing a little deaf in his right ear. He is keenly interested in English affairs and thinks Gladstone's policy with regard to the Irish question "one of the most extraordinary delusions ever seen in a statesman. It is so perfectly *1* evident that whatever power is granted to an Irish Parliament will be used to make the separation between the two countries more complete." Dr. Döllinger is convinced that "fear, and even *personal* fear," has a great deal to do with Gladstone's change of front, and that Mrs. Gladstone uses all her influence, which is very great, to induce her husband to adopt measures which will secure her husband from assassination. In this matter he believes that Gladstone is much under the influence of women. Moreover, "he has sunk down to the level of a mere demagogue : this attempt to set 'the masses' against 'the classes' is a common demagogue's trick." Dr. Döllinger also thought it quite true to say that Gladstone has become very sophistical. He added that Malcolm MacColl assures him that Gladstone is anxious to give up politics and devote himself to theology. It seems that he is to be the editor of the new edition of Palmer's *History of the Church*, about which Dr. *2* Döllinger has been several times consulted, and with respect to the execution of which he has made various suggestions. Dr. Döllinger said that all this tended to show that Gladstone is not so bent on retaining office as some people suppose. I replied that Gladstone might feel all that and mean all that, when he said it; and he had been saying it for the last fifteen years; but as soon as ever he had had a few weeks rest, his fingers itched to be in the midst of it all again. Dr. Döllinger laughed and said that he thought that that was very likely to be true.

He asked about my little sketch of the second and third centuries in the *Church of the Early Fathers*, and we had some talk about one or two points belonging to that period of ecclesiastical history. Dr. Döllinger is still convinced that the Muratorian Fragment is to be dated about A.D. 170 or earlier, and that the Shepherd of Hermas is of the date which the work itself indicates (A.D. 130-150). He does not at all believe in Bishop Lightfoot's proposal to identify 3 Caius with Hippolytus, and thinks that Caius is the earlier of the two. On the whole he is inclined to believe Jerome's statement that the presbyters of Alexandria ordained the bishop. Why should one suppose that Jerome is making a false statement in asserting this? There was no motive for a falsehood; and what he asserts is supported by later evidence. Dr. Döllinger does not think that episcopacy became universal in the Church until about the middle of the second century; but in some places, as in Asia Minor, it was certainly of Apostolic origin. He is convinced that the Angels of the Churches in the Apocalypse are bishops, and is disposed to adopt the earlier date for the Apocalypse, — which makes episcopacy in this form very early. He is still rather inclined to believe that the Apocalypse is by S. John the Apostle, but that the beloved disciple who wrote the Fourth Gospel is not the Apostle but another John.

While we were talking, a pamphlet was brought in;—*Der Episcopat in den drei ersten christlichen Jahrhunderten*, Toepliz und Deuticke,—a 4 present from the author, whose name was Winterstein. Dr. Döllinger at once lent it to me and I read a good deal of it in the course of the day, for I did not feel inclined to do much. He did not know anything of the author, and I am afraid that I did him no good by perusing his treatise; for when I reported to Dr. Döllinger what the drift of it was, he said, "Then I shall not read it: one has more than enough of that kind of thing from Harnack and his school." Dr. Döllinger also gave me several articles which he has been writing on *Die einflussreichste Frau der französischen Geschichte*—viz. Ma-5 dame de Maintenon, the wife of Louis XIV. "No woman," he remarked, "has ever had more influence on Church affairs; and that is why I have thought it worth while to write about her. There are some points in her history not generally known, which required to be pointed out." Her *bona fide* marriage to the king is one of these. But the whole essay is of immense interest and leaves one with very mixed feelings about her tragic career, constantly failing to move her husband, when she was certainly right, and not unfrequently succeeding when her advice, although well meant, was disastrous.

I went to Dr. Döllinger again at half past five for a walk in the Englischer Garten. He then gave me some particulars about the late King Ludwig II., whose suicide in the Starnberg lake caused such a sensation throughout Europe a few weeks ago. "The prevailing opinion," said Dr. Döllinger, "—and I agree with it myself,—is that the king had determined to destroy himself, and took the opportunity, when he was alone with his physician, to do so. He probably went first into the lake, and then was seized by the physician, who went in after him. The king was a very powerful man, the physician rather a weak one. The king held the head of the latter under water until he was unconscious, and then went out into deeper water and drowned himself. But we shall never know exactly what took place. The lower orders were slow to believe in his madness. When he met any of them in his rambles, he used to stop and say a few words to them. 'The masses' (to adopt Gladstonian language) know nothing of a man being partly sane and partly mad. That 'the classes' can understand, but not 'the masses'. Many of the peasants could tell from their own experience that the king talked sensibly enough; and so they believed that he was not mad at all. That gentleman who just passed us is a Staatsrath, a Counsellor of State. He was with the king for more than six years; and he has told me of a great many extraordinary sayings and doings of the king, which prove that at times he was quite mad, even when he first came to the throne. He was sometimes very violent and inflicted serious injury on persons with whom he was enraged. These things have been suppressed; but there can be no doubt that before now people have died from the treatment which they have received from him, — kicks in the stomach, and the like. He had long lucid intervals, in which he was quite reasonable; but of late these became shorter and the attacks more violent. Of late years he kept everyone but people of the lowest rank at a distance from him. He never saw a minister — never. He allowed no educated person to come near him. He knew that he was insane, and he was afraid of being found out. With the lower orders he thought that he was safe : people of education would detect the signs of madness in him. Yet he transacted all business quite properly. All state affairs had to pass through his hands; and he always signed the necessary documents. He never would see a physician, for the same reason as made him keep away from good society. He feared the discovery of his malady. When he had anything the matter with him, he would tell a servant his pains and other symptoms and order him to go to a doctor and tell him that he (the servant) had these symptoms; and in this way he would get advice and medicine. I was at Berg yesterday, where the king ended his life, and saw something which I had never seen before — the chapel which he had had built there for his own use. It was very characteristic. It had room for just *two* people : — the priest, of course, and the king. There was a little space about the altar, and the king's seat and kneeling-stool filled up all the rest. But the king himself was an infidel, and had been so for years. A long time ago some one lent him the works of Feuerbach, and they made a great impression on him, which he never got over.

He took no interest in religious matters. Only once have I known him show any curiosity about a religious question. He once sent to ask me what I thought of a particular *Life of Christ*. I have forgotten the writer's name : he was a Swiss, a Professor at Zurich. Though he did not go so far as Strauss, yet he rejected the Fourth Gospel; and so I told the king that I thought that there were other works on the subject more worthy of his attention. The physicians are of opinion that, if he had lived, he would have become as insane as his brother, the present king, who has for years been quite incapable."

I asked whether there had been any ceremony of state, when Prince Otto succeeded to the Crown. "It was merely announced to him that he was now king; but he took hardly any notice beyond appearing to be a little pleased at his new dignity. It is said that a slight look of gratification sometimes crosses his features, when he hears himself addressed as 'Your Majesty'; but that is all. He takes very little notice of anything. The Prince Regent Luitpold is very popular. The ultramontanes will not gain much by grumbling at him. They hoped for a change of government at the death of the king; but the Prince Regent at once announced his intention of making no changes."

Dr. Döllinger returned to the subject of female influence upon Gladstone. He said that he knew Mrs. Gladstone and one of her daughters, and he was sure that their fears had a great deal to do with the Premier's policy about Ireland. He laughed at Manning's amazing audacity in asserting that Roman Catholics have never persecuted Protestants in the past, and therefore are not likely to do so in the future. "One of the first things that the Irish Parliament would do would be to take possession of Trinity College, Dublin, and turn it into a Roman Catholic University." In connexion with this I pointed out to him the enormous majority for the Unionist candidates at Dublin University, in spite of there being Roman Catholics in the constituency. Under the secrecy of the ballot the Roman Catholics appeared to have voted against Home Rule, which they knew would be fatal to the University as well as to Ireland.

Dr. Döllinger told me a strange story, which he had heard on good authority from Liddon, and which for obvious reasons could not be published. Put very briefly, it comes to this. There are two Patriarchs at Alexandria, one Coptic, the other Melchite, one Monophysite, the other Orthodox. Negociations went on between them, and there was a fair prospect of this ancient schism being healed. An English political agent got wind of it and pointed out to the English government that the healing of the schism would increase the influence of Russia. Orders came from England that he was to endeavour to stop the negociations. As the best means of doing so he told the Pasha. The Pasha made very short work of it. He invited the Coptic Patriarch to an interview, and the invitation was accepted. At the interview the usual cup of coffee was offered to the visitor. It was poisoned; and with the death of the Coptic Patriarch the whole thing came to an end [1].   7

"Talking of Liddon," said Dr. Döllinger, "it would be a good thing if he would put a few critical drops into his orthodox wine." I replied that I thought that he had never been able quite to free himself from the influence of Dr. Pusey. "That is just it," said Dr. Döllinger; "it is Pusey's influence." "He himself said to me," I replied, "that he never quite liked to own it to himself, when he found himself differing from Dr. Pusey." "But in these days one must look facts in the face, and not ignore them, or force them to agree with one's own ideas."

In connexion with the Greek Church I asked him how their parish priests were appointed. He replied, "The congregations elect them. They choose their man and get him ordained. I heard of a case in which the man who was elected could not read the liturgy. This was the cause of the breach between Bulgaria and the Patriarchate of Constantinople : the Patriarch used to compel the people to accept Greek clergy who did not even know the Bulgarian language; and at last they would stand it no longer. The Patriarch of Jerusalem took their side."

It was a quarter to eight when we reached Dr. Döllinger's door. We had been walking, without once sitting down, for three hours and a quarter. I don't know whether he was tired : I know that I was. But he still commonly walks for two hours or more daily, or at least very frequently. I was glad to sit on the pedestal of the old King Ludwig's statue in the Odeon Platz, and wait for a tram to take me home.

Wednesday, July 14th. At one o'clock I was once more at Dr. Döllinger's to dine with him and his nieces. All the simple arrangements, which one knew so well, were repeated. And there were the dear old salt-cellars in the form of swans, which I have known these fifteen years and more. As they are of china, it is a credit to his servants that the swans' necks have not been broken. Perhaps his housekeeper keeps them for "company". When dinner was over, something—I don't at all know what—went wrong as coffee was brought in. Dr. Döllinger held up both his hands in momentary surprise or anger. The housekeeper muttered something by way of excuse or explanation, and then all went on as before. The nieces looked uncomfortable, as if something awkward had happened, but what it was I have no notion. We talked a mixture of German and English, the latter language prevailing, although the nieces were a little shy of attempting it. One of the officials at the Royal Library (which is to Munich what the British Museum Library

1. Very much the same story was told to me in June 1890 by Bishop Smythies of Central Africa.

is to London) had told Dr. Döllinger that morning that the late King Ludwig had some 1500 volumes out of the Library at the time of his death, and these were now all scattered about in the different royal residences. The king never bought books. *That* was not the way in which he got so heavily into debt. When he wanted books he sent to the Royal Library for them; and those which he borrowed from it were chiefly works on Art and the History of the reign of Louis XIV., some of whose ideas and projects he was very fond of imitating. He was building a magnificent imitation of Versailles at Chiemsee, when he died. It will never be finished; but even in its present incomplete state it is said to be well worth a visit. The Castle of Berg, where he died, is not at all a magnificent place, but is quite simply — indeed almost meanly furnished. Lindenhof and Hohenschwangau are the two other residences on which he has squandered so much money. The royal income is some 4,000,000 or 5,000,000 marks — some £200,000 or more. The poor insane King Otto and the Prince Regent do not require nearly the whole of this income, and the surplus will be devoted to paying the late king's very heavy debts.

Dr. Döllinger commented on Cardinal Newman's silence respecting the Home Rule question. "It is not often that he allows a great subject like this to arise without expressing an opinion upon it." "I suspect that he agrees with you, Sir, about it, but does not like to say what he thinks." "But the Roman Catholic hierarchy in England generally have not made themselves heard so much of late years. Manning himself has become more cautious." "Perhaps he does not feel so sure of his ground with the present Pope as with Pius IX." Dr. Döllinger laughed. "With Pius IX. everything that Manning said was right. — The present Pope prides himself on having made things more sure by being less pronounced. He fancies that his moderation is causing the Roman Church to be more firmly established. It remains to be seen whether he is right in thinking this. I fancy he is rather a vain man." "But not so vain as his predecessor." "Oh, dear no," laughed the Doctor, "certainly not so vain as that."

He told me that a fair amount of use was being made of the facilities which the present Pope had given for consulting the Archives of the Vatican. One or two governments had sent scholars to investigate, and it would now be very difficult for the Curia to draw back and close the Archives again. It was probably fear which induced the Pope to yield this point. The Curia was afraid that the Italian government would seize the Vatican Library as belonging to the nation quite as much as to the Church. Now that it is thrown open to everybody, there is no such good pretext for depriving the Pope of it.

The two nieces retired directly after coffee had been served, and I left soon afterwards, Dr. Döllinger asking me to call for him again

at six for one more walk. He had letters to write and would not be ready
much before then. I had writing to do also, and remained indoors until
it was time to go to him again. Directly we started he began asking
me about theological colleges in England, wether there were such
things, and what handbooks of dogmatic theology were used in them.
I told him that we had a good many such colleges; but one could
hardly say that such a thing as an English handbook of dogmatic
theology existed. The translations of Osterzee and Martensen were used. 8
Dr. Döllinger said that the former's work was a poor production;
the latter's writings were held in much estimation throughout Germany.
Besides these the work of Frank of Erlangen on *Christliche Gewissheit*
was much esteemed in South Germany and that of Dorner in the
North. The former was rather technical, the latter more free and liberal. 9
Dr. Döllinger expatiated on the "inconvenience" (i.e. grave evil) of
having no recognized work on dogmatics in England. The want of
stability in the teaching of the clergy is the consequence. In any question
that is at all out of the common track, the clergy, who ought to be
leaders, are waverers. They do not know what has been taught in the
Church in former times on the subject. They do not know whether
certainty, or anything like certainty, is attainable on the point, whether
Scripture gives any clue to a solution, and so forth. This places the
English Church at a great disadvantage, especially in relation to dissenters. This great defect ought to be remedied. He spoke much on
this subject, and pointed out how such a book ought to be written, —
in the main *historically*. The danger in writing such handbooks was
that the authors were tempted to close questions which ought to be
left open, because from the nature of the case no certainty was attainable,
and because the general consensus of the Church had been different
at different times. He gave as instances of such open questions the fall
of Satan : was it through pride or not? and the nature of Angels : have
they an etherial body, or are they pure spirit? On both these questions
the teaching of the medieval theologians still continues to hold its
ground at the present day, although it is quite different from the teaching
of the earliest Fathers of the Church; and certainly the medieval view
that Satan fell through pride, and that Angels have nothing analogous
to a body but are pure spirit, has no support from Scripture.

Dr. Döllinger also asked whether the ranks of the clergy were well
supplied with men. I said, on the whole, yes. Some incumbents found
a difficulty in obtaining curates, but as a rule men could be found
for the places that could be paid. What was wanted was more money
to pay more men. I asked him the same question with regard to Germany.
He replied that in the Roman Church there were many vacant places.
Some parishes had no priest. In others, in which there used to be one
or two curates, now there was none; the incumbent had to do all the

work himself. I asked whether this was owing to want of money or want of men. "Oh! want of men : there is no want of money. Any young man who will take Orders is forthwith provided for. Indeed as soon as he enters the Knaben-seminar — the boys-school for candidates for Orders — he has nothing further to care about as regards money. His career is secure. The intellectual requirements are not great and he is almost certain to pass the examinations. It is a common saying in Bavaria — at least in South Bavaria, — that a man, when he has become a priest, never opens a book again. He reads his newspaper, — of course a clerical one, — and that is his Gospel. That is all he knows. And he likes it well peppered — well peppered. He doesn't care for temperate language. His peppery newspaper is what he believes and talks and preaches[2]."

2. Deutscher Merkur – June 7. 1890 :
"MÜNCHEN. Die 'Köln. Ztg.' vom 22. Mai bringt unter der Ueberschrift 'Der Kampf der niedern gegen die höhere Geistlichkeit' einen Artikel über die klerikalen Zustände in Bayern, welcher die thatsächlichen Verhältnisse durchaus richtig gibt und recht instruktiv ist, wenn man hiebei nicht übersieht, daß diese klerikale Demagogie durch Rom und die Jesuiten behufs Durchführung des Unfehlbarkeitsdogmas gegen die nicht unters kaudinische Joch sich begeben wollenden Bischöfe eigens gezüchtet, gehätschelt und gefördert wurde und bis zum heutigen Tage die mächtigste Stütze der kurialpapistischen Politik bildet. Nicht mit den Bischöfen, nur mit dieser klerikalen Demagogie war und ist der Papalismus durchführbar. Wie im politischen Leben Demagogie und Cäsarismus einander auf die Beine helfen, so auch im kirchlichen. Eine Aristokratie, wie sie im Episkopat repräsentiert ist, kann nur wahrhaft wirken und gedeihen auf monarchischem Boden und sie verkümmert unter der Demagogie wie unter dem Cäsarismus. Wer also eine Heilung der nachfolgend geschilderten kirchlichen Zustände in Bayern bezielt, muß sich vor allem darüber klar sein, daß die Wurzel des Uebels im buchstäblichen Sinne ultramontan ist und tief im Nährboden des 18. Juli 1870 ruht. Hic Rhodus, hic salta! Es ist also ganz falsch, wenn die K. Z. meint, daß schon durch die Worte des Prinzregenten an den Erzbischof von München den besonnenen maßvollen obern kirchlichen Behörden ein Sieg über die erbitterten, verbissenen und verhetzenden Elemente des niedern Klerus
10 gelungen sei. Die Zukunft wird das Gegenteil lehren. Um den Jesuitismus zu besiegen, bedarf's schärferer Waffen. Und nun, wie sieht's in Bayern aus? Die K. Z. schreibt :
'Im Laufe der 50er und 60er Jahre wußte die niedere Geistlichkeit sich in den Diözesen Bayerns, namentlich auf dem Lande, einen fast uneingeschränkten Einfluß in ihren Gemeinden zu verschaffen, der auf alle Gebiete des staatlichen und kommunalen Lebens sich ausdehnte. In dieser Zeit schuf die niedere Geistlichkeit eine wirksame Waffe gegen ihre Gegner, die heute noch in Bayern so verderblich wirkende kleine ultramontane Presse. In den Städten und Städtchen aller Diözesen wuchsen sogenannte katholische Blätter, durch den Einfluß der geistlichen Leiter und Mitarbeiter sofort lebensfähig, aus dem Boden heraus; in ihnen bereiteten Pfarrer und Kapläne jene geistlose, mit groben Kraftausdrücken gepfefferte Kost, die heute noch die geistige Nahrung der Mehrzahl der Katholiken Bayerns bildet. Der Weizen dieser Presse blühte, als der Kulturkampf in Preußen kam; da konnten die Preßkapläne ungefährdet außerhalb der preußischen Grenzpfähle gegen jede staatliche Autorität zu Felde ziehen. Damals vergiftete die hetzende klerikale Presse das ganze politische Leben in Bayern und legte den Grund zu den beklagenswerten Zuständen, die in den letzten Monaten in der bayrischen Kammer in so greller Beleuchtung zu Tage getreten sind.'"

From that Dr. Döllinger passed on to another clerical topic. "Is the practice of auricular confession as much advocated in England as it was in Dr. Pusey's lifetime? Here the 'inconvenience' of regular confession is very great. People go to confession quite mechanically, and commit the same sins again, and confess them again, and so on *ad infinitum*. Contrition is not insisted upon; and the person who confesses perhaps knows at the very moment of confession that in a few days, or perhaps hours, the very same sins will be committed again. In some cases it even happens that the prostitutes go to confession and still continue their sinful life. Although as a rule confession is required before communion, yet no one is ever refused communion for not having confessed, because it is always possible that the confession has been made to another priest. Only those who are publicly excommunicated are ever refused communion; and such persons are rare, and are not likely to present themselves at the altar." That was a pathetic remark as coming from him.

When we got back to his door again he said, "Now reflect on what I have been saying about a handbook of dogmatic theology. Write to me when you get home; and if you want a list of the best books, I will send one." And I did reflect, and came to the conclusion that this meant that Dr. Döllinger wanted *me* to undertake the writing of such a handbook. Coming from him it was a most flattering proposal. But it was too flattering: such a task seemed beyond my strength, and I could not bring myself to think seriously of undertaking it. The list of the best books on the subject I should dearly have liked to get—but not by promising to use it for the purpose for which it was offered.

Shortly before I left England to pay this visit to Dr. Döllinger I had a letter from him in which he wrote as follows respecting the policy of Gladstone's Home Rule scheme for Ireland (translation):—

"Gladstone is to me a riddle, which I can solve only on the supposition that he knows little of Irish history and still less of Irish national character and of the spirit of the Irish priesthood. If he succeeds, what a frightful legacy will he leave behind to the generations which come after him! It is indeed the most threatening crisis which has occurred in England during the present century. God grant that she may surmount it happily."

This letter arrived during the general election on the question. After thinking the matter over for a day or two I decided on sending the letter to the *Times*. While I was in Munich a correspondent of the London press called on Dr. Döllinger and interviewed him about this letter to me. In speaking to me about it afterwards he did not blame me for publishing the letter, but merely remarked that it might cause an awkwardness, a *Spannung*, between him and Gladstone. He spoke just as decidedly to the newspaper correspondent, knowing of course that whatever he said would be given to the world. This is the interviewer's account of what Dr. Döllinger said to him. "It would have been a calamity for England and for the entire civilized world, if Mr. Gladstone's Bill had passed. I have made a special study of Irish history and have always shown sympathy for Ireland, sharing the general indignation for the injustice with which England formerly treated that country. But, as regards the claims at present put forward by the Irish, they are inconsistent with England's sovereign dominion, and the fate of Ireland is of secondary importance compared to that dominion ... An Irish Parliament would not bring peace, but civil war. The Irish people should be asked which they prefer,— a Parliament of their own, or the possession of the land they live on,— and it would be seen that only the extreme element would ask for the former. The purchase of land by the government, and its distribution among the people is not feasible. The Irish must be content with a fair and equitable reform in the system of land tenure."

Some weeks after this Dr. Döllinger and Gladstone were together at Tegernsee and were able to have many talks on the subject. So far as I am aware neither of them succeeded in convincing the other. Döllinger knew too much of what Ireland had been in the past, especially what Roman Catholicism in Ireland had been in the past, to believe that both priests and people would entirely change their natures under the beneficent influences of Gladstone's Irish Parliament. Gladstone, who "can convince many men of many things and himself of almost anything," had too completely convinced himself that his policy is the only right one, to change again.

1889

Once more two years passed by without my seeing Dr. Döllinger. Neither in 1887 nor in 1888 did we go either to Munich or to Tegernsee. In February 1889 he reached the age of ninety and we made a point of going to Munich on purpose to visit him in July. We were greeted by two changes immediately. The old portier at Hotel Leinfelder is gone, not dead but retired to live with his daughter at Ratisbon. He was the last of the old staff of servants that was there when we first began to go to the hotel. And the Englisches Café—one of the best known places of entertainment in Munich for the last twenty or thirty years—is gone. And when we arrived at Dr. Döllinger's we found that his housekeeper, who had been with him for I know not how many years, is gone also. But everything else was unchanged. His familiar rooms looked the same as ever; and he himself is wonderfully unchanged; and he gave us his usual hearty greeting. For a man of ninety he is quite marvellous. His hair is still far from being quite white; his eye is as bright and as keen as ever; his hearing has improved; and though he stoops rather more than of old and has grown *very* spare in figure, he has full control of his limbs, and his mental faculties are still keen and active. He said that he was very well, excepting the remains of a cold; and for a man of ninety with remains of a cold about him he seemed to be very lightly clad. The weather is the reverse of summerlike —quite damp and chill. He had written to me a few weeks before, and told me that he was hard at work on Church history, and that he would give me particulars when we met. I now asked him for them. He is at the thirteenth century, and on a favourite subject of his, one upon which he has been at work off and on for many years,—the suppression of the Knights Templar. He has all along been persuaded of their innocence. He said that he is glad now that he has never published anything previously. Very important materials have in the last few years been published from the archives at Paris and at Rome, *11* giving very full particulars of the trials of the Templars in different parts of Europe and of the methods by which their condemnation was accomplished. Oddly enough the Roman materials have been published by the Pope's orders, who must have been in ignorance of what he was giving forth to the world, or he would never have caused such things to be dragged into light. They afford very full material for forming a judgment of Pope Clement V., and they are very damaging to his character. "I confess," said Dr. Döllinger, "that even I was not prepared to find his conduct so bad as it is proved to be." A good deal of this new material was published in Berlin in 1887 by Schottmüller

12 in his *Untergang des Templer-Ordens*. But unfortunately, Dr. Döllinger remarked, the book is not well arranged and moreover is spun out to three times the necessary length; so that it has not been very well received by the reading public. Yet the value of the new material,— obtained in a large measure with the help of the late Emperor of Germany when he was Crown Prince,—abides, in spite of the uninviting form in which it is presented. With this and the evidence derived from the Parisian archives the question can now be definitely settled to the satisfaction of any reasonable person. Years ago Dr. Döllinger believed that the innocence of the Templars, as regards the gross charges brought against the whole Order, was certain; i.e. he had demonstrated it to his own satisfaction. He now thinks that he is in a position to convince everyone that they were guiltless.

He said that he had just had a long letter from Gladstone. But Gladstone's letters take a great deal of deciphering, and as yet Dr. Döllinger had not brought himself to the state of mind necessary for grappling with the familiar difficulty, so that he was quite in ignorance as to what Gladstone had written to him. "Usually I read a letter from him once, and get a faint impression here and there as to what he is writing about. Then I read it a second time, and am able to make out most of it. At the third reading I am able to read it all, or nearly all."

I had brought Dr. Döllinger a copy of Bishop Lightfoot's *Essays on*
13 '*Supernatural Religion*', which came out shortly before I left Durham. He enquired after the bishop's health and was glad to learn that he was decidedly better. "That is important," was his brief comment; but it meant a good deal with him. When we took our leave, it was arranged that I should call for him at six o'clock for a walk. He had had one the day before and was thinking of taking another. That seems to be a way in which his great age is telling : his walks are becoming both less frequent and shorter.

Rain fell so frequently during the afternoon and the temperature was so low that I doubted whether Dr. Döllinger would venture upon a walk. However he did do so, and we started soon after six, keeping to the pavement all the way, and just making the circuit along the north edge of the English Garden, round the University buildings, and back by the Ludwigstrasse. He walks very slowly now, and this circuit of scarcely a mile took us nearly an hour. He enquired after Manning and Newman, remarking that they were keeping very quiet. He said that he had heard that Newman was losing his memory. He thinks that the talk about the Pope's leaving Rome is a mere diplomatic device; it is not a project that is seriously contemplated. To the Pope, and perhaps still more to the Curia, life outside Italy would be utterly intolerable. The Italian cardinals would use all their influence to prevent the Pope from migrating to Spain. Owing to correspondence of the

Duc de Gramont which has recently been published, it is now known *14*
that Pius IX. did at one time seriously think of leaving Rome, and
had actually ordered a steamer to come to Civita Vecchia to take
him away to some other part of Italy. The Duke did all he could to
dissuade him from the step, but could not induce the self-willed Pope
to yield. So then he quietly ordered that the engines of the steamer
which was waiting to take the Pope away should be removed; and
before they could be replaced and the steamer made ready for service,
Pius IX., who was as capricious as he was self-willed, had changed
his mind.

After Dr. Döllinger had told me this, I remarked that it was reported
that the late Pope had actually negociated with the English government,
with a view to taking up his residence at Malta. "Yes," Dr. Döllinger *15*
replied, "there were formal negociations; but it was never intended that
the Pope should really go. Just as in the fatal year 1870 there were
negociations with the Prussian government for the Pope's migrating
to Germany. Prussia was quite willing, and would have been glad to *16*
have him; but he would not come. Bismarck's opinion was that it would
be an excellent thing for German ultramontanes to come to close quarters
with the Pope and his cardinals. Then they would know from their
own experience what the Papal court is like; and the result could not
fail to be beneficial to Germany. That remark of his is recorded in
the extracts from the late Emperor's journal which were published by
Dr. Geffcken." "I suppose that the late Emperor really *intended* his *17*
diary to be published." "Oh dear no," said Dr. Döllinger; "not at all.
Geffcken told me so himself; and he now admits that he did wrong
in publishing them. The late Emperor allowed him to read the diary,
and he made extracts from it; but without any permission to make
them public. Geffcken has established himself in Munich; but he suffers
from insomnia, and the doctors have ordered him to go to the Lake
of Constance. *If* there is anything serious in the present proposal of
the Pope to leave Rome, it is the result of the recent erection of a
statue to the heretic Giordano Bruno. I don't think that the significance *18*
of that event has been properly recognized in England: it is really
immense. During all these centuries such a thing has never been heard
of; and down to the present year such a thing has never been even
possible. It marks in the most emphatic way the antagonism which
exists between the Italian laity and the Roman hierarchy. The Italians
know or suspect that the Pope and the Curia would like to see Italy
once more split up into a number of small kingdoms, and they will
not tolerate the idea of having the Italian kingdom destroyed. And
in this matter the large majority of the Italian clergy are with the
laity and against the Papal court. The condition of many of the country
clergy in Italy at the present time is a very cruel one."

I asked Dr. Döllinger whether he thought that there was any chance of the next Pope being other than an Italian. (At the present time there are 35 Italian cardinals and 30 foreign cardinals; several hats being vacant.) He replied that he believed there was not the least likelihood of such a thing as the election of a foreign cardinal. The next Pope would probably be the Cardinal de Valetta, who was a thorough ultramontane. There was no danger of a double election, even if the Pope should decide on the highly improbable step of migrating to Spain. The cardinals were pretty unanimous — i.e. a sufficient majority were so; and an election made by the cardinals in Spain would not be disputed by those who remained in Rome.

I asked a question about the bishopric of Münster, respecting which
19 a controversy is going on at the present time. He said that the dispute between the Church and the State on the question arose in this way. "The usual course is that the Chapter should submit a number of names to the government, and that the government should then strike out the names of those whom it would not like to see elected. The election is then made by the Chapter from the remainder. In the case of the see of Münster it is said that the government struck out so many names that the freedom of the election was destroyed. The end of the dispute will very likely be that the Pope will decide. These collisions between Church and State are endless both in Prussia and in Bavaria. We generally have one about once every quarter of a year. The government might say of the hierarchy what a Roman consul once said of women — 'It is impossible to live without them, and it is impossible to live with them'."

When we were in front of the palace of Prince Karl, which was specially richly decorated for the great Turn-fest which began in Munich that same evening, a country cleric, who evidently did not in the least know who Dr. Döllinger was, came up and asked a lot of questions in rather an off hand way; — what that building was, why it was decorated in that way, who Prince Karl was, and so forth. Dr. Döllinger answered all his questions very amiably, and the man went off to rejoin another cleric. I looked about for him afterwards, for I should have liked to have told him that he had been talking to the arch-heretic Döllinger : he would no doubt have been glad to know this himself. But there are said to be about 18,000 visitors in Munich at the present time, mainly on account of the Turn-fest; and to look for a particular person in the streets is very like looking for the proverbial "needle in a bundle of hay". The number of visitors is calculated in a very characteristic way, — by the amount of *beer* which has been consumed. Prince Karl, Dr. Döllinger said, is not in Munich at the present time. He is a remarkable person, for in spite of being a prince and cousin to the Regent, he practises as a physician and a surgeon and does a great deal of good.

Previous to this encounter with the brusque cleric we had been talking
of the authorship of the Fourth Gospel. Dr. Döllinger had had a letter
from Watkins in reference to his Bampton lectures which he showed
me, saying that he had not yet answered it. He wanted to know what
the subject of the Bamptons was to be. I told him that it was the Fourth
Gospel. Dr. Döllinger said that unless fresh evidence was discovered,
which of course was possible, the problem of authorship could never be
settled with absolute certainty. "The confusion between John the Apostle
and John the Presbyter in the earliest witnesses is so great and so
inextricable. As a rule one cannot be sure which of the two the writer
means, or whether he himself is not in error about it. The earliest
witness of all, the Muratorian Fragment, seems to give the Gospel to the
Presbyter : it says *ex discipulis*, not *ex apostolis*. Have you remarked
that?" He had himself pointed it out to me six years before. He still
holds firmly to the early date for the Muratorian Fragment and does
not at all believe in Dr. Salmon's suggestion that it may be placed
as late as A.D. 220. He also holds to the correspondingly early date 20
for the Shepherd of Hermas[3].

Before we parted he said, "My niece has promised me that there
shall be a good dinner to-morrow; so I hope that you will come and
dine with us at one o'clock. We shall be just among ourselves; — you
and Mrs. Plummer, my two nieces, and myself. I think that your
wife looks younger than ever : still quite like a girl." I told him that
we were still taken for bride and bridegroom at times when we were
travelling; and he said that he could quite believe it. He did not seem
to be at all over tired when we parted, and he wanted no aid in getting
up the stairs to the flat on which he has lived for so long. But even
one flight of stairs might well be trying to a man of his years.

Sunday, 6th after Trinity, July 28th. We spent part of the morning
in walking about and looking at the decorations, which were really
very fine and effective. But the weather was effective without being
fine, and we had to take refuge in the arcades of the Hofgarten before
going to dine with Dr. Döllinger and his nieces. Soon after we had
reached No. 11 and had sat down to have a little talk before dinner,
Dr. Döllinger said to me, "I have a great favour to ask of you. Are
you in a granting mood?" "I hope so," I replied. "Well, an English
lady wrote to me some time ago and asked leave to translate my

---

3. Dr. Döllinger wrote to Watkins a few days later (Aug. 5th), "I regard it as certain
that the Fragm. Muritorianum is to be placed in the period between 150 and 175, and
that the Pastor of Hermas falls in the period from 130 to about 150. This is moreover
the prevailing and best supported view among German theologians whether Catholic
or Protestant." See *Bampton Lectures* p. 45.

Akademische Vorträge." "I am very glad to hear it," I interposed. "Ah! that is favourable then so far. She has already translated a work by Professor Holzendorf, and he expresses himself as being well satisfied with her translation of his book. She has sent me a considerable portion of her translation of the *Vorträge* and has asked me to revise it. I do not like to refuse and I do not like to accept. It is not work for which I am at all fitted, and I really cannot well afford the time that it would take me. You would do it much better. There will be some wet days while you are at Schliersee, when you will be able to get something done. If you would undertake it for me, you would free me from a great burden." Of course I said that I would gladly undertake it; and I took possession of the manuscript, which seemed to be very legible. The lady's name is Warre, Miss Warre of Melksham in Whiltshire, a sister of the Head Master of Eton. Dr. Döllinger gave me Vol. I. of the *Akademische Vorträge* to work with. He had already given me both volumes, but they were at home in England. I asked if it was only the first volume that was being translated. "Yes, only the first volume."

22   The second is of less general interest.

He said that he expected to be at Tegernsee, as usual, this August, and spoke quite with sprightliness of coming over to see us at Schliersee from thence — always provided that we are still there when he reaches Tegernsee. Three years ago, — when he was eighty-seven, therefore — he and Gladstone drove over from Tegernsee to Schliersee and *walked back* over the Prinzenweg, a heavy walk of four hours for good pedestrians and which no doubt took the two old men much longer. It involves an ascent and descent of about 2000 feet between the two lakes. Gladstone was none the worse for it; but Dr. Döllinger said that he came in at the end of it quite exhausted, and that he was unwell for a day or two afterwards. And no wonder : he called it a *tour de force*. One of the nieces hinted that the amount of talking which Gladstone did in going up hill added not a little to the amount of exertion. But Gladstone is ten years and ten months younger than Döllinger. The latter appeared to be as much puzzled as the rest of us about the state of French politics. He does not believe in Boulanger, and he does

23   not think that those who make use of Boulanger believe in him. He quoted with amusement some Frenchman's account of French parties. "There are only two — the satisfied and the discontented; and the latter have the large majority."

Dr. Döllinger could not tell me where he had lived when he was in Aschaffenburg (1823-1826), where he began his work as a university teacher. He was there for three years as Lyceal professor (for Aschaffenburg had only a Lyceum) before coming as university professor to Munich, when the University was moved hither from Landshut in 1826. All that he could remember of his home there was that windows looked out upon the bridge.

After dinner he gave me a new production of that indefatigable worker Reusch—a demonstration of the forgeries which, thanks to Thomas Aquinas, so long imposed upon the Western Church. *He* prob- 24 ably believed them to be genuine and used them in good faith; and his influence caused them to become widely known and accepted. What were put forth as quotations from Greek Fathers and Councils were really translations into Greek made from Latin inventions. Reusch prints the Latin and Greek side by side in parallel columns. The pamphlet is published by the Munich Academy; and like so many of their publications it is in inconvenient quarto form. After taking away from the Roman system all that is built upon forged interpolations into Fathers and Councils and all that is deduced by questionable logic from questionable interpretations of Scripture, how much is left? Dr. Döllinger told us of an interesting book of which a second edition, much improved, has recently appeared in Italy;—an account of the election of the present Pope by De Cesare. Dr. Döllinger said that he believed 25 it to be quite accurate.

At the end of dinner he ventured to take ice, and quite as a matter of course : his nieces made no suggestion that perhaps it would not be good for him. It made him very glad to have his cup of coffee afterwards, as one could see from the eager way in which he took it. We left before three o'clock, and our farewells were not much more than ordinary, for there was the possibility of our meeting again soon at Schliersee. But it was the last we ever saw of him. We left Schliersee before he left Munich and we came home by quite another route.

Döllinger gave his last address to Munich Academy, 15th November, 1889, on a subject which he had studied almost from a boy, and about which he had talked to me nearly twenty years before, soon after I had begun to know him—The Destruction of the Templars. 26 There are notes of his on the subject taken as early as 1840. And yet, in 1889, his address on the subject was not complete. That was very characteristic. The amount of material which he collected was always out of all proportion to the small amount which he produced. Towards the end of the address it was noticed that he spoke very slowly, and some of his hearers thought that the wonderful old man was suffering from bodily fatigue after standing and speaking for so long. But that was not the cause of his slow delivery. He had come to the end of his manuscript and had to finish his subject from memory.

When he got home he wrote—for the last time—to Professor Reusch of Bonn, "to let him know that he was alive" (Ihnen ein Lebenszeichen zu geben). He was still full of his subject, which he said had such a powerful attraction for him, because it gave one such opportunities of seeing into the strange corners and sidetracks, which lie at a distance from the great highroads of history. He intended to elaborate his subject still further, and show how little love of truth there was in the ultramontane manner of treating history. But his work-days were almost ended. In the middle of December he developed a distressing cough, which compelled him to shorten his daily walks more and more, and at last to give them up altogether. Yet he continued to work and on the last Saturday in the year he was asking Friedrich to get a new French work on the Templars for him from the Public Library, and yet another book on the Redemptorists from the University Library. His housekeeper, whom he had pensioned when his two nieces came to keep house for him (we had known her for years), had written to send him her best wishes for the New Year. He wrote back to her that like herself he was living on in quiet and contentment, and still getting some work done, so far as his strength allowed (Auch ich lebe ruhig und vergnügt fort, und arbeite noch, soviel meine Kräfte es gestatten). But his strength had greatly abated. The address was written in a very feeble and shaky hand.

TODES-ANZEIGE.

Tief erschüttert geben wir Kunde, dass es Gott dem Allmächtigen gefallen hat, unseren geliebten Oheim, den

Hochwürdigsten Herrn

Dr. Johann Joseph Ignaz von Döllinger,

Stiftspropst des Collegiat-Stifts zum heiligen Cajetan, lebenslänglicher Reichsrath der Krone Bayern, Vorstand der K. Akademie der Wissenschaften, General-Conservator der wissenschaftlichen Sammlungen des Staates, o. ö. Professor der Kirchengeschichte an der K. Ludwig-Maximilians-Universität, Vorsitzender des Capitels des K. Maximilians-Ordens für Wissenschaft und Kunst, Gross-Comthur des Verdienst-Ordens der Bayerischen Krone,

in seinem 91. Lebensjahre gestern Abend 8³/₄ Uhr nach Empfang der heiligen Ölung durch einen sanften Tod aus diesem Leben abzurufen.

München, den 11. Januar 1890.

Die tieftrauernden Nichten

**Jeannette Döllinger,
Elisabeth Döllinger**

zugleich im Namen der übrigen
Hinterbliebenen.

Die Beerdigung findet **Montag** den **13. Januar** Nachmittags 4 Uhr vom Leichenhause des südlichen Friedhofes aus, der Trauer-Gottesdienst am **Donnerstag** den **16. diess** Vormittags 10 Uhr in der altkatholischen Kirche (Kaulbachstrasse) statt.

Druck der Hübschmann'schen Buchdruckerei (E. Lintner).

1890

On New Year's Day, 1890, the Influenza, which was then very prevalent in Munich, seized him, and he had to take to his bed. No one saw him but his two nieces and the two doctors, Hofrath Stieler and Professor Bauer, who said that he must have no visitors, but soon said that there was good hope that his wonderful constitution would probably get the better of the malady; and he sometimes got up and sat in his armchair. He was sitting up on the 9th January, when he had a stroke which paralysed his right side and deprived him of consciousness. He continued to breathe till the evening of the next day, and about a quarter to nine passed to his well-earned rest[4].

On the second day of the influenza-attack, the parish-priest of St. Ludwig sent to offer his services. It would, of course, be a magnificent triumph for the ultramontanes if it could be said that the great heretic, on his deathbed, had been "reconciled to the Church." But long before this Döllinger had provided against any such thing happening, and had charged a friend, that, if he fell ill, no Roman Catholic priest was to be allowed to see him : they were to send for Professor Friedrich, who would see to everything that was necessary. And they acted on these instructions. In reply to the priest of St. Ludwig's the elder niece, Johanna, sent word that her uncle was not so very seriously ill, and that he had not asked for his services. She added to Friedrich, "Now they want to come, after having maltreated uncle in every possible way all these years! Not one of them shall come near him." Friedrich administered extreme unction, and remained with the nieces and a few friends until the end came. After death his features resumed their usual aspect, as if he was peacefully asleep. It was Frau von Sicherer who exclaimed, as they watched him through their tears : "How like he is to Dante!" And it was really so.

He was buried on Monday, 13th January, at 4 p.m. in the South Friedhof near his parents and brothers and sisters. There was an immense concourse of people of all classes, the Roman clergy excepted, and

---

27   4. "Dr. Stieler schreibt: 'Ich behandelte den nun verstorbenen Herrn Stiftspropst, Reichsrat I. v. Döllinger, vom 1.—11. Januar 1890. Derselbe war an Influenza Tags vorher erkrankt und die Entfieberung des Patienten erfolgte bereits am 5. Krankheitstage. Schon in der Rekonvalescenz begriffen, wurde Herr v. Döllinger, welcher schon zeitweilig das Bett verließ, ganz plötzlich, und zwar in seinem Lehnstuhle, von einem Schlaganfalle betroffen, den er zwar noch zwei Tage überlebte, dem er aber schließlich um so mehr erliegen mußte, als, wie die Sektion erwies, sich zu dem apoplektischen Insult, welcher den Kranken wegen der damit verbundenen Lähmung der rechten Körperhälfte natürlich wieder ganz ans Bett bannte, eine Berstung des Herzmuskels gesellte, welche für sich allein schon die Möglichkeit der Lebenserhaltung ausschloß.'"

expressions of condolence came to the nieces from all quarters. On Thursday 16th there was a memorial service in the Old Catholic church.

On the 30th January Johanna Döllinger wrote to me (translated) : "You were for so many years such a good friend of our dear uncle, and you know therefore how much we have lost in him. The sacrifice which God demands from us could not be greater, for indeed he has been a father to us, since we lost our own. Every year his tenderness and goodness of heart became more and more conspicuous. He was not only one of the greatest theologians and scholars of our century, he was also one of the best men that ever lived, excelling in beautiful traits of character. Never shall I be able to console myself for this loss. He was the dearest possession that I had in this world! Our distress is all the greater, but he had nearly got the better of the dreadful influenza, and then quite unexpectedly fell a victim to a stroke of paralysis. On the 1st January he took to his bed, and from the 4th January was better every day. On the 8th January he was allowed to sit for three hours at his writing-table, which he so dearly longed to do. On Thursday morning also, the 9th January, he sat there again. But he did not do any work, as English newspapers have stated; and on the evening of that day between five and six o'clock he lost the power of speech. The doctor who came first told us, to our great consternation, that our dear uncle had had a stroke, and that one side was paralysed. Half an hour later he lost consciousness also, and remained in this condition till the next evening, Friday, towards nine o'clock. Without pain or death-struggle, he fell asleep quite peacefully, and just ceased to breathe. After he had passed away, his features seemed to be glorified and his face assumed a look of rest and peace.

How often in these sad hours did I think of you and the many English friends, who, after all, were always the ones he liked best. How dearly I should have liked to have had them once more gathered together round his deathbed! The sympathy with our sorrow is truly universal. The whole city, the whole country, and in a special way England, mourns with us. How kind it is of you and your dear wife, who were in such high favour with my lamented uncle, to invite me to stay with you! In my calamity, I am doubly grateful for your kindness and friendship. I should be indeed glad to pay you a visit, if ever my fortune should take me to England. In the summer I should like very much to take the post companion for travel or otherwise, as I once had some years ago, and should be quite ready to come to England, if such a post were offered me. My sister, however, will stay here with my mother.

As my poor uncle has left no directions respecting his literary remains, this difficult undertaking falls upon us. There is an enormous amount of material, as you may suppose. I have asked Professor Reusch to come here and look through everything, and he has promised to do so. His whole library is left to the University, along with 1000 marks, for the purpose of a foundation, which is to bear my uncle's name. The University must print a catalogue and then sell the library by auction. I wish very much indeed, that, if possible, it may not be dispersed. Perhaps after all some rich Englishman or American may be found, or perhaps some institution, who would offer a large sum for the whole. There are about 15,000 volumes.

All articles in the English newspapers speak of the great veneration and sympathy which was felt in England respecting him.

Like you and your dear wife, I am so very glad that you saw my dear uncle again last summer. But I do not give up the hope that you will perhaps still pass through here next summer. We should be so glad to see you here with us, and should have so much to tell you. The old friends of our dear uncle will be ever dearer to us; and it would be a great consolation to us, if, with the loss of our uncle, we were not to lose them also.

Begging you to give our best greetings to your dear wife and to thank her for her kind invitation,

I remain always yours very sincerely

Johanna Doellinger."

On the 13th February she wrote again from Munich (translation).

"How grateful I am for your kind words and for the great trouble which you are taking about our dear uncle's library. I have now heard that the Minister wishes that the University itself should buy it. But it must in any case be sold by auction; the only question is whether piecemeal or as a whole; and whoever bids most will get it. It will probably be some months before I can send you a catalogue, for it is not yet begun. Mr. Gladstone and Dr. Liddon have also promised me their help.

The photograph which I send you with this is the last that was taken of him. It was shortly after his 90th birthday, in the month of March or April, that it was taken, and every one thinks it very good. I think that you and your dear wife will also be pleased with it.

The Munich friends of my poor uncle are talking a great deal about a biography of him; and so I have asked Lord Acton whether he will not write one; for in my opinion he would be more competent than any one else to do so. He had known uncle for forty years, and every year spent some time with him. He accompanied him on his travels, and knows all his foreign connexions. To my great sorrow, however, he has given me many reasons why he cannot grant my request. It will be hard to find a really suitable person, to whom one could entrust the extensive and important correspondence.

Now it is once more still and quiet in our house; but with this stillness there comes back also a painful feeling of loneliness. The rooms in which my good uncle lived for fifty years, — how desolate and empty are they now! From day to day I feel the loss of him more. Professor Reusch will come here next month and look through all papers and manuscripts. There will then no doubt be plenty for me to do; so that before autumn or winter I must not think of a long journey. It would rejoice us greatly to see you and your dear wife here. And if I should really one day come to England, I should consider it a great happiness to pay you a visit. How good and kind it is of you to think of finding a post for me! From the bottom of my heart I thank you for this true friendship, which you gave originally to my never-to-be-forgotten uncle, and now have transferred to me. With what delight should I be ready to render you some service in return! Please give my *best greetings* to your wife. With heartfelt gratitude,

J. Doellinger."

On the 13th April she wrote again from Von der Tann Strasse (translation) :

"My heartiest thanks to you for sending me your most interesting article in the 'Expositor'. How much affection, love, and veneration for the dead is expressed in every line! You tell us so much that is important and interesting in these few pages; and how conscientiously you reproduce his words and views I gather from the fact, that often, while I read these lines, I have the feeling that I am listening to him himself. Not only I, but also a number of friends, among whom my copy goes the round, as Cornelius, Friedrich, Lossen, etc., are grateful to you for publishing this. We are all wishing that your diary may contain a great many such sketches!

Professor Reusch has been spending three weeks with us, but is now gone back again to Bonn. You will, like many others, be astonished, when I tell you how few manuscripts he has found that are ready for printing. Among a huge mass of material he found only an historical account of the Council of Trent, and a fragment of a biography of Pius IX., which, however, only reaches to the year 1854, besides a few unpublished addresses. These last will, I dare say, make a third volume; the rest also a volume. But beyond that there will be nothing that can be published. The dear uncle had worked out in his own head the greater part of his notes and excerpts into a complete whole, but the working of it out on paper was not so much as begun. And even the accumulated material is suited only for his own extraordinary powers of memory. Professor Reusch will himself prepare the biography of Pius IX. for the press, and will include in the same volume three or *28* four letters which the dear uncle in the last years of his life wrote to the Nuncio here, to the Archbishop, to the Duchess of the Braganza

29 and to a nun. All four had written to bring him over — exhorting him
to be converted; and his replies, of which he himself had kept a copy,
are very fine and interesting. The volume of addresses Dr. Lossen will
30 again see to, and the Tridentinum will make a treatise by itself. Lord
Acton was very surprised and disappointed, as assuredly we all were,
when I told him the result of Prof. Reusch's visit. He thinks of coming
here next month, and I shall be very glad to have a talk with him.

We have been at work on the Catalogue for nearly three weeks, but
have not got further than 2000 volumes. According to our estimate, the
number will probably exceed 20,000, so that it will probably take several
months more to complete the Catalogue. It is still not decided whether
the sale by auction will be of the whole or volume by volume.

You will have received the two newspapers. Cornelius's speech in
31 the Academy made a great impression, and the audience were moved,
32 we are told, to tears. The obituary notice also contains much that is
interesting.

I am already counting the weeks to the time of seeing you again; and
I hope that I am not making a miscalculation in expecting you early
in July. I am immensely delighted at the prospect of seeing you and
your most lovable wife again; and I should so have liked to propose
that you should occupy the rooms of our poor uncle. But the place
is so completely blocked with books, that we should in that case have
to empty the little house into the yard. Besides this, next month the
place passes into the possession of the University, so that actually we
ourselves shall henceforth be only guests. It is sad to think that you
will never again find the rooms of your old friend, our never-to-be-
forgotten uncle, in their old condition; but you will certainly find there
the same friendly and hearty welcome.

Please give my best regards to your dear wife.

I am, in true friendship, yours very sincerely

J. Doellinger."

During this period I was also in correspondence with Lord Acton,
but I reserve his letters for the present. On the 6th July, 1890, Fräulein
Johanna wrote to me from Munich (translation) :

"I have just received your lines, which bring me the long wished
for news of seeing you again. I can therefore only tell you how immensely
delighted I am about it; and the time till the 26th will indeed be very
long to me. My delight at seeing you again is as great as if you were
a part of my dear uncle himself, and I were to have this opportunity
of seeing him. How much we shall have to say to one another and
to tell one another! I shall in any case be here to receive you, and
should prefer to refuse the invitation of friends to come to them in
the country.

Our Catalogue has got beyond no. 8000, which means that we have already reached 15000 to 16000 volumes; and yet we have scarcely done half.

Everything else I reserve till I can tell it you by word of mouth. But let these lines merely tell you once more how immensely I rejoice at the thought of seeing you and your wife again.

With heartiest greetings, yours very sincerely

J. Doellinger."

We left England on the evening of Wednesday, 23rd July, crossing from Harwick to Rotterdam, and on the evening of the next day were in Bonn, where we had not stayed since the Second Reunion Conference presided over by Döllinger in the summer of 1875. The next morning (25 July) I called on Prof. Reusch, who was most kind, and told me much that was very interesting. Döllinger, although by no means rich, had left more money than was expected. He had had a pretty good income for many years as University Professor and Stiftspropst of St. Cajetan; and his expenditure, excepting for books, had been very small. He had been generous to relations, but his own wants were of the simplest. An income is left to his house-keeper, the capital returning to the family after her death. Sums of money are left to his relations, the *younger* of the two nieces being his heiress after all legacies are paid. She will be comfortably off; but Johanna will hardly be able to live alone on what she receives, unless she gets a post to augment it. Not one word is said about Döllinger's literary remains, so that by law they go to the heiress. Of the sadly small amount that can be published Reusch is editing half and Prof. Berthold in Munich the other half. Reusch could begin printing at once, but he has to wait for his colleague. In his lifetime Döllinger published two volumes of Academical Addresses, both of which he gave me, the first volume twice; and there is material for two more volumes. In these 33 will be published the long promised Vindication of the Templars, in finishing which he died, and the life of Boniface VIII. Döllinger's note-books are to be preserved in some public place for the use of scholars. Reusch, like myself, used to urge him for the sake of the world at large to work into shape some of his enormous stores of material. Of some things he said that they were already in shape; but that meant in his head, — he knew exactly what he meant to say. Of late years, as might be expected of a man of his age, the disinclination to set to work to produce grew on him; and it became less and less likely that any considerable work would be written. Some of his former works are to be republished by Friedrich, especially "The Church and the Churches", the "Fables respecting the Popes", and "Janus". A few 34 notes will be added to make these books a little more adequate to his latest researches. The first of the three needs special editing in this respect, for in some places it contains views which he had entirely ceased to hold; *e.g.* his rather severe criticisms on the English Church. Reusch spoke of the loss, the unspeakable loss, caused by his death. "But we must be very thankful that we were allowed to have him for so many years. That he was preserved for ninety years we must regard as a very special blessing granted to us by God." That, rather than his death, is the marvel; and his death was a very merciful one.

I asked Reusch how things were going with the Old Catholics. He said, on the whole not badly : they could be well content. The progress was certainly not all that they could wish, but they were not going back. There were a number of earnest and capable students preparing themselves to keep up the supply of clergy. The great change which had been made in Bavaria since Döllinger's death had caused a great panic at first, but the real consequences would not be very serious. It did not make much difference whether or no the Bavarian government rec-
35 ognized them officially as Catholics. Catholics they certainly were, and true Catholics. Almost the only substantial difference which had been made by this stroke of the government was that Prof. Friedrich lost a small income which he had for a post which he held in the Church of St. Cajetan, of which Döllinger had been Provost. As the government no longer held Friedrich to be a Catholic, he could not of course hold a position in one of the Royal Churches. If the government had made this change in Döllinger's lifetime, *he* could not have retained the post of Provost. But that would have caused too much out-cry. The whole thing, said Reusch, was simply a money transaction : the Old Catholics were sacrificed for financial reasons. The government was in great need of funds for educational and other purposes, and without the ultra-montane vote they could not get it. The support of the ultramontane party was promised on condition that the government ceased to regard the Old Catholics as Catholics; and so the thing was done. Von Lutz was an indifferentist in religion, a man of no convictions; and there-fore he was not very likely to make any stand on behalf of the Old Catholics, who are not a very influential party. "And after all," I said, "he has gone to the wall and has had to retire." "Yes, on account of his health." "I thought that was a mere pretext." "No, he is seriously ill, and it is not expected that he will live many weeks[5]." His successor

36 5. "DER RÜCKTRITT DES MINISTERS VON LUTZ.

X. München, den 3. Juni. Das wichtige Ereignis, mit welchem der Monat Mai abschloß, —der fast plötzlich, aus Gesundheitsrücksichten erfolgte freiwillige Rücktritt des Ministers v. Lutz, nach mehr als zwanzigjähriger Führung des Kultusministeriums und fast ebenso langer Leitung der bayerischen Politik überhaupt— muß auch die bayerischen Altkatholiken auf's tiefste erregen und zu ernsten Betrachtungen stimmen. Herr v. Lutz selbst hat wiederholt öffentlich geäußert, daß er nicht glaube in besonderer Gunst bei uns zu stehen; Herr v. Crails-heim, als sein Stellvertreter, hat dieser Meinung noch jüngst in einer über das thatsächlich

as Premier, Kreilsheim, is an ultramontane. His successor as Cultus-
minister is not much more serious in religious matters than himself,
— Müller, formerly head of the police.

Richtige hinausgehenden Weise Worte geliehen. — Das Richtige ist einfach dieses : wir glaub-
ten seiner Zeit überzeugt sein zu dürfen, Herr v. Lutz betrachte uns als treue Bundes-
genossen im Kampf für die Freiheit der deutschen Kirche und für die Rechte des Staates
gegen römische Usurpation. Dann mußten wir erfahren, wie die Freundschaft nach und
nach erkaltete. Einzelne Altkatholiken hatten zu empfinden, daß man in den Kreisen der
Politiker enttäuscht darüber war, daß die altkatholische Bewegung nicht sofort eine mehr
volkstümliche, die Massen mit fortreißende geworden war. Die Politiker wußten nicht
oder hatten vergessen, daß die raschen Erfolge, welche vor 350 Jahren die protestantische
Reformation errungen hat, zu drei Vierteilen vielleicht der Mitwirkung der damaligen
Staatsgewalt zu verdanken war. Sie bedachten nicht, daß rein religiöse und sittliche
Reformideen, welche nicht durch politische Macht unterstützt werden, zwar auch das
Angesicht der Erde erneuern können, aber nur in Jahrhunderte langer stiller Arbeit und
unter Kämpfen, welche mehr von schweigendem Dulden, als von lautem Siegesjubel zu
berichten wissen. So hat das Christentum seinen Weg gefunden in den drei ersten Jahrhunderten, ehe Kaiser Constantin das Kreuz auf seine Fahnen heftete, — so auch hat
sich die Idee der Gewissensfreiheit nur in Jahrhunderte langem Ringen erst Duldung
verschafft, dann einen, übrigens auch heute noch unvollständigen Sieg in der christlichen
Welt errungen.

Der katholischen Reformbewegung scheint ein ähnliches Schicksal bestimmt. — Inzwischen wurde sie dem praktischen Politiker unbequem. Er hätte am liebsten seine Ruhe
gehabt. Da nun der grimmige Haß der Ultramontanen gegen die kleine 'Sekte', die
doch mit der Anmaßung auftrat, die wahre, auf dem alten Traditionsprinzip ruhende
katholische Kirche zu sein, nicht nachließ, sondern noch immer wuchs, so laut sie auch
jubelten, daß unsere Bewegung im Sande verlaufe, — als dann auch die klugen liberalen
Parteimänner nichts mehr wissen wollten von dem 'Streit um Dogmen', der ihnen
das Essen und den Mittagsschlaf verdarb, da entschloß sich Herr von Lutz, vor die
Frage gestellt, ob er fernerhin neben den Altkatholiken auf dem schmalen Steg gehen
könne, der über den Strom von religiösem Vorurteil und Fanatismus auf den festen
Boden kirchlichen Friedens führt, dem unbequemen Nachbar einen Stoß zu geben, der
ihn hinunter stürzte, während er selbst auf dem Stege sicher voranzuschreiten gedachte.
— Nun, wir haben schwimmen gelernt, und denken auch ohne den Steg der Staatshilfe
aus jenem Strom ans feste Ufer zu gelangen; aber der Minister ist auch, nachdem er
uns von sich gestoßen, nicht an sein Ziel gelangt. Ihn freilich hat keine Menschenhand
herabgestoßen, sondern eine höhere Macht, welche die Geschicke auch der Könige und
Machthaber leitet, ließ seine Körperkräfte vor der Zeit erlahmen.

Wir können den Rücktritt des Staatsministers, der aus Schwäche, oder in der Meinung
selbst dem Staate unentbehrlich zu sein, den treuesten Freund des Staates kirchlichem
Fanatismus preisgab, nicht beklagen; mit dem Manne aber empfinden wir aufrichtiges
Mitleid. Nachdem er zwanzig Jahre hindurch um den bayerischen Staat, um das Reich
und nicht am wenigsten, in der großen Katastrophe des Sommers 1886, um das bayerische 37
Königshaus sich hervorragende Verdienste erworben hat, hätte er ein besseres Ende seiner
politischen Laufbahn verdient, als daß er sie mit einer auf innere Unwahrheit gegründeten
Entscheidung beschließen mußte, jener Entscheidung der Iden des März, die seiner eigenen
und des gesamten bayerischen Ministeriums feierlichen früheren Zusage widersprach,
'nicht nur den einzelnen Anhänger der alten katholischen Lehre fortwährend als Katholiken betrachten zu wollen, sondern auch die altkatholischen Gemeinden als katholische
anzuerkennen.'   38

Was weiter kommen wird, steht in Gottes Hand. Wir hören wohl die Botschaft :
nicht das System, nur die Person sei geändert, aber wir glauben nicht daran; denn wir
kennen kein System, welches nicht von einer lebendigen, überzeugten Persönlichkeit

As regards Döllinger's ecclesiastical position, Reusch said that Döllinger himself had told him that, so far as his conscience allowed him, he meant to submit to authority, even though the authority was unjustly exercised. It was not against his conscience to abstain from celebrating and communicating. With the exception of the Reunion Conference at Bonn—a very exceptional occasion—Döllinger never attended an
39 Old Catholic service, and he *never* celebrated privately in his own room. On the other hand, Döllinger never blamed Reusch or others for doing otherwise. "When I have been in Munich, I have never hesitated to tell him that I had been preaching and celebrating at the Old Catholic church; and he never took offence. But the subject was a delicate one, and I did not like to question him about it. What he says in the letter to the Nuncio is the exact fact : he was 'isolated'[6]."

I remarked that Döllinger had considered the abolition of the celibacy of the clergy by the Old Catholics as a fatal mistake. Reusch of course knew this, and he had himself opposed it. "Schulte," I said, "was very eagerly in favour of it, was he not?" "Yes," said Reusch; "Schulte thought that if we allowed the clergy to marry, a great many priests would come over to us. I never thought that this was the case; and even if it had been, what would have been the worth of men who joined us for such a reason? It would be a shameful thing to avow that one had left one's communion in order to be able to marry. And, as a matter of fact, none have been attracted by the change." He added that scarcely any of the Old Catholic clergy had availed themselves of the leave. He seemed to know of only one, a priest at Düsseldorf, where the congregation were not averse to the priest's marrying. In most places it would be very much disapproved.

We had some talk about books, and he gave me one or two articles which he had written for cyclopedias, and which had been printed separately; and I then took my leave of him. I never saw him again.

We went on by an evening train and travelled all night to Munich, which we reached punctually at 8 a.m., Saturday 26th July. After break-

getragen wäre. Wir wünschen und hoffen zwar, daß der neue Kultusminister sich als ein Mann zugleich von festen Grundsätzen und von unbeugsamem Charakter erweisen werde, aber nicht auf fremde Hilfe, sondern auf unsere gute Sache und unsere eigene Kraft wollen wir vertrauen, und auf die diesen beiden Eigenschaften nicht fehlende Hilfe Gottes."

6. After speaking of the bishops who had opposed the dogma of Infallibility, Döllinger goes on to say to the Nuncio Ruffo Scilla : "Il est vrai que tous ces prélats ont fait leur soumission; tous s'accordaient à dire pour excuse : 'nous ne voulons pas faire un schisme.' Moi aussi, je ne veux pas être membre d'une societé schismatique; *je suis isolé*. Persuadé que la sentence lancée contre moi est injuste et nulle de droit, je persiste à me regarder comme membre de la grande église catholique, et c'est l'église elle-même qui, par la bouche des saints pères, me dit, qu'une telle excommunication ne peut pas
40 nuire à mon âme."

fast we went to the well-known house, Von der Tann Strasse 11/1, to see Döllinger's nieces, and they gave us a very hearty welcome. There was a very great deal to talk about. They gave us further details about their uncle's death. After the fatal stroke came, he never spoke, but he remained conscious for some time. He shook his head, when they asked whether he was in pain, but he groaned at times, perhaps at finding himself helpless. He evidently wanted something to be brought to him, but to their great distress they never found out what it was. Everything which they did bring was rejected. In their alarm they sent for three doctors, but it was a quarter of an hour or more before one came. The patient was then able to put out his tongue, when asked to show it; but he soon became unconscious, and remained so for the last 24 hours. The doctors were surprised at his living so long. A Roman priest came and said that he had in his pocket the formal revocation of the sentence of excommunication, sent apparently express from Rome : it would take effect, he said, immediately, if the dying man retracted. The elder niece requested him to retire, and he did so; and he has since been appointed Stiftspropst of St. Cajetan in Dr. Döllinger's place. This was not the parish priest of St. Ludwig, but Türk, then Stiftsdekan of St. Cajetan. The change is immense, for he is quite an insignificant person, and an out-and-out ultramontane. The nieces were not at the end of their difficulties when they rejected the spiritual services of Roman Catholic clergy, which would have led to the assertion that Döllinger had recanted on his deathbed. Ought they to send for an Old Catholic, when their uncle had steadfastly kept aloof from all Old Catholic services and ministrations? Would he, if he had been able to express his wishes, have accepted such ministrations now? On the whole, it was thought that to let their uncle die without any Christian office, — 'like a dog', as his enemies would say, — would be worst of all, and Friedrich was sent for, who administered extreme unction. It could do their uncle no harm; would commit him to nothing, as he could not speak; and might make his end more peaceful. To their great relief, the nieces afterwards were told by an intimate friend that Döllinger had said, "In my last illness, I should like Friedrich to be sent for." But it was strange, that, when he was suffering from the influenza, he never said anything on the subject to his nieces.   *41*

They were still busy cataloguing the library, which amounts to 30,000 volumes or more, and is valued at £ 5000 at least. One or two enquiries have come from America, and it may go there bodily. No library or society in Munich can afford to buy it, and many of the books which it contains are in Munich libraries already.

The nieces asked me to select something which had been their uncle's, and suggested one of his pictures, or one of the two book-rests which always stood before him on his writing-table, a small one immediately in front of him, and a large one for folios a little further off. I chose the small one, which he had used daily, when at home, for perhaps half a century. It will be a precious possession, and a worthy companion to the carved book-slide that formerly belonged to Bishop Lightfoot, who had died 21st December, 1889.

The nieces also placed at my disposal all Döllinger's manuscript notes, and they took my wife into their own room while I looked at some of the note-books. There were three cupboards full of them! Note-books of all sizes, with many portfolios containing loose sheets. It would be the work of years to do any justice to them. I found one from which it was possible to make a few extracts, but that was all that was possible in the time. I sat at his table and in his chair, where he has done years and years of work. He has lived in that same house for fifty years, and I believe that where I sat to take a few notes of his notes has always been his place of working. I can speak for nearly twenty years as to his habits in this respect and in others.

We left for mid-day table d'hôte, and returned at 5 p.m. to go for a walk in the Englischer Garten with the nieces. It was his favourite place for exercise. B. walked with the younger, and I with the elder niece. She told me that it was a very significant thing that, at her uncle's funeral, every confession was represented, *excepting his own*. Besides the mixed multitude, which was immense, there were clergy and other representatives of the Old Catholics, the English Church, the Greek Church, German and other Protestants, but no Roman Catholics. The City of Munich, which now has a majority of ultra-montanes in the municipal council, did, however, send a wreath with the inscription, "The City of Munich to its great Citizen". The black and yellow streamers, with these words upon them, the nieces now have in the house. The number of wreaths of all kinds was enormous, and some of them were gigantic. The grave was quite heaped up with them. The lamentations among the poor were very touching : "Ah! he was a good man; no one ever asked help from him and was refused;" and so forth.

During the attack of influenza he took very little interest in the numerous enquiries which came from the highest personages. "The Grand Duke of Baden has telegraphed to know how you are." "The Prince Regent has sent to enquire." "The Empress has telegraphed to say how grieved she is to hear of your illness, and to ask how you are going on." Of all these, and many more, he took little notice; he merely said, "please send my best thanks," and then sank back again in bed. It was very different with the congratulations which poured in from all parts of the world for his 90th birthday. In these he took full interest; and they went on for about three days. The nieces were not sorry when they were over.

They told us nothing about the will, but they did tell us something which makes the preference of the younger niece very intelligible. She has lived with her uncle for nine years, whereas Johanna has been with him only four or five; and the younger one did and does most of the house-work.

The accounts given of the Old Catholics in Munich were not very encouraging. The priest in charge of the little church is neither a good preacher nor a person of tact. He unsettles his congregation by making frequent changes, and where his changes are for the better he introduces them without sufficient caution as to the conservative predilections of old-fashioned people. These changes give Roman Catholic critics too much handle for saying: "Those who leave us never know when to stop. They go on surrendering one thing after another till they cease to be Christian at all. There *is* no logical standpoint between Rome and Atheism." This is a way of terrifying people which is worked with considerable success.

Next day, Sunday, 27th July, we dined with the sisters. After an American professor named Evans, who dined with us, had taken his leave, they took us to the Friedhof to visit their uncle's grave. He is buried near his parents and his brother and sister, of whom the sister died first. There were five or six brothers and three sisters. He was the eldest, and he outlived them all. There is no other family of Döllingers in Germany, as he told me years ago; but in Hungary the name is not uncommon. A lot of the Hungarian Döllingers wrote after his death and claimed to be his relations, hoping to get a share of whatever he might leave.

The nieces had tea with us at Hotel Leinfelder, and then we walked back with them to Von der Tann Strasse. On our way we met Lady Blennerhasset for the second time during our stay, and both times she was very pleasant. She was one of Döllinger's most intimate friends, and in former years we had more than once met her at his table. She told me that in reading what I had said about his conversation in the "Expositor" she seemed to hear the tone of his voice. It is to be hoped that she herself will write something about him. No one, *42* not even Lord Acton, would do it better. Perhaps not even to him did Döllinger talk so unreservedly as to her. Just then she was much worried about her own affairs and was hardly equal to writing anything.

Monday, 28th July. Dr. Lossen called soon after breakfast with the bronze medal of Döllinger which the Royal Academy of Bavaria had had executed in his honour. The likeness is excellent, and we were glad to be allowed to possess one. We then went to Julius Zumbusch (Teresien Strasse 54), the artist who took the mask of Döllinger after his death and executed the medal. We saw the cast made from the mask, and very peaceful the impression looked, — much as if he were asleep. Herr Zumbusch had medallion-portraits of Döllinger, much larger than the medal, and we ordered one. We then took leave of our friends, and an hour later we took leave of Munich. It may easily be a long time before we see it again. It was exactly a year since we saw Dr. Döllinger last. On the 28th July last year we parted from him, he talking of meeting us again at Tegernsee or Schliersee; but this was never accomplished. There was just a chance of our meeting Johanna Döllinger again that summer. Towards the end of August she expected to be with friends at Brixlegg, and there or elsewhere in the Tyrol we might possibly see her again. But on 17th August she wrote to me from Munich to cancel this (translation).

"Unhappily I must give up the hope of seeing you and your dear wife again; for of late we have been working harder than ever to get the Catalogue ready by October. The University urges us most strongly to have it ready by then. Consequently we must give up our fortnight's holiday. We have now reached 13,000. To the four American universities that may possibly buy the library as a whole may now be added that of Strasburg.

My sister is in Bonn by the invitation of Prof. Reusch. So I am alone with the dear books, which make very sweet company for me. I have not nearly told you what a delight your visit was to us. It was a couple of days of bright sunshine, lighting up our loneliness. If only you·could have stayed a few days longer! For you no doubt the return to Munich was a sad and painful one; but in later years you will not be sorry to remember the last visit which you paid to the forsaken abode.

I am doubly sorry not to see you again, because I did not take a long farewell of either of you. God knows when we may see one another again! Yet perhaps I may see you in your own home. But in any case I shall ever be grateful to you for your visit to us and for your true friendship. With a thousand greetings,

J. Doellinger."

On the 28th September she wrote again from Munich to say how sorry she was that an *un*framed medallion of Döllinger had been sent to us. Zumbusch had sent it off while she was away for ten days at Brixlegg. Since her return they had been working hard at the Catalogue of the library (translation).

"We have now catalogued 17,000, and by the end of October expect to reach the end, that is 20,000. As soon as we are finished I shall go to the Actons at Tegernsee for a fortnight. ...

Professor Friedrich has commissioned me to ask you whether he cannot get your articles in the 'Expositor'. Would you be so kind as to commission the publisher to send them to him? He was very sorry not to have seen you himself and had some talk with you.

How greatly I have lamented the death of our dear and venerated Dr. Liddon, I need hardly tell you. How quickly the two old friends have met again in the other world[7]! The shock would have been still greater to me, when I read of his death in the newspapers, if I had not been in some measure prepared for it by yourself. In him a truly excellent man has gone from the world.

Lady Blennerhasset is at present at Reichenhall, where her husband also spent a few days. He has just got a government-post in Dublin, and must be there by 1st October.

Our best greetings to you and your wife. Your grateful

J. Doellinger."

On 17th November she wrote from Munich (translation):

"The day before yesterday I came back from Tegernsee and found the copy of the 'Critical Review' which you had the kindness to send me[8], and I return you my best thanks for it. Besides your excellent criticism of the Letters I have also read the article on Dr. Liddon with great interest.

Lord Acton will stay two or three more days here in order to work in this house, and then will go on with his two eldest daughters to Cannes. I was nearly five weeks with them at Tegernsee, and they were very happy and satisfying days for me, for I am enthusiastically fond of the two charming girls. But I must confess that my stay there had also many sad memories for me. Especially painful to me was the return to our desolate, sad, and forsaken dwelling, where I shall not be able to remain much longer. If at all possible, I should like to be in England for Christmas, for as yet I have heard nothing from America. Lord Acton has promised to give letters of introduction, and so I shall not be altogether forsaken over there. The printing of the Catalogue is still not yet begun, for another copy has to be made. $\qquad$ 43

Professor Reusch will no doubt have sent you a copy of the volume

---

7. Liddon, born 1829, died 9th September, 1890, eight months after Döllinger. Newman, born 1801, died 11th August, 1890.

8. This was the first number of the "Critical Review", edited by Prof. S.D.F. Salmond of Aberdeen and published by T. & T. Clark, Edinburgh. Oddly enough, it has no date, not even the year. The second article was by myself on the *Briefe und Erklärungen von I. von Döllinger über die Vaticanischen Decrete, 1869-1887.* The eleventh article was by Professor Gibb, D.D., on *Canon Liddon. A Memoir, with his last Five Sermons.* As I happen to have a proof of my own article on the Letters and Declarations, I may as well paste it into this note-book [reproduced in appendix, pp. 264-267]. A translation of these Letters and Declarations on the Vatican Decrees was published by T. & T. Clark in 1891, and it is a small volume well worth possessing.

of uncle's writings which has just appeared. (*Kleinere Schriften*, Cotta, Stuttgart, 1890.)

Have you read Lord Acton's article in the 'Historical Review'? What colossal knowledge is exhibited in it! How grateful all uncle's friends and admirers would be to him, if he would really carry out his purpose and publish a larger work about him. I have had much conversation with him on the subject and have come to the conviction that no one is more competent to do that than himself. I think that uncle scarcely had a single friend that Lord Acton did not also know personally. He can look over the whole life of the man who forty years was his friend, and can do this with so much intelligence. With every circumstance and event he is fully acquainted.

I hope that these lines will find you and your dear wife in the best of health. Please accept once more the heartfelt thanks of yours very sincerely

J. Doellinger."

On the 26th December she wrote again :

"I have been so overwhelmed with Christmas business that not until to-day have I been able to thank you for sending the last number of the 'Expositor'. I thank you very specially for the passage which describes our relation to our dear good uncle, a relation which you know how to state in such kind terms. It was painful to me that in England, where uncle had so many friends who at least knew us personally, we should be placed in such an unfavourable light owing to some misunderstood words of Friedrich. Besides, uncle's last letter to Prof. Reusch is the best and fullest testimonial which he has ever given us, no doubt without any idea that his end was so close at hand.

I was greatly shocked to hear from you that now Dean Church is also dead. It almost seems as if I was to lose all my uncle's friends in England before I get over there myself. Lord Acton had told me a great deal about Dean Church, whom he knew very well, and to whom he was going to give a letter of introduction.

As you may suppose, these days are full of sad memories, and I have to pull myself together to avoid giving way to my distress. I mean to spend the 10th January here, and then on the 14th to set off. I shall stay a couple of days with Prof. Reusch in Bonn; so that it will probably be the 20th before I reach London. ...

J. Doellinger."

I had in the course of 1890 written five articles on Döllinger in the "Expositor". In March, on the Vatican Council; in April, on Roman Difficulties; in June on English Topics; in August on Continental Topics; in December on Biographical Topics. The passage in the last article

to which Fräulein Johanna refers runs as follows : "During the last
nine or ten years of his life one of his nieces devoted herself to taking
care of him, and during the last six years a second niece joined her
sister in this willing and constant devotion. A translation of a letter
from Dr. Friedrich has been published, in which he is made to imply
that there had been a time in which the nieces had not been on good
terms with their uncle, and had not done their duty towards him.
What Professor Friedrich actually wrote I do not know; but I have
good means of knowing that the translator must have given a meaning
to the original which it neither expressed nor implied."

In March 1890 I published in the "Churchman" a review of Döllinger's
work on Mediaeval Sects, *Beiträge zur Sektengeschichte des Mittelalters*,
published by Beck of Munich that same year. The "Churchman" had
previously contained other reviews, by the same hand, of works by
Dr. Döllinger. March 1887, on Madame de Maintenon; May 1887,
on Cardinal Bellarmine (in this work Reusch cooperated); April 1889, *44*
on the Jesuits and Casuistical Morality (in this also Reusch cooperated
and probably did most of the work). This last treatise, in two volumes,
is a mine of information on the subject. Its full title is : *Geschichte
der Moralstreitigkeiten in der römisch-katholischen Kirche seit dem sechzehnten Jahrhundert mit Beiträgen zur Geschichte und Characteristic
des Jesuitenordens. Auf Grund ungedruckter Aktenstücke bearbeitet
und herausgegeben von Ignaz von Döllinger und Fr. Heinrich Reusch.
Nördlingen, 1889.*

On the 17th March 1890 the Munich publisher Beck wrote to me
(translation) :
"Please forgive us for not having written till now in response to your
esteemed letter of 2nd February. We waited so long in the hope that
the Obituary Notice which Professor Friedrich was preparing would
appear in the Allgemeine Zeitung; but strange to say it is still not
yet published. As we have heard, some misunderstanding is the cause
of the inconceivably long delay. The *Sektengeschichte* we have sent
you at the express wish of the late Döllinger. You would greatly oblige
us, if you would have the kindness to tell us the number of the "Churchman" in which your review appears.
Whether in what Döllinger has left there are Manuscripts ready for
publication, we cannot at present say, but we cannot help doubting
it. No doubt Döllinger has left a large amount of learned material,
from which, had he been allowed to live, as he himself hoped, some
years longer, he could have produced a great deal. But, with his extraordinary memory, his habit always was to put down no more than
key-words, references to books, and the like; the main points he had
in his head. Whether, therefore, anything will be made of these is very

questionable. Professor Reusch of Bonn is at present engaged in looking through the literary remains.

Genehmigen Sie die Versicherung ausgezeichneter Hochachtung, mit der wir zeichnen

Ihre ergebenste

C.H. Beck'sche Verlagsbuchhandlung   Oskar Beck."

On the 31st July Père Hyacinthe wrote to me from 27 Boulevard d'Inkermann, Parc de Neuilly, près Paris.

"J'ai été bien touché de votre bonne lettre et de l'envoi si intéressant qui l'a suivie de près, Révérend et cher Monsieur, mais le temps et un peu aussi les forces m'ont manqué pour vous le dire. Mes occupations ne diminuent pas, elles augmentent plutôt, malgré l'âge qui se fait sentir et qui réclamerait du repos. J'éprouve parfois des fatigues telles que je n'ai pas le courage de prendre la plume pour écrire à mes meilleurs amis.

Je me souviens pourtant de nos bonnes rencontres, et je ne désespère pas de vous revoir encore en Angleterre ou en France.

Nous avons fait une perte immense en la personne de l'illustre Döllinger. Toutefois sa journée était finie et elle avait été bien remplie. Il se repose maintenant dans le sein de cette Vérité qu'il a servie et aimée, et pour laquelle il a souffert.

45   *Exoriatur aliquis ex ossibus ultor*!

Je compte assister au congrès international des Vieux-Catholiques, qui doit avoir lieu à Cologne, les 12, 13 et 14 du prochain mois de septembre.

La cause est grande, mais les événements ne lui ont point été favorables, et les hommes n'ont pas été à la hauteur de la cause qu'il fallait servir et des événements qu'il fallait vaincre.

Recevez, cher et Révérend Monsieur, l'assurance de mon fidèle et affectueux souvenir.

Madame Loyson et Paul ne veulent pas être oubliés près de vous.

Hyacinthe Loyson."

And now I pass on to Lord Acton's letters mentioned above. He wrote from Villa Arco, Tegernsee, 30th May, 1890.

"I have just come to these parts, and the first thing I read was your paper in the Churchman on the Sektengeschichte.

The ladies who gave it to me tell me that you are writing something more upon Doellinger, and that you have notes of his conversations. All his earlier letters to me are lost or mislaid; and I have promised a paper, if possible for July. Nothing would help me more than the help you could give me, if you have anything ready. Should you be generously able to let me see, in print or MS., notes or letters, I would undertake to return them to you *by the next days post.* I venture to make this appeal to your kindness in the belief that what you are writing will appear before my paper, which should be published in the middle of July, and must be out of my hands about the 20th of June. In that case I should incur no risk of anticipating you.

Forgive my request, and be sure that I know well the value of his confidential communications to you.

I remain, yours very truly

Acton."

On the 7th June he wrote again from Tegernsee.

"I return the letters, and keep the reminiscences, with sincerest thanks. The conversations recalled many things to my mind; and I am sorry to be obliged to write, if possible, for the next number, too soon for your fourth article. In spite of your very flattering allusion to me, I think I once or twice recognized that X stands for A[9]. Doellinger had forgotten, when he spoke to you about it, what passed with Wiseman touching Boniface VIII. I mention it now, because I had thought of telling the story as I seem to remember it. If I do so, don't think that I am contradicting you.

I wonder what your impression was, when he said what you have related at the top of p. 426 in the Expositor[10]. It may be read to mean that he was not greatly interested in pure Theology (Th. in the strict sense), and spoke of it as Bossuet or Liddon or Thiersch would not have spoken. I so interpret it, at this moment, by the light of what he wrote to the archbishop of Munich in 1887[11].

This leads me to another topic. Reusch is on the point of publishing a volume of 160 pages, containing the letters he (Döllinger) wrote, on

9. This refers to the paper in the "Expositor" for April 1890, on Roman Difficulties. In places where Döllinger had quoted Acton, I put 'X.', so as not to commit Lord Acton to anything which he might perhaps not wish to be publicly connected with him. Lord Acton's attitude towards the Roman Church was a difficult one.

10. The passage to which Lord Acton refers runs thus: "Few people," said Döllinger, "would insist upon rigid agreement with formulas in a matter of such inscrutable mystery as the Trinity. In some particulars it is impossible to know the meaning of the terms used. The most subtle philosopher and the most profound theologian cannot explain the difference between 'generation' and 'procession' in the 'generation of the Son' and the 'procession of the Spirit'. I believe that the Athanasian Creed is as old as the sixth century. When it was composed Arianism was abroad. Whole nations were converted to Arianism, and every one was keenly alive to the doctrine of the Trinity. The questions which perplex *us*, and which *we* have to try to solve, are of a very different kind. The Reformers made a great mistake in putting this creed in the public service."

11. In that letter Döllinger asked for a public conference, in which he should dispute with theologians who accepted the Infallibility dogma, and if possible be convinced of his errors. "For it is not a question of the mysteries of the faith, as the Trinity and the Incarnation, about which we can dispute until doomsday, and to no purpose. We here stand on the firm foundation of history, of evidences and of facts."

his own position, to certain official, and other, persons. Several of the known manifestoes are included. The most important letter, however, is the one above mentioned, which had never been published, and is extremely remarkable. It is so largely printed that it is 'en [?], really, than the Bonn Discourses in bulk.

A young Englishman at Munich, who knew Doellinger, and is on friendly terms with his literary representatives, wishes to translate this volume. He has not begun, for the sheets are not yet fully revised. His name is Swallow, and he is from Owens and not a Churchman, otherwise quite competent and trustworthy. Of course, if, on your own account, you would think of undertaking it, that would be best for the book itself, if not, eventually, for the family. Your name and position would be worth a great deal; not to speak of your experience of his style, also, the congruity of such a thing, not history, but manifesto, ἀγώνισμα, being in the hands of an ecclesiastical dignitary.

Let me or Reusch know your wishes, and pray send me No. 4, if you can.

Believe me, yours most sincerely

Acton."

On the 14th June he wrote once more from Tegernsee :

"I obey your directions, and inform our friends that you leave the translation to Mr. Swallow. Lossen will revise it, and will see that it is faithful.

Very many thanks indeed for your kindness in sending me the desired information, de locis. Reusch will tell you about Boniface VIII. He examined the papers and took with him what he thought he could make something of. When I looked them over, I had no means of knowing what Reusch had taken, though he had left a receipted list in the proper hands. I do not think that much will be found regarding any of the topics which last occupied his thoughts.

I am just leaving for a week or two in London; and my direction will be at the Athenaeum until the end of the month.

Should there be other letters, which you did not care to send half across Europe, but would be ready to trust *for a day* in faithful hands, in London, remember me there. Even, for instance, if, instead of Doellinger's own, you would allow me to see some of Newman's on Doellinger, which you must possess.

And, if this cannot be for good reasons which I appreciate beforehand, can you tell me where I could get, perchance, at his letters to Oxenham?

All this, NB. not for publicity, but for private guidance and information.

I remain very truly yours

Acton."

I was able to send him some letters that were worth his perusal as will be seen from the following letter, which was written from the Athenaeum on the 18th June.

"I return Newman's most interesting and characteristic letters with most sincere thanks. I am not at all sure that, in the case of Hippolytus, *48* Doellinger is quite free from reproach, or even that he would have stood by everything he wrote in the volume of 1853. There is no doubt that at that time of his life he would have been glad to be able to make out a case favourable to Rome, just as Newman would, though certainly not by aid of the same assumptions.

I remain yours very truly

Acton."

Lord Acton returned to Tegernsee and wrote to me from there on the 3rd October.

"I did not write to thank you for the last instalment, which you were so good as to send me, and which added, with its predecessors, more than I found I could use. I have sent Creighton a paper on the professor's (Döllinger's)[12] 'Historische Leistung', which you will consider very inadequate. But you will be the best judge of it, and if you can get a good word in the Guardian, you will do me good with a public I much wish to reach, but which I don't address in the Historical Review. Oxenham and Liddon are gone, and *nobody knew Doellinger as well as you do*.

You will find that I contradict one thing that he told you. I remember distinctly that story about Boniface VIII., which he had forgotten. It is of no consequence, but it serves to put him in his relations with a certain class of men.

I remain ever yours

Acton."

What follows is taken from Lord Acton's article on "Doellinger's Historical Work" in the "English Historical Review" for October 1890, Vol. V. p. 700. I have, as a rule, kept his wording, but not quite *49* invariably. The sentences are often condensed by omitting words.

When Dr. Doellinger obtained a chair in the reorganized University of Munich, his own country, Bavaria, at that time furnished no master or model to the young professor. Exempt, by date and position, from the discipline of a theological party, he so continued, and never turned elsewhere for the dependence he escaped at home. No German theologian

12. Lord Acton used commonly to speak of Döllinger as "the Professor"; my wife and I commonly called him "the Doctor".

bent his course, and he derived nothing from the powerful writer then dominant in the north. To a friend who described Herder as the one unprofitable classic he replied, "Did you ever learn anything from Schleiermacher?"

He knew modern languages well, and devoted himself systematically to the study of foreign divines. The characteristic universality of his later years sprang from the inadequacy of the national supply, and the search for truth in every century naturally became a professor, whose range extended over all Christian ages and who felt the inferiority of his own. Doellinger's conception of his science differed from the average by being more comprehensive. *Savigny* had expounded law and society in that historic spirit which soon pervaded other sciences; and Doellinger continued to recognise him as an originator of true scientific methods when his influence on jurisprudence was on the wane.

The first eminent thinker whom Doellinger heard was *Baader*[13], the poorest of writers, but the most instructive and impressive talker in Germany, and the one man who seems to have influenced the direction of his mind. Bishop Martensen has described his amazing powers; and Doellinger bore equal testimony to the wealth and worth of his religious philosophy. He probably owed to him his persistent disparagement of Hegel. Baader was full of the praises of *De Maistre*, and impressed upon his earnest listener the importance of the books on the Pope and on the Gallican Church[14], and assured him that their spirit is the genuine Catholicism. These conversations were the origin of Doellinger's ultramontanism. It governed one half of his life, and his interest in De Maistre outlasted the assent which he once gave to some of his opinions. It divided him from *Moehler*, whom he never ceased to venerate as the finest theological intellect he had known. The publication of the "Symbolik"[15] made it difficult for the author to remain in Wirtemberg, and having made Doellinger's acquaintance, he conceived an ardent desire to become his colleague in Munich. Doellinger negotiated the appointment, and Moehler took the supreme chair of ecclesiastical history by right of seniority. How came it to pass that a man who was eminently intelligent in the exposition of doctrines, but who in

13. Franz Xavier Baader (1765-1841) was a student of medicine and mineralogy before he became a theologian. He was director of the mining department at Munich and afterwards (1826) Professor of Speculative Theology. He took a free line respecting the Papacy, which he did not regard as essential to the Church.

14. *Du Pape* (1819); *De l'Église Gallicane dans ses rapports avec le Souverain Pontife* (1821).

15. "Symbolism, or the Doctrinal Differences between Catholics and Protestants". Translated by J.R. Robertson, 1843. The original work (1832) provoked a long controversy with Möhler's colleague at Tübingen, F.C. Baur, and hence Möhler's desire to migrate to Munich, which he did in 1835. The climate did not suit him, and he died at Würzburg, 12 April 1838.

narrative, description, and knowledge of character, was neither first nor second, resolved that his mission was history?

Doellinger was more earnest than others in regarding Christianity as history, and in pressing the affinity between Catholic and historical thought. He dreaded the predominance of great names which stop the way, and everything that interposes a school between the Church and the observer. To an Innsbruck professor, lamenting that there was no philosophy which he could heartily adopt, he replied that philosophies do not subsist in order to be adopted. A Thomist or a Cartesian seemed to him a captive, and he prized metaphysicians for the pearls which they drop outside the seclusion of their system. His colleague, *Schelling*, no friend of the friends of Baader, stood aloof from him. *Hegel* remained in Doellinger's eyes the strongest of all the enemies of religion, the reasoner who made a generation of clever men incapable of facing facts. The dogmas of pantheistic history offended him too much to give them deep study, and Hegelians said of him that he lacked the constructive unity of idea, and knew the way from effect to cause, but not from cause to law. He always assigned to original speculation a subordinate place, as a good servant but a bad master, without the certainty and authority of history. He alarmed Archer Gurney by saying that all hope of an understanding is at an end, if logic be applied for the rectification of dogma, and to Dr. Plummer, who acknowledged him as the most capable of modern theologians and historians, he spoke of the hopelessness of trying to discover the meaning of terms used in definitions. To his archbishop he wrote that men may discuss the mysteries of the faith to the last day without avail; and it was his inmost conviction that religion exists to make men better, and that the ethical quality of dogma constitutes its value[16]. In theology, apart from its action on the soul, he took less interest, and those disputes satisfied him most which can be decided by appeal to the historian.

From his early reputation and his position at the outpost he was expected to make up his mind over a large area of unsettled thought and disputed fact, and to be provided with a reasoned answer to every difficulty. The suspense of mind, which is the privilege of every un-professional scholar, was forbidden him. Students could not wait for the master to complete his studies; they flocked for something final to their keen unemotional professor, who sometimes said more than he could be sure of, but who did not give aphorism for argument. He accepted the situation. Everybody was invited once a week to put questions, and he at once replied[17]. This served less to promote care

16. He once said of theology: *tantum valet quantum ad corrigendum, purgandum, sanctificandum hominem confert.*   *50*
17. Rio, writing of Döllinger in 1830, speaks of his passion for theological study as if he   *51*

than premature certainty. But for this, his views would have been less decided, and therefore less liable to change.

As an historian, Doellinger regarded Christianity as a force more than as a doctrine, and displayed it as it expanded and became the soul of later history. It was the mission and occupation of his life to discover and to disclose how this was accomplished, and to understand the history of civilized Europe, religious and profane, by the aid of sources which yielded certainty. In his vigorous prime he thought that he could complete the narrative of the conquest of the world by Christ in a single massive work. Experience slowly taught him that he who takes all history for his province is not the man to write a compendium.

The four volumes of "Church History" which gave him a name in literature appeared between 1833 and 1838, and stopped short of the Reformation[18]. While Catholics objected that he was a candid friend, Lutherans observed that he resolutely held his ground wherever he could, and as resolutely abandoned every position that he found untenable. He has since said of himself that he always spoke sincerely, but that he spoke as an advocate — an advocate who pleaded for a cause which he had convinced himself was just. The cause he pleaded was the divine government of the Church, the fulfilment of the promise that it would be preserved from error, though not from sin, the uninterrupted employment of the powers committed by Christ for the salvation of man. A Tyrolese divine spoke of him as the most chivalrous of Catholic celebrities.

Taking his survey from the elevation of general history, he gives less space to all the early heresies together than to the rise of Mahometanism. His way lies between Neander, who cares for no institutions, and Baur, who cares for no individuals[19]. Setting life and action above theory, he omitted the progress of doctrine. The object of religion upon earth is saintliness, and its success is shown in holy individuals. He leaves law and doctrine, to hold up great men as examples of Christian virtue.

Doellinger was always reserved in his use of the supernatural. He deplored the uncritical credulity of the author of the "Monks of the
52 West". Historians, he said, have to look for natural causes : enough

was nothing but a priest, and his passion for ancient and modern writers as if he was nothing but a *littérateur*; added to which there was the gift of a lucid and almost affectionate delivery, as if he had accumulated all this knowledge only for the pleasure of communicating it.

18. "Lehrbuch der Kirchengeschichte", 1836-1838. Translated by E. Cox, 1839. An attempt was made to republish the translation after Döllinger's death; but those who knew that the work utterly misrepresented Döllinger's mature opinions protested, and the project was abandoned.

53   19. "*Alle/geschichtlichen Personen sind für uns blosse Namen*," Baur.

will remain for the action of Providence, where we cannot penetrate. He told of the mediaeval saints and their illusions when they spoke of the future, and described them, as he described Carlyle and Ruskin to Dr. Plummer, as prophets without the gift of prediction. At Frankfort, where he spoilt his watch by depositing it in holy water and it was whispered that he had put it there to mend it, everybody knew that there was hardly a Catholic in the Parliament, of whom such a fable could be told with more felicitous unfitness[20].

Doellinger owed much to the *Italians*, whose ecclesiastical literature was the first that he mastered. Here were the stupendous records of the religious orders, their biography and bibliography. In this world of patient, accurate, wide-reaching research, Doellinger laid the deep foundations of his historical knowledge. Beginning with Baronius and Muratori, he gave a large portion of his life to Noris, and to the solid and enlightened scholarship that surrounded Benedict XIV., down to the compilers Borgia, Fantuzzi, and Marini. He thought that Orsi and Saccarelli were the best writers on the general history of the Church. Afterwards, he relied much on the canonists Ballerini and Berardi. Italy possessed the largest extant body of Catholic learning; the whole sphere of Church government was within its range.

Next to the Italians he gave systematic attention to the *French*. The conspicuous Gallicans are absent from his pages. He never overcame his distrust of Pascal, for his methodical scepticism and his endeavour to dissociate religion from learning. He esteemed the French Protestants of the seventeenth century who transformed the system of Geneva and Dort. *English* theology did not come much in his way until he had made himself at home with the Italians and the primary French. Then it abounded. He gathered it in quantities on two journeys in 1851 and 1858, and he possessed the English divines in perfection, at least down to Whitby and the nonjurors. Few writers interested him more deeply than Stapleton, Davenport, Barclay, the adversary and friend of Bellarmine, and Ramsay, the convert and recorder of Fénelon.

He seldom quotes contemporary *Germans*, unless to dispute with them, he prefers old books to new, and speaks of the necessary revision of history. He suspected foregone conclusions even in Neander, and he missed no opportunity of showing his dislike for Gieseler — that accomplished artificer in mosaic. In later years the proportion of things was changed. There was a religious literature to be proud of, to rely upon : other nations had lost their superiority. Doellinger's cosmopolitan char-

---

20. Some of us have seen in the bed-rooms of hotels on the continent little vessels for holy water. They are hung against the wall, often by the side of the bed, and both in size and shape they resemble watch-pockets. When they are empty they can be used as watch-pockets. The one into which Döllinger put his watch, when he attended the Parliament at Frankfort in 1848, had the water in it.

acteristic diminished, he became more absorbed in the national thought, and he called himself the most German of Germans.

Doellinger came early to the belief that history ought to be impersonal, that the historian does well to be humble and self-effacing, making it a religious duty to prevent the intrusion of all that betrays his own position, quality, hopes, and wishes. Without aspiring to the calm indifference of Ranke, he was conscious that in early life he had been too positive and too eager to persuade. He has been thought to resemble Fénelon, and the comparison is partly true. In reasonableness, moderation, and charity, in general culture of mind and the sense of the demands of the progress of civilisation, he was more in harmony with Fénelon than with many others who resembled him in the character of their work.

He deemed it Catholic to take ideas *from* history, and heresy to take them *into* it. He felt that sincere history was the royal road to religious union, and he specially cultivated those who saw both sides. He would cite with complacency what clever Jesuits, Raynaud and Faure, said for the Reformation, Mariana and Cordara against their Society[21]. When a Rhenish Catholic and a Genevese Calvinist drew two portraits of Calvin which were virtually the same, or when, in Ficker's revision of Boehmer, the Catholic defended the Emperor Frederic II. against the Protestant, he rejoiced as over a sign of the advent of science. Wiseman consulted Doellinger as to what Pope there was whose good name had not been vindicated, and Doellinger's reply, that Boniface VIII. wanted a friend, prompted both Wiseman's article and Tosti's book[22].

In politics, as in religion, he made the past a law for the present, and resisted doctrines which are ready made and not derived from experience. Consequently, he undervalued work which would never have been done from disinterested motives; and there were three of his most eminent contemporaries whom he decidedly underestimated, Thiers, Stahl, and Macaulay. Having known *Thiers* and heard him speak, he felt profoundly the talent of the extraordinary man. But Doellinger, disgusted with Thiers' advocacy, whether of the revolution, of Napoleon, or of France, neglected his work[23]. *Stahl* claims to be accounted

54

---

21. Juan Mariana (1537-1624) became a Jesuit in 1554. His "De las enfermedadas de la Compañía de Jesús" got into the hands of a French bookseller, who at once published it in Spanish, French, Italian and Latin (Bordeaux, 1625); and the General of the Society got it condemned by Urban VIII.

Giulio Cesare Cordara (1704-1785) was an Italian poet who wrote a history of the Jesuits.

22. Döllinger told Plummer that he had no recollection of giving this advice to Wiseman. L. Tosti wrote the "Storia di Bonifazio VIII.", Monte Cassino, 1846.

23. Döllinger thought Thiers such a 'phrase-maker'; and the temptation to sacrifice truth for the sake of making a neat phrase he considered to be a common snare to French writers.

an historian by his incomparably able book on the Church government of the Reformation. As a professor at Munich, and afterwards as a 55 parliamentary leader at Berlin, he was always an avowed partisan. Doellinger depreciated him accordingly. Once, when I spoke of Stahl as the greatest man born of a Jewish mother since Titus, he thought me unjust to Disraeli[24]. Most of all he misjudged *Macaulay*, of whom even Ranke said that he could hardly be called an historian at all. Doellinger was not attracted by the author of so many pictures and so much bootless decoration. He desired more generous treatment of the Jacobites and the French king. He deemed it hard that a science happily delivered from the toils of religious passion should be involved in political by the most brilliant example in literature.

In 1865 Doellinger was invited to prepare a new edition of his Church History. He had begun it when Niebuhr was lecturing at Bonn; before Tischendorf unfolded his first manuscript; before Baur discovered the Tuebingen hypothesis in the congregation of Corinth; before Rothe had planned his treatise on the primitive Church, or Ranke had begun to 56 pluck the plums for his modern Popes. The application of instruments of precision was just beginning. None had worked harder at his science and at himself than Doellinger; and the change around him was not greater than the change within. In his early career he had often shrunk from books which bore no stamps of orthodoxy. The book which he had written in that state of mind, and with that conception of science and religion, had only a prehistoric interest for its author. He refused to reprint it, and *declared that there was hardly a sentence fit to stand unchanged*[25].

Doellinger could impart knowledge better than the art of learning. Thousands of his pupils acquired connected views of religion passing through the ages, and gathered some notion of the meaning of history; but nobody ever learnt from him the mechanism by which it is written. His own assistants were many, but the masters were few, and he looked up with extraordinary gratitude to men like Sigonius, Antonius Augustinus, Blondel, Petavius, Leibniz, Burke, and Niebuhr, who had opened the passes for him as he groped in the illimitable forest.

24. Friederich Julius Stahl (1802-1861) was Privatdocent at Munich 1826 and Professor at Erlangen 1832, at Berlin 1840, where he made a great name. Döllinger's neglect of him is the more remarkable, because, like Döllinger, he was opposed to Hegelianism. His aim was to base everything on authority, the authority of the Christian Revelation. Hence his two sayings : 'Die Wissenschaft muss umkehren', and 'Autorität nicht Majorität'; that is, human reason is impotent for the attainment of truth and therefore must accept revelation; and the individual must render passive obedience to the powers which be. Döllinger would have accepted neither principle.

25. In Sept. 1864 he wrote that he must always go on learning a great deal. Not without some humiliation he was often having the experience, that his conclusions and judgments on historical matters were too often drawn from insufficient premisses, and therefore turned out to be untenable.

Of his work on the Reformation he completed only that part of his plan which included Lutheranism and the sixteenth century. *The third volume* (1848), *containing the theology of the Reformation, is the most solid of his writings.* He had miscalculated, not his resources, of which only a part had come into action, but the possibilities of compression. The book was left a fragment.

He contracts the Reformation into a history of the doctrine of justification. He found that this alone was the essential point in Luther's mind, that he made it the basis of his argument, the motive of his separation, the root and principle of his religion. He believed that Luther was right in the cardinal importance which he attributed to this doctrine in his system, and he in his turn recognised that it was the cause of all that followed, the source of the Reformer's success, and the sole insurmountable obstacle to every scheme of restoration. It was also, for Doellinger, the centre and basis of his antagonism. That was the point that he attacked when he combated Protestantism, deeming all other elements of conflict to be not supremely serious. Apart from this, there was much in Protestantism that he admired, much in its effects for which he was grateful. With the Lutheran view of imputation, Protestant and Catholic were separated by an abyss[26]. Without it, there was no lasting reason why they should be separate at all. Against the communities that hold it he stood in order of battle. But he distinguished very broadly the religion of the Reformers from the religion of Protestants. The root dogma had been repudiated by the most eminent Protestants; and since so many of the best writers resist or modify that which was the sole ultimate cause of disunion, it cannot be logically impossible to discover a reasonable basis for discussion. Therefore conciliation was always in his thoughts. In 1881, when Ritschl, the author of the

57   chief work on the subject, spent some days with Doellinger, he found him still full of these ideas, and possessing Luther at his fingers' ends.

This is the reason why Protestants have found him so earnest an opponent and so warm a friend. It was this that attracted him towards Anglicans, and made very many of them admire a Roman dignitary who knew the Anglo-Catholic library better than De Lugo. In the same spirit he said to Pusey : *Tales cum sitis, jam nostri estis,* always spoke of Newman's "Justification"[27] as the greatest masterpiece of theology that England had produced in a hundred years, and described Baxter and Wesley as the most eminent of English Protestants, — meaning Wesley as he was after 1 Dec. 1767, and Baxter as the life-long opponent

---

26. Döllinger wrote in July 1888 of Luther: "Meinerseits habe ich noch eine andere schwere Anklage gegen ihn zu erheben, nämlich die, dass er durch seine falsche Imputationslehre das sittlich-religiöse Bewusstseyn der Menschen auf zwei Jahrhunderte hinaus
58   verwirrt und corrumpirt hat."
    27. Newman's "Lectures on Justification", 1838; 2nd ed. 1840.

of that theory which was the source and soul of the Reformation. In a later letter to Pusey he wrote: "I am convinced by reading your "Eirenicon" that we are united inwardly in our religious convictions, although externally we belong to different Churches." He welcomed 59 the overtures which came to him from eminent historians. When they were old men, he and Ranke lived on terms of mutual goodwill. In 1865, after a visit to Munich, Ranke allowed that in religion there was no dispute between them, and that he had no fault to find with the Church as Doellinger understood it. Doellinger's growing belief that an approximation of part of Germany to sentiments of conciliation was only a question of time, had much to do with his attitude in Church questions after 1860. If history cannot confer faith or virtue, *it can clear away the misconceptions that turn men against one another.* He learnt to think more favourably of the religious influence of Protestantism, and of its efficacy in the defence of Christianity; but he thought as before of the spiritual consequences of Lutheranism proper. When people said of Luther that he does not come well out of his matrimonial advice to Henry and to Philip, or his exhortations to exterminate the revolted peasantry, or his passage from a confessor of toleration to a teacher of intoleration, Doellinger would not have the most powerful conductor of religion that Christianity has produced in eighteen centuries condemned for two pages in a hundred volumes. As early as 1848, in addressing the bishops of Germany in secret session at Würzburg, he had exhorted them to avail themselves of the new 60 atmosphere of liberty. He told them that freedom is the breath of the Catholic life, that it belongs to the Church by right divine, and that what they claimed must be claimed for others. The Church claims no superiority over the State. When Doellinger made persecution answer both for the decline of Spain and the fall of Poland, he appeared to deliver the common creed of the Whigs; and he did not protest when he was called the acknowledged head of the liberal Catholics. His hopefulness in the midst of the troubles of 1848, his ready acquiescence in the fall of ancient institutions, his trust in Rome, and in the abstract rights of Germans, suggested a reminiscence of the *Avenir* in 1830[28].

Lamennais, returning with *Montalembert* after his appeal to Rome, met Lacordaire at Munich, and during a banquet given in their honour learnt privately that he was condemned. The three friends spent that afternoon in Doellinger's company, and it was after he had left them that Lamennais produced the encyclical and said: *Dieu a parlé.* The fame of the Bavarian school of thought spread in France among those who belonged to the wider circles of the *Avenir*; and priests and laymen

28. *L'Avenir* was founded on democratic principles, which were condemned by Gregory XVI. 15 Aug. 1832; *L'Avenir* was silenced, and Lamennais retired.

followed, as to a scientific shrine. Doellinger used to visit his former visitors in various parts of France. One day at the seminary at Paris he enquired who were the most promising students. Dupanloup pointed out a youth who was the hope of the Church, and whose name was Ernest Renan.

An unimpassioned German like Doellinger, who had no taste for ideas released from controlling fact, took little pleasure in the impetuous declamation of Lamennais, and afterwards pronounced him inferior to Loyson. Neither Lacordaire nor Montalembert has intimated that Doellinger made any lasting impression on Lamennais, who took leave of him without discussing the action of Rome. Doellinger never sought to renew acquaintance with Lacordaire, when he had become the most important man in the Church of France. He saw more of Dupanloup, without feeling as deeply as Renan did, the rare charm of the combative prelate[29]. To an exacting scholar there was incongruity in the attention paid to one of whom he heard that he promoted the Council, and that he gave the memorable advice: *Surtout méfiez-vous des sources*. Doellinger depreciated the attainments of the French clergy, a habit which was confirmed by the writings of the most eminent of them, Darboy, and lasted until the appearance of Duchesne. The politics of Montalembert were so heavily charged with conservatism that he pronounced in favour of the *coup d'état*, saying: *Je suis pour l'autorité contre la révolte*; and there were many things, human and divine, on which he and Doellinger could not think alike; but as the most eloquent and persevering of Doellinger's Catholic friends, gifted with knowledge and experience of affairs, he influenced the working of Doellinger's mind. Yet the plausible reading of Doellinger's life, which explains it by his connexion with such men as Montalembert, De Decker, and Mr. Gladstone, is profoundly untrue. To deem him a liberal in any scientific sense is to miss the keynote of his life. He had all the liberality which consists of common sense, justice, humanity, and enlightenment, the wisdom of Canning or Guizot. But revolution, as the breach of continuity, as the renunciation of history, was hateful to him.

Doellinger was too much absorbed in distant events to be always a close observer of what went on near him, and he was not so much

29. Renan writes in his "Souvenirs de Jeunesse" (p. 323) : "Je trouvai chez M. Dupanloup cette grande et chaleureuse entente des choses de l'âme qui faisait sa supériorité. Je fus avec lui d'une extrême franchise. Le côté scientifique lui échappa tout à fait; quand je lui parlai de critique allemande, il fut surpris. L'Écriture, à ses yeux, n'était utile que pour fournir aux prédicateurs des passages éloquents; or l'hébreu ne sert de rien pour cela. Mais quel bon, grand et noble cœur ! J'ai là sous mes yeux un petit billet de sa main : 'Avez-vous besoin de quelque argent ? Ma pauvre bourse est à votre disposition. Mon offre, toute simple, ne vous blessera pas, j'espère.' Je le remerciai, et n'eus à cela aucun mérite." This was just before Renan left St. Sulpice, because he saw that he had ceased to be a Catholic. He left 6 Oct. 1845. Three days later Newman entered the Roman Church at Littlemore.

influenced by contemporary history as men who were less entirely at home in other centuries. He knew nearly all that could be known of the ninth : in the nineteenth his superiority deserted him. He had lived in many cities, and had known many important men; he had sat in three parliamentary assemblies, and had been consulted about the making of ministries; but as an authority on recent history he was hardly equal to himself.

At Oxford in 1851, when James Mozley asked whom he would like to see, he said, the men who had written in the "Christian Remembrancer" on Dante and Luther. Mozley himself had written on Luther, and he introduced him to Church at Oriel. After thirty-two years, when Church was Dean of St. Paul's and might have been Primate, the visit was returned. But Church had no idea that he had once received Doellinger at Oriel.

In "Hippolytus und Kallistus" (1853)[30] Doellinger undertook to vindicate the insulted see of Rome. He was glad of the opportunity to strike a blow at three men of whom he thought ill both in science and religion. He spoke of Gieseler as the flattest and most leathern of historians; he accused Baur of frivolity and want of theological conviction; and he wished that he knew as many circumlocutions for untruth as there Arabian synonyms for a camel, that he might do justice to Bunsen without violation of courtesy. The "Philosophumena" was a gross attack on Pope Kallistus, and it was attributed to Hippolytus, the foremost European writer of the time, venerated as a saint and a Father of the Church. Doellinger admitted the authorship, but defended the Roman Church from the inference that might be drawn from such an attack upon Popes by such a man. *This controversial work is the high-water mark of Doellinger's official assent and concurrence.* His next book showed the ebb.

"Heidenthum und Judenthum", which came out in 1857, is designed as an introduction to Christian history. The difference between the moral teaching of the later pagan writers and the early Christian writers is not the key to the future. The true problem is to expose the ills and errors which Christ, the Healer, came to remove. The measure must be taken from the depth of evil from which Christianity had to rescue mankind. Newman, who sometimes agreed with Doellinger in the letter, but seldom in the spirit, and who distrusted him as a man in whom the divine lived at the mercy of the scholar, so much liked what he heard of the book that, being unable to read it, he had it translated at the Oratory[31].

30. "Hippolytus and Callistus; or the Church of Rome in the First Half of the Third Century, with special reference to the Writings of Bunsen, Wordsworth, Baur, and Gieseler", by J.J. Ign. von Döllinger, translated by Alfred Plummer. Edinburgh, T. & T. Clark, 1876.

31. "The Gentile and the Jew in the Courts of the Temple of Christ : an Introduction

Doellinger inclined to apply the observation of domestic life to public affairs, to reduce the level of the heroic and sublime; and history in his hands lost something both in terror and in grandeur. He acquired his art in the long study of earlier times, where materials are scanty. All that can be known of Charlemagne or Gregory VII. could be held in a dozen volumes. A library would not suffice for Charles V. or Lewis XIV. Extremely few of the ancients are known [to] us in detail, as we know Cicero or St. Augustine. The science of character comes in with modern history. Doellinger had lived too long in the ages during which men are seen mostly in outline, and his historical psychology was that of private experience. But great men are something different from an enlarged repetition of average types, and the working of their minds is sometimes the exact contrary of ordinary men. We cannot understand Cromwell or Shaftesbury by studies made in the parish. The study of subtle character was not habitual with Doellinger, and the result was an extreme dread of unnecessary condemnation. He resented being told that Henry III. and Lewis XIII. were assassins; that Elizabeth tried to have Mary made away with, and that Mary had no greater scruples. When he met men less merciful than himself, he said that they were hanging judges. This indefinite generosity did not disappear when he had long outgrown its early cause.

Doellinger used to commemorate his visit to Rome in 1857 as an epoch of emancipation[32]. He was received with civility, if not with cordiality, and his days were spent profitably between the Minerva and the Vatican, where he was initiated into the mysteries of Galileo's tower. In Rome he was not in contact with the sinister side of things, scandal in the spiritual order, suffering in the temporal, tyranny in both. But the persuasion that government by priests could not maintain itself in the world as it is, grew in force and definiteness as he meditated at home on the things that he had seen and heard[33]. He was despondent and

to the History of Christianity". From the German of John J.I. Döllinger, Professor of Eccles. Hist. to the University of Munich. By N. Darnell, M.A., Late Fellow of New College, Oxford. Longmans, 1862.

32. Acton accompanied Döllinger on this journey. His appearance in Rome was not very welcome. Reisach, seeing him in the street, said to a companion, "Why there's Döllinger with his long nose, come to stick it into our affairs here!" Döllinger wrote that, on the whole, people had received him very well, and been far better than he expected in allowing him access to manuscripts. His work on them had interfered with his seeing people; and "one can't serve two masters. Nevertheless, I don't regret it." When he had an audience, the Pope showed no interest in the condition of things in Germany, but made a mysterious remark about national Churches not being wanted. Döllinger found out that Reisach had told the Pope that Döllinger wanted to set up an independent German Church.

62   33. Flix, afterwards Rector of the Anima in Rome, said that it was delightful to hear Döllinger arguing with Theiner. At Frankfort he had thought Döllinger cold, but now he thought his quiet manner a dignified contrast to the restless and impetuous Theiner. When they discussed learned subjects, the knowledge displayed by both was amazing. When one of apprehensive; but he had no suspicion of what was so near. For more than a year he remained silent and uncertain, watching the use France would make of the irresistible authority acquired by the defeat of Austria and the collapse of government in Central Italy. In this country, Newman did not share the animosity of conservatives against Napoleon III. and his action in Italy. He preserved an embarassed silence, refusing to commit himself even in private. An impatient M.P. took train to Edgbaston, and began, trying to draw him : "What times we live in, Father Newman! Look at all that is going on in Italy." "Yes, indeed! And look at China too, and New Zealand!" Lacordaire favoured the cause of the Italians more openly, and craved religious liberty at Rome. "*Qu'y puis-je? Me déclarer contre l'Italie parce que ses chaînes tombent mal à propos? Non assurément.*" This was written 22 February 1861. In April Doellinger spoke on the Roman question in the Odeon at Munich, and explained himself more fully in the autumn in the most popular of all his books.

The argument in "Kirche und Kirchen" is that the Churches which are without the Pope drift into many troubles, whereas the Church which energetically preserves the principle of unity has a vast superiority, which would prevail, but for its discrediting failure in civil government [34]. *He exposed the faults of the papal government through many centuries, and the hopelessness of all efforts to save it unless it was reformed.* But it was easy to draw from his premises the conclusion that the temporal power could not be reformed, but must be swept away. His indictment of its misdeeds justified the conduct of those who would put an end to it.

His exaltation of the spiritual authority, though at the expense of the temporal, the side blow at the Protestants, filling more than half the volume, disarmed for the moment the resentment of Rome. But it was a step in the process of detachment; the historian was beginning to prevail over the divine. In his "Hippolytus" he began by surrendering the main point, that this writer who so vilified the Papacy was an undisputed saint. In his "Heidenthum" he flung away a favourite argument, by avowing that Paganism developed by its own laws, untouched by Christianity, until the second century. And he believed so far in Protestantism, that it was idle to talk of reconciliation until its providential mission had borne all its fruit. He exasperated a Munich colleague by refusing to decide whether Gregory and Innocent had the

them mentioned a point, the other at once showed that he knew all about it. Flix declared that the greatest political genius in the world could not reform the papal government; the means did not exist. Walking by moonlight in the Colosseum, Döllinger told Acton that the temporal power was near its end, but the Papacy itself would undergo very great change. He never visited Rome again.

34. "The Church and the Churches; or The Papacy and the Temporal Power. An Historical and Political Review". By Dr. Döllinger. Translated, with the Author's permission, by William Bernard Mac Cabe. Hurst & Blackett, 1862.

right to depose Emperors, or Otho and Henry to depose Popes : historians should not fit theories to facts, but show how things worked. He pursued a line of his own, was always learning and revising, and seemed to others to be incalculable. When he first addressed the University as Rector, he said that he would use the opportunity to speak what was closest to his heart, he told the students *to be always true to their convictions and not to yield to surroundings*; and he invoked the example of *Burke, his favourite among public men*, who, turning from his associates to obey the light within, carried the nation with him. At that time Doellinger was nearly the only German who knew Newman well and appreciated the grace and force of his mind. But Newman, even when he was angry, assiduously distinguished the pontiff from his court : — "There will necessarily," he said, "be round the Pope second-rate people, who are not subjects of that supernatural wisdom which is his prerogative. For myself, certainly I have found myself in
63 a different atmosphere, when I have left the Curia for the Pope himself." Montalembert said there were things in "Kirche und Kirchen" that he would not have liked to have said in public : — "Il est certain que la seconde partie de votre livre déplaira beaucoup, non seulement à Rome, mais encore à la très grande majorité des Catholiques. Je ne sais donc [pas] si j'aurais eu le courage d'infliger cette blessure à mon père
64 et à mes frères." Doellinger judged that the prerogative even of *natural* wisdom was often wanting in the government of the Church[35].

Doellinger did not care to travel over ground which was already occupied by specialists, and where he had nothing of his own to tell. He preferred to be a pathfinder. In treating the history of the Papacy, he began by eliminating legend. He found so much that was legendary, that his critical preliminaries took the shape of a history of fables relating to the Papacy. Many of these were harmless : *others were devised for a purpose, and he fixed his attention more and more on those which were the work of design.* How far had the persistent production of spurious matter affected the genuine constitution and theology of the Church? In his "Papstfabeln des Mittelalters" he indicated the problem without discussing it[36]. The threatening import of the volume was perceived, and twenty-one hostile critics sent reviews of it to one theological journal.

The "Pope Fables" carried the critical inquiry a little way; but he went on with the subject. After the Donation of Constantine came

35. In 1865 Döllinger wrote to Montalembert that his illusions were leaving him : "I am very much sobered (*ernüchtert*) : so much in the Church has turned out very differently from what 20 or 30 years ago I had anticipated, and depicted in such rosy colours."

36. "Fables respecting the Popes [of the Middle Ages]". A Contribution to Ecclesiastical History by John J. Ign. von Döllinger. Translated by Alfred Plummer. Rivingtons, 1871. This was my first book. The second was "Prophecies and the Prophetic Spirit in the Christian Era". An Historical Essay by John J. Ign. von Döllinger. Rivingtons, 1873.

the False Decretals, just then printed for the first time in a critical edition. Doellinger began to be absorbed in the long train of fictions, 65 which had deceived men like Gregory VII., Aquinas, Bellarmine, which Doellinger traced up to the false Areopagite, and down to the Laminae Granatenses. These studies became the chief occupation of his life, 66 and they led to his excommunication in 1871; for it was the history of Church government which so profoundly altered his position. Some trace of his researches appears in "Janus"; but the history itself, which was the main work of his life, was never completed or published. He died without making known the exact extent to which his earlier ideas were changed by his later studies.

Whilst he pursued his isolating investigations on hitherto unpublished materials collected by himself in Vienna and Venice, or sent to him from many countries by friends and strangers, he remained aloof from a disturbing question. Persecution was a problem which had never troubled him. The gravity of the question had not been brought home to him. At first he treated the intolerance of Catholics as a bequest from Imperial Rome, in no way involving the true practice and spirit of the Church. But Newman would admit no such compromise. "Is not," he said, "the miraculous infliction of judgments upon blasphemy, lying, profaneness, etc., in the Apostles' days a sanction of infliction upon the same by a human hand in the times of the Inquisition? Ecclesiastical rulers may punish with the sword, if they can, and if it be expedient to do so. The Church has a right to make laws and to enforce them with temporal punishments." 67

Liberal defenders of the temporal power of the Popes were in a difficulty. That power persecuted on principle. If they approved this, where was their liberality; if they condemned it, where was their Catholicity? Gratry welcomed Doellinger's "Kirche und Kirchen". So at last did Montalembert. Nothing better, he said, had been written since Bossuet. The judgment on the Roman government was just. He was coming to regard toleration as the supreme affair. At Malines he solemnly declared that the Inquisitor was as horrible as the Terrorist. A journey to Spain in 1865 made him more vehement than ever. "There you can see," he said, "what an exclusive Catholicism has made of one of the most heroic nations in the world." Before his death he declared that to send human beings to the stake, with a crucifix before them, was the act of a monster or a maniac.

Doellinger wrote a popular account of the Inquisition, and it appeared in the newspapers in 1867. There is no uncertainty as to the author's feeling towards the infliction of torture and death for religion, and the purpose of his treatise is to prevent the nailing of the Catholic colours to the stake. But compared with the sweeping vehemence of the Frenchmen who preceded, there is a restrained moderation of language. In 1879 he prepared materials for a paper on the massacre of St. Bartholomew. The discourse was never delivered, never composed; but the subject of toleration was absent no more from his thoughts.

His collections of materials constantly prompted new and attractive schemes, but *his way was strewn with promise unperformed, and abandoned for want of concentration.* He would not write with imperfect materials, and the materials were always imperfect. Perpetually engaged in going over his own life and reconsidering his conclusions, he was not depressed with unfinished work. When a sanguine friend hoped that all the contents of his hundred note-books would come into use, he answered that perhaps they might, if he lived for hundred and fifty years. He seldom wrote a book without compulsion, or the aid of energetic assistants. The account of mediaeval sects, dated 1890, was on the stocks for half a century. The discourse on the Templars, delivered at his last appearance in public, had been always before him since a conversation with Michelet about the year 1841.

Everybody has felt that his power was out of all proportion to his work, and that *he knew too much to write. It was so much better to hear him than to read all his books, that the memory of what he was will pass away with the children whom he loved.* Hefele called him the first theologian of Germany, and Hoefler said that he surpassed all men in the knowledge of historical literature. Martensen describes him as he talked with equal knowledge and certainty of every age, and understood all characters and all situations as if he had lived in the midst of them. Harnack has declared that no man had the same knowledge and intelligence of history in general, and of religious history which is its most essential element, and he affirms, what some have doubted, that he possessed the rare faculty of entering into alien thought. None of those who knew Doellinger best will ever qualify these judgments[37].

It is right to add that, in spite of boundless reading, *there was no lumber in his mind*, and, in spite of his classical learning, little ornament.

---

37. Von Sybel has given an admirable account of Döllinger's unique powers in conversation. Whatever subject came up, he seemed to have the details all in order in his prodiguous memory. And he never talked as if he was giving instruction, however instructive what he said might be. He was a master of fascinating conversation, a master of the first rank, in one respect far superior to such excellent talkers as Alex. Humbolt and Macaulay. Döllinger could be a good listener, and preferred a dialogue to having all the talk to himself. He would always listen to an objection, and you could always tell by his face whether he thought your objection worth anything. His eye would twinkle and he would look rather roguish when a good point was made against him. And then he would carry all before him with his wealth of knowledge and clearness of vision. "In my long life," says Sybel, "I have had the good fortune to be intimate with many remarkable men, but I have come across only one who in conversation has given me such delight—delight, it is true, of a very different texture,—and that was Prince Bismarck."

Among the men to be commemorated here, he stands alone. Throughout the measureless distance which he traversed, his movement was against his wishes, under no attraction but historical research alone. It was given to him to form his philosophy of history on the largest induction ever available to man; and while he owed more to divinity than any other historian, he owed more to history than any other divine.

APPENDIX

reprinted from *The Critical Review* 1 (1891) 21-28 :

BRIEFE UND ERKLÄRUNGEN VON I. VON DÖLLINGER ÜBER DIE VATICANISCHEN DECRETE, 1869-1887.

München, Beck'sche Verlagsbuchhandlung, 1890. Edinburgh,
Williams & Norgate.

It is natural at the present time, when the deaths of two such men as Döllinger and Newman are so recent, to compare the two together; and the making of such a comparison is almost inevitable in the case of those who have had the happiness of knowing both of them. Within a few months of one another both have gone to a well-earned rest, the one in his ninety-first, the other in his ninetieth year. Their ends were in some respects strikingly similar. Each until within a few days of his death was in his usual state of health, which, in Döllinger's case, was one of extraordinary vigour. Each was unconscious for some time before the end came, and was able to receive extreme unction only without the *viaticum*. Both of them carried with them to the grave an amount of veneration and affection such as is earned by few, and won by still fewer; and this veneration and affection, in the case of Döllinger certainly, and in the case of Newman probably, is most widely felt and cherished among those who are not members of the communion to which the objects of it belonged. It is equally obvious to remark that their ends were in one respect strikingly different. The one died as a prince of that Church which in his earlier days he had ferociously attacked as anti-Christian; the other died excommunicated by the same Church, of which he had for half a century been the most distinguished ornament.

A comparison of the lives and work of the two theologians would carry this article far beyond its proper limits: but a perusal of the little volume before us will convince anyone who is acquainted with the later writings of Cardinal Newman, how impossible it was that the two should agree about the recent developments of doctrine and practice which have taken place in the Church of Rome. The present writer on more than one occasion has acted as a means of communication between the two, each writing or saying to him what it was tacitly understood was to be conveyed to the other, although neither cared to write to the other direct; and he long ago came to the conclusion that the difference between the point of view of each was too fundamental for either to come over to the other, or for any half-way house to be found. The one took his stand upon historical facts, which for every competent student of history are indisputable, and which admit of only one reasonable interpretation. The other staked everything upon the inerrancy of a divinely guided authority; and for him the fact that this authority had given a decision, at once made well attested historical facts disputable, or made what would otherwise have been strained and improbable interpretations of them reasonable. The present intensely interesting collection of declarations and letters gives us in a short compass the main historical facts which Dr. Döllinger considered to be absolutely fatal to the truth of the dogma respecting the infallibility of the pope, and the reasons which for nineteen years prevented him from "submitting" even to the pope with the whole of the Roman episcopate at his back, when this authority required him to believe as necessary to salvation a *new* article of faith, and an article which reason and lifelong study convinced him *could* not be true.

Of the twenty-eight documents in this collection, the editing of which we owe to
Professor Reusch, four (1, 2, 3, 10) are already well known; and one or more of them may
be found in Quirinus, or Pomponio Leto, or *The New Reformation*, as well as elsewhere. *69*
Several others have appeared in newspapers and periodicals. But the editor has done well
to give all these once more to the world to explain and complete that which now appears for
the first time. The four well-known documents are—the pamphlet of "Considerations
for the Bishops of the Council respecting the question of Papal Infallibility," which
appeared anonymously (October, 1869); two articles in the *Allgemeine Zeitung* on the
address which certain members of the Vatican Council made to the pope requesting him to
declare his own infallibility, and on the new order of business in the Council and its
theological significance (January 21st and March 11th, 1870); and lastly, the famous
reply to Archbishop Scherr of Munich, when the latter, himself a former opponent of
the dogma, called upon Döllinger, on pain of excommunication, to submit to it (March
28th, 1871). These four we must do no more than mention, in the hope that those who cannot
read them in the original in the present volume will take note of them as authorities
to be sought for in one or other of the volumes mentioned above. They are indispensable
to every one who would have an intelligent grasp of the infallibility question. The
extracts for which space can be found here shall be taken from the letters in this
collection which have never been published before.

Of the various persons who write to Dr Döllinger with a view to his "conversion,"
or "submission," or "reconciliation with the Church," the only one who uses anything that
is worthy of being called argument is Archbishop Scherr. His successor Archbishop
Steichele, Bishop Hefele, the Papal Nuncio Ruffo Scilla, and a lady of rank, whose
name is not given, content themselves with urging him to save his soul from inevitable
damnation, or to make angels and men rejoice by abandoning his errors. Even Bishop
Hefele, whose submission was an amazement to all who knew how much he knew
of Church history, does not give a word of explanation as to how a student of history
could accept the dogma, but has only weak entreaties to send. The revelation of this fact
must be a blow to the infallibilists. It was known that Hefele had written to Döllinger,
June, 1886, and that Döllinger had sent him no answer; and it was confidently asserted,
in more than one ultramontane paper, that Döllinger's friends would not dare to
publish this unanswered, and (it was supposed) unanswerable letter. The appeal which it
contains is almost grotesque in its feebleness.

The red thread which runs through Döllinger's replies to the four other correspondents
is the following :—

"Since the beginning of the Vatican Synod I have publicly and repeatedly maintained
the opposite doctrine, and have supported it with many arguments. I should, therefore,
have both to refute myself and publicly prove that the doctrine which I have taught
both in former days, and with special emphasis in recent times, is a false and perverted
doctrine. Were I not to do this, assuredly no human being, no one at any rate who knows
anything of my writings and public declarations, would believe in the sincerity of my
submission. The whole world, both near and far (a few nuns perhaps excepted), would
stigmatize me as a gross, conscienceless hypocrite, who, out of fear for himself and his
position, was willing to deny his convictions."

To the lady of rank he writes in 1880, that it might suffice to refer a correspondent
of the other sex to the facts and arguments which he had published in 1871, when he
was requested to submit to the Vatican decrees; "facts and arguments of which, according to
a conviction that is more strongly confirmed in me than ever, every one remains unrefuted
and irrefutable." But she has probably never seen the document, or has never thought
it worthy of inspection : which is natural enough, for of course she has been told that
all he has maintained is untrue. Yet he ventures to direct her attention to one or two
circumstances, which may possibly moderate her judgment respecting him.

"I am now in my eighty-first year, and for forty-seven years I have been a public
teacher of theology; and in all this long time not a single censure or even a demand

for explanation has ever reached me from any ecclesiastical authority at home or abroad. The new articles of faith, which have been set up by Pius IX. with his council, I *never* taught. In my youth, when I was a student at Bamberg and Würzburg, they were regarded as theological opinions, and many added that they were badly founded opinions. For me, who for nearly half a century had had to work day by day at these subjects and the questions connected with them, the conviction grew stronger and stronger, that these doctrines and claims are not only biblically, traditionally, and historically baseless and erroneous, but also long before they were raised to the rank and binding force of articles of faith, had had the most pernicious effects upon Church, State, and society. Then came the fatal year 1870. If I obeyed the demand that I should swear to the new dogma, I thereby declared myself a teacher of error, and not only myself, but my teachers now dead, and a number of friends and colleagues, who found themselves in the like situation. In vain I begged that I might be left with the faith and confession to which I had hitherto without blame or contradiction remained loyal. Yesterday still orthodox, I was to-day a heretic worthy of excommunication, not because I had changed my doctrine, but because others had thought proper to institute a change and to turn opinions into articles of faith." She will tell him that he must make a "sacrifice of his intellect." But what then becomes of his belief in Christianity? That too is based upon historical facts. If he cannot trust his intellect respecting the facts which convince him of the falsehood of the new dogma, how can he trust it respecting the facts which convince him of the truth of Christianity? "If my bishop would declare to me, 'I will release you from excommunication on condition that you will believe and confess what Bossuet and Fénelon and hundreds of the most saintly and learned bishops with them have taught respecting the pope,' who would be more ready than I?"

To Archbishop Steichele, an old pupil of his, whose letters, although devoid of strength, are at least affectionate and reverential, he writes that he had been at work on a detailed reply, but that the material had grown to such an extent (it is to be hoped that it is in existence), that he could not venture to inflict it on him. He must content himself with mentioning a few facts.

"The curse of excommunication, which the Chapter of this cathedral in the name of your predecessor caused to be published against me from every pulpit, I am still unable to recognize as anything but an act of violence and injustice. I had expressly offered myself for instruction and public refutation. That I at the same time begged to be allowed to speak and to have my misgivings heard was more than reasonable, and would have been in accordance with ecclesiastical precedent. The counsellors of the archbishop were of course certain of victory : in their eyes the falseness of all that I maintain was, and is, clear as day; they were therefore convinced that the discussion could only lead to my public discomfiture and confusion, and that for me there would then naturally remain no alternative, but to accept the bestowed instruction with gratitude and humility, and to profess my submission. *Pertinacia*, therefore, on my side manifestly did not exist ; and your Grace knows that, where this is wanting, a sentence of excommunication for dogmatic dissent is null and void. The way in which I was treated is in truth a proceeding *without a parallel* in ecclesiastical history. It has never before come to pass, that an old man, who in forty-five years of public teaching has never incurred even a single episcopal reproof or censure, whose orthodoxy previously had never been subjected to a single authenticated suspicion, has been forthwith, without so much as being heard in his defence, handed over — according to the formula in vogue — to Satan." He assures the archbishop that there was a time when he sincerely *wished* to be able to accept and prove the papal system. He worked hard for many years, and collected an amount of material far more complete than is to be found in any printed work. "I do not believe that a single witness of any importance has escaped me." The result amounted to demonstration, so far as demonstration is possible in history; and he saw that he must abandon the idea of writing a history of the papacy. For his work would at once be placed on the Index; and then he must either make a hypocritical submission or abandon his work as university professor, "to which I clung with my whole soul. ... I say it to myself daily, that I am a frail mortal, perpetually going wrong in many ways. My whole intellectual life has been in the main a continual correcting and laying aside of opinions and views previously formed and embraced. I am not conscious that I have ever obstinately closed my mind against a better insight, — at least I cannot recall any such case. Even my most cherished opinions, although at first with a heavy heart, I have surrendered, so soon as it became clear to me that they were untenable."

Every Roman priest at his ordination takes an oath that he will interpret Scripture according to the tradition of the Church and the unanimous consensus of the Fathers. It is notorious that the Vatican decrees are based on interpretations of Scripture which are utterly at variance with patristic exegesis, and which not a single Father of the first four or five centuries admits. Döllinger says that he has asked a number of his brother clergy how they reconcile acceptance of the decrees with their oath. The answer was always either evasive or an awkward shrug of the shoulders. They said that this was a matter of detail, with which individual priests had no need to meddle; or that it was of the very essence of faith to surrender oneself blindly and without examination to the hierarchy *now living*, and to leave it to them to reconcile contradictions. "I need not tell you what impression such pitiable evasions made upon me."

In his reply to the Nuncio Ruffo Scilla (October 12th, 1887), Döllinger says : —

"I know from a number of irreproachable witnesses, from statements which they have let fall, that the council of the Vatican was not free, that the means there used were menaces, intimidations, and seductions. I know it from bishops, whose letters I hold, or who have told it to me by word of mouth. The very Archbishop of Munich who excommunicated me, came to me the day after his return from Rome, and told me certain details which left in me no doubt. It is true that all these prelates have made their submission : they all agreed to say, by way of excuse, 'We do not wish to make a schism.' *I also do not wish to be a member of a schismatical society : I am isolated.*"

This last sentence seems to settle the question whether Dr Döllinger was a member of the Old Catholic communion. A little further on he writes : —

"And here, Monseigneur, I venture to bring before you a characteristic fact. When the archbishop, obeying (as he stated) the orders of the pope, communicated to me the sentence pronounced against me, he conveyed to me the information that I was subject to all the penalties which are imposed by canon law upon excommunicated persons. The first and the most important of these penalties is contained in the celebrated bull of Pope Urban II., which decides that any one in the world may kill an excommunicated person, when his motive for doing so is zeal for the Church. At the same time he caused sermons to be preached against me in all the pulpits in Munich; and the effect of these declamations was such, that the head of the police informed me that attacks on my person were being planned, and that I should do well to avoid going out without company. May I venture to raise the question, Monseigneur, whether, in the event of my submission, I should be obliged to declare to the world that I find this decision of the infallible pope to be in perfect conformity with the morality of the Gospel?"

These extracts will probably suffice to prove the value and the interest of this small collection of documents. It tends to show that the Church of Rome does *not* always know what to do with men of genius and exceptional force of character. That she should have made no use of Newman, and should have cast away Döllinger, are dark blots in her history, in a century which for her is full of grievous stains.

EXPLANATORY NOTES

ABBREVIATIONS

ADB	*Allgemeine Deutsche Biographie*, 56 vols., Leipzig, 1875-1912.
AHC	*Annuarium Historiae Conciliorum. Internationale Zeitschrift für Konzilienforschung*, Amsterdam, 1969-70; Paderborn, 1971 ff.
AUBERT	R. AUBERT, *Le pontificat de Pie IX* (Histoire de l'Église depuis les origines jusqu'à nos jours, 21), Paris, 1952, ²1963.
BENTLEY	J. BENTLEY, *Ritualism and Politics in Victorian Britain. The Attempt to Legislate for Belief* (Oxford Theological Monographs), Oxford, 1978.
Bericht 1874	*Bericht über die am 14., 15. und 16. September zu Bonn gehaltenen Unions-Conferenzen. Im Auftrag des Vorsitzenden Dr. v. Döllinger herausgegeben von Fr. Heinr. REUSCH*, Bonn, 1874.
Bericht 1875	*Bericht über die vom 10. bis 16. August 1875 zu Bonn gehaltenen Unions-Conferenzen. Im Auftrag des Vorsitzenden Dr. v. Döllinger herausgegeben von Fr. Heinr. REUSCH*, Bonn, 1875.
BN	*Biographie Nationale*, 28 vols., Brussels, 1866-1944; supps., 1957 ff.
BOASE	F. BOASE, *Modern English Biography. Containing many thousand concise memoirs of persons who have died between the years 1851-1900 with an index of the most interesting matter*, 6 vols., Truro, 1892-1921; reprint, London, 1965.
BOSL	*Bosls Bayerische Biographie. 8000 Persönlichkeiten aus 15 Jahrhunderten*, ed. K. BOSL, Ratisbon, 1983.
BRANDMÜLLER	W. BRANDMÜLLER, *Die Publikation des 1. Vatikanischen Konzils in Bayern. Aus den Anfängen des bayerischen Kulturkampfes*, in *ZBLG* 31 (1968) 197-258, 575-634.
BRHE	*Bibliothèque de la Revue d'histoire ecclésiastique*, Louvain, 1927 ff.
BWDG	*Biographisches Wörterbuch zur deutschen Geschichte*, ed. H. RÖSSLER and G. FRANZ; new ed. by K. BOSL, G. FRANZ, and H.H. HOFMANN, 3 vols., Munich, 1973-75.
Cath	*Catholicisme. Hier, aujourd'hui, demain*, ed. G. JACQUEMET, continued by G. MATHON, G.-H. BAUDRY, and P. GUILLUY, Paris, 1947 ff.
CHADWICK, *Victorian Church*	O. CHADWICK, *The Victorian Church* (An Ecclesiastical History of England, 7-8), 2 vols., London, 1966-70.
CHADWICK, *Catholicism*	O. CHADWICK, *Catholicism and History. The Opening of the Vatican Archives*, Cambridge/London/New York/Melbourne, 1976.
ColLac	*Acta et decreta sacrorum conciliorum recentiorum. Collectio Lacensis*, 7 vols., Freiburg i/Br., 1870-90.
CWIEKOWSKI	F.J. CWIEKOWSKI, *The English Bishops and the First Vatican Council* (BRHE, 52), Louvain, 1971.

DAB   *Dictionary of American Biography*, 20 vols., New York, 1928-37.

DAH   J. B. CODE, *Dictionary of the American Hierarchy (1789-1964)*, New York, 1964.

DBF   *Dictionnaire de biographie française*, ed. J. BALTEAU, M. BARROUX, and M. PRÉVOST, continued by M. PRÉVOST, J. R. D'AMAT, and H. T. DE MOREMBERT, Paris, 1933ff.

DBI   *Dizionario Biografico degli Italiani*, Rome, 1960ff.

DE   *Dizionario Ecclesiastico*, ed. A. MERCATI and A. PELZER, 3 vols., Turin, 1953-58.

DE FRANCISCIS   P. DE FRANCISCIS (ed.), *Discorsi del Sommo Pontefice Pio IX, pronunziati in Vaticano ai fedeli di Roma e dell'Orbe dal principio della sua prigionia fino al presente*, 3 vols., Rome, 1872-75.

DENZLER   G. DENZLER, *Das I. Vatikanische Konzil und die Theologische Fakultät der Universität München*, in *AHC* 1 (1969) 412-455.

DHGE   *Dictionnaire d'histoire et de géographie ecclésiastiques*, ed. A. BAUDRILLART *et al.*, continued by A. DE MEYER, E. VAN CAUWENBERGH, and R. AUBERT, Paris, 1912ff.

DNB   *Dictionary of National Biography*, ed. L. STEPHEN and S. LEE, new ed., 22 vols., London, 1908-09; supps., 1912ff.

DSpir   *Dictionnaire de spiritualité ascétique et mystique. Doctrine et histoire*, ed. M. VILLER, F. CAVALLERA, and J. DE GUIBERT, continued by Ch. BAUMGARTNER, A. PAYEZ, A. DERVILLE, and A. SOLIGNAC, Paris, 1932ff.

DTC   *Dictionnaire de théologie catholique, contenant l'exposé des doctrines de la théologie catholique, leurs preuves et leur histoire*, ed. A. VACANT and E. MANGENOT, continued by É. AMANN, 15 vols., Paris, 1903-50; vol. XVI: B. LOTH and A. MICHEL, *Tables générales*, 3 vols., 1951-72.

EC   *Enciclopedia Cattolica*, 12 vols., Vatican City, 1949-54.

EI   *Enciclopedia Italiana di scienze, lettere ed arti*, 36 vols., Rome, 1929-39; supps., 1938ff.

EUI   *Enciclopedia Universal Ilustrada Europeo-Americana*, 70 vols., Madrid/Barcelona, 1905-30; supps., 1930ff.

Exp   *The Expositor*, London, 1875ff.

ExpT   *The Expository Times*, London, 1889ff.

FRIEDBERG, *Sammlung*   E. FRIEDBERG, *Sammlung der Aktenstücke zum ersten vaticanischen Concil mit einem Grundrisse der Geschichte desselben*, Tübingen, 1872.

FRIEDBERG, *Aktenstücke*   E. FRIEDBERG, *Aktenstücke die altkatholische Bewegung betreffend, mit einem Grundriss der Geschichte derselben. Zugleich als Fortsetzung und Ergänzung der "Sammlung der Aktenstücke zum ersten vatikanischen Concil"*, Tübingen, 1876.

FRIEDRICH   J. FRIEDRICH, *Ignaz von Döllinger. Sein Leben auf Grund seines schriftlichen Nachlasses dargestellt*, 3 vols., Munich, 1899-1901.

FRIES-SCHWAIGER   H. FRIES and G. SCHWAIGER (eds.), *Katholische Theologen Deutschlands im 19. Jahrhundert*, 3 vols., Munich, 1975.

GATZ   E. GATZ (ed.), *Die Bischöfe der deutschsprachigen Länder 1785/1803 bis 1945. Ein biographisches Lexikon*, Berlin, 1983.

GE   *La grande encyclopédie. Inventaire raisonné des sciences, des lettres et des arts*, 31 vols., Paris, 1886-1902.

GGT   *Gothaisches genealogisches Taschenbuch der gräflichen, freiherrlichen, adeligen und briefadeligen Häuser.*

HASLER   A. B. HASLER, *Pius IX. (1846-1878). Päpstliche Unfehlbarkeit und 1. Vatikanisches Konzil. Dogmatisierung und Durchsetzung einer Ideologie* (Päpste und Papsttum, 12), 2 vols., Stuttgart, 1977.

Hierarchia   R. RITZLER and P. SEFRIN, *Hierarchia Catholica medii et recentioris aevi.* Vol. VIII: *A pontificatu Pii PP. IX (1846) usque ad pontificatum Leonis PP. XIII (1903)*, Padua, 1978.

HUBER   E. R. HUBER, *Deutsche Verfassungsgeschichte seit 1789.* Vol. IV: *Struktur und Krisen des Kaiserreichs*, Stuttgart/Berlin/Cologne/Mainz, 1969.

HUBER-HUBER   E. R. HUBER and W. HUBER, *Staat und Kirche im 19. und 20. Jahrhundert. Dokumente zur Geschichte des deutschen Staatskirchenrechts.* Vol. II: *Staat und Kirche im Zeitalter des Hochkonstitutionalismus und des Kulturkampfs 1848-1890*, Berlin, 1976.

IKZ   *Internationale Kirchliche Zeitschrift*, Bern, 1911 ff. Continuation of *RIT*.

JANUS   *Der Papst und das Concil von JANUS*, Leipzig, 1869 (see p. LIII).

JL   L. KOCH, *Jesuiten-Lexikon. Die Gesellschaft Jesu einst und jetzt*, Paderborn, 1934; reprint, 2 vols., Louvain, 1962.

JTS   *The Journal of Theological Studies*, London/New York, 1900-05; Oxford, 1906 ff.

KAHLE   W. KAHLE, *Westliche Orthodoxie. Leben und Ziele Julian Joseph Overbecks* (Oekumenische Studien, 9), Leiden/Cologne, 1968.

KÜRY   U. KÜRY, *Die altkatholische Kirche. Ihre Geschichte, ihre Lehre, ihr Anliegen* (Die Kirchen der Welt, 3), 2nd ed. by Chr. OEYEN, Stuttgart, 1978, [3]1982.

Letters and Diaries *The Letters and Diaries of John Henry Newman*, ed. Ch. S. DESSAIN *et al.*, London, 1961-72; Oxford, 1973 ff.

LIDDON   H. P. LIDDON, *Life of Edward Bouverie Pusey, Doctor of Divinity, Canon of Christ Church, Regius Professor of Hebrew in the University of Oxford*, ed. J. O. JOHNSTONE, R. J. WILSON, and W. C. E. NEWBOLT, 4 vols., London/New York/Bombay, 1897.

LÖSCH   S. LÖSCH, *Döllinger und Frankreich. Eine geistige Allianz 1823-1871. Im Lichte von 56 bisher meist unbekannten Briefen, mit zwei Döllingerbildnissen nebst Döllinger-Bibliographie* (Schriftenreihe zur bayerischen Landesgeschichte, 51), Munich, 1955.

LTK   *Lexikon für Theologie und Kirche*, 2nd ed. by J. HÖFER and K. RAHNER, 11 vols., Freiburg i/Br., 1957-67.

MCCLELLAND   V. A. MCCLELLAND, *English Roman Catholics and Higher Education 1830-1903*, Oxford, 1973.

MCELRATH   D. MCELRATH, *The Syllabus of Pius IX. Some Reactions in England* (BRHE, 39), Louvain, 1964.

MANSI   G. D. MANSI, *Sacrorum conciliorum nova et amplissima collectio*, 2nd ed., 35 vols., Paris/Leipzig, 1901-04, with continuation by L. PETIT and J. B. MARTIN, *Collectio conciliorum recentiorum Ecclesiae universae*, 20 vols., 1911-27.

MBM   Miscellanea Bavarica Monacensia, Munich, 1967 ff.

MHP   Miscellanea Historiae Pontificiae, Rome, 1939 ff.

MOSS   C. B. MOSS, *The Old Catholic Movement, Its Origins and History*, London, 1948, ²1964.

MOURRE   M. MOURRE, *Dictionnaire d'histoire universelle*, 2 vols., Paris, 1968.

NCE   *New Catholic Encyclopedia*, 15 vols., New York/St. Louis/San Francisco/Toronto/London/Sydney, 1967; supps., 1974 ff.

NDB   *Neue deutsche Biographie*, Berlin, 1953 ff.

NEUNER   P. NEUNER, *Döllinger als Theologe der Ökumene* (Beiträge zur ökumenischen Theologie, 19), Paderborn/Munich/Vienna/Zurich, 1979.

NORMAN   E. R. NORMAN, *The Catholic Church and Ireland in the Age of Rebellion 1859-1873*, London, 1965.

ÖBL   *Österreichisches Biographisches Lexikon 1815-1950*, ed. E. OBERMAYER-MARNACH, Graz/Cologne, 1957 ff.

ODCC   *The Oxford Dictionary of the Christian Church*, 2nd ed. by F. L. CROSS and E. A. LIVINGSTONE, Oxford, 1974; rev. ed., 1983.

PALANQUE   J.-R. PALANQUE, *Catholiques libéraux et gallicans en France face au Concile du Vatican 1867-1870* (Publication des Annales de la Faculté des Lettres, Aix-en-Provence. Nouvelle Série, 34), Aix-en-Provence, 1962.

PATELOS   C. G. PATELOS, *Vatican I et les évêques uniates. Une étape éclairante de la politique romaine à l'égard des orientaux (1867-1870)* (BRHE, 65), Louvain, 1981.

QUIRINUS   *Römische Briefe vom Concil von QUIRINUS*, Munich, 1870 (see p. LIII).

RE   *Realencyklopädie für protestantische Theologie und Kirche*, 3rd ed. by A. HAUCK, 24 vols., Leipzig, 1896-1913.

RGG   *Die Religion in Geschichte und Gegenwart. Handwörterbuch für Theologie und Religionswissenschaft*, 3rd ed. by K. GALLING, 6 vols., Tübingen, 1957-62.

RIT   *Revue internationale de Théologie*, Bern, 1893-1910. From 1911 on: *IKZ*.

RQ   *Römische Quartalschrift für christliche Altertumskunde und Kirchengeschichte*, Rome/Freiburg/Vienna, 1887 ff.

RUMMEL   F. VON RUMMEL, *Das Ministerium Lutz und seine Gegner 1871-1882. Ein Kampf um Staatskirchentum, Reichstreue und Parlamentsherrschaft in Bayern* (Münchener historische Abhandlungen. Erste Reihe: Allgemeine und politische Geschichte, 9), Munich, 1935.

SCHÄRL W. SCHÄRL, *Die Zusammensetzung der bayerischen Beamten-schaft von 1806 bis 1918* (Münchener historische Abhand-lungen. Abteilung Bayerische Geschichte, 1), Kallmünz Opf., 1955.

SCHULTE J.F. VON SCHULTE, *Der Altkatholicismus. Geschichte seiner Entwicklung, inneren Gestaltung und rechtlichen Stellung in Deutschland. Aus den Akten und andern authentischen Quellen dargestellt*, Giessen, 1887.

SIVRIĆ I. SIVRIĆ, *Bishop J.G. Strossmayer. New Light on Vatican I*, Rome/Chicago, 1975.

THIEME-BECKER *Allgemeines Lexikon der bildenden Künstler von der Antike bis zur Gegenwart*, ed. U. THIEME and F. BECKER, continued by H. VOLLMER, 37 vols., Leipzig, 1907-50.

Thrèskeutikè Θρησκευτικὴ καὶ ἠθικὴ ἐγκυκλοπαιδεία, 12 vols., Athens, 1962-68.

TQ *Theologische Quartalschrift*, Tübingen, 1831-1928; various places, 1929 ff.

TRE *Theologische Realenzyklopädie*, ed. G. KRAUSE and G. MÜL-LER, Berlin/New York, 1976 ff.

Verhandlungen *Die Verhandlungen des zweiten Altkatholiken-Congresses zu Köln. Officielle Ausgabe*, Cologne/Leipzig, 1872.

WEBER M. WEBER, *Das I. Vatikanische Konzil im Spiegel der bayeri-schen Politik* (MBM, 28), Munich, 1970.

ZBLG *Zeitschrift für bayerische Landesgeschichte*, Munich, 1928 ff.

ZKG *Zeitschrift für Kirchengeschichte*, Gotha, 1876-1930; Stuttgart/ Berlin/Cologne/Mainz, 1931 ff.

NOTES TO VOLUME I

1. *Die neue Geschäftsordnung des Concils und ihre theologische Bedeutung*, declaration of March 9, 1870, published in the March 11 issue of the *Augsburger Allgemeine Zeitung*, reproduced in *Briefe und Erklärungen*, pp. 40-57 (Eng. trans., pp. 46-64), *ColLac* VII, cols. 1499d-1506a, and FRIEDBERG, *Sammlung*, p. 422-432.

2. See QUIRINUS, pp. 554-570 (61st letter, dated June 24; Eng. trans., pp. 712-731). This letter contains Pius IX's well-known "la tradizione son'io" (p. 555).

3. All information and quotations contained in note 1 are from QUIRINUS, pp. 407-408, 221, 252, 362, 388 (Eng. trans., pp. 526, 285, 326, 470, 502). In *Exp* 4/1, p. 216, Plummer replaces the note with another quotation from QUIRINUS, p. 107 (Eng. trans., p. 132): "He said, 'As to the Infallibility, as a simple clergyman, I always believed it; now as Pope, I *feel* it.' (*Per l'infallibilità, essendo l'Abbate Mastai l'ho sempre creduto; adesso, essendo Papa Mastai, la sento.*)".

4. Note 4 is an excerpt from the printer's proofs of *Exp* 4/1, p. 217. The complete text of Newman's letter to Ullathorne, dated Jan. 28, 1870, can be found in *Letters and Diaries* XXV, pp. 18-20.

5. Senestrey published this prohibition in a decree dated March 2, 1870. In a secret consistory held on March 21, Pius IX praised him for this measure. See P. MAI, *Bischof Ignatius' von Senestréys Aufzeichnungen vom I. Vatikanischen Konzil*, in *AHC* 1 (1969) 399-411; FRIEDRICH III, pp. 541-542. The text of the decree can be found in *ColLac* VII, col. 1490a, and in FRIEDBERG, *Sammlung*, p. 131.

6. The quotation from the *Allgemeine Zeitung* is from the printer's proofs of *Exp* 4/2, pp. 218-219. See QUIRINUS, pp. 570-580 (62nd letter, dated June 30; Eng. trans., pp. 732-742).

7. Plummer refers to the 63rd letter from Rome, dated July 2, published in the *Allgemeine Zeitung* on Wednesday, July 13 (No. 194); see QUIRINUS, pp. 580-585 (Eng. trans., pp. 743-748).

8. In *Exp* 4/1, p. 221, Plummer adds: "It has sometimes been stated that he was there during the Vatican Council; and this error seems still to prevail in some quarters (see the obituary notice in the Stuttgard *Neues Tagblatt*, Jan. 12th, 1890)".

9. The incident took place on June 22, 1870, when Stanley invited the Unitarian Dr. G. Vance Smith to receive holy communion with him in Westminster Abbey. For reactions to this event, see CHADWICK, *Victorian Church* II, p. 46.

10. In *Exp* 4/1, p. 223, Plummer adds a quotation from QUIRINUS, p. 453 (Eng. trans., p. 586): "'*Si cambia la religione*' is the good-humoured scoff of the Roman populace on the subject".

11. Cf. QUIRINUS, p. 71 (Eng. trans., p. 83).

12. In *Exp* 4/1, p. 224, Plummer adds: "The names sent to Rome by the Westminster chapter were Errington, Clifford, and Grant. Errington had been

Wiseman's coadjutor with *right of succession*; but the Pope ignored that and the chapter's nominations, and appointed Manning".

13. Ferdinand A. GREGOROVIUS, *Geschichte der Stadt Rom im Mittelalter. Vom fünften bis zum sechzehnten Jahrhundert*, 8 vols., Stuttgart, 1859-72.

14. During an audience, probably on Jan. 25 in the evening, Patriarch Joseph Audo was required by Pius IX to endorse the appointment of two bishops and thus recognize Rome's authority (see V. CONZEMIUS, in *Briefwechsel* II, pp. 115-116, n. 2; HASLER, pp. 116-117, differs as to the date of the audience). This event was only one of the many conflicts between Rome and Audo in the controversy on the independence and jurisdictional powers of the Chaldean Church (cf. p. 58). See PATELOS, pp. 268-285, 441-447.

15. The essay on *Dante als Prophet* was only made public in an address to the Bavarian Academy of Sciences on Nov. 15, 1887. It first appeared in the *Allgemeine Zeitung*, 1887, No. 287, and in 1888 was included in *Akademische Vorträge* I, pp. 78-117 (Eng. trans. in *Studies in European History*, pp. 80-118).

16. The Burials Bill dealt with the Dissenters' right to be buried in Anglican cemeteries with their own ceremonies. Nonconformists protested against the requirement that every burial be performed according to the Anglican ritual led by the incumbent of the local parish which owned the cemetery. From 1862 Gladstone supported the dissenting Burials Bills and in so doing elicited strong reactions among High Churchmen, who considered the admission of dissenting ministers to cemeteries as the first step in the Dissenters' penetration of the Church of England. The conflict reached a high point in the 1870's but was solved during Gladstone's second term in part as a result of the intervention of Canterbury's Archbishop Tait (see p. 161). The Burial Laws Amendment Act, dated Sept. 7, 1880, satisfied the Dissenters' principal demands. See W.H. MACKINTOSH, *Disestablishment and Liberation. The Movement for the Separation of the Anglican Church from State Control*, London, 1972, pp. 107-109, 199-202, 274-282; CHADWICK, *Victorian Church* II, pp. 202-207.

17. The University Tests required all students to sign the Thirty-Nine Articles at registration. Nonconformists and Oxford Radicals under the leadership of Benjamin Jowett worked for the abolition of this obligation. In 1870 they succeeded in urging Gladstone to take the matter firmly in hand. On June 16, 1871, the University Tests Act was approved for the universities and colleges of Oxford, Cambridge, and Durham. It stipulated that no signing of any formula of faith be required for any academic or collegiate degree or office (except for degrees in divinity). Conservatives feared that non-denominational colleges could no longer provide a decent religious education. Their opposition to the University Tests Bill lead to the establishment of Keble College at Oxford (1870) and Selwyn College at Cambridge (1879-82). See W.H. MACKINTOSH, *op. cit.*, pp. 263-273; CHADWICK, *Victorian Church* II, pp. 439-444.

18. In *Exp* 4/1, pp. 423-424, Plummer adds: "'Even if an establishment had no advantage but this, it would be worth keeping.' He was most anxious on the subject, especially during the clamour for disestablishment a few years ago. At that time he brought me a copy of the *Guardian*, and pointed out a letter in which the writer expressed the opinion that if disestablishment could be staved off for a year or two longer, the Church would be safe from this disaster for an indefinite period. 'What do you think of that?' said Dr. Döllinger. 'I believe that there is a great deal of truth in it. Englishmen always respect hard and

disinterested work. And there is such an immense amount of really splendid work being done by all sections of the clergy, that the Church is steadily regaining its hold of the masses.' 'I am delighted to hear that you can think so,' he replied. 'I have been so long accustomed to regard the disestablishment of the English Church as only a question of time, that the opinion that it may still be averted—at least for a very long time—is quite a new light to me. No one will rejoice more than I shall, if it would be well grounded'".

Plummer adds a footnote: "When I returned to England I told Bishop Light-foot of the conversation, and asked him his opinion of the view propounded by the writer in the *Guardian*. 'I do not know that I should venture to say that "a year or two" would suffice; but give us twelve years, and then I think that we are safe'".

19. Note 7 is a clipping from an unidentified newspaper.

20. See *Lectures on the Reunion of the Churches*, pp. 127-129.

21. The exchange of letters between Scherr and Döllinger can be found in *Briefe und Erklärungen*, pp. 69-92 (Eng. trans., pp. 78-104). The main documents, also concerning Friedrich's excommunication and the reactions in Munich which followed, are published in FRIEDBERG, *Sammlung*, pp. 61, 170-198, 688-710. See further the overview in WEBER, pp. 208-219.

22. Döllinger was excommunicated on April 17, Friedrich on April 18. The excommunications were proclaimed from the pulpit in Munich on April 23. See FRIEDBERG, *Sammlung*, pp. 179-180; *Briefe und Erklärungen*, p. 103 (Eng. trans., p. 116).

23. The complete text of Newman's letter can be found in *Letters and Diaries* XXV, pp. 308-310. The letter was an answer to a letter from Plummer on April 1, in which the latter had given a summary of Döllinger's declaration of March 28 to Scherr. On April 9, when writing to Döllinger himself to introduce the Rev. Alexander Gordon, Newman took the opportunity to express his feelings: "I hope I am not wrong to intrude upon you just now, when you have so overpowering an anxiety upon you. At least, in doing so, I am able to assure you that you are continually in my thoughts, and in my prayers. I am sure you must have many hearts, feeling and praying for you, and astonished that so true a servant and son of the Catholic Church should be so tried", *ibid.*, p. 311.

24. The declaration of the parish priests is published in FRIEDBERG, *Samm-lung*, pp. 184-187.

25. The pastoral letter to the faithful, together with a letter to the clergy, was composed during the German bishops' conference held in Eichstätt on May 7-9, 1871. Both texts are included in MANSI LIII, cols. 923B-934A (where the conference is incorrectly called the second Fulda convention) and in FRIED-BERG, *Sammlung*, pp. 713-725. Hefele refused to sign the texts, especially the letter to the faithful, in which it was said that modern German science could not be united with Catholic faith (cf. p. 22). See BRANDMÜLLER, pp. 236-244.

26. In *Exp* 4/1, p. 271, Plummer adds: "It will be remembered that the Old Catholics were not yet organized as a party, still less as a Church. The attitude of those who rejected the Vatican decrees was simply one of protest".

27. In *Exp* 4/1, pp. 271-272, Plummer adds: "He had refused to join with the seventeen bishops who had issued a pastoral from Fulda in September, 1870, in which they declared that it was incompatible with the Catholic religion

to say that the doctrine of papal infallibility is not contained in Scripture and tradition. In Rome he had spoken of resigning his diocese rather than publish the Infallibility dogma. And yet the refusal to renew his quinquennial faculties forthwith brought him to his knees".

Hefele's letter of April 10, 1871, *An den hochwürdigen Clerus*, is published in MANSI LIII, cols. 1058C-1059D, and in FRIEDBERG, *Sammlung*, pp. 711-712. It is reproduced in facsimile in *TQ* 150 (1970) 164-165.

28. The *Münchener Erklärung* of Pentecost 1871 was composed by a group of prominent Catholic laymen and theologians who came together in Munich on May 28-30 at Döllinger's invitation to make known their position in the ecclesial situation. The text, which appeared in the *Beilage* to the *Allgemeine Zeitung*, No. 164, and in the *Rheinischer Merkur*, pp. 238-240, was largely written by Döllinger. It contained a rejection of the Vatican decrees, a protest against the Church's measures taken after the Council, and indications for a true Church reform in the direction of the reunification of Christians. The names of Acton and Blennerhassett were among those who signed. However, in a letter to the *Times* on June 18, 1871, Blennerhassett declared that these signatures were not authentic. See SCHULTE, pp. 338-340; the text is reproduced in SCHULTE, pp. 16-22; FRIEDBERG, *Sammlung*, pp. 725-731; and KÜRY, pp. 445-450. The position of Acton and Blennerhassett is made clear in R. K. BULIN, *Zur Unterzeichnung der Münchener Pfingsterklärung 1871*, in *IKZ* 74 (1984) 158-169.

29. Frederick MEYRICK, *Moral and Devotional Theology of the Church of Rome According to the Authoritative Teaching of S. Alfonso de' Liguori*, 5 vols., London, 1855-57. Meyrick also wrote *On Dr. Newman's Rejection of Liguori's Doctrine of Equivocation*, London, 1864.

30. Louis BAILLY, *Theologia dogmatica et moralis ad usum seminariorum*, 8 vols., Dijon, 1789, was the classic handbook in the first half of the 19th century, used in all the seminaries of France. Between 1804 and 1852 it was reprinted 18 times, including a number of revisions by Receveur and Gerbet. On Dec. 7, 1852, it was put on the Index because of Gallicanism. Bailly also wrote a *Tractatus de Ecclesia Christi* (2 vols., Dijon, 1776) and a *Tractatus de vera religione* (2 vols., Dijon, 1771). His *Tractatus theologicus de matrimonio* was revised by Receveur in 1830. See J. DEDIEU, *Bailly (L.)*, in *DHGE* 6 (1932) 263-264.

31. With the Disruption of May 18, 1843, 451 of the 1203 Scottish ministers, under the leadership of Thomas Chalmers, separated from the Established Church. The schism of the Free Church of Scotland was the culmination of the 'Ten Years Conflict' concerning the presbyteries' right of veto about the appointment of ministers. The question remained contentuous until 1869, when the General Assembly of the Established Church decided to submit to Parliament the elimination of patronage. With the Patronage Act of 1874 the congregations finally received the right to elect their own ministers. See J.H.S. BURLEIGH, *A Church History of Scotland*, London/New York/Toronto, 1960, pp. 334-369.

32. This letter from Hefele has not been preserved. Plummer's mention of it invalidates R. Reinhardt's supposition (based on FRIEDRICH III, p. 597) that correspondence between Hefele and Döllinger ceased after April 10, 1871, the date of Hefele's submission to the Vatican decrees. See R. REINHARDT, *Johannes Joseph Ignaz von Döllinger und Carl Joseph von Hefele*, in *ZBLG* 33 (1970) 439-446, p. 444.

33. In *Exp* 4/1, p. 273, Plummer adds: "It was well understood that the king was entirely with his provost, and would certainly have stood by him if he had defied the archbishop and continued to celebrate in the royal churches. But Döllinger always lived and died a loyal member of the Church. Rome's cruel treatment of him never drove him into rebellion against lawful authority. When Rome said to him, 'Believe the new dogma,' he said, 'I cannot, for it is not true; and I will not submit, because you have no authority to impose it.' When she said, 'Cease to celebrate mass,' he obeyed at once: it was possible to do so; and, although he believed the command to be unjust, he submitted to it as coming from one who had authority to give it".

34. In *Exp* 4/1, pp. 274-275, Plummer comments more extensively on his visit to Hyacinthe Loyson: "Through him I became acquainted with three cases of submission to the dogma, which are so typical that no excuse is needed for introducing them here. 1. Archbishop Darboy, of Paris, had been one of the most strenuous opponents of the dogma. He was one of the eighty-eight who voted *non placet* at the final division, June 13th, 1870, and he was the inspirer and almost the author of *La Dernière Heure du Concile*, in which it was shown that the Council had been coerced, and that its decrees were *forced* upon its members ('*Les évêques ont été appelés à sanctionner ce que les Jésuites avaient écrit; voilà toute l'histoire du concile*', p. 4). Yet he submitted to them. A few days before his tragic death in 1871 Père Hyacinthe was with him, and the archbishop said to him: *Ce dogme n'a pas l'importance que vous lui attribuez, et au fond il ne décide rien. Je n'y étais pas opposé comme théologien, car il n'est pas faux, mais comme homme, parce qu'il est inepte. On nous a fait jouer à Rome le rôle de sacristains, et pourtant nous étions au moins deux cents qui valions mieux que cela.'* — This then was one method of submitting: The dogma means nothing. It is silly, but not false. Therefore it may be accepted. 2. While I was in Paris in August, 1871, I visited Père Gratry, the author of the four famous letters against the definition. He had not yet publicly submitted; but it was certain that the ultramontane Guibert, the new Archbishop of Paris, would call upon him to submit, and his friends knew that he would comply. Père Gratry deplored the active line taken by Hyacinthe, an activity '*nuisible et stérile*'; he was now quite in the wrong. 'But what Père Hyacinthe has written is not more strong than what you have written.' 'You mean in my letters to the Archbishop of Malines? They were written before the Council.' 'But are they true?' 'Yes, in the main. Some errors of detail there may well be; but the position maintained in them is correct, and I maintain it still. I still hold that the infallibility of the Pope is neither independent (*séparée*), nor personal, nor absolute.' 'That is the very negation of the dogma.' 'Not necessarily. There is a sense in which both may be true; and I find in my conscience that I can accept the dogma and still hold to what I wrote in my letters to the Archbishop of Malines. I have heard the archbishop himself say that the personal and absolute infallibility of the Pope was a blasphemy.' This therefore was a second method of submitting: Assert that the dogma means the very opposite of what it plainly states, and then say that you accept it. 3. The third instance was that of a priest who visited Hyacinthe at Passy, and told him that he had two convictions, an external and an internal. 'With the external I accept the dogma; with the internal I reject it.' And this was said quite calmly, as if there were

nothing strange or scandalous in such an avowal.— Third method of submission : Profess to accept the dogma, although you believe it to be false".
On *La dernière heure du Concile*, see p. 298, n. 20. The four letters of Gratry
were published separately under the title, *Mgr l'Évêque d'Orléans et Mgr l'Arche-
vêque de Malines*, in Jan., Feb., April, and May 1870.

35. Newman's letter goes on : "and whatever be the sins, the intrigues, the
cruelties of individuals, Securus judicat orbis terrarum", *Letters and Diaries*
XXVI, p. 120. The work mentioned in the text, translated by Oxenham, is
The First Age of Christianity and the Church.

36. Between 1864 and 1889 William Stubbs edited 19 large vols. with chronicles,
gesta, and historical works from the mediaeval period of British history in
the series *Rerum Britannicorum Medii Aevi Scriptores* (which also bore the
title *Chronicles and Memorials of Great Britain and Ireland during the Middle
Ages*). This collection is known as the *Rolls Series*, derived from the Master
of the Rolls, head of the Public Record Office, who was in charge of the
organization of the series. See M.D. KNOWLES, *Great Historical Enterprises.
IV : The Rolls Series*, in *Transactions of the Royal Historical Society* 5/11 (1961)
137-159.

37. Isidor Silbernagl was not, in fact, a professor of Civil law but of Canon
law. In the winter semester of 1871 he took over Döllinger's chair in Church
history. See DENZLER, pp. 450-455.

38. Note 12 is an unidentified paper cutting.

39. In *Exp* 4/1, p. 277, Plummer adds a footnote: "In connexion with this
argument the following passage in Dr. Newman's essay on the 'Trials of
Theodoret' is of interest. It looks as if it were written with an eye to the
Vatican Council. 'Cyril had on his side the Pope, the monks, the faithful everywhere, tradition, and the truth; and he had not much tenderness for the
scruples of literary men, for the *rights of councils*, or for *episcopal minorities*'
(*Historical Sketches*, iii., p. 349. Pickering, 1873)".

40. Heinrich VON SYBEL, *Geschichte der Revolutionszeit von 1789 bis 1795*,
5 vols., Düsseldorf, 1853-77.

41. Antonio ROSMINI-SERBATI, *Delle Cinque Piaghe della Santa Chiesa*,
Lugano, 1848. Rosmini had already written the book in 1832 but did not
consider it opportune to publish it then. In 1849 the book was put on the Index.

42. The letter, dated Aug. 23, 1870, was addressed to Hefele. Haneberg had
also made it public during the meeting of a number of Catholics under Döllinger's
leadership which took place in Nuremberg on Aug. 25. The letter was published
in the *Rheinischer Merkur*, 1871, pp. 171-172, without Haneberg's permission.
Haneberg replied with a letter in the *Bayerischer Kurier* of June 4-5, 1871,
pp. 1150-1151, in which he pointed out that he had already submitted twice
to the Vatican decrees. See SCHULTE, pp. 98-102; FRIEDBERG, *Aktenstücke*,
p. 51.

43. In *Exp* 4/1, p. 276, n. 1, Plummer adds : "This is stated to be the view
of the present Pope. It is said that more than once he has informally sent
kind messages to Döllinger. 'Tell him to come back to us : there is a new Pope.'
'Yes,' said Döllinger; 'but the old Papacy'".

44. During their Congress in Cologne on Sept. 21, 1872, the Old Catholics
recommended as an "urgent necessity" to the German governments that civil
marriage be mandatory (*Verhandlungen*, p. XXI ; FRIEDBERG, *Aktenstücke*, p. 105;

cf. SCHULTE, p. 356). It was first introduced in Prussia in 1874. A year later, via the law of Feb. 6, the requirement was extended to the whole German Empire. On Jan. 1, 1876, the law went into effect. See HUBER, pp. 723-724; HUBER-HUBER, pp. 630-631.

45. *Zur Geschichte des vaticanischen Conciles*, Munich, 1871, was an expanded translation of Acton's article on *The Vatican Council* in *The North British Review* 105 (1870) 183-229. The translation was placed on the Index on Sept. 20, 1871. From Acton's correspondence with Döllinger it appears that he was not satisfied with the translation and had planned to publish a very extensive revision of the text. This revision was never carried out. See *Briefwechsel* III, pp. 14-15, 34-35, where Conzemius, from a comparison of the English and German versions, notes no fundamental differences and calls Acton's essay the "bestinformierter Beitrag zur Vorkonzilsgeschichte" (p. 35, n. 4).

46. *The Homilies of S. John Chrysostom, Archbishop of Constantinople* (Library of Fathers), 16 vols., Oxford, 1839-52. The translation of the homilies was completed in 1883. Work had been interrupted in anticipation of the new edition of the Greek text which was completed in 1862.

47. Speculation on the existence of the bull reached a climax in Jan. 1874, when the *Kölnische Zeitung* published the text of a supposed bull *Apostolicae Sedis munus* (dated May 28, 1873) in which the Pope directed the immediate election of his successor. This document was a forgery, inspired by measures taken by Pius VI in 1798, and was formally disclaimed as such by the Vatican. But such a bull of Pius IX did indeed exist. On Aug. 23, 1871, in the bull *In hac sublimi*, he authorized the cardinals who would be present at his death to proceed immediately to the determination of the place and manner of the papal election. In exceptional circumstances the customary ten day interval between the Pope's death and the beginning of the conclave could be omitted, but for the validity of the election the presence of at least one half plus one of the members of the Sacred College was mandatory. These and other provisions were given in greater detail later on by Pius IX in the bulls *Licet per Apostolicas* (Sept. 8, 1874) and *Consulturi* (Oct. 10, 1877) and in a regulation dated Jan. 10, 1878. See L. LECTOR, *Le Conclave. Origines, histoire, organisation, législation ancienne et moderne*, Paris, [1894], pp. 716-779.

48. Henri Marie Gaston de Bonnechose, Archbishop of Rouen, was named cardinal in 1863. Ferdinand François Auguste Donnet, Archbishop of Bordeaux, became a cardinal in 1852.

49. Quotation from QUIRINUS, p. 100 (Eng. trans., p. 123).

50. Probably Döllinger's *History of the Church* (1840-42), the translation of *Geschichte der christlichen Kirche* (1833-35).

51. In passing the law against the Jesuits on July 4, 1872, the *Reichstag* decided to exclude the Jesuit and related orders and congregations from the German state. Their institutions had to be dissolved within six months, foreign nationals among the orders' members could be deported, and assigned residences could be imposed on German members. On July 5 a decree of the *Bundesrat* forbade all activities of the Jesuit order, especially in Church and school, and the preaching of missions. On Sept. 28 these activities were specified as every priestly and pastoral activity, particularly preaching, confession, absolution, mass, and administration of the sacraments. A decision taken on Feb. 22 and made public on May 20, 1873, considered four congregations as affiliated with

the Jesuits: Redemptorists, Lazarists, Holy Ghost Fathers, and the Dames du Sacré Cœur. See HUBER-HUBER, pp. 545-550.

52. The 'Declaration of the Archbishops and Bishops of The Roman Catholic Church in Ireland' was composed on Jan. 25, 1826, as an answer to the 1825 Government Inquiry, with the intention of rectifying erroneous interpretations of the Catholic faith. The standpoint on infallibility is part of art. XI which determines that Irish Catholics "declare, on oath, their belief, that 'no act in itself unjust, immoral, or wicked, can ever be justified or excused by or under pretence or colour that it was done either for the good of the Church, or in obedience to any ecclesiastical power whatsoever;' 'that it is not an article of the Catholic faith, neither are they thereby required to believe, that the pope is infallible;' and that they do not hold themselves 'bound to obey any order in its own nature immoral, though the pope or any ecclesiastical power should issue or direct such an order; but, on the contrary, that it would be sinful in them to pay any respect or obedience thereto'". The parts between single commas are verbatim quotations from a declaration of a R.C. committee which was sent to Rome in 1758 as the act and deed of the Irish Catholics. This text was republished in 1792 as an authentic exposition of the views of the Irish R.C. body. See W.D. KILLEN, *The Ecclesiastical History of Ireland. From the Earliest Period to the Present Times*, vol. II, London, 1875, pp. 277-281; 560-565 (text). Conzemius quotes a Latin version of this text in *Briefwechsel* II, p. 250, n. 3.

53. On Aug. 12, 1870, Robert Cornthwaite, Bishop of Beverley, wrote in a letter to the clergy of his diocese: "The doctrine which, but a few weeks ago, it was only not heresy to call in question, is now a matter of Catholic faith, a condition of Catholic membership; it takes rank with the doctrines of the real presence of our Divine Lord in the Holy Eucharist, and the existence of God: to deny it, or to doubt it consciously and wilfully, is to make shipwreck of the faith", quoted in CWIEKOWSKI, pp. 276-277.

54. Heinrich VON SYBEL, *Was wir von Frankreich lernen können*, Bonn, 1872. Reprinted in ID., *Vorträge und Aufsätze*, Berlin, 1879, pp. 331-347.

55. It concerns Acton's letter of July 5, 1872: "Was meinen Sie davon dem Pusey ein Ehrendiplom zu geben?", *Briefwechsel* III, p. 83.

56. The confessional separation of education in history, introduced in 1854, was abrogated by the *Schulordnung* of Aug. 20, 1874. In 1882 a suggestion to reintroduce separation would be rejected in the Bavarian lower house thanks to Döllinger's intervention. See FRIEDRICH III, pp. 644-648.

57. Cf. QUIRINUS, p. 225 (Eng. trans., p. 291).

58. See *Briefe und Erklärungen*, pp. 73-74 (Eng. trans., pp. 82-83).

59. Johann FRIEDRICH, *Zur Vertheidigung meines Tagebuches. Offener Brief an den Herrn P. Rudolf Cornely, Priester der Gesellschaft Jesu*, Nördlingen, 1872. Cornely was at that moment professor of exegesis and oriental languages in the Jesuit college of Maria Laach. His critical review of Friedrich's diary appeared in the Jan. issue of *Stimmen aus Maria Laach* 2 (1872) 86-89. Cornely answered Friedrich's open letter in *Stimmen aus Maria Laach* 3 (1872) 278-287.

60. The vicissitudes of Gonzalez' book, or better of his books, are extensively described by Döllinger and Reusch in *Geschichte der Moralstreitigkeiten* I, pp. 120-273; II, pp. 19-219 (documents). In 1673 Gonzalez wrote a book entitled *Fundamentum theologiae moralis, id est tractatus de recto usu opinionum pro-*

babilium, but he was forbidden to publish it. After he was elected General of the Jesuits in 1687, he wrote a new book, conceived as a *prodromus* for a new edition of the first book; it was called *Tractatus succinctus de recto usu opinionum probabilium* and was printed in Dillingen in 1691. This book also met with much opposition in his order and was never published. After much discussion Gonzalez finally wrote a completely reworked text which was corrected by the censors and which again bore the title *Fundamentum theologiae moralis, id est tractatus de recto usu opinionum probabilium*. It was published in 1694 in Rome, Antwerp, Dillingen, and Naples. Only this edition has been preserved.

61. (1) The seven lectures *Über die Wiedervereinigung der christlichen Kirchen*, held in 1872, appeared on the basis of stenographer's notes in the *Allgemeine Zeitung* in 1872. In the same year H.N. Oxenham translated them into English using the MS: *Lectures on the Reunion of the Churches*. Döllinger only published the German original in 1888 (LÖSCH, p. 544).

(2) Döllinger never published the historical letters to the German bishops. It is possible that they related to a planned revision of his *Erwägungen für die Bischöfe des Conciliums über die Frage der päpstlichen Unfehlbarkeit*, which appeared anonymously in 1869. In Nov. 1869 Döllinger had written to Reusch that he would shortly add documents, witnesses, and historical digressions to this text. But he never carried out this project. Reusch republished the *Erwägungen* in 1890 in *Briefe und Erklärungen*, pp. 1-28 (the letter, dated Nov. 25, 1869, is quoted on p. 1). Years later Döllinger seems to have worked on a similar plan. On Oct. 2, 1886, he wrote to Reusch that he was planning to publish an extensive historical overview, entitled *Die Vaticanischen Decrete im Lichte der Geschichte*, in the form of a series of letters to a highly placed prelate. Reusch found preliminary studies for these letters among Döllinger's papers. But it seems that Döllinger had not begun on the text (see Reusch's preface in *Briefe und Erklärungen*, pp. III-IV).

Döllinger and Reusch gave extensive attention to Liguori's person and work in *Geschichte der Moralstreitigkeiten* I, pp. 356-476.

(3) For the essay on Dante, see p. 275, n. 15.

(4) The essay on the *Vaticinium Lehninense* was not published by Döllinger. Plummer himself treated the prophecy in *Prophecies and the Prophetic Spirit in the Christian Era*, Appendix A: "The Prophecies of Hermann of Lehnin" (pp. 171-212).

(5) The vindication of the Knights Templar would occupy Döllinger for years. It was the subject of his last lecture before the Bavarian Academy in 1889 (see p. 225).

(6) Döllinger never published a major study on the authorship of the False Decretals, although he had already discussed them briefly in his *Lehrbuch der Kirchengeschichte* II, pp. 44-49, and in JANUS, pp. 100-106. But he did remain interested in the question (cf. pp. 164, 261). In 1887 he informed Prof. B. von Simson that he hoped soon to treat the matter in a book. See B. VON SIMSON, *Ein Schreiben Döllingers über die Entstehung der Pseudoisidorischen Dekretalen*, in ZKG 12 (1890-91) 208-209.

62. See Louis BLANC, *Histoire de la révolution française*, 12 vols., Paris, 1847-62.

63. Pedro de Arbués and Archbishop Josaphat Kunczewicz were canonized

on June 29, 1867; Marguerite-Marie Alacoque was beatified on Sept. 18, 1864. See also pp. 119, 132.

64. In 1870 Wilhelm von Kaulbach painted *Peter Arbues, Grossinquisitor, verurteilt eine Ketzerfamilie zum Feuertod,* inspired by indignation at the canonization of Pedro de Arbués. The immediate occasion for the work was a rousing series of articles written by Döllinger himself in the *Allgemeine Zeitung* and in the *Neue Freie Presse* (see p. 119, n. 14). In this period Kaulbach became Döllinger's friend. See *Briefwechsel* IV, p. 453, n. 12.

65. *Martyrologium Romanum ad novam Kalendarii rationem et ecclesiasticae historiae veritatem restitutum. Gregorii XIII. Pont. Max. iussu editum.* In 1583 two defective editions appeared in Rome. They were followed by a corrected edition in 1584, one on which Baronius had cooperated. In 1586 a new edition appeared in Rome, including Baronius' extensive *Notationes* and his *Tractatio de Martyrologio Romano.* Other glosses, to the third Vatican edition of 1589, were added to the 1630 edition. See A. PINCHERLE, *Baronio, C.,* in *DBI* 6 (1964) 470-478, p. 472.

66. Julius CORDARA, *Historiae Societatis Jesu Pars sexta, complectens res gestas sub Mutio Vitellescho,* vol. I, Rome, 1750. The second part, covering the period 1625-33, was published in 1859 by P. Ragazzini. Among the papers found after Cordara's death were various reflections on the reasons which had led to the suppression of the order. Döllinger published excerpts from these notes in *Beiträge zur politischen, kirchlichen und Cultur-Geschichte der sechs letzten Jahrhunderte* III, pp. 1-74: "Denkwürdigkeiten des Jesuiten Julius Cordara zur Geschichte von 1740-1773. Rom, die Päpste, der Jesuiten-Orden" (esp. pp. 64-74).

67. Thomas VOGAN, *The True Doctrine of the Eucharist,* London, 1871. The book was originally published in 1849 under the title, *Nine Lectures on the Holy Sacrament of the Lord's Supper.*

68. The speeches mentioned were published in DE FRANCISCIS I. The address to the charitable society was delivered on July 5, 1872 (pp. 475-476). The challenge directed against Bismarck dates from June 24, 1872 (pp. 456-458) and can be found in a German translation in FRIEDBERG, *Aktenstücke,* pp. 52-53. The allusion to the O.T. was made in a speech delivered on June 15 and repeated in an address on June 16, 1872 (pp. 437-438, 440-442). De Franciscis also corrected the faulty reference. Gladstone published a critique of this edition in 1875 (see p. 124).

69. Wilhelm DRUMANN, *Geschichte Roms in seinem Uebergange von der republikanischen zur monarchischen Verfassung, oder Pompejus, Caesar, Cicero und ihre Zeitgenossen. Nach Geschlechtern und mit genealogischen Tabellen,* 6 vols., Königsberg, 1834-44 (2nd ed. by P. GROEBE, 1899-1929).

70. ID., *Geschichte Bonifacius des Achten,* 2 vols., Königsberg, 1852.

71. In *Exp* 4/1, p. 282, Plummer writes: "Apparently Newman saw through it; at any rate the flattering request was declined". In fact, on Sept. 14, 1857, Newman accepted Wiseman's proposal to assume direction over the translation. He contacted possible translators, wrote an introduction and sent Wiseman a cost estimate. A year later he was informed that the American bishops were also preparing a new translation of the Bible and that they had proposed continuing the work in common, which made a separate English translation

seem superfluous. After this notice, Westminster had no further contact on the subject either with Newman or with the Americans, who decided to complete their own translation. In the end Newman abandoned the project. See W. WARD, *The Life of John Henry Cardinal Newman, Based on His Private Journals and Correspondence*, vol. I, London, 1912, pp. 417-429; M. TREVOR, *Newman. Light in Winter*, London, 1962, pp. 169-173.

72. Wiseman's article on *Anglican Claims of Apostolical Succession* appeared in *The Dublin Review* 7 (1839) 138-180, as an unsigned review article of the *Tracts for the Times*. It was reprinted in his *Essays on Various Subjects*, vol. II, London, 1853, pp. 201-262, under the title, "The Catholic and Anglican Churches". Newman read the text in Sept. 1839. Initially he was not much influenced by Wiseman's suggested parallel between the Anglicans and the Donatists concerning their place in the *Una Sancta*. But when his friend Robert Williams showed him the formula with which Augustine sought to settle the controversy (*securus judicat orbis terrarum*), he underwent what he himself called "the first real hit from Romanism". With these words, he wrote in his *Apologia*, "the theory of the *Via Media* was absolutely pulverized". See W. WARD, *op. cit.*, pp. 67-70; E.C. MESSENGER, *Wiseman, the Donatists, and Newman: A "Dublin" Centenary*, in *The Dublin Review* 205 (1939) 110-119.

73. Note 31 is a cutting from a book catalogue.

74. The Anglican controversialist Edward Tatham, around 1802, defended in a famous sermon the authenticity of 1 Jn 5,7 (called the 'Three Heavenly Witnesses' or the *Comma Johanneum*). See W.P. COURTNEY, *Tatham, E.*, in *DNB* 19 (1909) 382-384.

75. Nicholas WISEMAN, *Two Letters on some Parts of the Controversy Concerning the Genuineness of 1 John v. 7. Containing also an enquiry into the origin of the first Latin version of Scripture, commonly called "the Itala"*, Rome, 1835 (originally published in the *Catholic Magazine* in 1832-33; reprinted in ID., *Essays on Various Subjects*, vol. I, London, 1853, pp. 1-70).

76. Ἡ Παλαιὰ καὶ ἡ Καινὴ Διαθήκη. *Vetus et Novum Testamentum ex antiquissimo codice Vaticano edidit Angelus MAIUS*, 5 vols., Rome, 1857. The text had existed in print since 1838 but was not made available until three years after Mai's death (Sept. 1854). An edition of the N.T. followed in 1859, Ἡ Καινὴ Διαθήκη. *Novum Testamentum ex vetustissimo codice Vaticano secundis curis editum studio Angeli MAII*, Rome, 1859.

77. *Novum Testamentum Vaticanum. Post Angeli Maii aliorumque imperfectos labores ex ipso codice edidit Aenoth. Frid. Constant. TISCHENDORF*, Leipzig, 1867; appendix, 1869.

78. *Relazioni degli Ambasciatori Veneti al Senato*, ed. E. ALBÈRI, vol. IV, Florence, 1840, p. 213.

79. A. KURTZEL, *Der Jesuit Girard und seine Heilige. Ein Beitrag zur geistlichen Geschichte des vorigen Jahrhunderts*, in *Historisches Taschenbuch* n.s. 4 (1843) 413-485.

80. By the new General of the Dominicans, Döllinger meant Vincent Jandel, who was Magister General from 1855 until 1872. Cf. QUIRINUS, p. 67 (Eng. trans., p. 77).

81. Edmond DE PRESSENSÉ, *Le Concile du Vatican. Son histoire et ses conséquences politiques et religieuses*, Paris, 1872, p. 276. In fact, Pressensé does not refer to the declaration by the Irish bishops in 1826: he believes that there had

been a declaration by English and Irish bishops in 1829 (the year of Catholic Emancipation). However, this belief is based on a misinterpretation of a text in Prosper GUÉRANGER, *De la définition de l'infaillibilité papale. À propos de la Lettre de Mgr d'Orléans à Mgr de Malines*, Paris, 1870, pp. 46-47, where the author speaks of "des déclarations faites, avant 1829, au gouvernement et au Parlement anglais par plusieurs prélats catholiques d'Angleterre et d'Irlande". Guéranger is the "French ultramontane" referred to in Plummer's text.

82. By "Denz" Plummer means the handbook written by the Belgian theologian Pierre DENS, *Theologia ad usum seminariorum et sacrae theologiae alumnorum*, 14 vols., Louvain, 1777 (published posthumously). A reworked version with many additional Roman documents was published in Dublin in 1832 under the title, *Theologia moralis et dogmatica*, 8 vols. Since then Dens had been used in Ireland primarily as a handbook of moral theology—thus long before Bailly was forbidden. See D.A. KERR, *Peel, Priests and Politics. Sir Robert Peel's Administration and the Roman Catholic Church in Ireland, 1841-1846* (Oxford Historical Monographs), Oxford, 1982, pp. 232-233, 236-237.

83. On the contrary, there seemed to be a decrease in the tension between Patriarch Audo and Rome at the time. On July 29, 1872, Audo submitted to the decisions of the Vatican Council, even though it was with the express reservation that he would maintain all the rights and privileges of the Eastern patriarchates. The conflict reached its high point in 1876 when Audo, who had meanwhile consecrated four bishops on his own initiative, was threatened by Rome with excommunication. Audo avoided a schism by submitting on March 1, 1877. See PATELOS, pp. 526, 536.

84. In his address delivered May 19 (MANSI LII, cols. 112A-125C), Cardinal Cullen tried to show that the Irish Church agreed with the doctrine of infallibility by referring to the Acts of the synod of Thurles of 1850 in which adherence to the papal prescriptions regarding faith had been expressed. These Acts were signed by various bishops present at the Council, including the Archbishop of Tuam who, he was certain, would speak in favour of infallibility. However, MacHale, in his address delivered May 20 (MANSI LII, cols. 144C-151C), declared that he could not agree with the proposed schema because it played down the bishops' role in doctrinal definitions. The Irish Catholics would find little advantage in a declaration of infallibility; they had little interest in strict definitions. A definition would only elicit sharper reactions among the opponents of Catholicism. In his second address to the Council on June 20 (MANSI LII, cols. 784D-790C), MacHale stated that the question of papal infallibility did not as such arise at the synod of Thurles. Cf. NORMAN, pp. 412-413.

85. Because of illness Heinrich von Hofstätter had not participated in the Council or the bishops' conference of Fulda. On Dec. 12, 1870, Pius IX sent him a letter in which he expressed his unease at Hofstätter's silence regarding the Vatican decrees. An explanation of the Council decisions and a personal declaration of loyalty to the new teaching were his urgent pastoral duty. Hofstätter defended his stance in an emotional letter, dated Jan. 15, 1871, in which he declared that he had wanted to wait with the publication of the decrees until more precise norms for carrying them out were made known. As proof of his agreement with the Council he added to the letter a copy of his diocesan newspaper dated Jan. 15, 1871. This contained the constitution *Pastor Aeternus* together with an introductory text in which the clergy were directed to teach the dogma to the people. See BRANDMÜLLER, pp. 212-215.

86. The cutting contained in note 35 is from an unidentified newspaper. In the corresponding text in *Exp* 4/2, p. 463, Plummer refers explicitly to the coincidence of the facts: the declaration of Minister von Lutz in 1890 and the date suggested by Archbishop von Scherr in 1871 both fall on March 15, "the Ides of March; which was another coincidence, like the definition of the dogma on the *dies Alliensis*". For the consequences of Lutz' declaration, see p. 311, n. 35.

87. As has become evident from the publications of V. Conzemius, Lord Acton and Duke Louis Arco were Döllinger's primary sources for his *Letters from Rome*. In fact, Acton himself wrote the text of 15 of these letters. During the Council Döllinger most likely had no direct contact with any bishop. Among the various bishops who kept Acton and Arco informed Conzemius mentions in the first place Strossmayer and further Dupanloup. All important documents were passed on to Acton by a Roman prelate whose name is unknown. Conzemius suspects that it was Canon Nikola Voršak, Strossmayer's theologian. See V. CONZEMIUS, *"Römische Briefe vom Konzil"*, in *TQ* 140 (1960) 427-462; ID., *Die Verfasser der "Römischen Briefe vom Konzil" des "Quirinus"*, in *Festschrift für H. Foerster* (Freiburger Geschichtsblätter, 52), Freiburg/Schw., 1963-64, pp. 229-256; ID., *Die "Römischen Briefe vom Konzil". Eine entstehungsgeschichtliche und quellenkritische Untersuchung zum Konzilsjournalismus Ignaz v. Döllingers und Lord Actons*, in *RQ* 59 (1964) 186-229; 60 (1965) 76-119.

88. *Ce qui se passe au Concile*, published anonymously in 1870 in Paris, was highly critical of the conciliar procedure. In mentioning the author Jules Galliard, Plummer probably means Léopold de Gaillard, editor-in-chief of *Le Correspondant*, whom Dupanloup is thought to have commissioned to write the brochure; see J. GADILLE, *Gaillard, L. de*, in *DHGE* 19 (1981) 680-681. However, it is also often presumed that the brochure was written by someone in Mgr. Maret's entourage. On July 13, 1870, 42 Council Fathers presented a protest against the book and another brochure, *La dernière heure du Concile* (see p. 298, n. 20) (MANSI LII, cols. 1260A-1261B). Both works were condemned during the general session of July 16 (MANSI LII, cols. 1318B-1319B; *ColLac* VII, cols. 1750b-1752a). Döllinger was involved in the German translation of *Ce qui se passe au Concile*, which appeared under the title, *Wie es auf dem Konzile hergeht*, Munich, 1870. See PALANQUE, pp. 130-131; *Briefwechsel* IV, pp. 479-480.

89. In *Exp* 4/2, pp. 465-466, Plummer adds: "People are apt to think that excommunication is an obsolete and ridiculous weapon, incapable of injuring the object of it. That certainly was not Dr. Döllinger's view of his own sentence. He fully believed that it was iniquitous and therefore invalid, and that it left him spiritually unharmed; but he was profoundly sensible of other effects. A Roman Catholic friend, who to a large extent shared his views, said to him, 'Well, at any rate, they cannot burn us at the stake.' 'No,' said Döllinger sternly; 'they cannot burn us at the stake. But they can inflict an amount of moral torture, to which the stake would perhaps be preferable.' To another he said, 'I am the fascine, which is flung into the ditch, to help the others to cross.' And even the stake was not so far off. The penalty which was inflicted on him was 'the greater excommunication, *with all the canonical consequences which are attached to it*.' Among these 'canonical consequences' is this, that any

zealot may slay the excommunicated person. It is laid down that any one who out of genuine zeal kills such an one [*sic*] *nullam meretur pænitentiam*. And the Munich police formally warned Dr. Döllinger that violence was contemplated, and that he ought to be cautious and not go out unattended. This will to some seem incredible; but he himself states it both in his letter to Archbishop Steichele and in that to the nuncio, Ruffo Scilla (*Briefe und Erklärungen*, pp. 140, 153)".

90. "Seien Sie ohne Sorgen, nach Canossa gehen wir nicht, weder körperlich noch geistlich". Bismarck gave his famous Canossa speech in the *Reichstag* on May 14, 1872, during the discussions on Rome's refusal to accept the Imperial nominee Cardinal von Hohenlohe as ambassador to the Holy See. The representation of the German Empire in Rome remained unfilled and formally ceased to exist in 1874. See HUBER-HUBER, pp. 536-543.

91. *Hymns Ancient and Modern, for Use in the Service of the Church*, one of the most popular hymn-books in the Church of England, was first published in London in 1861 by H.W. Baker. The collection was expanded in 1868 and revised in 1875 (with further supplements in 1889 and 1916).

The Christian Year. Thoughts in Verse for the Sundays and Holidays throughout the Year, Oxford, 1827, was written by John Keble. See *ODCC*, pp. 684, 280.

92. Newman's letter was written on July 19 (*Letters and Diaries* XXVI, pp. 138-139). In a letter from Munich, dated July 14, Plummer had already written to Newman that Döllinger did not understand his position regarding the dogma of papal infallibility: "I believe he is fairly puzzled to know how one who is in uprightness and ability what he knows you to be could think and say what you thought and said of the Dogma before it was passed and yet can defend it now", *ibid.*, p. 139, n. 3. Döllinger alluded to Newman's letter of Jan. 28, 1870, to Ullathorne. For Döllinger's reaction to Newman's letter of July 19, see pp. 66-67.

93. Plummer copied incorrectly: Newman did not deliver his lectures at the Birmingham Corn Exchange in 1851 but rather in 1850; see, also for the other references, *Letters and Diaries* XVI, p. 138.

94. Wiseman's article on *Pope Boniface VIII* was a review of J.C.L. DE SISMONDI, *A History of the Italian Republics* (London, 1832) and appeared in *The Dublin Review* 11 (1841) 505-549. It was republished in Wiseman's *Essays on Various Subjects*, vol. III, London, 1853, pp. 159-222.

95. Marie-Joseph Henri OLLIVIER, *Le Pape Alexandre VI et les Borgia*. Première partie: *Le Cardinal de Llançol y Borgia*, Paris, 1870.

96. In *Exp* 4/1, p. 278, Plummer replaces the preceding sentence with a footnote: "Dean Stanley used to speculate how different things would have been if Newman had read German".

97. John Henry NEWMAN, *Affairs of Rome*, in *The British Critic* 21 (1837) 261-283; republished in ID., *Essays Critical and Historical*, vol. I, London, 1871, pp. 102-136, under the title, "Fall of De la Mennais".

98. The reference in note 39, which has been taken over from QUIRINUS, p. 212 (Eng. trans., p. 274), is incorrect. The quotation is not found in vol. I but in vol. II of the *Œuvres posthumes de F. Lamennais. Correspondance*, ed. E.D. FORGUES, Paris, 1859, p. 247 (letter to Countess de Senfft, dated Nov. 1, 1832; cf. Lamennais' *Correspondance générale*, ed. L. LE GUILLOU, vol. V, Paris, 1974, p. 209).

Notes to Volume II

1. See A BAVARIAN CATHOLIC, *Catholicism in Bavaria*, in *The Contemporary Review* 14 (1870) 495-510; *Döllinger and the Catholic Church-Crisis in Bavaria*, ibid. 17 (1871) 261-273; *The Crisis in the Catholic Church in Bavaria*, ibid. 19 (1871-72) 120-144.

2. Probably Jacob FROHSCHAMMER, *Die Unfehlbarkeit des Papstes. Offenes Sendschreiben an den Erzbischof von München-Freising Gregor von Scherr betreffend den Hirtenbrief vom 26. Dezember 1870*, Munich, 1871.

3. Lola Montez did not die on June 30, but on Jan. 17, 1861. She spent the last years of her life in the USA where she turned toward religion. Using the name Fanny Gibbons, she devoted herself to good works, among them an institute for wayward women. See *Notable American Women 1607-1950. A Biographical Dictionary*, ed. E.T. JONES, vol. II, Cambridge, Mass., 1971, pp. 564-566.

4. Regarding Acton's honorary degree, see *Briefwechsel* III, pp. 84-85.

5. In the years 1860-70 the practice of auricular confession met with strong resistance among the opponents of the ritualist movement in the Church of England. It was not only considered as a romanizing tendency but was also experienced as an intrusion into the privacy of prudish Victorian family life. See BENTLEY, pp. 30-35.

6. *A Charge to the Clergy of the Diocese of St. David's by Connop, Lord Bishop of St. David's, Delivered at His Eleventh Visitation, Oct. & Nov. 1872*, London, 1872. Reprinted in *Remains Literary and Theological of Connop Thirlwall*, ed. J.J. STEWART PEROWNE, vol. II, London, 1877, pp. 290-357. Plummer had, in a letter to Newman dated Feb. 20, 1873, quoted this fragment from Döllinger's letter in translation (*Letters and Diaries* XXVI, p. 259, n. 1). For Newman's answer, see p. 289, n. 13.

7. The book on which Döllinger and Acton were working is the edition of *Ungedruckte Berichte und Tagebücher zur Geschichte des Concils von Trient*, which would only appear in 1876. See also pp. 148, 158, and the references in *Briefwechsel* III, pp. 105-161.

8. Johann Nepomuk HUBER, *Der Jesuiten-Orden nach seiner Verfassung und Doctrin, Wirksamkeit und Geschichte characterisirt*, Berlin, 1873.

9. *Der alte und der neue Glaube. Ein Bekenntnis*, Leipzig, 1872, was David Friedrich Strauss' last book. It contained a justification of his position and a last reckoning with Christian theology. The book was a best-seller but received a nearly unanimous negative reception. A variety of replies were published, among them the famous one by Friedrich Nietzsche, who ridiculed Strauss as "Bildungsphilister" in his *Unzeitgemäße Betrachtungen*, Leipzig, 1873 (part 1). See H. HARRIS, *David Friedrich Strauss and His Theology*, Cambridge, 1973, pp. 238-255.

10. Probably Döllinger does not refer to Holbach's *Système de la nature* but to *Le Bon-Sens, ou Idées naturelles opposées aux idées surnaturelles*, Paris, 1772, a popular version of his philosophy, which became his most widely read work.

11. Most likely the work of Johann Nepomuk HUBER, *Der alte und der neue Glaube. Ein Bekenntnis von Dav. Frdr. Strauß kritisch gewürdigt*, Nördlingen, 1873 (first published in the *Allgemeine Zeitung*).

12. Gladstone's proposal of establishing an open National University for Ireland with affiliated denominational colleges was rejected by Parliament in March 1873. The Bill met with resistance both among the Conservatives as well as among a group of Liberals led by Henry Fawcett, and among the Irish Catholic M.P.'s. On Feb. 17, 1874, Gladstone resigned. He was convinced that the Irish M.P.'s, in rejecting the Bill, were bound by the standpoint of the Irish episcopate which, under Archbishop Cullen's leadership, had rejected it because it sanctioned 'mixed education' and did not provide for an endowment for a Catholic college. See NORMAN, pp. 444-454. Döllinger also believed that the bishops' rejection had "muzzled" the Irish M.P.'s, *Briefwechsel* III, pp. 105 and 106-109 (Acton's opinion).

13. In his answer to Plummer, Newman wrote on Feb. 21: "I am always glad to hear about Dollinger, much as I grieve at what he has felt it a duty to do. He knows more of the Bishop of St D.'s [St David's] charge than I do — but I think it plain that the Irish University Bill has been affected by the Vatican decrees. As it stands, I don't see how Cardinal Cullen can accept it without a great inconsistency; but I suppose it will be cut about in committee", *Letters and Diaries* XXVI, pp. 258-259.

14. Leopold VON RANKE, *A History of England Principally in the Seventeenth Century*, 6 vols., Oxford, 1875. Plummer was one of the eight translators.

15. ID., *Englische Geschichte vornehmlich im siebzehnten Jahrhundert*, 8 vols., Berlin, 1859-66; ID., *Deutsche Geschichte im Zeitalter der Reformation*, 6 vols., Berlin, 1839-47; ID., *Geschichte Wallensteins*, Leipzig, 1869.

16. ID., *Die römischen Päpste, ihre Kirche und ihr Staat im sechzehnten und siebzehnten Jahrhundert*, vols. 2-4 of his *Fürsten und Völker von Süd-Europa im sechzehnten und siebzehnten Jahrhundert*, Berlin, 1834-36.

17. See *Letters and Diaries* XXVI, p. 328. As for Döllinger's reply, *ibid.*, p. 328, n. 2.

18. In his answer to the invitation to the congress, Wordsworth summarized in two points his reservations regarding the position of the Old Catholics, as it was expressed in their Munich confession of faith (1871), namely, their acceptance of Pius IV's confession of faith (1564) and the decrees of the Council of Trent. If they really wanted to call themselves Old Catholics, then they should only accept the Councils of the undivided Church. On Sept. 20 Wordsworth declared in an address that the Roman Church, in excommunicating Anglicans, excommunicated the primitive Church itself. He advised his audience to restore the primitive Church by reintroducing Holy Scripture in the vernacular, as well as the ancient symbols and the unfalsified sacraments of Christ. They must also call upon the Kaiser. If they were really Old Catholics, he would undoubtedly recognize them. Again, he recommended to the Old Catholics that they reject the Tridentine Church which logically evolved into the Vatican Church. See *Verhandlungen*, pp. 16-19; part 2, pp. 94-100.

19. In fact, Bishop Place had insisted in a pastoral letter dated Aug. 4, 1870, that the faithful submit to the Vatican decrees for the sake of peace and unity in the Church. He repeated this call during the diocesan synod of Marseilles in 1876. See MANSI LIII, cols. 1035D-1036C.

20. The French priest Eugène Michaud, after his break with Rome in Feb. 1872, tried unsuccessfully to initiate an Old Catholic movement in Paris. In 1876 he left his small community and joined the Old Catholics in Switzerland.

See R. DEDEREN, *Un réformateur catholique au XIXe siècle. Eugène Michaud (1839-1917). Vieux-catholicisme - Œcuménisme* (Travaux d'histoire éthico-politique, 2), Geneva, 1963, pp. 93-112; corrections found in V. CONZEMIUS, *Eugène Michaud, ein katholischer Reformator des 19. Jahrhunderts? Zu einer Michaud-Biographie*, in *Zeitschrift für schweizerische Kirchengeschichte* 58 (1964) 177-204, esp. pp. 195-196. Conzemius published Michaud's letters to Döllinger, *ibid.*, pp. 309-356; Michaud himself published the letters Döllinger wrote to him in *RIT* 7 (1899) 233-255.

21. Alexandre HERCULANO, *História de Portugal, desde o começo da monarquia até o fem do reinado de Afonso III*, 4 vols., Lisbon, 1846-53; ID., *História da origem e estabelecimento da Inquisição em Portugal*, 3 vols., Lisbon, 1854-59. Döllinger discussed both works in his memorial lecture on Herculano before the Bavarian Academy on March 28, 1875, published in *Akademische Vorträge* II, pp. 254-279.

22. ID., *Opusculos*. Tomo I : *Questões publicas*, vol. I, Lisbon, 1873.

23. The Seven Weeks War between Prussia and Austria broke out on June 15, 1866, as a result of the dispute over the Schleswig-Holstein question. On July 3 the outcome was decided by the battle of Königgrätz, the consequence of which was Austria's surrender to Prussia. In early Aug. Prussia defeated the South German states. On Aug. 22, the day before the Peace Treaty of Prague, Bavaria made a secret defensive and offensive alliance with Prussia, which guaranteed the integrity of its territory and obliged it to place its armed forces under Prussian command in time of war. See also p. 85, n. 6.

24. Not William but Edgar Edmund ESTCOURT, *The Question of Anglican Ordinations Discussed. With an Appendix of Original Documents and Facsimiles*, London, 1873.

25. In *Exp* 4/1, pp. 427-428, Plummer further elaborates the last sentence: "This grave blunder of Eugenius IV. is a more serious difficulty with regard to Roman orders than anything which can be urged against Anglican orders; and if Anglican controversialists always met the attack on their orders by pointing out the confusion introduced by Eugenius IV., such attacks would probably become less frequent. The Nag's Head fable is of course exploded. The consecration of Bishop Barlow, Parker's consecrator, was never called in question until 1616, eighty years after the event; and the validity of Parker's consecration is so strongly attested that Lingard does not venture to question it. Bossuet also admitted it; and it cannot be questioned excepting upon sceptical grounds which would render history impossible".

The decree of Eugenius IV is the *Decretum pro Armeniis*, enacted in the bull *Exsultate Deo*, dated Nov. 22, 1439 (MANSI XXXI, cols. 1047E-1060D).

26. The emissary from the British Museum was Joseph Stevenson, a clergyman who had converted to Roman Catholicism in 1863 and was ordained priest in 1872. From Oct. 1872 until the end of 1876 (with a few interruptions) he worked in the Vatican Archives on commission from the Public Record Office. At the beginning of 1877 he continued to work there in a private capacity. See CHADWICK, *Catholicism*, pp. 77-87.

27. Doubtless Plummer means Guglielmo Acton, Acton's nephew and Minghetti's brother-in-law. From Jan. 1870 to Aug. 1871 he served as minister of the navy in the Lanza cabinet. But he had no ministry post in the new Minghetti cabinet. In 1879 he became head of the Naval General Staff and

president of the Naval Supreme Council. See R. BERNOTTI, *Acton, G.*, in *DBI* 1 (1960) 206.

The difficult finance portfolio was in the end taken by Minghetti himself; he established reforms which resulted in the first balanced budget since 1860. See M. MENGHINI, *Minghetti, M.*, in *EI* 23 (1934) 362-363.

28. MacHale and Moriarty, the two Irish bishops who had voted *non placet* at the Council, appear never to have been called upon to give formal assent to the dogma of infallibility. There were rumours, particularly about MacHale, that he continued to oppose infallibility. Cardinal Cullen expected a clear and unambiguous answer from him; he was of the opinion that MacHale, in keeping silence, was allowing his name to be used as an excuse for heresy (see D. BOWEN, *Paul Cardinal Cullen and the Shaping of Modern Irish Catholicism*, Dublin, 1983, pp. 206-207). Yet it is difficult to assert, as Plummer does, that MacHale did not accept the dogma. Immediately after his return from Rome, he had already declared that his opposition during the Council was not directed against the doctrine of infallibility but only against the dogma's expediency. During the Maynooth bishops' synod in 1875, both MacHale and Moriarty signed the joint pastoral which ratified the dogma of infallibility as an article of faith. However, it was only on March 29, 1880, that MacHale sent Rome a personal declaration accepting the Vatican decrees (MANSI LIII, col. 953). See NORMAN, p. 414.

29. The Sydow case belonged to King Wilhelm I's struggle against Minister Falk's liberal policy about the Evangelical Church. In 1879 the conflict would finally lead to Falk's resignation (p. 183). See HUBER, pp. 856-862.

30. *The Sling and the Stone* was a book written by the Anglican clergyman Charles Voysey. In 1871 Voysey was removed from office on the charge of heresy by the Judicial Committee of the Privy Council. He was accused of denying that Christ's death was sacrificial, of rejecting original sin, of regarding justification by faith as contrary to the teaching of Christ, and of deeming spurious long passages in the N.T. for purely subjective reasons. See CHADWICK, *Victorian Church* II, pp. 133-134.

31. The Bennett case refers to the discussions about an open letter published in 1867 by the Anglican clergyman William James Early BENNETT, *A Plea for Toleration in the Church of England in a Letter to Dr. Pusey*. Because of the opinion expressed in this letter on the Real Presence in the Eucharist, the Protestant Church Association accused Bennett of heresy before the Court of Arches. The Court decided in July 1870 that Bennett had not contravened the ecclesiastical law, a decision which the Privy Council upheld in appeal in 1872. See W.P. COURTNEY, *Bennett, W.J.E.*, in *DNB* 22 (1909) 169-171.

32. In Italy the Law of Guarantees of May 13, 1871, abrogated the *Exequatur*, the royal *Placet*, and other forms of governmental authorization for the publication and execution of the acts of ecclesiastical authorities, except when these acts related to the disposal of ecclesiastical goods and the provision of benefices. Ecclesiastics who were provided with benefices had to submit their appointment bill for approval by the state authorities. Because the majority of new bishops ignored this regulation, a growing number of them had to turn to the Holy See for financial support. The conflict was resolved in 1876, when the Vatican authorized the bishops to comply with the demands of the *Exequatur*. See G. PENCO, *Storia della Chiesa in Italia*, vol. II, Milan, 1978, pp. 336-338.

33. George SALMON, *Some Notes on the Chronology of Hippolytus*, in *Hermathena* 1 (1873) 82-128. Plummer discussed Salmon's article in his translation of *Hippolytus und Callistus*, Appendix A: "Dr. Salmon on the chronology of Hippolytus" (pp. 333-340).

34. The law respecting the education of the clergy, announced on May 11, 1873, was the first 'May Law' (see p. 294, n. 57). It made appointment to a clerical office dependent on German citizenship and a scientific education at a German university. Explicit recognition by the State was required for the formation at a diocesan seminary to be made equivalent to the studies at a theological faculty. Theology students were also required to take a complementary 'culture examination' in philosophy, history, and German literature.

35. See Pius' speech on July 6, 1873, to Roman officials of the Prelature and the Supreme Tribunal, in DE FRANCISCIS II, p. 371.

36. Heinrich August Wilhelm MEYER, *Kritisch exegetischer Kommentar über das Neue Testament*, 16 vols., Göttingen, 1832-59. Meyer published a text and translation of the N.T. and wrote commentaries on the Gospels and all the Pauline Epistles except Thess. The latter and the remaining vols. were prepared by younger colleagues. Meyer himself published several revised editions of his commentaries.

37. Hermann OLSHAUSEN, *Biblischer Commentar über sämmtliche Schriften des Neuen Testaments zunächst für Prediger und Studirende*, 7 vols., Königsberg, 1830-62. Olshausen was the author of the first four vols.; the work was completed by J.A.H. Ebrard and A. Wiesinger.

38. By "Sprengel" Plummer means Leonard Spengel, who was professor of classical languages at the University of Munich from 1847.

39. The difference of opinion between Bishop Krementz of Ermland and the Prussian government was one of the first conflicts during the *Kulturkampf*. Without first consulting the state authorities, Krementz denied permission to teach to the religion teacher Wollmann and the theology professor Michelis, who were later excommunicated because of their opposition to the definition of infallibility. Since in addition to being clergymen both were civil servants, the government considered Krementz' act illegal. On Sept. 25, 1872, Krementz' state salary was withheld, because he refused to submit unconditionally to state laws. Krementz tried repeatedly to have this disciplinary measure revoked. But it was finally upheld by the High Court in Berlin, which rejected Krementz' appeal on July 14, 1873, because the bishop had no civil claim to the state subsidy on account of his episcopal position. See HUBER-HUBER, pp. 474-484, 490-521.

40. The succession to Samuel Wilberforce as Bishop of Winchester did not go to Richard W. Church but to Edward H. Browne, Bishop of Ely.

41. *Ueberblick über die geschichtliche Entwicklung und die gegenwärtige Aufgabe unsrer Akademie*, Munich, 1873; reprinted in *Akademische Vorträge* II, pp. 327-340.

42. See p. 77, n. 4.

43. Ernest RENAN, *Questions contemporaines*, Paris, 1868, p. 259 (cf. *Akademische Vorträge* II, p. 332).

44. Quotation from LUCRETIUS, *De rerum natura*, II, 79.

45. Wilhelm VON BEETZ, *Der Antheil der k. bayerischen Akademie der Wissenschaften an der Entwickelung der Electricitätslehre*, Munich, 1873.

46. By "S. Pellau" Plummer means the Austrian Sankt Pölten, which was made an independent diocese on Jan. 28, 1785.

47. Christopher WORDSWORTH, *St. Hippolytus and the Church of Rome in the Earlier Part of the Third Century. From the Newly-Discovered Philosophumena*, London, 1853; enl. ed., 1880.

48. After King Amadeo I's abdication on Feb. 11, 1873, the Republic was proclaimed in Spain. The country was in danger of falling apart because of civil disorder until, in 1875, the monarchy was reinstated under Alfonso XII.

49. On Feb. 21, 1874, Newman had written to Plummer: "Is not the new move of getting an episcopal succession for the Old Catholics contrary to the policy which Dollinger intended? and can he come into it? I thought he recognized the duty, nay necessity, of communion with Rome, and only denied the fact that the Vatican decrees were legitimate and valid, or that the disunion was more than accidental and temporary", *Letters and Diaries* XXVII, p. 20. Plummer had informed Döllinger of this last part of Newman's letter and, on April 9, passed Döllinger's comments on to Newman in translation.

50. In total William Palmer wrote eight letters to Wiseman in the years 1841-42. They were collected under the title, *Letters to N. Wiseman, D.D., on the Errors of Romanism, in Respect to the Worship of Saints, Satisfactions, Purgatory, Indulgences, and the Worship of Images and Relics*, Oxford, 1842; London, 1851.

51. *Hus redivivus oder die Kirche der Zukunft. Eine Vision*, Münster, 1874; the book was published anonymously.

52. Rhossis referred to the Second Council of Nicaea (787), already mentioned on p. 106 (cf. *Bericht 1874*, p. 44). In the Conference of 1875 it would come up again in the tense discussion on the number of ecumenical councils (see pp. 140-141, 146).

53. *Sendschreiben der St. Petersburger Sektion des Vereins der Freunde Geistlicher Aufklärung in St. Petersburg an Herrn Professor Dr. Langen*, St. Petersburg, 1874; published under the title *Ein russisches Verzeichnis der Unterscheidungslehren* on Feb. 28, 1874, in the *Deutscher Merkur*, No. 9, pp. 65-67. The text was composed as a preparation of the First Reunion Conference. See NEUNER, pp. 183-184.

54. Frederick MEYRICK (ed.), *Correspondence between the Secretaries of the Friends of Spiritual Enlightenment and the Anglo-Continental Society, Containing Statements on the Validity of Anglican Orders, the Eternal Procession of the Holy Ghost, the Intercession and Invocation of the Saints*, London/Oxford/Cambridge, 1875.

55. Johann FRIEDRICH, *Ueber kirchliche Reformen. Rede gehalten auf dem Alt-Katholiken-Congress zu Köln am 22. September 1872*, Cologne/Leipzig, 1872; also in *Verhandlungen*, part 2, pp. 48-56 (esp. pp. 54-55). According to *Bericht 1874*, pp. 56-57, the discussion was not abruptly terminated after Reusch's and Döllinger's replies to Tatschaloff, as Plummer further suggests, but continued briefly with interventions by Knoodt, Rhossis, Janyschew, and Reinkens.

56. The Public Worship Regulation Act of Aug. 7, 1874, was designed to restrict the spread of ritualism in the Church of England. It allowed the Archbishops of Canterbury and York to appoint a lay judge to head the provincial courts to decide upon irregularities in ritual practice. A final appeal to the Judicial Committee of the Privy Council was allowed, and the bishops

reserved the right to veto the proceedings under the Act. The Act became discredited when five clergymen were imprisoned for contumacy in the years 1877-87, because they refused to recognize the decisions against them taken by the court. To avoid such disciplinary measures against their clergy, the bishops exercised their right of veto in all other cases. See BENTLEY, pp. 46-128, 129-142 (text); CHADWICK, *Victorian Church* II, pp. 322-325, 348-352, 361-362.

57. The Falk Laws or May Laws (*Maigesetze*) of 1873 were developed by Adalbert Falk, the Prussian minister of public worship. The law of May 11 enlarged the State's influence on the training and appointment of the clergy (see p. 292, n. 34). The law of May 12 limited ecclesiastical disciplinary power over clerics, introduced the possibility of appeal, gave government functionaries the authority to initiate a process to remove clerics from their office, and instituted a Royal Tribunal of Ecclesiastical Affairs to carry out these measures. The law of May 13 forbade ecclesiastical disciplinary and penal measures against Church members if these affected the civil domain. The law of May 14 made secession from the Church easier. The R.C. bishops of Germany rejected the laws in a collective petition on May 26 and forbade all co-operation in putting them into effect. In the years 1874-75 the laws were expanded and made harsher via additional punishments. Pius IX, in his encyclical *Quod numquam* of Feb. 5, 1875, declared the entire body of *Kulturkampf* legislation invalid, because it contravened the constitution and rights of the Church. See HUBER, pp. 710-767; texts in HUBER-HUBER, pp. 580-622.

58. The Bavarian election campaign in July 1875 placed the National Liberals, supported by the Lutz cabinet, in opposition to the Patriotic party, which argued that a greater openness toward the Prussians would invite the introduction of the Prussian *Kulturkampf* legislation into Bavaria. In pastoral letters the bishops also called on the faithful to vote for candidates who would defend throne and country, religion and Church, law and order. These interventions elicited a sharp reaction from Lutz who tried in vain to obtain sanctions against bishops such as Scherr and Senestrey. In the elections the Patriots won 79 seats and the Liberals 77. After vigorous discussions in the new House, the Lutz cabinet did in the end remain in office, after the king had rejected its attempt to resign. See RUMMEL, pp. 72-89.

59. The controversy in the Church of Ireland concerned the revision of the Prayer Book. A revision committee had made a number of recommendations which were passed in the 1875 session of the general synod. William Lee, Archdeacon of Dublin and a strong High Churchman, was a sharp opponent of the 'protestantizing' tendencies of the proposed changes. To strengthen the position of the anti-revisionists, he asked Pusey, in May 1875, to make public his opinion. In his answer Pusey expressed the hope that the new Prayer Book would be rejected. Church members who feared such a rejection would bring about a schism should recognize that "this faith-destroying Prayer-book" in itself was schismatic. See LIDDON IV, p. 282; R.B. McDOWELL, *The Church of Ireland 1869-1969* (Studies in Irish History, 2/10), London/Boston, 1975, pp. 61-66.

60. On Feb. 18, 1875, after a period of vigorous ecclesiastical disputes, the clergy of the Greek-Ruthenian diocese of Chelm (Poland), under the leadership of its administrator Marceli Popiel, had expressed the desire to be reunited

with the Orthodox Church. Czar Alexander II agreed to their request on March 25. On May 11 the diocese of Chelm was incorporated in the Orthodox diocese of Warsaw. The members of the Church who opposed this transition were persecuted in the years that followed. In 1905 they received permission to return to the Catholic Church of the Latin rite. See X. W. MEYSZTOWICZ, *Chelm*, in *DHGE* 12 (1953) 605-614, cols. 609-614.

61. In the Roman Catholic Relief Act of April 13, 1829, no further directives were included concerning the Crown Veto over episcopal appointments or the *Exequatur*, the previously much discussed 'securities' which were to guarantee Catholic allegiance after Emancipation. The only remaining reservation with regard to the Catholic bishops was the prohibition of their use of the titles of the ancient episcopal sees. See E. NORMAN, *The English Catholic Church in the Nineteenth Century*, Oxford, 1984, pp. 63-66. For the situation in Italy, see p. 87.

62. In *Exp* 4/2, p. 122, Plummer adds a quotation from QUIRINUS, pp. 433-434 (Eng. trans., p. 562) in a footnote: "As a French politician of the Left said, when asked to back up a protest against the proceedings of the Vatican Council, '*Rome fait trop bien nos affaires pour qu'il soit de notre intérêt de lui créer des embarras*'".

63. Between May 6 and Aug. 3, 1867, Döllinger published eleven articles on *Rom und die Inquisition* in the *Allgemeine Zeitung*. Because of a veto from its publisher Cotta, the newspaper could not continue the series. In 1868 there followed four anonymous articles on *Die spanische Inquisition* and *Die römische Inquisition, ihre Erneuerung und Erweiterung* in the *Neue Freie Presse* in Vienna. The articles were reprinted in *Kleinere Schriften*, pp. 286-404. See LÖSCH, pp. 541-542, and *Briefwechsel* III, p. 98.

64. In a circular dated May 14, 1872, Bismarck had commissioned the representatives of the German Empire to begin negotiations with interested European governments in order to exercise influence over the coming papal election. The existence of the dispatch became known in Dec. 1874 as a result of a court case against Count Arnim, former ambassador to the Holy See. On Dec. 29 the text was published in the *Staatsanzeiger*. In Jan. 1875 the German episcopate published a collective declaration rejecting every intervention by a state in the election of the Pope. See HUBER, pp. 731-732; texts in HUBER-HUBER, pp. 645-650.

65. In *Exp* 4/2, p. 127, Plummer adds a footnote: "The conclave lasted three months, February to May, 1769, and there were 185 scrutinies".

66. *Commentary on the Gospel According to S. John by S. Cyril, Archbishop of Alexandria*. Vol. I: *S. John I-VIII* (Library of Fathers), Oxford, 1874. The text was edited by Pusey's son, Philip E. Pusey. Pusey himself wrote the greater part of the preface (pp. X-LX). It was intended as a contribution to the anticipated discussion on the procession of the Spirit at the Bonn Reunion Conferences. Pusey feared that the representatives of the Western Churches, and more particularly Döllinger, would, in their efforts at reunion with the Orientals, abandon the affirmation of the *Filioque*. A year later, he sent the text of the preface to the Second Conference at Bonn. See LIDDON IV, pp. 294-295.

67. W. E. GLADSTONE, *Is the Church of England Worth Preserving?*, in *The Contemporary Review* 26 (1875) 193-220.

68. ID., *Rome and the Newest Fashions in Religion. Three Tracts. The Vatican*

Decrees. – Vaticanism. – Speeches of the Pope. Collected Edition, with a Preface, London, 1875. The first two tracts are Gladstone's famous pamphlets, *The Vatican Decrees in Their Bearing on Civil Allegiance: A Political Expostulation* (Nov. 1874) and *Vaticanism: An Answer to Reproofs & Replies* (Feb. 1875). Döllinger had read the proof-sheets of the first pamphlet and had sent Gladstone text corrections as well as some suggestions regarding the contents of the second pamphlet. The third text is a review article of DE FRANCISCIS which originally appeared in *The Quarterly Review* 138 (1875) 266-304. In a letter dated June 4, 1875, Gladstone, with a view to a new edition, asked Döllinger to give his comments on these texts. See MCELRATH, pp. 225-323. Döllinger had Max Lossen translate the three texts into German (FRIEDRICH III, pp. 656-658).

69. *Ignaz Döllingers Briefe an eine junge Freundin*, pp. 197-198 (letter dated Jan. 27, 1865). See LÖSCH, pp. 253-254, who also discusses the contacts between Döllinger and Dupanloup in the years preceding the Council (pp. 255-281). The expectations of the French bishops of liberal and Gallican sympathies regarding the coming Council are described by PALANQUE, pp. 61-103.

70. Maret had visited Döllinger in Munich in July 1868 to consult him about the second part of his notorious book, *Du Concile général et de la paix religieuse*. See LÖSCH, pp. 215-216.

71. The Pope referred to Jakob FROHSCHAMMER, *Über den Ursprung der menschlichen Seelen. Rechtfertigung des Generatianismus*, Munich, 1854, which had been placed on the Index at the insistance of Kleutgen.

72. The law on higher education of July 12, 1875, marked the pinacle of the Catholic struggle for freedom of education. Every institution with at least three faculties was entitled to call itself a free university. To obtain a degree the students of free faculties had to present themselves to a mixed jury consisting half of professors of state faculties and half of professors of free faculties. See A. DANSETTE, *Histoire religieuse de la France contemporaine. De la Révolution à la Troisième République*, Paris, ²1948, pp. 461-463.

73. There was no episcopal seminary in Louvain. Plummer most likely refers to the diocesan college, a secondary school institution.

74. In the years 1864-67 Newman had conceived the plan to found a house of the Oratory in Oxford, with the intention of offering spiritual guidance to Catholic students at the University. At the end of 1864 he initially abandoned the plan after the English bishops had decided to discourage Catholics from attending the University. In 1867 Newman definitively abandoned his project when, in response to a second request, Propaganda permitted the establishment of the house only on the condition that Newman himself did not take up residence in Oxford. See MCCLELLAND, pp. 194-234.

75. See *Bericht 1875*, pp. 18-24.

76. The letters of Edward H. Browne, Bishop of Winchester, and of Gladstone are included, in German translation, in *Bericht 1875*, pp. 30-37. The original English texts are added in an appendix.

77. See *Bericht 1875*, pp. 43-52.

78. Note 18 is a printed text taken from a non-identified source.

79. The synod of Antioch in 268, which condemned Paul of Samosata, rejected the term because Paul employed it to deny the subsistent personhood of the Logos.

NOTES TO VOLUME III

1. See *Bericht 1875*, pp. 77-83.

2. The discussion on the number of ecumenical councils grew into a personal confrontation between Overbeck and Döllinger (cf. *Bericht 1875*, pp. 83-86). After the discussion Overbeck felt very hurt and abandoned by the Russians. From that moment he gave up his hopes for closer bonds with the Old Catholics and, in fact, later endeavoured to create a negative attitude towards them in the Eastern Churches. See KAHLE, pp. 145-157, 243-251.

3. See *Bericht 1875*, pp. 91-113.

4. The six articles taken from the writings of John of Damascus are quoted in *Bericht 1875*, pp. 92-93 (cf. MOSS, p. 269).

5. The causes for the suspension of the Conferences, particularly the influence of Overbeck and Pusey, are more expansively explained in NEUNER, pp. 211-219. See also pp. 184-185.

6. The letter by 45 bishops, dated July 7, was published in a German translation in the *Deutscher Merkur* on July 29, 1876, No. 31, p. 268; the letter by 347 clergymen and 277 laymen, dated Aug. 1, on Sept. 21, No. 36, p. 308.

7. Pomponio LETO, *Otto mesi a Roma durante il Concilio Vaticano. Impressioni di un contemporaneo*, Florence, 1873. The author was the Marquis Francesco Nobili Vitelleschi, an Italian politician and literator. His brother Salvatore was Archbishop of Osimo and Cingoli. In 1875 he was made cardinal. A year later the book was put on the Index.

8. Manning had most strongly denied Cardinal Vitelleschi's contribution to the editing of Leto's book in *The Vatican Council and Its Definitions: A Pastoral Letter*, London, 1870. Later, in *The True Story of the Vatican Council*, London/New York, 1877, he wrote: "As to the true authorship of Pomponio Leto various things are affirmed. It belongs to the anonymous school of *Janus* and *Quirinus*, and seems to be the work of more hands than one, and to betray both a German and an English contributor" (p. 165).

9. In fact, Silvestre Guevara had been Archbishop of Caracas since 1852. In 1871 he was banned from Venezuela after a conflict with the new president Guzmán Blanco. In 1873 the Holy See appointed an apostolic vicar to administer the archdiocese. But after a short while, Guzmán no longer accepted this solution. In 1876 the nuncio Rocco Cocchia convinced Guevara to resign, and Rome accepted the nomination of José Ponte, a connection of Guzmán, as the new archbishop. See J. L. SÁNCHEZ, *Historia general de la Iglesia en América latina*, vol. VII, Salamanca, 1981, pp. 460-479.

10. Carl Paul CASPARI, *Ungedruckte, unbeachtete und wenig beachtete Quellen zur Geschichte des Taufsymbols und der Glaubensregel. Herausgegeben und in Abhandlungen erläutert*, 3 vols., Christiania, 1866-75; reviewed by Plummer in his translation of *Hippolytus und Callistus*, Appendix F: "Professor Caspari's contributions to the subject" (pp. 355-360).

11. Gottfried THOMASIUS, *Die Christliche Dogmengeschichte als Entwicklungs-Geschichte des kirchlichen Lehrbegriffs*. Erster Band: *Die Dogmengeschichte der alten Kirche. Periode der Patristik*; Zweiter Band: *Die Dogmengeschichte des Mittelalters und der Reformationszeit*, 2 vols., Erlangen, 1874-76; 2nd ed. by G. N. BONWETSCH (vol. I) and R. SEEBERG (vol. II), 1886-89.

12. Pierre LANFREY, *Histoire de Napoléon Ier*, 5 vols., Paris, 1867-75.

13. Johannes FRIEDRICH, *Döllinger und Platen*, in *Studien zur Kultur- und Litteraturgeschichte Altbayerns* 1 (1892) 69-102.

14. As did Enzler, Käs in the end also requested that his proposed appointment be withdrawn. The episcopal sees of Würzburg and Speyer remained vacant for two years. It was only in 1878, under the new Pope Leo XIII, that two new bishops were appointed. See RUMMEL, pp. 94-96.

15. E. B. PUSEY, *On the Clause "And the Son," in Regard to the Eastern Church and the Bonn Conference. A Letter to the Rev. H. P. Liddon*, Oxford, 1876. Originally Pusey had the intention of rewriting his preface to the Commentary of Cyril (see p. 122). Liddon, however, had asked him instead to compose a public letter, indicating how the propositions of the Second Reunion Conference could be amended. In his letter Pusey said that the Bonn propositions were too ambiguous and incomplete and added numerous amendments in an appendix. Liddon discussed Pusey's objections extensively in his preface to the *Proceedings at the Reunion-Conference Held at Bonn between 10th and 16th of August, 1875*, London, 1876. See LIDDON IV, pp. 293-302.

16. Ernst TRUMPP, *Nānak, der Stifter der Sikh-Religion*, Munich, 1876. The address was delivered on July 25, 1876.

17. Eduard ZELLER, *Geschichte der deutschen Philosophie seit Leibniz* (Geschichte der Wissenschaften in Deutschland. Neuere Zeit, 13), Munich, 1873.

18. Rochus Freiherr VON LILIENCRON, *Ueber den Inhalt der allgemeinen Bildung in der Zeit der Scholastik*, Munich, 1876; delivered before the Bavarian Academy on March 28, 1876.

19. *Gedächtnißrede auf König Johann von Sachsen*, Munich, 1874; delivered before the Academy on March 28, 1874; reprinted in *Akademische Vorträge* II, pp. 228-240.

20. *La dernière heure du Concile* appeared in Munich in early July 1870. The anonymous brochure contained sharp attacks on the course of events at the Council, culminating in accusations against the Jesuits, Propaganda, and Pius IX himself (PALANQUE, pp. 133-134). Döllinger suspected that the brochure was written by someone close to Dupanloup, Place, or Darboy; according to Acton, Albert Du Boÿs or Darboy himself was the author (*Briefwechsel* II, pp. 430-435). *La dernière heure du Concile* together with *Ce qui se passe au Concile*, was condemned by the Council Fathers on July 16 (see p. 286, n. 88).

21. In *Exp* 4/1, pp. 432-433, Plummer adds: "'—An English clergyman once called on me, who evidently thought that I should be very pleased to know that, in celebrating the eucharist, he wore vestments closely resembling those of our own clergy. And some time afterwards I received a photograph of him in this costume: beretta, chasuble, lace, and all the rest of it. It amused me much, and (I confess) rather disgusted me: first, that he should care to be photographed in such attire; and, secondly, that he should suppose that I should care to have the photograph'".

22. During the first two synods of the German Old Catholics (1874-75), the abandoning of compulsory celibacy for clerics was rejected. The third synod (1876) decided that the matter should be treated after a decision had been reached on other more essential reforms. It was decided at the same time that no further objection would be made to giving ecclesiastical blessing to a civil marriage contracted by an Old Catholic priest, provided the latter had given up his pastoral activity. The fourth synod (1877) decided that the question

of mandatory celibacy must be further investigated, more particularly with a view to the possible implications of marriage with regard to the laws of the State, and that suggestions should be prepared for the following synod. During the fifth synod in 1878, compulsory celibacy was finally abolished (pp. 171-172). See SCHULTE, pp. 625-649.

23. Acton's notice appeared in *The Academy*, May 20, 1876, pp. 473-474.

24. The Russian-Turkish War broke out on April 24, 1877. Great Britain adopted a neutral position on the condition that its interests be respected, such as Russian recognition of Constantinople's inviolability and the guarantee of navigation in the Straits. As the war progressed, anti-Russian feelings grew in England. When, in Jan. 1878, Russian troops occupied Adrianople, the British government dispatched its Mediterranean fleet to Constantinople. A week later, on Jan. 31, armistice was declared between Russia and Turkey.

25. Gladstone's "bag and baggage" policy favoured self-government as the solution to the problems in the Balkans. The expression comes from his famous pamphlet, *The Bulgarian Horrors and the Question of the East* (Sept. 1876), in which he protested against the mass murders by the Turks in Bulgaria in May-June, 1876. He demanded that the Turks withdraw from the province "one and all, bag and baggage", J. MORLEY, *The Life of William Ewart Gladstone*, vol. II, London, 1903, p. 554.

26. Their efforts resulted in the foundation of Wycliffe Hall, Oxford, in 1877, and Ridley Hall, Cambridge, in 1880 (opened in 1881). Robert Payne Smith, the Dean of Canterbury, was chairman of the council of Wycliffe Hall from 1877 until the end of his life. See J.S. REYNOLDS, *The Evangelicals at Oxford 1735-1871. A Record of an Unchronicled Movement, with the Record Extended to 1905*, Oxford, 1975, p. 182; part 2, pp. 26-27.

27. *Justin Martyr's Epistle to Diognetus and the Oration to the Gentiles*, in *The Church Quarterly Review* 4 (1877) 42-76. The Stephanus mentioned in the text is Henri Estienne who published the letter in 1592.

28. B. G. NIEBUHR, *Ueber das Alter des Dialogus Philopatris*, in ID., *Kleine historische und philologische Schriften*, vol. II, Bonn, 1843, pp. 73-78.

29. Heinrich WESSIG, *De aetate et auctore Philopatridis dialogi (qui una cum Lucianeis edi solet)*, Koblenz, 1868.

30. It was Acton who, while studying the massacre of St. Bartholomew, discovered that Theiner had omitted passages detrimental to the Church in his continuation of Baronius' *Annales*. In 1869 he mentioned this in a letter to Döllinger (*Briefwechsel* I, p. 501). In 1881-82 he strongly condemned such manipulation of historical evidence (*Briefwechsel* III, pp. 283-291). See further p. 198, and CHADWICK, *Catholicism*, pp. 58-61.

31. *Annales ecclesiastici, quos post Caesarem S.R.E. Baronium, Odoricum Raynaldum ac Iacobum Laderchium ab an. MDLXXII ad nostra usque tempora continuat Augustinus* THEINER, 3 vols., Rome, 1856. On the dedication, see H. JEDIN, *Gustav Hohenlohe und Augustin Theiner 1850-1870*, in *RQ* 66 (1971) 171-186, p. 180.

32. Giuseppe CARDONI, *Elucubratio de dogmatica Romani Pontificis infallibilitate eiusque definibilitate*, Rome, 1870. Cardoni was adviser to the theological commission which prepared the Council. His book is almost identical to the votum *De Romani Pontificis infallibilitate*, which he had presented to the preparatory commission, and which had played a central role in the genesis of

the ultimate definition of the dogma. See U. BETTI, *La costituzione dommatica "Pastor aeternus" del Concilio Vaticano I* (Spicilegium Pontificii Athenaei Antoniani, 14), Rome, 1961, esp. pp. 44-50 (text), 208, n. 8.

33. Augustin THEINER, *Geschichte des Pontificats Clemens' XIV. Nach unedirten Staatsschriften aus dem geheimen Archive des Vaticans*, 2 vols., Leipzig/ Paris, 1853. A French translation had already appeared in 1852 in Paris. This rehabilitation of the Pope who had suppressed the Jesuit order made Theiner the order's enemy. From that moment he nourished a veritable "anti-Jesuit psychosis", H. JEDIN, *Augustin Theiner. Zum 100. Jahrestag seines Todes am 9. August 1874*, in *Archiv für schlesische Kirchengeschichte* 31 (1973) 134-176, p. 154. See also H.H. SCHWEDT, *Augustin Theiner und Pius IX*, in E. GATZ (ed.), *Römische Kurie. Kirchliche Finanzen. Vatikanisches Archiv. Studien zu Ehren von Hermann Hoberg* (MHP, 46), vol. II, Rome, 1979, pp. 825-868 (esp. pp. 835-838).

34. By the History of the Council of Trent, Plummer means Theiner's project to publish the Acts of the Council. In 1857 he received permission from Pius IX to publish them, but a year later—thus already a long time before the conflict at the Vatican Council—the authorization was withdrawn. Finally Theiner had a part of the collection printed with Strossmayer's help and without papal authorization, but he died on Aug. 9, 1874, before the publication was completed. It appeared under the title, *Acta genuina SS. Oecumenici Concilii Tridentini sub Paulo III, Julio III et Pio IV PP.MM., ab Angelo Massarello episcopo Thelesino eiusdem Concilii secretario conscripta, nunc primum integra edita ab Augustino THEINER. Accedunt acta eiusdem Concilii sub Pio IV a Cardinale Gabriele Paleotto archiepiscopo Bononiensi digesta, secundis curis expolitiora*, 2 vols., Zagreb/Leipzig, 1874-75. See H. JEDIN, *Das Publikationsverbot der Monumenta Tridentina Augustin Theiners im Jahre 1858*, in *AHC* 3 (1971) 89-97; CHADWICK, *Catholicism*, pp. 46-53, 68-69.

35. The additional material on the Council of Trent was published in 1882 in *Beiträge zur politischen, kirchlichen und Cultur-Geschichte der sechs letzten Jahrhunderte* III, pp. 283-339: "Documente zur Geschichte des Concils von Trient". For the sketch of the Council, see p. 310, n. 30.

36. The *Decretum Magistri Gratiani* was the first part of the second Leipzig edition of the *Corpus iuris canonici*, prepared by Emil Friedberg; it was completed in 1879. A second part, with *Decretalium collectiones*, appeared in 1881.

37. Note 11 is a quotation from QUIRINUS, p. 306 (Eng. trans., p. 399).

38. Gladstone had referred to the Gordon case in the preface of *Rome and the Newest Fashions in Religion* (pp. v-viii), the republication of his pamphlets against Vaticanism (see p. 295, n. 68), as an illustration of the illegitimate interference of the R.C. law in civil legislation. More details on the case in MCELRATH, pp. 318-320.

39. J. FRIEDRICH, *Geschichte des Vatikanischen Konzils*. Erster Band: *Vorgeschichte bis zur Eröffnung des Konzils*, Bonn, 1877.

40. James Anthony FROUDE, *Life and Times of Thomas Becket*, in *The Nineteenth Century* 1 (1877) 548-562, 843-856; 2 (1877) 15-27, 217-229, 389-410, 669-691. Reprinted in ID., *Short Studies on Great Subjects. New Edition in Four Volumes*, vol. IV, London, 1883, pp. 1-230.

41. See *Christenthum und Kirche in der Zeit der Grundlegung*, pp. 103-104.

42. In his turn Plummer confuses Johann Strauss, the composer of "An

der schönen blauen Donau", with his younger brother Eduard. Eduard Strauss worked in his brother Josef's orchestra and himself composed more than 318 dances.

43. On July 30 and Aug. 8, Bismarck and Gaetano Aloisi Masella, nuncio in Munich, had held confidential discussions in Kissingen with the intention of reinstating a regular exchange of views between Rome and the Prussian government. During the discussions, the divergent goals of both parties became evident: Bismarck only wanted to create, via an armistice, the possibility of reaching a practical agreement or modus vivendi; the Vatican stood on principle and wanted a peace ensured by a concordat (including the abrogation of the May Laws). The discussions were discontinued because of the death of Secretary of State Franchi, but the exchange of letters which followed between Bismarck and Lorenzo Nina, Franchi's successor, opened the way to a solution of the conflict. See R. LILL, *Die Wende im Kulturkampf*, in *Quellen und Forschungen aus italienischen Archiven und Bibliotheken* 50 (1970) 227-283; documents in ID. (ed.), *Vatikanische Akten zur Geschichte des deutschen Kulturkampfes. Leo XIII*, vol. I, Tübingen, 1970, pp. 1-131. See also HUBER-HUBER, pp. 770-775.

44. The immediate cause of the law against the socialist movement was the second attack on Kaiser Wilhelm I on June 2, 1878. Bismarck counted on the fact that German public opinion would consider that the socialists bore intellectual responsibility for the attack and succeeded, on July 11, in dissolving the *Reichstag*. The Right emerged victorious from the elections. The government immediately formulated a second stronger *Sozialistengesetz* (the first was rejected in May 1878). The law was approved by the *Reichstag* on Oct. 18 and came into force on Oct. 21. It forbade all assemblies, gatherings, writings, and the collecting of funds which aimed at the overthrow of the existing state or social order by giving support to the social democrat, socialist, or communist movements. The *Sozialistengesetz* was valid only until March 31, 1881; thereafter it was extended four times until 1890. See HUBER, pp. 1153-1166.

45. During the fifth synod of the German Old Catholics in June 1878, it was decided that the existing canonical prohibition of clerical marriages was no longer in effect. The proposition was adopted 75 votes to 22. On Nov. 8, 1878, Bishop Reinkens published an ordinance with practical norms for carrying out the new ruling: a cleric who wanted to marry must demonstrate to the bishop that his marriage was compatible with the dignity of the priesthood and that it would not interfere with his further activities in his community. See SCHULTE, pp. 636-649.

46. Friedrich and Reusch had, just as Bishop Reinkens, opposed the removal of compulsory celibacy because they did not consider the synod authorized to make such reforms. After the voting, Friedrich declared that he was withdrawing from the Old Catholic movement directed by Bonn. He no longer took part in the synod's activities, and the Bavarian delegation was absent from the Bonn meetings for several years. However, Friedrich continued to participate, albeit less actively, in the life of the Old Catholic community in Munich. See V. CONZEMIUS, *Friedrich (J.)*, in *DHGE* 19 (1981) 76-82, cols. 80-81.

Reusch declared that the decision introduced directions totally foreign to the origin and true character of the Old Catholic movement. As early as 1876 he had written in a letter to a friend what his position would be in the case of the abandonment of celibacy: "Ich bleibe Altkatholik, aber einer à la

Doellinger, jedenfalls will ich dann nicht mehr Generalvikar, Synodalrepräsentant und Pfarrverweser sein", quoted in L. K. GOETZ, *Franz Heinrich Reusch 1825-1900. Eine Darstellung seiner Lebensarbeit*, Gotha, 1901, p. 73. Therefore, after 1878, Reusch resigned all his offices in the Old Catholic Church but continued to participate in Church activities. See SCHULTE, pp. 647-648.

47. The new edition of Newman's *Essay on the Development of Christian Doctrine* is the thoroughly revised one of 1878, "greatly superior in form and coherence to the original edition", J. M. CAMERON, in the introduction to the Pelican edition of the text of 1845, Harmondsworth, 1974, p. 8.

48. Michael O'Connor was not present at the Council. After his resignation, he entered the Jesuit order. During the Council he was living in his religious community. See J. HENNESEY, *The First Council of the Vatican: The American Experience*, New York, 1963, p. 25.

49. William Makepeace THACKERAY, *The History of Henry Esmond, Esquire*, 3 vols., London, 1852. On Taine's work, see further pp. 176-177, and n. 53 below.

50. Steichele wrote various studies on the history of the diocese of Augsburg, especially *Das Bisthum Augsburg, historisch und statistisch beschrieben*, 7 vols., Augsburg, 1861-1909 (continued, after his death in 1889, by A. Schröder).

51. By signing the secret Anglo-Turkish Convention of June 4, 1878, concluded shortly before the Congress of Berlin, Great Britain committed itself to defend Asiatic Turkey against the Russians. In his turn the Sultan promised to pursue reforms in the area, protect the Christian population, and allow Cyprus to come under British occupation and administration.

52. Johannes HUBER, *Savonarola. Ein Kulturbild aus der Renaissancezeit*, in *Historisches Taschenbuch* 5/5 (1875) 35-106.

53. Hippolyte TAINE, *La Révolution*, vol. I, Paris, 1878, was the second part of *Les origines de la France contemporaine*. The first part (called further on in the text the "introductory volume") treated *L'Ancien Régime*, Paris, 1876. Later, vols. II and III on *La Révolution* appeared (1881-85) as did two vols. on *Le régime moderne* (1891-95).

54. Adolphe THIERS, *Histoire de la Révolution française*, 10 vols., Paris, 1823-27; François Auguste MIGNET, *Histoire de la Révolution française, depuis 1789 jusqu'en 1814*, 2 vols., Paris, 1824. Döllinger discussed the relationship between Thiers and Mignet in his memorial lecture on Mignet before the Bavarian Academy on March 28, 1885, published in *Akademische Vorträge* II, pp. 310-324.

55. Hippolyte TAINE, *Voyage en Italie*, 2 vols., Paris, 1866.

56. Louis DUCHESNE, *Étude sur le Liber pontificalis* (Bibliothèque des Écoles françaises d'Athènes et de Rome, 1/1), Paris, 1877.

57. *Real-Encyklopädie für protestantische Theologie und Kirche*. Unter Mitwirkung vieler protestantischer Theologen und Gelehrten in zweiter durchgangig verbesserter und vermehrter Auflage herausgegeben von J. J. HERZOG und G. L. PLITT, 18 vols., Leipzig, 1877-88. After the deaths of Plitt (1880) and Herzog (1882) Albert Hauck continued the publication.

58. Louis DUCHESNE, *Le Liber pontificalis. Texte, introduction et commentaire* (Bibliothèque des Écoles françaises d'Athènes et de Rome, 2/3), 2 vols., Paris, 1886-92 (2nd ed., with addition of vol. III, by C. VOGEL, 1955-57); ID. (ed.),

Vita Sancti Polycarpi Smyrnaeorum episcopi auctore Pionio. Primum graece edita, Paris, 1881; ID., *Les Origines chrétiennes. Leçons d'histoire ecclésiastique professées à l'École supérieure de théologie de Paris en 1878/79 et en 1880/81*, Paris, [1881?].

59. Gustav Leopold PLITT, *Einleitung in die Augustana*. 1. Hälfte: *Geschichte der evangelischen Kirche bis zum Augsburger Reichstage*; 2. Hälfte: *Entstehungsgeschichte des evangelischen Lehrbegriffs bis zum Augsburger Bekenntnisse*, 2 vols., Erlangen, 1867-68.

60. By "Weltzer and Wette" Plummer means *Wetzer und Welte's Kirchenlexikon oder Encyklopädie der katholischen Theologie und ihrer Hilfswissenschaften*. Zweite Auflage, in neuer Bearbeitung, unter Mitwirkung vieler katholischer Gelehrten begonnen von Joseph Cardinal HERGENRÖTHER, fortgesetzt von Dr. Franz KAULEN, 13 vols., Freiburg i/Br., 1882-1903.

61. Kensington University College was opened in Jan. 1875 under the rectorship of Mgr. Thomas James Capel. Capel had to resign after only four years. The college carried on from 1878 to 1882 in Cromwell Place, South Kensington, and was thereafter associated with St. Charles's College, Bayswater, as its department of higher studies. In 1879 the English bishops agreed to Capel's demand for indemnification in order to avoid a public law suit. Meanwhile Capel had to appeal to Rome against a charge of immorality. In 1882 Manning suspended him from his office as priest in the diocese of Westminster. See MCCLELLAND, pp. 277-332; ID., *Cardinal Manning. His Public Life and Influence 1865-1892*, London/New York/Toronto, 1962, pp. 104-126.

62. Benjamin DISRAELI, *Lothair*, 3 vols., London, 1870. In the novel Capel and Manning were portrayed as Mgr. Catesby and Cardinal Grandison. See M. BUSCHKÜHL, *Die irische, schottische und römische Frage. Disraeli's Schlüsselroman "Lothair" (1870)* (Kirchengeschichtliche Quellen und Studien, 11), St. Ottilien, 1980.

63. The text of Döllinger's letter to Nevin is from an unidentified newspaper cutting. The letter is also published in *Briefe und Erklärungen*, pp. 111-113 (Eng. ed., pp. 124-125).

64. *Garcin de Tassy und Indien*, a lecture delivered before the Academy on March 28, 1879, reprinted in *Akademische Vorträge* II, pp. 280-309 (p. 297).

65. The Bulgarian bishops had established an independent exarchate on Jan. 20, 1871. They were excommunicated, together with the entire Bulgarian population, on Sept. 29, 1872, by a general council in Constantinople under the leadership of Patriarch Anthimos VI. They were accused of the heresy of philetism, i.e. church nationalism. However, this decision was only accepted by the Greeks; the other autocephalous Churches retained contacts with the Bulgarians. Cyril, the Patriarch of Jerusalem mentioned, had kept distant from the council probably under pressure from the Russians, who supported his patriarchate and protected the Holy Places. See R. JANIN, *Bulgarie*, in *DHGE* 10 (1938) 1120-1194, cols. 1153-1161.

66. J. FRIEDRICH, *Geschichte des Vatikanischen Konzils*, vol. III, Bonn, 1877, p. 394, quotes a letter from Strossmayer, dated June 10, 1870, in which he himself mentions the rumour. See also Giovanni Giuseppe FRANCO, *Appunti storici sopra il Concilio Vaticano*, ed. G. MARTINA (MHP, 33), Rome, 1972, p. 265. After the Council, on Nov. 30, 1873, Pius IX indeed sent Strossmayer a letter admonishing him for his behaviour (HASLER, p. 436).

67. Most historians, basing themselves on MANSI LIII, cols. 997D-998A, generally accept that Strossmayer submitted to the Vatican decrees in Dec. 1872 or Jan. 1873, when *Pastor Aeternus* was published in his diocesan paper (see, e.g., AUBERT, p. 364). SIVRIĆ, pp. 247, 251-266, however, shows that, during Pius IX's pontificate, Strossmayer never unequivocally expressed his acceptance of papal infallibility. Only under Leo XIII did he explicitly express, in a pastoral letter dated Feb. 4, 1881, his agreement with the dogma (MANSI LIII, cols. 998D-1001A).

68. In the address of July 1, 1867, 500 bishops in Rome expressed their gratitude to the Pope for the allocution of June 26, in which he had announced the Council. Haynald was commissioned by a committee to compose the text. It was not the Jesuits but Manning who insisted on including the word 'infallible' in the text, and Haynald conceded. Dupanloup arranged for the word to be removed from the text, but an implicit recognition of papal infallibility was still clear (MANSI XLIX, cols. 247D-262C; *ColLac* VII, cols. 1033a-1042b). See C. BUTLER, *The Vatican Council. The Story Told from Inside in Bishop Ullathorne's Letters*, vol. I, London, 1930, pp. 85-88. In Feb. 1870 Acton wrote to Döllinger that Haynald in a discussion with him regretted the way in which the address was later used (*Briefwechsel* II, p. 165).

69. The modification of the May Laws was the first *Milderungsgesetz* of July 14, 1880. It replaced the previous right of the State to remove clergymen from office with the possibility of declaring them unqualified to hold public office (which included the loss of their government salary). It further gave the executive a number of discretionary powers, by which the *Kulturkampf* legislation could be made less severe. See HUBER, pp. 778-780; text in HUBER-HUBER, pp. 817-819.

70. Paul Melchers, Archbishop of Cologne, had lived in Holland since 1874 in order to avoid imprisonment. In 1875 the Prussian government removed him from office. Only in 1885 he was succeeded by Philipp Krementz.

71. Frederick Rymer, president of St. Edmund's College, Ware, had, in the summer of 1870, committed his stance regarding the new dogma to writing in a private paper entitled *Reasons why we are not yet bound to receive the definition of Papal Infallibility*, which he sent to Newman and Bishop Clifford among others. In the beginning of Sept. Manning removed him from his post because of his inopportunist views. See CWIEKOWSKI, pp. 286-289.

72. In *Exp* 4/2, p. 124, Plummer adds a footnote: "In April, 1879, he had written to me: 'In Rome "they have caught a Tartar" in making Newman a cardinal. If only the good people there knew how fundamentally anti-Romish —in spite of all protestations of submission (*Unterwerfungs-demonstrationen*)— Newman's theological modes of thought are! With all their curialistic cunning (*Pfiffigkeit*) there is *sancta simplicitas*.' On another occasion he said that if Newman's writings had been known and understood in Rome, they would have put him on the Index instead of making him cardinal".

73. In 1880 only the first vol. of Friedrich's *Geschichte des Vatikanischen Konzils* had appeared (see p. 165). In 1883 he published the second vol., *Die Geschichte des Konzils*. But it too remained limited to the discussion of the preparations for the Council. Finally in 1887 the third vol. (in two parts) followed, *Die Geschichte des Konzils bis zum 18. Juli 1870*.
Eugenio CECCONI, *Storia del Concilio Ecumenico Vaticano scritta sui documenti*

originali. Parte prima: *Antecedenti del Concilio*; Parte seconda: *Documenti*, 4 vols., Rome, 1873-79. Cecconi was asked by Pius IX to write the official history of the Council, but he could not complete the project because he was named Archbishop of Florence in 1875.

74. Döllinger delivered his study on Boniface VIII before the Bavarian Academy on Jan. 5, 1878. In the Academy's *Sitzungsberichte* it was entitled, *Die Gefangennahme und der Tod des Papstes Bonifaz VIII.* After Döllinger's death, it was published in *Akademische Vorträge* III, pp. 223-244, under the title *Anagni* (as in the MS); Eng. trans. in *Addresses on Historical and Literary Subjects*, pp. 181-201. For the other texts, see p. 310, n. 26; p. 275, n. 15; p. 300, n. 35.

75. *Das Haus Wittelsbach und seine Bedeutung in der deutschen Geschichte*, Munich/Nördlingen, 1880; reprinted in *Akademische Vorträge* I, pp. 25-55 (Eng. trans. in *Studies in European History*).

76. The Prince Imperial was Eugène Louis Napoléon Bonaparte, son of Napoleon III. He was in the service of the British army in 1879 when he was killed during the Zulu War. Queen Victoria supported the plan to erect a statue to him in Westminster Abbey, but the House of Commons passed a resolution against it. It was feared that the monument would be taken as a political act against the French Republic. See CHADWICK, *Victorian Church* II, pp. 394-395.

77. In *Exp* 4/1, p. 435, Plummer adds: "But I have seldom, if ever, heard him speak with greater admiration of any book than he expressed to me last July [1889] for Dr. Salmon's *Infallibility of the Church*. He had read it with the keenest delight. Its humour, *good* humour, dialectical skill, and thorough knowledge of the ins and outs of the controversy, had given him immense enjoyment. And of the whole subject treated in the volume there was no critic who could at all equal Dr. Döllinger. If the knowledge of his admiration for the book induces any reader of this article to study the volume, he will thank me for having mentioned the fact". On Salmon's book, see p. XXVI.

78. *Usury. A Reply and a Rejoinder*, in *The Contemporary Review* 37 (1880) 316-333. The Bishop of Manchester was James Fraser.

79. In the years 1878-84 Littledale wrote nine review articles concerning the Petrine claims in *The Church Quarterly Review*. A corrected version was published under the title, *The Petrine Claims: A Critical Inquiry*, London, 1889.

80. Richard Frederick LITTLEDALE, *Plain Reasons against Joining the Church of Rome*, London/New York, 1880.

81. Leo XIII had recommended the study of Thomas Aquinas in the encyclical *Aeterni Patris* of Aug. 4, 1879.

82. The "ultramontane professor" was Georg von Hertling. His nomination, in 1882, coincided with Friedrich's transfer from the theology faculty to that of philosophy. This transfer had also been made at the insistence of the ultramontane party. For reactions to these measures, see E. KESSLER, *Johann Friedrich (1836-1917). Ein Beitrag zur Geschichte des Altkatholizismus* (MBM, 55), Munich, 1975, pp. 459-465.

83. The addresses on *Die Politik Ludwig's XIV* (March 28, 1882) and on *Die Juden in Europa* (July 25, 1881) were published in 1888 in *Akademische Vorträge* I, pp. 265-325, 209-241 (Eng. trans. in *Studies in European History*, pp. 265-324, 210-242).

84. Émile DE LAVELEYE, *Lettres d'Italie. 1878-1879*, Brussels, 1880. See

M. DUMOULIN, *Émile de Laveleye et l'Italie*, in *Risorgimento* (Brussels) 18 (1976) 59-91, esp. pp. 86-87.

85. Theiner's papers consisted of transcripts of documents regarding the Council of Trent, his correspondence (containing letters from Pius IX on his *Life of Clement*), and other written material. Immediately after Theiner's death, Canon Nikola Voršak took possession of the papers. The Court of Vienna had officially appointed him executor of Theiner's last will. Voršak was put under pressure by the Pope and the curia to return the papers after the posthumous publication of a part of the Acts of Trent (see p. 300, n. 34). In early 1878 he surrendered to this pressure. It is possible that Döllinger learned of this at the time of Voršak's death in Feb. 1880, when the Vatican newspaper *L'Aurora* in an obituary notice remarked that it was to his merit that he had returned Theiner's papers to the Vatican. See SIVRIĆ, pp. 195-199.

86. Eleven letters to Friedrich and four letters to Döllinger from the years 1867-73 were separately published by Friedrich in various journals: the *Kölnische Zeitung*, 1874, Nos. 237, 239, 240, the *Allgemeine Zeitung*, 1874, No. 241 (*Beilage*), and the *Deutscher Merkur*, 1874, No. 39 (*Beilage*), 1875, No. 8 (*Beilage*). They were republished together in Hermann GISIGER, *P. Theiner und die Jesuiten. Rückerinnerungen an P. Theiner, Präfekten des vatikanischen Archivs, mit Zusätzen von Prof. Friedrich* (Bilder aus der Geschichte der katholischen Reformbewegung des 18. und 19. Jahrhunderts, ser. 1, 1/5-6), Mannheim, 1875, pp. 77-106.

87. Plummer seems to have erred. He may not be speaking of a professor of ecclesiastical history at Marburg (where there no longer was a R.C. faculty of theology in 1883) but rather of the already mentioned F.X. Kraus, professor in Freiburg (see p. 181), who frequently visited the Vatican Archives.

88. The famous letter *Saepenumero considerantes* has been published in *Acta Sanctae Sedis* 16 (1883) 49-57. The three cardinals heeded the Pope's call by forming a commission and appointing a sub-commission with the intention of publishing the documents in the Archives and, on this basis, of writing a true history of the Catholic Church. However, they did not succeed in accomplishing their plans. See CHADWICK, *Catholicism*, pp. 100-106, where one also finds a summary of the letter's content and an account of some contemporary reactions.

89. Cesare CANTÙ, *Storia universale*, 35 vols., Turin, 1838-46.

90. See Carl August CREDNER, *Geschichte des Neutestamentlichen Kanon*, ed. G. VOLKMAR, Berlin, 1860, pp. 158-159.

91. See Theodor ZAHN, *Papias von Hierapolis, seine geschichtliche Stellung, sein Werk und sein Zeugnis über die Evangelien*, in *Theologische Studien und Kritiken* 39 (1866) 649-696, esp. pp. 663-666.

92. ID., *Der Hirt des Hermas*, Gotha, 1868, pp. 14-20.

93. See Ewald's review of Credner's *Geschichte des Neutestamentlichen Kanon*, in *Göttingische Gelehrte Anzeigen* 113 (1860) 978-995.

94. *A Dictionary of Christian Biography, Literature, Sects and Doctrines; Being a Continuation of 'The Dictionary of the Bible'*, ed. William SMITH and Henry WACE, 4 vols., London, 1877-87; reprint, New York/Milwood, N.Y., 1974.

95. Quotation from Theophilus' apology *Ad Autolycum*, II, 20.

96. It would be Friedrich who published the new edition of the *Papstfabeln* after Döllinger's death (see p. 311, n. 34).

97. The sixth edition of Meyer's commentary on John, in his *Kritisch exegetischer Kommentar über das Neue Testament*, was published in a fully revised version by Bernhard Weiss under the title, *Kritisch exegetisches Handbuch über das Evangelium des Johannes*, Göttingen, 1880.

98. Bernhard WEISS, *Das Leben Jesu*, 2 vols., Berlin, 1882.

NOTES TO VOLUME IV

1. Plummer refers to Gladstone's conversion to the principle of Home Rule. On April 8, 1886, he introduced his Home Rule Bill to Parliament. After a second reading the Bill was rejected on June 7; the following day Parliament was dissolved. In the subsequent elections, the Conservatives and the Liberal Unionists, who had separated from Gladstone, gained a working majority of 113 over Gladstone's Liberals and the Irish Nationalists. On July 20 Gladstone's cabinet resigned. See N. MANSERGH, *The Irish Question 1840-1921. A Commentary on Anglo-Irish Relations and on Social and .Political Forces in Ireland in the Age of Reform and Revolution*, Toronto/Buffalo, ³1975, pp. 135-174.

2. Plummer means William PALMER, *A Treatise on the Church of Christ: Chiefly Designed for the Use of Students in Theology*, 2 vols., London, 1838, rev. ed., 1842, a book which Gladstone considered one of the best defenses of the position of the Anglican Church. In the years 1882-83 first Palmer himself, then later MacColl, had asked Döllinger to collaborate in a revision. However, a new edition of the book never appeared. See *Briefwechsel* III, pp. 294, 318, 326.

3. J.B. LIGHTFOOT, *Caius or Hippolytus?*, in *The Journal of Philology* 1 (1868) 98-112; partly reprinted in ID., *The Apostolic Fathers*. Part I: *S. Clement of Rome. A Revised Text with Introductions, Notes, Dissertations, and Translations*, vol. II, London/New York, 1890, pp. 374-380. In this publication he moderated his standpoint (pp. 380-388).

4. Richard WINTERSTEIN, *Der Episcopat in den drei ersten christlichen Jahrhunderten*, Leipzig, 1886.

5. On March 25, 1886, Döllinger delivered the address on Madame de Maintenon before the Bavarian Academy. The expanded text appeared in *Akademische Vorträge* I, pp. 326-417 (Eng. trans. in *Studies in European History*, pp. 325-415).

6. Possibly the German theologian Theodor Keim, who was professor in Zurich from 1860 to 1873. Keim wrote *Die Geschichte Jesu von Nazara, in ihrer Verhaltung mit dem Gesamtleben seines Volkes frei untersucht und ausführlich erzählt*, 3 vols., Zurich, 1867-72. In 1872 he published a shorter version, *Geschichte Jesu nach den Ergebnissen heutiger Wissenschaft für weitere Kreise übersichtlich erzählt* (rev. ed., 1875).

7. The Coptic Patriarch was Cyril IV, the 'Father of Coptic reform', Metropolitan of Cairo since 1854. In his endeavours to promote reunification he was not only congenial toward the Melchite Greek Patriarch Kallinikos, but he also sought closer relations with the Russian Orthodox Church and the Church of England. Said Pasha, Khedive of Egypt, who feared foreign interference in such contacts, had Cyril poisoned during an audience on Jan, 29, 1861. He died the following day. See A.S. ATIYA, *A History of Eastern Christianity*, London, 1968, p. 106.

8. Jan Jacob VAN OOSTERZEE, *Christian Dogmatics. A Text-Book for Academical Introduction and Private Study* (Theological and Philosophical Library), 2 vols., New York/London, 1874; original Dutch ed., *Christelijke dogmatiek. Een handboek voor academisch onderwijs*, 2 vols., Utrecht, 1870-72.

Hans Lassen MARTENSEN, *Christian Dogmatics. A Compendium of the Doctrines of Christianity* (Clark's Foreign Theological Library, 4/12), Edinburgh, 1865; transl. of *Die christliche Dogmatik. Vom Verfasser selbst veranstaltete deutsche Ausgabe*, Berlin, 1856. The original Danish ed., *Den christelige dogmatik*, was published in 1849 in Copenhagen.

9. Franz Hermann Reinhold FRANK, *System der christlichen Gewissheit*, 2 vols., Erlangen, 1870-73; rev. ed., 1881-84.

Isaac August DORNER, *System der christlichen Glaubenslehre*. 1. Band: *Grundlegung oder Apologetik*; 2. Band: *Specielle Glaubenslehre*, 3 vols., Berlin, 1879-81.

10. In a letter dated May 15, 1890, Prince Regent Luitpold asked Antonius von Thoma, the new Archbishop of Munich-Freising, to abandon, for the sake of peace, the planned organization of the German *Katholikentag* in Munich. The moderate Catholic leaders succeeded in removing the *Katholikentag* to Koblenz. See HUBER, pp. 808-809. On the "regrettable circumstances", mentioned further in the note, see pp. 60 (n. 35), 234.

11. The text from the Roman Archives is the *Regestum Clementis Papae V ex Vaticanis archetypis domini nostri Leonis XIII pontificis maximi iussu et munificenta nunc primum editum cura et studio monachorum ordinis S. Benedicti*, 8 vols., Rome, 1885-88. By the French documents Döllinger seems to mean the *Livre de Guillaume le Maire*, edited by C. PORT in *Mélanges historiques. Choix de documents*, vol. II, Paris, 1877, pp. 107-569; more precisely the *Modus procedendi contra singulas personas Templariorum* (pp. 446-448), a text which Döllinger, in his Templar address of 1889, called "ein wichtiges, viel Licht gebendes Document" (*Akademische Vorträge* III, p. 258). This document, however, was not preserved in Paris but in Angers. Döllinger may also have referred to other documents, published in studies by H. Prutz, E. Boutaric, or A. Baudouin; see M. DESSUBRÉ, *Bibliographie de l'ordre des Templiers (imprimés et manuscrits)* (Bibliothèque des Initiations Modernes, 5), Paris, 1928, Nos. 853, 118-121, 73.

12. Konrad SCHOTTMÜLLER, *Der Untergang des Templer-Ordens. Mit urkundlichen und kritischen Beiträgen*, 2 vols., Berlin, 1887; reprint, Wiesbaden/New York, 1970.

13. J.B. LIGHTFOOT, *Essays on the Work Entitled Supernatural Religion. Reprinted from The Contemporary Review*, London, 1889. The essays, written between Dec. 1874 and May 1878, were highly critical of the anonymous work, *Supernatural Religion. An Inquiry into the Reality of Divine Revelation*, 3 vols., London, 1874-77, which contained a strong attack on the books of the N.T. The author of this work answered Lightfoot's criticism in *A Reply to Dr. Lightfoot's Essays*, London, 1889. See CHADWICK, *Victorian Church* II, pp. 70-72.

14. L. THOUVENEL (ed.), *Le secret de l'Empereur. Correspondance confidentielle et inédite échangée entre M. Thouvenel, le duc de Gramont et le général comte de Flahault 1860-1863. Publiée avec notes et index biographique*, 2 vols., Paris, 1889, esp. vol. I, pp. 227-229. Pius IX had considered departing in an Austrian ship for Spain or Trieste after the defeat of the papal army in Castel-

fidardo on Sept. 18, 1860. This defeat allowed the Piedmontese armies to occupy Umbria and the Marches. See AUBERT, pp. 91-92.

15. Pius IX was offered asylum on Malta by Lord John Russell, British minister of foreign affairs, on March 23, 1862. For the reaction to this proposition, see information provided by his nephew Odo Russell, who resided in Rome as member of the diplomatic service, in N. BLAKISTON (ed.), *The Roman Question. Extracts from the Despatches of Odo Russell from Rome 1858-1870*, London, 1962, pp. 241-256. See also p. 12.

16. During negotiations in Aug.-Oct. 1870 on possible Prussian intervention to protect the Pope, Bismarck indicated that he was prepared to provide Pius IX with a refuge in Fulda. However, King Wilhelm I opposed accepting the Pope in Prussian territory. See HUBER, pp. 670-672; documents in HUBER-HUBER, pp. 451-459.

17. Heinrich Geffcken published in the *Deutsche Rundschau* of Sept. 20, 1888, selections from the war diary of the recently deceased Kaiser Friedrich III, who had taken part in the Franco-Prussian War as Crown Prince Friedrich Wilhelm. The selections caused much controversy: they suggested disagreements between the Crown Prince, Kaiser Wilhelm I, and Bismarck, and revealed that Friedrich had defended the use of violence against the South German states during the negotiations on the formation of the German Empire. Immediately following the publication Bismarck reacted with a sharp rejoinder in which he accused the publisher of betraying state secrets. Geffcken was arrested on Sept. 30, but in early 1889 the court decided that his treason had not been demonstrated. See HUBER, pp. 190-194.

18. The unveiling of Giordano Bruno's statue on the Campo dei Fiori during Pentecost 1889 was the high point of the anti-papal demonstrations in Rome. Afterwards, Leo XIII discussed, in the secret consistory of June 30, the possibility of fleeing to Monaco, Malta, or Spain in case of war. Meanwhile, contacts were renewed with Austria with a view to possible emigration. See J. SCHMIDLIN, *Papstgeschichte der neuesten Zeit*, vol. II, Munich, 1934, pp. 416-417.

19. Kultusminister Gossler, in particular, pleaded that the chapter forego its right of selection and sought direct negotiations with Rome. But in the end, the chapter was still given the right to select the bishop. On Aug. 14, 1889, to everyone's surprise, it choose as bishop the unknown teacher Hermann Dingelstad. See H. BÖRSTING, *Geschichte des Bistums Münster*, Bielefeld, 1951, pp. 166-170.

20. According to Salmon, the fragment belonged to the pontificate of Zephyrinus (198-217); see his article on the *Muratorian Fragment* in *A Dictionary of Christian Biography* 3 (1882) 1000-1003.

21. Henry William WATKINS, *Modern Criticism Considered in Its Relation to the Fourth Gospel. Being the Bampton Lectures for 1890*, London, 1890.

22. Margaret Warre's translation, *Studies in European History, Being Addresses Delivered by John Ignatius Döllinger*, appeared in 1890. In 1894 Miss Warre prepared a second vol., *Addresses on Historical and Literary Subjects [in Continuation of 'Studies in European History']*. This collection contains one address from vol. II and seven addresses from vol. III of the *Akademische Vorträge* (these are not mentioned in Lösch's bibliography).

23. The retired general Georges Boulanger, after entering politics in 1888, had gathered around himself all the anti-governmental factions in France. He

achieved spectacular election victories, but he did not succeed, at the beginning of 1889, in keeping control over the protest movement he had created. On April 1 he fled to Brussels in fear of arrest. In the following period his political influence diminished rather rapidly as would appear in the July 28 elections, to which Plummer most likely refers. See É. FRANCESCHINI, *Boulanger (G.E.J.M.)*, in *DBF* 6 (1954) 1342-1344.

24. F. H. REUSCH, *Die Fälschungen in dem Tractat des Thomas von Aquin gegen die Griechen (Opusculum contra errores Graecorum ad Urbanum IV.)*, Munich, 1889 (from the *Abhandlungen* of the Bavarian Academy of Sciences, *Historische Classe*, 18/3, pp. 673-742).

25. Raffaele DE CESARE, *Il conclave di Leone XIII, con aggiunte e nuòvi documenti, e Il futuro conclave*, Città di Castello, 1888. The first edition was published in 1887.

26. The address on *Der Untergang des Tempelordens* was published in the *Augsburger Abendzeitung*, 1889, No. 219, on the basis of stenographer's notes. Using this text and Döllinger's MS, Max Lossen republished it in *Akademische Vorträge* III, pp. 245-263, adding further material Döllinger had written after his address: "Anhang. Stücke aus der erweiterten Bearbeitung des Vortrags über den Tempelorden", pp. 263-273 (see the editor's preface, pp. V-VI; Eng. trans. in *Addresses on Historical and Literary Subjects*, pp. 202-228).

27. Note 4 is a clipping from an unidentified newspaper.

28. The text *Pius IX. Ein Fragment* was included in *Kleinere Schriften*, pp. 558-602. According to Reusch's explanation in the preface (p. VI), Döllinger had written the text after the Pope's death in 1878 at the request of the *Allgemeine Zeitung*'s editors. When it appeared that the sketch was too lengthy for the newspaper, Döllinger wanted to publish it as an independent work, but he did not complete the text and never returned to it. However, even in later years he never gave up his plan to publish the biography.

29. Reusch did not, in fact, publish the letters to Nuncio Ruffo Scilla, to Archbishop von Steichele, and to the Duchess with the biography of Pius IX, but in *Briefe und Erklärungen*, together with their letters to Döllinger. In the preface (p. V) Reusch says that he had not found the letter to a nun among Döllinger's papers.

30. Döllinger's *Geschichtliche Uebersicht des Konzils von Trient*, written in 1866, was intended for the broader reading public. His plan to revise the text once more was not fulfilled. The overview was not, as Johanna Döllinger writes, published as a separate treatise but rather included in *Kleinere Schriften*, pp. 228-263. To it were added a conclusion, missing in the MS, and comments by August von Druffel (see the editor's preface, pp. V-VI). On the addresses, see p. 233.

31. Carl Adolf CORNELIUS, *Gedächtnisrede auf I. von Döllinger, gehalten in der öffentlichen Sitzung der k.b. Akademie der Wissenschaften zu München am 28. März 1890*, Munich, 1890. Also in *Deutscher Merkur*, May 24, No. 21, pp. 161-163, and May 31, No. 22, pp. 169-171.

32. The obituary notice, written by Friedrich, appeared in the *Beilage* to the *Allgemeine Zeitung* of April 9, 1890, No. 98.

33. The remaining *Akademische Vorträge* were published together in one vol. by Max Lossen in 1891. The Prof. Berthold mentioned earlier by Plummer is Josef Berchtold, professor of law at the University of Munich. He never published a text of Döllinger.

In addition to the writings mentioned, Reusch published a number of selections from Döllinger's papers, primarily consisting of letters from 16th-century Jesuits: F. Heinrich REUSCH, *Archivalische Beiträge zur Geschichte des Jesuitenordens*, in *ZKG* 15 (1894-95) 98-107, 261-282. Reusch himself used this material in his *Beiträge zur Geschichte des Jesuitenordens*, Munich, 1894.

34. Friedrich only republished the latter two works: the *Papstfabeln des Mittelalters* in Stuttgart, 1890, and JANUS in Munich, 1892, under the title, *Das Papstthum von I. von Döllinger*.

35. On March 15, 1890, under pressure of the house of representatives, the Lutz cabinet declared that the Old Catholics were no longer considered members of the Catholic Church (see p. 60, n. 35). This measure cost the Old Catholic community its status as a legitimate public corporation; from then on it could only claim the rights of a private religious community. See HUBER-HUBER, pp. 911-916; W. GRASSER, *Johann Freiherr von Lutz (eine politische Biographie) 1826-1890* (MBM, 1), Munich, 1967, pp. 130-135.

36. Note 5 is a clipping from the *Deutscher Merkur* of June 7, 1890, No. 23, p. 177.

37. The catastrophe in the summer of 1886 was the crisis in the Bavarian monarchy. On June 7 the Lutz cabinet decided to put Ludwig II under medical supervision; on June 10 he was removed from office and Luitpold became regent; on June 13 Ludwig committed suicide. See HUBER, pp. 387-391.

38. The article refers to Lutz's standpoint expressed in a speech to the Bavarian *Landtag* on Oct. 14, 1871. See FRIEDBERG, *Sammlung*, p. 873, and WEBER, pp. 277-284.

39. At the end of his *Expositor* article (4/2, pp. 471-472), Plummer supports his contention that "*he* [Döllinger] *was not a member of the Old Catholic communion*" by appealing to three pieces of evidence: Reusch's declaration, Johanna Döllinger's comment on the occasion of Döllinger's funeral (see p. 238), and Döllinger's declaration to Nuncio Ruffo Scilla (quoted in note 6). Plummer adds his own reflections to Reusch's comment: "At Bonn the service was exceptional. It was an earnest of the reunion for which those who went thither were working. If attendance at that service proved Döllinger to be a member of the Old Catholic body, then various members of the English, American, and Lutheran Churches are proved to be so also by precisely the same fact. At Munich he never entered the Old Catholic church, although his relations attended the services. To explain this by saying that he was an old man, and that he lived some distance from the church, is strangely to impugn his religious earnestness. He could walk for two or three hours without resting, and he was well enough off to afford a carriage whenever he needed one. His reason for absenting himself from Old Catholic services had nothing to do with the distance between his house and the building in which they were held".

40. Letter dated Oct. 12, 1887, in *Briefe und Erklärungen*, pp. 150-151 (Eng. trans., p. 163).

41. Cf. p. 228 and FRIEDRICH III, p. 593, who, however, adds that Döllinger had also instructed his nieces in the 1880's that when he should become seriously ill, no Roman clergyman, but only Friedrich, should be summoned.

42. Charlotte Blennerhassett published only a short memorial article on Döllinger on the occasion of his 100th birthday: *In Memoriam. I. von Döllinger. – 28. Februar 1799. – 10. Januar 1890*, in *Deutsche Rundschau* 93 (1899) 459-463.

43. In 1893 the catalogue was published by the bookseller J. Lindauer in Munich: *Bibliotheca Döllingeriana. Katalog der Bibliothek des verstorbenen kgl. Universitäts-Professors J.J.I. von Döllinger*. It contained 18,495 titles, including about 10,000 on theology and Church history.

44. The work on Bellarmine is the edition of his *Selbstbiographie*, published by Döllinger and Reusch in 1887.

45. Quotation from VERGILIUS, *Aeneis*, IV, 625.

46. According to Acton, Döllinger had suggested to Wiseman that he write a defense of Boniface VIII (see p. 252). Plummer, however, says that Döllinger could not remember ever having said any such thing to Wiseman (see pp. 65-66, taken up in *Exp* 4/1, p. 284). See also p. 247.

47. Letter dated March 1, 1887, to Archbishop von Steichele, in *Briefe und Erklärungen*, p. 137 (Eng. trans., p. 150). See also p. 249.

48. Newman discussed Döllinger's standpoint on Hippolytus in his letters to Plummer, dated Oct. 17, 1876, and Oct. 11, 1877, in *Letters and Diaries* XXVIII, pp. 125-126, 246-247.

49. ACTON, *Doellinger's Historical Work*, in *The English Historical Review* 5 (1890) 700-744; reprinted in ID., *The History of Freedom and Other Essays*, ed. J.N. FIGGIS and R.V. LAURENCE, London, 1907, pp. 375-435 (reprint, Freeport, N.Y., 1967). The article, together with other material for the unpublished biography of Döllinger, is quoted by S.J. TONSOR, *Lord Acton on Döllinger's Historical Theology*, in *Journal of the History of Ideas* 20 (1959) 329-352. V. Conzemius published two letters in which Acton responded to Charlotte Blennerhassett's critical reactions to his article, in *Der Tod Ignaz v. Döllingers in den Briefen der Freunde*, in *Kurtrierisches Jahrbuch* 8 (1968) 300-316, pp. 309-316. The importance of the article in the development of Acton's thought is shown by D. MATHEW, *Lord Acton and His Times*, London, 1968, pp. 343-350.

50. Quotation from a letter to Acton, dated May 7, 1886, in *Briefwechsel* III, p. 354.

51. See A.-F. RIO, *Épilogue à l'Art chrétien*, vol. I, Paris, 1892, p. 366.

52. Le Comte de MONTALEMBERT, *Les moines d'Occident, depuis saint Benoît jusqu'à saint Bernard*, 7 vols., Paris, 1860-77.

53. Quotation from Ferdinand Christian BAUR, *Die christliche Lehre von der Dreieinigkeit und Menschwerdung Gottes in ihrer geschichtlichen Entwicklung. Erster Theil: Das Dogma der alten Kirche bis zur Synode von Chalcedon*, Tübingen, 1841, p. XX.

54. *Regesta Imperii. V: Die Regesten des Kaiserreichs unter Philipp, Otto IV., Friedrich II., Heinrich (VII.), Conrad IV., Heinrich Raspe, Wilhelm und Richard 1198-1272*. Nach der Neubearbeitung und dem Nachlasse Joh. Frdr. Böhmers neu herausgegeben und ergänzt von Jul. FICKER, parts 1-3, Innsbruck, 1879-82 (parts 4-9, ed. J. FICKER and E. WINCKELMANN, completed by F. WILHELM, 1901; additions by P. ZINSMAIER, 1983).

55. Friedrich Julius STAHL, *Die Kirchenverfassung nach Lehre und Recht der Protestanten*, Erlangen, 1840; enl. ed., 1862.

56. Richard ROTHE, *Die Anfänge der christlichen Kirche und ihrer Verfassung. Ein geschichtlicher Versuch*, Wittenberg, 1837.

57. Albrecht RITSCHL, *Die christliche Lehre von der Rechtfertigung und Versöhnung. Erster Band: Die Geschichte der Lehre; Zweiter Band: Der biblische*

Stoff der Lehre; Dritter Band : *Die positive Entwicklung der Lehre*, 3 vols., Bonn, 1870-74.

58. Quotation from a letter to Acton, dated July 3, 1888, in *Briefwechsel* III, p. 375. This letter brought to an end a very extensive, fundamental discussion which Döllinger and Acton carried on between 1882 and 1888 on historical personages (*ibid.*, pp. 257-376). See further pp. 255, 258, and T. MURPHY, *Lord Acton and the Question of Moral Judgments in History: The Development of His Position*, in *The Catholic Historical Review* 70 (1984) 225-250, pp. 245-250.

59. Quotation from a letter dated May 30, 1866, published in LIDDON IV, p. 118.

60. *Gutachten, auf der Konferenz der deutschen Bischöfe zu Würzburg im Oktober und November 1848 abgegeben*, in *Kleinere Schriften*, pp. 53-71.

61. Ernest RENAN, *Souvenirs d'Enfance et de Jeunesse*, Paris, 1883, p. 323 (in Renan's *Œuvres complètes*, ed. H. PSICHARI, vol. II, Paris, 1948, p. 882).

62. By "Flix" Plummer means Alois Flir, who describes Döllinger's conversations with Theiner in *Briefe aus Rom*, ed. L. RAPP, Innsbruck, 1864, p. 80.

63. Quotation from a letter to Acton, dated July 5, 1859, in *Letters and Diaries* XIX, p. 167. Cf. H.A. MACDOUGALL, *The Acton-Newman Relations. The Dilemma of Christian Liberalism*, New York, 1962, p. 60.

64. Letter to Döllinger, dated Nov. 28, 1861, quoted in V. CONZEMIUS, *Montalembert et l'Allemagne*, in *Revue d'histoire de l'Église de France* 56 (1970) 17-46, p. 39. The letter is not included in the selection from the correspondence between Döllinger and Montalembert published in LÖSCH, pp. 374-498; nor is Döllinger's letter, quoted in note 35 (on this see V. CONZEMIUS, *art. cit.*, p. 41).

65. *Decretales Pseudo-Isidorianae et Capitula Angilramni. Ad fidem librorum manuscriptorum recensuit, fontes indicavit, commentationem de collectione Pseudo-Isidori praemisit Paulus HINSCHIUS*, Leipzig, 1863. Cf. FRIEDRICH III, pp. 341-342.

66. The *Laminae Granatenses*, discovered in 1588 in Granada, contained Arabic texts, alleged to date from apostolic times. In 1682 Rome definitively rejected them as forgeries. See V. CONZEMIUS, in *Briefwechsel* I, p. 472, n. 3.

67. Quotation from a letter to Acton, dated July 19, 1862, in *Letters and Diaries* XX, p. 231. Cf. H.A. MACDOUGALL, *op. cit.*, p. 150.

68. Heinrich VON SYBEL, *Giesebrecht und Döllinger*, in ID., *Vorträge und Abhandlungen* (Historische Bibliothek, 3), Munich/Leipzig, 1897, pp. 321-335 (esp. pp. 331-332).

69. *The New Reformation. A Narrative of the Old Catholic Movement from 1870 to the Present Time. With a Historical Introduction by THEODORUS* [J. B. MULLINGER], London, 1875.

INDEX OF PERSONS

ANTHIMOS VI, Joannidès (c. 1790-1878), Patriarch of Constantinople (1845-48, 1853-55, 1871-73). *DHGE* 3 (1924) 533-534. *185, 213, 303*[65]

ANTONELLI, Giacomo (1806-76), cardinal secretary of state. Under Gregory XVI he was delegate to Orvieto (1835), Viterbo (1837), Macerata (1839), and assistant in the Department of the Interior (1841). He was ordained to the diaconate but never advanced to the priesthood. He was appointed head of the financial administration in 1845, and in 1847, named cardinal and minister of finance. In 1848 he headed the papal government in exile, and that same year he was appointed prosecretary of state. From 1850 until his death he was secretary of state. Antonelli has often been suspected of duplicity on the political level, esp. regarding the relations between the Holy See and Napoleon III. His powerful position in the papal administration led many to try to win his favour, but he had no friends. *DBI* 3 (1961) 484-493. *12, 65, 164, 186*

ARBUÉS, Pedro de, St. (1441-85), Spanish theologian, regular canon of the Cathedral of Zaragoza (1474), inquisitor for Aragon (1484). *LTK* 8 (1963) 348. *48, 119, 132, 282*[63]*, 283*[64]

ARCO-VALLEY, Anna Margareta, Gräfin v. (1813-85), *née* Contessa Marescalchi, married Count J. M. v. Arco-Valley (1832). *GGT*, Gräfliche Häuser, 1910, p. 31. *169, 173-174, 176, 180, 182, 200*

ARCO-VALLEY, Johann Maximilian, Graf v. (1806-75), Bavarian chamberlain and senator, Grand Chancellor of the Bavarian Order of St. George. *GGT*, Gräfliche Häuser, 1910, p. 31. *176*

ARCO-VALLEY, Leopoldine Maria Gabriele, Gräfin v. (1847-1911), daughter of the above-mentioned, sister-in-law of J. Acton. *GGT*, Gräfliche Häuser, 1913, p. 33. *169, 180, 182*

ARNIM, Bettina v. (1785-1859), *née* Elisabeth Brentano, German Romantic writer, sister of Clemens Brentano, married the poet Achim v. Arnim (1811). *NDB* 1 (1953) 369-371. *53*[30]*, 84*

ARNIM-SUCKOW, Harry Kurt Eduard Carl, Graf v. (1824-81), German diplomat, served in Lisbon, Kassel, and Munich (1862), appointed Prussian ambassador to the Holy See (1864), and to France (1872). During the Council he attempted to organize a common protest of the secular states against the infallibility dogma. In 1874 he was condemned for withholding and later publishing confidential dispatches from that period. *NDB* 1 (1953) 373-375. *165*

AUDO, Joseph (1780-1878), Chaldean Bp. of Mossoul (1824), and Amadiyah (1833), elected Patriarch of Babylon (1847). *DHGE* 5 (1931) 317-357. *11, 58, 275*[14]*, 285*[83]

AUGUSTA (1811-90), daughter of Grand-Duke Karl August v. Sachsen-Weimar and Grand-Duchess Maria Pawlowna of Russia, married Prince Wilhelm of Prussia (1829), Queen of Prussia and German Empress (1861). *NDB* 1 (1953) 451-452. *41, 194-195*

AUGUSTINE, St. (354-430), Bp. of Hippo (c. 396). *4*[2]*, 123, 129-130, 258*

AUGUSTINUS, Antonius, latinized name of Antonio Agustín (1517-86), Spanish humanist scholar, Bp. of Alife (1556), and Lérida (1561), Abp. of Tarragona (1576). *DHGE* 1 (1912) 1077-1080. *253*

BAADER, Benedikt Franz Xaver v. (1765-1841), German philosopher, prof. of philosophy and speculative theology in Munich (1826). FRIES-SCHWAIGER I, pp. 274-302. *248, 249*

BAILLY, Louis (1730-1808), French theologian, prof. of dogmatic theology in Dijon (1763-85). *DBF* 4 (1948) 1355-1356. *21, 58, 277*[30]

BALLERINI, Pietro (1698-1769), Italian canonist and patristic scholar, published works on usury, papal primacy, and the history of probabilism. *DBI* 5 (1963) 575-587. *251*

BARCLAY, William (*c.* 1543-1608), Scottish R.C. jurist, prof. of civil law in Pont-à-Mousson (1578) and Angers (1604), held Gallican views. *DNB* 1 (1908) 1093-1094. *251*

BARLOW, Henry Clark (1806-76), English Dante scholar. *DNB* 1 (1908) 1141-1142. *14*

BARLOW, William (d. 1568), Bp. of St. Asaph (1535), St. David's (1536), Bath and Wells (1548), and Chichester (1559). *DNB* 1 (1908) 1149-1151. *107, 290*[25]

BARONIUS, Caesar, latinized name of Cesare Baronio (1538-1607), Italian R.C. historian, entered the Oratory of St. Philip Neri (1557), ordained priest (1564), succeeded Neri as superior (1593). He was created cardinal (1596) and became prefect of the Vatican Library (1597). His *Annales ecclesiastici* (1588-1607) were a reply to the anti-Roman 'Centuries of Magdeburg', by Matthias Flacius and other Lutheran historians. *DBI* 6 (1964) 470-478. *35, 49, 163, 251, 283*[65]

BAUER, Karl Josef v. (1845-1912), German physician, prof. of internal medicine (1876), and head of the clinic for internal medicine in Munich (1892). *NDB* 1 (1953) 641-642. *228*

BAUR, Ferdinand Christian (1792-1860), German Protestant theologian, founder of the Tübingen School, taught history and philology at Blaubeuren (1817), prof. of historical theology at Tübingen (1826). *TRE* 5 (1980) 352-359. *153, 248*[15]*, 250, 253, 257*

BAXTER, Richard (1615-91), English Puritan divine, favoured latitudinarian views and an attitude of tolerance towards Romanists in order to advance the unity of the English Church. *DNB* 1 (1908) 1349-1357. *254-255*

BEACONSFIELD, *see* DISRAELI, Benjamin

BECK, Oskar (1850-1924), Bavarian printer and scientific publisher, transferred C.H. Beck's Publishing House from Nördlingen to Munich (1889). BOSL, p. 53. *243-244*

BECKET, Thomas, St. (*c.* 1118-70), chancellor to Henry II (1155), Abp. of Canterbury (1162). *166*

BEETZ, Friedrich Wilhelm Hubert v. (1822-86), German physicist, prof. in Berlin (1850), Bern (1856), Erlangen (1858), and Munich (1868), where he was also director of the Technical Academy (1874-77); member of the Bavarian Academy (1869). *NDB* 1 (1953) 743-744. *95*

BELLARMINE, Robert, St. (1542-1621), Italian controversialist and cardinal (1599), Abp. of Capua (1602-05). *35, 103, 243, 251, 261*

BENEDICT XIII (*c.* 1328-1423), Pedro de Luna, Antipope at Avignon (1394-1417). *175*

BENEDICT XIV (1675-1758), Prospero Lorenzo Lambertini, Pope from 1740. *57, 251*

BENNETT, William James Early (1804-86), Anglican High Churchman, minister of St. Paul's, Knightsbridge (1840), vicar of Frome, Somerset (1852). *DNB* 22 (1909) 169-171. *85, 291*[31]

BERARDI, Carlo Sebastiano (1719-68), Italian canonist, prof. in Turin (1754). *DBI* 8 (1966) 750-755. *251*

BERCHTOLD, Josef (1833-94), German jurist, prof. of civil law in Munich (1867), member of the Old Catholic Church. *ADB* 46 (1902) 367-368. *233, 310*[33]

BEUST, Friedrich Ferdinand, Graf v. (1809-86), German statesman, Saxon foreign minister (1849), minister of interior (1853), and prime minister (1858), later appointed Austrian foreign minister (1866), prime minister (1867), and imperial chancellor of the Habsburg monarchy (1867-71). After his dismissal he became ambassador in London (1871), and Paris (1878-82). *NDB* 2 (1955) 198-200. *159*

BISMARCK-SCHÖNHAUSEN, Otto Eduard Leopold, Graf v. (1815-98), German statesman, founder of modern Germany, was Prussian representative at the Frankfurt Parliament

BONIFACE VIII (c. 1234-1303), Benedetto Caetani, Pope from 1294. *11*[5], *51, 65-66, 191, 233, 245, 246, 247, 252*

BONNECHOSE, Henri Marie Gaston de (1800-83), Bp. of Carcassonne (1847), Bp. of Évreux (1855), Abp. of Rouen (1858), created cardinal and elected senator (1863). During the Council he belonged to the so-called 'Third-Party'. *DBF* 6 (1954) 996-997. *37, 280*[48]

BORGIA, Stefano (1731-1804), Italian cardinal (1789), prefect of various curia congregations, published many antiquarian and historical writings. *DBI* 12 (1970) 739-742. *251*

BOSSUET, Jacques-Bénigne (1627-1704), noted French orator and churchman, Bp. of Condom (1669), tutor to the Dauphin (1670), Bp. of Meaux (1681). He drew up the Four Gallican Articles (1682). *DHGE* 9 (1937) 1339-1391. *54-55, 124*[16]*, 131, 245, 261, 266, 290*[25]

BOSSUET, Jacques-Bénigne (1664-1743), nephew of the above-mentioned, Bp. of Troyes (1716). *DHGE* 9 (1937) 1391-1395. *54*

BOULANGER, Georges Ernest Jean Marie (1837-91), French general, minister of war (1886), expelled from office (1887), and later pensioned (1888). His subsequent election victories (1888-89) threatened the Third Republic. *DBF* 6 (1954) 1342-1344. *224, 309*[23]

BRAGANZA, Adelheid, Duchess of (1831-1909), *née* Prinzessin zu Löwenstein-Wertheim-Rosenberg, married Miguel de Braganza (1851). *ZBLG* 33 (1970) 442 n. 16. *231-232, 265-266*

BRAVO-MURILLO, Juan (1803-73), Spanish statesman, minister of justice (1847), production, education and public works (1848), and finance (1849). In 1851 he became minister of finance and minister president. He signed a concordat with Rome (Oct. 1851) but was forced to resign after he had proposed an anti-liberal revision of the constitution (1852). *EUI* 9 (n.d.) 708-709. *148*

BRAY-STEINBURG, Otto Camillus Hugo Gabriel, Graf v. (1807-99), Bavarian statesman and diplomat, ambassador in St. Petersburg (1843), Berlin (1859), and Vienna (1860), and minister of foreign affairs (1846-49). He later became prime minister (1870) but resigned due to his opposition to the *Kulturkampf* policy (1871) and returned to his post in Vienna (1871-97). *NDB* 2 (1955) 564. *21*

BRENTANO, Clemens Wenzel Maria (1778-1842), German Romantic poet, novelist, and dramatist. During his studies in Jena he became acquainted with the Schlegel brothers, L. Tieck and F. Savigny. In Heidelberg he met J. Görres and A. v. Arnim, with whom he published the collection of folk songs *Des Knaben Wunderhorn* (1805-08). Later he returned to Roman Catholicism (1817), recorded the visions of A. K. Emmerick (1819-24), and finally retired in Munich (1833). *NDB* 2 (1955) 589-593. *53, 54, 84*

BRENTANO, Sophie (1761-1806), *née* Schubart, German writer, married Cl. Brentano (1803). *NDB* 2 (1955) 589. *53*[30]

BRIGHT, William (1824-1901), English Church historian and hymn-writer, Regius prof. of ecclesiastical history and Canon of Christ Church in Oxford (1868). *DNB 1901-1911* 1 (1912) 224-225. *26*

BRINZ, Alois, Ritter v. (1820-87), German jurist and politician, prof. of civil law in Erlangen (1851), Prague (1857), Tübingen (1866), and Munich (1871), member of the Bohemian *Landtag* (1861-66). *NDB* 2 (1955) 617. *65*

BROWNE, Edward Harold (1811-91), Bp. of Ely and later, of Winchester. He was educated at Eton and Emmanuel College, Cambridge, where he became a fellow and tutor. He was ordained priest in 1837. After filling pastoral positions in Stroud and Exeter, he became vice-principal of St. David's College, Lampeter, in 1843. He was appointed

Norrisian prof. of divinity at Cambridge in 1854, was consecrated Bp. of Ely in 1864, and succeeded S. Wilberforce as Bp. of Winchester in 1873. He regularly functioned as a moderate figure between the opposing parties in the Church of England. He published *An Exposition of the Thirty-Nine Articles* (1850-53). *DNB* 22 (1909) 304.   *80, 100-101, 102-105, 130*

BRYCE, James, Viscount Bryce (1838-1922), English jurist, historian, and politician, Regius prof. of civil law at Oxford (1870-93), Liberal M.P. (1880), ambassador to the USA (1907-13). *DNB 1922-1930* (1937) 127-135.   *26*

BRYENNIOS, Philotheos (1833-1914), Greek Orthodox churchman and patristic scholar. He was educated in Halki and continued his studies at the universities of Leipzig, Berlin, and Munich. In 1861 he was appointed prof. of Church history and exegesis in Halki, and in 1867 he became director of the School of the Phanar in Constantinople. He was elected Metropolitan of Serrae (Macedonia) in 1875 and Metropolitan of Nicomedia in 1877. In 1880 he was sent as an exarch to Bucarest. *ODCC*, p. 206.   *141*

BUNSEN, Christian Karl Josias, Freiherr v. (1791-1860), German diplomat and Protestant theologian, Prussian envoy in Rome (1824) and Bern (1839), ambassador in London (1841-54). *RGG* 1 (1957) 1525-1526.   *257*

BURKE, Edmund (1729-97), British political theorist and Whig politician, published an influential work against the French Revolution (1790). *DNB* 3 (1908) 345-365.   *253, 260*

CADIÈRE, Marie-Catherine (b. 1709), confided to her spiritual director J.-B. Girard that she received visions and the stigmata. After Girard had dissociated himself from her (1730), she accused him of sorcery. *DBF* 7 (1956) 798-799.   *56*

CAETANI, Michelangelo (1804-82), duca di Sermoneta, man of letters and liberal politician, advocate of Italian unity. *DBI* 16 (1973) 189-192.   *11*[5]

CAIUS, or Gaius (early 3rd cent.), Roman presbyter.   *210*

CALLISTUS I, St. (d. *c.* 222), Bp. of Rome (*c.* 217).   *257*

CALVIN, Jean (1509-64), French theologian and Protestant Reformer.   *111, 121, 123, 252*

CANNING, George (1770-1827), British Liberal statesman, foreign secretary (1807-09, 1822-27), and prime minister (1827). *DNB* 3 (1908) 872-883.   *256*

CANTÙ, Cesare (1804-95), Italian writer and historian, taught literature in Sondrio, Como, and Milan, served in Parliament (1860-67), appointed director of the State Archives at Milan (1873). *DBI* (1975) 336-344.   *202*

CAPEL, Thomas John (1836-1911), English R.C. prelate, chaplain of a mission for English speaking Catholics in Pau, Southern France (1860-68), founded a R.C. public school in Kensington (1873), and was elected rector of the University College there (1874). After the failure of the College and the subsequent conflict with Manning, he migrated to the USA (1883), where he was appointed prelate in charge of the R.C. Church for the district of Northern California. *DNB 1901-1911* 1 (1912) 312-313.   *181, 303*[61,62]

CARDONI, Giuseppe (1802-73), Italian prelate, tit. Bp. of Caristo (1852), Bp. of Recanati and Loreto (1863), tit. Abp. of Edessa (1867), prefect of the Vatican Archives (June 9, 1870). *Hierarchia*, pp. 187, 256, 478.   *163, 299*[32]

CARLYLE, Thomas (1795-1881), Scottish historian, essayist, and moralist, whose Romantic, anti-intellectualistic ideas exerted an enormous influence in Victorian Britain. He viewed history as the development of a divine plan and propounded the need for the hero-ruler. *DNB* 3 (1908) 1020-1036.   *91, 193, 251*

CASPARI, Carl Paul (1814-92), German-Norwegian theologian and orientalist of Jewish descent, converted to Protestantism (1838), lecturer (1847), and prof. of theology at the University of Christiania, Oslo (1857). *RE* 3 (1897) 737-742. *1/50, 190*

CAVALLI, Marino (1500-73), Venetian diplomat, ambassador to Germany, France, Rome, and Turkey. *DBI* 22 (1979) 749-754. *55-56*

CECCONI, Eugenio (1834-88), Abp. of Florence (1875), published works on the Council of Florence (1869), the Vatican Council (1873-79), and Luther (1883). *DBI* 23 (1979) 291-293. *190, 191*

CHARLEMAGNE (*c.*742-814), first Holy Roman Emperor (800). *102, 128, 258*

CHARLES I (1600-49), King of Great Britain and Ireland (1625). *37*

CHARLES V (1500-58), Holy Roman Emperor (1519). *55-56, 121, 258*

CHRIST, Wilhelm v. (1831-1906), German classical philologist, member of the Bavarian Academy (1858), prof. and protector of the Antiquarium in Munich (1860), member of the Old Catholic Church. *NDB* 3 (1957) 216. *65*

CHURCH, Richard William (1815-90), Dean of St. Paul's. He was educated at Wadham College, Oxford, and elected fellow of Oriel College in 1838. He became Newman's follower and took part in the Tractarian Movement. He was ordained priest in 1852 and in 1853 began pastoral work in Whatley, Somerset. In 1871 he was appointed Dean of St. Paul's. He was a leading figure in the High Church party and a renowned preacher. He was one of the founders of the *Guardian* (1846) and authored the classical work on the Oxford Movement (published in 1891). On the political level he considered himself Conservative but nevertheless supported Gladstone up to the moment the latter adopted Home Rule (1886). *DNB* 22 (1909) 431-434. *22, 93, 242, 257*

CLARKE, Richard Frederick (1839-1900), English philosopher, fellow of St. John's College, Oxford (1860-69), and master of Radley School (1861-63). In 1869 he joined the R.C. Church and in 1871 entered the Jesuit order. He was appointed headmaster of the Jesuit school at Wimbledon in 1892, and in 1896, founded Clarke's Hall at Oxford. BOASE IV, col. 679. *19*

CLEMENT V (1264-1314), Bertrand de Got, Pope from 1305. *205, 219*

CLEMENT XII (1652-1740), Lorenzo Corsini, Pope from 1730. *176*

CLEMENT XIV (1705-74), Giovanni Vincenzo Antonio Ganganelli, Pope from 1769. *46, 66, 92, 120*

CLIFFORD, William Joseph Hugh (1823-93), R.C. Bp. of Clifton (1857), one of the most learned English bishops. During the Council he was regarded as the leader of the English Minority group. He submitted to the Vatican decrees in Dec. 1870. BOASE IV, col. 690. *4, 10, 274*[12]

COCCHIA, Rocco (1830-1900), Italian Capuchin prelate, apostolic delegate to S. Domingo, Haiti and Venezuela (1874), Abp. of Otranto and vicar apostolic in S. Domingo (1883), apostolic internuncio in Brasil (1884), Abp. of Chieti and Vasto (1887). *Hierarchia*, pp. 311, 428, 522, 545. *148*[3]*, 297*[9]

COLOMBIÈRE, Claude la (1641-82), French Jesuit, superior of the college in Paray-le-Monial (1875), spiritual director of M.-M. Alacoque. *DSpir* 2 (1953) 939-943. *48, 56*

COLONNA, Sciarra (Giacomo) (*c.* 1270-1328), enemy of Boniface VIII, excommunicated and deprived of some of his estates (1297); took Boniface prisoner at Anagni (1303). *DBI* 27 (1982) 314-316. *65*

CONNOLLY, Thomas Louis (1815-76), Irish-born Capuchin, Bp. of St. John's, New Brunswick (1852), and Abp. of Halifax (1859). *NCE* 4 (1967) 182. *172*[13]

COPELAND, William John (1804-85), Anglican divine, scholar and fellow at Trinity College, Oxford, friend of Newman. After his ordination (1829) he was curate of Hackney

(1829-32) and later returned to Oxford. He became Newman's curate at Littlemore (1840) and accepted the college living of Farnham, Essex (1849). *DNB* 4 (1908) 1093-1094. *67*

CORDARA, Giulio Cesare (1704-85), Italian Jesuit historian and writer, taught in Macerata (1735) and at the Collegio Romano (1739), appointed historiographer of the Jesuit order (1742). *DBI* 28 (1983) 789-792. *49, 252*

CORNELIUS, Carl Adolf Wenzeslaus v. (1819-1903), German historian, studied in Bonn and Berlin, prof. in Münster (1854), Bonn (1855), and Munich (1856). In 1858 he became member of the Bavarian Academy, and was secretary of the Historical Commission from 1890 to 1898. His conversion to the Old Catholic Church was not only inspired by religious, but also by national considerations. He wrote works on humanism, the anabaptists, and Calvin. *NDB* 3 (1957) 363. *231, 232*

CORNELY, Karl Joseph Rudolf (1830-1908), German Jesuit biblical scholar, prof. in Maria Laach (1867). After the expulsion of the Jesuits from Germany he worked in Belgium (1872), Rome (1879), and Holland (1889), and then retired in Trier (1902). *DHGE* 13 (1956) 897-899. *45*

CORNTHWAITE, Robert (1818-90), R.C. Bp. of Beverley (1861) and of Leeds (1878). BOASE IV, col. 761. *39-40, 281*[53]

COTTERILL, Joseph Mortland, British theologian. *162*

CRAILSHEIM, Friedrich Krafft, Freiherr v. (1841-1926), Bavarian minister of foreign affairs (1880), and minister president (1890-1903). *NDB* 3 (1957) 387-388. *234-235*

CRANMER, Thomas (1489-1556), Abp. of Canterbury (1532). *111*

CREDNER, Karl August (1797-1857), German Protestant theologian, associate prof. in Jena (1830), full prof. of N.T. exegesis and Church history in Giessen (1832). *NDB* 3 (1957) 404. *203*[29]

CREIGHTON, Mandell (1843-1901), Anglican historian, Dixie prof. of ecclesiastical history at Cambridge (1884), Bp. of Peterborough (1891), and London (1897), first editor of *The English Historical Review* (1886-91) and first president of the Church Historical Society (1894-1901). *DNB* 22 (1909) 507-513. *247*

CROMWELL, Oliver (1599-1658), Lord Protector of England, Scotland and Ireland (1653). *258*

CULLEN, Paul (1803-78), Bp. of Armagh (1850), and Abp. of Dublin (1852), Ireland's first cardinal (1866). At the Council he worded the definition of papal infallibility finally accepted by the Council Fathers. He presided at the synod of Maynooth (1875). *DNB* 5 (1908) 277-278. *58*[34], *79, 285*[84], *289*[12,13]

CYRIL, St. (d. 444), Patriarch of Alexandria (412). *5, 12, 28, 122, 279*[39]

CYRIL II (1792-1877), Greek Orthodox Patriarch of Jerusalem (1845-72). *Thrèskeutikè* 7 (1965) 1205-1207. *184, 213, 303*[65]

CYRIL IV (1816-61), Coptic Patriarch, Metropolitan of Cairo (1854). *212-213, 307*

DANTE ALIGHIERI (1265-1321), Italian poet and philosopher. *14, 24, 47, 191, 228, 257*

DARBOY, Georges (1813-71), Bp. of Nancy (1859) and Abp. of Paris (1863). His doctrinal differences of opinion with Pius IX were the cause of the Pope's refusal to create him cardinal. During the Council he was the leader of the French resistance to the declaration of infallibility, but he submitted to the Council's decisions in March 1871. During the Commune revolt he was taken prisoner and shot. *DHGE* 14 (1960) 84-86. *37, 155, 256, 278*[34]

DAVENPORT, Christopher (1598-1680), English Franciscan theologian, attempted to show the conformity of the 39 Articles with Catholic tradition (1634). *DNB* 5 (1908) 558-559. *251*

DE CESARE, Raffaele (1845-1918), Italian journalist and politician of the Right, opposed the Papal States and the *non expedit* policy. *EI* 12 (1931) 459. *225*

DECHAMPS, Victor Auguste (1810-83), Abp. of Malines (1867). *278*[34]

DE DECKER, Pieter (1812-91), Belgian liberal Catholic publicist and politician, representative (1839-66), and prime minister (1855-57). He supported Unionism and defended equal rights for the Flemish population. *Nationaal Biografisch Woordenboek* 1 (1964) 385-392. *256*

DE LUCA, Antonino Xaverio (1805-83), Italian prelate, Bp. of Aversa (1845), nuncio in Munich (1853) and Vienna (1856), created cardinal (1863), appointed prefect of the congregations of the Index (1864) and of Studies (1878), Bp. of Palestrina and vicechancellor of the Roman Church (1878). *Hierarchia*, pp. 16, 45, 537. *201, 202*

DENS, Pierre (1690-1775), Belgian theologian, president of the archdiocesan seminary at Malines (1735). *DTC* 4 (1911) 421-423. *58, 285*[82]

DENTON, William (1815-88), Anglican priest (1845), graduated from Worcester College, Oxford, vicar of St. Bartholomew, Cripplegate (1850). He published religious works and championed the Eastern populations under Turkish rule. *DNB* 22 (1909) 555-556. *127*

DE VALETTA, *see* MONACO LA VALLETTA, Raffaele

DISRAELI, Benjamin (1804-81), 1st Earl of Beaconsfield, British statesman of Italian-Jewish descent, converted to Christianity (1817). He was elected to Parliament in 1837 and became the leader of the Tories in the Commons in 1849. He served as chancellor of the exchequer in 1852, 1858-59, and 1865-67, and in 1868 became prime minister for 10 months. During his second administration (1874-80) he introduced important social reforms. He took a pro-Turkish line in the Eastern Crisis (1876-78) and returned in triumph from the Congress of Berlin (1878). He resigned after a defeat in the elections of 1880. He was the author of many novels, political writings, and satire. *DNB* 5 (1908) 1006-1022. *55-56, 181, 188, 253, 303*[62]

DÖLLINGER, Elisabeth Christine (1861-1917), the daughter of Döllinger's brother Moritz. After her father's death (1882) she was taken under protection by Döllinger and later ran his household. In 1895 she married the physician Karl Uhl. *ZBLG* 33 (1970) 441 n. 12. *213-214, 223, 225-226, 228-229, 233, 237-240, 242-243*

DÖLLINGER, Ignaz v. (1799-1890). *XI-XXIV, XXVI-XXXV*; youth in Würzburg, *150-151, 187*; curacy in Markt Scheinfeld, *161*; in Aschaffenburg, *224*; visits to Oxford, *22, 257*; visit to Rome, *8, 125, 258-259*; excommunication, *18, 28, 60-61, 91, 278*[33]*, 286*[89]; lectures, *5-7, 21, 26, 27, 31, 47, 64*; rector of the University of Munich, *71-72, 74-75, 260*; addresses to the Bavarian Academy, *93-95, 154, 191, 204-205, 225-226*; at the Reunion Conferences in Bonn, (1874) *99-116*, (1875) *127-145*; early wishes, *191-192*; literary undertakings, *14, 45-47, 164, 191, 204-205, 219-220, 225-226*; works, *LII-LIV, 14, 15, 16*[18]*, 23-24, 45, 61, 73*[2]*, 78, 95*[8]*, 158, 164, 167, 205, 243, 250, 253, 254, 257, 259, 260-262*; library, *30, 150, 191, 230, 232, 233, 237, 240, 241*; letters to Plummer, *23*[10]*, 77*[4]*, 93*[7]*, 99*[9]*, 169, 217, 304*[72]; last illness, *228-229, 237*; death, *228-229, 230, 234, 237*; funeral, *228-229, 238*; will, *233, 239*; literary remains, *229-230, 231-232, 233-234, 238, 241-242, 243-244, 245-246*; and Gladstone, *124, 185, 188, 209, 212, 217-218, 220, 224, 256*; and Manning, *9-10, 38, 148, 181*; and Newman, *4-5, 18*[8]*, 25-26, 28, 29, 38, 64-65, 66-67, 80, 99*[9]*, 147, 172, 190, 214, 247, 254, 257, 260, 261, 264, 267, 304*[72]; and Pius IX, *4, 48-49, 50, 125, 156-157, 202*; and the Old Catholics, *29, 57, 75, 99*[9]*, 171-172, 234, 236, 311*[39]; view of theology, *29, 245, 249*

DÖLLINGER, Johanna, sister of Elisabeth. She was secretary and companion to the Marquise de Forbin d'Oppède in St. Marcel near Marseilles from 1879 to 1884, and then joined Döllinger's household. After Döllinger's death she moved to England where she married an Anglican clergyman. *Briefwechsel* III, p. 226 n. 4. *213-214, 223, 225-226, 228-233, 237-243, 311*[39]

DOMENEC, Michael (1816-78), Spanish-born R.C. Bp. of Pittsburgh (1860), later Bp. of Allegheny (1876-77). *NCE* 4 (1967) 960-961. *172*[13]

DONNET, Ferdinand François Auguste (1795-1882), Abp. of Bordeaux (1837), created cardinal and appointed senator (1852). At the Council he was a member of the Majority. *DHGE* 14 (1960) 666-668. *37, 280*[48]

DORNER, Isaak August (1809-84), German Lutheran theologian, prof. of theology in Tübingen (1838), Kiel (1839), Königsberg (1843), Bonn (1847), Göttingen (1853), and Berlin (1862). *TRE* 9 (1982) 155-158. *215*

DRUMANN, Wilhelm Carl August (1786-1861), German historian, prof. (1817) and librarian (1820) in Königsberg. *NDB* 4 (1959) 140. *51*

DUCHESNE, Louis Marie Olivier (1843-1922), French Church historian and priest (1867), prof. of Church history at the Institut Catholique (1877-85) and the École des Hautes Études (1887-95), director of the École française de Rome (1895), prothonotary apostolic (1900), and member of the French Academy (1910). His *Histoire ancienne de l'Église* (1906-10) was placed on the Index (1912). *DHGE* 14 (1960) 965-984. *177, 256*

DUPANLOUP, Félix Antoine Philibert (1802-78), Bp. of Orléans (1849). In France he was the most prominent defender of the Church's rights, esp. in the area of education. During the Council he became one of the leaders of the Minority party due to his desire to avoid any decision which could elicit a conflict between the Church and modern society. After repeated insistence, he submitted to the Vatican decrees on Feb. 18, 1871. He was active in French politics as a member of the National Assembly (1871) and the senate (1875). *DHGE* 14 (1960) 1070-1122. *57, 124, 125, 256, 286*[87], *304*[68]

ELIZABETH I (1533-1603), Queen of England (1558). *258*

EMMERICK, Anna Katharina (1774-1824), German stigmatic and mystic, lived in the Augustinian convent Agnetenberg in Dülmen (1802), and then with a French priest (1812). Her visions (1812-18) were recorded by Cl. Brentano and published in 1833, 1852, 1858-60. *DSpir* 4 (1960) 622-627. *53, 54*

ENZLER, Leonhard (1817-93), Bavarian priest (1841), Canon (1859) and Dean (1874) of St. Cajetan in Munich, later Dean of the Metropolitan chapter of the Frauenkirche (1883). HUBER, p. 753 n. 46. *151-152, 166, 298*[14]

ERRINGTON, George (1804-86), coadjutor to N. Wiseman, Abp. of Westminster (1855). *274*[12]

ESTCOURT, Edgar Edmund (1816-84), Anglican clergyman, converted to the R.C. Church (1845), ordained priest (1848), Canon of St. Chad's Cathedral, Birmingham (1848). *DNB* 6 (1908) 872-873. *82*

EUGENIUS IV (1383-1447), Gabriele Condulmer, Pope from 1431. *61, 82, 141, 290*[25]

EVANS, Edward Payson (1831-1917), American author, prof. of modern languages at the University of Michigan (1863), lived in Munich as private scholar and free-lance journalist (1870-1914). *DAB* 6 (1931) 197-198. *239*

EWALD, Georg Heinrich August (1803-75), German Protestant orientalist and biblical scholar, prof. in Göttingen (1827), Tübingen (1838), and again, in Göttingen (1848-67), co-founder of the *Protestantenverein* (1863), and deputy to the *Reichstag* (1867-74). *TRE* 10 (1982) 694-696. *153, 204*

FALK, Paul Ludwig Adalbert (1827-1900), German jurist and politician, Bismarck's 'Kulturkampfminister', appointed minister of public worship in 1872. He resigned his post in 1879 and in 1882 exchanged all his duties for an appointment as president of the Superior District Court in Hamm. *NDB* 5 (1961) 6-7. *183*

FANTUZZI, Gaetano (1708-78), Italian cardinal (1758), prefect of the Congregation of Immunity. He organized in his palace a sort of academy to discuss juridical questions. *DHGE* 16 (1967) 488. *251*

FAURE, Giovanni Battista (1702-79), Italian Jesuit, anti-Jansenist polemist, wrote also against the Inquisition. *NCE* 5 (1967) 858-859. *252*

FAWCETT, Henry (1833-84), English politician, prof. of political economy in Cambridge (1863), Liberal M.P. (1865), later appointed postmaster-general (1880). *DNB* 6 (1908) 1116-1121. *78, 289*[12]

FÉNELON, François de Salignac de la Mothe- (1651-1715), French theologian and man of letters, tutor of the Duke of Burgundy (1689), later named Abp. of Cambrai (1695). His *Explication des maximes des saints* (1697) was condemned by Rome for quietism (1699). *DHGE* 16 (1967) 958-987. *54-55, 251, 252, 266*

FEUERBACH, Ludwig Andreas (1804-72), German philosopher, prof. in Erlangen (1828), retired to a life of private study (1832). *TRE* 11 (1983) 144-157. *211*

FICKER, Johann Kaspar Julius (1826-1902), German historian, prof. of history in Innsbruck (1852), retired to devote himself entirely to scholarly research (1879). *NDB* 5 (1961) 133. *252*

FLIR, Alois Kasimir (1805-59), Austrian theologian and writer, prof. of classical philology and aesthetics in Innsbruck (1835), member of the Frankfurt Parliament (1848), appointed rector of the S. Maria dell'Anima in Rome (1853), later named auditor of the Rota (1858). *ÖBL* 1 (1957) 330. *258*[33], *313*[62]

FORBES, Alexander Penrose (1817-75), Bp. of Brechin, known as the 'Scottish Pusey'. He studied at Brasenose College, Oxford, where he came under the influence of the Oxford Movement. He was ordained priest in 1844. After performing pastoral duties in Oxford, Stonehaven, and Leeds, he was named Bp. of Brechin in 1847. He took up residence in Dundee where he accomplished much by way of stimulating the life of the Church. He was a friend of Gladstone and Döllinger and sympathized with the Old Catholic Movement. He wrote *A Short Explanation of the Nicene Creed* (1852), *An Explanation of the Thirty-Nine Articles* (1867-68), and published many sermons, manuals of devotion, liturgical and hagiographical texts. *DNB* 7 (1908) 378-379. *15, 21*

FRANCHI, Alessandro (1819-78), Italian cardinal (1873), prefect of the Propaganda (1874), appointed secretary of state by Leo XIII (March 1878). *DHGE* 18 (1977) 576-581. *190*

FRANCIS OF ASSISI, St. (1181/2-1226), founder of the Franciscan order. *32*

FRANK, Franz Hermann Reinhold v. (1827-94), German Protestant theologian, prof. of Church history and systematic theology in Erlangen (1857). *TRE* 11 (1983) 322-324. *215*

FRASER, James (1818-85), Bp. of Manchester (1870), whose efforts for the working classes earned him the title 'bishop of all denominations'. *DNB* 7 (1908) 649-651. *193, 305*[78]

FREDERICK II (1194-1250), King of Sicily (1198) and Germany (1212), Holy Roman Emperor (1220). *252*

FREDERICK III (1415-93), German King (1440), Holy Roman Emperor (1452). *61*

FREEMAN, Edward Augustus (1823-92), English historian, fellow of Trinity College (1845), prof. of modern history at Oxford (1884). *DNB* 22 (1909) 672-676. *26*

FREYBERG-EISENBERG, Maximilian Prokop, Freiherr v. (1789-1851), German archivist and historian, president of the Bavarian Academy (1842-48). *NDB* 5 (1961) 421. *94*

FRIEDRICH, Johannes (1836-1917), German Church historian, obtained his theological formation in Bamberg, appointed chaplain in Markt Scheinfeld after his ordination (1859). He continued his theological studies in Munich, where he became Döllinger's assistant. He became lecturer in 1862 and prof. of homiletics in 1865. He accompanied Cardinal v. Hohenlohe to Rome as his theological adviser for the Council but returned to Munich in May, 1870, and worked with the movement protesting the Council. He was excommunicated in 1871 yet appointed prof. of theology in Munich in 1872. Ten years later he was transferred to the faculty of philosophy where he remained as prof. until his retirement in 1905. In 1869 he became a member of the Bavarian Academy. He played a leading role in organizing the Old Catholic Movement but withdrew from Church activities after the abolition of mandatory celibacy for priests (1878). By the end of his life he was isolated. *DHGE* 19 (1981) 76-84. *18, 19[8], 27, 45, 65, 114, 165-166, 172, 190, 226, 228, 231, 233, 234, 237, 240-241, 242, 243, 276[22], 298[13], 301[46], 305[82], 310[32], 311[41]*

FRIEDRICH WILHELM (1831-88), the son of Wilhelm I, married Princess Royal Victoria of England in 1858. As Prussian Crown Prince (1861) he was a commander in the wars against Denmark (1864), Austria (1866) and France (1870-71). On March 9, 1888, he became German Emperor and King of Prussia as Friedrich III. *NDB* 5 (1961) 487-489. *43, 149, 194-195, 220, 221, 309[17]*

FROHSCHAMMER, Jakob (1821-93), German philosopher, theologian, and priest (1847). He was lecturer (1850) and prof. of philosophy in Munich (1855). His philosophical ideas were condemned in the papal letter *Gravissimas inter* (Dec. 11, 1862). Because he refused to submit, he was suspended (1863) and later excommunicated (1871). In the last period of his life he devoted himself to the development of his philosophical system which had little influence. FRIES-SCHWAIGER III, pp. 169-189. *72, 125, 296[71]*

FROUDE, James Anthony (1818-94), English historian and man of letters, wrote a history of England in the 16th cent. (1856-70) and a biography of Th. Carlyle (1882-84). *DNB* 22 (1909) 679-687. *166*

GAILLARD, Léopold de (1820-93), French liberal Catholic publicist, collaborator (1843) and later editor-in-chief of *Le Correspondant*. *DBF* 15 (1982) 89-90. *61, 286[88]*

GANGANELLI, *see* CLEMENT XIV

GEFFCKEN, Friedrich Heinrich (1830-96), German jurist and politician, worked in the diplomatic service in Hamburg (1854) and London (1866), magistrate in the Hamburg senate (1869), prof. of political science and civil law in Strassburg (1872-82). *NDB* 6 (1964) 127-128. *221, 309[17]*

GEIGER, German R.C. preacher. *39*

GENNADIOS, Roumanian Orthodox Bp. of Argesh. *140, 141*

GFRÖRER, August Friedrich (1803-61), German historian, librarian in Stuttgart (1830), prof. of history in Freiburg (1846), converted to Roman Catholicism (1853). *RGG* 2 (1958) 1565. *162*

GIBB, John (1835-1915), Scottish Presbyterian theologian, prof. of Church history at the Theological College of the Presbyterian Church of England in Cambridge (1877). *Who was Who* 1 ([5]1966) 271. *241[8]*

GIESEBRECHT, Friedrich Wilhelm Benjamin v. (1814-89), German historian, prof. of history in Königsberg (1857) and Munich (1862), member (1858) and secretary (1873) of the Historical Commission of the Bavarian Academy. *NDB* 6 (1964) 379-382. *71, 74*

HOWSON, John Saul (1816-85), Anglican divine, attended Giggleswick School and Trinity College, Cambridge, and was ordained priest in 1846. He taught at the Liverpool Collegiate Institute and in 1849 succeeded W. J. Conybeare as headmaster. In 1866 he became vicar in Wisbech and from 1867 he was Dean of Chester. *DNB* 10 (1908) 130-132. *103, 105, 108, 109, 127, 141-142*

HUBER, Johann Nepomuk (1830-79), German theologian and philosopher, studied in Munich, where he became lecturer (1855) and prof. of philosophy and pedagogy (1859). In 1859 his book *Die Philosophie der Kirchenväter* (1859) was put on the Index. After his refusal to submit, theology students were forbidden to attend his courses. In the controversy around the Vatican Council he sided with Döllinger. He helped in the publication of *Janus* and forwarded the *Quirinus* letters to the *Allgemeine Zeitung*. In the Old Catholic Church he was an avid opponent of 'Jesuitism'. *NDB* 9 (1972) 695-696. *78, 91, 176, 288*[11]

HUGO, Victor Marie (1802-85), French writer, leader of the Romantic Movement in France, also active in politics as member of the Legislative Assembly (1848). After a lengthy exile (1851-70), he returned to Paris to become the leader of the Left in the National Assembly (1871-72), and later a senator (1876). *GE* 20 (n.d.) 355-360. *193*

HUMBOLDT, Alexander, Freiherr v. (1769-1859), famous German explorer and scientist, made expeditions to Central and South America (1799-1804), lived in Paris (1807-27) and later in Berlin, where he served as a tutor to the Crown Prince, a member of the privy council, and a court chamberlain. *NDB* 10 (1974) 33-43. *262*[37]

HUMBOLDT, Wilhelm, Freiherr v. (1767-1835), elder brother of Alexander, Prussian statesman, linguistic scholar, and educational reformer, resident and minister plenipotentiary in Rome (1801), minister of education (1809-10), ambassador in Vienna (1812) and minister of interior (1819). *NDB* 10 (1974) 43-51. *32*[14]

HUNT, John (1827-c. 1908), Britisch theologian, converted from the Presbyterian to the Established Church, staff member of *The Contemporary Review* (1867-77), vicar of Otford, Kent (1877), sympathized with the Old Catholic Church. *EUI* 28/1 (1925) 730-731. *111*

HYACINTHE, Père, *see* LOYSON, Charles

INCE, William (1825-1910), Anglican theologian, Regius prof. of divinity and Canon of Christ Church, Oxford (1878). *DNB 1901-1911* 2 (1912) 337-338. *173*

INNOCENT III (1160/61-1216), Lotario de' Conti di Segni, Pope from 1198. *50, 128, 202, 259*

INNOCENT XI (1611-89), Benedetto Odescalchi, Pope from 1676. *46*

INNOCENT XII (1615-1700), Antonio Pignatelli, Pope from 1691. *46*

JACOBI, Friedrich Heinrich, Ritter v. (1743-1819), German philosopher, together with J. G. Hamann a leading figure of the *Gefühlsphilosophie*, lived in Munich from 1805, president of the Bavarian Academy (1807-12). *NDB* 10 (1974) 222-224. *94*

JANDEL, Vincent-Alexandre (1810-72), French Dominican, elected vicar-general (1850) and appointed magister-general by Pius IX (1855). *Cath* 6 (1967) 310. *56, 284*[80]

JANYSCHEW, Johannes Leontewitsch (1826-1910), Russian Orthodox theologian, was priest of the Orthodox communities in Wiesbaden (1851-56, 1858-66) and Berlin (1858). In 1866 he became prof. of moral theology and rector of the Spiritual Academy of St. Petersburg. From 1883 he was the confessor for the imperial family, protopresbyter of the court clergy, and a member of the Holy Synod. He attended the Old Catholic Congress at Cologne (1872) and both Reunion Conferences at Bonn. *DE* 2 (1955) 515. *108-109, 112, 115, 130, 141, 142, 143, 144-145*

JEROME, St. (c. 345-c. 420), Latin Church Father. *4*², *8*³, *129, 167, 210*
JOHN OF DAMASCUS, St. (c. 675-c. 749), Greek Church Father. *142*
JOHN LACKLAND (1167-1216), King of England (1199). *56*
JOSEPH II (1741-90), German King (1764), Holy Roman Emperor (1765). *95*
JOWETT, Benjamin (1817-93), Anglican theologian and priest (1845), student, fellow, tutor, and later master (1870) of Balliol College, Oxford. In 1855 he became Regius prof. of Greek at Oxford. Inspired by his Greek studies and German (esp. Hegelian) philosophy, his theological thinking evolved in a liberal direction. After his commentaries on the Epistles of St. Paul appeared (1855), suspicion began to develop concerning his orthodoxy, esp. regarding his view of atonement. His contribution in the *Essays and Reviews* (1860) on the interpretation of Scripture caused still further suspicion. From then on he ceased writing on theological subjects and applied himself to the study of the Greek classics. *DNB* 22 (1909) 921-928. *117, 275*¹⁷

KÄS, Ambrosius (1815-90), German R.C. priest (1841), prior of the Carmelite monastery in Würzburg, theologian to the General of his order, but dismissed during the Council because of his anti-infallibilist views. HUBER, p. 753 n. 47. *151*⁵, *166, 298*¹⁴
KALLINIKOS (1800-89), Greek Orthodox Metropolitan of Mytilene (1843) and Patriarch of Alexandria (1858-61). *Thrèskeutikè* 7 (1965) 250-251. *212, 307*⁷
KALLISTUS, *see* CALLISTUS
KARL THEODOR (1795-1875), Prince of Bavaria, commander-in-chief of the 7th German army corps in the German-Danish War (1860), and of the Bavarian army in the Seven Weeks War (1866). After the defeat of the Bavarians he resigned all his military dignities and retired to his castle at Tegernsee. *ADB* 15 (1882) 258-260. *81-82, 169, 180, 222*
KAULBACH, Wilhelm v. (1805-74), German artist, received his training in Düsseldorf and Munich. He was appointed court painter by Ludwig I (1837), after which he moved to Rome (1838-39) and then returned to Munich, where he became director of the Academy (1849). *NDB* 11 (1977) 356-357. *48-49, 119, 283*⁶⁴
KEIM, Karl Theodor (1825-78), German Protestant Church historian and biblical scholar, prof. of theology in Zurich (1860) and Giessen (1873). *NDB* 11 (1977) 410. *212, 307*⁶
KERFOOT, John Barrett (1816-81), Irish-born Bp. of the Episcopal Diocese of Pittsburgh (1865). Although he was a High Churchman, he opposed the advance of ritualism in his diocese. He attended the first two Lambeth Conferences (1867, 1878), the Old Catholic Congress at Freiburg (1874), and the Bonn Conference of 1874. *DAB* 10 (1933) 354. *100, 102, 105, 107, 108, 109*
KIRÉEFF, Alexander Alekseevich (1832-1910), Russian general and liberal theologian, associated with the University of St. Petersburg, representative for the district of Moscow, and secretary of the Society of the Friends of Spiritual Enlightenment. He sought to approach the Old Catholics in the hope of spreading Orthodoxy in the West. He took part in numerous Old Catholic Congresses and was co-founder of and regular contributor to the *RIT*. *EC* 7 (1951) 704-705. *141*
KIRKPATRICK, Alexander Francis (1849-1940), Anglican theologian, ordained priest in 1875, fellow of Trinity College, Cambridge (1871), later examining chaplain to E. H. Browne, Bp. of Winchester (1878), and to R. Davidson, Bp. of Rochester (1890), Winchester (1895), Abp. of Canterbury (1903-28). He was Regius prof. of Hebrew (1882) and Lady Margaret prof. of divinity (1903) in Cambridge, Canon (1882) and Dean (1906) of Ely, and master of Selwyn College (1898-1907). *Who was Who* 3 (²1967) 760. *127*

defended modern freedoms and the separation of Church and State. His program was condemned by Gregory XVI in the encyclical *Mirari vos* (1832). After an initial submission, Lamennais published the controversial *Paroles d'un croyant* (1834), which brought about a new condemnation in *Singulari nos* (1834). After breaking with the R.C. Church, he was primarily occupied with the social question and the defense of democracy. In 1848 he was elected to the National Assembly, but after the coup in 1851, he withdrew in disillusionment. *Cath* 6 (1967) 1713-1723. *57, 64, 67, 255-56*

LANFREY, Pierre (1828-77), French historian and politician, member of the National Assembly (1871), ambassador in Bern (1871-73), senator (1875). *GE* 21 (n.d.) 887. *150*

LANGE, Bavarian artist. *175-176*

LANGEN, Joseph (1837-1901), German theologian and priest (1859), prof. of N.T. exegesis in Bonn (1864). In 1872 he was excommunicated for his rejection of the Vatican decrees. He played an important role in the establishment of the Old Catholic Church and was president of the sub-commission which, in view of the Reunion Conference at Bonn, had to prepare negotiations with the Orthodox. After the abolition of compulsory celibacy (1878), he resigned his positions in the Old Catholic Church. *RE* 11 (1902) 268-271. *127*

LAVELEYE, Émile Louis Victor de (1822-92), Belgian economist, historian, philologist, and author, prof. of political economy in Liège (1863). *BN* Supp. 6 (1968) 528-549. *197*

LEE, William (1815-83), Irish divine, prof. of ecclesiastical history in Dublin (1857), rector of Arboe (1862), archdeacon and rector of St. Peter's, Dublin (1864), member of the N.T. Revision Company (1870). *DNB* 11 (1909) 826. *118*, *294*[59]

LEIBNIZ, Gottfried Wilhelm (1646-1716), German philosopher, mathematician, and court adviser. *253*

LENBACH, Franz Seraph v. (1836-1904), German artist, prof. at the Academy of Weimar (1863), later devoted himself to portrait painting, living in Munich, Vienna, and Berlin. His works include portraits of Döllinger, Bismark, Gladstone, Lord and Lady Acton, Lady Blennerhassett, and many others. THIEME-BECKER 23 (1929) 43-45. *147*

LEO III, St. (d. 816), Pope from 795. *102, 128*

LEO X (1475-1521), Giovanni de'Medici, Pope from 1513. *8*

LEO XIII (1810-1903), Vincenzo Gioacchino Pecci, nuncio in Brussels (1843), Bp. of Perugia (1846), created cardinal (1853), elected Pope on Feb. 20, 1878. Although he pursued the policy of his predecessor in many aspects, his pontificate was characterized by a more reconciliatory attitude regarding civil governments, a greater openness to scholarly research, and a deeper concern for the pastoral and social problems of the modern time. *Cath* 7 (1975) 331-335. *173, 189-190, 196, 197-198, 201-203, 214, 219, 220-221, 222, 225, 279*[43]*, 309*[18]

LESSING, Gotthold Ephraim (1729-81), German critic and dramatist. *74*

LETO, Pomponio, *see* NOBILI VITELLESCHI, Francesco

LIAS, John James (1834-1923), Anglican divine, scholar of Emmanuel College, Cambridge, ordained priest in 1860. He was curate of Shaftesbury, Dorset (1858-60), and Folkestone (1865-66), vicar of Eastbury, Berks (1866-68), and minor canon of Llandaff Cathedral (1868-71). He was appointed prof. of modern literature and lecturer in theology and Hebrew at St. David's College, Lampeter (1871), vicar of St. Edwards, Cambridge (1880), and preacher at the Royal Chapel, Whitehall (1884). Later he became examining chaplain to the Bp. of Llandaff (1887-1900) and rector of East Bergholt (1892-1903). *Who was Who* 2 (³1962) 630. *127*

LIDDON, Henry Parry (1829-90), Canon of St. Paul's. He was educated at King's College

School, London, and Christ Church, Oxford, where he became a close associate with J. Keble and E. B. Pusey. He was ordained priest in 1853. From 1852 until 1854 he was curate in Wantage. He was appointed first vice-principal of Cuddesdon Theological College in 1854, vice-principal of St. Edmund's Hall, Oxford, in 1859, and in 1864 named prebendary of Salisbury. From 1870 to 1882 he was Dean Ireland prof. of exegesis at Oxford, during which period he played a prominent role in university politics. In 1870 he was appointed Canon of St. Paul's Cathedral. After resigning his professorship, he devoted himself to writing a biography of Pusey. Liddon was a famous preacher and a convinced defender of High Church principles. In 1871 he worked for the preservation of the Athanasian Creed, and in 1889 he sharply opposed *Lux Mundi*, edited by Ch. Gore, for containing a new critical interpretation of the O.T. He sympathized with the Old Catholic Movement and was interested in the Eastern Churches. He was a friend of Ch. Loyson and visited Döllinger several times in Munich. *DNB* 11 (1909) 1102-1107. *8-12, 16[7], 100, 102, 105, 107-108, 109-110, 115-116, 117, 118, 124, 127, 133-134, 135, 142, 152, 212-213, 230, 241, 245, 247, 298[15]*

LIEBIG, Justus, Freiherr v. (1803-73), German chemist, prof. of chemistry in Giessen (1824) and Munich (1852), president of the Bavarian Academy (1859). *ADB* 18 (1883) 589-605. *94, 95*

LIEBKNECHT, Wilhelm (1826-1900), German socialist leader, member of the *Reichstag* (1867), founded, together with August Bebel, the Social Democrat Party (1869), editor-in-chief of *Vorwärts*, the party organ, member of the Saxon lower house (1879-92). *BWDG*, cols. 1650-1651. *171*

LIGHTFOOT, Joseph Barber (1828-89), Bp. of Durham. He was fellow (1852) and tutor (1857) of Trinity College, Cambridge, and was named Hulsean prof. of divinity at Cambridge in 1861. In 1871 he became Canon of St. Paul's, and in 1875 Lady Margaret prof. of divinity at Cambridge. He was a member of the N.T. Company of Revisors (1870-80), and published important works on the Epistles of St. Paul and the Apostolic Fathers. In 1879 he was named Bp. of Durham. *DNB* 11 (1909) 1111-1119. *210, 220, 238, 276[18]*

LIGUORI, Alfonso Maria de', St. (1696-1787), Italian moral theologian, founder of the Redemptorists (1732), Bp. of Sant'Agata dei Goti (1762-75). *21, 47, 58, 126*

LILIENCRON, Rochus, Freiherr v. (1820-1912), German musicologist and philologist, prof. of German language and literature in Kiel (1851) and Jena (1852), theatrical manager and librarian in Meiningen (1855), editor of German historical folk songs and the *ADB* while living in Munich (1869-76). Later he was a free-lance writer in Schleswig (1908). *RGG* 4 (1960) 378. *154*

LINDWURM, Josef v. (1824-74), German physician, director of the University clinic for internal medicine in Munich (1869). BOSL, pp. 482-483. *65*

LINGARD, John (1771-1851), English R.C. historian. *290[25]*

LITTLEDALE, Richard Frederick (1833-90), Anglican liturgical writer and controversialist, curate in Thorpe Hamlet, Norfolk (1856-57), and London (1857-61). *DNB* 11 (1909) 1243-1244. *195*

LONGFELLOW, Henry Wadsworth (1807-82), American poet and translator, prof. of modern languages at Bowdoin College (1826) and Harvard (1835-54). *DAB* 11 (1933) 382-387. *14*

LOOS, Henricus (1813-73), Old Catholic Abp. of Utrecht (1858). In July 1872 he administered confirmation in several communities in Bavaria. In Sept. 1872 he was present at the Old Catholic Congress in Cologne, and in April 1873, raised two German sub-deacons to the priesthood at Utrecht. He died the same day that J.

was minister of justice from 1867 until 1871 and minister of public worship from 1869 until 1890. Although he only became prime minister in 1880, he was the leading figure in the Bavarian government from 1872, so that it came to be called the 'System Lutz'. He initiated the Pulpit clause (*Kanzelparagraph*) in the German Empire (1871), and carried out an 'underhanded' *Kulturkampf* in Bavaria, for which he occasionally consulted Döllinger. He continued to consider the Old Catholics part of the Catholic Church, but in 1890, just before he stepped down, he was compelled to revise this standpoint. *ADB* 55 (1910) 555-558. *21, 22, 27, 42, 60[35], 117, 196, 234-235, 286[86], 311[35,38]*

LYKURGOS, Alexander (1827-75), Greek Orthodox Abp. of Syros, Melos and Tenos. He studied in Athens and at the universities of Leipzig, Halle and Berlin. From 1860 on he was prof. at the theological faculty in Athens. In 1862, during a pilgrimage to Jerusalem, he was ordained priest and became an archimandrite. In 1866 he was named Abp. of the Cyclad islands Syros, Melos and Tenos. At the end of 1869 he travelled for 3 months in England, where he had an audience with Queen Victoria, became acquainted with W. E. Gladstone and received honorary doctorates in Oxford and Cambridge. In 1872 he represented the Greek Church at the synod of Constantinople which excommunicated the Bulgarians. Because of his great prestige in the field of ecumenism, his participation to the second Reunion Conference at Bonn increased the interest from the Eastern Churches. *Thrèskeutikè* 2 (1963) 112-113. *127[17], 130-131, 132, 143, 144*

MACAULAY, Thomas Babington, Baron Macaulay (1800-59), English historian and politician, commissioner and secretary of the Indian board of control (1832), legal adviser to the supreme council of India (1834-38), secretary for war (1839-41), and paymaster-general (1846-47). His *History of England to the Death of William III* (1848-61) made him one of the founders of the Whig interpretation of history. *DNB* 12 (1909) 410-418. *79, 252, 253, 262[37]*

MACCOLL, Malcolm (1831-1907), Scottish divine and author, studied at the Episcopalian college at Glenalmond, ordained priest in 1857, filled pastoral positions in Scotland, England, and Southern Italy. He was an admirer and assistant of W. E. Gladstone and defended his policy in several pamphlets. In 1876 he visited Eastern Europe with H. P. Liddon, where he witnessed the Bulgarian atrocities. In 1884 he became residentiary canon of Ripon. *DNB 1901-1911* 2 (1912) 508. *99[9], 127, 134, 135, 209*

MACHALE, John (1791-1881), R.C. Bp. of Killala (1834), Abp. of Tuam (1834), ardent Irish nationalist. He did not favour any system of non-denominational education and was strongly opposed to Newman's appointment as rector of the R.C. University in Dublin. From 1854 his influence declined in the Irish Church, and he withdrew from political activity. *NCE* 9 (1967) 29-30. *58[34], 84, 285[84], 291[28]*

MACNAMARA, Mr., Scotchman, a friend of Bp. Forbes of Brechin. *21-22*

MAI, Angelo (1782-1854), Italian Jesuit palaeographer, scriptor at the Ambrosian Library in Milan (1813), left the Jesuits to become prefect of the Vatican Library (1819), later created cardinal (1838). *Cath* 8 (1979) 168-169. *55*

MAINTENON, Françoise d'Aubigné, marquise de (1635-1719), second wife of Louis XIV (1697). *210, 243*

MAIR, John (1822-1902), Scottish theologian, minister of Southdean Parish, Roxburghshire. *Who was Who* 1 ([5]1964) 467. *95*

MAISTRE, Joseph Marie, comte de (1753-1821), French diplomat and political writer, member of the Savoy senate (1788), exiled after the French annexation of Savoy

(1792). He became Sardinian envoy in St. Petersburg (1802-17) and later lived in Turin. Together with L. de Bonald he was the leading proponent of the traditionalist reaction to the French Revolution. *Cath* 8 (1979) 208-210. *248*

MANNING, Henry Edward (1808-92), Abp. of Westminster. He was ordained priest of the Anglican Church in 1833 and appointed Archdeacon of Chichester in 1840. He converted to the R.C. Church in 1851, was again ordained priest, and studied in Rome at the request of Pius IX. In 1857 he became provost of the Westminster chapter and founded the Oblates of St. Charles in London. In 1865 he was named Abp. of Westminster. During the Council he was the most active member of the group favouring infallibility, esp. as organizer of the Majority committee. In 1875 he was created cardinal. *DNB* 12 (1909) 947-953. *9-10, 11, 37-38, 90-91, 121, 124, 126, 147-148, 157, 181, 212, 214, 220, 275[12], 297[8], 303[61,62], 304[68]*

MARET, Henri Louis Charles (1805-84), prof. (1841) and dean (1853) of the theological faculty of the Sorbonne, tit. Abp. of Sura and member of the chapter of St. Denys (1861). He favoured a reconciliation between the Church and the modern world and tried to dissuade Pius IX from publishing the Syllabus. During the Council he was a leading spokesman of the Minority group, but he accepted the Council's decisions in Aug. 1870. In 1882 he was named tit. Abp. of Lepanto. *Cath* 8 (1979) 435-439. *124-125, 296[70]*

MARIANA, Juan de (1536-1624), Spanish Jesuit theologian and historian (called the 'Spanish Livy'), lectured on theology in Rome (1561), Sicily (1564), and Paris (1569), preached in Italy, France, and Flanders. He later returned to Toledo and devoted himself to writing (1574). *JL*, cols. 1163-1165. *48, 252*

MARINI, Gaetano Luigi (1740-1815), Italian epigraphist, archivist, and archaeologist, coadjutor (1772) and prefect (1782) of the Vatican Archives, head custodian of the Vatican Library (1800). *EC* 8 (1952) 158. *251*

MARINI, Marino (1783-1855), Italian archivist, succeeded his uncle Gaetano Marini as prefect of the Vatican Archives (1814). Through his efforts (1815-17) the papal archives were returned to Rome from Paris, where they had been deported under Napoleon (1810). CHADWICK, *Catholicism*, pp. 14-38. *163[10]*

MARTENSEN, Hans Lassen (1808-84), Danish Lutheran theologian, prof. of systematic theology in Copenhagen (1840), court preacher (1845), Bp. of Seeland (1854). *RE* 12 (1903) 373-379. *215, 248, 262*

MARY STUART (1542-87), Queen of Scotland (1543-67). *147*

MARY TUDOR (1516-58), Queen of England (1553). *258*

MAXIMILIAN I (1756-1825), Elector of Bavaria as Maximilian IV Joseph (1799), crowned himself King of Bavaria (1806). He concluded a treaty with Austria (1813), joined the German League (1815), sealed a concordat with Rome (1817), and approved a liberal constitution for Bavaria (1808, 1818). *ADB* 21 (1885) 31-39. *152*

MAXIMILIAN II (1811-64), King of Bavaria (1848). Regarding the German Question he defended the idea of a 'triad', *viz.* the establishment of a league of smaller German states under Bavarian leadership to balance the strength of Prussia and Austria. After 1850 he leaned more toward Austria. In Bavaria he introduced a number of liberalizing reforms and encouraged the arts and sciences. *ADB* 21 (1885) 39-53. *32, 35-36, 47, 123, 148*

MELANCHTHON, Philipp (1497-1560), German humanist and Reformer. *192*

MELCHERS, Paul Ludolf (1813-95), Bp. of Osnabrück (1857), Abp. of Cologne (1866), and president of the German bishops' conference at Fulda (1867-85). At the Council he defended the inopportunist viewpoint, but later he was the first of the German

Minority bishops to subscribe to the Vatican decrees. During the *Kulturkampf* he was imprisoned for 6 months (1874) and then left Germany to govern his diocese from Maastricht (Netherlands). In 1885 he resigned his see at Leo XIII's request to facilitate a settlement of the *Kulturkampf*. He was created cardinal and went to Rome, where he entered the Jesuit order (1892). GATZ, pp. 493-497. *93*

MEYER, Heinrich August Wilhelm (1800-73), German Protestant N.T. scholar, superintendent in Hoya (1837), member of the consistory in Hanover (1841). After his retirement (1865) he devoted himself to his exegetical work. *RE* 13 (1903) 39-42. *91, 205*

MEYER, Fräulein, German actress. *98*

MEYRICK, Frederick (1827-1906), Anglican theologian, studied at Trinity College, Oxford, where he was elected fellow in 1847. In 1853 he was one of the founders of the Anglo-Continental Society, of which he served as secretary for 46 years. In 1852 he was ordained priest, became tutor of Trinity College, and actively participated in discussions on university reform. In 1859 he was named inspector of schools, and in 1868 he became rector of Blickling. From 1868 until 1885 he was examining chaplain to Chr. Wordsworth, Bp. of Lincoln, and non-residentiary canon of Lincoln. He visited Döllinger during his period of excommunication and was involved in organizing the Bonn Reunion Conferences. *DNB 1901-1911* 1 (1912) 617-618. *21, 100-101, 112, 127, 130-131, 134*

MIALL, Edward (1809-81), English M.P. (1852-57, 1869-74), opponent of the Established Church. *DNB* 13 (1909) 324-326. *167*

MICHAUD, Philibert Eugène (1839-1917), French theologian. After a short stay with the Dominicans, he became a secular priest at St. Roch in Paris, and later was vicar in the Madeleine. In 1867 he was promoted under Döllinger in theology *in absentia*. In 1872 he left the R.C. Church and tried to organize the Old Catholic Church in Paris. He took part in the Congress at Cologne (1872) and the Reunion Conferences at Bonn. In 1876 he was named prof. of dogmatic theology and Church history in the Bern theological faculty. In Sept. of that year, he was appointed vicar-general for French Switzerland, but in 1878 Bp. Herzog removed him from this position. Michaud published numerous books and polemical writings in which he praised increasingly liberal positions. He was a friend of A. Kiréeff and sympathized with the Eastern Churches. In 1880 he became a correspondent to the Russian ministry of education, and in 1889 prof. of French literature in Bern. From 1893 to 1910 he edited the *RIT*. *Zeitschrift für schweizerische Kirchengeschichte* 58 (1964) 177-204. *80, 101, 105, 118, 146, 289²⁰*

MICHELET, Jules (1798-1874), French historian, taught at the École normale supérieure (1827), head of the historical section of the national Record Office (1831), prof. at the Sorbonne (1832) and the Collège de France (1838-52). *Cath* 9 (1982) 117-119. *262*

MIGNET, François Auguste Marie (1796-1884), French historian, archivist at the foreign ministry (1830), member (1832) and permanent secretary (1837) of the Académie des sciences morales et politiques, member of the French Academy (1836). MOURRE, p. 1377. *177*

MILL, John Stuart (1806-73), British empiricist philosopher and political economist, who systematized the utilitarianism of Jeremy Bentham. He was an employee of the East India Co. (1823-58) and a M.P. for Westminster (1865-68). *DNB* 13 (1909) 390-399. *75*

MINGHETTI, Marco (1818-86), Italian statesman and economist, minister of public works in the Papal States (1848), soon resigned after Pius IX took a distance from the Italian struggle for freedom. In 1859 Cavour appointed him secretary general of the foreign office in Piedmont-Sardinia. In 1860 he was appointed minister of interior and in 1862, finance minister. As prime minister of Italy he sealed the September Convention (1864) which aimed at a regulation of the Roman Question. In exchange for the withdrawal of French troops from Rome, Minghetti was prepared to move the capital to Florence. He soon resigned as a result of protest against this measure. Form 1873 to 1876 he was again prime minister of the last moderate liberal cabinet of the 'historic Right'. *EC* 8 (1952) 1025-1026. *37, 83, 119, 290*[27]

MÖHLER, Johann Adam (1796-1838), German theologian and Church historian, representative of the Catholic Tübingen School, prof. of Church history in Tübingen (1828) and Munich (1835), Dean of Würzburg Cathedral (1838). His *Gesammelte Schriften und Aufsätze* were edited by Döllinger (1839-40). FRIES-SCHWAIGER II, pp. 70-98. *248*

MOMMSEN, Christian Matthias Theodor (1817-1903), leading German historian, jurist, and philologist, prof. of law in Leipzig (1848), Zurich (1852), and Breslau (1854), member of the Prussian Academy (1858), and prof. of ancient history in Berlin (1861). He was also deputy in the Prussian *Landtag* (1863-66, 1873-79) and in the German *Reichstag* (1881-84). *BWDG*, cols. 1925-1926. *51*

MONACO LA VALLETTA, Raffaele (1827-96), Italian cardinal (1868), vicar of Rome (1876), and abbot of Subiaco (1873-84). *Hierarchia*, p. 18. *222*

MONTALEMBERT, Charles René Forbes, comte de (1810-70), French publicist, politician, and historian. He worked to spread liberal Catholicism in France as contributor to *L'Avenir* (1830) and, after his break with Lamennais, to *L'Univers religieux* (1833). As member of the House of Peers (1831) he defended the freedom of religion and education. After the Revolution of 1848, he became a representative of the Assembly where, under Napoleon III, he belonged to the opposition (1851-57). He later fought the absolutism of the Second Empire as member of the French Academy (1851) and as editor of *Le Correspondant* (1855). His plea for "L'Église libre dans l'État libre", uttered at the Congress of Belgian Catholics at Malines (1863), elicited strong reactions in ultramontane circles and in Rome. He was Döllinger's friend from 1832. *DTC* 10/2 (1929) 2344-2355; *Tables*, col. 3246. *250, 255-256, 260, 261, 312*[52]

MONTEZ, Lola, stage name of Marie Dolores Eliza Rosanna Gilbert (1818-61), Irish dancer and adventuress. *DNB* 7 (1908) 1210-1212. *72-73, 288*[3]

MOZART, Wolfgang Amadeus (1756-91), Austrian composer. *154*

MOZLEY, James Bowling (1813-78), Canon of Worcester. He was educated at Oriel College, Oxford, and became fellow at Magdalen in 1840. He was actively involved in the Oxford Movement but modified his views after the Gorham case (1847-50). In 1847 he was elected M.P. for Oxford University, and in 1869 became Canon of Worcester. He was Regius prof. of divinity at Oxford from 1871 until his death. *DNB* 13 (1909) 1146-1148. *22, 173, 175, 257*

MÜLLER, Friedrich Max (1823-1900), German orientalist and linguist, one of the founders of the modern comparative study of religion, lived in England from 1846. In 1850 he was appointed associate prof. and in 1854 full Taylorian prof. of modern European languages at Oxford. He was named a member of Christ Church in 1851 and obtained a life fellowship from All Souls in 1858. In 1868 he was appointed prof. of comparative philology. From 1875 he devoted himself completely to editing the *Sacred Books of the East*, a 51 vols. series translating Eastern non-Christian religious literature. *DNB* 22 (1909) 1023-1029. *19, 65, 74, 153*

MÜLLER, Ludwig August v. (1846-95), Bavarian politician and jurist, cabinet secretary of

Finally Overbeck's plans to create a Western Orthodox rite failed, probably because of the opposition of the Patriarchate of Constantinople. His proposals, delivered in a petition in 1869, were definitively rejected by the Synod at St. Petersburg in 1892. KAHLE, pp. 10-30. *140-141, 142. 146, 297*[2]

OXENHAM, Henry Nutcombe (1829-88), English theologian, studied at Harrow and Balliol College, Oxford. In 1854 he was ordained priest in the Church of England, but in 1857 he converted to the R.C. Church. He received the minor orders, but his ordination to the priesthood was not taken into consideration because of his attacks on the seminary system. He joined the professorial staff of St. Edmund's College, Ware, and was later appointed master at the Oratory school in Birmingham. In 1863 Acton sent him to Germany to study under Döllinger. Oxenham was one of the founders of the Society for the Promotion of the Unity of Christendom (1857). He maintained good relations with members of the Church of England throughout his life. He was involved in the first discussions on rapprochement with the Old Catholics but later would distance himself from the movement. *DNB* 15 (1909) 13-15. *25*[11], *103. 107, 246, 247*

PALMER, William (1803-85), Tractarian theologian, fellow of Worcester College, Oxford (1831), vicar in Witchurch, Dorset (1846), and prebendary of Highworth (1849-58). In his *Treatise of the Church of Christ* (1838) he developed the 'Branch theory' to defend the position of the Church of England. *DNB* 15 (1909) 168-170. *99*[9], *209*

PALOMBA-CARACCIOLA, Joseph, Ritter v., secretary of the Austro-Hungarian diplomatic mission in Rome. *186*

PANTALEONI, Diomede (1810-85), Italian physician and politician, representative in the Roman Parliament (1848), where he repeatedly took part in the discussions concerning the Pope's flight from Rome. In 1861 Cavour commissioned him, together with C. Passaglia, to convince Pius IX to cede his temporal power. When his mission failed, Pantaleoni left Rome and settled in Paris, where he continued to seek a diplomatic solution for the Roman Question. In 1873 he became a senator. *EC* 9 (1952) 684. *40, 52*

PARKER, Matthew (1504-75), Abp. of Canterbury (1559). *107, 290*[25]

PASCAL, Blaise (1623-62), French scientist, religious and philosophical writer. *251*

PAUL III (1468-1549), Alessandro Farnese, Pope from 1534. *176*

PAUL IV (1476-1559), Gian Pietro Carafa, Pope from 1555. *167*

PAYNE SMITH, Robert (1819-95), Dean of Canterbury (1870), Regius prof. of divinity at Oxford (1865-71), member of the O.T. Revision Committee (1870-85). *DNB* 15 (1909) 570-572. *160, 299*[26]

PECCI, Giuseppe (1807-90), Leo XIII's brother, member of the Jesuit order (1824), taught philosophy in Perugia. In 1848 he left the Jesuits and in 1861 became lecturer of philosophy at the University of Rome. In 1870 he lost the chair because he refused to swear allegiance to the Italian government. In 1879 he was created cardinal, appointed vice-librarian of the Roman Church, and later prefect of the Vatican Archives. He was also chosen president of the Accademia romana di S. Tommaso d'Aquino. He returned to the Jesuit order in 1889. He contributed to the composition and practical application of the encyclical *Aeterni Patris* (1879). *EC* 9 (1952) 1041-1042. *190, 202*

PECCI, Vincenzo Gioacchino, *see* LEO XIII

PEEL, Sir Robert, 2nd Baronet (1788-1850), British statesman, founder of the Conservative party, M.P. from 1809. He was under-secretary for war and colonies (1810), chief secretary for Ireland (1812), and chairman of the currency committee (1819). As home secretary (1822-27, 1828-30) he introduced the Catholic Emancipation Bill (1829). He was prime minister in 1834-35 and 1841-46. *DNB* 15 (1909) 655-669. *119*

PETAVIUS, Dionysius, latinized name of Denys Petau (1583-1652), French Jesuit theologian and patrologist, prof. of positive theology (1621) and librarian (1644) at the Collège de Clermont in Paris. In his *Dogmatica theologica* (1644-50) he traced the continuity of the Church's doctrine to its sources in Scripture and Tradition. *DTC* 12/1 (1933) 1313-1337. *253*

PHILARET DROZDOV, b. Vasily Mikhailovich Drozdov (1782-1867), Metropolitan of Moscow. He was prof. of philosophy and theology (1808) and later rector (1812) of the Ecclesiastical Academy of St. Petersburg. He was elected Abp. of Tver and member of the Holy Synod (1819), transferred to the See of Jaroslav (1820), and a year later chosen as Abp. of Moscow. His *Christian Catechism of the Orthodox Catholic Eastern Greco-Russian Church* (1823) exercised widespread influence on 19th-cent. Russian theology. *DTC* 12/1 (1933) 1376-1395. *107*

PHILIP (1504-67), landgrave of Hesse (1509), confidant of Luther. *255*

PHILIP II (1527-98), King of Spain and Naples (1556), King of Portugal (1580). *56, 120-121, 179*

PHILIP IV THE FAIR (1268-1314), King of France (1285). *205*

PICCIRILLO, Carlo (1821-88), Italian Jesuit (1835), taught in Salerno, Benevento, and Naples, editor of *Civiltà Cattolica* (1852-76), later moved to the USA, where he was named prof. of Canon law, Church history, and Scripture, and prefect of studies at Woodstock. *Bibliothèque de la Compagnie de Jésus*, new ed. by C. SOMMERVOGEL, vol. VI, Brussels/Paris, 1895, cols. 698-699. *49*[29]

PICHLER, Aloys (1833-74), German R.C. Church historian, lecturer, and vicar of St. Cajetan (1863), associate member of the Bavarian Academy (1868). He was appointed librarian in St. Petersburg (1869), condemned to a Siberian exile for stealing books (1871), but later pardoned through the intervention of Prince Luitpold of Bavaria (1874). *ADB* 26 (1888) 103-104. *30*[13]

PITRA, Jean-Baptiste François (1812-89), French Benedictine scholar, created cardinal (1863), Librarian of the Roman Church (1869), Bp. of Frascati (1879), Bp. of Porto and S. Rufina (1884). He published important works on Christian archaeology, history of Church music, and Eastern Canon law. *DTC* 12/2 (1935) 2238-2245. *201, 202*

PIUS V, St. (1504-72), Antonio Michele Ghislieri, Pope from 1566. *36, 46*

PIUS VII (1740-1823), Barnaba Gregorio Chiaramonti, Pope from 1800. *46, 66, 92, 129, 150*[4]

PIUS IX (1792-1878), Giovanni Maria Mastai Ferretti, Abp. of Spoleto (1827), Bp. of Imola (1832), created cardinal (1840), elected Pope on June 16, 1846. In 1848, when Italian revolutionaries sieged the Quirinal, he fled to Gaeta where he called upon the European powers to reinstall the Papal States. When he returned to Rome (1850), he had abandoned his liberal ideas. His pontificate was characterized by the international expansion of the R.C. Church, the promotion of devotion, a distrust of modern thinking, and an increasing ecclesiastical centralization culminating in the procla-mation of papal primacy and infallibility at the Vatican Council. After Victor Emmanuel's occupation of Rome (1870), he considered himself prisoner of the Vatican. *NCE* 11 (1967) 405-408. *4, 5, 6, 11-12, 34, 36*[16]*, 37, 40, 48-49, 50, 52, 53, 54, 56, 64, 65, 66, 83, 87, 90, 91, 107, 119, 124-125, 126, 151*[5]*, 156-157, 163-164, 166, 173, 186, 190, 197-198, 202, 214, 221, 231, 258*[32]*, 260, 265, 266, 274*[3]*, 275*[12]*, 280*[47]*, 285*[85]*, 303*[66]*, 308*[14-16]

PLACE, Charles Philippe (1814-93), Bp. of Marseilles (1866), opponent of papal infallibility due to his Gallican tendencies. He refused appointments as Abp. of Lyons and coadjutor to Abp. Guibert of Paris. In 1878 he was named Abp. of Rennes and in 1886, created cardinal. *EC* 9 (1952) 1596-1597. *80, 289*[19]

PLANCK, Johann Julius Wilhelm (1817-1900), German jurist, prof. of law in Basel (1842), Greifswald (1845), Kiel (1850), and Munich (1867-95), member of the Bavarian Academy (1881). *EI* 27 (1935) 475-476. *65*

PLATEN-HALLERMÜNDE, August, Graf v. (1796-1835), German poet and dramatist, studied in Würzburg (1818) and Erlangen (1819), moved to Italy (1826) where he lived in Florence, Rome and Naples. *ADB* 26 (1888) 244-249. *161*[7]

PLITT, Gustav Leopold (1836-80), German Protestant Church historian, prof. of theology in Erlangen (1867). *ADB* 26 (1888) 304-307. *178, 204*

PLUMMER, Alfred (1841-1926). *XXIV-XXV*; N.T. commentator, *XXXVII-XLVI*; visits to Döllinger in Munich, (1870) *3-17*, (1871) *19-24*, (1872) *25-76*, (1873) *77-98*, (1875) *117-126*, (1876) *146-159*, (1877) *160-168*, (1880) *188-195*, (1882) *196-199*, (1886) *209-218*, (1889) *219-226*, at Tegernsee, (1878) *169-180*, (1879) *181-187*, (1883) *200-205*; at the Reunion Conferences in Bonn, (1874) *99-116*, (1875) *126-145*; visit to Ch. Loyson in Paris (1872), *25, 278*[34]; to F. H. Reusch in Bonn (1890), *233-236*; to Döllinger's nieces in Munich (1890), *236-240*; works, *XLVIII-LI*; *Recollections of Dr Döllinger* (1890), *231, 239, 240, 241, 242, 243, 245*; articles in *The Churchman*, *45*[25], *243*, in *The Critical Review*, *241, 264-267*

PLUMMER, Bertha Katharine, *née* Everest, married A. Plummer on Dec. 29, 1874. *116, 117-127, 133, 134, 142, 145, 146-152, 154, 158-159, 160-166, 169-171, 173-180, 187, 188-191, 195, 196-197, 199, 200-201, 203, 204-205, 209, 219-220, 223-225, 233, 236-240, 247*[12]

PLUMMER, Harold (b. 1879), A. Plummer's son. *187, 188*

PLUMMER, Matthew, A. Plummer's father. *204*

POEZL, Joseph v. (1814-81), German jurist, prof. of law in Würzburg (1845) and Munich (1847), member of the Frankfurt Parliament (1848), the Bavarian House of Representatives (1858-69), and the *Reichstag* (1872). *ADB* 26 (1888) 495-497. *65, 71*

PONTE, José Antonio (1832-83), Venezuelan cleric, prof. of theology at the seminary (1869) and the university (1872) of Caracas, Abp. of Caracas (1876). *Hierarchia*, p. 315. *148*[3], *297*[9]

POTTER, Henry Codman (1835-1908), American Episcopal priest (1858), rector of St. John's Church, Troy, N.Y. (1859), assistant minister of Trinity Church, Boston (1866), and rector of Grace Church, New York (1868). From 1866 until 1883 he was secretary for the House of Bishops of the General Convention, and it was in this capacity that he attended the Reunion Conference at Bonn (1875). In 1883 he was elected assistant Bp. of New York, assuming the factual administration of the diocese in place of his uncle, Bp. Horatio Potter, who had retired from active work. *DAB* 15 (1935) 127-129. *126*

PRESSENSÉ, Edmond Dehault de (1824-91), French politician and Protestant minister, vicar of the independent community of the Chapelle Taitbout in Paris (1847), founder of the *Revue Chrétienne* (1854), member of the National Assembly (1871-76) and senator for life (1883). *RE* 16 (1905) 20-25. *58, 284*[81]

PUSEY, Edward Bouverie (1800-82), Anglican theologian and High Churchman, elected fellow of Oriel College, Oxford, in 1823. In 1825-27 he studied biblical criticism and oriental languages in Germany, and in 1828 he became prof. of Hebrew and Canon of Christ Church in Oxford. He was one of the leading personalities in the Oxford Movement and after Newman's departure (1845), gave a more ritualistic direction to the movement. He repeatedly opposed the spread of liberalism in the Church, e.g. via his reaction against the *Essays and Reviews* (1860), his accusations against B. Jowett (1862), and his efforts to retain the Athanasian Creed. His expectations regarding an approach to the R.C. Church, written in 3 stages in his *Eirenicon* (1865, 1869, 1870), were dashed by the definition of papal infallibility. *DNB* 16 (1909) 496-504. *3, 14, 22, 34, 41, 118, 122, 146, 149, 152-153, 175, 213, 217, 254-255, 294*[59]*, 295*[66]*, 298*[15]

PUTTKAMER, Robert v. (1828-1900), Prussian statesman, president of Gumbinnen (1871), Metz (1875), and Silesia (1877), minister of public worship (1879), minister of interior and vice-president of the ministry of state (1881-88), president of Pomerania (1891-99). *BWDG*, cols. 2231-2232. *183*

RAMPF, Michael v. (1825-1901), German R.C. prelate, president and prof. of pastoral theology at the seminary of Freising (1855), vicar-general in Munich (1874), Bp. of Passau (1889). GATZ, pp. 592-593. *60*[35]

RAMSAY, Andrew Michael (1686-1743), Scottish writer, converted to the R.C. Church on Fénelon's persuasion (1710), and lived with him until Fénelon's death (1715). *DNB* 16 (1909) 681-682. *251*

RAMSAY, Edward Bannerman (1793-1872), Dean of Edinburgh (1841), wrote *Reminiscences of Scottish Life and Character* (1858). *DNB* 16 (1909) 684-685. *180*

RANKE, Leopold v. (1795-1886), German historian, the leading exponent of historicism, prof. of history in Berlin (1825-71), official Prussian historiographer (1841), and member of the Munich Historical Commission (1857). His History of the Popes was placed on the Index (1841). *ADB* 27 (1888) 242-269. *79, 252, 253, 255*

RAYNAUD, Théophile (1583-1663), French Jesuit theologian, taught philosophy and theology in Lyons (1615-31), later displeased both Richelieu and Urban VIII by refusing their request to author certain polemical works. *DTC* 13/2 (1937) 1823-1829. *252*

RAYNOUARD, François Juste Marie (1761-1836), French writer, philologist, and jurist, founder of the study of Old-Occitanian language and literature, member of the Legislative Assembly (1793-1813), member (1807) and secretary (1817-29) of the French Academy. *GE* 28 (n.d.) 1915. *177*[17]

REINKENS, Joseph Hubert (1821-96), first Bp. of the German Old Catholic Church. He studied philosophy and theology in Bonn, was ordained priest in 1848, and earned his doctorate in theology at Munich in 1849. In 1853 he was appointed prof. of Church history in Breslau. During the academical year 1867-68 he took a sabbatical, met Döllinger in Munich, and went to Rome, where he spent 4 months. Because of his opposition to papal infallibility, he was suspended in 1870 and excommunicated in 1872. He took part in the Old Catholic Congresses at Munich (1871) and Cologne (1872). He was elected Bp. of the German Old Catholic Church on June 4, 1872, and consecrated on Aug. 11, 1873, in Rotterdam by Bp. H. Heykamp of Deventer. He remained in contact with Döllinger, taking part in both Reunion Conferences at Bonn (1874-75). *RE* 16 (1905) 580-584. *100, 101, 104-105, 106, 107, 109, 110, 112, 115, 116, 127, 140, 144, 172, 198, 301*[45,46]

REISACH, Karl August, Graf v. (1800-69), Bp. of Eichstätt (1836), Abp. of Munich and Freising (1846), a strong proponent of the Church's freedom from the State. In 1855 he was transferred to Rome as curial cardinal as compensation for concessions made by King Maximilian II to the Bavarian hierarchy. He became member of various congregations and minister of education in the Papal States. From 1865 he was actively involved in the preparations of the Council, and in 1869 he was named first president of the Council, but he died before he could fulfill this function. GATZ, pp. 603-606. *36, 258*[32]

RENAN, Joseph Ernest (1823-92), French philosopher and historian of religions, received a seminary training but broke with the Church in 1845. In 1860-61 he carried out archaeological research in the Near East, and in 1862 he was named prof. of Hebrew at the Collège de France, but his teaching was immediately suspended because of his disputed remarks on the figure of Jesus. Ecclesiastical protest was exacerbated after the publication of his famous *Vie de Jésus* (1863). He was rehabilitated in 1870, became member of the French Academy in 1878, and administrator of the Collège de France in 1883. MOURRE, pp. 1801-1802. *94, 256*

REUSCH, Franz Heinrich (1825-1900), German theologian, studied in Bonn (1843), Tübingen (1845), and Munich (1846-47), entered the seminary in Cologne (1848), and was ordained R.C. priest in 1849. From 1849 until 1853 he was chaplain at St. Alban's in Cologne. In 1858 he was named prof. of O.T. exegesis in Bonn. From 1866 until 1877 he was editor of the *Theologisches Literaturblatt*. After his excommunication (1872), he became priest of the Old Catholic community in Bonn, vicar-general to Bp. Reinkens, and prof. of theology in Bern. In 1878, when mandatory celibacy for priests was abolished, he resigned his position. In the first half of his career he published works mainly concerning O.T. subjects; after joining the Old Catholic Church, he devoted himself to the history of the post-Reformation R.C. Church. *NCE* 12 (1967) 435-436. *100, 114, 172, 225, 229-232, 233-236, 240-244, 245-246, 265, 301*[46], *311*[39]

RHOSSIS, Zicos (1838-1933), Greek Orthodox theologian and philosopher, studied in Athens and from 1863, in Halle, Berlin, and Leipzig, where he obtained a doctorate in philosophy in 1866. He became prof. at the Rizarion seminary and lecturer in homiletics and introduction to theology at the theological faculty in Athens, where in 1875 he was appointed full prof. of dogmatics, Christian ethics, and introduction to theology. He resigned his chair at the university in 1911 and his post at the seminary in 1913. He attended the Old Catholic Congress at Freiburg (1874). His reports to the Synod on the Bonn Reunion Conferences were published in 1874 and 1876. Later he wrote several works on the relations between the Orthodox and Old Catholic Churches, in which, under J.J. Overbeck's influence, he took a less flexible stance towards the Old Catholics. His best-known work is the apologetical *Dogmatic System of the Orthodox Catholic Church* (1903). *Thrèskeutikè* 16 (1967) 973-976. *106, 110, 112, 133, 140*

RIARIO SFORZA, Sisto (1810-77), Italian prelate, Bp. of Aversa (1845), Abp. of Naples (1845), created cardinal (1846). From 1861 to 1866 he lived in exile in Civitavecchia. *EC* 10 (1953) 846-847. *90, 164*

RICCI, Lorenzo (1703-75), Italian Jesuit, elected 18th General of the Jesuit order (1758). *JL*, cols. 1535-1539. *46*

RICCIO (or Rizzio), David (*c.* 1533-66), born in Turin, secretary to Mary Stuart. *147*

RIEDEL, Valentin v. (1802-57), German prelate, director and prof. of pastoral theology and pedagogy at the seminary of Freising (1838), Bp. of Ratisbon (1842). GATZ, pp. 616-617. *36*

RIEHL, Wilhelm Heinrich (1823-97), German historian and writer, one of the founding fathers of modern study of folklore, worked as a journalist in Frankfurt, Karlsruhe, Wiesbaden, and Augsburg. In 1859 he was appointed prof. of history of culture and statistics in Munich, and in 1885 was named director of the Bavarian National Museum and general curator of the Kunstdenkmähler und Altertümer Bayerns. *ADB* 53 (1907) 362-383. *92, 93, 96*

Rio, Alexis-François (1797-1874), French writer and art critic, taught history at the Lycée Louis-le-Grand in Paris (1819), secretary in the ministry of foreign affairs in Rome (1830), prof. of history of art at the Sorbonne (1858). He visited Döllinger many times in 1830-69. Lösch, pp. 24-44. *249*[17]

Ritschl, Albrecht Benjamin (1822-89), German Protestant theologian, founder of *Kulturprotestantismus*, prof. of theology in Bonn (1851) and Göttingen (1864). *RE* 17 (1906) 22-34. *254*

Robespierre, Maximilien Marie Isidore de (1758-94), French Jacobine leader. *47*

Rosmini-Serbati, Antonio, conte di (1797-1855), Italian philosopher and liberal Catholic theologian, founder of the *Istituto della Carità* (1828). As Pius IX's adviser, he fled with him to Gaeta (1848) where he lost the Pope's favour and retired to Stresa. His works were put on the Index but later dismissed without censure (1854). Posthumously 40 propositions taken from his works were condemned under Leo XIII (1887-88). *DTC* 13/2 (1937) 2917-2952. *30*

Rothe, Richard (1799-1867), German Lutheran theologian, most important representative of the *Vermittlungstheologie*, prof. of theology in Heidelberg (1837-49, 1854-67), and Bonn (1849-54). *RE* 17 (1906) 169-178. *253*

Ruffo Scilla, Luigi, jr. (1840-95), Italian prelate, Abp. of Chieti and Vasto (1877), nuncio in Munich (1887), created cardinal (1891). *EC* 10 (1953) 1436. *231-232, 236, 265, 267, 287*[89], *311*[39]

Ruskin, John (1819-1900), English art critic and social reformer, Slade prof. of fine arts at Oxford (1870-79, 1883-84), champion of the Gothic Revival Movement in architecture, opponent of the laissez-faire economic policy of his days. *DNB* 22 (1909) 1177-1199. *193, 251*

Rymer, Frederick, English R.C. priest, prefect of studies (1857), vice-president (1861), and president (1868-70) of St. Edmund's College, Ware. Cwiekowski, pp. 286-289. *189, 304*[71]

Saccarelli, Gaspare (1723-1803), Italian Oratorian, librarian of the Bibliotheca Vallicelliana, published a 26 vols. Latin course of ecclesiastical history (1771). *EC* 10 (1953) 1524. *251*

Said Pasha, Mohammed (1822-63), 3rd Ottoman viceroy of Egypt (1854). *GE* 29 (n.d.) 171-172. *212, 307*[7]

Salisbury, Robert Arthur Talbot Gascoyne-Cecil, 3rd Marquis of (1830-1903), English statesman, secretary of state for India (1866-67, 1874-78), leader of the Conservatives (1881), prime minister (1885-86, 1886-92, 1895-1902), foreign secretary (1878-80, 1885-86, 1887-92, 1895-1900). After Bismarck's retirement he dominated European politics. *DNB 1901-1911* 1 (1912) 329-343. *181-182*

Salmon, George (1819-1904), Irish mathematician and theologian, student (1831) and fellow (1841) of Trinity College, Dublin. After his ordination (1845) he participated in the work of the Divinity School of Trinity. He was Donegal lecturer of mathematics (1848-66), Regius prof. of divinity (1866), and later provost of Trinity College (1888). He also held the position of examining chaplain to Abp. Whateley (1852) and took part in the reconstruction of the Irish Church after disestablishment (1870). *DNB 1901-1911* 3 (1912) 251-254. *87, 223, 305*[77]

Salmond, Stewart Dingwall Fordyce (1838-1905), Scottish Protestant theologian, assistant prof. of Greek in Aberdeen, minister of the Free Church of Barry, Forfarshire, prof. of systematic theology and exegesis (1876) and principal (1898) at the United Free Church College, Aberdeen. *Who was Who* 1 ([5]1966) 623. *241*[8]

SANDFORD, Charles Waldegrave (1828-1903), Bp. of Gibraltar. He was tutor, senior censor, and proctor of Christ Church, Oxford, preacher at Whitehall (1862-64), examining chaplain and commissary to the Abp. of Canterbury (1868-73), rector of Bishopsbourne, Kent (1870-74), and rural dean of Bridge (1872-74). In 1874 he was appointed Bp. of Gibraltar by diploma, and also Bp. of the British Congregations in Malta, Southern and Eastern Europe, Anatolia, and the seaboard of North Africa. *Who was Who* 1 (^{5}1966) 625. *127, 130, 133-134, 144*

SAVIGNY, Friedrich Karl v. (1779-1861), German jurist, founder of the German historical school of law, associate prof. of penal law in Marburg (1803), full prof. of Roman law in Landshut (1808) and Berlin (1810), head of the department for the revision of the Prussian statutes (1842-48). *ADB* 30 (1890) 425-452. *53[30], 84, 248*

SAVIGNY, Kunigunde v. (1780-1863), *née* Brentano, sister of Clemens and Bettina, married F. v. Savigny (1804). *53[30], 84*

SCHAFF, Philipp (1819-93), Swiss Protestant Church historian, studied in Tübingen, Halle, and Berlin. After his ordination (1844) he went to the USA where he was named prof. at the seminary of the German Reformed Church in Mercesburg, Pa. In 1870 he joined the Presbyterian Church and was appointed prof. at the Union Theological Seminary in New York. He played an important role in the development of American theology as organizer of various large theological projects and mediator between European theology and American scholarship. He was active in organizing the American branch of the Evangelical Alliance (1866) and in the formation of the Alliance of Reformed Churches (1875). *DAB* 16 (1935) 417-418. *44, 134*

SCHELLING, Friedrich Wilhelm Joseph v. (1775-1854), German philosopher, prof. in Jena (1798) and Würzburg (1803-06), member of the Bavarian Academy (1806), general secretary of the Academy of Plastic Arts in Munich (1807), lecturer in Erlangen (1820-26), prof. and president of the Bavarian Academy in Munich (1827), appointed prof. in Berlin to counteract the influence of Hegelian philosophy (1841). *ADB* 31 (1890) 6-27. *94, 95, 249*

SCHENKEL, Daniel (1813-85), Swiss Protestant theologian, prof. in Basel (1850) and Heidelberg (1851), co-founder of the *Protestantenverein* (1863), editor of the *Allgemeine kirchliche Zeitschrift* (1860-72). *RE* 17 (1906) 555-559. *72*

SCHERR, Gregor v. (1804-77), Abp. of Munich-Freising. He studied philosophy and theology in Landshut and Ratisbon, where he was ordained priest in 1829. After some years of pastoral ministry he entered the newly founded Benedictine abbey of Metten in 1832 and became abbot in 1840. In 1854 he played an important role in the foundation of the abbey of St. Bonifaz at Munich. In 1856 he was consecrated Abp. of Munich and Freising. During the Council he sided with those who opposed the definition of papal infallibility on principle. However, as early as Aug. 1870 he published *Pastor Aeternus* in his diocese for reasons of obedience. GATZ, pp. 654-656. *7, 9, 18, 22, 27, 28, 35-36, 45, 52, 59, 60-61, 149, 162, 265, 266, 267, 286[86]*

SCHILLER, Johann Christoph Friedrich v. (1759-1805), German dramatist, poet, and literary theorist. *147*

SCHLEIERMACHER, Friedrich Daniel Ernst (1768-1834), German Protestant theologian and philosopher, 'Church Father of the 19th century'. *248*

SCHMID, Alois v. (1825-1910), German R.C. theologian and philosopher, prof. of philosophy in Dillingen (1853), prof. of dogmatics (1866-94) and apologetics (1866-1903) in Munich. *LTK* 9 (1964) 432. *155*

SCHOTTMÜLLER, Conrad (1841-94), German historian, secretary of the Prussian Historical Institute in Rome (1881-90). *219-220, 308[12]*

Serbia (1851), played a central role in the cultural and political life of Croatia. During the Council he fought against the definition of papal infallibility because he feared that it would make reunion with the Slavic Churches impossible. After the Council he continued to oppose the dogma for a long time and maintained contact with the Old Catholics who tried in vain to win him for their cause. Finally, under Leo XIII, he demonstrated his unequivocal acceptance of the dogma. *Neue Österreichische Biographie* 9 (1956) 73-83. *20, 186, 198, 286*[87], *303*[66], *304*[67]

STUBBS, William (1825-1901), English Church historian, librarian at Lambeth (1862), Regius prof. of modern history at Oxford (1866), later Bp. of Chester (1884), and Oxford (1888). He founded the systematic study of English mediaeval constitutional history. *DNB 1901-1911* 3 (1912) 444-451. *26, 191*

SWALLOW, Mr., English translator. *246*

SYBEL, Heinrich v. (1817-95), German historian and politician, one of the leaders of the Prussian historical school, prof. of history in Bonn (1844), Marburg (1845), Munich (1856), and again, in Bonn (1861). He was secretary (1858) and president (1886) of the Historical Commission of the Bavarian Academy, founded the *Historische Zeitschrift* (1859), and was appointed director of the Prussian State Archives (1875). For several years he maintained a liberal seat in the Prussian House of Representatives. Opposed to the views of his teacher Ranke, he believed that the historian, through his work, must participate in political life. *ADB* 54 (1908) 645-667. *30, 40, 262*[37]

SYDOW, Karl Leopold Adolf (1800-82), German Protestant theologian, preacher in Potsdam (1836). After a stay in England, he defended freedom of confession in the Church, which brought him in conflict with King Friedrich Wilhelm IV (1846). Consequently, he was named pastor of the Neue Kirche in Berlin (1846-76). He was co-founder of the *Protestantenverein* (1863). *ADB* 37 (1894) 275-279. *84-85, 291*[29]

TAINE, Hippolyte Adolphe (1828-93), French philosopher, historian, and critic, prof. of aesthetics and history of art at the École des Beaux Arts in Paris (1864), member of the French Academy (1878). He gave up his professorship to write a History of France, in which he showed himself an opponent of the Revolution and an advocate of conservative power. *GE* 30 (n.d.) 881-883. *19, 174, 176-177*

TAIT, Archibald Campbell (1811-82), Anglican Broad Churchman, fellow and tutor of Balliol College, Oxford (1835), where in 1841 he protested against *Tract 90*. He later became headmaster of Rugby (1842), Dean of Carlisle (1849), Bp. of London (1856), and Abp. of Canterbury (1868). *DNB* 19 (1909) 292-299. *161*

TALBOT, Edward Stuart (1844-1934), Anglican divine, educated at Christ Church, Oxford. In 1870 he was ordained priest, and became the first warden of Keble College, Oxford. A moderate High Churchman, he contributed to *Lux Mundi* (1889). He was vicar of Leeds (1888) and later became Bp. of Rochester (1895), Southwark (1905), and Winchester (1911-24). *DNB 1931-1940* (1949) 844-845. *100, 105*

TATHAM, Edward (1749-1834), Anglican controversialist, rector of Lincoln College, Oxford (1792). *DNB* 19 (1909) 382-384. *55*

TATSCHALOFF, Arsenius, provost of the Russian Orthodox community in Wiesbaden. *111, 114*

TAUFFKIRCHEN-GUTTENBERG, Karl, Graf v. (1826-95), Bavarian diplomat, envoy in St. Petersburg and Stockholm (1867), to the Holy See (1869), in Stuttgart and Darmstadt (1874), and in Karlsruhe (1887). SCHÄRL, No. 663. *65*

THACKERAY, William Makepeace (1811-63), English novelist. *DNB* 19 (1909) 570-586. *302*[49]

THROCKMORTON, Miss, the daughter of Robert George Throckmorton, Acton's uncle. *182*

TISCHENDORF, Lobegott Friedrich Constantin v. (1815-74), German Protestant theologian and biblical text critic, nominally prof. of theology (1845) and biblical palaeography (1859) in Leipzig, gained fame for his discovery of the Codex Sinaiticus (1859; ed. 1862), and as editor of a standard critical edition of the N.T. (8th ed., 1869-72). *RE* 19 (1907) 788-797. *55, 253*

TOCQUEVILLE, Alexis Charles Henri Maurice Clérel, comte de (1805-59), French political scientist, historian, and politician, member of the French Academy (1841), member of the Chamber of Deputies (1839-48), and minister of foreign affairs (1849). He gave a perceptive description of American society in *De la démocratie en Amérique* (1835-40). MOURRE, pp. 2143-2144. *94*

TORQUEMADA, Juan de (1388-1468), Spanish Dominican theologian, *Magister Palatii* (1431), Eugenius IV's theologian at the Councils of Basel (1432-37) and Ferrara-Florence (1438-43), created cardinal (1439), appointed Bp. of Cádiz (1440), Orense (1442), Palestrina (1455), Sabina (1463), and León (1466). He defended papal supremacy in his influential *Summa de Ecclesia* (1448-49, printed 1480). *DTC* 15/1 (1946) 1235-1239. *82*

TOSTI, Luigi (1811-97), Italian Benedictine historian, lecturer (1834-42) and titular abbot (1858) of Montecassino, vice-archivist of the Vatican Archives (1879-91). He committed himself to a diplomatic solution of the Roman Question and the conciliation of Church and State in Italy. *EC* 12 (1954) 367-369. *252*

TRINDER, Daniel (1828-88), Anglican priest (1856), founder and principal of Probus School (1853-57), perpetual curate of St. Michael's, Highgate (1878), member of Hornsey School board and rural dean of Highgate (1887). BOASE VI, cols. 708-709. *108*

TRUMPP, Ernst (1828-85), German orientalist, lecturer of oriental languages in Tübingen (1873), member of the Bavarian Academy (1873), prof. of semitic languages in Munich (1874). His life work was the translation of the *Adi Granth*, the holy book of the Sikhs (1877). *ADB* 38 (1894) 687-689. *153, 154*

TÜRK, Ritter v. (1826-1912), Bavarian cleric, Dean of St. Cajetan, succeeded Döllinger as provost. *237*

TUIGG, John (1820-89), Irish-born R.C. Bp. of Pittsburgh (1876), administrator of the diocese of Allegheny (1877). *DAH*, pp. 285-286. *172*[13]

TZETZES, Greek student of philology in Munich. *88, 89-90, 91-92*

ULLATHORNE, William Bernard (1806-89), R.C. Bp. of Birmingham (1850), tit. Abp. of Cabasa (1888). At the Council he adopted a middle position. *DNB* 20 (1909) 19-21. *4*

URBAN VIII (1568-1644), Maffeo Barberini, Pope from 1623. *252*[21]

VANCE SMITH, George (*c*. 1816-1902), English Unitarian theologian. *9, 274*[9]

VEUILLOT, Louis (1813-83), French ultramontane journalist, editor of *L'Univers* (1843), which became the mouthpiece of those favouring infallibility during the Council. *DTC* 15/2 (1950) 2799-2835. *6*

VICTOR EMMANUEL II (1820-78), King of Sardinia-Piedmont (1849), first King of a united Italy (1861). *50, 121*

VICTORIA Adelaide Mary Louise (1840-1901), Princess Royal of Great Britain, married Prince Friedrich Wilhelm of Prussia (1858), German Empress and Queen of Prussia (1888). *DNB 1901-1911* 3 (1912) 560-568. *195*

VIGFÚSSON, Gutbrandr (1828-89), Icelandic scholar, research fellow in Copenhagen (1854-

and Abp. of Westminster. *NCE* 14 (1967) 976-977. *53, 55, 65-66, 245, 252, 275*[12], *283*[71], *284*[72]

WORDSWORTH, Christopher (1807-85), Bp. of Lincoln. He was a student and fellow of Trinity College, Cambridge, was ordained priest in 1835, and in 1836 became public orator in Cambridge and headmaster of Harrow. In 1844 he was named Canon of Westminster Abbey and in 1865 Archdeacon. He was consecrated Bp. of Lincoln in 1869. He was a conservative High Churchman and was sympathetic toward the Old Catholic Movement. He wrote a History of the Church until 451 (1881-83), an extensive commentary on the Bible (1856-70), and a collection of Church hymns, *The Holy Year* (1862). *DNB* 21 (1909) 924-926. *80, 95*[8], *99*[9], *122, 289*[18]

ZAHN, Theodor v. (1838-1933), German Protestant N.T. and patristic scholar, prof. in Göttingen (1871), Kiel (1877), Erlangen (1878), Leipzig (1888), and again, in Erlangen (1892-1909). *ODCC*, p. 1510. *204*

ZELLER, Eduard (1814-1908), German philosopher and Protestant theologian, lecturer of theology in Tübingen (1840), prof. of theology in Bern (1847) and Marburg (1849, later transferred to the faculty of philosophy), prof. of philosophy in Heidelberg (1862) and Berlin (1872-95). He was editor of the *Theologische Jahrbücher*, the organ of the Tübingen School (1842-57), and wrote an unsurpassed *Philosophie der Griechen* (1844-52). *RGG* 6 (1962) 1892. *154*

ZUMBUSCH, Julius (1832-1908), German sculptor, lived as a lay brother in the monastery of Altötting (1858-66), and then settled in Munich, where he worked esp. as a portrait-sculptor. THIEME-BECKER 36 (1947) 595-596. *239-240.*

INDEX OF SUBJECTS

BIBLIOTHECA EPHEMERIDUM THEOLOGICARUM LOVANIENSIUM

LEUVEN UNIVERSITY PRESS / UITGEVERIJ PEETERS LEUVEN

* Out of print

1. *Miscellanea dogmatica in honorem Eximii Domini J. Bittremieux*, 1947. 235 p. FB 450.
*2-3. *Miscellanea moralia in honorem Eximii Domini A. Janssen*, 1948.
*4. G. PHILIPS, *La grâce des justes de l'Ancien Testament*, 1948.
*5. G. PHILIPS, *De ratione instituendi tractatum de gratia nostrae sanctificationis*, 1953.
6-7. *Recueil Lucien Cerfaux*, 1954. 504 et 577 p. FB 800 par tome. Cf. *infra*, n° 18.
8. G. THILS, *Histoire doctrinale du mouvement œcuménique*. Nouvelle édition, 1963. 338 p. FB 135.
*9. J. COPPENS et al. *Études sur l'Immaculée Conception. Sources et sens de la doctrine*, 1955. 110 p.
*10. J.A. O'DONOHOE, *Tridentine Seminary Legislation. Its Sources and its Formation*, 1957.
*11. G. THILS, *Orientations de la théologie*, 1958.
*12-13. J. COPPENS, A. DESCAMPS, É. MASSAUX (éd), *Sacra Pagina, Miscellanea Biblica Congressus Internationalis Catholici de Re Biblica*, 1959.
*14. *Adrien VI, le premier Pape de la contre-réforme. Sa personnalité — sa carrière — son œuvre*, 1959.
*15. F. CLAEYS BOUUAERT, *Les déclarations et serments imposés par la loi civile aux membres du clergé belge sous le Directoire (1795-1801)*, 1960.
*16. G. THILS, *La « Théologie Œcuménique ». Notion-Formes-Démarches*, 1960.
17. G. THILS, *Primauté pontificale et prérogatives épiscopales. « Potestas ordinaria » au Concile du Vatican*, 1961. 104 p. FB 50.
*18. *Recueil Lucien Cerfaux*, t. III, 1961. Cf. *supra*, n°ˢ 6-7.
*19. *Foi et réflexion philosophique. Mélanges F. Grégoire*, 1961.
*20. *Mélanges G. Ryckmans*, 1963.
21. G. THILS, *L'infaillibilité du peuple chrétien « in credendo »*, 1963. 66 p. FB 50.
*22. J. FÉRIN et L. JANSSENS, *Progestogènes et morale conjugale*, 1963.
*23. *Collectanea Moralia in honorem Eximii Domini A. Janssen*, 1964.
24. H. CAZELLES (éd.), *L'Ancien Testament et son milieu d'après les études récentes. De Mari à Qumrân* (Hommage J. Coppens, I), 1969. 158*-370 p. FB 800.
25. I. DE LA POTTERIE (éd.). *De Jésus aux évangiles. Tradition et rédaction dans les évangiles synoptiques* (Hommage J. Coppens, II) 1967. 272 p. FB 600.

26. G. THILS et R.E. BROWN (éd.), *Exégèse et théologie* (Hommage J. Coppens, III), 1968. 328 p. FB 600.

27. J. COPPENS (éd.), *Ecclesia a Spiritu sancto edocta. Hommage à Mgr G. Philips*, 1970. 640 p. FB 580.

28. J. COPPENS (éd.), *Sacerdoce et Célibat. Études historiques et théologiques*, 1971. 740 p. FB 600.

29. M. DIDIER (éd.), *L'évangile selon Matthieu. Rédaction et théologie*, 1971. 432 p. FB 900.

*30. J. KEMPENEERS, *Le Cardinal van Roey en son temps*, 1971.

*31. F. NEIRYNCK, *Duality in Mark. Contributions to the Study of the Markan Redaction*, 1972.

*32. F. NEIRYNCK (éd.), *L'évangile de Luc. Problèmes littéraires et théologiques. Mémorial Lucien Cerfaux*, 1973.

*33. C. BREKELMANS (éd.), *Questions disputées d'Ancien Testament. Méthode et théologie*, 1974.

*34. M. SABBE (éd.), *L'évangile selon Marc. Tradition et rédaction*, 1974.

*35. *Miscellanea Albert Dondeyne. Godsdienstfilosofie. Philosophie de la religion*, 1974.

*36. G. PHILIPS, *L'union personnelle avec le Dieu vivant*, 1974.

37. F. NEIRYNCK, in collaboration with T. HANSEN and F. VAN SEGBROECK, *The Minor Agreements of Matthew and Luke against Mark with a Cumulative List*, 1974. 330 p. FB 800.

*38. J. COPPENS, *Le Messianisme et sa relève prophétique*, 1974.

39. D. SENIOR, *The Passion Narrative according to Matthew. A Redactional Study*, 1975; new impression, 1982. 440 p. FB 1000.

*40. J. DUPONT (éd.), *Jésus aux origines de la christologie*, 1975.

*41. J. COPPENS (éd.), *La notion biblique de Dieu*, 1976.

42. J. LINDEMANS – H. DEMEESTER (éd.), *Liber Amicorum Monseigneur W. Onclin*, 1976. 396 p. FB 900.

43. R.E. HOECKMAN (éd.), *Pluralisme et œcuménisme en recherches théologiques. Mélanges offerts au R.P. Dockx, O.P.*, 1976. 316 p. FB 900.

44. M. DE JONGE (éd.), *L'Évangile de Jean*, 1977. 416 p. FB 950.

45. E.J.M. VAN EIJL (éd.), *Facultas S. Theologiae Lovaniensis 1432-1797. Bijdragen tot haar geschiedenis. Contributions to its History. Contributions à son histoire*, 1977. 570 p. FB 1500.

46. M. DELCOR (éd.), *Qumrân. Sa piété, sa théologie et son milieu*, 1978. 432 p. FB 1550.

47. M. CAUDRON (éd.), *Faith and Society. Foi et Société. Geloof en maatschappij. Acta Congressus Internationalis Theologici Lovaniensis 1976*, 1978. 304 p. FB 1150.

48. J. KREMER (éd.), *Les Actes des Apôtres. Traditions, rédaction, théologie*, 1979. 590 p. FB 1600.

49. F. NEIRYNCK, avec la collaboration de J. DELOBEL, T. SNOY, G. VAN BELLE, F. VAN SEGBROECK, *Jean et les Synoptiques. Examen critique de l'exégèse de M.-É. Boismard*, 1979. XII-428 p. FB 950.

50. J. COPPENS, *La relève apocalyptique du messianisme royal. I. La royauté – Le règne – Le royaume de Dieu. Cadre de la relève apocalyptique*, 1979. 325 p. FB 848.

51. M. GILBERT (éd.), *La Sagesse de l'Ancien Testament*, 1979. 420 p. FB 1700.

52. B. DEHANDSCHUTTER, *Martyrium Polycarpi. Een literair-kritische studie*, 1979. 296 p. FB 950.

53. J. LAMBRECHT (éd.), *L'Apocalypse johannique et l'Apocalyptique dans le Nouveau Testament*, 1980. 458 p. FB 1400.

54. P.-M. BOGAERT (éd.), *Le Livre de Jérémie. Le prophète et son milieu. Les oracles et leur transmission*, 1981. 408 p. FB 1500.

55. J. COPPENS, *La relève apocalyptique du messianisme royal. III. Le Fils de l'homme néotestamentaire*, 1981. XIV-192 p. FB 800.

56. J. VAN BAVEL & M. SCHRAMA (éd.), *Jansénius et le Jansénisme dans les Pays-Bas. Mélanges Lucien Ceyssens*, 1982. 247 p. FB 1000.

57. J.H. WALGRAVE, *Selected Writings – Thematische geschriften. Thomas Aquinas, J.H. Newman, Theologia Fundamentalis*. Edited by G. DE SCHRIJVER & J.J. KELLY, 1982. XLIII-425 p. FB 1000.

58. F. NEIRYNCK & F. VAN SEGBROECK, avec la collaboration de E. MANNING, *Ephemerides Theologicae Lovanienses 1924-1981. Tables générales. (Bibliotheca Ephemeridum Theologicarum Lovaniensium 1947-1981)*, 1982. 400 p. FB 1600.

59. J. DELOBEL (éd.), *Logia. Les paroles de Jésus – The Sayings of Jesus. Mémorial Joseph Coppens*, 1982. 647 p. FB 2000.

60. F. NEIRYNCK, *Evangelica. Gospel Studies – Études d'évangile. Collected Essays*. Edited by F. VAN SEGBROECK, 1982. XIX-1036 p. FB 2000.

61. J. COPPENS, *La relève apocalyptique du messianisme royal. II. Le Fils d'homme vétéro- et intertestamentaire*. Édition posthume par J. LUST, 1983. XVII-272 p. FB 1000.

62. J.J. KELLY, *Baron Friedrich von Hügel's Philosophy of Religion*, 1983. 232 p. FB 1500.

63. G. DE SCHRIJVER, *Le merveilleux accord de l'homme et de Dieu. Étude de l'analogie de l'être chez Hans Urs von Balthasar*, 1983. 344 p. FB 1500.

64. J. GROOTAERS & J.A. SELLING, *The 1980 Synod of Bishops: « On the Role of the Family ». An Exposition of the Event and an Analysis of Its Texts*. Preface by Prof. emeritus L. JANSSENS, 1983. 375 p. FB 1500.

65. F. NEIRYNCK & F. VAN SEGBROECK, *New Testament Vocabulary. A Companion Volume to the Concordance*, 1984. XVI-494 p. FB 2000.

66. R.F. COLLINS, *Studies on the First Letter to the Thessalonians*, 1984. XI-415 p. FB 1500.

67. R. BOUDENS (ed.), *Alfred Plummer, Conversations with Dr. Döllinger 1870-1890*. With the collaboration of L. KENIS, 1985. LIV-372 p. FB 1800.

68. N. LOHFINK (ed.), *Das Deuteronomium. Entstehung, Gestalt und Botschaft / Origin, Form and Message*, 1985. XI-382 p. FB 2000.

69. P.F. FRANSEN, *Hermeneutics of the Councils and Other Studies*. Collected by H.E. MERTENS and F. DE GRAEVE, 1985. 543 p. FB 1800.

In preparation:
70. J. DUPONT, *Études sur les Évangiles synoptiques*.

ORIENTALISTE, P.B. 41, B-3000 Leuven